The
Unfinished
Nation

A CONCISE HISTORY
OF THE AMERICAN PEOPLE

Volume One: To 1877

The Unfinished Nation

A CONCISE HISTORY
OF THE AMERICAN PEOPLE

Volume One: To 1877

Alan Brinkley
Columbia University

OVERTURE
BOOKS

McGraw-Hill, Inc.

New York   St. Louis   San Francisco   Auckland   Bogotá   Caracas
Lisbon   London   Madrid   Mexico   Milan   Montreal   New Delhi
Paris   San Juan   Singapore   Sydney   Tokyo   Toronto

THE UNFINISHED NATION: A Concise History of the American People
Volume One: To 1877

Adapted from *American History: A Survey*, by Brinkley, Current, Freidel, and Williams.

2 3 4 5 6 7 8 9 0 DOC DOC 9 0 9 8 7 6 5 4 3

ISBN 0-07-007871-8

This book was set in Janson by Black Dot, Inc.
R. R. Donnelley & Sons Company was printer and binder.
Maps were prepared by David Lindroth Inc.

Publisher: Roth Wilkofsky
Sponsoring Editor: Peter Labella
Associate Editor: Niels Aaboe
Editing Supervisor: Larry Goldberg
Designer: Wanda Siedlecka
Production Supervisor: Kathryn Porzio
Photo Editor: Elyse Rieder

Cover Photo: New Bedford Fifty Years, Ago, 1858. I.N. Phelps Stokes Collection of American Historical Prints. Miriam and Ira D. Wallach Division of Art, Prints, and Photographs, The New York Public Library, Astor, Lenox, and Tilden Foundations.

Library of Congress Cataloging-in-Publication Data

Brinkley, Alan.
    The unfinished nation: a concise history of the American people /
    Alan Brinkley.
        p.   cm.
    "Overture books."
    Includes bibliographical references and index.
    Contents: v. 1. To 1877—v. 2. From 1865.
    ISBN 0-07-007871-8 (v. 1)—ISBN 0-07-007872-6 (v. 2)
    1. United States—History.   I. Title.
    E178.1.B827   1993
    973—dc20   92-44995

Contents

AMERICAN VOICES

DEBATING THE PAST

APPENDICES

List of Illustrations

List of Maps

Preface

T he story of the American past, which is the subject of this book, is
as contested today as it has been at any moment in its history. As
the population of the United States becomes ever more diverse and as
groups that once stood outside the view of scholarship thrust themselves
into its center, historians are revealing the immense and, until recently,
inadequately understood complexity of their country's past. The result has
been the slow emergence of a richer and fuller history of the United States,
but also a more fragmented and contentious one. That history offers a
picture of a highly diverse people. It also provides a picture of a great nation.

Threading one's way through the many, conflicting demands of contemporary scholars and contemporary readers is no easy task. But I have
tried in this book to find an acceptable middle ground between the claims
of diversity and the claims of unity. The United States is, indeed, a nation
of many cultures. We cannot understand its history without understanding
the experiences of all the different groups that have shaped American society,
without understanding the particular worlds that have developed within it
based on race, gender, ethnicity, religion, class, or region.

But the United States is more than just a collection of different cultures.
It is also a nation. And as important as understanding its diversity is
understanding the forces that have drawn it together and allowed it to
survive and flourish despite division. The United States has constructed a
remarkably stable and enduring political system that touches the lives of all
Americans. It has developed an immense, highly productive national economy that affects the working and consuming lives of virtually everyone. It
has created a mass popular culture that colors the experiences and assumptions of almost all the American people, and the people of much of the rest
of the world as well. One can admire these unifying forces for their
contributions to America's considerable success as a nation, or condemn
them for the ways they have contributed to inequality, injustice, and failure.
But no one proposing to understand the history of the United States can
afford to ignore them.

In the great historical narratives of the nineteenth and early twentieth
centuries, the story of America moved smoothly and triumphantly from one

clearly defined era to another, focusing on great events and great men and tracing the rise of national institutions. The late twentieth century has produced a different narrative, with frequent, sometimes jarring, changes of focus and direction. It devotes attention to private as well as public events, to failure as well as success, to difference as well as to unity. And yet it remains, in the end, a narrative, a story—newly complicated, perhaps, by our understanding of the many worlds of historical experience that once eluded us—but no less remarkable and compelling for those complications.

This book is an effort to tell this newer story of America for students of history and for general readers in a single, reasonably concise volume. It has its origins in a considerably larger book by Alan Brinkley, Richard N. Current, Frank Freidel, and T. Harry Williams, *American History: A Survey*, now in its eighth edition. But it is not simply an abridgment of that longer work. I have tried here to craft a new, more thematic, and more selective narrative that preserves the central elements of the larger text but presents a clearer and more readily accessible story. In addition to the central narrative (and the maps and illustrations that accompany it), readers will also find a collection of essays examining major interpretive debates among scholars; and they will find a series of excerpts from important or emblematic American autobiographies, journals, memoirs, and other works. Together, I hope, these elements will serve to introduce readers to enough different approaches to and areas of American history to make them aware of its extraordinary richness and diversity. I hope they will also give readers some sense of the shared experiences of Americans.

The title of this book, *The Unfinished Nation*, is meant to suggest several things. It is a reminder of America's exceptional diversity: of the degree to which, despite all the many efforts to build a single, uniform definition of the meaning of American nationhood, that meaning remains contested and diverse. It is a reference to the centrality of change in American history: to the way in which the nation has continually transformed itself and to how it continues to do so in our own time. And it is a description of the writing of American history itself, of the way historians are engaged in a continuing, ever unfinished, process of asking new questions of the past.

Many people contributed to this book: Chris Rogers, David Follmer, Niels Aaboe, Larry Goldberg, Roth Wilkofsky, and Peter Labella at McGraw-Hill; Ashbel Green at Knopf; Yanek Mieczkowski, my research assistant at Columbia; and several anonymous scholars who read and commented on the manuscript and saved me from many errors and inelegancies. I am grateful to them all. I will also be grateful to any readers who wish to offer comments, criticisms, and corrections as I prepare future editions. Suggestions can be sent to me in care of the Department of History, Columbia University, New York, NY 10027; I will respond to them as fully and constructively as I can.

ALAN BRINKLEY

CHAPTER ONE

The Meeting of Cultures

America Before Columbus ~ *Europe Looks Westward*
The Arrival of the English

HE DISCOVERY OF America did not begin with Christopher Columbus. It started many thousands of years earlier when human beings
first crossed an ancient land bridge over the Bering Strait into what is now
Alaska and—almost certainly without realizing it—began to people a new
continent.

AMERICA BEFORE COLUMBUS

No one is certain when these migrations began; recent estimates suggest
that they started between 14,000 and 16,000 years ago. They were probably
a result of the development of new stone-tipped spears and other hunting
implements that made it possible for humans to pursue the large animals
that regularly crossed between Asia and North America. Year after year, a
few at a time, these nomadic peoples—apparently drawn from a Mongolian
stock similar to that of modern-day eastern Siberia—entered the new
continent and moved deeper into its heart. Perhaps as early as 8000 B.C., the
migrations reached the southern tip of South America. By the end of the
fifteenth century A.D., when the first important contact with Europeans
occurred, America was the home of many millions of men and women.
Scholars estimate that well over 10 million people lived in South America
by 1500 and that perhaps 4 million lived in the territory that now constitutes
the United States.

The Civilizations of the South

The most elaborate of these societies emerged in South and Central America and in Mexico. In Peru, the Incas created a powerful empire of perhaps 6 million people. They developed a complex political system and a large network of paved roads that welded together the populations of many tribes under a single government. In Central America and on the Yucatan peninsula of Mexico, the Mayas built a sophisticated culture with a written language, a numerical system similar to the Arabic, an accurate calendar, and an advanced agricultural system. They were succeeded by the Aztecs, a once-nomadic warrior tribe from the north. In the late thirteenth century, the Aztecs established a precarious rule over much of central and southern Mexico and built elaborate administrative, educational, and medical systems comparable to the most advanced in Europe at the time. The Aztecs also developed a harsh religion that required human sacrifice. Their Spanish conquerors discovered the skulls of 100,000 victims in one location when they arrived in 1519.

The economies of these societies were based primarily on agriculture, but there were also substantial cities. Tenochtitlán, the Aztec capital built on the site of present-day Mexico City, had a population of over 100,000 in 1500, which was comparable to some of the largest European cities of the time. The Mayas (at Mayapan and elsewhere) and the Incas (in such cities as Cuzco and Machu Picchu) produced elaborate settlements with striking religious and ceremonial structures. These civilizations accomplished all this without some of the important technologies that Asian and European civilizations possessed. As late as the sixteenth century, no American society had yet developed wheeled vehicles.

The Civilizations of the North

The peoples north of Mexico—in the lands that became the United States and Canada—developed less elaborate but still substantial civilizations and political systems. Inhabitants of the northern regions of the continent subsisted on hunting, gathering, fishing, or some combination of the three. They included the Eskimos of the Arctic Circle, who fished and hunted seals and whose civilization spanned thousands of miles of largely frozen land; the big-game hunters of the northern forests, who led nomadic lives based on pursuit of moose and caribou; the tribes of the Pacific Northwest, whose principal occupation was salmon fishing and who created substantial permanent settlements along the coast; and a group of tribes spread through

relatively arid regions of the Far West who developed successful communities, many of them quite wealthy and densely populated, based on fishing,
hunting small game, and gathering edible seeds, roots, and other plant
materials.

Other societies in North America were primarily agricultural. Among
the most developed were those in the Southwest. The people of that arid
region built large irrigation systems, and they constructed substantial towns
of stone and adobe structures. In the Great Plains region, too, most tribes
were engaged in sedentary farming (corn and other grains) and lived in large
permanent settlements, although there were some small nomadic tribes that
subsisted by hunting buffalo.

The Eastern third of what is now the United States—much of it covered
with forests and inhabited by the Woodland Indians—had the greatest food
resources of any area of the continent. The many tribes of the region engaged
in farming, hunting, gathering, and fishing simultaneously. In the South
there were substantial permanent settlements and large trading networks
based on the corn and other grains grown in the rich lands of the Mississippi
River valley. The city of Cahokia (near present-day St. Louis), was a large
trading center. At its peak in A.D. 1200 it had a population of 40,000.

The agricultural societies of the Northeast were less stationary. Farm-
ing techniques there were designed to exploit the land quickly rather than
to develop permanent settlements. Many of the tribes living east of the
Mississippi River were linked together loosely by common linguistic roots.
The largest of these language groups consisted of the Algonquin tribes,
which lived along the Atlantic seaboard from Canada to Virginia; the
Iroquois Confederation, which was centered in what is now upstate New
York; and the Muskogean, which consisted of the tribes in the southernmost
region of the Eastern seaboard. Alliances among the various Indian societies
(even among those with common languages) were fragile, since the peoples
of the Americas did not think of themselves as members of a single civilization. When Europeans arrived and began to threaten their way of life, tribes
only rarely were able to unite in opposition to white encroachments.

In the last centuries before the arrival of Europeans, native Americans—
like peoples in other areas of the world—were experiencing an agricultural
revolution. In all areas of what is now the United States (if in varying degrees
from place to place), tribes were becoming more sedentary and were
developing new sources of food, clothing, and shelter. Most regions were
experiencing significant population growth. And virtually all were developing the sorts of elaborate social customs and rituals that only relatively
stationary societies can produce. Religion was as important to Indian society

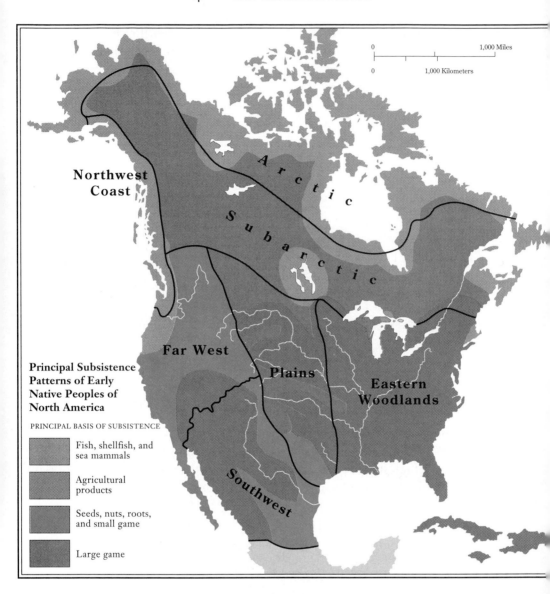

Principal Subsistence Patterns of Early Native Peoples of North America

PRINCIPAL BASIS OF SUBSISTENCE

Fish, shellfish, and sea mammals

Agricultural products

Seeds, nuts, roots, and small game

Large game

as it was to most other cultures and was usually closely bound up with the natural world on which the tribes depended. Native Americans worshiped many gods, whom they associated variously with crops, game, forests, rivers, and other elements of nature.

All tribes assigned women the jobs of caring for children, preparing meals, and gathering certain foods. But the allocation of other tasks varied from one society to another. Some tribal groups (notably the Pueblos of the

Southwest) reserved farming tasks almost entirely for men. Among others (including the Algonquins, the Iroquois, and the Muskogean), women tended the fields, while men engaged in hunting, warfare, or clearing land. Iroquois women and children were often left alone for extended periods while men were away hunting or fighting battles. As a result, women tended to control the social and economic organization of the settlements and played powerful roles within families.

EUROPE LOOKS WESTWARD

Europeans were almost entirely unaware of the existence of the Americas before the fifteenth century. A few early wanderers—Leif Ericson, an eleventh-century Norse seaman, and perhaps others—had glimpsed parts of the New World on their voyages. But even if their discoveries had become common knowledge (and they did not), there would have been little incentive for others to follow, for Europe in the Middle Ages (roughly A.D. 500–1500) was so divided and decentralized, so limited in its commerce, and

INDIANS OF NEW FRANCE The drawing is by the cartographer Charles Bécard de Granville, who was employed by the French government to make maps of their territories in North America. This depiction of Indian hunters traveling by river dates from approximately 1701.

so lacking in powerful political leaders that interest in great ventures re-mained limited. By the end of the fifteenth century, however, conditions in Europe had changed, and the incentive for overseas exploration had grown.

Commerce and Nationalism

Two changes in particular helped produce incentives for Europeans to look toward new lands. One was a result of the significant growth in Europe's population in the fifteenth century. The Black Death, a catastrophic epi-demic of the bubonic plague that began in Constantinople in 1347, had killed (according to some estimates) as many as half the people of the Continent. But a century and a half later, the population had rebounded. With that growth came a reawakening of commerce and a general increase in prosperity. A new merchant class was emerging to meet the rising demand for goods from abroad. As trade increased, and as advances in navigation and shipbuilding made long-distance sea travel more feasible, interest in expanding trade even further grew quickly.

At the same time, new governments were emerging that were more united and powerful than the feeble political entities of the feudal past. In the western areas of Europe in particular, strong new monarchs were emerging, creating centralized nation-states, and growing eager to enhance the commercial growth of their nations.

Ever since the early fourteenth century, when Marco Polo and other adventurers had returned from the Orient bearing exotic goods (spices, cloths, dyes) and even more exotic tales, Europeans who craved commercial glory had dreamed above all of trade with the East. For two centuries, that trade had been limited by the difficulties of the long overland journey to the Asian courts. But in the fourteenth century, as the maritime talents of several western European societies increased, there began to be talk of finding a faster, safer route to the Orient by sea. In the late fifteenth century, some of the new monarchs were ready to finance daring voyages of exploration.

The first to do so were the Portuguese. Their maritime preeminence in the fifteenth century was in large part the work of Prince Henry the Navigator, who devoted much of his life to the promotion of exploration. Some of Henry's mariners went as far south as Cape Verde, on Africa's west coast. After his death in 1460, Portuguese explorers advanced farther still. In 1486, Bartholomeu Díaz rounded the southern tip of Africa (the Cape of Good Hope); and in 1497–1498 Vasco da Gama proceeded all the way around the cape to India. In 1500, the next Portuguese fleet bound for India, under the command of Pedro Cabral, was blown off course and happened upon the coast of Brazil. But by then, another man, in the service of another country, had already encountered the "New World".

Christopher Columbus

Christopher Columbus was born and reared in Genoa, Italy, and spent his early seafaring years in the service of the Portuguese. As a young man, he became interested in trying to reach the Orient by going west, across the Atlantic, rather than east, around Africa. Columbus's optimism rested on several basic misconceptions. He thought the world was far smaller than it actually is. He also believed that the Asian continent extended farther eastward than it actually does. Most important, he did not realize that anything lay to the west between Europe and the lands of Asia.

Columbus failed to convince the leaders of Portugal of the value of his plan, so he turned instead to Spain. Although the Spaniards were not yet as advanced a maritime people as the Portuguese, they were just as energetic and ambitious. And in the fifteenth century they were establishing a strong nation-state. The marriage of Spain's two most powerful regional rulers, Ferdinand of Aragon and Isabella of Castile, had produced the strongest monarchy in Europe, one that was eager to demonstrate its strength by sponsoring new commercial ventures.

Columbus appealed to Queen Isabella for support for his proposed westward voyage, and in 1492, after consolidating her position at home, she agreed. Commanding ninety men and three ships—the *Niña*, the *Pinta*, and the *Santa Maria*—Columbus left Spain in August 1492 and sailed west into the Atlantic. Ten weeks later, he sighted land and assumed he had reached an island off Asia. In fact, he had landed on an island in the Bahamas. When he pushed on and encountered Cuba, he assumed he had reached China. He returned to Spain, bringing with him several captured natives as evidence of his achievement. (He called the natives "Indians" because he believed they were from the East Indies in the Pacific.)

Columbus did not, however, bring back news of the great khan's court in China or any samples of the fabled wealth of the Indies. And so a year later, he tried again, this time with a much larger expedition. As before, he headed into the Caribbean, discovering several other islands and leaving a small and short-lived colony on Hispaniola. On a third voyage, in 1498, he finally reached the mainland and cruised along the northern coast of South America. He then realized, for the first time, that he had encountered not a part of Asia but a separate continent. Still, he remained convinced that Asia was only a short distance away.

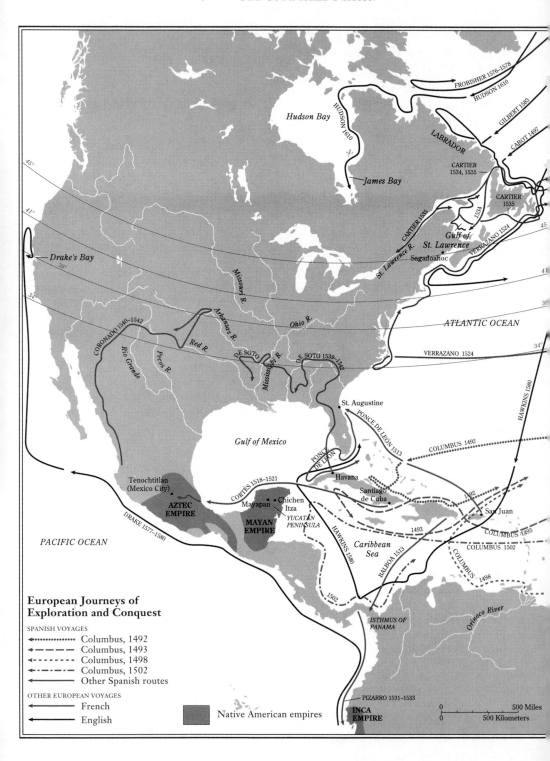

FROBISHER 1576–1578

HUDSON 1610

GILBERT 1583

CABOT 1497

LABRADOR

CARTIER 1534, 1535

CARTIER 1535

VERRAZANO 1524

Hudson Bay

HUDSON 1610

James Bay

45°

41°

CARTIER 1535

Gulf of
St. Lawrence

Sagadahoc

45

Drake's Bay

38°

34°

Missouri R.

St. Lawrence R.

CARTIER 1534

41

CORONADO 1540–1542

Arkansas R.

Ohio R.

ATLANTIC OCEAN

Rio Grande

Red R.

Pecos R.

DE SOTO

Mississippi R.

DE SOTO 1539–1542

34

VERRAZANO 1524

HAWKINS 1580

St. Augustine

PONCE DE LEÓN 1513

COLUMBUS 1492

Gulf of Mexico

PONCE
DE LEÓN

Havana

1492

Tenochtitlán
(Mexico City)

CORTÉS 1518–1521

Mayapan

Chichen
Itza

Santiago
de Cuba

San Juan

**AZTEC
EMPIRE**

1493

COLUMBUS 1493

DRAKE 1577–1580

**MAYAN
EMPIRE**

*YUCATAN
PENINSULA*

HAWKINS 1580

COLUMBUS 1502

PACIFIC OCEAN

*Caribbean
Sea*

COLUMBUS

1498

BALBOA 1513

Orinoco River

1502

*ISTHMUS OF
PANAMA*

European Journeys of
Exploration and Conquest

PIZARRO 1531–1533

**INCA
EMPIRE**

SPANISH VOYAGES

•••••••••• Columbus, 1492
— • — Columbus, 1493
— — — Columbus, 1498
— • — • Columbus, 1502
——— Other Spanish routes

OTHER EUROPEAN VOYAGES

——— French

——— English

Native American empires

0   500 Miles
0   500 Kilometers

Columbus's celebrated accomplishments made him a popular hero for a time, but he ended his life in obscurity. Ultimately he was even unable to give his name to the land he had revealed to the Europeans. That distinction went instead to a Florentine merchant, Amerigo Vespucci, a passenger on a later Portuguese expedition to the New World, who wrote a series of vivid (if largely fictitious) descriptions of the lands he visited.

Partly as a result of Columbus's initiative, Spain began to devote greater resources and energy to maritime exploration and gradually replaced Portugal as the foremost seafaring nation. In 1513 the Spaniard Vasco de Balboa fought his way across the Isthmus of Panama and became the first European to gaze westward upon the great ocean that separated America from China. Seeking access to that ocean, Ferdinand Magellan, a Portuguese in Spanish employ, found the strait that now bears his name at the southern end of South America, struggled through the stormy narrows and into the ocean (so calm by contrast that he christened it the Pacific), and then proceeded to the Philippines. There Magellan died in a conflict with the natives, but his expedition went on to complete the first known circumnavigation of the globe (1519–1522). By 1550, Spaniards had explored the coasts of North America as far north as Oregon in the west and Labrador in the east.

The Spanish Empire

In time, Spanish explorers in the New World stopped thinking of America simply as an obstacle to their search for a route to the East and began instead to consider it a possible source of wealth in itself. The Spanish claimed for themselves the whole of the New World, except for a piece of it (today's Brazil) that was reserved by a papal decree for the Portuguese; and by the mid-sixteenth century, they were establishing a substantial American empire.

The early Spanish colonists, beginning with those Columbus brought on his second voyage, settled on the islands of the Caribbean. But then, in 1518, Hernando Cortés, who had been an unsuccessful Spanish government official in Cuba for fourteen years, decided to lead a small military expedition (about 600 men) against the Aztecs in Mexico and their powerful emperor, Montezuma, after hearing stories of great treasures there. His first assault on Tenochtitlán, the Aztec capital, failed. But Cortés and his army had, unknowingly, unleashed an assault on the Aztecs far more devastating than military attack: they had exposed the natives to smallpox. An epidemic of that disease decimated the Aztec population and made it possible for the Spanish to triumph in their second attempt at conquest. Through his ruthless suppression of the surviving natives, Cortés established himself as the most brutal of the Spanish *conquistadores* (conquerors). Twenty years later, Francisco Pizarro conquered Peru, revealed to the world the wealth of the Incas, and opened the way for other advances into South America.

The story of the Spanish warriors is one of great military daring and achievement. It is also a story of remarkable brutality and greed. The conquistadores subjugated and, in some areas, virtually exterminated the native populations. In this horrible way, they made possible the creation of a vast Spanish Empire in the New World.

Although the conquistadores had cleared the way for Spanish colonization of America, the task of creating settlements remained difficult. Spaniards who wished to launch expeditions to the New World had to get licenses

CORTÉS IN THE NEW WORLD An Aztec artist created this image of Hernando Cortés in Mexico. Cortés is visible at upper left, on horseback, wielding a sword. Other images suggest the destruction his arrival produced among the Aztecs. One of the most brutal and successful of the Spanish *conquistadores*, Cortés burned his ships upon landing at Vera Cruz (where he founded a city) in 1519 to prevent his men from turning back. In 1521, he captured the Aztec capital, Tenochtitlán, after a long siege.

from the crown and pay the monarch a fifth of any wealth gathered in the new colonies. Colonizers then had to equip and finance their expeditions without help from the government and assume the full risk of loss or ruin. They might succeed and make a fortune; they might fail and lose everything, including their lives.

The first Spanish settlers in America were interested only in exploiting the American stores of gold and silver, and they were fabulously successful. For 300 years, beginning in the sixteenth century, the mines in Spanish America yielded more than ten times as much gold and silver as the rest of the world's mines together. These riches made Spain for a time the wealthiest and most powerful nation on earth.

After the first wave of conquest, however, most Spanish settlers in America traveled to the New World for other reasons. Many went in hopes of creating a profitable agricultural economy in America, and they helped establish elements of European civilization permanently in America. Other Spaniards went to America to spread the Christian religion; after the 1840s priests or friars accompanied all colonizing ventures. Through the work of zealous missionaries, the influence of the Catholic church ultimately extended throughout South and Central America and Mexico.

By the end of the sixteenth century, the Spanish Empire had become one of the largest in the history of the world. It included the Caribbean islands, Mexico, and southern North America, where a second wave of European colonizers had established outposts. The Spanish fort established in 1565 at St. Augustine, Florida, became the first permanent European settlement in the present-day United States. The Spanish Empire also spread into South America and included what is now Chile, Argentina, and Peru. In 1580, when the Spanish and Portuguese monarchies temporarily united, Brazil came under Spanish jurisdiction as well.

It was, however, a colonial empire very different from the one the English would later establish in North America. The earliest Spanish ventures in the New World had operated largely independently of the throne, but by the end of the sixteenth century the monarchy had extended its authority directly into the governance of local communities, leaving colonists few opportunities to establish political institutions independent of the crown. The Spanish were far more successful than the British would be in extracting great surface wealth—gold and silver—from their American colonies. But they concentrated relatively less energy on making agriculture and commerce profitable in their colonies. The strict and inflexible commercial policies of the Spanish government made the problem worse. The

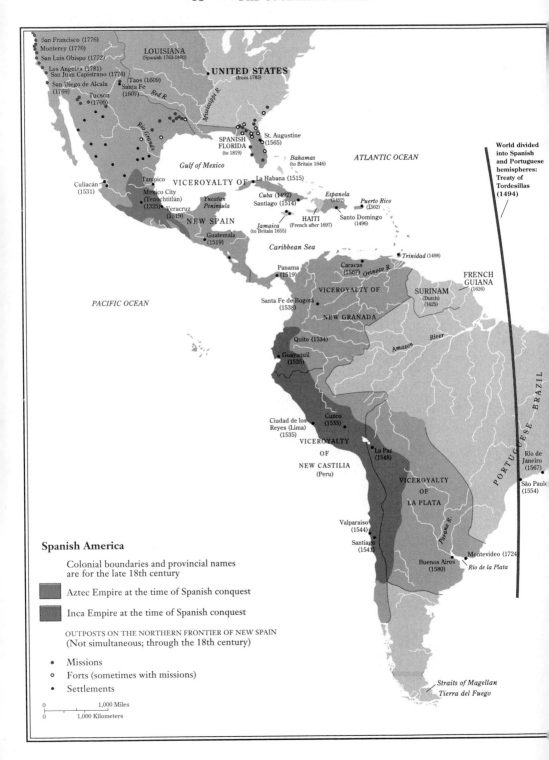

San Francisco (1776)
Monterey (1770)
San Luis Obispo (1772)
Los Angeles (1781)
San Juan Capistrano (1776)
San Diego de Alcala (1769)
Tucson (1709)
Taos (1609)
Santa Fe (1607)
Culiacán (1531)

LOUISIANA
(Spanish 1763–1800)

Red R.
Rio Grande
Mississippi R.

UNITED STATES
(from 1783)

SPANISH FLORIDA
(to 1819)
St. Augustine (1565)

Bahamas
(to Britain 1646)

ATLANTIC OCEAN

World divided
into Spanish
and Portuguese
hemispheres:
Treaty of
Tordesillas
(1494)

Gulf of Mexico

Tampico
VICEROYALTY OF
La Habana (1515)

Mexico City
(Tenochtitlán)
(1325)
Veracruz
(1519)

Yucatan
Peninsula

Cuba (1492)
Santiago (1514)

Española
(1492)

Puerto Rico
(1502)

NEW SPAIN

Jamaica
(to Britain 1655)

HAITI
(French after 1697)

Santo Domingo
(1496)

Guatemala
(1519)

Caribbean Sea

Trinidad (1498)

Panama
(1519)

Caracas
(1567)

Orinoco R.

FRENCH
GUIANA
(1626)

VICEROYALTY OF

SURINAM
(Dutch)
(1625)

PACIFIC OCEAN

Santa Fe de Bogotá
(1538)

NEW GRANADA

Quito (1534)

Amazon
River

Guayaquil
(1535)

PORTUGUESE BRAZIL

Ciudad de los
Reyes (Lima)
(1535)

Cuzco
(1535)

La Paz
(1548)

Rio de
Janeiro
(1567)

VICEROYALTY
OF
NEW CASTILIA
(Peru)

VICEROYALTY
OF
LA PLATA

São Paulo
(1554)

Valparaiso
(1544)

Paraná R.

Santiago
(1541)

Montevideo (1724)

Buenos Aires
(1580)

Rio de la Plata

Spanish America

Colonial boundaries and provincial names
are for the late 18th century

Aztec Empire at the time of Spanish conquest

Inca Empire at the time of Spanish conquest

OUTPOSTS ON THE NORTHERN FRONTIER OF NEW SPAIN
(Not simultaneous; through the 18th century)

• Missions
○ Forts (sometimes with missions)
• Settlements

Straits of Magellan
Tierra del Fuego

0   1,000 Miles
0   1,000 Kilometers

Spanish emphasis on surface riches ultimately had a stifling impact on Spain itself too. The supply of easy wealth from America weakened the incentive to promote domestic economic growth. That was one reason why Spain remained less developed than its northern European rivals and why its power declined so quickly in the seventeenth century.

But the biggest difference between the Spanish Empire and the later European colonization of North America was in the characters of the populations. The societies of English, French, and Dutch America were centered on farming and permanent settlement and emphasized family life. Hence, the Europeans in North America reproduced themselves rapidly after their first difficult years and in time came to outnumber the natives. The Spanish, by contrast, ruled their empire but did not people it. The number of European settlers in Spanish America always remained relatively small, and despite disease and war, the vast majority of the population continued to consist of natives. The Spanish Empire, therefore, was the product of a collision between and then a commingling of two cultures that had been developing for centuries along completely different lines.

Cultural Exchanges

European and native cultures never entirely merged in the Spanish Empire. Indeed, significant differences remain today between European and Indian cultures throughout South and Central America. Nevertheless, the arrival of whites launched a process of interaction between different peoples that left no one unchanged.

That Europeans were exploring the Americas at all was a result of their early contacts with the natives, from whom they had learned of the rich deposits of gold and silver. From then on, the history of the Americas became one of increasing levels of exchanges—some beneficial, some catastrophic—among different peoples and cultures. The first and perhaps most profound result of this exchange was the importation of European diseases to the New World. It would be difficult to exaggerate the consequences of the exposure of native Americans to such illnesses as influenza, measles, typhus, and above all smallpox—diseases to which Europeans had over time developed at least a partial immunity but to which Americans were tragically vulnerable. Millions died. In some areas, native populations were virtually wiped out within a few decades of their first contact with whites. On Hispaniola— where the Dominican Republic and Haiti are today and where Columbus landed and established a small, short-lived colony in the 1490s—the native population quickly declined from approximately 1 million to about 500. In the Mayan areas of Mexico, as much as 95 percent of the population perished within a few years of the natives' first contact with the Spanish. Some groups fared better than others; many (although not all) of the tribes north of Mexico, whose contact with European settlers came later and was often less intimate, were spared the worst of the epidemics. But for other areas of the New World, this was a catastrophe at least as grave as, and in some places far worse than, the Black Death that had killed as much as half the population of Europe two centuries before.

The decimation of native populations in the southern regions of the Americas was not, however, purely a result of exposure to infection. It was also a result of the conquistadores' quite deliberate policy of subjugation and extermination. Their brutality was in part a reflection of the ruthlessness with which Europeans waged war in all parts of the world. It was also a result of their conviction that the natives were "savages"—uncivilized peoples who could be treated as somehow not fully human. Ironically, it was also a consequence of the high level of development of some native societies. Had the natives truly been as primitive and disorganized as Europeans wanted to believe, there would have been little need to destroy them. But organized into substantial empires, they posed a serious threat to the conquistadores' ambitions. That, more than anything else, accounts for the thoroughness with which the Spanish set about obliterating native cultures. They razed cities and dismantled temples and monuments. They destroyed records and documents. They systematically killed Indian warriors, leaders, priests, and organized elites. By the 1540s, the combined effects of European diseases and European military brutality had all but destroyed the empires of Mexico and South America and allowed the Spanish to exert their authority with few organized challenges from the natives.

Not all aspects of the exchange were so disastrous to the Indians. The Europeans introduced to America important new crops (among them sugar and bananas), domestic livestock (cattle, pigs, and sheep), and perhaps most significantly the horse. Indians soon learned to cultivate the new crops, and European livestock spread widely among tribes that in the past had possessed virtually no domesticated animals other than dogs. The horse, in particular, became central to the lives of many natives and transformed their societies.

The exchange was at least as important (and more beneficial) to the Europeans. In both North and South America, the arriving white peoples learned from the natives new agricultural techniques appropriate to the demands of the new land. They discovered new crops, above all maize (corn), which Columbus took back to Europe from his first trip to America and which became an important staple in Europe itself as well as among European settlers in the New World. Such foods as squash, pumpkins, beans, sweet potatoes, tomatoes, peppers, and potatoes all found their way into European diets by way of native Americans. These and other American crops revolutionized European agriculture, enabling farmers to feed more people with more nutritious foods. That, in turn, facilitated the growth of the European population and the transformation of the European economy. Agricultural discoveries ultimately proved more important to Europe than the gold and silver the conquistadores valued so highly.

In South America, Central America, and Mexico, a society emerged in which Europeans and natives lived in intimate, if unequal, contact with one another. As a result, Indians adopted many features of European civilization, although seldom did those features survive the transfer to America unchanged. Many natives gradually came to speak Spanish or Portuguese, but they created a range of dialects fusing the European languages with elements of their own. Gradually, European missionaries—through a combination of persuasion and coercion—spread Catholicism through most areas of the Spanish Empire. But native Christians combined the new religion with features of their old ones.

Colonial officials were expected to take their wives with them to America, but among the ordinary settlers—the majority—European men outnumbered European women by at least ten to one. As a result, male Spanish immigrants had substantial sexual contact with native women. Intermarriage—sometimes forcible, sometimes with the agreement of native women responding to the shortage of native men—became frequent. Before long, the population of the colonies came to be dominated (numerically, at least) by people of mixed race, or *mestizos*.

Virtually all the enterprises of the Spanish and Portuguese colonists depended on an Indian work force. In some places, Indians were sold into slavery. More often, colonists used a coercive wage system by which Indians worked in the mines and on the plantations under duress for fixed periods, unable to leave without the consent of their employers. These indentured work forces survived in some areas of the South American mainland for many centuries. Yet even that was not, in the end, enough to meet the labor needs of the colonists—particularly since the native population had declined (and in some places virtually vanished) because of disease and war. As early as 1502, therefore, European settlers began importing slaves from Africa.

Africa and America

Over half of all the immigrants to the New World between 1500 and 1800 were Africans, virtually all of them sent to America against their will. Most came from a large region in west Africa below the Sahara Desert, known as Guinea.

Europeans and white Americans came to portray African society as primitive and uncivilized (in part to justify the enslavement of Africa's people). But most Africans were, in fact, civilized peoples with well-developed economies and political systems. The residents of upper Guinea had substantial commercial contact with the Mediterranean world—trading ivory, gold, and slaves for finished goods—and, largely as a result, became early converts to Islam. After the collapse of the ancient kingdom of Ghana around A.D. 1100, they created the even larger empire of Mali, which survived into the fifteenth century and whose trading center at Timbuktu became fabled as a meeting place of the peoples of many lands and a center of education.

Farther south, Africans were more isolated from Europe and the Mediterranean and were more politically fragmented. The central social unit was the village, which usually consisted of members of an extended family group. Some groups of villages united in small kingdoms. But no large empires emerged in the south comparable to the Ghana and Mali kingdoms farther north. Nevertheless, these southern societies developed extensive trade—in woven fabrics, ceramics, wooden and iron goods, as well as crops and livestock—both among themselves and, to a lesser degree, with the outside world.

African civilizations naturally developed economies that reflected the climates and resources of their lands. In upper Guinea, fishing and rice cultivation, supplemented by the extensive trade with Mediterranean lands, were the foundation of the economy. Farther south, Africans grew wheat and other food crops, raised livestock, and fished. There were some more nomadic tribes in the interior, who subsisted largely on hunting and gathering and developed less elaborate social systems. But most Africans were sedentary, farming people.

As in many Indian societies in America, but in contrast to the European tradition, African families tended to be matrilineal. That means that people traced their heredity through and inherited property from their mothers. Women played a major role, often the dominant role, in trade; in many areas, they were the principal farmers (while the men hunted, fished, and raised livestock); and everywhere, they managed child care and food preparation. Most tribes also divided political power by gender, with men choosing leaders and systems for managing male affairs and women choosing parallel leaders to handle female matters.

In those areas of west Africa where indigenous religions had survived the spread of Islam (which included most of the lands south of the empire of Mali), people worshiped many gods, whom they associated with various aspects of the natural world and whose spirits they believed lived in trees, rocks, forests, and streams. Most Africans also developed forms of ancestor worship and took great care in tracing family lineage; the most revered priests were generally the oldest people.

Small elites of priests and nobles stood at the top of African societies. Most people belonged to a large middle group of farmers, traders, crafts workers, and others. At the bottom of society were slaves—men and women who were put into bondage after being captured in wars, because of criminal behavior, or as a result of unpaid debts. Slavery was not usually permanent; people were generally in bondage for a fixed term, and in the meantime retained certain legal protections (including the right to marry). Children did not inherit their parents' condition of bondage. The slavery that Africans would experience at the hands of the Europeans was to be very different.

The African slave trade long preceded European settlement in the New World. As early as the eighth century, west Africans began selling slaves to traders from the Mediterranean. When Portuguese sailors began exploring the coast of Africa in the fifteenth century, they too bought slaves and took them back to Portugal, where there was a small but steady demand. In the sixteenth century, however, the market for slaves grew dramatically as a result of the growing European demand for sugar cane. The small areas of sugar cultivation in the Mediterranean were proving inadequate, and production soon moved to new areas: to the island of Madeira off the African coast, which became a Portuguese colony, and not long thereafter (still in the sixteenth century) to the Caribbean islands and Brazil. Sugar was a labor-intensive crop, and the demand for African workers in these new areas of cultivation was high. At first the slave traders were overwhelmingly Portuguese and, to a lesser extent, Spanish. By the seventeenth century, the Dutch had won control of most of the market. In the eighteenth century, the English dominated it; by then, slavery had spread well beyond its original locations in the Caribbean and South America and into the English colonies to the north.

THE ARRIVAL OF THE ENGLISH

England's first documented contact with the New World came only five years after Spain's. In 1497, John Cabot (like Columbus, a native of Genoa) sailed to the northeastern coast of North America on an expedition sponsored by King Henry VII. Other English navigators, continuing Cabot's unsuccessful search for a northwest passage through the New World to the Orient, explored other areas of North America during the sixteenth century. But nearly a century passed before the English made any serious efforts to establish colonies there. Like other European nations, England had to experience an internal transformation before it could begin settling new lands.

Incentives for Colonization

Interest in colonization grew in part as a response to the social and economic problems of sixteenth-century England. The English people suffered from frequent and costly European wars, and they suffered from almost constant religious strife within their own land. They suffered too from a harsh economic transformation of the countryside. Because the worldwide demand for wool was growing rapidly, many landowners were converting their land from fields for crops to pastures for sheep. The result was a significant growth in the wool trade—and a reduction in the amount of land available for growing food. Many of the displaced farmers became beggars or criminals. And England's food supply declined at the same time that the English population was growing—from 3 million in 1485 to 4 million in 1603. To some of the English, the New World began to seem attractive because it offered something that was growing scarce in England: land.

At the same time, new merchant capitalists were prospering from the expansion of foreign trade, particularly once merchants helped create a domestic cloth industry that allowed them to begin marketing finished goods. At first, most exporters did business almost entirely as individuals. In time, however, merchants developed more collective enterprises and formed enterprises that operated on the basis of charters from the monarch giving companies monopolies for trading in particular regions. Some were joint-stock companies, similar in some respects to modern corporations, with stockholders sharing risk and profit either on single ventures or, increasingly, on a permanent basis. These investors often made fantastic profits, and they were eager to continue the expansion of their profitable trade.

Central to this drive was the emergence of a new concept of economic life known as mercantilism. Mercantilism rested on the belief that the world's wealth was finite, that one person or nation could grow rich only at the expense of another, and that a nation's economic health depended, therefore, on extracting as much wealth as possible from foreign lands and exporting as little wealth as possible from home. The principles of mercantilism guided the economic policies of virtually all the great nation-states that were emerging in Europe in the sixteenth and seventeenth centuries and increased the competition among nations. Every European state was trying to find markets for its exports while trying to limit its imports. One result was the increased attractiveness of acquiring colonies, which could become the source of goods that a country might otherwise have to buy from other nations and could become a market for goods produced by the colonizing power.

In England, the mercantilistic program thrived at first on the basis of the flourishing wool trade with the European continent, and particularly with the great cloth market in Antwerp. In the 1550s, however, that glutted market began to collapse, and English merchants had to look elsewhere for overseas trade. The establishment of colonies seemed to be an answer to their problems. Some English also believed colonies would help alleviate poverty and unemployment by siphoning off the surplus population. Perhaps most important, colonial commerce would allow England to acquire products for which the nation had previously been dependent on foreigners—products such as lumber, naval stores, and silver and gold.

There were also religious motives for colonization. The Protestant Reformation began in Germany in 1517, when Martin Luther challenged some of the basic practices and beliefs of the Roman Catholic church—until then, the supreme religious authority. Luther quickly won a wide following among ordinary men and women in northern Europe. When the pope excommunicated him in 1520, Luther began leading his followers out of the Catholic church entirely.

As the spirit of the Reformation spread rapidly throughout Europe, other dissidents began offering other alternatives to Catholicism. The Swiss theologian John Calvin went even further than Luther had in rejecting the Catholic belief that human behavior or the church itself could affect an individual's prospects for salvation. Calvin introduced the doctrine of predestination. God "elected" some people to be saved and condemned others to damnation; each person's destiny was determined before birth, and no one could change that predetermined fate. But those who accepted Calvin's teachings came to believe that the way they led their lives might reveal to them their chances of salvation. A wicked or useless existence would be a sign of damnation; saintliness, diligence, and success could be signs of grace. Calvinism created anxieties among its followers, but it also produced a strong incentive to lead virtuous, productive lives. The new creed spread rapidly throughout northern Europe and produced (among other groups) the Huguenots in France and the Puritans in England.

At first, however, the English Reformation was less a result of these doctrinal revolts than of a political dispute between the king and the pope. In 1529 King Henry VIII, angered by the refusal of the pope to grant him a divorce from his Spanish wife (who had failed to bear him the son he desperately wanted), broke England's ties with the Catholic church and established himself as the head of the Christian faith in his country. After Henry's death, his Catholic daughter, Queen Mary, restored England's allegiance to Rome and persecuted those who resisted. But when Mary died in 1558, her half-sister, Elizabeth I, became England's sovereign and once again severed the nation's connection with the Catholic church, this time for good.

To many English people, however, the new Church of England—which differed little at first from the Catholic church—was not reformed enough. Some had been affected by the teachings of the European Reformation, and they complained that theirs was a church that had abandoned Rome without abandoning Rome's offensive beliefs and practices. They clamored for reforms that would "purify" the church, and thus they became known as "Puritans."

The most radical Puritans, known as Separatists, were determined to worship as they pleased in their own independent congregations, despite English laws that required all subjects to attend regular Anglican services. But most Puritans did not wish to leave the Church of England. They wanted, rather, to simplify Anglican forms of worship; reduce the power of the crown-appointed bishops, who were sometimes corrupt and extravagant; and reform the clergy, many of whom were uneducated men with little interest in or knowledge of theology. Like the Separatists, they grew increasingly frustrated by the refusal of either political or ecclesiastical authorities to respond to their demands.

Puritan discontent grew rapidly after the death of Elizabeth, the last of the Tudors, and the accession of James I, the first of the Stuarts, in 1603. Convinced that kings ruled by divine right, James quickly antagonized the Puritans, a group that included most of the rising businessmen, by resorting to illegal and arbitrary taxation, by favoring English Catholics in the granting of charters and other favors, and by supporting "high-church" forms of ceremony. By the early seventeenth century, some religious nonconformists were beginning to look for places of refuge outside the kingdom.

Many factors, therefore, combined to increase the interest of the English in peopling distant lands—social and economic instability, religious discontent, personal ambition, commercial greed. England's first experience with colonization, however, came not in the New World but in neighboring Ireland. The English had long laid claim to the island, but only in the late sixteenth century did serious efforts at colonization begin. The long, brutal process by which the English attempted (never entirely successfully) to subdue the Irish led to an important assumption about colonization that the English would take with them to America: the belief that settlements in foreign lands must retain a rigid separation from the native populations. Unlike the Spanish in America, the English in Ireland tried to build a separate society of their own, peopled with emigrants from England itself. They would take that concept with them to the New World.

The French and the Dutch in America

English settlers in North America were to encounter not only natives but also other Europeans who were, like them, driven by mercantilist ideas. There were scattered North American outposts of the Spanish Empire, whose residents looked on the English as intruders. More important, there were French and Dutch settlers.

France founded its first permanent settlement in America at Quebec in 1608, less than a year after the English started their first at Jamestown. The colony's population grew very slowly, but the French exercised an influence in the New World disproportionate to their numbers, because of their relationships with native Americans. Unlike the early English settlers, who hugged the coastline and traded with the Indians of the interior through intermediaries, the French forged close ties with natives deep inside the continent. French Jesuit missionaries established some of the first contacts between the two peoples. More important were the *coureurs de bois*—adventurous fur traders and trappers—who also penetrated far into the wilderness and developed an extensive trade that became one of the underpinnings of the French colonial economy. The French traders formed partnerships with the Indians and often became virtually a part of native society, living among the natives and at times marrying Indian women. The fur trade helped open the way for French agricultural estates (or *seigneuries*) along the St. Lawrence River and for the development of trade and military centers at Quebec and Montreal.

The English also faced competition from the Dutch in North America. Holland in the early seventeenth century was one of the leading trading nations of the world. In 1609 an English explorer in the employ of the Dutch, Henry Hudson, sailed up the river that was to be named for him in what is now New York State; and his explorations led to a Dutch claim on that territory and to the establishment of a permanent Dutch presence in the New World. In 1624, not long after the first two permanent English colonies took root in Jamestown and Plymouth, the Dutch created a wedge between them when the Dutch West India Company established a series of permanent trading posts on the Hudson, Delaware, and Connecticut rivers. The company actively encouraged settlement of the region, and the result was the colony of New Netherland and its principal town, New Amsterdam, on Manhattan Island. But the Dutch population remained relatively small.

The First English Settlements

The first permanent English settlement in the New World was established at Jamestown, in Virginia, in 1607. But for nearly thirty years before that, English merchants and adventurers had been engaged in a series of failed efforts to create colonies in America.

Through much of the sixteenth century, the English had harbored mixed feelings about the New World. They were intrigued by its possibilities, but they were also leery of Spain, which remained the dominant force in America and the dominant naval power in Europe. In 1588, however, King Philip II of Spain sent one of the largest military fleets in the history of warfare—the Spanish Armada—across the English Channel to attack England itself. The invasion failed. The smaller English fleet, taking advantage of its greater maneuverability, dispersed the Armada and, in a single stroke, ended Spain's domination of the Atlantic. The most important inhibition the English had retained about establishing themselves in the New World was now removed.

The pioneers of English colonization were Sir Humphrey Gilbert and his half-brother Sir Walter Raleigh—both friends of Queen Elizabeth, and both veterans of earlier colonial efforts in Ireland. In 1578 Gilbert obtained from Elizabeth a six-year patent granting him the exclusive right "to inhabit and possess any remote and heathen lands not already in the possession of any Christian prince." Five years later, after several setbacks, he led an expedition to Newfoundland and proceeded south looking for a good place to build a profitable colony. But a storm sank his ship, and he was lost at sea.

ROANOKE A drawing by one of the English colonists in the ill-fated Roanoke expedition of 1585 became the basis for this engraving by Theodore DeBry, published in England in 1590. A small European ship carrying settlers approaches the island of Roanoke, at left. The wreckage of several larger vessels farther out to sea and the presence of Indian settlements on the mainland and on Roanoke itself suggest some of the perils the settlers encountered.

Sir Walter Raleigh was undeterred. The next year, he secured his own six-year grant from the queen and sent a small group of men on an expedition to explore the North American coast. When they returned, Raleigh named the region they had explored Virginia, in honor of Elizabeth, who was unmarried and was known as the "Virgin Queen."

In 1585 Raleigh recruited his cousin, Sir Richard Grenville, to lead a group of men to the island of Roanoke, off the coast of what is now North Carolina, to establish a colony. Grenville deposited the settlers on the island, antagonized the natives by destroying an Indian village as retaliation for a minor theft, and returned to England. The following spring, with expected supplies and reinforcements from England long overdue, Sir Francis Drake unexpectedly arrived in Roanoke. The colonists boarded his ships and left.

Raleigh tried again in 1587, sending an expedition to Roanoke carrying ninety-one men, seventeen women (two of them pregnant), and nine children. The settlers attempted to take up where the first group of colonists had left off. (Shortly after arriving, one of the women—the daughter of the commander of the expedition, John White—gave birth to a daughter, Virginia Dare, the first American-born child of English parents.) White returned to England after several weeks, leaving his daughter and granddaughter behind, in search of supplies and additional settlers. Because of a war with Spain, he was unable to return to Roanoke for three years. When he did, in 1590, he found the island utterly deserted, with no clue to the fate of the settlers other than the cryptic inscription "Croatoan" carved on a post. No solution to the mystery of the "Lost Colony" has ever been found.

The Roanoke disaster marked the end of Sir Walter Raleigh's involvement in English colonization of the New World, and no later colonizer would receive grants of land in the New World as vast or undefined as those Raleigh and Gilbert had acquired. But despite the discouraging example of these first experiences, the colonizing impulse remained very much alive. In the early years of the seventeenth century, a group of London merchants to whom Raleigh had assigned his charter rights decided to renew the attempt at colonization in Virginia. A rival group of merchants, from the area around Plymouth, was also interested in American ventures and was sponsoring voyages of exploration farther north. In 1606 James I issued a new charter, which divided America between the two groups. The London group got the exclusive right to colonize in the south, and the Plymouth merchants received the same right in the north. Through the efforts of these and other companies, the first enduring English colonies would be established in America.

The English "Transplantations"

HE ROANOKE FIASCO dampened enthusiasm for colonization in England for a time. But the lures of the New World—the presumably vast riches, the abundant land, the promise of religious freedom, the chance to begin anew—were too strong to be suppressed for very long. By the early seventeenth century, the effort to establish permanent English colonies in the New World resumed.

The new efforts were much like the earlier, failed ones: private ventures, with little planning or direction from the English government; small, fragile enterprises led by people unprepared for the hardships they were to face. Unlike the Roanoke experiment, they survived, but not before experiencing a series of disastrous setbacks.

Three conditions in particular shaped the character of these English settlements. First, the colonies were business enterprises, and one of their principal concerns was to produce a profit for their corporate sponsors. Second, the English colonies, unlike the Spanish, were designed to be "transplantations" of societies from the Old World to the New. As in Ireland, there were few efforts to blend English society with the society of the natives. And third, because the colonies were tied only indirectly to the crown, they began from the start to develop their own political and social institutions.

THE EARLY CHESAPEAKE

Once James I had issued his 1606 charters to the London and Plymouth Companies, the Plymouth group floundered and largely abandoned its efforts at settling the northern regions of British America. But the London

Company moved quickly and decisively to launch a colonizing expedition headed for Virginia—a party of 144 men aboard three ships, the *Godspeed,* the *Discovery,* and the *Susan Constant,* which set sail for America early in 1607.

The Founding of Jamestown

Only 104 men survived the journey. They reached the American coast in the spring of 1607, sailed into Chesapeake Bay and up a river they named the James, and established their colony on a peninsula. They called it Jamestown.

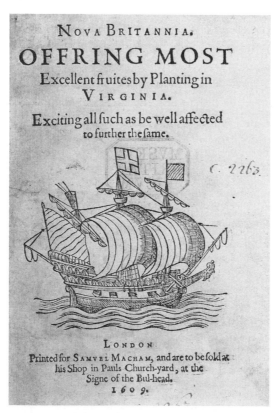

RECRUITING FOR THE COLONIES, 1609 This is the title page for a pamphlet that describes the attractions of settlement in the New World. Most accounts of the "excellent fruites" of life in Virginia were, like this one, written by people who had never seen America but who shared the excitement that the colonies inspired among the early-seventeenth-century English.

They chose an inland setting that they believed would offer them security from the natives. But they chose poorly. The site was low and swampy and subject to outbreaks of malaria. It was surrounded by thick woods, which were difficult to clear for cultivation. And it bordered the territories of powerful local Indians. The result could hardly have been more disastrous. For seventeen years, one wave of settlers after another attempted to make Jamestown a habitable and profitable colony. Every effort failed. The town became instead a place of misery and death, and the London Company found itself saddled with endless losses. All that could be said of Jamestown at the end of this first period of its existence was that it had survived.

The initial colonists ran into serious difficulties from the moment they landed. They had no prior exposure to the infections of the new land and were highly vulnerable to local diseases, particularly malaria. The promoters in London demanded a quick return on their investment and diverted the colonists' energies into futile searches for gold and only slightly more successful efforts to pile up lumber, tar, pitch, and iron for export. These energies would have been better spent on growing food. The promoters also had little interest in creating a family-centered community, and they sent virtually no women to Jamestown. Hence settlers could not establish real households and had difficulty feeling any sense of a permanent stake in the community.

By January 1608, when ships appeared with additional men and supplies, all but 38 of the first 104 colonists were dead. Jamestown, now facing extinction, survived largely as a result of the efforts of Captain John Smith, who at age twenty-seven was already a famous world traveler. Leadership in the colony had been bitterly divided until the fall of 1608, when Smith took control. He imposed work and order on the community. He also organized raids on neighboring Indian villages to steal food and kidnap natives. During the colony's second winter, fewer than a dozen (in a population of about 200) died. By the summer of 1609, when Smith returned to England, the colony was showing promise of survival. But Jamestown's ordeal was not over yet.

Reorganization and Expansion

As Jamestown struggled to survive, the London Company (now renamed the Virginia Company) was already dreaming of bigger things. In 1609, it obtained a new charter from the king, which increased its power and enlarged its territory. It raised money by selling additional stock. It offered stock in the company to planters who were willing to migrate at their own expense. And it provided free passage to Virginia for poorer people who would agree to serve the company for seven years. In the spring of 1609, confident that it was now poised to transform Jamestown into a successful venture, the company dispatched a fleet of nine vessels with about 600 people (including some women and children) to Virginia.

Disaster followed. One of the Virginia-bound ships was lost at sea in a hurricane. Another ran aground off Bermuda and was unable to free itself for months. Many of those who reached Jamestown, still weak from their long and stormy voyage, succumbed to fevers before winter came. The winter of 1609–1610 became known as the "starving time," a period worse than anything before. The local Indians, antagonized by the hostile actions of the early English settlers, killed off the livestock in the woods and kept the colonists barricaded within their palisade. The Europeans lived on what they could find: "dogs, cats, rats, snakes, toadstools, horsehides," and even the "corpses of dead men," as one survivor recalled. When the migrants who had run aground on Bermuda finally arrived in Jamestown the following May, they found about 60 emaciated people (out of 500 residents the previous summer) still alive. The new arrivals took the survivors onto their ship, abandoned the settlement, and set sail downriver for home. But as the refugees proceeded down the James, they met an English ship coming up the river—part of a fleet bringing supplies and the colony's first governor, Lord De La Warr. The departing settlers agreed to return to Jamestown. New relief expeditions with hundreds of colonists soon began to arrive, and the effort to turn a profit in Jamestown resumed.

Under the leadership of the first governors, Virginia survived and even expanded. New settlements began lining the river above and below Jamestown. That was partly because of the order and discipline the governors at times managed to impose and partly because of military assaults by the English on local Indian tribes to protect the new settlements. But it was also because the colonists had at last discovered a marketable crop—tobacco.

Europeans had become aware of tobacco soon after Columbus first returned from the West Indies, where he had seen the Cuban natives smoking small cigars (*tabacos*), which they inserted in the nostril. By the early seventeenth century, tobacco from the Spanish colonies was already in wide use in Europe. Then, in 1612, the Jamestown planter John Rolfe, noting that local Indians were growing a strain of tobacco, began trying to cultivate the crop in Virginia with seeds obtained from the Spanish colonies. Tobacco planting quickly spread up and down the James.

Almost immediately, tobacco cultivation created great pressure for territorial expansion. Tobacco growers needed large tracts of land to grow

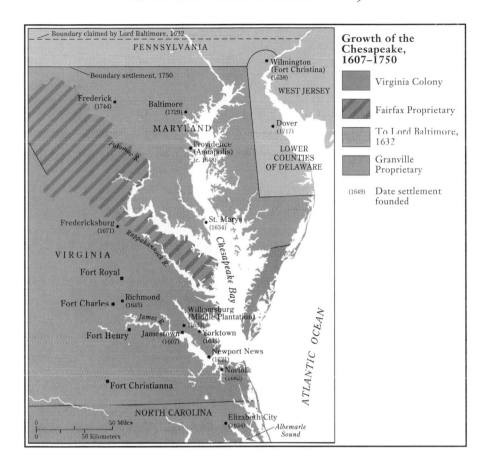

Growth of the Chesapeake, 1607–1750

Boundary claimed by Lord Baltimore, 1632

PENNSYLVANIA

Boundary settlement, 1750

Frederick (1744)

Baltimore (1729)

MARYLAND

Potomac R.

Providence (Annapolis) (c. 1648)

Wilmington (Fort Christina) (1638)

WEST JERSEY

Dover (1717)

LOWER COUNTIES OF DELAWARE

Fredericksburg (1671)

Rappahannock R.

St. Marys (1634)

Chesapeake Bay

VIRGINIA

Fort Royal

Fort Charles

Richmond (1645)

James R.

Williamsburg (Middle Plantation) (1633)

Fort Henry

Jamestown (1607)

Yorktown (1631)

Newport News (1621)

Norfolk (1682)

Fort Christianna

NORTH CAROLINA

Elizabeth City (1634)

Albemarle Sound

ATLANTIC OCEAN

0   50 Miles
0   50 Kilometers

Virginia Colony

Fairfax Proprietary

To Lord Baltimore, 1632

Granville Proprietary

(1649)   Date settlement founded

profitable crops; and because tobacco exhausted the soil very quickly, the demand for land increased even more. As a result, English farmers began establishing plantations deeper and deeper in the interior, isolating themselves from the center of European settlement at Jamestown and penetrating farther into the territory of the native tribes.

The tobacco economy also created a heavy demand for labor. To entice new workers to the colony, the Virginia Company established what it called the "headright" system. Headrights were fifty-acre grants of land. Those who already lived in the colony received two headrights (100 acres) apiece. Each new settler received a single headright for himself or herself. This system encouraged family groups to migrate together, since the more family members traveled to America, the more land the family would receive. In addition, anyone who paid for the passage of immigrants to Virginia would receive an extra headright for each arrival, an encouragement to the prosperous to import new laborers. As a result, some colonists were able to assemble large plantations.

The company also transported ironworkers and other skilled craftsmen to Virginia to diversify the economy. In 1619, it sent 100 Englishwomen to the colony (which was still overwhelmingly male) to become the wives of male colonists. It promised the male colonists the full rights of Englishmen (as provided in the original charter of 1606), an end to strict and arbitrary rule, and even a share in self-government. On July 30, 1619, delegates from the various communities met as the House of Burgesses. It was the first meeting of an elected legislature within what was to become the United States.

A month later, Virginia established another important precedent. As John Rolfe recorded, "about the latter end of August" a Dutch ship brought in "20 and odd Negroes." There is some reason to believe that the colonists did not consider these first Africans in Virginia slaves, that they thought of them rather as servants to be held for a term of years and then freed, like the white servants with whom the planters were already familiar. For a time, moreover, the use of black labor remained limited. Although Africans continued to trickle steadily into the colony, planters continued to prefer European indentured servants until at least the 1670s, when white servants began to become scarce and expensive. But the small group of blacks who arrived in 1619 marked the first step toward the enslavement of Africans within what was to be the American republic.

The European settlers in Virginia built their society not only on the coerced labor of imported Africans but also on the effective suppression of the local Indians. For two years, Sir Thomas Dale led unrelenting assaults against the Powhatan Indians and in the process kidnapped the great chief Powhatan's daughter Pocahontas. When Powhatan refused to ransom her, she converted to Christianity and in 1614 married John Rolfe. At that point, Powhatan ceased his attacks on the English in the face of overwhelming odds. But after his death several years later, his brother, Opechancanough, revived the effort to defend tribal lands and began secretly to plan the elimination of the English intruders. On a March morning in 1622, tribesmen called on the white settlements as if to offer goods for sale, and then suddenly attacked. Not until 347 whites of both sexes and all ages (including John Rolfe) lay dead were the Indian warriors finally forced to retreat. And not until over twenty years later were the Powhatans finally defeated.

By then, however, the Virginia Company in London was defunct. The company had poured virtually all its funds into its profitless Jamestown venture and in the aftermath of the 1622 Indian uprising faced imminent bankruptcy. In 1624, James I revoked the company's charter, and the colony at last came under the control of the crown. So it would remain until 1776.

With the stabilization of Virginia's English sponsorship, the suppression of the Indian threat, and the development of a profitable cash crop, the colony finally seemed secure. But this success had come at a terrible cost. In Virginia's first seventeen years, more than 8,500 white settlers had arrived in the colony. In 1624, the white population stood at 1,300. More than 80 percent had abandoned the colony or died.

Maryland and the Calverts

The Maryland colony ultimately came to look much like Virginia, but its origins were very different from those of its southern neighbor. George Calvert, the first Lord Baltimore, was a recent convert to Catholicism and a shrewd businessman, and he envisioned establishing a colony in America both as a great speculative venture in real estate and as a retreat for English Catholics oppressed by the Anglican establishment at home. Calvert died while still negotiating with the king for a charter to establish a colony in the Chesapeake region. But in 1632 his son Cecilius, the second Lord Baltimore, finally received the charter.

The Maryland charter was remarkable not only for the extent of the territory it granted to Calvert—an area that encompassed parts of what is now Pennsylvania, Delaware, and Virginia, in addition to present-day Maryland—but for the powers it bestowed on him. He and his heirs were to hold their province as "true and absolute lords and proprietaries." Their only obligation to the king was paying an annual fee to the crown.

Lord Baltimore named his brother, Leonard Calvert, as governor of the colony. In March 1634, two ships—the *Ark* and the *Dove*—bearing Calvert along with 200 or 300 other colonists, entered the Potomac River, turned into one of its eastern tributaries, and established the village of St. Mary's on a high, dry bluff. Neighboring Indians befriended the settlers and provided them with temporary shelter and with stocks of corn. The early Marylanders experienced no Indian assaults, no plagues, no starving time.

The Calverts needed to attract thousands of settlers to Maryland if their expensive colonial venture was to pay. As a result, they had to encourage the immigration of Protestants as well as their fellow English Catholics. The Calverts soon realized that Catholics would always be a minority in the colony, and so they adopted a policy of religious toleration, embodied in the 1649 "Act Concerning Religion," which assured freedom of worship to all Christians. Nevertheless, politics in Maryland remained plagued for years by tensions, and at times violence, between the Catholic minority and the Protestant majority.

The government in Maryland gradually came to resemble that of other English colonies in America in many ways. At the insistence of the first settlers, the Calverts agreed in 1635 to the calling of a representative assembly—the House of Delegates—whose proceedings were based on the rules of Parliament. But the proprietor retained absolute authority to distribute land as he wished; and since Lord Baltimore granted large estates to his relatives and to other English aristocrats, a distinct upper class soon established itself. By 1640, a severe labor shortage forced a modification of the land-grant procedure; and Maryland, like Virginia, adopted a headright system—a grant of 100 acres to each male settler, another 100 for his wife and each servant, and 50 for each of his children. But the great landlords of the colony's earliest years remained powerful even as the population grew larger and more diverse. Like Virginia, Maryland became a center of tobacco cultivation; and as in Virginia, planters worked their land with the aid, first, of indentured servants imported from England and then, beginning late in the seventeenth century, of slaves imported from Africa.

Turbulent Virginia

By the mid-seventeenth century, the Virginia colony had survived its early disasters. Its population was growing, and its economy was becoming more complex and profitable. Soon, factions began to emerge within the colony to compete for influence within the government, and particularly for influence over policies toward the natives.

For more than thirty years, one man—Sir William Berkeley, the royal governor of Virginia—dominated the politics of the colony. He took office in 1642 at the age of thirty-six and with but one interruption remained in control of the government until the 1670s. In his first years as governor, he helped open up the interior of Virginia by sending explorers across the Blue Ridge Mountains and crushing a 1644 Indian uprising. The defeated Indians agreed to a treaty ceding to England most of the territory east of the mountains and establishing a boundary west of which white settlement would be prohibited. But the rapid growth of the Virginia population made this agreement difficult to sustain. By 1650, Virginia's population of 16,000 was twice what it had been ten years before; by 1660, it had more than doubled again, to 40,000. By 1652, English settlers had established three counties in the territory set aside by the treaty for the Indians. Unsurprisingly, there were frequent clashes between natives and whites.

In the meantime, Berkeley was expanding his powers and making himself virtually an autocrat. By 1670, the vote for delegates to the House of Burgesses, once open to all white men, was restricted to landowners. Elections were rare, and the same burgesses, representing the established planters of the Eastern (or tidewater) region of the colony and subservient to the governor, remained in office year after year. The more recent settlers on the frontier were underrepresented in the assembly or not represented at all.

Resentment of the power of the governor and the tidewater aristocrats grew steadily in the newly settled lands of the west (often known as the "back country"). In 1676, this resentment helped create a major conflict, led by Nathaniel Bacon, a young, handsome aristocrat who had arrived in Virginia in 1673. Bacon had a good farm in the west and a seat on the governor's council. But like other members of the new back-country gentry, he was at odds in crucial ways with the governor and his tidewater allies, particularly over Indian policy. The frontier elite was in constant danger of attack from the tribes on whose lands they were encroaching, and they chafed at the governor's attempts to hold the line of settlement steady so as to avoid antagonizing the Indians. Bacon's rift with Berkeley was also a result of resentment that he was not part of the inner circle of the governor's council and that Berkeley refused to allow him a piece of the Indian fur trade, which the governor himself controlled.

Bloody events thrust Bacon into the role of leader of an anti-Berkeley faction. In 1675, a major conflict erupted in the west between whites and natives. As the fighting escalated, Bacon and other concerned landholders demanded that the governor send the militia. Berkeley, however, simply ordered the construction of several new forts along the western border. Bacon responded by offering to organize a volunteer army of back-country men who would do their own fighting. Berkeley, who saw Bacon as a potential rival and feared a needless slaughter of the natives, rejected the offer. Bacon ignored him and launched a series of vicious but unsuccessful pursuits of the Indian challengers.

When Berkeley heard of the unauthorized military effort, he dismissed Bacon from the governor's council and proclaimed him and his men to be rebels. Bacon now turned his army against the governor and, in what became known as Bacon's Rebellion, twice led his troops east to Jamestown. The first time he won a temporary pardon from the governor; the second time, after the governor reneged on the agreement, Bacon burned the city and drove the governor into exile. But then Bacon died suddenly of dysentery; and Berkeley, his position bolstered by the arrival of British troops, soon regained control. In 1677, the Indians (aware of their inability to defeat the white forces militarily) reluctantly signed a new treaty that opened new lands to white settlement.

Bacon's Rebellion was significant for several reasons. It was evidence of the continuing struggle to define the Indian and white spheres of influence in Virginia. It revealed the bitterness of the competition among rival elites and between easterners and westerners in particular. But it also demonstrated the potential for instability in the colony's large population of free, landless men. These men—most of them former indentured servants without property or prospects—had formed the bulk of Bacon's constituency during the rebellion. Their hatred of Indians drew them to Bacon, but they also harbored a deep animosity toward the landed gentry (of which Bacon himself was a part). One result was that landed elites in both eastern and western Virginia began to recognize a common interest in quelling social unrest from below. That was one of several reasons for their turning increasingly to the African slave trade to fulfill their need for labor. African slaves, unlike white indentured servants, did not need to be released after a fixed term and hence did not threaten to become an unstable, landless class.

THE GROWTH OF NEW ENGLAND

The northern regions of British North America were slower to attract settlers, in part because the Plymouth Company was never able to mount a successful colonizing expedition after receiving its charter in 1606. It did, however, sponsor exploration of the region. Captain John Smith, after his return from Jamestown, made an exploratory journey for the Plymouth merchants, wrote an enthusiastic pamphlet about the lands he had seen, and called them New England.

Plymouth Plantation

A discontented congregation of Puritan Separatists in England, not the Plymouth Company, established the first enduring European settlement in New England. In 1608, after years of persecution for attempting to practice their own religion, a congregation of Separatists from the hamlet of Scrooby began emigrating quietly (and illegally), a few at a time, to Leyden, Holland, where they could enjoy freedom of worship. But as foreigners in Holland, they could not join the Dutch guilds of craftsmen, and so they had to work at unskilled and poorly paid jobs. They also watched with alarm

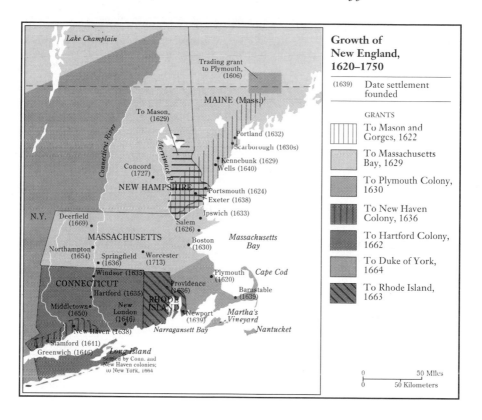

Growth of New England, 1620–1750

(1639) Date settlement founded

GRANTS

To Mason and Gorges, 1622

To Massachusetts Bay, 1629

To Plymouth Colony, 1630

To New Haven Colony, 1636

To Hartford Colony, 1662

To Duke of York, 1664

To Rhode Island, 1663

as their children began to speak Dutch, marry into Dutch families, and drift away from their church. Finally some of the Separatists decided to move again, across the Atlantic, where they hoped to create a stable, protected community and where they could spread "the gospel of the Kingdom of Christ in those remote parts of the world."

In 1620, leaders of the Scrooby group obtained permission from the Virginia Company to settle in Virginia and received informal assurances from the king that he would "not molest them, provided they carried themselves peaceably." Several English merchants advanced the necessary funds for the venture on the condition that the merchants share in the profits at the end of seven years. The "Pilgrims," as they saw themselves, sailed from Plymouth, England, in September 1620 aboard the *Mayflower*, with thirty-five "saints" (Puritan Separatists) and sixty-seven "strangers" (people who were not part of the congregation) aboard. In November, after a long and difficult voyage, they sighted land—the shore of what is now Cape Cod. That had not been their destination, but it was too late in the year to sail farther. So the Pilgrims chose a site for their settlement in the area just north of the cape, a place John Smith had labeled "Plymouth" on a map he had drawn during an earlier exploration of New England. Because Plymouth lay outside the London Company's territory, the settlers were not bound by the company's rules. So while still aboard ship, the "saints" in the group drew up an agreement, the Mayflower Compact, which established a civil government. Then, on December 21, 1620, they stepped ashore at Plymouth Rock.

The Pilgrims' first winter was a difficult one. Half the colonists perished from malnutrition, disease, and exposure. But the colony survived, in large part because of crucial assistance from local Indians, who showed them how to gather seafood and cultivate corn. After the first autumn harvest, the settlers invited the natives to join them in a festival, the original Thanksgiving. The Pilgrims could not create rich farms on the sandy and marshy soil around Plymouth, but they developed a profitable trade in fish and furs. New colonists arrived from England, and in a decade the population reached the modest total of 300.

The people of Plymouth Plantation chose as their governor the remarkable William Bradford, who in 1621 won them title to their land from the Council for New England (the successor to the old Plymouth Company, which had charter rights to the territory). He never succeeded in his efforts to obtain a royal charter giving the Pilgrims clear rights of self-government, but Bradford governed successfully for many years without any real interference from London.

The Pilgrims were always a poor community. As late as the 1640s, they had only one plow among them. But they were, on the whole, content to be left alone to live their lives in what they considered godly ways. At times, they spoke of serving as a model for other Christians. But the Pilgrims were less concerned about how they were viewed by others than were the Puritans who settled the larger and more ambitious English colonies to their north.

The Massachusetts Bay Experiment

Turbulent events in England in the 1620s generated a strong interest in colonization among other groups of Puritans. James I had been creating tensions for years by his effort to assert the divine right of kings and by his harsh, repressive policies toward Puritans. The situation grew worse when he was succeeded in 1625 by his son, Charles I, who was even more aggressively autocratic than his father. The new king tried to restore Roman Catholicism to England and to destroy religious nonconformity. The Puritans were particular targets of Charles's policies; many of them were impris-

A M E R I C A N   V O I C E S

WILLIAM BRADFORD

Safe Arrival of the Pilgrims at Cape Cod

BEING THUS ARRIVED in a good harbor, and brought safe to land, they fell upon their knees and blessed the God of Heaven who had brought them over the vast and furious ocean, and delivered them from all the perils and miseries thereof, again to set their feet on the firm and stable earth, their proper element. . . .

But here I cannot but stay and make a pause, and stand half amazed at this poor people's present condition; . . . they had now no friends to welcome them nor inns to entertain or refresh their weatherbeaten bodies; no houses or much less towns to repair to, to seek for succour. It is recorded in Scripture as a mercy to the Apostle and his shipwrecked company, that the barbarians showed them no small kindness in refreshing them, but these savage barbarians, when they met with them . . . were readier to fill their sides full of arrows than otherwise. . . . Besides, what could they see but a hideous and desolate wilderness, full of wild beasts and wild men—and what multitudes there might be of them they knew not. . . . Which way soever they turned their eyes (save upward to the heavens) they could have little solace or content in respect of any outward objects. For summer being done, all things stand upon them with a weatherbeaten face, and the whole country, full of woods and thickets, represented a wild and savage hue.

SOURCE: William Bradford, *Of Plymouth Plantation: 1620–1647*, ed. Samuel Eliot Morison, pp. 61–62. Copyright 1952 Samuel Eliot Morison. Reprinted by permission of Alfred A. Knopf, Inc.

oned for their beliefs. The king dissolved Parliament in 1629 (it was not to be recalled until 1640), ensuring that there would be no political redress.

In the midst of this turmoil, a group of Puritan merchants began organizing a new enterprise to take advantage of opportunities in America. At first, their interest was largely an economic one. They obtained a grant of land in New England for most of the area now comprising Massachusetts and New Hampshire; and they acquired a charter from the king (who was evidently unaware of their religious inclinations) allowing them to create the Massachusetts Bay Company and to establish a colony in the New World. In 1629, they were ready to dispatch a substantial group of settlers to New England.

Some members of the Massachusetts Bay Company, however, saw the enterprise as something more than a business venture. They decided to emigrate themselves and try to create in New England a refuge for Puritans. After buying out the interests of the company members who preferred to stay in England, the new owners elected a governor, John Winthrop, who commanded the expedition that sailed for New England in 1630: seventeen ships and 1,000 people, mostly family groups. It was the largest single migration of its kind in the seventeenth century. Winthrop carried with him the charter of the Massachusetts Bay Company, which meant that the colonists would be responsible to no company officials in England.

The Massachusetts migration quickly produced several settlements. The port of Boston, at the mouth of the Charles River, became the capital, but in the course of the next decade colonists established several other towns in eastern Massachusetts: Charlestown, Newtown (later renamed Cambridge), Roxbury, Dorchester, Watertown, Ipswich, Concord, Sudbury, and others. The Massachusetts Bay Company soon transformed itself into the Massachusetts colonial government. According to the terms of the original company charter, the "freemen" (the eight stockholders) formed the governing body (or "general court") of the colony. But the colonists redefined "freemen" to include all male citizens. John Winthrop continued to dominate the politics of Massachusetts Bay, but after 1634 he and most other officers of the colony had to face election each year.

Unlike the Separatist founders of Plymouth, the Puritan founders of Massachusetts had come to America with no intention of breaking away from the Church of England. Yet if they continued to feel any real attachment to the Anglican establishment, they gave little sign of it in their behavior. In every town, the community church had (in the words of the prominent minister John Cotton) "complete liberty to stand alone," without connection to Anglican hierarchy or ritual. Each congregation chose its own minister and regulated its own affairs. The result was what became the Congregational church, a church controlled by its own congregation.

The Massachusetts Puritans were not grim or joyless, as many critics would later come to believe, but they were serious and pious. They strove to lead useful, conscientious lives of thrift and hard work, and they honored material success as evidence of God's favor. Winthrop and the other founders of Massachusetts believed they were founding a holy commonwealth, a model—a "city upon a hill"—for the corrupt world to see and emulate. But if Massachusetts was to become a beacon to others, it had first to maintain its own purity and "holiness." And to that end, the ministers and the officers of the government worked closely together. Massachusetts dissidents had no more freedom of worship than the Puritans themselves had had in England.

Like other new settlements, the Massachusetts Bay colony had early difficulties. During the first winter (1629–1630), nearly 200 died and many others decided to leave. But more rapidly than Jamestown, the colony grew and prospered. The nearby Pilgrims and neighboring Indians helped with food and advice. Incoming settlers, many of them affluent, brought needed tools and other goods. The dominance of families in the colony (a sharp contrast to the early years at Jamestown) helped ensure a feeling of commitment to the community and a sense of order among the settlers, and it also ensured that the population would reproduce itself.

Spreading Settlement

It did not take long for English settlement to begin moving outward from Massachusetts Bay to other parts of New England and beyond. Some people migrated in search of more productive soil than the stony land around Boston provided. Others left because of the oppressiveness of the church-dominated government of Massachusetts. Tolerance for those who were not practicing Puritans was limited, and most had little choice but to conform or leave.

The Connecticut River valley, about 100 miles west of Boston, began attracting English families as early as the 1630s, despite the presence of powerful native tribes and despite claims to those lands by the Dutch. The Connecticut settlers were attracted by the valley's fertile lands and by its isolation from the religious character of Massachusetts Bay. In 1635, Thomas Hooker, a minister of Newtown (Cambridge), defied the Massachusetts government, led his congregation west, and established the town of Hartford. Four years later, the people of Hartford and of two other newly founded towns nearby established a colonial government of their own and adopted a constitution known as the Fundamental Orders of Connecticut. This created a government similar to that of Massachusetts Bay but gave a larger proportion of the men the right to vote and hold office. (Women were barred from voting virtually everywhere.) Another Connecticut colony grew up around New Haven on the Connecticut coast. Unlike Hartford, it reflected unhappiness with what its founders considered the increasing religious laxity in Boston. The Fundamental Articles of New Haven (1639) established a Bible-based government even stricter than that of Massachusetts Bay. New Haven remained independent until 1662, when a royal charter officially gave the Hartford colony jurisdiction over the New Haven settlements.

European settlement in what is now Rhode Island was a result of the religious and political dissent of Roger Williams, an engaging but controversial young minister who lived for a time in Salem, Massachusetts. Williams was a confirmed Separatist who argued that the Massachusetts church should abandon even its nominal allegiance to the Church of England. He was also friendly with the neighboring Indians and proclaimed that the land the colonists were occupying belonged to the natives and not to the king or to the Massachusetts Bay Company. The colonial government considered Williams dangerous and voted to deport him, but he escaped before they could do so. During the bitter winter of 1635–1636, he took refuge with Narragansett tribesmen; and the following spring he bought a tract of land from them, and with a few followers, created the town of Providence on it. Williams considered himself the proprietor of the region and he called for complete freedom of worship. In 1644, after obtaining a charter from Parliament, he established a government for Providence and the surrounding settlements—a government that was based on the Massachusetts pattern but that did not restrict the vote to church members or tax the people for church support. For a time, Rhode Island was the only colony in which all faiths (including Judaism) could worship without interference.

Another challenge to the established religious order in Massachusetts Bay came from Anne Hutchinson, an intelligent and charismatic woman from a substantial Boston family. Hutchinson argued that the faithful could communicate directly with God (as she claimed she herself had done) and gain from Him assurance of grace and salvation. Such teachings (known as the Antinomian heresy) were a serious threat to the spiritual authority of the established clergy. The belief that an individual could receive a revelation directly from God carried with it an implication that ministers were not essential to the task of discovering one's chance of salvation. Hutchinson also affronted prevailing assumptions about the proper role of women in

Puritan society. She was not a retiring, deferential wife and mother, but a powerful religious figure in her own right.

As Hutchinson's influence grew, and as she began to deliver open attacks on members of the clergy, the Massachusetts hierarchy mobilized to stop her. In 1638, she was convicted of heresy and sedition and banished. With her family and some of her followers, she moved to a point on Narragansett Bay not far from Providence. Later she moved south into New York, where in 1643 she and her family died during an Indian uprising.

METACOMET, OR KING PHILIP This eighteenth-century engraving by Paul Revere shows the Indian chieftain Metacomet, known to the English as King Philip of Mount Hope (the site of his tribe's principal stronghold). Metacomet, son of Massasoit, became chief of the Wampanoags in 1662 and inherited his tribe's resentment at having been forced from their lands along Narragansett Bay by European settlers.

The Hutchinson affair had an important impact on the settlement of the areas north of Massachusetts Bay. New Hampshire and Maine were established in 1629 by two English proprietors. But despite lavish promotional efforts, few settlers moved into these northern regions until the religious disruptions in Massachusetts Bay. In 1639, John Wheelwright, a disciple of Anne Hutchinson, led some of his fellow dissenters to Exeter, New Hampshire. Other groups—of both dissenting and orthodox Puritans—soon followed. The Massachusetts Bay Company tried to extend its authority over this entire northern territory, with partial success. New Hampshire became a separate colony in 1679, but Maine remained a part of Massachusetts until 1820.

Settlers and Natives

The first white settlers in New England generally maintained amicable relations with the natives and learned much from them. Indians taught whites how to grow vital food crops such as corn, beans, pumpkins, and potatoes; they also taught them crucial agricultural techniques, such as annual burning for fertilization and planting beans to replenish exhausted soil. European farmers also benefited from the extensive lands Indians had already cleared (and either abandoned or sold). White traders used Indians as partners in some of their most important trading activities (and particularly in the creation of the thriving North American fur trade). Indeed, commerce with the Indians was responsible for the creation of some of the first great fortunes in British North America. Other white settlers attempted to educate the Indians in European religion and culture. Protestant missionaries converted some natives to Christianity, and a few Indians became at least partially assimilated into white society.

But as in other areas of white settlement, tensions soon developed in New England between Europeans and natives—primarily as a result of the white colonists' insatiable appetite for land and their steady encroachments into Indian territory. The particular character of those conflicts—and the brutality with which whites assaulted their Indian foes—emerged as well out of Puritan attitudes toward the natives. The religious leaders of New England came to consider the tribes a threat to their hopes of creating a godly community in the New World, particularly once dissenters such as Roger Williams began forming close relationships with the tribes. Gradually, the image of Indians as helpful neighbors came to be replaced by the image of Indians as "heathens" and barbarians.

In 1637, hostilities broke out between English settlers in the Connecticut Valley and the Pequot Indians of the region, a conflict (known as the Pequot War) that ended disastrously for the natives. The Pequot tribe was almost wiped out. But the bloodiest and most prolonged encounter between whites and Indians in the seventeenth century began in 1675, a conflict that whites called King Philip's War. As in the Pequot War, an Indian tribe—the Wampanoags, under the leadership of a chieftain known to the white settlers as King Philip and among his own people as Metacomet—rose up to resist English encroachment on its lands and the efforts of the colonial government to impose English law on the natives. (A court in Plymouth had recently tried and hanged several Wampanoags for murdering a member of their own tribe.)

For three years, the natives inflicted terror on a string of Massachusetts towns, killing over a thousand people (including at least one-sixteenth of the white males in the colony). But the white settlers gradually prevailed, beginning in 1676. Massachusetts leaders recruited guides and spies from rival tribes, including a group of Mohawks who ambushed Metacomet, shot and killed him, and then bore his severed head to Boston to present to the colonial leaders. Without Metacomet, the fragile alliance among the tribes collapsed, and the white settlers were soon able to crush the uprising.

Yet these victories by the white colonists did not end the danger to their settlements. This was in part because other Indians in other tribes were still capable of launching wars. It was also because the New England settlers faced competition not only from the natives but also from the Dutch and the French, who claimed the territory on which some of the outlying settlements were established. The French, in particular, would pose a constant threat to the English through their alliance with the Algonquins. In later years, they would support hostile Indians in their attacks on the New England frontier.

THE RESTORATION COLONIES

By the end of the 1630s, then, English settlers had established the beginnings of what would eventually become six of the thirteen original states of the American republic: Virginia, Massachusetts, Maryland, Connecticut, Rhode Island, and New Hampshire. But for nearly thirty years after Lord Baltimore received the charter for Maryland in 1632, no new English colonies were established in America. England was preoccupied with troubles of its own at home.

The English Civil War

The unpopular James I had attracted widespread opposition in England before he died in 1625, but he never came into open conflict with Parliament. His son, Charles I, was not so fortunate. After he dissolved Parliament in 1629 and began ruling as an absolute monarch, he steadily alienated a growing number of his subjects—and the members of the powerful Puritan community above all. Finally, desperately in need of money, Charles called Parliament back into session in 1640 and asked it to levy new taxes. But he antagonized the members by dismissing them twice in two years; and in 1642, they organized a military force, thus beginning the English Civil War.

The conflict between the Cavaliers (the supporters of the king) and the Roundheads (the forces of Parliament, who were largely Puritans) lasted seven years. In 1649, the Roundheads defeated the king's forces, captured Charles himself, and beheaded the monarch. The stern Roundhead leader Oliver Cromwell replaced the king and assumed the position of "protector." But when Cromwell died in 1658, his son and heir proved unable to maintain his authority, and two years later, King Charles II, son of the beheaded monarch, returned from exile and seized the throne, thus completing what became known as the Stuart Restoration.

Among the results of the Restoration was the resumption of colonization in America. Charles II rewarded faithful courtiers with grants of land in the New World and in the twenty-five years of his reign issued charters for four additional colonies: Carolina, New York, New Jersey, and Pennsylvania. The new colonies were all proprietary ventures (modeled on Maryland rather than on Virginia and Massachusetts), in large part because private companies were no longer taking an interest in launching colonies, having finally realized that there were no quick profits to be had in the New World. The new colonies had different aims: not so much quick commercial success as permanent settlements that would provide proprietors with land and power.

The Carolinas

Carolina (a name derived from the Latin word for "Charles") was, like Maryland, carved in part from the original Virginia grant. In successive charters issued in 1663 and 1665, Charles II awarded eight proprietors joint title to a vast territory stretching south to the Florida peninsula and west to the Pacific Ocean. Like Lord Baltimore, they received almost kingly powers over their grant. They reserved tremendous estates for themselves and distributed the rest through a headright system similar to those in Virginia and Maryland, after which they collected annual payments from the settlers. Although committed Anglicans themselves, they welcomed settlers of all Christian faiths and guaranteed them religious freedom in the colonial charter. The proprietors also allowed a measure of political freedom, creating a representative assembly to make laws. They hoped to attract settlers from the existing American colonies and to avoid the expense of financing expeditions from England.

But their initial efforts to profit from settlement in Carolina failed dismally. A few early colonizing ventures were quickly abandoned, and most of the original proprietors soon concluded that the Carolina venture could not succeed. One man, however, persisted—Anthony Ashley Cooper. Cooper convinced the other proprietors to give up on attracting settlers from other colonies and to finance expeditions to Carolina from England, the first of which set sail with 300 people in the spring of 1670. Only 100 people survived the difficult voyage; those who did established a settlement at Port Royal on the Carolina coast. Ten years later they founded a city at the junction of the Ashley and Cooper rivers, which in 1690 became the colonial capital. They called it Charles Town (it was later renamed Charleston).

With the aid of the English philosopher John Locke, Cooper (now the Earl of Shaftesbury) drew up the Fundamental Constitution for Carolina in 1669 in an attempt to create a highly ordered society. It divided the colony into counties of equal size and divided each county into equal parcels. The largest number of parcels would be distributed among the proprietors themselves (who were to be known as "seigneurs"); a local aristocracy (consisting of lesser nobles known as "landgraves" or "caciques") would receive fewer parcels; and ordinary settlers ("leet-men") would receive less land still. At the bottom of this stratified society would be poor whites, who had no political rights, and African slaves, whose subjection would be complete. Proprietors, nobles, and other landholders would have a voice in the colonial parliament in proportion to the size of their landholdings.

In fact, however, Carolina developed along lines quite different from the carefully ordered vision of Shaftesbury and Locke. For one thing, the colony was never really united in anything more than name. The northern and southern regions of settlement were widely separated and socially and economically distinct from one another. The northern settlers were mainly backwoods farmers, scratching out a meager existence at subsistence agriculture. They developed no important aristocracy and for many years imported virtually no black slaves. In the south, fertile lands and the good harbor at Charles Town promoted a far more prosperous economy and a far more stratified, aristocratic society. Settlements grew up rapidly along the

Ashley and Cooper rivers, and colonists established a flourishing trade, particularly (beginning in the 1660s) in rice—which was to become the colony's principal commercial crop.

Southern Carolina very early developed close commercial ties to the large (and overpopulated) European colony on the Caribbean island of Barbados. During the first ten years of settlement, most of the new residents in Carolina were Barbadians, some of whom arrived with large groups of black workers and established themselves as substantial landlords. African slavery had taken root on Barbados earlier than in any of the mainland colonies; and the white Caribbean migrants—tough, uncompromising profit seekers—established a similar slave-based plantation society in Carolina.

For several decades, Carolina remained one of the most factious of all the English colonies in America. There were tensions between the small farmers of the Albemarle region in the north and the wealthy planters in the south. And there were conflicts between the rich Barbadians in southern Carolina and the smaller landowners around them. After Lord Shaftesbury's death, the proprietors proved unable to establish order. In 1719, the colonists seized control of the colony from them. Ten years later, the king divided the region into two royal colonies, North and South Carolina.

New Netherland and New York

In 1664, Charles II granted his brother James, the Duke of York, all the territory lying between the Connecticut and Delaware rivers. But the grant faced major challenges. The Massachusetts Bay Company claimed some of the territory, and, more importantly, the Dutch claimed the entire area and controlled settlements at New Amsterdam and other strategic points.

England and the Netherlands were already commercial rivals in Europe, and that rivalry now extended to America, where the Dutch served as a wedge between the northern and southern English colonies. In 1664, vessels of the English navy, under the command of Richard Nicolls, put in at New Amsterdam and extracted a surrender from the arbitrary and unpopular Dutch governor, Peter Stuyvesant. Several years later, in 1673, the Dutch reconquered and briefly held their old provincial capital. But they lost it again, this time for good, in 1674.

The Duke of York, now firmly in possession of his territory, renamed it New York and set out to govern the diverse region. New York contained not only Dutch and English but Scandinavians, Germans, French, a large number of Africans (imported as slaves by the Dutch West India Company), as well as members of several different Indian tribes. James wisely made no effort to impose his own Roman Catholicism on the colony. He delegated powers to a governor and a council but made no provision for representative assemblies.

Property holding and political power remained highly divided and highly unequal in New York. In addition to confirming the great Dutch "patroonships" already in existence, James granted large estates to some of his own political supporters in order to create a class of influential land-owners loyal to him. Power in the colony thus remained widely dispersed— among wealthy English landlords, Dutch patroons, fur traders, and the duke's political appointees. By 1685, when the Duke of York ascended the English throne as James II, New York contained about four times as many people (around 30,000) as when he had taken power over it twenty years before, and it was one of the most factious colonies in America.

Shortly after James received his charter, he gave a large part of the land south of New York to a pair of political allies, both Carolina proprietors, Sir John Berkeley and Sir George Carteret. Carteret named the territory New Jersey, after the island in the English Channel on which he had been born. But the venture in New Jersey generated few profits, and in 1674, Berkeley sold his half interest. The colony was divided into two jurisdictions, East and West Jersey, which squabbled with one another until 1702, when the two halves of the colony were again joined and became a single royal colony.

New Jersey, like New York (from which much of the population had come), was a colony of enormous ethnic and religious diversity, and the weak colonial government made few efforts to impose strict control over the fragmented society. But unlike New York, New Jersey developed no impor-tant class of large landowners; most of its residents remained small farmers. Nor did New Jersey (which, unlike New York, had no natural harbor) produce any single important city.

The Quaker Colonies

Pennsylvania was born out of the efforts of a dissenting English Protestant sect, the Society of Friends, to find a home for their own distinctive social order. The society began in the mid-seventeenth century under the leader-ship of George Fox, a Nottingham shoemaker, and Margaret Fell. Their followers came to be known as Quakers (from Fox's instruction to them to "tremble at the name of the Lord"). Unlike the Puritans, Quakers rejected the concept of predestination and original sin. All people, they believed, had divinity within themselves and need only learn to cultivate it; all could attain salvation. Also unlike the Puritans, Quakers granted women a position within the church generally equal to that of men.

The Quakers had no formal church government and no traditional church buildings, only meetinghouses. They had no paid clergy, and in their worship they spoke up one by one as the spirit moved them. Disregarding distinctions of gender and class, they addressed one another with the terms "thee" and "thou," words commonly used in other parts of English society only in speaking to servants and social inferiors. As confirmed pacifists, they would not take part in wars. Unpopular in England both with the government and with members of other religious orders (whose services Quakers occasionally disrupted), the Quakers began looking to America for asylum. A few migrated to New England or Carolina, but most Quakers wanted a colony of their own. As members of a despised sect, however, they could not get the necessary royal grant without the aid of someone influential at the court.

Fortunately for the Quaker cause, a number of wealthy and prominent men had converted to the faith. One of them was William Penn, whose father, Sir William Penn, was an admiral in the Royal Navy and a landlord of valuable Irish estates. Over his father's objections, the younger Penn converted to Quakerism, took up evangelism, and was sent repeatedly to prison. He soon began working with George Fox to create a Quaker colony in America.

Penn looked first to New Jersey, half of which (after 1674) belonged to two fellow Quakers. But in 1681, after the death of his father, he received from the king an even more valuable grant of lands. Penn had inherited his father's claim to a large debt from the king. Charles II paid the debt with an enormous grant of territory between New York and Maryland, which Penn was to control as both landlord and ruler. At the king's insistence, the territory was to be named Pennsylvania, after Penn's late father.

Through his informative and honest advertising, Penn soon made Pennsylvania the best-known and most cosmopolitan of all the English colonies in America, a place to which settlers flocked from England and the Continent. More than any other English colony, Pennsylvania prospered from the outset, because of Penn's successful recruiting, his thoughtful planning, and the region's mild climate and fertile soil. But the colony never became a great source of profit for Penn or his descendants. Indeed, Penn himself, near the end of his life, was imprisoned in England for debt and died in poverty in 1718.

But Penn was much more than a mere real-estate promoter, and he undertook in Pennsylvania what he called a "holy experiment." He personally sailed to Pennsylvania in 1682 to oversee the laying out, between the Delaware and the Schuylkill rivers, of the city he named Philadelphia ("Brotherly Love"), which with its rectangular streets helped set the pattern for most later cities in America. Penn recognized Indian claims to the land in the province, and he was scrupulous about reimbursing them for it. The Indians respected Penn, and during his lifetime the colony had no major battles with the natives.

But the colony was not without conflict. By the late 1690s, some residents of Pennsylvania were beginning to chafe at the nearly absolute power of the proprietor. Residents of the southern areas of the colony, in particular, complained that the government in Philadelphia was unresponsive to their needs. Pressure from these groups grew to the point that in 1701, shortly before he departed for England for the last time, Penn agreed to a Charter of Liberties for the colony. The charter established a representative assembly (consisting, alone among the English colonies, of only one house), which greatly limited the authority of the proprietor. The charter also permitted "the lower counties" of the colony to establish their own representative assembly. The three counties did so in 1703 and as a result became, in effect, a separate colony—Delaware—although until the Revolution it continued to have the same governor as Pennsylvania.

The Founding of Georgia

Not until 1733, decades after the founding of the Restoration colonies, did another new English settlement emerge in America: Georgia, the last English colony to be established in what would become the United States. Georgia was unlike any other colony. It was founded neither by a corporation nor by a wealthy proprietor. Its guiding purpose was neither the pursuit of profit nor the desire for a religious refuge. The founders of Georgia, led by General James Oglethorpe, were driven primarily by military and philanthropic motives. They wanted to erect a military barrier against the Spanish lands on the southern border of English America; and they wanted to provide a refuge for the impoverished, a place where English men and women without prospects at home could begin a new life.

The need for a military buffer between South Carolina and the Spanish settlements in Florida was growing urgent in the first years of the eighteenth century. There had been tensions between the Spanish and the English in

North America ever since the founding of Jamestown. And when hostilities broke out in Europe between Spain and England in 1701 (known in England as Queen Anne's War and on the Continent as the War of the Spanish Succession), fighting renewed in America as well. That war ended in 1713, but another European conflict with repercussions for the New World was continually expected.

Oglethorpe, a hero of Queen Anne's War, was very much aware of the military advantages of an English colony south of the Carolinas. Yet his interest in the settlement was primarily philanthropic. As head of a parliamentary committee investigating English prisons, he was moved by the plight of honest debtors rotting in confinement. Such prisoners, and other poor people in danger of succumbing to a similar fate, could, he believed, become the farmer-soldiers of the new colony in America.

A 1732 charter from King George II transferred the land between the Savannah and Altamaha rivers to Oglethorpe and his fellow trustees. Oglethorpe himself led the first colonial expedition to Georgia, which built a fortified town at the mouth of the Savannah River in 1733 and later constructed additional forts south of the Altamaha. The trustees organized the colony in part to make it militarily defensible. They limited the size of landholdings to make the settlement compact and easily defended against Spanish and Indian attacks. Blacks—free or slave—were excluded; rum was prohibited; Roman Catholics were excluded; and trade with the Indians was strictly regulated—all to limit the possibility of wartime insurrection or collusion with future enemies. In the end, only a few debtors were released from jail and sent to Georgia; but the trustees brought hundreds of needy tradesmen and artisans from England and Scotland and many religious refugees from Switzerland and Germany.

The strict rules governing life in the new colony helped stifle its development and create dissent in its early years. Settlers in Georgia needed a work force, and almost from the start they began demanding the right to buy slaves. Some opposed the restrictions on the size of individual property holdings. Many resented the nearly absolute political power of Oglethorpe and the trustees. As a result, newcomers to the region generally preferred to settle in South Carolina, where there were fewer restrictive laws. Eventually the trustees removed the limitation on individual landholding and later the ban on slavery and the prohibition of rum. In 1751, they returned control of the colony to the king, who immediately permitted the election of a representative assembly. Georgia continued to grow more slowly than the other southern colonies, but it now developed along lines roughly similar to those of South Carolina.

THE DEVELOPMENT OF EMPIRE

The English colonies in America had originated as quite separate projects, and for the most part they grew up independent of one another and subject to little more than nominal control from London. Yet by the mid-seventeenth century, the growing commercial success of the colonial ventures was producing pressure in England for a more rational, uniform structure to the empire.

The Drive for Reorganization

Reorganization, its advocates claimed, was necessary to ensure the success of the mercantile system, the foundation of the English economy. For the new possessions truly to promote mercantilist goals, England decided it would have to exclude foreigners (as Spain had done) from its colonial trade. But in that decision were the seeds of conflict, because many American colonists had developed a profitable trade with the Spanish, Dutch, and French and were likely to resist interference with it.

The English government began trying to regulate colonial trade in the 1650s, when Parliament passed laws to keep Dutch ships out of the English colonies. Later Parliament passed three important Navigation Acts. The first of them, in 1660, closed the colonies to all trade except that carried in by English ships and required that tobacco and other items be exported from the colonies only to England or to an English possession. The second act, in 1663, required that all goods sent from Europe to the colonies pass through England on the way, where they would be subject to English taxation. The third act, in 1673, imposed duties on the coastal trade among the English colonies, and it provided for the appointment of customs officials to enforce the Navigation Acts. These acts, with later amendments and additions, formed the legal basis of England's mercantile system in America for a century.

The Dominion of New England

Before the Navigation Acts, all the colonial governments (except that of Virginia, a "royal colony" with a governor appointed by the king) had operated largely independently of the crown, with governors chosen by the proprietors or by the colonists themselves and with powerful representative assemblies. Officials in London recognized that to increase their control over their colonies they would have to create an instrument separate from the independent-minded colonial governments, which were unlikely to enforce the new laws.

In 1675, the king created a new body, the Lords of Trade, to make recommendations for imperial reform. Following their advice, he moved in 1679 to increase his control over Massachusetts, the most defiant of the colonies. He stripped it of its authority over New Hampshire and chartered a separate, royal colony there whose governor he would himself appoint. He also began seeking legal grounds for revoking the colony's corporate charter and making Massachusetts itself a royal colony. He soon became convinced that he had found such grounds in the defiance of the Navigation Acts and the Lords of Trade by the Massachusetts General Court, which insisted that Parliament had no power to legislate for the colony. In 1684, the king finally succeeded in revoking the Massachusetts charter.

Charles II's brother, James II, who succeeded him to the throne in 1685, went further. He created a single Dominion of New England, which combined the government of Massachusetts with the governments of the rest of the New England colonies and later with those of New York and New Jersey as well. He eliminated the existing assemblies within the new Dominion and appointed a single governor, Sir Edmund Andros, to supervise the entire region from Boston. Andros's rigid enforcement of the Navigation Acts and his brusque dismissal of the colonists' claims to the "rights of Englishmen" made him quickly and thoroughly unpopular.

The "Glorious Revolution"

James II was not only losing friends in America; he was making powerful enemies in England by attempting to exercise autocratic control over Parliament and the courts and by appointing his fellow Catholics to high office. By 1688, his popular support had all but vanished, and Parliament invited his Protestant daughter Mary and her husband, William of Orange, ruler of the Netherlands, to assume the throne. James II (perhaps remembering what had happened to his father, Charles I) offered no resistance and fled to France. As a result of this bloodless coup, which the English called "the Glorious Revolution," William and Mary became joint sovereigns.

When Bostonians heard of the overthrow of James II, they moved quickly to unseat his unpopular viceroy in New England. Andros was arrested and imprisoned. The new sovereigns in England accepted the toppling of Andros, quickly abolished the Dominion of New England, and restored separate colonial governments. They did not, however, re-create them as they had been. In 1691, they combined Massachusetts with Plymouth and made it a royal colony. The new charter restored the General Court, but it gave the crown the right to appoint the governor. It also replaced church membership with property ownership as the basis for voting and officeholding.

Andros had been governing New York through a lieutenant governor, Captain Francis Nicholson, who enjoyed the support of the wealthy merchants and fur traders of the province. Other, less favored colonists—farmers, mechanics, small traders, and shopkeepers—had a long accumulation of grievances against Nicholson and his allies. The leadership of the New York dissidents fell to Jacob Leisler, a German immigrant and a prosperous merchant. He had married into a prominent Dutch family but had never won acceptance as one of the colony's ruling class. In May 1689, when news of the Glorious Revolution in England and the fall of Andros in Boston reached New York, Leisler raised a militia, captured the city fort, drove Nicholson into exile, and proclaimed himself the new head of government in New York. For two years, he tried in vain to stabilize his power in the colony amid fierce factional rivalry. In 1691, when William and Mary appointed a new governor, Leisler briefly resisted. He soon yielded, but his hesitation allowed his many political enemies to charge him with treason. He was convicted and executed. Fierce rivalry between what became known as the "Leislerians" and the "anti-Leislerians" dominated the politics of the factious colony for many years thereafter.

In Maryland, many people erroneously assumed when they heard news of the Glorious Revolution that their proprietor, the Catholic Lord Baltimore who was living in England, had sided with the Catholic James II and opposed William and Mary. So in 1689, an old opponent of the proprietor's government, the Protestant John Coode, led a revolt that drove out Lord Baltimore's officials and petitioned the crown for a charter as a royal colony. In 1691, William and Mary complied, stripping the proprietor of his authority. The colonial assembly established the Church of England as the colony's official religion and excluded Catholics from public office. Maryland became a proprietary colony again in 1715, but only after the fifth Lord Baltimore joined the Anglican church.

Thus the Glorious Revolution of 1688 in England touched off revolutions, mostly bloodless ones, in several colonies. Under the new king and queen, the representative assemblies that had been abolished were revived, and the scheme for colonial unification from above was abandoned. But the Glorious Revolution in America was not, as many Americans later came to believe, a clear demonstration of American resolve to govern itself or a clear victory for colonial self-rule. In New York and Maryland, in particular, the uprisings had more to do with local factional and religious divisions than with any larger vision of the nature of the empire. And while the insurgencies did succeed in eliminating the short-lived Dominion of New England, their ultimate results were governments that actually increased the crown's potential authority. As the first century of English settlement in America came to its end, the colonists were becoming more a part of the imperial system than ever before.

CHAPTER THREE

Life in Provincial America

The Colonial Population ~ The Colonial Economy
Patterns of Society ~ The Colonial Mind

A S THE EXTENT of settlement in North America grew, and as the economies of the colonies began to flourish, several distinctive ways of life emerged. The new American societies differed considerably from the society that most had attempted to re-create in the New World—the society of England. They differed as well from one another. Indeed, the pattern of society in some areas of North America seemed to resemble that of others scarcely at all. Americans would eventually decide that they had enough in common to enable them to join together and form a single nation. But regional differences would continue to shape their society throughout their history.

THE COLONIAL POPULATION

After uncertain beginnings at Jamestown and Plymouth, the non-Indian population of English North America grew rapidly and substantially, through continued immigration and through natural increase, until by the late seventeenth century European and African immigrants outnumbered the natives along the Atlantic coast.

A few of the early settlers were members of the English upper classes, but for the most part the early colonial population was decidedly unaristocratic. It included some members of the emerging English middle class, businessmen who migrated to America for religious or commercial reasons or both. But the dominant element was English laborers. Some came independently, such as the religious dissenters in early New England, who came as families, paid their own way, and settled on their own land. But in the Chesapeake, at least three-fourths of the immigrants in the seventeenth century arrived as indentured servants.

Indentured Servitude

The system of temporary servitude developed out of practices in England. Young men and women bound themselves to masters for fixed terms of servitude (usually four to five years) in exchange for passage to America, food, and shelter. Upon completion of their service, male indentures were supposed to receive clothing, tools, and occasionally land; in reality, however, many left service with nothing. Roughly one-fourth of the indentures in the Chesapeake were women, most of whom worked as domestic servants and could expect to marry when their terms of servitude expired, since men greatly outnumbered women in the region.

Most indentured servants came to the colonies voluntarily, but some did not. Beginning as early as 1617, the English government occasionally dumped shiploads of convicts in America to be sold into servitude. The government also transported prisoners taken in battles with the Scots and the Irish in the 1650s, as well as orphans, vagrants, and paupers. Other involuntary immigrants were victims of kidnapping, or "impressment," by unscrupulous investors and promoters.

By the late seventeenth century, the indentured servant population had become one of the largest elements of the population and was creating serious social problems. Some former indentures managed to establish themselves successfully as farmers, tradespeople, or artisans. Some women married propertied men. Others (mostly males) found themselves without land, without employment, without families, and without prospects; and there grew up in some areas, particularly the Chesapeake, a large floating population of young single men—such as those who supported Bacon's Rebellion—who served as a potential (and at times actual) source of social unrest. Even those free laborers who did find employment or land for themselves and settled down with families often did not stay put for very long. Many families simply pulled up stakes and moved to other, more promising locations every few years.

Beginning in the 1670s, a decrease in the birth rate and an improvement in economic conditions in England reduced the pressures on laboring men and women to emigrate, and the flow of indentured servants declined. Those who did travel to America as indentured servants generally avoided the Southern colonies, where working conditions were arduous and prospects for advancement were slim. In the Chesapeake, therefore, landowners were

A M E R I C A N   V O I C E S

GOTTLIEB MITTLEBERGER

An Indentured Servant's Voyage from Germany to America

 BOTH IN ROTTERDAM and in Amsterdam the people are packed densely, like herrings so to say, in the large sea-vessels. . . . During the voyage there is on board these ships terrible misery, stench, fumes, horror, vomiting, many kinds of sea-sickness, fever, dysentery, headache, heat, constipation, boils, scurvy, cancer, mouth-rot, and the like, all of which come from old and sharply salted food and meat, also from very bad and foul water, so that many die miserably. . . . Many sigh and cry, "Oh, that I were at home again, and if I had to lie in my pigsty!" . . . Many hundred people necessarily die and perish in such misery, and must be cast into the sea, which drives their relatives . . . to such despair that it is almost impossible to pacify and console them. . . .

When the ships have landed at Philadelphia after their long voyage, no one is permitted to leave them except those who pay for their passage or can give good security; the others, who cannot pay, must remain on board the ships till they are purchased, and are released from the ships by their purchasers. The sick always fare the worst, for the healthy are naturally preferred and purchased first; and so the sick and wretched must often remain on board in front of the city for 2 or 3 weeks, and frequently die. . . . Many parents must sell and trade away their children like so many head of cattle. . . . It often happens that such parents and children, after leaving the ship, do not see each other again for many years, perhaps no more in their lives.

beginning to rely much more heavily on African slavery as their principal source of labor.

Birth and Death

Although immigration remained for a time the greatest source of population increase, the most important long-range factor in the growth of the colonial population was its ability to reproduce itself. Marked improvement in the reproduction rate began in New England and the mid-Atlantic colonies in the second half of the seventeenth century, and after the 1650s natural increase became the most important source of population growth in those areas. The New England population more than quadrupled through reproduction alone in the second half of the seventeenth century. That was not just because families were having large numbers of children. It was also because life expectancy in New England was unusually high, both in comparison to that of other colonies and in comparison to that of England.

Conditions improved much more slowly in the South. The high mortality rates in the Chesapeake region did not begin to decline to the levels of those elsewhere until the mid-eighteenth century. Throughout the seventeenth century, the average life expectancy for men in the region was just over forty years, and for women slightly less. (In New England, life expectancy was up to thirty years longer.) One in four children died in infancy, and half died before the age of twenty. Children who survived infancy often lost one or both of their parents before reaching maturity. Widows, widowers, and orphans thus formed a substantial proportion of the Chesapeake population. Only after settlers developed immunity to local diseases (particularly malaria) did life expectancy increase significantly. Population growth was substantial in the region, but it was largely a result of immigration.

The natural increases in the population in the seventeenth century were in large part a result of a steady improvement in the balance between men and women in the colonies. In the early years of settlement, more than three-quarters of the white population of the Chesapeake consisted of men. And even in New England, which from the beginning had attracted more families (and thus more women) than the Southern colonies, 60 percent of the inhabitants were male in 1650. Gradually, however, more women began to arrive in the colonies; and increasing birth rates, which of course produced roughly equal numbers of males and females, contributed to shifting the sex ratio as well. By the late seventeenth century, the proportion of males to females in all the colonies was becoming more balanced.

Women and Families in the Colonies

The importance of reproduction in the labor-scarce society of seventeenth-century America had significant effects on both the status and the life cycles of women. The high sex ratio meant that few women remained unmarried for long. The average European woman in America married for the first time at twenty or twenty-one years of age, considerably earlier than in England.

In the Chesapeake, the extraordinarily high mortality rate made the traditional patriarchal family structure of England—by which husbands and fathers exercised firm, even dictatorial control over the lives of their wives and children—difficult to maintain. Because so few families remained intact for long, rigid patterns of familial authority were constantly undermined and sexual mores grew more flexible than in England or other parts of America.

Because of the large numbers of indentured servants who were forbidden to marry until their terms of service expired, premarital sexual relationships were frequent. Over a third of Chesapeake marriages occurred with the bride already pregnant. Bastard children were usually taken from their mothers and bound out as indentured servants at a young age.

Women in the Chesapeake could anticipate a life consumed with childbearing. The average wife experienced pregnancies every two years. Those who lived long enough bore an average of eight children apiece (up to five of whom typically died in infancy or early childhood). Since childbirth was one of the most frequent causes of female death, relatively few women survived to see all their children grow to maturity.

But Southern white women did enjoy certain advantages. Because men were plentiful and women scarce, females had considerable latitude in choosing husbands. Because women generally married at a much younger age than men, they also tended to outlive their husbands. Widows were generally left with several children and with responsibility for managing a farm or plantation, a circumstance of enormous hardship but one that also gave them significant economic power. Widows seldom remained unmarried for long, however. And since many widows married men who were themselves widowers, complex combinations of households were frequent.

By the early eighteenth century, the demographic character of the Chesapeake was beginning to change, and with it the nature and structure of the typical family. Life expectancy was increasing, and indentured servitude was in decline. Natural reproduction was becoming the principal source of white population growth. The sex ratio was becoming more equal. One result of these changes was that life for white people in the region became less perilous and less arduous. Another result was that women lost some of the power that their small numbers had once given them. As families grew more stable, traditional patterns of male authority revived. By the mid-eighteenth century, Southern families were becoming highly patriarchal.

In New England, where many more immigrants arrived with family members and where death rates declined far more quickly, family structure was much more stable than in the Chesapeake and hence much more traditional. Because the sex ratio was less imbalanced, most men could expect to marry. But women remained in the minority. As in the Chesapeake, they married young, began producing children early, and continued to do so well into their thirties. In contrast to the situation in the South, however, Northern children were more likely to survive (the average family raised six to eight children to maturity), and their families were more likely to remain intact. Fewer New England women became widows, and those who did generally lost their husbands later in life. Hence women were less often cast in roles independent of their husbands. Young women, moreover, had less control over the conditions of marriage, both because there were fewer unmarried men vying for them and because their fathers were more likely to be alive and able to exercise control over their choices.

The longer lives in New England meant that parents continued to influence their children's lives far longer than did parents in the South. They did not often actually "arrange" marriages for their children, but few sons and daughters could choose a spouse entirely independently of their parents' wishes. Men tended to rely on their fathers for land to cultivate—generally a prerequisite for beginning families of their own. Women needed dowries from their parents if they were to hope to attract desirable husbands. Stricter parental supervision of children meant, too, that fewer women became pregnant before marriage than was the case in the South (although even in Puritan New England, the premarital pregnancy rate was as high as 20 percent in some communities).

Puritanism placed a high value on the family, which was not only the principal economic unit but the principal religious unit within every community. In one sense, then, women played important roles within the family because the position of wife and mother was highly valued in Puritan culture. At the same time, however, Puritanism served to reinforce the idea of nearly absolute male authority and the assumption of female weakness and inferiority. Women were expected to be modest and submissive. A wife was expected to devote herself almost entirely to serving the needs of her husband. Yet however subservient they may have been, women were vital to the family economy. They were continuously engaged in tasks crucial to the functioning of the farm—gardening, raising poultry, tending cattle, spinning, and weaving, as well as cooking, cleaning, and washing.

Family life in the Chesapeake colonies grew more patriarchal in the late seventeenth and early eighteenth centuries. New England families were growing somewhat less so. As settlement spread beyond the early Puritan centers, as the authority of the church began gradually to decline, and as sons began increasingly to chafe under the control of their fathers, family life became somewhat more fluid, and the rigid division of authority between generations and between the sexes that had characterized seventeenth-century communities became less universal.

The Beginnings of Slavery in English North America

The demand for black servants to supplement the scarce Southern labor supply existed almost from the first moments of settlement. The supply of African laborers, however, remained relatively restricted during much of the seventeenth century because the Atlantic slave trade did not serve the English colonies in America then. Gradually, however, a substantial commerce in slaves grew up within the Americas, particularly between the Caribbean islands and the Southern colonies of English America. By the late seventeenth century, the supply of black workers in North America was becoming plentiful.

As the commerce in slaves grew more extensive and more sophisticated, it also grew more horrible. Before it ended in the nineteenth century, it was responsible for the forced immigration of as many as 11 million Africans to North and South America and the Caribbean. Indeed, until the late eighteenth century, the number of African immigrants to the Americas was higher than that of Europeans. In the flourishing slave marts on the African coast, native chieftains made large numbers of blacks available by capturing members of enemy tribes in battle and bringing them out of the forests and to the ports. The terrified victims were then packed into the dark, filthy holds of ships for the horrors of the "middle passage"—the long journey to America, during which the black prisoners were kept chained in the bowels of the slave ships and supplied with only minimal food and water. Women were often victims of rape and other sexual abuse. Those who died en route, and many did, were simply thrown overboard. Slave traders tried to cram as many Africans as possible into their ships to ensure that enough would survive to yield a profit at journey's end. Upon arrival in the New World,

AFRICANS BOUND FOR AMERICA Shown here are the below-deck slave quarters of a
Spanish vessel en route to the West Indies. A British warship captured the slaver,
and a young English naval officer (Lt. Francis Meynell) made this watercolor
sketch on the spot. The Africans seen in this picture appear somewhat more
comfortable than prisoners on other slave ships, some of whom were chained
and packed together so tightly that they had no room to stand or even sit.

slaves were auctioned off to white landowners and transported, frightened
and bewildered, to their new homes.

North America was a less important destination for African slaves than
were such other parts of the New World as the islands of the Caribbean and
Brazil; fewer than 5 percent of the Africans imported to the Americas arrived
first in the English colonies. At first, those blacks who were transported to
what became the United States came not directly from Africa but from the
West Indies. Not until the 1670s did traders start importing blacks directly
from Africa to North America. Even then the flow remained small for a
time, mainly because a single group, the Royal African Company of England, monopolized the trade and kept prices high and supplies low.

A turning point in the history of the black population in North America
was 1697, the year the Royal African Company's monopoly was broken. With

the trade now open to competition, prices fell and the number of blacks greatly increased. By 1700, about 25,000 black slaves lived in English North America. That was only 10 percent of the total non-Indian population. But because blacks were so heavily concentrated in a few Southern colonies, they were already beginning to outnumber whites in some areas. There were perhaps twice as many black men as black women in most areas, but in some places the African-American population grew by natural increase nevertheless. In the Chesapeake more new slaves were being born than were being imported from Africa. In South Carolina, by contrast, the arduous conditions of rice cultivation ensured that the black population would barely be able to sustain itself through natural increase until much later.

By 1760, the number of Africans in the colonies had increased to approximately a quarter of a million. A few (16,000 in 1763) lived in New England; slightly more (29,000) lived in the middle colonies. The vast majority, however, continued to live in the South. By then blacks had almost wholly replaced white indentured servants as the basis of the Southern work force.

For a time, the legal and social status of the African laborers remained somewhat fluid. In some areas—South Carolina, for example, where the number of black arrivals swelled more quickly than anywhere else—whites and blacks worked together at first on terms of relative equality. Some blacks were treated much like white hired servants, and some were freed after a fixed term of servitude. A few blacks themselves became landowners, and some apparently owned slaves of their own. By the late seventeenth century, however, a rigid distinction was emerging between blacks and whites. White workers could not be bound to a master indefinitely, but there was no legal requirement that masters free black workers after a term of service. Gradually, the assumption spread that blacks would remain in service permanently and that black children would inherit their parents' bondage. White beliefs about the inferiority of the black race reinforced the growing rigidity of the system. That slavery was developing in a society that was already multiracial also had an impact on its evolution. Whites had long ago defined themselves as a superior race in their relations with the native Indian population; the idea of subordinating an inferior race was, therefore, already part of European thinking by the time substantial numbers of Africans appeared in their midst.

The system of permanent servitude—American slavery—became legal in the early eighteenth century when colonial assemblies began to pass "slave codes" granting almost absolute authority to white masters over their slaves. One factor only determined whether a person was subject to the slave codes:

color. In the colonial societies of Spanish America, people of mixed race were granted a different (and higher) status than pure Africans. English America recognized no such distinctions. Any African ancestry was enough to classify a person as black.

Later Immigration

The most distinctive and enduring feature of the American population was that it brought together peoples of many different races, ethnic groups, and nationalities. North America was home to a substantial population of natives, to a growing number of English immigrants, to forcibly imported Africans, and to substantial non-English groups from Europe. When the flow of immigrants from England began to decline in the early eighteenth century, large numbers of whites continued to immigrate to North America from France, Germany, Switzerland, Ireland, Scotland, and Scandinavia.

The earliest of these non-English European immigrants were the French Calvinists, or Huguenots, escaping religious persecution in Roman Catholic France. A total of about 300,000 left France, a few of them for the English colonies of North America, after the Edict of Nantes, which had guaranteed them substantial liberties, was revoked in 1695. Many German Protestants suffered similarly from the arbitrary religious policies of their rulers, and all Germans suffered from the frequent wars between their principalities and France. Because of its proximity to France, the Rhineland of southwestern Germany, known as the Palatinate, was exposed to frequent invasion, which sent more than 12,000 Germans fleeing to England early in the eighteenth century; approximately 3,000 of them found their way to America. Most settled in Pennsylvania, where they ultimately became known to English settlers as the "Pennsylvania Dutch," (a corruption of the German term for their nationality, *Deutsch*). Other, later German immigrants headed to Pennsylvania as well, among them the Moravians and Mennonites, whose religious views were similar to those of the Quakers.

The most numerous of the newcomers were the so-called Scotch-Irish—Scotch Presbyterians who had settled in northern Ireland (in the county of Ulster) in the early seventeenth century. Most of the Scotch-Irish in America pushed out to the edges of European settlement and occupied land without much regard for who actually claimed to own it, whether absentee whites, Indians, or the colonial governments. They were as ruthless in their displacement and suppression of the Indians as they had been with the native Irish Catholics in Ireland.

There were also immigrants from Scotland itself and from southern

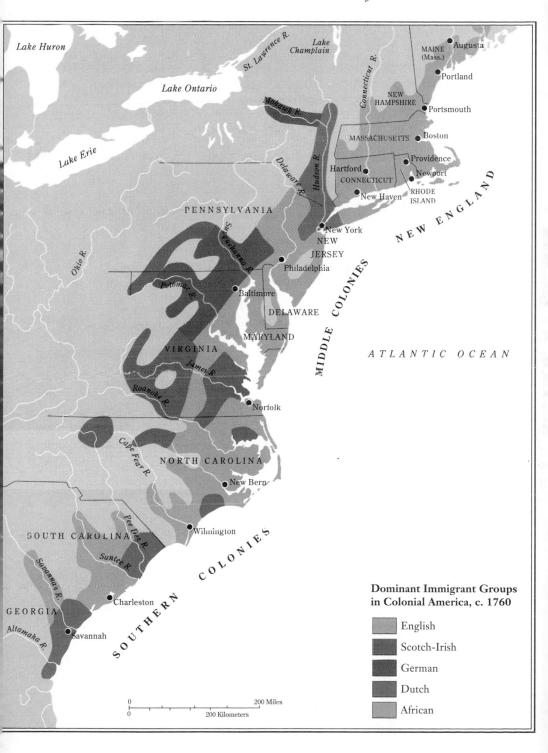

Lake Huron

Lake Ontario

Lake Erie

St. Lawrence R.

Lake
Champlain

Connecticut R.

Mohawk R.

MAINE
(Mass.) ● Augusta

● Portland

NEW
HAMPSHIRE   ● Portsmouth

MASSACHUSETTS ● Boston

Hudson R.

Delaware R.

PENNSYLVANIA

Susquehanna R.

Ohio R.

Potomac R.

● Baltimore

Philadelphia

DELAWARE

MARYLAND

VIRGINIA

James R.

Roanoke R.

● Norfolk

Cape Fear R.

NORTH CAROLINA

● New Bern

Pee Dee R.

SOUTH CAROLINA

Suntee R.

● Wilmington

Savannah R.

GEORGIA

Altamaha R.

● Savannah

● Charleston

Hartford
CONNECTICUT

● New Haven

● Providence
● Newport

RHODE
ISLAND

● New York

NEW
JERSEY

NEW ENGLAND

MIDDLE COLONIES

ATLANTIC OCEAN

SOUTHERN COLONIES

**Dominant Immigrant Groups
in Colonial America, c. 1760**

English

Scotch-Irish

German

Dutch

African

0   200 Miles
0   200 Kilometers

Ireland. Scottish Highlanders, some of them Roman Catholics, immigrated to North Carolina above all. Scottish Presbyterian Lowlanders, fleeing high rents and unemployment, left for America in large numbers shortly before the American Revolution. The Irish migrated steadily over a long period and by the time of the Revolution were almost as numerous as the Scots. Many of them had by then abandoned their Roman Catholic religion and much of their ethnic identity.

By 1775, the non-Indian population of the colonies was over 2 million—a nearly tenfold increase since the beginning of the century. Throughout the colonial period, the population nearly doubled every twenty-five years. Its continuing and increasing ethnic diversity became one of many factors dividing colonial society from the society of England.

THE COLONIAL ECONOMY

Farming dominated almost all areas of European and African settlement in North America throughout the seventeenth and eighteenth centuries. Even so, the economies of the different regions varied markedly from one another.

The Southern Economy

A strong European demand for tobacco enabled some planters in the Chesapeake (Maryland and Virginia) to grow enormously wealthy and at times allowed the region as a whole to prosper. But throughout the seventeenth and eighteenth centuries, production of tobacco frequently exceeded demand, and as a result the price of the crop could suffer severe declines. The result was a boom-and-bust cycle in the Chesapeake economy, with the first major bust occurring in 1640.

Most of the Chesapeake planters believed that the way to protect themselves from the instability of the market was to grow more tobacco. That only made the overproduction problem worse. It also encouraged those planters who could afford to do so to expand their landholdings, enlarge their fields, and acquire additional laborers. After 1700, tobacco plantations employing several dozen slaves or more were common.

South Carolina and Georgia relied on rice production, since the low-lying coastline with its many tidal rivers made it possible to build rice paddies that could be flooded and drained. Rice cultivation was arduous work—performed standing knee deep in malarial swamps—a task so difficult and unhealthy that white laborers generally refused to perform it. Hence planters in South Carolina and Georgia were far more dependent on slaves than were their Northern counterparts. African workers were adept at rice cultivation, in part because some of them had come from rice-producing regions of west Africa and in part because they were generally more accustomed to the hot and humid climate than were the Europeans.

Because of their dependence on large-scale cash crops, the Southern colonies developed less of a commercial or industrial economy than the colonies of the North. The trading in tobacco and rice was handled largely by merchants based in London and, later, in the Northern colonies. Few cities of more than modest size developed in the South. A pattern was established that would characterize the Southern economy, and differentiate it from that of other regions, for more than two centuries.

SELLING TOBACCO This late-seventeenth-century label was used in the sale of American tobacco in England. The drawing depicts Virginia as a land of bright sunshine, energetic slaves, and prosperous, pipe-smoking planters.

The Northern Economy

In the North, as in the South, agriculture continued to dominate, but it was agriculture of a more diverse kind. In addition to farming, there gradually emerged an important commercial sector of the economy.

One reason that agriculture did not remain the exclusive economic pursuit of the North was that conditions for farming were less favorable than in the South. In northern New England, in particular, colder weather and hard, rocky soil made it difficult for colonists to develop the kind of large-scale commercial farming system that Southerners were creating. Most New Englanders did not produce a staple crop that could become a major export item; they planted largely to meet the needs of their own families. Conditions for agriculture were better in southern New England and the middle colonies, where the soil was fertile and the weather more temperate. New York, Pennsylvania, and the Connecticut River valley were the chief suppliers of wheat to much of New England and to parts of the South.

Beginning with a failed effort to establish an ironworks in Saugus, Massachusetts, in the mid-seventeenth century, colonists in New England and the middle colonies embarked on industrial ventures as well. Almost every colonist engaged in a certain amount of industry at home. Occasionally these home industries provided families with goods they could trade or sell. Beyond these domestic efforts, craftsmen and artisans established themselves in colonial towns as cobblers, blacksmiths, riflemakers, cabinetmakers, silversmiths, and printers. In some areas, entrepreneurs harnessed water power to run small mills for grinding grain, processing cloth, or milling lumber. And in several places, large-scale shipbuilding operations began to flourish.

The largest industrial enterprise anywhere in English North America was the ironworks of the German ironmaster Peter Hasenclever in northern New Jersey. Founded in 1764 with British capital, it employed several hundred laborers, many of them imported from ironworks in Germany. There were other, smaller ironmaking enterprises in every northern colony (with particular concentrations in Massachusetts, New Jersey, and Pennsylvania), and there were ironworks as well in several of the southern colonies. But these and other growing industries did not become the basis for the kind of explosive industrial growth that Great Britain experienced in the late eighteenth century—in part because parliamentary regulations such as the Iron Act of 1750 restricted colonists from engaging in metal processing and stifled the development of a steel industry in America. Similar prohibitions reduced the manufacture of woolens, hats, and other goods. But the most important obstacles to industrialization in America were an inadequate labor supply, a small domestic market, and inadequate transportation facilities and energy supplies.

More important than manufacturing to the economy of the Northern colonies were extractive industries, which exploited the natural resources of the continent. By the mid-seventeenth century, the flourishing fur trade of earlier years was in decline; the supply of fur-bearing animals along the Atlantic seaboard had been nearly exhausted, and the interior fur trade was largely in the hands of the Algonquins and their French allies. More important now were lumbering, mining, and fishing, particularly in the waters off the New England coast. These industries provided commodities that could be exported to England in exchange for manufactured goods. And they helped, therefore, to produce the most distinctive feature of the Northern economy—a thriving commercial class.

The Rise of Commerce

Perhaps the most remarkable feature of colonial commerce in the seventeenth century was that it was able to survive at all. American merchants faced such bewildering and intimidating obstacles, and lacked so many of the basic institutions of trade, that they managed to stay afloat only with great difficulty. There was no commonly accepted money. The colonies had almost no gold or silver, and their paper currency was not acceptable as payment for goods from abroad. For many years, colonial merchants had to rely on barter or on money substitutes such as beaver skins.

A second obstacle was lack of information about supply and demand. Traders had no way of knowing what they would find in foreign ports; vessels sometimes stayed at sea for years, journeying from one port to another, trading one commodity for another, attempting to find some way to turn a profit. There were, moreover, an enormous number of small, fiercely competitive companies, which made the problem of rationalizing the system even more acute.

Nevertheless, commerce in the colonies survived and grew. There was an elaborate coastal trade, through which the colonies did business with one another and with the West Indies. The mainland colonies traded rum, agricultural products, meat, and fish. The islands offered sugar, molasses, and at times slaves in return. There was also trade with England, continental Europe, and the west coast of Africa. This commerce has often been described, somewhat inaccurately, as the "triangular trade," suggesting a neat process by which merchants carried rum and other goods from New

Overseas Trade During the Colonial Period

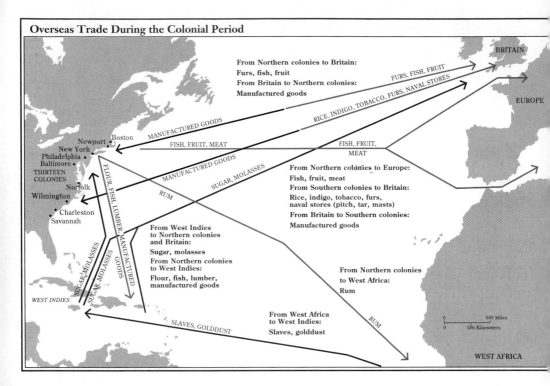

England to Africa, exchanged their merchandise for slaves, whom they then transported to the West Indies (hence the term "middle passage" for the dread journey—it was the second of the three legs of the voyage), and then exchanged the slaves for sugar and molasses, which they shipped back to New England to be distilled into rum. In fact, the so-called "triangular" trade in rum, slaves, and sugar was a maze of highly diverse trade routes.

Out of this risky trade emerged a group of adventurous entrepreneurs who by the mid-eighteenth century were beginning to constitute a distinct merchant class concentrated in the port cities of the North. The British Navigation Acts protected them from foreign competition in the colonies. They had ready access to the market in England for such colonial products as furs, timber, and American-built ships. But they also developed markets illegally outside the British Empire—in the French, Spanish, and Dutch West Indies, where prices were often higher than in the British colonies.

During the eighteenth century, the colonial commercial system began to stabilize. But the trading sector of the American economy remained open to newcomers, largely because it—and the society on which it was based— was expanding so rapidly.

PATTERNS OF SOCIETY

Although there were sharp social distinctions in the colonies, the well-defined and deeply entrenched class system of England failed to reproduce itself in America. In England, land was scarce and the population large, and the relatively few landowners had enormous power over the landless. In America, in contrast, land was abundant and people were scarce. Aristocracies emerged there, to be sure; but they tended to rely less on landownership than on control of a substantial work force, and they were generally less secure and less powerful than their English counterparts. More than in England, there were opportunities in America for social mobility both up and down. There were also new forms of community in America, and they varied greatly from one region to another.

The Plantation

The plantation system of the American South illustrated clearly the way in which colonial communities evolved in response to local conditions. The first plantations emerged in the tobacco-growing areas of Virginia and Maryland. Some of the early planters hoped to re-create in America the entrenched, landholding aristocracy of England, and in a few cases—notably in the great Maryland estates granted by Lord Baltimore to his relatives and friends—a semblance of such an aristocracy did emerge. On the whole, however, seventeenth-century colonial plantations were rough and relatively small estates. In the early days in Virginia, they were little more than crude clearings where landowners and indentured servants worked side by side in conditions so harsh that death was an everyday occurrence. Even in later years, when the death rate declined and the landholdings became more established, plantation work forces seldom exceeded thirty people. Most landowners lived in rough cabins or houses, with their servants or slaves nearby.

The economy of the plantation was a precarious one. Planters could not control their markets, so even the largest of them were constantly at risk. When prices fell—as tobacco prices did, for example, in the 1660s—they faced the prospect of ruin. The plantation economy created many new wealthy landowners, but it also destroyed many.

Because plantations were often far from cities and towns, they tended to become self-contained communities. Wealthier planters often created something approaching a full town on their plantations. Smaller planters lived more modestly, but still in a relatively self-sufficient world. On the larger estates, plantation mistresses, unlike the wives of small farmers, had servants to perform ordinary household chores, thus freeing up time they could devote to their husbands and children. But many also had to tolerate sexual liaisons between their husbands or sons and black women of the slave community.

Even though the fortunes of planters could rise and fall quickly, there were always particularly wealthy landowners who exercised great social and economic influence. A great landowner controlled not only the lives of those who worked his own plantation but the livelihood of poorer neighbors who could not compete with him and thus depended on him to market their crops and supply them with credit. Some whites were unable to own their land and rented their farms from wealthy planters. Such independent farmers, working with few or no slaves to help them, formed the majority of the Southern agrarian population; but the planters dominated the Southern agrarian economy.

The enslaved African-Americans, of course, lived very differently. On the smaller farms with only a handful of slaves, it was not always possible for a rigid separation to develop between whites and blacks. But over three-fourths of all blacks lived on plantations of at least ten slaves; nearly half lived in communities of fifty slaves or more. And in these places they began to develop a society and culture of their own. Although whites seldom encouraged formal marriages among slaves, blacks themselves developed a strong and elaborate family structure. Slaves attempted to construct nuclear families, and they managed at times to build stable households. But families were always precarious, because any member could be sold at any time to another planter, even to one in another colony. As a result, blacks placed special emphasis on extended kinship networks and created surrogate "relatives" for people separated entirely from their own families. There was also a distinctive slave religion, which blended Christianity with African folklore and which became a central element in the emergence of an independent black culture.

Nevertheless, black society was subject to constant intrusions from and interaction with white society. Black house servants, for example, were isolated from their own community and were under constant surveillance from whites. Black women were subject to the usually unwanted sexual advances from owners and overseers and hence to bearing mulatto children, who were rarely recognized by their white fathers but were generally accepted as members of the slave community. On some plantations, black workers were treated with kindness and sometimes responded with genuine devotion. On others, they encountered physical brutality and occasionally even sadism, against which they were virtually powerless.

There were several slave rebellions during the colonial period. The most important was the Stono Rebellion in South Carolina in 1739, during which about 100 blacks rose up, seized weapons, killed several whites, and attempted to escape south to Florida. The uprising was quickly crushed, and most participants were executed. A more frequent form of resistance was simply running away, but that provided no real solution either. There was nowhere to go. And so for most slaves, resistance took the form of subtle, and often undetected, defiance or evasion of their masters' wishes.

Most slaves, male and female, worked as field hands (with the women shouldering the additional burdens of cooking and child rearing). But on the larger plantations that aspired to genuine self-sufficiency, some slaves learned trades and crafts: blacksmithing, carpentry, shoemaking, spinning, weaving, sewing, midwifery, and others. These skilled crafts workers were at times hired out to other planters. Some set up their own establishments in towns or cities and shared their profits with their owners. A few were able to buy their freedom. There was a small free black population living in Southern cities by the time of the Revolution.

The Puritan Community

The characteristic social unit in New England was not the isolated farm but the town. In the early years of colonization, each new settlement drew up a "covenant" binding all residents together in a religious and social unit. The structure of the towns reflected the spirit of the covenant. Colonists laid out a village, with houses and a meetinghouse arranged around a central pasture, or "common." Thus families generally lived with their neighbors close by, reinforcing the strong sense of community. They divided up the outlying fields and woodlands among the residents; the size and location of a family's field depended on the family's numbers, wealth, and social station.

Once a town was established, residents held a yearly "town meeting" to decide important questions and to choose a group of "selectmen," who ran the town's affairs. Participation in the meeting was generally restricted to adult males who were members of the church. Only those who could give evidence of grace, of being among the elect (the "visible saints") assured of salvation, were admitted to full membership, although other residents of the town were required to attend church services.

New Englanders did not adopt the English system of primogeniture—the passing of all property to the firstborn son. Instead, a father divided up his land among all his sons. His control of this inheritance gave him great power over the family. Often a son would reach his late twenties before his father would allow him to move into his own household and work his own land. Even then, sons would usually continue to live in close proximity to their fathers. Young women were generally more mobile than their brothers, since they did not stand to inherit land.

The early Puritan community was, in short, a tightly knit organism. The town as a whole was bound together by the initial covenant, by the centralized layout of the village, by the power of the church, and by the town meeting. The family was held together by the rigid patriarchal structure that limited opportunities for younger members (males in particular) to strike out on their own. Yet as the years passed and the communities grew, this communal structure experienced strains. This was partly because of the increasing commercialization of New England society, which introduced new forces and new tensions into the communities of the region. It was also partly because of population growth. As towns grew larger, residents tended to cultivate lands farther and farther from the community center and, by necessity, to live at increasing distances from the church. Often, groups of outlying residents would apply for permission to build a church of their own, usually the first step toward creation of a wholly new town. Such applications could cause bitter quarrels between the original townspeople and those who proposed to break away.

The control of land by fathers also created strains. In the first generations, fathers generally controlled enough land to satisfy the needs of all their sons. After several generations, however, when such lands were being subdivided for the third or fourth time, there was often too little to go around, particularly in communities surrounded by other towns, with no room to expand outward. The result was that in many communities, groups of younger residents broke off and moved elsewhere—at times far away—to form towns of their own.

But it was only against the strict standards of the first years of settlement, and the even stricter standards of Puritan expectations, that New England towns were unraveling. Measured against most contemporary communities in England or other parts of America, the Puritan town remained remarkably communal.

The tensions building in Puritan communities could produce bizarre and disastrous events. One example was the widespread hysteria in the 1680s and 1690s over accusations of witchcraft (the human exercise of Satanic powers) in New England. The most famous outbreak (although by no means the only one) was in Salem, Massachusetts, where adolescent girls began to exhibit strange behavior and leveled charges of witchcraft against several West Indian servants steeped in voodoo lore. Hysteria spread throughout the town, and hundreds of people (most of them women) were accused of witchcraft. Nineteen residents of Salem were put to death before the trials finally ended in 1692; the girls who had been the original accusers later recanted and admitted that their story had been fabricated.

The Salem experience was not unique. Accusations of witchcraft spread through many New England towns in the early 1690s (and indeed had emerged regularly in Puritan society for many years before). Research into the background of accused witches reveals that most were middle-aged women, often widowed, with few or no children. Accused witches were, moreover, generally of low social position, were often involved in domestic conflicts, had frequently been accused of other crimes, and were considered abrasive by their neighbors. Many "witches" were women who were not

ACCUSATION OF A WITCH This picture, by an artist working with inlaid wood, conveys something of the terror that witchcraft accusations produced in New England communities in the seventeenth century.

securely lodged within a patriarchal family structure and who seemed to defy the passive norms Puritan society had created for them. That suggests that tensions over gender roles played a substantial role in generating the crisis. The witchcraft controversies were also a reflection of the highly religious character of New England societies. New Englanders believed in the power of Satan and his ability to assert his power in the world. Belief in witchcraft was not a marginal superstition, rejected by the mainstream. It was a common feature of Puritan religious conviction.

Cities

Even the largest colonial community was scarcely bigger than a modern small town. Yet by the standards of the eighteenth century, cities did exist in America. In the 1770s the two largest ports—Philadelphia and New York— had populations of 28,000 and 25,000, respectively, which made them larger than most English urban centers. Boston (16,000), Charles Town (later Charleston), South Carolina (12,000), and Newport, Rhode Island (11,000), were also substantial communities by the standards of the day.

Colonial cities served as trading centers for the farmers of their regions and as marts for international commerce. Their leaders were generally merchants who had acquired substantial estates. Sharp class divisions may not often have emerged in the cities, but more than in any other area of colonial life (except of course in the relationship between masters and slaves) social distinctions were real and visible in urban areas.

Cities were the centers of much of what industry there was in the colonies, such as the distilleries for turning imported molasses into exportable rum. They were the locations of the most advanced schools and sophisticated cultural activities and of shops where imported goods could be bought. In addition, they were communities with urban social problems: crime, vice, pollution, traffic. Unlike smaller towns, cities needed to set up constables' offices and fire departments and develop systems for supporting the urban poor, whose numbers became especially large in times of economic crisis—to which cities were particularly vulnerable.

Finally, cities became places where new ideas could circulate and be discussed. There were newspapers, books, and other publications from abroad, and hence new intellectual influences. The taverns and coffeehouses of cities provided forums in which people could gather and debate the issues of the day. That is one reason why the Revolutionary crisis, when it began to build in the 1760s and 1770s, manifested itself first in the cities.

THE COLONIAL MIND

Intellectual life in colonial America revolved around the conflict between the traditional outlook of the sixteenth and seventeenth centuries, with its emphasis on a personal God deeply involved in individual lives, and the new spirit of the Enlightenment, which was sweeping both Europe and America and which stressed the importance of science and human reason. The old views placed a high value on a stern moral code in which intellect was less important than faith. The Enlightenment suggested that people had substantial control over their own lives and societies.

The Pattern of Religions

Religious toleration flourished in America to a degree unmatched in any European nation, not because Americans deliberately sought to produce it, but because conditions virtually required it. Settlers in America brought with them so many different religious practices that it proved impossible to impose a single religious code on any large area.

The experience of the Church of England illustrated how difficult the establishment of a common religion would be in the colonies. By law, Anglicanism was established as the official faith in Virginia, Maryland, New York, the Carolinas, and Georgia. In these colonies everyone, regardless of belief or affiliation, was supposed to be taxed for the support of the church. Except in Virginia and Maryland, however, the laws establishing the Church of England as the official colonial religion were largely ignored. Missionaries of the Society for the Propagation of the Gospel, founded in 1701 to spread the Anglican faith, had some success in Massachusetts and Connecticut. But Anglicanism never succeeded in becoming a dominant religious force in America.

Even in New England, where the Puritans had originally believed that they were all part of a single faith, there was a growing tendency in the eighteenth century for different congregations to affiliate with different denominations, especially Congregationalism and Presbyterianism. In parts of New York and New Jersey, Dutch settlers had established their own Calvinist denomination, Dutch Reformed, which survived after the colonies became part of the British Empire. The American Baptists (of whom Roger Williams is considered the first) were also originally Calvinistic in their theology, but a great variety of Baptist sects emerged. They shared the belief that rebaptism, usually by total immersion, was necessary when believers reached maturity. But while some Baptists remained Calvinists, believers in predestination, others came to believe in salvation by free will.

Protestants extended toleration to one another more readily than they did to Roman Catholics. Many Protestants feared and hated the pope. New Englanders, in particular, viewed their Catholic neighbors in New France (Canada) not only as commercial and military rivals but as agents of Rome bent on frustrating their own divine mission. In most of the English colonies, however, Roman Catholics were too few to cause serious conflict. They were most numerous in Maryland, and even there they numbered no more than 3,000. Perhaps for that reason they suffered their worst persecution in that colony. After the overthrow of the original proprietors in 1691, Catholics in Maryland not only lost their political rights but were forbidden to hold religious services except in private houses.

Jews in provincial America totaled no more than about 2,000 at any time. The largest community lived in New York City. Smaller groups settled in Newport and Charleston, and there were scattered Jewish families in all the colonies. Nowhere could they vote or hold office. Only in Rhode Island could they practice their religion openly.

By the beginning of the eighteenth century, some Americans were growing troubled by the apparent decline in religious piety in their society. With so many diverse sects existing side by side, some people were tempted to doubt whether any particular denomination, even their own, possessed a monopoly of truth. The movement of the population westward and the wide scattering of settlements had caused many communities to lose touch with organized religion. The rise of commercial prosperity created a secular outlook in urban areas. The progress of science and free thought in Europe—and the importation of Enlightenment ideas to America—caused at least some colonists to doubt traditional religious belief.

Concerns about declining piety surfaced as early as the 1660s in New England, where the Puritan oligarchy warned of a deterioration in the power of the church. Sabbath after Sabbath, ministers preached sermons of despair (known as "jeremiads"), deploring the signs of waning piety. By the standards of other societies or other eras, the Puritan faith remained remarkably strong. But New Englanders measured their faith by their own standards, and to them the "declension" of religious piety seemed a serious problem.

The Great Awakening

By the early eighteenth century, similar concerns were emerging in other regions and among members of other faiths. Everywhere, colonists were coming to believe, religious piety was in decline and opportunities for spiritual regeneration were dwindling. The result was the first great American revival: the Great Awakening.

The Great Awakening began in earnest in the 1730s, reached its climax in the 1740s, and brought a new spirit of religious fervor that many believed was reversing the trend away from piety. The revival had particular appeal to women (who constituted the majority of converts) and to younger sons of the third or fourth generation of settlers—those who stood to inherit the least land and who faced the most uncertain futures. The rhetoric of the revival emphasized the potential for every person to break away from the constraints of the past and start anew in his or her relationship to God— which seemed to reflect the desire of many people to break away from their families or communities and start a new life in the world.

Powerful evangelists from England helped spread the revival. John and Charles Wesley, the founders of Methodism, visited Georgia and other colonies in the 1730s. George Whitefield, a powerful open-air preacher and for a time an associate of the Wesleys, made several evangelizing tours through the colonies and drew tremendous crowds. But the evangelizers from abroad were less important to American revivalism in the long run than the colonial ministers attempting to restore religious fervor in America. The outstanding preacher of the Great Awakening was the New England Congregationalist Jonathan Edwards—a deeply orthodox Puritan but a highly original theologian. From his pulpit in Northampton, Massachusetts, Edwards attacked the new doctrines of easy salvation for all. He preached anew the traditional Puritan ideas of the absolute sovereignty of God, predestination, and salvation by God's grace alone. His vivid descriptions of hell could terrify his listeners.

The Great Awakening led to the division of existing congregations (between "New Light" revivalists and traditionalists) and to the founding of new ones. It also affected areas of society outside the churches. Some of the revivalists denounced book learning as a hindrance to salvation, and some communities repudiated secular education altogether. But other evangelists saw education as a means of furthering religion, and they founded or led schools for the training of New Light ministers.

Education

Many colonists placed a high value on education, despite the difficulties they confronted in gaining access to it. Some families tried to teach their children to read and write at home, although the heavy burden of work in most agricultural households limited the time available for schooling. In Massachusetts, a 1647 law required that every town support a public school; and while many communities failed to comply, a modest network of institutions emerged as a result. The Quakers and other sects operated church schools; and in some communities, widows or unmarried women conducted "dame schools" by holding private classes in their homes. In cities, master craftsmen set up evening schools for their apprentices.

White male Americans, at least, achieved a high degree of literacy in the eighteenth century. By the time of the Revolution, well over half of all white men could read and write, a rate substantially higher than that in most European countries. The literacy rate for women lagged behind the rate for men until the nineteenth century; and while opportunities for education beyond the primary level were scarce for men, they were almost nonexistent for women. Nevertheless, the literacy rate for females was also substantially higher than that of their European counterparts.

African-Americans, most of whom were enslaved, had virtually no access to education. Occasionally a master or mistress would teach slave children to read and write; but as the slave system became more firmly

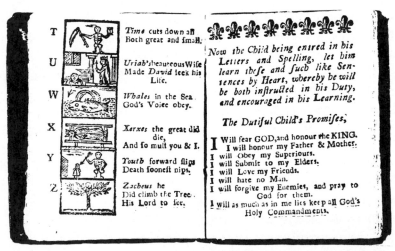

A "DAME SCHOOL" PRIMER More than the residents of any other region of North America (and far more than those of most of Europe), the New England colonists strove to educate their children and achieved perhaps the highest level of literacy in the world. Throughout the region, young children attended institutions known as "dame schools" (because the teachers were almost always women) and learned from primers such as this one.

entrenched, strong social (and ultimately legal) sanctions developed to discourage such efforts, lest literacy encourage slaves to question their stations. Indians, too, remained largely outside the white educational system—to a large degree by choice: most tribes preferred to educate their children in their own way. But some white missionaries and philanthropists established schools for Native Americans and helped create a small but significant population of Indians literate in spoken and written English.

Nowhere was the intermingling of traditional religiosity and the new spirit of the Enlightenment clearer than in the colleges and universities of colonial America. Of the six colleges in operation by 1763, all but two were founded by religious groups primarily for the training of preachers. Yet in almost all, the influences of the new scientific, rational approach to knowledge could be felt.

Harvard, the first American college, was established in 1636 by Puritan theologians who wanted to create a training center for ministers. (The college was named for a Charlestown minister, John Harvard, who had left his library and half his estate to the college). Decades later, in 1693, William and Mary College (named for the English king and queen) was established in Williamsburg, Virginia, by Anglicans; like Harvard, it was conceived as an academy to train clergymen. And in 1701, conservative Congregationalists, dissatisfied with the growing religious liberalism of Harvard, founded Yale (named for one of its first benefactors, Elihu Yale) in New Haven, Connecticut. Out of the Great Awakening emerged the College of New Jersey, founded in 1746 and known later as Princeton (after the town in which it was located); one of its first presidents was Jonathan Edwards. Despite the religious basis of these colleges, most of them offered curricula that included not only theology but logic, ethics, physics, geometry, astronomy, rhetoric, Latin, Hebrew, and Greek. King's College, founded in New York in 1754 and later renamed Columbia, was specifically devoted to the spread of secular knowledge; it had no theological faculty and was interdenominational from the start. The Academy and College of Philadelphia, which became the University of Pennsylvania, was from its birth in 1755 a completely secular institution, founded by a group of laymen under the inspiration of Benjamin Franklin.

After 1700, most colonial leaders received their entire education in America (rather than attending university in England, as had once been the case). But the advantages of higher education were not widely shared. Women, blacks, and Indians were excluded from all colleges and universities. And among white men, only those from relatively affluent families could afford to attend.

Concepts of Law and Politics

In law and politics, as in other parts of their lives, Americans in the seventeenth and eighteenth centuries believed that they were re-creating in the New World the practices and institutions of the Old. But as in other areas, they in fact created something very different.

Changes in the law in America resulted in part from the scarcity of English-trained lawyers, who were almost unknown in the colonies until after 1700. Although the American legal system adopted most of the essential elements of the English system, including such ancient rights as trial by jury, significant differences developed in court procedures, punishments, and the definition of crimes. In England, for example, a printed attack on a public official, whether true or false, was considered libelous. At the 1734 trial of the New York publisher John Peter Zenger, who was powerfully defended by the Philadelphia lawyer Andrew Hamilton, the courts ruled that criticisms of the government were not libelous if factually true—a verdict that removed some colonial restrictions on the freedom of the press.

More significant for the future of the relationship between the colonies and England were differences emerging between the American and British political systems. Because the royal government—in theory the ultimate authority over the colonies— was so far away, Americans created a group of institutions of their own that gave them a large measure of self-government. In most colonies, local communities grew accustomed to running their own affairs with minimal interference from higher authorities. The colonial assemblies came to exercise many of the powers that Parliament exercised in England. Provincial governors (appointed by the king after the 1690s) had broad powers on paper, but in fact their influence was sharply limited. Control over appointments and contracts resided largely in England or with local colonial leaders. A governor could be removed any time his patron in England lost favor. And in some cases, governors were not even familiar with the colonies they were meant to govern; most governors were Englishmen who came to the colonies for the first time to assume their offices.

The result of all this was that the focus of politics in the colonies became a local one, the provincial governments became accustomed to acting more or less independently of Parliament, and a set of assumptions and expectations about the rights of the colonists took hold in America that was not shared by policymakers in England. These differences caused few problems before the 1760s, because the British did little to exert the authority they believed they possessed. But when, beginning in 1763, the English government began attempting to tighten its control over the American colonies, a historic crisis resulted.

D E B A T I N G T H E P A S T

The Origins of Slavery

HE DEBATE AMONG historians over how and why white Americans created a system of slave labor in the seventeenth century—and how and why they determined that African-Americans and no others should populate that system—has been an unusually lively one. At its center is a debate over whether slavery was a result of white racism, or whether racism was a result of slavery.

In 1950, Oscar and Mary Handlin published an influential article comparing slavery to other systems of "unfreedom" in the colonies. What separated slavery from other conditions of servitude, they argued, was that it was restricted to people of African descent, that it was permanent, and that it passed from one generation to the next. The unique characteristics of slavery, the Handlins argued, were part of an effort by colonial legislatures to increase the available labor force. White laborers needed an incentive to come to America; black laborers, forcibly imported from Africa, did not. The distinction between the conditions of white workers and the conditions of black workers was, therefore, based on legal and economic motives, not on racism.

Winthrop Jordan was one of a number of historians who later challenged the Handlins' thesis and argued that white racism, more than economic interests, produced African slavery. In *White Over Black* (1968), Jordan argued that Europeans had long viewed people of color—and black Africans in particular—as inferior beings appropriate for serving whites. Those attitudes migrated with white Europeans to the New World, and white racism shaped the treatment of Africans in America—and the nature of the slave labor system—from the beginning. Even without the economic

(continued on next page)

incentives the Hanlins described, in other words, whites would have been likely to oppress blacks in the New World.

Peter Wood's *Black Majority* (1974), a study of seventeenth-century South Carolina, was one of a number of works that moved the debate back towards social and economic conditions in the 1970s and after. Wood demonstrated that blacks and whites often worked together on relatively equal terms in the early years of settlement; that racism, in other words, did not inevitably shape the relationships between blacks and whites. But as rice cultivation expanded, it became more difficult to find white laborers willing to do the arduous work. The increase in the forcible importation of African workers, and the creation of a system of permanent bondage, was a response to this growing demand for labor. It was also a response to fears among whites that without slavery it would be difficult to control a labor force brought to America against its will. Edmund Morgan's *American Slavery, American Freedom* (1975) argued similarly that the southern labor system was at first relatively flexible and later grew more rigid. In colonial Virginia, he claimed, white settlers did not at first intend to create a system of permanent bondage for blacks or whites. But as the tobacco economy grew and created a high demand for cheap labor, white landowners began to feel uneasy about their dependence on a large group of dependent white workers. Such workers were difficult to recruit and control. Slavery, therefore, was less a result of racism than of the desire for whites to find a reliable and stable labor force.

In recent years, the debate over the origins of slavery has become part of a larger debate over the nature of racism in American (and world) history. Some scholars continue to argue, as Winthrop Jordan did in the 1960s, that racism is a powerful, autonomous part of white culture, which exists independent of other factors. Others argue that race as a category of distinction among human beings is itself meaningless; since there are no significant biological or genetic distinctions separating the races, the belief that there are important differences is always an invention, or "construction," designed to serve other needs. Just as historians have argued that eighteenth-century racism was a product and not a cause of slavery, so other scholars argue that racism in other times is an ideology created to justify systems of oppression that serve economic, political, or other needs.

CHAPTER FOUR

The Empire Under Strain

Origins of Resistance ~ *The Struggle for the Continent*
The New Imperialism ~ *Stirrings of Revolt* ~ *Cooperation and War*

A s LATE AS the 1750s, few Americans objected to their membership in the British Empire. The imperial system had commercial and political benefits for the Americans. And it had few costs, because for the most part, the English government left the colonies alone. By the mid-1770s, however, the relationship between the American colonies and their British rulers had become so strained, so poisoned, so characterized by suspicion and resentment that the empire was on the verge of unraveling. And in the spring of 1775, the first shots were fired in a war that would ultimately win America its independence. How had it happened? And why so quickly?

ORIGINS OF RESISTANCE

In one sense, it had not happened quickly at all. Ever since the first days of English settlement in North America, the ideas and institutions of the colonies had been diverging from those in Britain in countless ways. In another sense, however, the Revolutionary crisis emerged in response to important and relatively sudden changes in the administration of the em pire. Because in 1763, the English government began to enforce a series of policies toward its colonies that brought the differences between the two societies into sharp focus.

A Loosening of Ties

In the fifty years after the Glorious Revolution, the English Parliament (which became the British Parliament after the union of England and Scotland in 1707) established a growing supremacy over the king. During the reigns of George I (1714–1727) and George II (1727–1760), both of whom were German-born and unaccustomed to English ways, the prime minister and his cabinet became the nation's real executives. They held their positions not by the king's favor but by their ability to control a majority in Parliament.

These parliamentary leaders were less inclined than the seventeenth-century monarchs had been to try to tighten control over the empire. They depended politically on the great merchants and landholders, most of whom feared that any such efforts would reduce the profitability of the colonial trade. As a result, administration of colonial affairs remained decentralized and inefficient, with no single office or agency responsible for colonial affairs.

The character of the royal officials in America—the governors and other officers of the royal colonies and (in all the colonies) the naval officers and collectors of customs—contributed further to the looseness of the imperial system. Some of these officeholders were able and intelligent; most were not. Many, perhaps most, colonial officials had used bribery to obtain their offices; many, perhaps most, accepted bribes once they assumed their offices. Some appointees remained in England and hired substitutes to take their places in America.

Resistance to imperial authority centered in the colonial legislatures. By the 1750s the assemblies had become accustomed to levying taxes, making appropriations, approving appointments, and passing laws for their respective colonies. The assemblies came to look upon themselves as little parliaments, each practically as sovereign within its colony as Parliament itself was in England.

Intercolonial Disunity

Even so, the colonists continued to think of themselves as loyal English subjects. Many felt stronger ties to England than they did to one another, so great were the differences among the societies of the various colonies. Yet for all their differences, the colonies could not avoid forging connections with one another. As settlement became almost continuous along the seacoast, people of the different colonies came into closer contact. The gradual construction of roads, the rise of trade, and the creation of a colonial postal service also forged intercolonial ties.

Still, the colonists were reluctant to cooperate even when, in 1754, they faced a common threat from their old rivals, the French, and France's Indian allies. A conference of colonial leaders—with delegates from Pennsylvania, Maryland, New York, and New England—was meeting in Albany in that year to negotiate a treaty with the Iroquois. The delegates tentatively approved a plan offered by Benjamin Franklin to set up a "general government" in America to manage relations with the Indians on behalf of all the colonies. War with the French and Indians was already beginning when this Albany Plan was presented to the colonial assemblies. None approved it.

THE STRUGGLE FOR THE CONTINENT

The war that raged in North America through the late 1750s and early 1760s was part of a larger struggle between England and France for dominance in world trade and naval power. The British victory in that struggle, known in Europe as the Seven Years' War, confirmed England's commercial supremacy and cemented its control of the settled regions of North America.

In America, however, the conflict was also the final stage in a long struggle among the three principal powers in northeastern North America: the English, the French, and the Iroquois. For more than a century prior to the conflict—known in America as the French and Indian War—these three groups had maintained a precarious balance of power. The events of the 1750s upset that balance, produced a prolonged and open conflict, and established a precarious dominance for the English societies throughout the region. The war also brought English America into closer contact with British authority than ever before and raised to the surface some of the underlying tensions in the colonial relationship.

New France and the Iroquois Nation

The French and the English had coexisted relatively peacefully in North America for nearly a century. But by the 1750s, as both English and French settlements expanded, religious and commercial tensions began to produce new frictions and new conflicts.

By the end of the seventeenth century, the French Empire in America comprised a vast territory. In the 1680s, French explorers journeyed as far south as the delta of the Mississippi, claimed the surrounding country for France, and named it Louisiana in honor of King Louis XIV. Subsequent traders and missionaries wandered southwest as far as the Rio Grande and west to the Rocky Mountains. The French had by then revealed the outlines of, and laid claim to, the whole continental interior.

To secure their hold on these enormous claims, they founded a string of widely separated communities, strategically located fortresses, and far-flung missions and trading posts. Fort Louisbourg, on Cape Breton Island, guarded the approach to the Gulf of St. Lawrence. Would-be feudal lords established large estates *(seigneuries)* along the banks of the St. Lawrence River. And on a high bluff above the river stood the fortified city of Quebec, the center of the French Empire in America. Montreal to the south and Sault Sainte Marie and Detroit to the west marked the northern boundaries of French settlement. On the lower Mississippi emerged plantations much like those in the Southern colonies of English America, worked by black slaves and owned by "Creoles" (white immigrants of French descent). New Orleans, founded in 1718 to service the French plantation economy, was soon as big as some of the larger cities of the Atlantic seaboard; Biloxi and Mobile to the east completed the string of French settlement.

But the French, of course, shared the continental interior with a large and powerful Indian population. Both the French and the English were aware that the battle for control of North America would be determined in part by which group could best win the allegiance of native tribes—as trading partners and, at times, as military allies. The English—with their more advanced commercial economy—could usually offer the Indians better and more plentiful goods. But the French offered something that was often more important: tolerance. Unlike the English settlers, who strove constantly to impose their own social norms on the Indians they encountered, the French settlers in the interior generally adjusted their own behavior to Indian patterns. French fur traders frequently married Indian women and adopted tribal ways; Jesuit missionaries interacted comfortably with the natives and converted them to Catholicism by the thousands without challenging most of their social customs. By the mid-eighteenth century, therefore, the French had better and closer relations with most of the Indians of the interior than did the English.

The most powerful native group, however, had a different relationship with the French. The Iroquois Confederacy—five Indian nations (Mohawk, Seneca, Cayuga, Onondaga, and Oneida) that had formed a defensive alliance in the fifteenth century—had been the most powerful native presence in the Ohio Valley and a large surrounding region since the 1640s. For nearly a century, neither the French nor the English raised any serious challenge to Iroquois control of the region, and the Iroquois maintained their autonomy by avoiding too close a relationship with either group. They traded successfully with both the English and the French and astutely played the two groups off against each other. As a result, they maintained an uneasy balance of power in the Great Lakes region.

Anglo-French Conflicts

As long as England and France remained at peace and as long as the precarious balance in the North American interior survived, English and French colonists coexisted without serious difficulty. But after the Glorious Revolution in England, a series of Anglo-French wars erupted and continued intermittently in Europe for nearly eighty years.

The wars had important repercussions in America. King William's War (1689–1697) produced only a few, indecisive clashes between the English and the French in northern New England. Queen Anne's War, which began in 1701 and continued for nearly twelve years, generated more substantial conflicts: border fighting with the Spaniards in the south as well as with the French and their Indian allies in the north. The Treaty of Utrecht, which brought the conflict to a close in 1713, transferred substantial territory from the French to the English in North America, including Acadia (Nova Scotia) and Newfoundland.

Two decades later, disputes over British trading rights in the Spanish colonies produced a war between England and Spain that soon merged with a much larger European war, in which England and France lined up on opposite sides. The English colonists in America were soon drawn into the struggle, which they called King George's War, and between 1744 and 1748 they engaged in a series of conflicts with the French. New Englanders captured the French bastion at Louisbourg on Cape Breton Island; but the peace treaty that finally ended the conflict forced them to abandon it.

In the aftermath of King George's War, relations among the English, French, and Iroquois in North America quickly deteriorated. The Iroquois (in what appears to have been a major blunder) granted trading concessions in the interior to English merchants for the first time. The French, fearful (probably correctly) that the English were using the concessions as a first step toward expansion into French lands, began in 1749 to construct new fortresses in the Ohio Valley. The English interpreted the French activity as a threat to their western settlements, protested, and began making military preparations and building fortresses of their own. The balance of power that the Iroquois had carefully and successfully maintained for so long rapidly disintegrated.

For the next five years, tensions between the English and the French increased. In the summer of 1754 the governor of Virginia sent a militia force (under the command of an inexperienced young colonel, George Washington) into the Ohio Valley to challenge French expansion. Washington built a crude stockade (Fort Necessity) not far from Fort Duquesne, the larger outpost the French were building on the site of what is now Pittsburgh. After the Virginians staged an unsuccessful attack on a French detachment, the French countered with an assault on Fort Necessity, trapping Washington and his soldiers inside. After a third of them died in the fighting, Washington surrendered. The clash marked the beginning of the French and Indian War.

The Great War for the Empire

The French and Indian War lasted nearly nine years, and it moved through three distinct phases. During the first of these phases, from the Fort Necessity debacle in 1754 until the expansion of the war to Europe in 1756, it was primarily a local, North American conflict. The English colonists managed the war mainly on their own, and they focused largely on defending themselves against raids on their western settlements by the Indians of the Ohio Valley. Virtually all the tribes except the Iroquois were now allied with the French; they had interpreted the defeat of the Virginians at Fort Duquesne as evidence of British weakness. Even the Iroquois, who were nominally allied with the British, feared antagonizing the French. They remained largely passive in the conflict. By late 1755, many English settlers along the frontier had withdrawn to the east of the Allegheny Mountains to escape the hostilities.

The second phase of the struggle began in 1756, when the governments of France and England formally opened hostilities and a truly international conflict (the Seven Years' War) began. The fighting now spread to the West Indies, India, and Europe itself. But the principal struggle remained the one in North America, where so far England had suffered nothing but frustration and defeat. Beginning in 1757, William Pitt, the English secretary of state (and future prime minister), began to transform the war effort in America by bringing it for the first time fully under British control. Pitt himself planned military strategy, appointed commanders, and issued orders to the colonists. Military recruitment had slowed dramatically in America, and to replenish the army British commanders began forcibly enlisting colonists (a practice known as "impressment"). Officers also seized supplies from local farmers and tradesmen and compelled colonists to offer shelter to British troops—all generally without compensation. The Americans resented these new impositions and firmly resisted them—at times, as in a 1757 riot in New York City, violently. By early 1758, the friction between the British authorities and the colonists was threatening to bring the war effort to a halt.

Beginning in 1758, therefore, Pitt initiated the third and final phase of the war by relaxing many of the policies that Americans had found obnoxious.

He agreed to reimburse the colonists for all supplies requisitioned by the army. He returned control over recruitment to the colonial assemblies (which resulted in an immediate and dramatic increase in enlistments). And he dispatched large numbers of additional British troops to America. Finally, the tide of battle began to turn in England's favor. The French, who had always been outnumbered by the British colonists and who, after 1756, suffered from a series of poor harvests, were unable to sustain their early military successes. By mid-1758, the British regulars in America (who did the bulk of the actual fighting) and the colonial militias were seizing one French stronghold after another. Two brilliant English generals, Jeffrey Amherst and James Wolfe, captured the fortress at Louisbourg in July 1758; a few months later Fort Duquesne fell without a fight. The next year, at the end of a siege of Quebec, supposedly impregnable atop its towering cliff,

RECRUITING FOR THE FRENCH AND INDIAN WAR The extravagant promises in this recruiting poster, distributed to colonists during the French and Indian War, suggests how difficult it sometimes was to persuade Americans to fight in the British army.

the army of General Wolfe struggled up a hidden ravine under cover of darkness, surprised the larger forces of the Marquis de Montcalm, and defeated them in a battle in which both commanders were slain. The dramatic fall of Quebec on September 13, 1759, marked the beginning of the end of the American phase of the war. A year later, in September 1760, the French army formally surrendered to Amherst in Montreal.

Peace finally came in 1763, with the Peace of Paris. Under its terms, the French ceded to Great Britain some of their West Indian islands, most of their colonies in India and Canada, and all other French territory in North America east of the Mississippi. They ceded New Orleans and their claims west of the Mississippi to Spain, thus surrendering all title to the mainland of North America.

The French and Indian War had profound effects on the British Empire and the American colonies. It greatly expanded England's territorial claims in the New World. At the same time, the cost of the war greatly enlarged Britain's debt and substantially increased British resentment of the Americans. English leaders were contemptuous of the colonists for what they considered American military ineptitude during the war; they were angry that the colonists had made so few financial contributions to a struggle waged largely for American benefit; they were particularly bitter that some colonial merchants had been selling food and other goods to the French in the West Indies throughout the conflict. All these factors combined to persuade many English leaders that a major reorganization of the empire, giving London increased authority over the colonies, would be necessary in the aftermath of the war.

The war had an equally profound but very different effect on the American colonists. It was an experience that forced them, for the first time, to act in concert against a common foe. And it seemed to establish certain precedents. The friction of 1756–1757 over British requisition and impressment policies and the 1758 return of authority to the colonial assemblies seemed to many Americans to confirm the illegitimacy of English interference in local affairs.

For the Indians of the Ohio Valley, the third major party in the French and Indian War, the British victory was disastrous. Those tribes that had allied themselves with the French had earned the enmity of the victorious English. The Iroquois Confederacy, which had allied itself with Britain, fared only slightly better. English officials saw the passivity of the Iroquois during the war (a result of their effort to hedge their bets and avoid antagonizing the French) as evidence of duplicity. In the aftermath of the peace settlement, the Iroquois alliance with the British quickly unraveled, and the Iroquois Confederacy itself began to crumble from within. The tribes would continue to contest the English for control of the Ohio Valley for another fifty years; but increasingly divided and increasingly outnumbered, they would seldom again be in a position to deal with their European rivals on terms of military or political equality.

THE NEW IMPERIALISM

With the treaty of 1763, England found itself truly at peace for the first time in more than fifty years. Undistracted by war, the British government could now turn its attention to the organization of its empire. And after the difficult experiences of the previous decade, many English leaders were convinced that the question of imperial organization could no longer be ignored. Saddled with enormous debts from the many years of fighting, England was desperately in need of new revenues from its empire. And responsible for vast new lands in the New World, the imperial government felt compelled to expand its involvement in its colonies.

Burdens of Empire

The experience of the French and Indian War, however, suggested that such increased involvement would not be easy to establish. Not only had the colonists proved so resistant to British control that Pitt had been forced to relax his policies in 1758, but the colonial assemblies had continued after that to respond to British needs slowly and grudgingly. Unwilling to be taxed by Parliament to support the war effort, the colonists were generally reluctant to tax themselves as well. Defiance of imperial trade regulations and other British demands continued.

With the territorial annexations of 1763, the area of the British Empire was suddenly twice as great as it had been, and the problems of governing it thus became many times more complex. Some English officials argued that the empire should restrain rapid settlement and development of the Western territories to avoid further costly conflicts with the Indians and perhaps even the French. Restricting settlement would also keep the land available for hunting and trapping. Others wanted to see the new territories opened for immediate development, but they disagreed among themselves about who should control the Western lands. The existing colonial governments made fervent, and often conflicting, claims of jurisdiction. Some officials in London wanted control to remain in England and wanted the territories to be considered entirely new colonies, unlinked to the existing settlements.

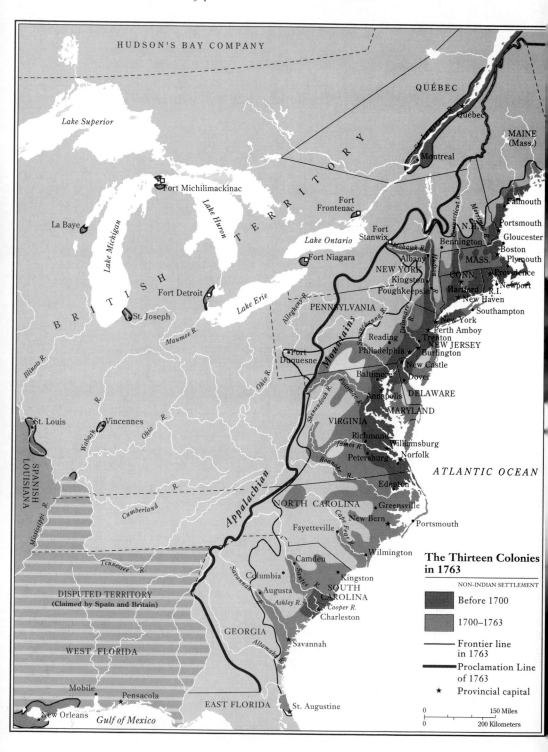

HUDSON'S BAY COMPANY

QUÉBEC

Lake Superior

MAINE
(Mass.)

Fort Michilimackinac

Québec

Lake Huron

La Baye

Montreal

Fort
Frontenac

Falmouth

Lake Michigan

Lake Ontario

Fort
Stanwix

N.H.

Portsmouth
Gloucester

B R I T I S H   T E R R I T O R Y

Fort Niagara

Mohawk R.

Bennington

Boston

Albany

MASS.

Plymouth

Fort Detroit

Lake Erie

NEW YORK

CONN.

Providence

Kingston

Hartford

R.I.

Newport

St. Joseph

Allegheny R.

Poughkeepsie

New Haven

Maumee R.

PENNSYLVANIA

Susquehanna R.

Southampton

New York

Illinois R.

Fort
Duquesne

Reading

Perth Amboy
Trenton
NEW JERSEY

Delaware R.

Philadelphia

Burlington

Ohio R.

Appalachian Mountains

New Castle

Baltimore

Dover

R.

Potomac R.

Annapolis

DELAWARE

St. Louis

Vincennes

Wabash R.

Ohio R.

Shenandoah R.

MARYLAND

SPANISH
LOUISIANA

VIRGINIA

Richmond

Williamsburg

James R.

Norfolk

Petersburg

Roanoke R.

ATLANTIC OCEAN

R.

Mississippi R.

Cumberland R.

Edenton

NORTH CAROLINA

Greensville

New Bern

Tennessee R.

Fayetteville

Portsmouth

Cape Fear R.

Wilmington

**The Thirteen Colonies
in 1763**

Camden

NON-INDIAN SETTLEMENT

Columbia

Saltee R.

DISPUTED TERRITORY
(Claimed by Spain and Britain)

Kingston

Before 1700

Savannah R.

Augusta

SOUTH
CAROLINA

1700–1763

Ashley R.

Cooper R.

Charleston

Frontier line
in 1763

GEORGIA

Proclamation Line
of 1763

WEST   FLORIDA

Altamaha R.

Savannah

★ Provincial capital

Mobile

Pensacola

EAST FLORIDA

St. Augustine

0   150 Miles

New Orleans

Gulf of Mexico

0   200 Kilometers

At the same time, the government in London was running out of options in its effort to deal with its staggering war debt. Landlords and merchants in England itself were objecting strenuously to tax increases. And the reluctance of the colonial assemblies to pay for the war effort had suggested that England could not rely on any cooperation from them in its search for revenues. Only a system of taxation administered by London, the leaders of the empire believed, could effectively meet England's needs.

At this crucial moment in Anglo-American relations, with the imperial system in need of redefinition, the government of England was thrown into turmoil by the accession to the throne of a new king, George III, who assumed power in 1760. He brought two particularly unfortunate qualities to the office. First, he was determined, unlike his two predecessors, to reassert the authority of the monarchy. Pushed by his ambitious mother, he removed from power the relatively stable coalition of Whigs who had governed the empire for much of the century and replaced them with a new coalition of his own, assembled through patronage and bribes. The new ministries that emerged as a result of these changes were very unstable, each lasting in office an average of only about two years.

The king also had serious intellectual and psychological limitations. He suffered, apparently, from a rare mental disease that produced intermittent bouts of insanity. (Indeed, in the last years of his long reign he was, according to most accounts, a virtual lunatic, confined to the palace and unable to perform any official functions.) Yet even when George III was lucid and rational, which was most of the time in the 1760s and 1770s, he was painfully immature (he had been only twenty-two when he ascended the throne) and insecure. The king's personality, therefore, contributed both to the instability and to the intransigence of the British government during these critical years.

More directly responsible for the problems that soon emerged with the colonies, however, was George Grenville, whom the king made prime minister in 1763. Grenville, though a brother-in-law of William Pitt, did not share Pitt's sympathy with the American point of view. He agreed instead with the prevailing opinion within Britain that the colonists had been too long indulged and that they should be compelled to obey the laws and to pay a part of the cost of defending and administering the empire.

The British and the Tribes

With the defeat of the French, frontiersmen from the English colonies had begun immediately to move over the mountains and into tribal lands in the upper Ohio Valley. An alliance of Indian tribes, under the Ottawa chieftain

Pontiac, struck back. To prevent an escalation of the fighting that might threaten Western trade, the British government issued a ruling—the Proclamation of 1763—forbidding settlers to advance beyond the mountains that divided the Atlantic coast from the interior.

The Proclamation of 1763 gave London, rather than the provincial governments and their land-hungry constituents, power to control (and slow) the westward movement of the white population. Slower Western settlement would limit costly wars with the Indians. It would also slow the population exodus from the coastal colonies, where England's most important markets and investments were. And it would reserve opportunities for land speculation and fur trading for English rather than colonial entrepreneurs.

Although Native Americans had few illusions about the Proclamation, which required them to cede land east of the mountains to the white settlers, many Indian groups supported the agreement as the best bargain available to them. The Cherokee, in particular, worked actively to hasten the drawing of the boundary, hoping finally to put an end to white encroachments. Relations between the Western tribes and the British improved in at least some areas after the Proclamation, partly as a result of the work of the Indian superintendents the British appointed, who were sympathetic to tribal needs.

In the end, however, the Proclamation of 1763 failed to meet even the modest expectations of the Indians, because on the crucial point of the line of settlement, it was almost completely ineffective. White settlers continued to swarm across the boundary and continued to claim lands farther and farther into the Ohio Valley. The British authorities tried repeatedly to establish limits to the expansion. In 1768, new agreements with the Western tribes created a supposedly permanent boundary (which, as always, increased the area of white settlement at the expense of the Indians). But these treaties (signed respectively at Hard Labor Creek, South Carolina, and Fort Stanwix, New York) also failed to stop the white advance. Within a few years, the 1768 agreements were replaced with new ones, which pushed the line of settlement still farther west.

The Colonial Response

The Grenville ministry soon increased its authority in the colonies more directly. Regular British troops were stationed permanently in America; and under the Mutiny Act of 1765 the colonists were required to help provision and maintain the army. Ships of the British navy patroled American waters to search for smugglers. The customs service was reorganized and enlarged.

Royal officials were required to take up their colonial posts in person instead of sending substitutes. Colonial manufacturing was restricted, so that it would not compete with rapidly expanding industies in Great Britain.

The Sugar Act of 1764, designed in part to eliminate the illegal sugar trade between the continental colonies and the French and Spanish West Indies, established new vice-admiralty courts in America to try accused smugglers—thus cutting them off from sympathetic local juries. The Currency Act of 1764 required that the colonial assemblies stop issuing paper money. Most momentously, the Stamp Act of 1765 imposed a tax on every printed document in the colonies: newspapers, almanacs, pamphlets, deeds, wills, licenses. British officials were soon collecting more than ten times as much annual revenue in America as they had been before 1763. But the new policies created many more problems than they solved.

It was difficult for the colonists to resist these unpopular new laws. For one thing, Americans continued to harbor as many grievances against one another as they did against the authorities in London. In 1763, for example, a band of Pennsylvania frontiersmen known as the Paxton Boys descended on Philadelphia to demand tax relief and financial support for their defense against Indians; bloodshed was averted only by concessions from the colonial assembly. In 1771, a small-scale civil war broke out in North Carolina when the Regulators, farmers of the Carolina upcountry, organized and armed themselves to resist the high taxes that local sheriffs (appointed by the colonial governor) collected. An army of militiamen, most of them from the eastern counties, crushed the revolt in the Battle of Alamance. Nine on each side were killed and many others wounded. Afterward, six Regulators were hanged for treason.

Despite the conflicts, however, the new policies of the British government began after 1763 to create common grievances among virtually all colonists. For under the Grenville program, as Americans saw it, all people in all colonies would suffer. Northern merchants would suffer from restraints on their commerce, from the closing of the West to land speculation and fur trading, from the restriction of opportunities for manufacturing, and from the increased burden of taxation. Southern planters, in debt to English merchants, would now have to pay additional taxes and would be unable to ease their debts by speculating in Western land. Small farmers, the largest group in the colonies, would suffer from increased taxes and from the abolition of paper money, which had been the source of most of their loans. Workers in towns faced the prospect of narrowing opportunities, particularly because of the restraints on manufacturing and currency. The new restrictions came, moreover, at the beginning of a postwar economic depression.

The British government had poured money into the colonies to finance the war, but that flow stopped after 1763. Now the authorities in London proposed to aggravate the problem by taking money out of the colonies.

In reality, most Americans soon found ways to live with (or circumvent) the new British laws. The American economy was not being destroyed. But there was still a deep sense of unease, particularly in the cities—the places most directly affected by British policies. Periodic and increasingly frequent economic slumps, the frightening depression of the early 1760s, the growth of a large group of unemployed or semiemployed—all combined to produce great distress in some colonial cities, and particularly in Boston, the city suffering the worst economic problems.

Whatever the economic burdens of the imperial program, colonists considered the political burdens worse. Americans were accustomed (and deeply attached) to wide latitude in self-government. The key to it, they believed, was the right of the colonial assemblies to control appropriations for the costs of government within the colonies. By attempting to circumvent the colonial assemblies and raise extensive revenues directly from the public, the British government was challenging the basis of colonial political power.

STIRRINGS OF REVOLT

By the mid-1760s, therefore, a hardening of positions had begun in both England and America that would bring the colonies into increasing conflict with the mother country. The result was a progression of events that, more rapidly than anyone could have imagined, destroyed the English empire in America.

The Stamp Act Crisis

Grenville could not have devised a better method for antagonizing and unifying the colonies than the Stamp Act of 1765 if he had tried. Unlike the Sugar Act of a year earlier, which affected only a few New England merchants, the tax on printed documents fell on all Americans. The actual economic burdens of the Stamp Act were relatively light, but the precedent it seemed to set was ominous. In the past, taxes and duties on colonial trade had always been presented as measures to regulate commerce, not raise money. The Stamp Act, however, was a direct attempt by England to raise revenue in the colonies without the consent of the colonial assemblies. If

Americans accepted this new tax without resistance, the door would be open for more burdensome taxation in the future.

Few colonists believed that they could do anything more than grumble until the Virginia House of Burgesses sounded a "trumpet of sedition" that aroused Americans to action almost everywhere. Foremost among the Virginia malcontents was Patrick Henry, who made a dramatic speech to the House in May 1765, concluding with a vague prediction that if present policies were not revised, George III, like earlier tyrants, might lose his head. There were shocked cries of "Treason!" and, according to one witness, an immediate apology from Henry (although many years later he was quoted as having made the defiant reply: "If this be treason, make the most of it"). Henry introduced a set of resolutions declaring that Americans possessed the same rights as the English, especially the right to be taxed only by their own representatives; that Virginians should pay no taxes except those voted by the Virginia assembly; and that anyone advocating the right of Parliament to tax Virginians should be deemed an enemy of the colony. The House of Burgesses defeated some of Henry's resolutions, but all of them were printed and circulated as the "Virginia Resolves."

In Massachusetts at about the same time, James Otis persuaded his fellow members of the colonial assembly to call an intercolonial congress to take action against the new tax. And in October 1765, the Stamp Act Congress, as it was called, met in New York with delegates from nine colonies and petitioned the king and Parliament. Their petition denied that the colonies could rightfully be taxed except through their own provincial assemblies.

Meanwhile, in several colonial cities mobs began taking the law into their own hands. During the summer of 1765 serious riots broke out up and down the coast, the largest of them in Boston. Men belonging to the newly organized Sons of Liberty terrorized stamp agents and burned stamps. The agents, themselves Americans, hastily resigned. In Boston, the mob also attacked such pro-British "aristocrats" as the lieutenant governor, Thomas Hutchinson (who had privately opposed passage of the Stamp Act but who felt obliged to support it once it became law). Hutchinson's elegant house was pillaged and virtually destroyed.

At last the crisis subsided, largely because England backed down. The authorities in London were less affected by the political protests than by economic pressure. Many New Englanders had stopped buying English goods to protest the Sugar Act of 1764. Now the colonial boycott spread, and the Sons of Liberty intimidated reluctant colonists to participate in it.

The merchants of England, feeling the loss of much of their colonial market, begged Parliament to repeal the unpopular law. On March 18, 1766, the Stamp Act was repealed at the urging of the new prime minister, the Marquis of Rockingham. To satisfy his strong and vociferous opponents, Rockingham also pushed through the Declaratory Act, which confirmed parliamentary authority over the colonies "in all cases whatsoever." In their rejoicing over the repeal, most Americans paid little attention to this sweeping declaration of Parliament's power, but the Declaratory Act was clear evidence of how large a gulf had emerged between the English and American views of the imperial relationship.

The Townshend Program

The Rockingham government's policy of appeasement met substantial opposition in England. English landlords, a powerful political force, feared that not taxing the colonies would result in imposing new taxes on them. The king finally dismissed the Rockingham ministry, and replaced it with a new government led by the aging but still powerful William Pitt (now Lord Chatham). Chatham had been a critic of the Stamp Act and had a reputation in America as a friend of the colonists. Once in office, however, he was so hobbled by gout and at times so incapacitated by mental illness that the actual leadership of his administration fell to the chancellor of the exchequer, Charles Townshend (pronounced "Townsend").

Townshend had to deal with imperial problems and colonial grievances left over from the Grenville ministry. With the Stamp Act repealed, the greatest American grievance involved the Mutiny (or Quartering) Act of 1765, which required the colonists to provide quarters and supplies for the British troops in America. The colonists did not object to quartering or supplying the troops; but they resented that these contributions were now mandatory, and they considered them another form of taxation without their consent. The Massachusetts and New York assemblies refused to vote the mandated supplies to the troops.

To enforce the law and to try again to raise revenues in the colonies, Townshend steered two measures through Parliament in 1767. First, the New York Assembly was disbanded until the colonists agreed to obey the Mutiny Act. (By singling out New York, Townshend thought he would avoid Grenville's mistake of arousing all the colonies at once.) Second, new taxes (known as the Townshend Duties) were levied on various goods imported to the colonies from England—lead, paint, paper, and tea. Townshend reasoned that since these were taxes purely on "external" transactions (imports from overseas) as opposed to the internal transactions the Stamp Act had taxed, the colonists could not object.

But the distinction between external and internal taxation meant little to the colonists. The purpose of the new duties, they claimed, was the same as that of the Stamp Act: to raise revenue from the colonists without their consent. And the suspension of the New York Assembly aroused the resentment of all the colonies. They considered this assault on the rights of one provincial government a threat on all of them.

The Massachusetts Assembly took the lead in opposing the new measures by circulating a letter to all the colonial governments urging them to stand up against every tax imposed by Parliament. At first, the document evoked little response outside Massachusetts. Then Lord Hillsborough, secretary of state for the colonies in London, warned that assemblies endorsing the Massachusetts letter would be dissolved. Massachusetts defiantly reaffirmed its support for the circular, and the other colonies supported Massachusetts.

Besides persuading Parliament to levy import duties and suspend the New York Assembly, Townshend took steps to enforce commercial regulations in the colonies more effectively. The most important of these steps was the establishment of a board of customs commissioners in America to stop the rampant corruption in the colonial customs houses. To some extent the plan worked. The new commissioners virtually ended smuggling in Boston, where they established their headquarters, although smugglers continued to carry on a busy trade in other colonial seaports.

The Boston merchants—accustomed to loose enforcement of the Navigation Acts and aggrieved now that the new commission was diverting the lucrative smuggling trade elsewhere—took the lead in organizing another boycott. Merchants in Philadelphia and New York joined them in a nonimportation agreement in 1768, and later some Southern merchants and planters also agreed to cooperate. The colonists boycotted British goods that were subject to the Townshend Duties; and throughout the colonies, American homespun and other domestic products became suddenly fashionable, while English luxuries fell from favor.

Late in 1767, Charles Townshend died—before the consequences of his ill-conceived program had become fully apparent. In March 1770, the new prime minister, Lord North, hoping to break the nonimportation agreement and divide the colonists, repealed all the Townshend Duties except the tea tax.

The Boston Massacre

Before news of the repeal reached America, an event in Massachusetts had electrified colonial opinion. The harassment of the new customs commissioners in Boston had grown so intense that the British government had placed four regiments of regular troops in the city—a constant affront to the colonists' sense of independence. Everywhere they went, Bostonians encountered British "redcoats," some of whom were arrogant, coarse, or provocative. Many poorly paid British soldiers wanted jobs in their off-duty hours, and they thus competed with local workers in an already tight market. Clashes between them were frequent.

On the night of March 5, 1770, a few days after a particularly intense skirmish between workers at a ship-rigging factory and British soldiers who were trying to find jobs there, a mob of dockworkers, "liberty boys," and others began pelting the sentries at the customs house with rocks and

THE BOSTON MASSACRE (1770), BY PAUL REVERE This is one of many engravings, by Revere and others, of the conflict between British troops and Boston laborers that became important as propaganda for the Patriot cause in the 1770s. Among the victims of the massacre listed by Revere was Crispus Attucks, probably the first black man to die in the struggle for American independence.

snowballs. Hastily, Captain Thomas Preston of the British regiment lined up several of his men in front of the building to protect it. There was some scuffling; one of the soldiers was knocked down; and in the midst of it all, apparently, several British soldiers fired into the crowd, killing five people (among them a mulatto sailor, Crispus Attucks).

This murky incident, almost certainly the result of panic and confusion, was quickly transformed by local resistance leaders into the "Boston Massacre"—a graphic symbol of British oppression and brutality. The victims became popular martyrs; the event became the subject of such lurid (and inaccurate) accounts as the widely circulated pamphlet *Innocent Blood Crying to God from the Streets of Boston*. A famous engraving by Paul Revere portrayed the massacre as a carefully organized, calculated assault on a peaceful crowd. The British soldiers, tried before a jury of Bostonians, were found guilty only of manslaughter and given token punishment. But colonial pamphlets and newspapers convinced many Americans that the soldiers were guilty of official murder. Year after year, resistance leaders marked the anniversary of the massacre with demonstrations and speeches.

The leading figure in fomenting public outrage over the Boston Massacre was Samuel Adams, the most effective radical in the colonies. He spoke frequently at Boston town meetings; and as one unpopular English policy followed another, his message attracted increasing support. England, he argued, had become a morass of sin and corruption; only in America did public virtue survive. In 1772, he proposed the creation of a "committee of correspondence" in Boston to publicize the grievances against England throughout the colony, and he became its first head. Other colonies followed Massachusetts's lead, and a loose inter-colonial network of political organizations was soon established that kept the spirit of dissent alive through the 1770s.

The Philosophy of Revolt

Although a superficial calm settled on the colonies for approximately three years after the Boston Massacre, the crises of the 1760s had helped arouse enduring ideological excitement and had produced instruments for publicizing colonial grievances. Gradually a political outlook took hold in America that would ultimately serve to justify revolt.

The ideas that would support the Revolution emerged from many sources. Some were indigenous to America, drawn from religious (particularly Puritan) sources or from the political experiences of the colonies. But these native ideas were enriched and enlarged by the importation of powerful arguments from abroad. Of most importance, perhaps, were the "radical" ideas of those in Great Britain who stood in opposition to their government. Some were Scots, who viewed the English state as tyrannical. Others were embittered "country Whigs," who felt excluded from power and considered the existing system corrupt and oppressive. Drawing from some of the great philosophical minds of earlier generations—most notably John Locke—these English dissidents framed a powerful argument against their government.

Central to this emerging ideology was a new concept of what government should be. Because humans were inherently corrupt and selfish, government was necessary to protect individuals from the evil in one another. But because any government was run by corruptible people, it needed safeguards against abuses of power. In the eyes of most English and American people, the English constitution was the best system ever devised to meet these necessities. By distributing power among the three elements of society—the monarchy, the aristocracy, and the common people—the English political system ensured that no individual or group could exercise authority unchecked by another. Yet by the mid-seventeenth century, dissidents in both England and America had become convinced that the constitution was in danger. A single center of power—the king and his ministers—was emerging, and the system was becoming a corrupt and dangerous tyranny.

Such arguments found little sympathy in most of England. The English constitution was not a written document; nor was it a fixed set of unchangeable rules. It was a general sense of the "way things are done," and most people in England were willing to accept evolutionary changes in it. Americans, by contrast, drew from their experience with colonial charters, in which the shape and powers of government were permanently inscribed on paper. They resisted the idea of a flexible, changing set of basic principles. Many colonists argued that the English constitution should itself be written down, to prevent fallible politicians from tampering with its essence.

Part of that essence, Americans believed, was their right to be taxed only with their own consent. When Townshend levied his external duties, the Philadelphia lawyer John Dickinson published a widely circulated pamphlet, *Letters of a Pennsylvania Farmer*, which argued that even external taxation was legal only when designed to regulate trade and not to raise a revenue. Gradually, most Americans ceased to accept even that distinction, and they finally took an unqualified stand: "No taxation without representation." Whatever the nature of a tax—whether internal or external, whether designed to raise revenue or to control trade—it could not be levied without the consent of the colonists themselves.

This clamor about "representation" made little sense to the English. According to the prevailing English theory, members of Parliament did not represent individuals or particular geographical areas. Instead, each member represented the interests of the whole nation and indeed the whole empire, no matter where the member happened to come from. The many unenfranchised boroughs of England, the whole of Ireland, and the colonies thousands of miles away—all were thus represented in the Parliament at London, even though they elected no representatives of their own. This was the theory of "virtual" representation. But Americans, drawing from their experiences with their town meetings and their colonial assemblies, believed in "actual" representation. Every community was entitled to its own representative, elected by the people of that community and directly responsible to them. Since they had none of their own representatives in Parliament, it followed that they were not represented there. According to the emerging American view of the empire, the colonial assemblies played the same role within the colonies—had the same powers, enjoyed the same rights—that Parliament did within England. The empire, the Americans argued, was a sort of federation of commonwealths, each with its own legislative body, all tied together by common loyalty to the king.

What may have made the conflict between England and America ultimately insoluble was a fundamental difference of opinion over the nature of sovereignty. By arguing that Parliament had the right to legislate for England and for the empire as a whole, but that only the provincial assemblies could legislate for the individual colonies, Americans were in effect arguing for a division of sovereignty. Parliament would be sovereign in some matters; the assemblies would be sovereign in others. To the British, such an argument was absurd. In any system of government there must be a single, ultimate authority. And since the empire was, in their view, a single, undivided unit, there could be only one authority within it: the English government of king and Parliament. Ultimately, that presented the colonists with a stark choice: between complete subordination to England and complete independence from it. Slowly, cautiously, they began moving toward independence.

The Tea Excitement

The apparent calm in America in the first years of the 1770s masked a growing sense of frustration and resentment in response to the continued and increasingly heavy-handed enforcement of the Navigation Acts. Popular anger was visible in occasional acts of rebellion. At one point, colonists seized a British revenue ship on the lower Delaware River. And in 1772, angry residents of Rhode Island boarded the British schooner *Gaspée*, set it afire, and sank it in Narragansett Bay.

What finally revived the Revolutionary fervor of the 1760s, however, was a new act of Parliament—one that the English government had expected to be relatively uncontroversial. It involved the business of selling tea. In 1773, Britain's East India Company (which possessed an official monopoly on trade with the Far East) was sitting on large stocks of tea that it could not sell in England. It was on the verge of bankruptcy. In an effort to save it, the government passed the Tea Act of 1773, which gave the company the right to export its merchandise directly to the colonies without paying any of the regular taxes that were imposed on the colonial merchants, who had traditionally served as the middlemen in such transactions. With these privileges, the company could undersell American merchants and monopolize the colonial tea trade.

The act proved inflammatory for several reasons. First, it angered influential colonial merchants, who feared being replaced and bankrupted by a powerful monopoly. More important, however, the Tea Act revived American passions about the issue of taxation without representation. The law provided no new tax on tea. But the original Townshend duty on the commodity—the only one of the original duties that had not been repealed—survived. It was the East India Company's exemption from that duty that put the colonial merchants at such a grave disadvantage in competition with the company. Lord North assumed that most colonists would welcome the new law because it would reduce the price of tea to consumers by removing the middlemen. But resistance leaders in America resented the monopolistic privileges of the company and, more important, argued that the law in effect represented an unconstitutional tax. The colonists responded by boycotting tea.

Unlike earlier protests, most of which had involved relatively small numbers of people, the tea boycott mobilized large segments of the population. It also helped link the colonies together in a common experience of mass popular protest. Particularly important to the movement were the activities of colonial women, who were among the principal consumers of tea and now became the leaders of the effort to boycott it. The Daughters of Liberty—a women's patriotic organization which, like the Sons of Liberty, was committed to agitating against British policies, proclaimed "that rather than Freedom, we'll part with our Tea."

In the last weeks of 1773, with strong popular support, leaders in various colonies made plans to prevent the East India Company from landing its cargoes in colonial ports. In Philadelphia and New York, determined colonists kept the tea from leaving the company's ships; and in Charleston, they stored it away in a public warehouse. In Boston, after failing to turn three ships away from the harbor, local patriots staged a spectacular drama. On the evening of December 16, 1773, three companies of fifty men each, masquerading as Mohawks, passed through a crowd of spectators, went aboard the three ships, broke open the tea chests, and heaved them into the harbor. As the electrifying news of the Boston "tea party" spread, other seaports staged similar acts of resistance of their own.

Parliament retaliated in four acts of 1774, closing the port of Boston, drastically reducing the powers of self-government in Massachusetts, permitting royal officers to be tried in other colonies or in England when accused of crimes, and providing for the quartering of troops by the colonists. These Coercive Acts—or, as they were more widely known in America, "Intolerable Acts"—were followed by the Quebec Act, which was unrelated to them but also provocative to English Americans. The law extended the boundaries of Quebec to include the French communities between the Ohio and Mississippi rivers. It also granted political rights to Roman Catholics and recognized the legality of the Roman Catholic church within the enlarged province. Many Americans feared that a plot was afoot in London to subject Americans to the authority of the pope. Those interested in Western lands, moreover, believed that the act would hinder westward expansion.

The Coercive Acts, far from isolating Massachusetts, made it a martyr in the eyes of residents of other colonies and sparked new resistance up and down the coast. Colonial legislatures passed a series of resolves supporting Massachusetts. Women's groups throughout the colonies mobilized to extend the boycotts of British goods and to create substitutes for the tea, textiles, and other commodities they were shunning. In Edenton, North Carolina, fifty-one women signed an agreement in October 1774 declaring their "sincere adherence" to the anti-British resolutions of their provincial assembly and proclaiming their duty to do "every thing as far as lies in our power" to support the "publick good."

COOPERATION AND WAR

Revolutions do not simply happen. They must be organized and led. Beginning in 1765, colonial leaders developed a variety of organizations for converting popular discontent into action—organizations that in time formed the basis for an independent government.

New Sources of Authority

The passage of authority from the royal government to the colonists themselves began on the local level. In colony after colony, local institutions responded to the resistance movement by simply seizing authority on their own. At times, entirely new institutions emerged and began to perform some of the functions of government.

The most effective of these new groups were the committees of correspondence that Adams had inaugurated in Massachusetts in 1772. Virginia later established the first intercolonial committees of correspondence, which made possible continuous cooperation among the colonies. And Virginia took the greatest step of all toward united action in 1774. After the royal governor dissolved the assembly, a rump session met in the Raleigh Tavern at Williamsburg, declared that the Intolerable Acts menaced the liberties of every colony, and issued a call for a Continental Congress.

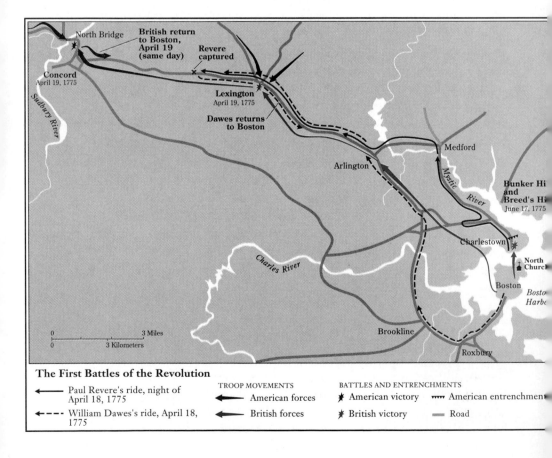

The First Battles of the Revolution

TROOP MOVEMENTS

◄——— Paul Revere's ride, night of April 18, 1775
◄——— American forces

◄--- William Dawes's ride, April 18, 1775
◄——— British forces

BATTLES AND ENTRENCHMENTS

✱ American victory   ⩘ American entrenchment
✱ British victory   ——— Road

Delegates from all thirteen colonies except Georgia were present when, in September 1774, the First Continental Congress convened in Philadelphia. They made five major decisions. First, in a close vote, they rejected a plan for a colonial union under British authority. Second, they endorsed a statement of grievances that reflected the influence of moderates by seeming to concede Parliament's right to regulate colonial trade and by addressing the king as "Most Gracious Sovereign," but it also included a more extreme demand for the repeal of all oppressive legislation passed since 1763. Third, they approved a series of resolutions from a Massachusetts convention recommending that military preparations be made for defense against possible attack by the British troops in Boston. Fourth, they agreed to a series of boycotts that they hoped would stop all trade with Great Britain, and they formed a "Continental Association" to see that these agreements were enforced. And fifth, the delegates agreed to meet again the following spring, indicating that they saw the Continental Congress as a continuing organization.

During the winter, the Parliament in London debated proposals for conciliating the colonists. Lord North finally won approval early in 1775 for a series of measures known as the Conciliatory Propositions. Parliament proposed that the colonies, instead of being taxed directly by Parliament, would tax themselves at Parliament's demand. With this offer, Lord North hoped to divide the American moderates, whom he believed represented the views of the majority, from the extremist minority. But his offer was too little and too late. It did not reach America until after the first shots of war had been fired.

Lexington and Concord

For months, the farmers and townspeople of Massachusetts had been gathering arms and ammunition and training as "minutemen," preparing to fight on a minute's notice. The Continental Congress had approved preparations for a defensive war, and the citizen-soldiers only waited for an aggressive move by the British regulars in Boston.

In Boston, General Thomas Gage, commanding the British garrison, considered his army too small to do anything without reinforcements. He resisted the advice of less cautious officers, who assured him that the Americans would never dare actually to fight, that they would back down quickly before any show of British force. When General Gage received orders to arrest the rebel leaders Sam Adams and John Hancock, known to be in the vicinity of Lexington, he still hesitated. But when he heard that the

THE BRITISH RETREAT FROM CONCORD, 1775 This American cartoon satirizes the retreat of British forces from Concord after the battle there on April 19, 1775. Patriot forces are lined up on the left, and the retreating British forces (portrayed with dog heads, perhaps because many of the soldiers were "wild" Irish) straggle off at right—some fleeing in panic, others gloating over the booty they have plundered from the burning homes above.

minutemen had stored a large supply of gunpowder in Concord (eighteen miles from Boston), he decided to act. On the night of April 18, 1775, he sent a detachment of about 1,000 men out from Boston on the road to Lexington and Concord. He hoped to surprise the colonials and seize the illegal supplies without bloodshed.

But patriots in Boston were watching the British movements closely; and during the night two horsemen, William Dawes and Paul Revere, were dispatched to warn the villages and farms. When the redcoats arrived in Lexington the next day, several dozen minutemen awaited them on the town common. Shots were fired and minutemen fell; eight of them were killed and ten more were wounded. Advancing to Concord, the British discovered that the Americans had hastily removed most of the powder supply, but the redcoats burned what was left of it. All along the road from Concord back to Boston, the British were harassed by the gunfire of farmers hiding behind trees, rocks, and stone walls. By the end of the day, the British had lost almost three times as many men as the Americans.

The first shots—the "shots heard round the world," as Americans later called them—had been fired. But who had fired them first? According to one of the minutemen at Lexington, the British commander, Major Thomas Pitcairn, had shouted to the colonists on his arrival, "Disperse, ye rebels!" When they ignored him, he ordered his troops to fire. British officers and soldiers claimed that the minutemen had fired first and that only after seeing the flash of American guns had they begun to shoot. Whatever the truth, the rebels succeeded in circulating their account well ahead of the British version, adorning it with tales of British atrocities. The effect was to rally to the rebel cause thousands of colonists, North and South, who previously had had little enthusiasm for it.

It was not immediately clear to the British, and even to many Americans, that the skirmishes at Lexington and Concord were the first battles of a war. But whether they recognized it at the time or not, the War for Independence had begun.

CHAPTER FIVE

The American Revolution

The States United ~ The War for Independence ~ War and Society
The Creation of State Governments ~ The Search for a National Government

TWO STRUGGLES OCCURRED simultaneously during the seven years of war that began in April of 1775. One was the military conflict with Great Britain. The second was a political conflict within America.

The military conflict was, by the standards of later wars, a relatively modest one. Battle deaths on the American side totaled fewer than 5,000. By the standards of its own day, however, it was an unusually savage conflict, pitting not only army against army but the civilian population against a powerful external force. The shift of the war from a traditional, conventional struggle to a new kind of conflict—a revolutionary war for liberation—is what made it possible for the United States to defeat the more powerful British.

At the same time, Americans were wrestling with the great political questions that the conflict necessarily produced: first, whether to demand independence from Britain; then, how to structure the new nation they had proclaimed. Only the first of these questions had been resolved by the time of the British surrender at Yorktown in 1781.

THE STATES UNITED

Although many Americans had been expecting a military conflict with Britain for months, even years, the actual beginning of hostilities in 1775 found the colonies generally unprepared. A still-unformed nation faced the task of mobilizing for war against the world's greatest armed power. Americans faced that task deeply divided about what they were fighting for.

Defining American War Aims

Three weeks after the battles of Lexington and Concord, when the Second Continental Congress met in Philadelphia, delegates from every colony except Georgia (which was not represented until the following autumn) agreed to support the war. But they disagreed about its purpose. At one extreme was a group led by the Adams cousins (John and Samuel), Richard Henry Lee of Virginia, and others, who already favored independence; at the other extreme was a group led by such moderates as John Dickinson of Pennsylvania, who hoped for a quick reconciliation with Great Britain. Most of the delegates tried to find some middle ground between these positions. They voted for one last appeal to the king: the so-called Olive Branch Petition. Then, on July 6, 1775, they adopted a Declaration of the Causes and Necessity of Taking Up Arms. It proclaimed that the British government had left the American people with only two alternatives: "unconditional submission to the tyranny of irritated ministers or resistance by force."

Most Americans still believed they were fighting not for independence but for a redress of grievances within the British Empire. During the first year of fighting, however, many of them began to change their minds. The costs of the war—human and financial—were so high that the original war aims began to seem too modest to justify them. What lingering affection they retained for the mother country greatly diminished when the British began trying to recruit Indians, black slaves, and German mercenaries (the hated "Hessians") against them. When the British government rejected the Olive Branch Petition and instead enacted the Prohibitory Act, which closed the colonial ports (through a naval blockade) to all overseas trade and made no concessions to American demands except an offer to pardon repentant rebels, many colonists concluded that independence was the only remaining option.

An impassioned pamphlet crystallized these feelings in January 1776: *Common Sense*, by Thomas Paine, who had emigrated from England to America less than two years before. Paine wanted to persuade Americans that no reconciliation with Britain was possible. He wanted to turn the anger of Americans away from particular parliamentary measures and toward what he considered the root of the problem—the English constitution itself. It was simple common sense for Americans to break completely with a political system that could produce so corrupt a monarch as George III and could inflict such brutality on its own people.

Common Sense sold more than 100,000 copies in only a few months. To many of its readers it was a revelation. Although sentiment for independence was still far from unanimous, the first months of 1776 saw a rapid growth of support for the idea.

The Decision for Independence

In the meantime, the Continental Congress in Philadelphia was moving toward a complete break with England. It opened American ports to the ships of all nations except Great Britain, began negotiating with other nations, and recommended to the colonies that they establish governments independent of the empire, as in fact most already were doing.

At the beginning of the summer, finally, Congress appointed a committee to draft a formal declaration of independence. And on July 2, 1776, it adopted a resolution: "That these United Colonies are, and, of right, ought to be, free and independent states; that they are absolved from all allegiance to the British crown, and that all political connexion between them and the state of Great Britain is, and ought to be, totally dissolved." Two days later, on July 4, Congress approved the Declaration of Independence itself, which provided formal justifications for the actions the delegates had taken two days earlier.

The Declaration was largely the work of Thomas Jefferson, a thirty-three-year-old Virginian, although it was substantially revised by other delegates. (Among other changes, Congress struck out a passage condemning the slave trade to placate Southern slaveowners.) The final document was in two parts. In the first, Jefferson restated the familiar contract theory of John Locke: the theory that governments were formed to protect what Jefferson called "life, liberty and the pursuit of happiness." In the second part, he listed the alleged crimes of the king, who, with the backing of Parliament, had violated his contract with the colonists and thus had forfeited all claim to their loyalty. Little of what Jefferson wrote was new to the document's readers; the power of the Declaration lay in the eloquence with which it expressed beliefs already widespread in America.

Having asserted their independence, the individual colonies now began to call themselves states—a reflection of their belief that each province was now a sovereign entity. By 1781, most states had produced written constitutions for themselves that established republican governments. At the national level, however, the process was more uncertain and less immediately successful. For a time, Americans were not sure whether they even wanted a real national government; virtually everyone considered the individual colonies (now states) the real centers of authority. Yet fighting a war required a certain amount of central direction. In November 1777, finally, Congress adopted a plan for union. The document was known as the Articles of Confederation, and it confirmed the weak, decentralized system already in operation. (See pp. 136–137.)

Mobilizing for War

Organizing the war effort was a formidable task for the frail Congress and the new state governments. They had to find the money to pay for the war, and they had to raise and equip an army to fight it.

Financing the war was particularly difficult, because Congress lacked the authority and the states generally lacked the inclination to impose taxes on the public. Hard currency (gold and silver) had always been scarce in America. And when Congress requisitioned money from the state governments, none contributed more than a small part of its expected share. Congress had little success borrowing from the public, since few Americans could afford to buy bonds and those who could preferred to invest in more profitable ventures, such as privateering. So there was no alternative in the end but to issue paper money. Continental currency came from the printing presses in enormous batches, and the states printed currencies of their own. The result, predictably, was soaring inflation. Many American farmers and merchants began to prefer doing business with the British, who could pay for goods in gold or silver coin. (That was one reason why George Washington's troops suffered from food shortages at Valley Forge in the winter of 1777–1778; many Philadelphia merchants would not accept the paper money the army offered them.) Congress was unable to stop the inflation, and ultimately it was able to finance the war only by borrowing from other nations.

Raising and equipping the army was little easier. After the first surge of patriotism in 1775, only a small proportion of eligible men were willing to volunteer. States had to pay bounties or use a draft to recruit the needed men. At first, militiamen remained under the control of their respective states. But Congress recognized the need for a centralized military command, and it created a Continental army with a single commander in chief: George Washington. A forty-three-year-old Virginia planter-aristocrat who had commanded colonial forces during the French and Indian War, Washington had considerable military experience and was an early advocate of independence; he was admired, respected, and trusted by nearly all Patriots. He took command of the new army in June 1775.

Washington was not without shortcomings as a military commander.

Indeed, he lost more battles than he won. But whatever his faults and failures, he was indisputably a great war leader. With the aid of foreign military experts such as the Marquis de Lafayette from France and the Baron von Steuben from Prussia, he built a force that prevailed against the mightiest power in the world. Even more important, perhaps, Washington's steadiness, courage, and dedication to his cause provided the army—and the people—with a symbol of stability around which they could rally.

THE WAR FOR INDEPENDENCE

On the surface, all the advantages in the military struggle between America and Great Britain appeared to lie with the British. They had the greatest navy and the best-equipped army in the world. They had the resources of an empire. They had a coherent structure of command. The Americans, by contrast, were struggling to create an army and a government at the same time that they were trying to fight a war. Yet the United States had advantages too. Americans were fighting on their own ground. They were

REVOLUTIONARY SOLDIERS Jean Baptiste de Verger, a French officer serving in America during the Revolution, kept a journal of his experiences illustrated with watercolors. Here he portrays four American soldiers carrying different kinds of arms: a black infantryman with a light rifle, a musketman, a rifleman, and an artilleryman.

more committed to the conflict than the British. And beginning in 1777, they were receiving substantial aid from abroad.

But the American victory was not simply the result of these advantages, or even of the spirit and resourcefulness of the people and the army. It was a result, too, of a series of blunders and miscalculations by the British in the early stages of the fighting, when England could (and probably should) have won. And it was, finally, a result of the transformation of the war—through three distinct phases—into a new kind of conflict that the British military, for all its strength, was unable to win.

The First Phase: New England

For the first year of the conflict—from the spring of 1775 to the spring of 1776—the British were not entirely sure that they were fighting a war. Many English authorities thought that British forces were simply quelling pockets of rebellion in the contentious area around Boston.

American forces besieged the British army in Boston (under the command of General Thomas Gage) after the redcoats withdrew from Lexington and Concord. In the Battle of Bunker Hill (actually fought on Breed's Hill) on June 17, 1775, the Patriots suffered severe casualties and withdrew. But they inflicted even greater losses on the enemy (indeed, the heaviest casualties the British were to suffer in the entire war) and continued the siege. Early in 1776, the British decided that Boston was a poor place from which to fight. It was in the center of the most anti-British part of America, and it was also tactically indefensible, easily isolated and besieged. And so, on March 17, 1776, the redcoats left Boston for Halifax with hundreds of Loyalist refugees.

In the meantime, a band of Patriots to the south, at Moore's Creek Bridge in North Carolina, crushed an uprising of Loyalists (Americans still loyal to England and its king) on February 27, 1776, and discouraged a British plan to invade the Southern states. And to the north, the Americans began an invasion of Canada—hoping to remove the British threat and to win the Canadians to their cause. Generals Benedict Arnold and Richard Montgomery threatened Quebec in late 1775 and early 1776. Montgomery was killed in the assault on the city; and although a wounded Arnold kept up the siege for a time, the Quebec campaign ended in failure. Canada did not become the fourteenth state.

By the spring of 1776, it had become clear to the British that the conflict was not just a local phenomenon in the area around Boston. The American campaigns in Canada, the agitation in the South, and the growing evidence

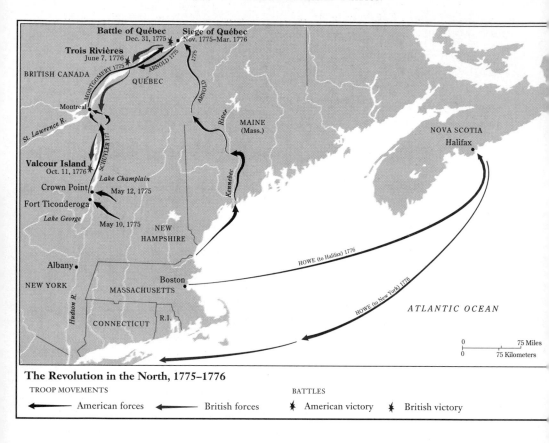

The Revolution in the North, 1775–1776

TROOP MOVEMENTS

⟵——— American forces   ⟵—— British forces

BATTLES

✸ American victory   ✸ British victory

of colonial unity all suggested that England must prepare to fight a much larger conflict.

The Second Phase: The Mid-Atlantic Region

It was during the next phase of the war, which lasted from 1776 until early 1778, that the British were in the best position to win. Indeed, had it not been for a series of blunders and misfortunes, they probably would have crushed the rebellion then.

The British regrouped quickly after their retreat from Boston. During the summer of 1776, in the weeks immediately following the Declaration of Independence, hundreds of British ships and 32,000 British soldiers arrived in New York, under the command of William Howe. Howe wanted to avoid an armed conflict with the Americans and hoped simply to awe them into submission. He offered Congress a choice between surrender with royal pardon and a battle against overwhelming odds.

A M E R I C A N V O I C E S

JOSEPH P. MARTIN

A Soldier's View of the Battle of Long Island

[T]HE REGIMENT WAS ordered to Long Island, the British having landed in force there . . . I went to the top of the house where I had a full view of that part of the island . . . The horrors of battle there presented themselves to my mind in all their hideousness. . . . We were soon ordered to our regimental parade, from which, as soon as the regiment was formed, we were marched off for the ferry. At the lower end of the street were placed several casks of sea-bread . . . nearly hard enough for musket flints. As my good luck would have it, there was a momentary halt made; I improved the opportunity thus offered me, as every good soldier should upon all important occasions, to get as many of the biscuit as I possibly could. . . .

Our officers . . . pressed forward to the creek, where a large party of Americans and British were engaged. By the time we arrived, the enemy had driven our men into the creek . . . where such as could swim got across. Those that could not swim, and could not procure anything to buoy them up, sunk. . . . There was in this action a regiment of Maryland troops (volunteers), all young gentlemen. When they came out of the water and mud, looking like water rats, it was a truly pitiful sight. Many of them were killed in the pond, and more were drowned. Some of us went into the water . . . and took out a number of corpses and a great many arms that were sunk in the pond and creek.

To oppose Howe's great array, Washington could muster only about 19,000 inadequately armed and poorly trained soldiers, and no navy at all. Yet the Americans instantly rejected Howe's offer and chose continued war—which meant inevitably a succession of defeats. The British pushed the Patriot forces off Long Island, forced them to abandon Manhattan, and then drove them in slow retreat over the plains of New Jersey, across the Delaware River, and into Pennsylvania.

The British settled down for the winter in northern and central New Jersey, with an outpost of Hessians at Trenton on the Delaware River. But Washington did not sit still. On Christmas night 1776, he daringly recrossed the icy river, surprised and scattered the Hessians, and occupied Trenton. Then he advanced to Princeton and drove a force of redcoats from their base in the college there. But Washington was unable to hold either Princeton or Trenton and finally took refuge for the rest of the winter in the hills around Morristown. As the campaign of 1776 came to an end, the Americans could console themselves with the thought that they had won two minor victories, that their main army was still intact, and that the invaders were no nearer than before to the decisive triumph that Howe had so confidently anticipated. But the British retained their heavy advantages in men and supplies.

For the campaigns of 1777 the British devised a strategy that, if Howe had stuck to it, might have cut the United States in two and prepared the way for final victory by Great Britain. Howe would move from New York up the Hudson to Albany, while another force would come down from Canada to meet him. John Burgoyne secured command of this northern force and prepared a two-pronged attack to the south along both the Mohawk and the upper Hudson approaches to Albany.

But after setting the plan in motion, Howe inexplicably abandoned his part of it. Instead of moving north to meet Burgoyne, he went south and attacked Philadelphia, in the hope that capturing the rebel capital would discourage the Patriots, rally the Loyalists, and bring the war to a speedy conclusion. He moved most of his forces by sea from New York to the head of the Chesapeake Bay, brushed Washington aside at the Battle of Brandywine Creek on September 11, and proceeded north to Philadelphia, which he took with little resistance. After launching an unsuccessful Patriot attack on October 4 at Germantown (just outside Philadelphia), Washington went into winter quarters at Valley Forge. The Continental Congress reassembled at York, Pennsylvania.

Howe's move to Philadelphia left Burgoyne to carry out the campaign in the north alone. Burgoyne sent Colonel Barry St. Leger up the St. Lawrence River toward Lake Ontario and the Mohawk, while he himself

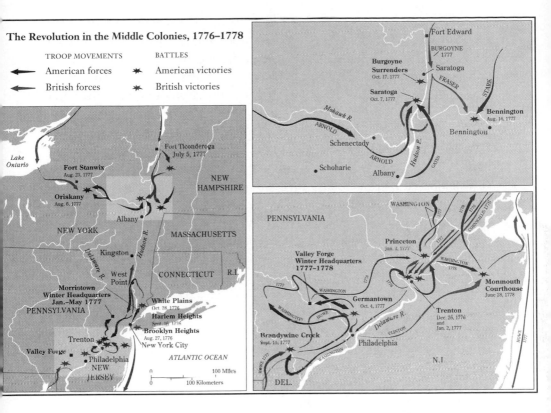

The Revolution in the Middle Colonies, 1776–1778

TROOP MOVEMENTS

American forces

British forces

BATTLES

American victories

British victories

advanced directly down the upper Hudson Valley. At first, all went well. Burgoyne easily seized Fort Ticonderoga and its large store of powder and supplies; Congress was so dismayed by the loss that it removed General Philip Schuyler from command of American forces in the north and replaced him with Horatio Gates.

By the time Gates took over, Burgoyne had already experienced two staggering defeats. In one of them—at Oriskany, New York, on August 6—Patriots held off a force of Indians and Tories commanded by St. Leger. That gave Benedict Arnold time to close off the Mohawk Valley to St. Leger's advance. In the other battle—at Bennington, Vermont, on August 16—New England militiamen mauled a detachment that Burgoyne had sent to seek supplies. Short of materials, with all help cut off, Burgoyne fought several costly engagements and then withdrew to Saratoga, where Gates surrounded him. On October 17, 1777, Burgoyne surrendered—an event that became a major turning point in the war.

The campaign in upstate New York was not just a British defeat. It was a setback for the ambitious efforts of several Iroquois leaders. Although the

Iroquois Confederacy had declared its neutrality in the Revolutionary War in 1776, not all of its members were content to remain passive. Among those who worked to expand the Indian role in the war were a Mohawk brother and sister, Joseph and Mary Brant. The Brants persuaded their own tribe to contribute to the British cause and attracted the support of the Seneca and Cayuga as well.

The alliance had unhappy consequences for the Iroquois. It further divided their already weakened Confederacy; only three of the Iroquois nations supported the British. Then, a year after their defeat at Oriskany, Indians joined British troops in a series of raids on outlying white settlements in upstate New York. Patriot forces under the command of General John Sullivan harshly retaliated, wreaking such destruction on Indian settlements that large groups of Iroquois fled north into Canada to seek refuge. Many never returned.

Securing Aid from Abroad

The leaders of the American effort knew that victory would not be likely without aid from abroad. And their most promising ally, they realized, was France, still smarting from its defeat by the British in 1763. The astute French foreign minister, the Count de Vergennes, understood that France had much to gain from seeing Britain lose a crucial part of its empire.

From the beginning, therefore, there was interest in an alliance on both the American and the French sides. At first, France provided the United States with badly needed supplies but remained reluctant to grant formal diplomatic recognition to the United States. After the Declaration of Independence, Benjamin Franklin himself went to France to lobby for aid and diplomatic recognition. Franklin and his cause became popular among the French, but Vergennes wanted some evidence that the Americans had a real chance of winning before he would agree to open French intervention. That evidence soon appeared in the form of reports of the British defeat at Saratoga.

That news arrived in London and Paris in early December 1777. In London, the news persuaded Lord North to make a new peace offer: complete home rule within the empire for Americans if they would quit the war. That worried Vergennes, who feared the Americans might accept the offer and thus destroy France's opportunity to weaken Britain. Prompted by Franklin, he decided that French assistance might persuade the Americans to continue the struggle. And on February 6, 1778, he reached agreement with American diplomats on formal recognition of the United States as a sovereign nation and on the groundwork for greatly expanded French assistance to the American war effort.

The entrance of France into the war made it an international conflict. In the course of the next two years, France, Spain, and the Netherlands all drifted into another general war with Great Britain in Europe. That contributed indirectly to the ultimate American victory by complicating England's task. All three nations contributed directly by offering financial and material assistance. But France was America's indispensable ally. It furnished the new nation with most of its money and munitions, and it provided a navy and an expeditionary force that were vital to the final, successful phase of the revolutionary conflict.

The Final Phase: The South

The failure of the British to crush the Continental army in the mid-Atlantic states, combined with the stunning American victory at Saratoga, transformed the war and ushered it into a new and final phase. This last phase of the military struggle in America was fundamentally different from either of the first two. After the defeat at Saratoga and the intervention of the French, the British government placed new limits on its commitment to the conflict. Instead of mounting a full-scale military struggle against the American army, the British tried to enlist the support of those elements of the American population—a majority, they continued to believe—who were still loyal to the crown; they worked, in other words, to undermine the Revolution from within. Since Loyalist sentiment was thought to be strongest in the South, and since the English also hoped slaves would rally to their cause, the main focus of the British effort shifted there.

The new strategy was a dismal failure. British forces spent three years (from 1778 to 1781) moving through the South, fighting small battles and large, and attempting to neutralize the territory through which they traveled. But they had badly overestimated the extent of Loyalist sentiment. Even where Loyalists were most numerous, they were often afraid to help the British because they feared reprisals from the Patriots around them. There were also logistical problems. Patriot forces could move at will throughout the region, living off the resources of the countryside, blending in with the civilian population, and leaving the British unable to distinguish friend from foe. The British, by contrast, suffered all the disadvantages of an army in hostile territory.

It was this phase of the conflict that made the war "revolutionary"—not only because it introduced a new kind of warfare, but because it had the effect of mobilizing and politicizing large groups of the population who had previously remained aloof from the struggle. With the war expanding into previously isolated communities, with many civilians forced to involve themselves whether they liked it or not, the political climate of the United States grew more heated than ever. And support for independence, far from being crushed as the British had hoped, greatly increased.

Against that backdrop occurred the important military encounters of the last years of the war. In the North, where significant numbers of British troops remained, the fighting settled into a stalemate. Sir Henry Clinton replaced the hapless William Howe in 1778 and moved what had been Howe's army from Philadelphia back to New York. There the British troops stayed for more than a year, with Washington and his army keeping watch around them. During that same winter, George Rogers Clark, on orders from the state of Virginia, led an expedition over the mountains that captured settlements in the Illinois country from the British and their Indian allies.

During this period of relative calm, the American forces were shocked by the exposure of treason on the part of General Benedict Arnold. Arnold had been one of the early heroes of the war; but now, convinced that the American cause was hopeless, he conspired with British agents to betray the Patriot stronghold at West Point on the Hudson River. When the scheme was exposed and foiled, Arnold fled to the safety of the British camp, where he spent the rest of the war.

The British did have some significant military successes during this period. On December 29, 1778, they captured Savannah, on the coast of Georgia. On May 12, 1780, they took the port of Charleston, South Carolina. And they inspired some Loyalists to take up arms and advance with them into the interior. But although the British were able to win conventional battles, they were constantly harassed as they moved through the countryside by Patriot guerrillas led by such resourceful fighters as Thomas Sumter, Andrew Pickens, and Francis Marion, the "Swamp Fox." Penetrating to Camden, South Carolina, Lord Cornwallis (Clinton's choice as British commander in the South) met and crushed a Patriot force under Horatio Gates on August 16, 1780. Congress recalled Gates, and Washington replaced him with Nathanael Greene, probably the ablest of all the American generals of the time next to Washington himself.

Even before Greene arrived in the war theater, the tide of battle had already begun to turn against Cornwallis. At King's Mountain (near the North Carolina–South Carolina border) on October 7, 1780, a band of Patriot riflemen from the backwoods killed, wounded, or captured an entire force of 1,100 New York and South Carolina Tories, upon whom Cornwallis

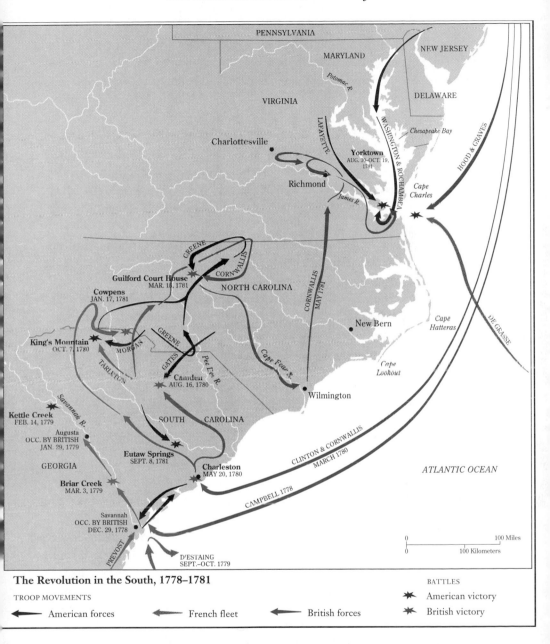

The Revolution in the South, 1778–1781

TROOP MOVEMENTS

← American forces ← French fleet ← British forces

BATTLES

✹ American victory
✹ British victory

had depended as auxiliaries. Once Greene arrived, he confused and exasperated Cornwallis by dividing the American forces into fast-moving contingents while avoiding an open, conventional battle. One of the contingents inflicted what Cornwallis admitted was "a very unexpected and severe blow" at Cowpens on January 17, 1781. Finally, after receiving reinforcements,

Greene combined all his forces and maneuvered to meet the British at Guilford Court House, North Carolina. After a hard-fought battle there on March 15, 1781, Greene was driven from the field; but Cornwallis had lost so many men that he decided to abandon the Carolina campaign.

Cornwallis withdrew to the port town of Wilmington, North Carolina, to receive supplies. Later he moved north, hoping to carry on raids in the interior of Virginia. But Clinton, fearful that the southern army might be destroyed, ordered him to take up a defensive position on the peninsula between the York and James rivers and wait for transport to New York or Charleston. Cornwallis retreated to Yorktown and began to build fortifications there.

At that point, American and French forces descended on Yorktown in an effort to trap Cornwallis. Washington and the Count de Rochambeau marched a French-American army from New York to join the Marquis de Lafayette in Virginia, while Admiral de Grasse took a French fleet with additional troops up Chesapeake Bay to the York River. These joint operations caught Cornwallis between land and sea. After a few shows of resistance, he surrendered on October 17, 1781. Two days later, as a military band played the old tune "The World Turn'd Upside Down," he surrendered his whole army of more than 7,000.

Winning the Peace

Cornwallis's defeat provoked outcries in England against continuing the war. Lord North resigned as prime minister; Lord Shelburne emerged from the political wreckage to succeed him; and British emissaries appeared in France to talk informally with the American diplomats there, of whom the three principals were Benjamin Franklin, John Adams, and John Jay.

The Americans were under instructions to cooperate fully with France in their negotiations with England. But Vergennes, the French foreign minister, insisted that France could not agree to any settlement of the war with England until its ally Spain had achieved its principal war aim: winning back Gibraltar from the British. There was no real prospect of that happening soon, and the Americans began to fear that the alliance with France might keep them at war indefinitely. As a result, Franklin, Jay, and Adams began proceeding on their own, without informing Vergennes, and soon drew up a preliminary treaty with Great Britain, which was signed on November 30, 1782. Franklin, in the meantime, skillfully pacified Vergennes and avoided an immediate rift in the French-American alliance.

The final treaty was signed September 3, 1783, when both Spain and

France agreed to end hostilities. It was, on the whole, remarkably favorable to the United States in granting a clear-cut recognition of independence and a generous, though ambiguous, cession of territory—from the southern boundary of Canada to the northern boundary of Florida and from the Atlantic to the Mississippi. With good reason the American people celebrated as the last of the British occupation forces embarked from New York and General Washington, at the head of his troops, rode triumphantly into the city.

WAR AND SOCIETY

Historians have long debated whether the American Revolution was a social as well as a political revolution. But whatever the intentions or desires of those who produced and fought the War for Independence, the conflict had important effects on the nature of American society.

Loyalists and Minorities

Estimates differ as to how many Americans remained loyal to England during the Revolution, but it is clear that there were many—at least a fifth (and some estimate as much as a third) of the white population. Some were officeholders in the imperial government. Others were merchants whose trade was closely tied to the imperial system (although most merchants supported the Revolution). Still others were people who lived in relative isolation and had simply retained their traditional loyalties. There were also cultural and ethnic minorities who feared that an independent America would not offer them sufficient protection. And there were those who, expecting the British to win the war, were simply currying favor with the anticipated victors.

Hounded by Patriots in their communities, harassed by legislative and judicial actions, many of these Loyalists found themselves in an intolerable position during the war. Up to 100,000 fled the country. Those who could afford to—for example, the hated Tory governor of Massachusetts, Thomas Hutchinson—fled to England, where many lived in difficult and lonely exile. Others of more modest means moved to Canada, establishing the first English-speaking community in the province of Quebec. Some returned to America after the war and, as the early passions and resentments faded, managed to reenter the life of the nation. Others remained abroad for the rest of their lives.

The war had a significant effect on other minorities as well. No sect suffered more than the Anglicans, many of whose members were Loyalists and all of whom were widely identified with England. In Virginia and Maryland, the new Revolutionary regimes removed Anglicanism as the official religion and stopped funding it. In other states, Anglicans lost the economic aid they were accustomed to receiving from England. By the time the fighting ended, many Anglican parishes could no longer even afford clergymen. Anglicanism was permanently weakened from its losses during the Revolution. Also weakened were the Quakers in Pennsylvania and elsewhere, whose pacifism won them widespread unpopularity when they refused to support the war. The church was never to recover fully. Other Protestant denominations, however, grew stronger as a result of their enthusiastic support for the war. Presbyterian, Congregationalist, and Baptist churches successfully tied themselves to the Patriot cause.

Most American Catholics also supported the Patriots during the war and won increased popularity as a result. The church did not greatly increase its numbers as a result of the Revolution, but it did strengthen itself considerably as an institution. Shortly after the peace treaty was signed, the Vatican provided the United States with its own hierarchy and, in 1789, its first bishop. Hostility toward Catholics had not disappeared from American life, but the church had established a footing from which to withstand future assaults.

For the largest of America's minorities—the black population—the war had limited, but nevertheless significant, effects. For some, the Revolution meant freedom. Because so much of the fighting occurred in the South during the last years of the war, many slaves came into contact with the British army, which—in the interests of disrupting and weakening the American cause—emancipated thousands of them and took them out of the country. For other blacks, the Revolution meant exposure to the idea, although not the reality, of liberty. In towns and cities in particular, even blacks who could not read had exposure to the new ideas of liberty; and in some cases, they attempted to apply those ideas to themselves.

That was one reason why Revolutionary sentiment was more restrained in South Carolina and Georgia than in other colonies. Blacks constituted a majority in South Carolina and almost half the population in Georgia, and whites in both places feared that revolution would foment slave rebellions. The same fears discouraged English colonists in the Caribbean islands (who were even more greatly outnumbered by black slaves) from joining with the continental Americans in the revolt against Britain.

Native Americans and the Revolution

Indians viewed the American Revolution with considerable uncertainty. The American Patriots tried to persuade them to remain neutral in the conflict, which they insisted had nothing to do with the tribes. The British too generally sought to maintain Indian neutrality, fearing that native allies would prove unreliable and uncontrollable. Most tribes ultimately chose to stay out of the war.

But many Indians feared that the Revolution would replace a ruling group in which they had developed at least some measure of trust (the British) with one they considered generally hostile to them (the Patriots). The British had consistently sought to limit the expansion of white settlement into Indian land, even if unsuccessfully the Americans had spearheaded the encroachments. Thus some Indians, among them those Iroquois who participated in the Burgoyne campaign in upper New York, chose to join the English cause. Still others took advantage of the conflict to launch attacks of their own.

In the western Carolinas and Virginia, the Cherokee, led by Chief Dragging Canoe, launched a series of attacks on outlying white settlements in the summer of 1776. Patriot militias responded in great force, ravaging Cherokee lands and forcing the chief and many of his followers to flee west across the Tennessee River. Those Cherokee who remained behind agreed to a new treaty by which they gave up still more land. Some Iroquois, despite the setbacks at Oriskany, continued to wage war against Americans in the West and caused widespread destruction in large agricultural areas of New York and Pennsylvania—areas whose crops were of crucial importance to the Patriot cause. And although the retaliating American armies inflicted heavy losses on the Indians, the attacks continued throughout the war.

In the end, however, the Revolution generally weakened the position of Native Americans in several ways. The Patriot victory increased white demand for Western lands. Many whites resented the assistance such nations as the Mohawk had given the British and insisted on treating them as conquered people. Others derived from the Revolution a paternalistic view of the tribes that was only slightly less dangerous to the Native Americans than open hostility. Thomas Jefferson, for example, came to view the Indians as "noble savages," uncivilized in their present state but redeemable if they were willing to adapt to the norms of white society.

Among the Indians themselves, the Revolution increased the deep divisions that made it difficult for them to form a common front to resist the growing power of whites. In 1774, for example, the Shawnee Indians in western Virginia could attract no support from neighboring tribes when they attempted to lead a widespread uprising against white settlers moving into the lands that would later become Kentucky. They were defeated by the colonial militia and forced to cede still more land to white settlers. The Cherokee generated little support from surrounding tribes in their 1776 battles. The Iroquois, whose power had been eroding since the end of the French and Indian War, were unable to act in unison in the Revolution; and the nations that chose to support the British attracted little support from tribes outside the Confederacy (many of whom resented the long Iroquois domination of the interior).

Women's Rights and Women's Roles

The long Revolutionary War had a profound effect on American women. The departure of so many men to fight in the Patriot armies left wives, mothers, sisters, and daughters in charge of farms and businesses. Often, women handled these tasks with great success. But in many cases, inexperience, inflation, the unavailability of male labor, or the threat of enemy troops led to failure. Other women whose husbands or fathers were called away to war did not have even a farm or shop to fall back on. Cities and towns developed significant populations of impoverished women, who on occasion led protests against price increases or rioted and looted for food. On several other occasions (in New Jersey and Staten Island), women launched attacks on occupying British troops, whom they were required to house and feed at considerable expense.

Not all women stayed behind when the men went off to war. Sometimes by choice, more often by necessity, women flocked to the camps of the Patriot armies to join their male relatives. Despite the disapproval of many officers of these female "camp followers," the women were of significant value to the new army, which had not yet developed an adequate system of supply and auxiliary services; the women increased army morale and provided a ready source of volunteers to do cooking, laundry, nursing, and other necessary tasks. In the rough environment of the camps, traditional gender distinctions proved difficult to maintain. Considerable numbers of women became involved, at least intermittently, in combat—including the legendary "Molly Pitcher" (so named because she carried pitchers of water to soldiers on the battlefield), who watched her husband fall during one encounter and immediately took his place at a field gun. A few women even disguised themselves as men so as to be able to fight.

After the war, of course, the soldiers and the women who had accompanied them returned home. The experience of combat had little visible lasting impact on how society (or women themselves) defined female roles in peacetime. The Revolution did, however, call certain assumptions about women into question in other ways. The emphasis on liberty and the "rights of man" led some women to begin to question their position in society as well. "By the way," Abigail Adams wrote to her husband John Adams in 1776, "in the new code of laws which I suppose it will be necessary for you to make, I desire you would remember the ladies and be more generous and favorable to them than your ancestors. Do not put such unlimited power into the hands of the Husbands." Adams was calling for a relatively modest expansion of women's rights: for new protections against abusive and tyrannical men. A few women, however, went further. Judith Sargent Murray, one of the leading essayists of the late eighteenth century, wrote in 1779 that women's minds were as good as those of men and that girls as well as boys therefore deserved access to education.

Nevertheless few concrete reforms were enacted into law or translated into practice. Under English common law, an unmarried woman had certain legal rights, but a married woman had virtually no rights at all. Everything she owned and everything she earned belonged to her husband. She had no legal authority over her children. Because she had no property rights, she could not engage in any legal transactions on her own (buying or selling, suing or being sued, writing wills). She could not vote. Nor could she obtain a divorce; that too was a right reserved almost exclusively to men. The Revolution did little to change any of these legal customs. In some states, it did become easier for women to obtain divorces. And in New Jersey, women obtained the right to vote (although that right was repealed in 1807). Otherwise, there were few advances and some setbacks—including the loss of the right of widows to regain their dowries from their husbands' estates. The Revolution, in other words, did not really challenge the patriarchal legal system. In many ways, it actually confirmed and strengthened it.

But the Revolution did encourage people of both sexes to reevaluate the contribution of women to the family and society. Part of this change was a result of the participation of women in the Revolutionary struggle itself. And part was a result of the reevaluation of American life after the war. As the new republic searched for a cultural identity for itself, it attributed a higher value to the role of women as mothers. The new nation was, many Americans liked to believe, producing a new kind of citizen, steeped in the principles of liberty. Mothers had a particularly important task, therefore, in instructing their children in the virtues that the republican citizenry was expected now to possess. Wives were still far from equal partners in marriage, but their ideas and interests were receiving some respect.

The War Economy

The Revolution also produced important changes in the structure of the American economy. After more than a century of dependence on the British imperial system, American commerce suddenly found itself on its own. English ships no longer protected American vessels, but tried to drive them from the seas. British imperial ports—including those in England itself— were closed to American trade. But this disruption in traditional economic patterns served in the long run to strengthen the American economy. The end of imperial restrictions on American shipping opened up enormous new areas of trade to the nation. Colonial merchants had been violating British regulations for years, but the rules of empire had nevertheless served to inhibit American exploration of many markets. Now, enterprising merchants in New England and elsewhere began to develop new commerce in the Caribbean and South America. By the mid-1780s, American merchants were developing an important trade with the Orient. There was also a substantial increase in trade among the American states.

When English imports to America were cut off—first by the prewar boycott, then by the war itself—there were desperate efforts throughout the states to stimulate domestic manufacturing of certain necessities. No great industrial expansion resulted, but there was a modest increase in production and an even greater increase in expectations. Having broken politically with the British Empire, citizens of the new nation began to dream of breaking economically with it too—of developing a strong economy to rival that of the Old World.

THE CREATION OF STATE GOVERNMENTS

At the same time that Americans were struggling to win their independence on the battlefield, they were also struggling to create new institutions of government to replace the British system they had repudiated. That struggle continued for more than fifteen years, but its most important phase occurred during the war itself, at the state level.

The formation of state governments began early in 1776. At first, the new state constitutions reflected primarily the fear of bloated executive power that had done so much to produce the break with England. Gradually, however, Americans became equally concerned about the instability of a government too responsive to popular will. In a second phase of state constitution writing, therefore, they gave renewed attention to the idea of balance in government.

The Assumptions of Republicanism

If Americans agreed on nothing else when they began to build new governments for themselves, they agreed that those governments would be republican. To them, that meant a political system in which all power came from the people, rather than from some supreme authority (such as a king). The success of any government, therefore, depended on the nature of its citizenry. If the population consisted of sturdy, independent property owners imbued with civic virtue, then the republic could survive. If it consisted of a few powerful aristocrats and a great mass of dependent workers, then it would be in danger. From the beginning, therefore, the ideal of the small freeholder (the independent landowner) was basic to American political ideology.

Another crucial part of that ideology was the concept of equality. The Declaration of Independence had given voice to that idea in its most ringing phrase: "All men are created equal." It was a belief that stood in direct contrast to the old European assumption of an inherited aristocracy. The innate talents and energies of individuals, not their positions at birth, would determine their roles in society. Some people would inevitably be wealthier and more powerful than others. But all people would have to earn their success. There would be no equality of condition, but there would be equality of opportunity.

In reality, of course, the United States was never a nation in which all citizens were independent property holders. From the beginning, there was a sizable dependent labor force—the white members of which were allowed many of the privileges of citizenship, the black members of which were allowed virtually none. American women remained both politically and economically subordinate. Native Americans were systematically exploited and displaced. Nor was there ever full equality of opportunity. American society was more open and more fluid than that of most European nations, but wealth and privilege were often passed from one generation to another. The condition of a person's birth was almost always a crucial determinant of success.

Nevertheless, in embracing the assumptions of republicanism, Americans were adopting a powerful, even revolutionary ideology, and their experiment in statecraft became a model for many other countries. It made the United States for a time the most admired and studied nation on earth.

The First State Constitutions

Two states, Connecticut and Rhode Island, did not write new constitutions. They already had governments that were republican in all but name, and they simply deleted references to England and the king from their charters and adopted them as constitutions. The other eleven states, however, produced new documents.

The first and perhaps most basic decision was that the constitutions were to be written down. In England, the constitution was simply a vague understanding about the nature of government. Americans believed that the vagueness had produced corruption, so they insisted that the structures of their own governments be clearly recorded so no one could pervert them. The second decision was that the power of the executive, which Americans believed had grown bloated in England, must be limited. Pennsylvania eliminated the executive altogether. Most other states inserted provisions limiting the power of the governor over appointments, reducing or elimi- nating his right to veto bills, and preventing him from dismissing the legislature. Most important, every state forbade the governor or any other executive officer from holding a seat in the legislature, thus ensuring that, unlike in England, the two branches of government would remain wholly separate.

But the new constitutions did not move all the way toward direct popular rule. In Georgia and Pennsylvania, the legislature consisted of one popularly elected house. But in every other state, there was an upper and a lower chamber; and in most cases, the upper chamber was designed to represent the "higher orders" of society. There were property requirements for voters—some modest, some substantial—in all states.

The initial phase of constitution writing proceeded rapidly. Ten states completed the process before the end of 1776. Georgia and New York finished by the end of 1777. Massachusetts did not finally adopt a constitu- tion until 1780, by which time the construction of state governments had moved into a new phase.

Revising State Governments

By the late 1770s, Americans were growing concerned about the apparent factiousness and instability of their new state governments, which were having trouble accomplishing anything at all. Many believed the problem was one of too much democracy. As a result, most of the states began to revise their constitutions to limit popular power. Massachusetts was the first to act on the new concerns. By waiting until 1780 to ratify its first constitution, Massachusetts allowed these changing ideas to shape its government; and the state produced a constitution that served as a model for others.

Two changes in particular characterized the Massachusetts and later constitutions. The first was a change in the process of constitution writing itself. Most of the first documents had been written by state legislatures and thus could easily be amended (or violated) by them. By 1780, sentiment was growing to find a way to protect the constitutions from those who had written them, to make it difficult to change the documents once they were approved. The solution was the constitutional convention: a special assembly of the people that would meet only for the purpose of writing the constitution and that would never (except under extraordinary circumstances) meet again. The constitution would be the product of the popular will; but once approved, it would be protected from the whims of public opinion and the political moods of the legislature.

The second change was a significant strengthening of the executive, a reaction to what many believed was the instability of the original state governments that had weak governors. The 1780 Massachusetts constitution made the governor one of the strongest in any state. He was to be elected directly by the people; he was to have a fixed salary (in other words, he would not be dependent on the good will of the legislature each year for his wages); he would have significant appointment powers and a veto over legislation. Other states followed. Those with weak or nonexistent upper houses strengthened or created them. Most increased the powers of the governor. Pennsylvania, which had had no executive at all at first, now produced a strong one. By the late 1780s, almost every state had either revised its constitution or drawn up an entirely new one in an effort to produce stability in government.

Toleration and Slavery

The new states moved far in the direction of complete religious freedom. Most Americans continued to believe that religion should play some role in government, but they did not wish to give special privileges to any particular denomination. The privileges that churches had once enjoyed were now largely stripped away. New York and the Southern states stopped subsidizing the Church of England, and the New England states stripped the Congregational church of many of its privileges. Boldest of all was Virginia. In 1786, it enacted a Statute of Religious Liberty, written by Thomas Jefferson, which called for the complete separation of church and state.

More difficult to resolve was the question of slavery. In areas where slavery was already weak—in New England, where there had never been many slaves, and in Pennsylvania, where the Quakers opposed slavery—it was abolished. Even in the South, there were some pressures to amend the institution; every state but South Carolina and Georgia prohibited further importation of slaves from abroad, and South Carolina banned the slave trade during the war. Virginia passed a law encouraging the freeing of slaves (manumission). Nevertheless, slavery survived in all the Southern and border states. There were several reasons: racist assumptions among whites about the inferiority of blacks; the enormous economic investments many white southerners had in their slaves; and the inability of even such men as Washington and Jefferson, who had deep moral misgivings about slavery, to envision any alternative to it. If slavery were abolished, what would happen to the black people in America? Few whites believed blacks could be integrated into American society as equals. In maintaining slavery, Jefferson once remarked, Americans were holding a "wolf by the ears." However unappealing it was to hold on to it, letting go would be even worse.

THE SEARCH FOR
A NATIONAL GOVERNMENT

Americans were much quicker to agree on state institutions than they were on their national government. At first, most believed that the central government should remain a relatively weak and unimportant force and that each state would be virtually a sovereign nation. Such beliefs reflected the assumption that were a republican government to attempt to administer too large and diverse a nation, it would founder. It was in response to such ideas that the Articles of Confederation emerged.

The Confederation

The Articles of Confederation, which the Continental Congress had adopted in 1777, provided for a national government much like the one already in place. Congress would remain the central—indeed the only—institution of national authority. Its powers would expand to give it authority to conduct wars and foreign relations and to appropriate, borrow, and issue money. But it would not have power to regulate trade, draft troops, or levy taxes directly on the people. For troops and taxes it would have to make formal requests to the state legislatures, which could refuse them. There was to be no separate executive; the "president of the United States" would be merely the presiding officer at the sessions of Congress. Each state would have a single vote in Congress, and at least nine of the states would have to approve any important measure. All thirteen state legislatures would have to approve before the Articles could be ratified or amended.

The ratification process revealed broad disgreements over the plan. The small states had insisted on equal state representation, but the larger states wanted representation to be based on population. The smaller states prevailed on that issue. More important, the states claiming Western lands wished to keep them, but the rest of the states demanded that all such territory be turned over to the Confederation government. When New York and Virginia agreed to give up their Western claims, Maryland (the only state still holding out) approved the Articles of Confederation. They went into effect in 1781.

The Confederation, which existed from 1781 until 1789, was not the complete failure that subsequent accounts often describe. But it was far from a success. Lacking adequate powers to deal with interstate issues or to enforce its will on the states, and lacking sufficient stature in the eyes of the world to be able to negotiate effectively, it suffered a series of damaging setbacks.

Diplomatic Failures

Evidence of the low esteem in which the rest of the world held the Confederation was its difficulty in persuading Great Britain (and to a lesser extent Spain) to live up to the terms of the peace treaty of 1783.

The British had promised to evacuate American soil, but British forces continued to occupy a string of frontier posts along the Great Lakes within the United States. Nor did the British honor their agreement to make restitution to slaveowners whose slaves the British army had confiscated. There were also disputes over the Northeastern boundary of the new nation and over the border between the United States and Florida, which Britain had ceded back to Spain in the treaty. There were other diplomatic problems. American commerce, freed from imperial regulations, was expanding in new directions, but most American trade remained within the British Empire. Americans wanted full access to British markets; England, however, placed sharp postwar restrictions on that access.

In 1784, Congress sent John Adams as minister to London to resolve these differences, but Adams made no headway with the English, who could never be sure whether he represented a single nation or thirteen different ones. Throughout the 1780s, the British government refused even to return the courtesy of sending a minister to the American capital.

In dealing with the Spanish government, the Confederation demonstrated similar weakness. Its diplomats agreed to a treaty with Spain in 1786 that accepted the American interpretation of the Florida boundary in return for American recognition of Spanish possessions in North America and an agreement that the United States would limit its right to navigate the Mississippi for twenty years. But the Southern states, incensed at the idea of giving up their access to the Mississippi, blocked ratification.

The Confederation and the Northwest

The Confederation's most important accomplishment was its resolution of some of the controversies involving the Western lands—although even this was a partial and ambiguous achievement.

When the Revolution began, only a few thousand whites had lived west of the Appalachian divide; by 1790 their numbers had increased to 120,000. The Confederation had to find a way to include these new settlements in the political structure of the new nation. The Western settlers were already often in conflict with the established centers of the East over Indian policies, trade provisions, and taxes. And Congress faced the additional difficulty of competing with state governments for jurisdiction over the trans-Appalachian region. The landed states began to yield their claims to the Confederation in 1781, and by 1784 the states had ceded enough land to the Confederation to permit Congress to begin making policy for the national domain.

The Ordinance of 1784, based on a proposal by Thomas Jefferson, divided the Western territory into ten self-governing districts, each of which could petition Congress for statehood when its population equaled the number of free inhabitants of the smallest existing state. Then, in the Ordinance of 1785, Congress created a system for surveying and selling the Western lands. The territory north of the Ohio River was to be surveyed and marked off into neat rectangular townships. In every township four sections were to be set aside for the United States; the revenue from the sale of one of the others was to support creation of a public school. Sections were to be sold at auction for no less than one dollar an acre.

The original ordinances proved highly favorable to land speculators and less so to ordinary settlers, many of whom could not afford the price of the land. Congress compounded the problem by selling much of the best land to the Ohio and Scioto companies before making it available to anyone else. Criticism of these policies led to the passage in 1787 of another law governing Western settlement—legislation that became known as the "Northwest Ordinance." The 1787 Ordinance abandoned the ten districts established in

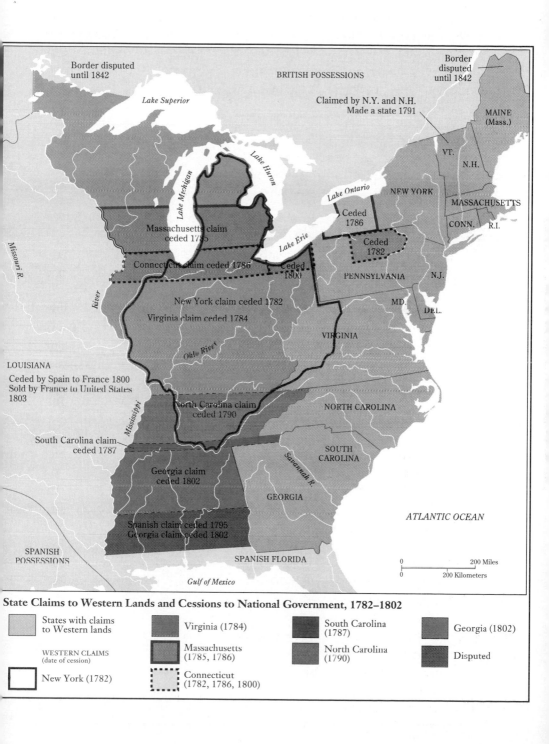

Border disputed until 1842

Lake Superior

BRITISH POSSESSIONS

Border disputed until 1842

Claimed by N.Y. and N.H.
Made a state 1791

MAINE
(Mass.)

Lake Michigan

Lake Huron

VT.

N.H.

Lake Ontario

NEW YORK

MASSACHUSETTS

Missouri R.

Massachusetts claim
ceded 1785

Ceded
1786

Lake Erie

CONN.

R.I.

Connecticut claim ceded 1786

Ceded
1800

Ceded
1782

River

New York claim ceded 1782

PENNSYLVANIA

N.J.

Virginia claim ceded 1784

MD.

DEL.

Ohio River

VIRGINIA

LOUISIANA

Ceded by Spain to France 1800
Sold by France to United States
1803

Mississippi

North Carolina claim
ceded 1790

NORTH CAROLINA

South Carolina claim
ceded 1787

SOUTH
CAROLINA

Georgia claim
ceded 1802

Savannah R.

GEORGIA

ATLANTIC OCEAN

Spanish claim ceded 1795
Georgia claim ceded 1802

SPANISH
POSSESSIONS

SPANISH FLORIDA

0   200 Miles

0   200 Kilometers

Gulf of Mexico

State Claims to Western Lands and Cessions to National Government, 1782–1802

States with claims
to Western lands

Virginia (1784)

South Carolina
(1787)

Georgia (1802)

WESTERN CLAIMS
(date of cession)

Massachusetts
(1785, 1786)

North Carolina
(1790)

Disputed

New York (1782)

Connecticut
(1782, 1786, 1800)

1784 and created a single Northwest Territory out of the lands north of the Ohio; the territory might subsequently be divided into between three and five territories. It also specified a population of 60,000 as a minimum for statehood, guaranteed freedom of religion and the right to trial by jury to residents of the Northwest, and prohibited slavery throughout the territory.

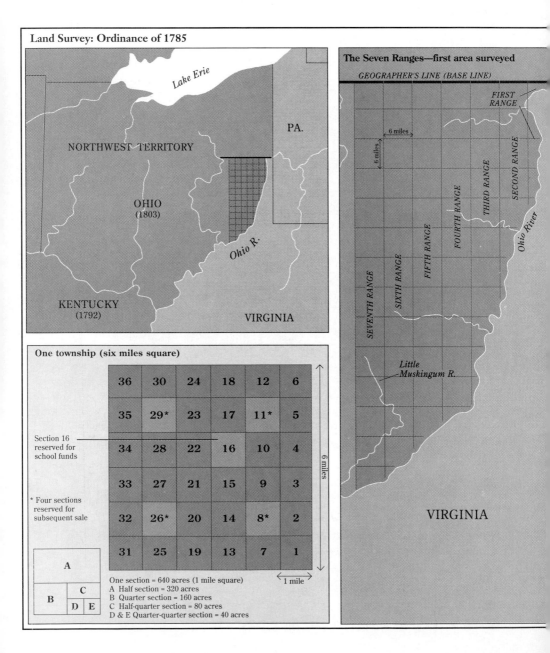

Land Survey: Ordinance of 1785

Lake Erie

PA.

NORTHWEST TERRITORY

OHIO
(1803)

Ohio R.

KENTUCKY
(1792)

VIRGINIA

The Seven Ranges—first area surveyed

GEOGRAPHER'S LINE (BASE LINE)

FIRST RANGE

6 miles

6 miles

SECOND RANGE

THIRD RANGE

FOURTH RANGE

FIFTH RANGE

SIXTH RANGE

SEVENTH RANGE

Ohio River

Little Muskingum R.

VIRGINIA

One township (six miles square)

36	30	24	18	12	6
35	29*	23	17	11*	5
34	28	22	16	10	4
33	27	21	15	9	3
32	26*	20	14	8*	2
31	25	19	13	7	1

Section 16 reserved for school funds

* Four sections reserved for subsequent sale

6 miles

1 mile

One section = 640 acres (1 mile square)
A Half section = 320 acres
B Quarter section = 160 acres
C Half-quarter section = 80 acres
D & E Quarter-quarter section = 40 acres

The Western lands south of the Ohio River received less attention from Congress, and development was more chaotic there. The region that became Kentucky and Tennessee developed rapidly in the late 1770s, and in the 1780s speculators and settlers began setting up governments and asking for recognition as states. The Confederation Congress was never able successfully to resolve the conflicting claims in that region.

Indians and the Western Lands

On paper at least, the Western land policies of the Confederation created a system that brought order and stability to the process of white settlement in the Northwest. But in reality, order and stability came slowly and at great cost, because much of the land the Confederation was neatly subdividing and offering for sale consisted of territory claimed by the Indians of the region.

Congress tried to resolve that problem in 1784, 1785, and 1786 by persuading Iroquois, Choctaw, Chickasaw, and Cherokee leaders to sign treaties ceding substantial Western lands in the North and South to the United States. But those agreements proved ineffective. In 1786, the leadership of the Iroquois Confederacy repudiated the treaty it had signed two years earlier and threatened to attack white settlements in the disputed lands. Other tribes had never really accepted the treaties affecting them and continued to resist white movement into their lands.

Violence between whites and Indians on the Northwest frontier reached a crescendo in the early 1790s. In 1790 and again in 1791, the Miami, led by the famed warrior Little Turtle, defeated United States forces in two major battles near what is now the western border of Ohio; in the second of those battles, on November 4, 1791, 630 white Americans died in fighting at the Wabash River (the greatest military victory Indians had ever or would ever achieve in their battles with whites). Efforts to negotiate a settlement foundered on the Miami insistence that no treaty was possible unless it forbade white settlement west of the Ohio River. Negotiations did not resume until after General Anthony Wayne led 4,000 soldiers into the Ohio Valley in 1794 and defeated the Indians in the Battle of Fallen Timbers.

A year later, the Miami signed the Treaty of Greenville, ceding substantial new lands to the United States (which was now operating under the Constitution of 1789) in exchange for a formal acknowledgment of their claim to that portion of their territory they retained. This was the first time the new federal government recognized the sovereignty of Indian nations; in doing so, the United States was affirming that Indian lands could be ceded

LITTLE TURTLE Little Turtle led the Miami confederacy
in its wars with the United States in what is now Ohio
and Indiana in the early 1790s. For a time he seemed
almost invincible, but in 1794 Little Turtle was defeated
in the Battle of Fallen Timbers.

only by the tribes themselves. That hard-won assurance, however, proved a
frail protection against the pressure for white expansion westward in later
years.

Debts, Taxes, and Daniel Shays

The postwar depression, which lasted from 1784 to 1787, increased the
perennial American problem of an inadequate money supply, a problem
that bore particularly heavily on debtors. In dealing with the serious problem of debts, Congress most clearly demonstrated its weakness.

The Confederation itself had an enormous outstanding debt and few means with which to pay it. It had sold bonds during the war that were now due to be repaid; it owed money to its Revolutionary soldiers; it had substantial debts abroad. But it had no power to tax. It could only make requisitions of the states, and it received only about one-sixth of the money it requisitioned—barely enough to meet the government's ordinary operating expenses, too little to pay the debts. The fragile new nation was faced with the prospect of defaulting on its obligations.

This alarming prospect brought to the fore a group of leaders who would play a crucial role in the shaping of the republic for several decades. Committed nationalists, they sought ways to increase the powers of the central government and to permit it to meet its financial obligations. Robert Morris, the head of the Confederation's treasury; Alexander Hamilton, his young protégé; James Madison of Virginia; and others called for a "continental impost"—a 5 percent duty on imported goods, to be levied by Congress and used to fund the debt.

But the scheme met with substantial opposition. Many Americans feared that the impost plan would concentrate too much financial power in the hands of Morris and his allies in Philadelphia. Congress failed to approve the impost in 1781 and again in 1783. Angry and discouraged, the nationalists largely withdrew from any active involvement in the Confederation.

The states themselves generally relied on increased taxation to pay their own debts. But poor farmers, already burdened by debt and now burdened again by new taxes on their lands, considered such policies unfair, even tyrannical. They demanded that the state governments issue paper currency to increase the money supply and make it easier for them to meet their obligations. Resentment was especially high among farmers in New England, who felt that the states were squeezing them to enrich already wealthy bondholders in Boston and other towns. Debtors who failed to pay their taxes found their mortgages foreclosed and their property seized; sometimes they found themselves in jail.

Throughout the late 1780s, therefore, mobs of distressed farmers rioted periodically in various parts of New England. They caused the most serious trouble in Massachusetts. Dissidents in the Connecticut Valley and the Berkshire Hills, many of them Revolutionary veterans, rallied behind Daniel Shays, a former captain in the Continental army. Shays issued a set of demands that included paper money, tax relief, a moratorium on debts, the removal of the state capital from Boston to the interior, and the abolition of imprisonment for debt. During the summer of 1786, the Shaysites concentrated on preventing the collection of debts, private or public, and used force to keep courts from sitting and sheriffs from selling confiscated property. In Boston, members of the legislature, including Samuel Adams, denounced Shays and his men as rebels and traitors.

When winter came, the rebels advanced on Springfield hoping to seize weapons from the arsenal there. An army of state militiamen, financed by a loan from wealthy merchants who feared a new revolution, set out from Boston to confront them. In January 1787, this army met Shays's band and dispersed his ragged troops.

As a military enterprise, Shays's Rebellion was a failure. But it had important consequences for the future of the United States. In Massachusetts, it resulted in a few immediate gains for the discontented groups. Shays and his lieutenants, at first sentenced to death, were later pardoned; and Massachusetts offered the protesters some tax relief and a postponement of debt payments. More significantly, however, the rebellion added urgency to a movement already gathering support throughout the new nation—the movement to produce a new, national constitution.

D E B A T I N G   T H E   P A S T

The American Revolution

HE LONGSTANDING DEBATE over the origins of the American Revolution has tended to reflect two broad schools of interpretation. One sees the Revolution largely as a political and intellectual event and argues that the revolt against Britain was part of a defense of ideals and principles. The other views the Revolution as a social and economic phenomenon and contends that material interests were at the heart of the rebellion.

The Revolutionary generation itself portrayed the conflict as a struggle over ideals, and this interpretation prevailed through most of the nineteenth century. But in the early twentieth century, historians influenced by the reform currents of the progressive era began to identify social and economic forces that they believed had contributed to the rebellion. Carl Becker, for example, wrote in a 1909 study of New York that two questions had shaped the Revolution: "The first was the question of home rule; the second was the question . . . of who should rule at home." The colonists were not only fighting the British; they were also engaged in a kind of civil war, a contest for power between radicals and conservatives that led to the "democratization of American politics and society."

Other "progressive" historians elaborated on Becker's thesis. J. Franklin Jameson, writing in 1926, argued, "Many economic desires, many social aspirations, were set free by the political struggle, many aspects of society profoundly altered by the forces thus let loose." Arthur M. Schlesinger maintained in a 1917 book that colonial merchants, motivated by their own interest in escaping the restrictive policies of British mercantilism, aroused American resistance in the 1760s and 1770s.

Beginning in the 1950s, a new generation of scholars began to reem-

(continued on next page)

phasize the role of ideology and de-emphasize the role of economic interests. Robert E. Brown (in 1955) and Edmund S. Morgan (in 1956) both argued that most eighteenth-century Americans shared common political principles and that the social and economic conflicts the progressives had identified were not severe. The rhetoric of the Revolution, they suggested, was not propaganda but a real reflection of the ideas of the colonists. Bernard Bailyn, in *The Ideological Origins of the American Revolution* (1967), demonstrated the complex roots of the ideas behind the Revolution and argued that this carefully constructed political stance was not a disguise for economic interests but a genuine ideology, rooted in deeply held convictions about rights and power, that itself motivated the colonists to act. The Revolution, he claimed, "was above all else an ideological, constitutional, political struggle and not primarily a controversy between social groups undertaken to force changes in the organization of the society or the economy."

By the late 1960s, however, a group of younger historians—many of them influenced by the New Left—were challenging the ideological interpretation again by illuminating social and economic tensions within colonial society that they claimed helped shape the Revolutionary struggle. Jesse Lemisch and Dirk Hoerder pointed to the actions of mobs in colonial cities as evidence of popular resentment of both American and British elites. They noted, for example, that Revolutionary crowds were likely to attack all symbols of wealth and power, whether British or American; that they displayed a range of class-based grievances not rooted in elite ideologies. Joseph Ernst reemphasized the significance of economic pressures on colonial merchants and tradesmen. Gary Nash, in *The Urban Crucible* (1979), emphasized the role of growing economic distress in colonial cities in creating a climate in which Revolutionary sentiment could flourish. Edward Countryman and Rhys Isaac both pointed to changes in the nature of colonial society and culture, and in the relationship between classes in eighteenth-century America, as a crucial prerequisite for the growth of the Revolutionary movement. Many of these newer social interpretations of the Revolution do not argue that the rebellion was a class conflict or that economic interests inevitably *determined* a person's stance toward the struggle. They argue, rather, that the relationship between interests and ideology must be a part of any workable explanation of the conflict.

CHAPTER SIX

The Constitution
and the New Republic

Toward a New Government ~ *Adoption and Adaptation*
Federalists and Republicans ~ *Asserting National Sovereignty*
The Downfall of the Federalists

Y THE LATE 1780s, many Americans had grown dissatisfied with the Confederation. It was factious and unstable, unable to deal effectively with economic problems, and frighteningly powerless in the face of Shays's Rebellion. A decade earlier, Americans had deliberately avoided creating a genuine national government. Now they reconsidered. In 1787, in a burst of great political creativity, the nation created a new constitution and a new government consisting of three independent branches.

The American Constitution derived most of its principles from the state documents that had preceded it. But it was also a remarkable achievement in its own right. It created a system of government that has survived for more than two centuries as one of the stablest and most successful in the world. William Gladstone, the great nineteenth-century British statesman, once called the Constitution the "most wonderful work ever struck off at a given time by the brain and purpose of man." The American people generally agreed. Indeed, to many the Constitution took on some of the characteristics of a sacred document, an unassailable "fundamental law" from which all public policies and all political principles must spring.

Yet the adoption of the Constitution did not complete the creation of the republic. For while most Americans agreed that the Constitution was a nearly perfect document, they disagreed—at times fundamentally—on what that document meant. Out of those disagreements emerged the first great political battles of the new nation.

147

TOWARD A NEW GOVERNMENT

So unpopular and ineffectual had the Confederation Congress become by the mid-1780s that it began to lead an almost waiflike existence. In 1783, its members timidly withdrew from Philadelphia to escape army veterans demanding their back pay. They took refuge for a while in Princeton, New Jersey, then moved on to Annapolis, and in 1785 settled in New York. Through all of this, delegates were often scarce. Only with great difficulty could Congress produce a quorum to ratify the treaty with Great Britain ending the Revolutionary War. Only eight state delegations voted on the Confederation's most important piece of legislation, the Northwest Ordinance.

Advocates of Centralization

Weak and unpopular though the Confederation was, a great many citizens—probably a majority—remained wary of a strong central government. They had, they believed, fought the Revolutionary War to abolish remote and tyrannical authority; now they wanted to keep political power centered in the states, where it could be carefully and closely controlled. But some of the wealthiest and most powerful groups in the population were beginning to clamor in the 1780s for a more genuinely national government capable of dealing more effectively with the country's problems. By 1786, such demands had grown so intense that even defenders of the existing system reluctantly agreed that the government needed strengthening at its weakest point—its lack of power to tax.

The most resourceful advocate of centralization was Alexander Hamilton, the illegitimate son of a Scottish merchant in the West Indies, who had become a successful New York lawyer and had once served as an aide to George Washington. Hamilton had been unhappy with the Articles of Confederation, and the weak central government they had created, from the start. He now called for a national convention to overhaul the entire document.

He found an important ally in James Madison of Virginia, who persuaded the Virginia legislature to convene an interstate conference on commercial questions. Only five states sent delegates to the meeting, which was held at Annapolis, Maryland, in 1786; but the conference approved a proposal drafted by Hamilton (representing New York) for a convention of special delegates from all the states to meet in Philadelphia the next year and consider ways to "render the constitution of the Federal government adequate to the exigencies of the union."

At that point, in 1786, there seemed little reason to believe the Philadelphia convention would generate much wider interest than the Annapolis meeting had attracted. Only by winning the support of George Washington, the centralizers believed, could they hope to prevail. But Washington at first showed little interest in joining the cause. Then, early in 1787, the news of Shays's Rebellion spread throughout the nation. Thomas Jefferson, then the American minister in Paris, was not alarmed. "I hold," he confided in a letter to James Madison, "that a little rebellion, now and then, is a good thing, and as necessary in the political world as storms in the physical." But Washington took the news less calmly. "There are combustibles in every State which a spark might set fire to," he exclaimed. "I feel infinitely more than I can express for the disorders which have arisen. Good God!" He promptly made plans to travel to Philadelphia for the Constitutional Convention. His support gave the meeting wide credibility.

A Divided Convention

Fifty-five men, representing all the states except Rhode Island, attended one or more sessions of the convention that sat in the Philadelphia State House from May to September 1787. These "Founding Fathers," as they later became known, were relatively young men; the average age was forty-four, and only one delegate (Benjamin Franklin, then eighty-one) was genuinely aged. They were well educated by the standards of their time. Most represented the great property interests of the country, and many feared what one of them called the "turbulence and follies" of democracy. Yet all were also products of the American Revolution and retained the Revolutionary suspicion of concentrated power.

The convention unanimously chose Washington to preside over its sessions and then closed its business to the public and the press. (If James Madison had not kept a diary chronicling the proceedings, historians might know little about what happened in Philadelphia.) It then ruled that each state delegation would have a single vote and that major decisions would require not unanimity, as they did in Congress, but a simple majority. Almost all the delegates agreed that the United States needed a stronger central government. But there agreement ended.

Virginia, the largest state in population, sent a well-prepared delegation to Philadelphia. James Madison (thirty-six years old) was its intellectual leader. He had devised in some detail a plan for a new "national" government; the Virginians used it to control the agenda of the convention from the start.

Edmund Randolph of Virginia opened the debate by proposing a central element of the Virginia Plan: that "a national government ought to be established, consisting of a supreme Legislative, Executive, and Judiciary." It was a drastic proposal, calling for a government fundamentally different from the existing Confederation. But so committed were the delegates to fundamental reform that they approved the resolution after only brief debate. Then Randolph introduced the details of Madison's Virginia Plan. It called for a national legislature of two houses. In the lower house, states would be represented in proportion to their population; thus the largest state (Virginia) would have about ten times as many representatives as the smallest (Delaware). Members of the upper house were to be elected by the lower house under no rigid system of representation; thus some of the smaller states might at times have no members at all in the upper house.

The proposal aroused immediate opposition among delegates from Delaware, New Jersey, and other small states. Some responded by arguing that the convention had authority to do no more than revise the existing Articles of Confederation. William Paterson of New Jersey offered an alternative (the New Jersey Plan) that would have retained the essence of the existing system. It preserved the existing one-house legislature of the Confederation, in which each state had equal representation; but it gave Congress expanded powers to tax and to regulate commerce. The majority of the delegates voted to table Paterson's proposal.

Supporters of the Virginia Plan now realized they would have to make concessions to the small states if the delegations were ever to agree. They conceded an important point by agreeing that the members of the upper house would be elected by the state legislatures, thereby ensuring that every state would be represented.

But many questions remained unresolved. Among the most important was the question of slavery. Would slaves be counted as part of the population in determining representation in Congress? Or would they be considered property, not entitled to representation? Delegates from the states with large slave populations wanted to have it both ways. They argued that slaves should be considered persons in determining representation but as property if the new government were to levy taxes on the states on the basis of population. Representatives from states where slavery had disappeared or was expected soon to disappear argued that slaves should be included in calculating taxation but not representation. No one argued seriously for giving slaves the right to vote or citizenship.

Compromise

The delegates bickered for weeks. By the end of June, as both temperature and tempers rose to uncomfortable heights, the convention seemed in danger of collapsing. But the delegates refused to give up (partly because of the patient urging of Benjamin Franklin). Finally, on July 2, the convention created a "grand committee," chaired by Franklin and with one delegate from each state, to resolve the remaining disagreements. The committee produced a proposal that became the basis of the "Great Compromise." Its most important achievement was resolving the difficult problem of representation. The proposal called for a legislature in which the states would be represented in the lower house on the basis of population; each slave would be counted as three-fifths of a free person in determining the basis for both representation and direct taxation. And the proposal called for an upper house in which the states would be represented equally with two members apiece. On July 16, 1787, the convention voted to accept the compromise.

In the next few weeks, the convention agreed to another important compromise on the explosive issue of slavery. The representatives of the Southern states feared that if the national government were granted power to regulate trade, it might interfere with slavery. The convention agreed to bar the new government from stopping the slave trade for twenty years. This was a large and difficult concession from the delegates who opposed slavery, but they agreed to it because they feared that without it the Constitution would fail.

Some important issues remained unaddressed. Most important was the absence of a list of individual rights, which would restrain the powers of the national government in the way that bills of rights restrained the state governments. Madison opposed the idea, arguing that specifying rights that were reserved to the people would, in effect, limit those rights. Others, however, feared that without such protections the national government might abuse its new authority.

The Constitution of 1787

Many people contributed to the creation of the American Constitution, but the most important person in the process was James Madison. Madison had devised the Virginia Plan, from which the final document ultimately emerged, and he did most of the drafting of the Constitution itself. Madison's most important achievement, however, was in helping resolve two important philosophical questions that had served as obstacles to the creation of an effective national government: the question of sovereignty and the question of limiting power.

The creation of the federal Constitution had required the resolution of difficult questions associated with sovereignty. How could a national government exercise sovereignty concurrently with state governments? Where did ultimate sovereignty lie? The answer, Madison and his contemporaries decided, was that all power, at all levels of government, flowed ultimately from the people. Thus neither the federal government nor the state governments were truly sovereign. All of them derived their authority from below. The opening phrase of the Constitution—"We the people of the United States of America"—is an expression of the belief of most of the framers that the new government derived its power not from the states but from the public at large.

The resolution of the problem of sovereignty made possible one of the distinctive features of the Constitution—its division of powers between the national and state governments. The Constitution and the government it created were to be the "supreme law" of the land; no state would have the authority to defy it. The federal government would have the power to tax, to regulate commerce, and to control the currency. At the same time, the Constitution left certain important powers in the hands of the states.

In addition to solving the question of sovereignty, the Constitution produced a distinctive solution to the problem of concentrated authority. Nothing so frightened the leaders of the new nation as the prospect of creating a tyrannical government. Indeed, that fear had been one of the chief obstacles to the creation of a national government at all. Drawing from the ideas of the French philosopher Baron de Montesquieu, most Americans had long believed that the best way to avoid tyranny was to keep government close to the people. A republic must remain confined to a relatively small area; a large nation would breed corruption and despotism because the rulers would be so distant from most of the people that there would be no way to control them. In the new American nation, these assumptions had led to the belief that the individual states must remain sovereign and that a strong national government would be dangerous.

Madison, however, helped break the grip of these assumptions by arguing that a large republic would be less, not more, likely to produce tyranny, because it would contain so many different factions that no single group would ever be able to dominate it. This idea of many centers of power "checking each other" and preventing any single, despotic authority from emerging also helped shape the internal structure of the federal government. The Constitution's most distinctive feature was its "separation of powers" within the government, its creation of "checks and balances" among the legislative, executive, and judicial branches. The forces within the government would constantly compete with (and often frustrate) one another. Congress would have two chambers, each checking the other, since both would have to agree before any law could be passed. The president would have the power to veto acts of Congress. The federal courts would be protected from both the executive and the legislature, because judges, once appointed by the president and confirmed by the Senate, would serve for life.

The "federal" structure of the government was designed to protect the United States from the kind of despotism that Americans believed had emerged in England. But it was also designed to protect the nation from another kind of despotism: the tyranny of the people. Shays's Rebellion, most of the founders believed, had been only one example of what could happen if a nation did not defend itself against the unchecked exercise of popular will. Thus in the new government, only the members of the House of Representatives would be elected directly by the people. Senators, the president, federal judges—all would be insulated in varying degrees from the public.

On September 17, 1787, thirty-nine delegates signed the Constitution, doubtless sharing the feelings that Benjamin Franklin expressed at the end: "Thus I consent, Sir, to this Constitution, *because I expect no better, and because I am not sure that it is not the best.*"

ADOPTION AND ADAPTATION

The delegates at Philadelphia had greatly exceeded their instructions from Congress and the states. Instead of making simple revisions in the Articles of Confederation, they had produced a plan for a completely different form of government. They feared, therefore, that the Constitution would not be ratified under the rules of the Articles of Confederation, which required unanimous approval by the state legislatures. So the convention changed the rules, proposing that the new government come into being when nine of the thirteen states ratified the Constitution and recommending that state conventions, not state legislatures, be called to ratify it.

Federalists and Antifederalists

The Congress in New York, demoralized and overshadowed by the events in Philadelphia, passively accepted the convention's work and submitted it to the states for approval. All the state legislatures except Rhode Island elected delegates to ratifying conventions, most of which had begun meeting by early 1788. Even before the ratifying conventions adjourned, however, a great national debate on the new Constitution had begun—in the state legislatures, in public meetings, in newspapers, and in ordinary conversations.

Supporters of the Constitution had a number of advantages. They were better organized. They had the support of the two most eminent men in America, Franklin and Washington. And they seized an appealing label for themselves: "Federalists"—a term that opponents of centralization had once used to describe themselves—thus implying that they were less committed to a "nationalist" government than in fact they were. The Federalists had the support of some of the ablest political philosophers of their time: Alexander Hamilton, James Madison, and John Jay. Those three men, under the joint pseudonym "Publius," wrote a series of essays—widely published in newspapers throughout the nation—explaining the meaning and virtues of the Constitution. The essays were later issued as a book, and they are known today as *The Federalist Papers*. They are among the greatest American contributions to political theory.

The Federalists called their critics "Antifederalists," which suggested that their rivals had nothing to offer except opposition. But the Antifederalists had serious and intelligent arguments of their own. They saw themselves as the defenders of the true principles of the Revolution. The Constitution, they believed, would betray those principles by establishing a strong, potentially tyrannical, center of power in the new national government. The new government, they claimed, would increase taxes, obliterate the states, wield dictatorial powers, favor the "well born" over the common people, and abolish individual liberty. Among their biggest complaint was that the Constitution lacked a bill of rights, a concern that revealed one of the most important reasons for their opposition: their basic mistrust of human nature and of the capacity of human beings to wield power. The Antifederalists argued that any government that placed authority in the hands of a few powerful people would inevitably produce despotism. Their demand for a bill of rights was a product of this belief: no government could be trusted to protect the liberties of its citizens; only by enumerating the rights of the people could there be any certainty that those rights would be protected.

Despite the efforts of the Antifederalists, ratification proceeded quickly (although not without difficulty in several states) during the winter of 1787–1788. The Delaware convention was the first to act. It ratified the Constitution unanimously, as did New Jersey and Georgia. New Hampshire ratified the document in June 1788—the ninth state to do so. It was now theoretically possible for the Constitution to go into effect.

A new government could not hope to succeed, however, without Virginia and New York, whose conventions remained closely divided. But by the end of June, first Virginia and then New York had consented to the Constitution by narrow margins. The New York convention yielded to expediency—even some of the most staunchly Antifederalist delegates feared that the state's commercial interests would suffer if New York were to remain outside the new union. Massachusetts, Virginia, and New York all ratified on the assumption that a bill of rights would be added in the form of amendments to the Constitution. North Carolina's convention adjourned without taking action, waiting to see what happened to the amendments. Rhode Island did not even consider ratification.

Completing the Structure

The first elections under the Constitution were held in the early months of 1789. Almost all the newly elected members of Congress had favored ratification, and many had served as delegates to the Philadelphia convention. There was never any doubt about who would be the first president. George Washington had presided at the Constitutional Convention, and many who had favored ratification did so only because they expected him to preside over the new government as well. Washington received the votes of all the presidential electors. John Adams, a leading Federalist, became vice president. After a journey from his estate at Mount Vernon, Virginia, marked by elaborate celebrations along the way, Washington was inaugurated in New York on April 30, 1789.

The first Congress served in many ways almost as a continuation of the Constitutional Convention, because its principal responsibility was filling in the various gaps in the Constitution. Its most important task was drafting a bill of rights. By early 1789, even Madison had come to agree that some sort of bill of rights would be essential to legitimize the new government in the eyes of its opponents. On September 25, 1789, Congress approved twelve amendments, ten of which were ratified by the states by the end of 1791. What we know as the Bill of Rights is these first ten amendments to the Constitution. Nine of them placed limitations on Congress by forbidding it to infringe on certain fundamental rights: freedom of religion, speech, and the press; immunity from arbitrary arrest; trial by jury; and others. The Tenth Amendment reserved to the states all powers except those specifically withheld from them or delegated to the federal government.

THE INAUGURATION OF GEORGE WASHINGTON, APRIL
30, 1789 Washington took the oath of office as
the first president of the United States under the
new Constitution at Federal Hall in New York
City, which was then the nation's capital city.

On the subject of federal courts, the Constitution said only: "The
judicial power of the United States shall be vested in one Supreme Court,
and in such inferior courts as the Congress may from time to time ordain
and establish." It was left to Congress to determine the number of Supreme
Court judges to be appointed and the kinds of lower courts to be organized.
In the Judiciary Act of 1789, Congress provided for a Supreme Court of six
members and a system of lower district courts and courts of appeal. In the
same act, Congress gave the Supreme Court the power to make the final
decision in cases involving the constitutionality of state laws.

The Constitution referred indirectly to executive departments but did
not specify which ones or how many there should be. The first Congress
created three such departments—state, treasury, and war—and also estab-

lished the offices of the attorney general and postmaster general. To the office of secretary of the treasury Washington appointed Alexander Hamilton of New York, who at age thirty-two was an acknowledged expert in public finance. For secretary of war he chose a Massachusetts Federalist, General Henry Knox. As attorney general he named Edmund Randolph of Virginia, sponsor of the plan on which the Constitution had been based. As secretary of state he chose another Virginian, Thomas Jefferson.

FEDERALISTS AND REPUBLICANS

The resolution of these initial issues, however, did not resolve the disagreements about the nature of the new government. The framers of the Constitution had dealt with many controversies not by solving them but by papering them over with a series of vague compromises; as a result, the disagreements survived to plague the new government, and the first twelve years under the Constitution produced a politics of unusual acrimony.

At the heart of the controversies of the 1790s was the same basic difference in philosophy that had been at the heart of the debate over the Constitution. On one side stood a powerful group who believed that America required a strong, national government: that the country's mission was to become a genuine nation-state, with centralized authority, a complex commercial economy, and a proud standing in world affairs. On the other side stood another group—a minority at first, but one that gained strength during the decade—whose members envisioned a more modest central government. American society should not, this group believed, aspire to be highly commercial or urban. It should remain predominantly rural and agrarian. The centralizers became known as the Federalists and gravitated to the leadership of Alexander Hamilton. Their opponents acquired the name Republicans and gathered under the leadership of James Madison and Thomas Jefferson.

Hamilton and the Federalists

For twelve years, the Federalists retained firm control of the new government. That was in part because George Washington had always envisioned a strong national government and as president did little to stop those attempting to create one. But the president, Washington believed, should stand above political controversies, and so he avoided any personal involvement in the deliberations of Congress. As a result, the dominant figure in his administration became Alexander Hamilton, who exerted more influence than anyone else on domestic and foreign policy.

Of all the national leaders of his time, Hamilton was one of the most aristocratic in personal tastes and political philosophy; he believed that a stable and effective government required an elite ruling class. Thus the new government needed the support of the wealthy and powerful; and to get that, it needed to give elites a stake in its success. Hamilton proposed, therefore, that the existing public debt be "funded": that the various certificates of indebtedness that the old Congress had issued during and after the Revolution—many of them now in the possession of wealthy speculators—be called in and exchanged for interest-bearing bonds. He also recommended that the Revolutionary state debts be "assumed," taken over by the United States, to cause state as well as federal bondholders to look to the central government for eventual payment. Hamilton did not envision paying off and thus eliminating the debt; he wanted to create a large and permanent national debt, with new bonds being issued as old ones were paid off. The result, he believed, would be that the wealthy classes, who were the most likely to lend money to the government, would have a permanent stake in seeing the government survive.

Hamilton also wanted to create a national bank. It would provide loans and currency to businesses. It would give the government a safe place for the deposit of federal funds. It would facilitate the collection of taxes and the disbursement of the government's expenditures. And it would provide a stable center to the nation's small and feeble banking system. The bank would be chartered by the federal government and would have a monopoly of the government's own banking business, but much of its capital would come from private investors.

The funding and assumption of debts would require new sources of revenue for the national government. Hamilton recommended two kinds of taxes to complement the receipts anticipated from the sales of public land. One was an excise tax on alcoholic beverages, a tax that would be most burdensome to the whiskey distillers of the back country, especially those in Pennsylvania, Virginia, and North Carolina—small farmers who converted part of their corn and rye crop into whiskey. The other was a tariff on imports, which Hamilton saw not only as a way to raise money but as a way to protect domestic industries from foreign competition. In his famous "Report on Manufactures" of 1791, he outlined a plan for stimulating the growth of industry in the United States and spoke glowingly of the advantages to society of a healthy manufacturing sector.

The Federalists, in short, offered more than a vision of a stable new government. They offered a vision of the sort of nation America should become—a nation with a wealthy, enlightened ruling class, a vigorous, independent commercial economy, and a thriving industrial sector; a country able to play a prominent role in world economic affairs.

Enacting the Federalist Program

Few members of Congress objected to Hamilton's plan for funding the national debt; but many did oppose his proposal to fund the debt at par, that is, to exchange new bonds for old certificates of indebtedness on a dollar-for-dollar basis. The old certificates had been issued to merchants and farmers in payment for war supplies during the Revolution and to officers and soldiers of the Revolutionary army in payment for their services. Many of these holders had been forced to sell their bonds during the hard times of the 1780s to speculators, who had bought them at a fraction of their face value. James Madison, now a representative from Virginia, argued for a plan by which the new bonds would be divided between the original holders and the speculators. But Hamilton's allies insisted that such a plan was impracticable and that the honor of the government required a literal fulfillment of its earlier promises to pay. Congress finally passed the funding bill Hamilton wanted.

Hamilton's proposal that the federal government assume the state debts encountered greater difficulty. Its opponents argued that if the federal government took over the state debts, the states with few debts would have to pay taxes to service the states with large ones. Massachusetts, for example, owed much more money than did Virginia. Only by striking a bargain with the Virginians were Hamilton and his supporters able to win passage of the assumption bill.

The deal involved the location of the national capital. The Virginians wanted to create a new capital near them in the South. Hamilton met with Jefferson and Madison and agreed to provide Northern support for placing the capital in the South in exchange for Virginia's votes for the assumption bill. The bargain called for the construction of a new capital city on the banks of the Potomac River, which divided Maryland and Virginia, on land to be selected by George Washington. The government would move its operations by the beginning of the new century.

Hamilton's bank bill produced the most heated debates. Madison, Jefferson, Randolph, and others argued that because the Constitution made no provision for a national bank (or for Congress's issuing of articles of incorporation), Congress had no authority to create one. But Congress agreed to Hamilton's bill despite these objections, and Washington, despite some apparent reservations, signed it. The Bank of the United States began operations in 1791, under a twenty-year charter.

Hamilton also had his way with the excise tax, although protests from farmers later forced revisions to reduce the burden on the smaller distillers. He failed to win passage of a tariff as highly protective as he had hoped for, but the tariff law of 1792 did raise the rates somewhat.

Once enacted, Hamilton's program won the support of manufacturers, creditors, and other influential segments of the population, as he had hoped. But others found the Hamilton program less appealing. Small farmers, who formed the majority of the population, complained that they were being taxed excessively. They and others began to argue that the Federalist program served the interests not of the people but of small, wealthy elites. Out of this feeling an organized political opposition arose.

The Republican Opposition

The Constitution made no reference to political parties, and the omission was not an oversight. Most of the framers—and George Washington in particular—believed that organized parties were dangerous and to be avoided. Disagreement was inevitable on particular issues, but most of the founders believed that such disagreements need not and should not lead to the formation of permanent factions.

Yet not many years had passed after the ratification of the Constitution before Madison and others became convinced that Hamilton and his followers had become a dangerous, self-interested faction. Not only had the Federalists enacted a program that many of these leaders opposed, more ominously, Hamilton himself had, they believed, worked to establish a national network of influence that embodied all the worst features of a party. The Federalists had used the powers of their offices to reward their supporters and win additional allies. They had encouraged the formation of local associations—largely aristocratic in nature—to strengthen their standing in local communities. They were doing many of the same things, their opponents believed, that the corrupt British governments of the early eighteenth century had done.

Because the Federalists appeared to their critics to be creating such a menacing and tyrannical structure of power, there was no alternative but to organize a vigorous opposition. The result was the emergence of an alternative political organization, whose members called themselves "Republicans." (These first Republicans are not related to the modern Republican party, which was born in the 1850s.) By the late 1790s, the Republicans were going to even greater lengths than the Federalists to create an apparatus of partisan influence. In every state they had formed committees, societies, and caucuses; Republican groups were corresponding with one another across state lines; they were banding together to influence state and local elections. And they were justifying their actions by claiming, just as Hamilton and his supporters claimed, that they and they alone represented the true interests of the nation. Neither side was willing to admit that it was acting as a party; nor would either concede the right of the other to exist. This institutionalized factionalism is known to historians as the "first party system."

From the beginning, the preeminent figures among the Republicans were Thomas Jefferson and James Madison. Jefferson, the more politically magnetic of the two, became the most prominent spokesman for the cause. He promoted a vision of an agrarian republic, in which most citizens would farm their own land. Jefferson did not scorn commercial activity; farmers would, he assumed, market their crops through national and even international trade. Nor did he oppose industrial activity; Americans should, he believed, develop a certain amount of manufacturing capacity. But Jefferson did believe that the nation should be wary of too much urbanization and industrialization.

Although both parties had supporters in all parts of the country and among all classes, there were regional and economic differences. The Federalists were most numerous in the commercial centers of the Northeast and in such Southern seaports as Charleston; the Republicans were most numerous in the rural areas of the South and the West. The difference in their philosophies was visible in, among other things, their reactions to the progress of the French Revolution. As that revolution grew increasingly radical in the 1790s, with its attacks on organized religion, the overthrow of the monarchy, and eventually the execution of the king and queen, the Federalists expressed horror. But the Republicans applauded the democratic, antiaristocratic spirit they believed the French Revolution had displayed.

When the time came for the nation's second presidential election in 1792, both Jefferson and Hamilton urged Washington to run for a second term. The president reluctantly agreed. But while Washington had the respect of both factions, he was, in reality, more in sympathy with the Federalists than with the Republicans. And during his presidency, Hamilton remained the dominant figure in government.

ASSERTING NATIONAL SOVEREIGNTY

The Federalists consolidated their position—and attracted wide public support for the new national government—by acting effectively in two areas in which the old Confederation had been largely unsuccessful: the Western frontier and diplomacy.

Securing the West

Despite the Northwest Ordinance, the old Congress had largely failed to tie the outlying Western areas of the country firmly to the national government. Farmers in western Massachusetts had rebelled; settlers in Vermont, Kentucky, and Tennessee had flirted with seceding from the Union. At first, the new government under the Constitution faced similar problems.

In 1794, farmers in western Pennsylvania raised a major challenge to federal authority when they refused to pay the new whiskey excise tax and began terrorizing the tax collectors in the region. But the federal government did not leave settlement of the so-called Whiskey Rebellion to the authorities of Pennsylvania as Congress had left Shays's Rebellion to the authorities of Massachusetts. At Hamilton's urging, Washington called out the militias of three states and assembled an army of nearly 15,000, a larger force than he had commanded against the British during most of the Revolution; and he personally accompanied the troops into Pennsylvania. At the approach of the militiamen, the rebellion quickly collapsed.

The federal government won the allegiance of the whiskey rebels through intimidation. It won the loyalties of other Western people by accepting new states as members of the Union. The last of the original thirteen colonies joined the Union once the Bill of Rights had been appended to the Constitution—North Carolina in 1789 and Rhode Island in 1790. Vermont became the fourteenth state in 1791 after New York and New Hampshire agreed to give up their claims to it. Next came Kentucky, in 1792, when Virginia gave up its claim to that region. After North Carolina ceded its Western lands to the Union, Tennessee became a state in 1796.

The new government faced a greater challenge in more distant areas of the Northwest and the Southwest. The ordinances of 1784–1787, establishing the terms of white settlement in the West, had produced a series of border conflicts with Indian tribes resisting white settlement in their lands. The new government inherited these clashes, which continued with few interruptions for nearly a decade.

These clashes revealed another issue the Constitution had done little to

WASHINGTON IN COMMAND, 1794 When Pennsylvania farmers rose up in the Whiskey Rebellion in 1794, President Washington decided at once on a strong military response. This painting, credited to Frederick Kemmelmeyer, shows Washington reviewing troops in Cumberland, Maryland, as they prepare to march against the insurgents.

resolve: the place of the Indian nations within the new federal structure. The Constitution made almost no mention of Native Americans. It gave Congress power to "regulate Commerce . . . with the Indian tribes." And it bound the new government to respect treaties negotiated by the Confederation, most of which had been with the tribes. But none of this did very much to clarify the precise legal standing of Indians or Indian nations within the United States. The tribes received no direct representation in the new government. Above all, the Constitution did not address the major issue that would govern relations between whites and Indians: land. Indian nations lived within the boundaries of the United States, yet they claimed (and the white government at times agreed) that they had some measure of sovereignty over their own land. But neither the Constitution nor common law offered any clear guide to the rights of a "nation within a nation" or to the precise nature of tribal sovereignty, which ultimately depended on control of land. Thus, the relationship between the tribes and the United States remained to be determined by a series of treaties, agreements, and judicial decisions in a process that has continued for more than two centuries.

Maintaining Neutrality

Not until 1791 did Great Britain send a minister to the United States, and then only because Madison and the Republicans were threatening to place special trade restrictions on British ships. A new crisis in Anglo-American relations emerged in 1793 when the new French government established after the revolution of 1789 went to war with Great Britain. Both the president and Congress took steps to establish American neutrality in the conflict, but that neutrality was severely tested.

Early in 1794, the Royal Navy began seizing hundreds of American ships engaged in trade in the French West Indies, outraging public opinion in the United States. Anti-British sentiment rose still higher at the report that the governor general of Canada had delivered a warlike speech to the Indians on the Northwestern frontier. Hamilton was deeply concerned. War would mean an end to imports from England, and most of the revenue for maintaining his financial system came from duties on those imports.

Hamilton and the Federalists did not trust the State Department, now in the hands of the ardently pro-French Edmund Randolph, to find a solution to the crisis. So they persuaded Washington to name a special commissioner to go to England and negotiate a solution: the staunch New York Federalist and chief justice of the Supreme Court, John Jay. Jay was instructed to secure compensation for the recent British assaults on American shipping, to demand withdrawal of British forces from their posts on the frontier of the United States, and to negotiate a commercial treaty with Britain compatible with America's 1778 treaty with France.

The long and complex treaty Jay negotiated in 1794 failed to achieve these goals. But it was not without merit. It settled the conflict with Britain, avoiding a likely war. It provided for undisputed American sovereignty over the entire Northwest. It produced a reasonably satisfactory commercial relationship with a nation whose trade was important to the United States. Nevertheless, when the terms became known in America, criticism was intense and Jay was burned in effigy in some places. Opponents of the treaty—who included almost all the Republicans and even many Federalists—went to great lengths to defeat it in the Senate, cheered on by agents of France. But in the end the Senate ratified what was by then known as Jay's Treaty.

Jay's Treaty paved the way for a settlement of important American disputes with Spain. Under Pinckney's Treaty (negotiated by Thomas Pinckney and signed in 1795), Spain recognized the right of Americans to navigate the Mississippi to its mouth and to deposit goods at New Orleans for reloading on ocean-going ships; agreed to fix the northern boundary of Florida where Americans always had insisted it should be, along the 31st parallel; and commanded its authorities to prevent the Indians in Florida from launching raids north across the border.

THE DOWNFALL OF THE FEDERALISTS

Since almost everyone in the 1790s agreed that there was no place in a stable republic for organized parties, the emergence of the Republicans as a powerful and apparently permanent opposition seemed to the Federalists a grave threat to national stability. And so when major international perils

BURNING JOHN JAY IN EFFIGY Popular opposition to the treaty John Jay negotiated with Great Britain in 1794, which many considered more favorable to the English than the Americans, was eagerly exploited by Republicans in their effort to discredit the Federalists.

confronted the government in the 1790s, the temptation to move forcefully against this "illegitimate" opposition was strong. Facing what they believed was a stark choice between respecting individual liberties and preserving stability, the Federalists chose stability. Largely as a result of that decision, the Federalists never won another presidential election after 1796.

The Election of 1796

George Washington refused to run for a third term as president in 1796, thus removing the last impediment to open expression of the partisan rivalries that had been building over the previous eight years. Jefferson was the obvious candidate of the Republicans for president that year, but the Federalists faced a more difficult choice. Hamilton had created too many enemies to be a credible candidate. Vice President John Adams, directly associated with none of the controversial Federalist achievements, received the party's nomination for president at a caucus of the Federalists in Congress.

The Federalists were still clearly the dominant party. But without Washington to mediate, they fell victim to fierce factional rivalries that almost led to their undoing. Hamilton and many other Federalists (especially in the South) were not reconciled to Adams's candidacy and supported Thomas Pinckney. Adams defeated Jefferson by only three electoral votes and assumed the presidency as head of a divided party facing a powerful opposition. Jefferson became vice president as a result of finishing second. (Not until the adoption of the Twelfth Amendment in 1804 did electors vote separately for president and vice president.)

The Quasi War with France

American relations with Great Britain and Spain improved as a result of Jay's and Pinckney's treaties. But the nation's relations with revolutionary France quickly deteriorated. French vessels captured American ships on the high seas and at times imprisoned the crews. And when the South Carolina Federalist Charles Cotesworth Pinckney, brother of Thomas Pinckney, arrived in France, the government refused to receive him as the official representative of the United States.

In an effort to stabilize relations, Adams appointed a bipartisan commission to negotiate with France. When the Americans arrived in Paris in 1797, three agents of the French foreign minister, Prince Talleyrand, demanded a loan for France and a bribe for French officials before any negotiations could begin. Pinckney, now a member of the commission, responded succinctly and angrily: "No! No! Not a sixpence!"

When Adams heard of the incident, he sent a message to Congress denouncing the French insults and urging preparations for war. Before delivering the commissioners' report over to Congress, he deleted the names of the three French agents and designated them only as Messrs. X, Y, and Z. When the report was published, the "XYZ Affair," as it quickly became known, provoked an even greater reaction than Adams had expected. There was widespread popular outrage at France's actions and strong popular support for the Federalists' response. For nearly two years, 1798 and 1799, the United States found itself engaged in an undeclared war with France.

Adams persuaded Congress to cut off all trade with France, to abrogate the treaties of 1778, and to authorize American vessels to capture French armed ships on the high seas. In 1798, Congress created the Department of the Navy and appropriated money for the construction of new warships. The navy soon won a number of duels and captured a total of eighty-five French ships, including armed merchantmen. The United States also began cooperating so closely with the British as to be virtually a cobelligerent in England's war with France. The British provided the American navy with ammunition, furnished officers to help with the training and direction of American crews, and offered signaling information so that British and American ships could communicate readily with one another.

The French, taking note of all this, tried to conciliate the United States. Adams sent another commission to Paris in 1800, and the new French government (headed now by "first consul" Napoleon Bonaparte) agreed to a treaty with the United States that canceled the old agreements of 1778 and established new commercial arrangements. As a result, the "quasi war" came to a reasonably peaceful end, and the United States at last freed itself from the entanglements and embarrassments of its "perpetual" alliance with France.

Repression and Protest

The conflict with France helped the Federalists increase their majorities in Congress in 1798. Armed with this new strength they began to consider ways to silence the Republican opposition. The result was some of the most controversial legislation in American history: the Alien and Sedition Acts.

The Alien Act placed new obstacles in the way of foreigners who wished to become American citizens, and it strengthened the president's hand in dealing with aliens. The Sedition Act allowed the government to prosecute those who engaged in "sedition" against the government. In theory, only libelous or treasonous activities were subject to prosecution; but since such activities were defined in widely varying terms, the law in effect gave the government authority to stifle virtually any opposition. The Republicans interpreted the new laws as part of a Federalist campaign to destroy them and fought back.

President Adams signed the new laws but was cautious in implementing them. He did not deport any aliens, and he prevented the government from launching a broad crusade against the Republicans. But the legislation did have a significant repressive effect. The Alien Act discouraged immigration and encouraged some foreigners already in the country to leave. And the administration used the Sedition Act to arrest and convict ten men, most of them Republican newspaper editors whose only crime had been criticism of the Federalists in government.

Republican leaders pinned their hopes for a reversal of the Alien and Sedition Acts on the state legislatures. (The right of the Supreme Court to

CONGRESSIONAL PUGILISTS, 1798 This cartoon was inspired by the celebrated fight on the floor of the House of Representatives between Matthew Lyon, a Republican representative from Vermont, and Roger Griswold, a Federalist from Connecticut. Griswold (at right) attacks Lyon with his cane, and Lyon retaliates with fire tongs. Other members of Congress seem to be enjoying the battle.

nullify congressional legislation had not yet been established.) They laid out a theory for state action in two sets of resolutions in 1798–1799, one written (anonymously) by Jefferson and adopted by the Kentucky legislature and the other drafted by Madison and approved by the Virginia legislature. The Virginia and Kentucky Resolutions, as they were known, used the ideas of John Locke and the Tenth Amendment to the Constitution to argue that the federal government had been formed by a "compact" or contract among the states and possessed only certain delegated powers. Whenever a party to the contract, a state, decided that the central government had exceeded those powers, it had the right to "nullify" the appropriate laws.

The Republicans did not win wide support for the nullification idea; only Virginia and Kentucky declared the congressional statutes void. They did, however, succeed in elevating their dispute with the Federalists to the level of a national crisis. By the late 1790s, the entire nation was as deeply and bitterly politicized as at any time in its history. State legislatures at times resembled battlegrounds. Even the United States Congress was plagued with violent disagreements. In one celebrated incident in the chamber of the House of Representatives, Matthew Lyon, a Republican from Vermont, responded to an insult from Roger Griswold, a Federalist from Connecticut, by spitting in Griswold's eye. Griswold attacked Lyon with his cane, Lyon fought back with a pair of fire tongs, and soon the two men were wrestling on the floor.

The "Revolution" of 1800

The 1800 presidential election was shaped by these bitter controversies. The presidential candidates were the same as four years earlier: Adams for the Federalists, Jefferson for the Republicans. But the campaign of 1800 was very different from the one preceding it. Indeed, it was probably the ugliest in American history. Adams and Jefferson themselves displayed reasonable dignity, but their supporters showed no such restraint. The Federalists accused Jefferson of being a dangerous radical and his followers of being wild men who, if they should come to power, would bring on a reign of terror comparable to that of the French Revolution. The Republicans portrayed Adams as a tyrant conspiring to become king, and they accused the Federalists of plotting to subvert human liberty and impose slavery on the people. There was considerable personal invective as well.

The election was close, and the crucial contest was in New York. There, Aaron Burr mobilized an organization of Revolutionary War veterans, the

Tammany Society, to serve as a Republican political machine. And through Tammany's efforts, the party carried the city by a large majority, and with it the state. Jefferson was, apparently, elected.

But an unexpected complication soon jeopardized the Republican victory. The Constitution called for each elector to "vote by ballot for two persons." The normal practice was that an elector would cast one vote for his party's presidential candidate and another for the vice presidential candidate. To avoid a tie, the Republicans had intended that one elector would refrain from voting for Burr. But the plan went awry. When the votes were counted, Jefferson and Burr each had 73. No candidate had a majority, and—in accordance with the Constitution—the House of Representatives had to choose between the two top candidates, Jefferson and Burr. Each state delegation would cast a single vote.

The new Congress, elected in 1800 with a Republican majority, was not to convene until after the inauguration of the president, so it was the Federalist Congress that had to decide the question. Some Federalists hoped to use the situation to salvage the election for their party; others wanted to strike a bargain with Burr and elect him. But after a long deadlock, several leading Federalists, most prominent among them Alexander Hamilton, concluded that Burr (whom many suspected of having engineered the deadlock in the first place) was too unreliable to trust with the presidency. On the thirty-sixth ballot, Jefferson was elected.

After the election of 1800, the only branch of the federal government left in Federalist hands was the judiciary. The Adams administration spent its last months in office taking steps to make the party's hold on the courts secure. By the Judiciary Act of 1801, passed by the lame duck Congress, the Federalists reduced the number of Supreme Court justiceships by one but greatly increased the number of federal judgeships as a whole. Adams quickly appointed Federalists to the newly created positions. Indeed, there were charges that he stayed up until midnight on his last day in office to finish signing the new judges' commissions. These officeholders became known as the "midnight appointments."

Even so, the Republicans viewed their victory as almost complete. The nation had, they believed, been saved from tyranny. A new era could now begin, one in which the true principles of America would once again govern the land. The exuberance with which the victors viewed the future—and the importance they ascribed to the defeat of the Federalists—was evident in the phrase Jefferson himself later used to describe his election. He called it the "Revolution of 1800." It remained to be seen how revolutionary it would really be.

CHAPTER SEVEN

The Jeffersonian Era

The Rise of Cultural Nationalism ~ *Stirrings of Industrialism*
Jefferson the President ~ *Doubling the National Domain*

THOMAS JEFFERSON AND his followers assumed control of the national government in 1801 as the champions of a distinctive vision of America. They favored a society of sturdy, independent farmers, happily free from the workshops, the industrial towns, and the city mobs of Europe. They celebrated localism and republican simplicity. Above all, they proposed a federal government of sharply limited power, with most public authority remaining at the level of the states.

Almost nothing worked out as they had planned, for during their years in power the young republic was developing in ways that made much of their vision obsolete. The American economy in the period of Republican ascendancy became steadily more diversified and complex, making the ideal of a simple, agrarian society impossible to maintain. American cultural life was dominated by a vigorous and ambitious nationalism reminiscent of (and often encouraged by) the Federalists. The Republicans did manage to translate some of their political ideals into reality. Jefferson dismantled much of the bureaucracy that the Federalists had erected in the 1790s and helped keep the federal government small and relatively weak. Yet at the same time, he frequently encountered situations that required him to exercise strong national authority.

The Republicans did not always like these nationalizing and modernizing trends, and on occasion they resisted them. For the most part, however, they had the sense to recognize what could not be changed. In adjusting to the new realities, they themselves began to become agents of the very transformation of American life they had once resisted.

THE RISE OF CULTURAL NATIONALISM

In many respects, American cultural life in the early nineteenth century reflected the Republican vision of the nation's future. Opportunities for education increased, the nation's literary and artistic life began to free itself from European influences, and American religion began to adjust to the spread of Enlightenment rationalism. In other respects, however, the new culture was posing a serious challenge to Republican ideals.

Educational and Literary Nationalism

Central to the Republican vision of America was the concept of a virtuous and enlightened citizenry. An ignorant electorate could not be trusted to preserve democracy; education was essential. Republicans believed, therefore, in the creation of a nationwide system of public schools, in which all male citizens would receive free education.

Such hopes were not fulfilled. No state actually created an effective system of free schools (although several endorsed the idea). In 1789, Massachusetts reaffirmed the colonial laws by which each town was obliged to support a school, but there was little enforcement. In Virginia, the state legislature ignored Jefferson's call for universal elementary education and for advanced education for the gifted. As late as 1815, not a single state had a comprehensive public school system.

Instead, schooling became primarily the responsibility of private institutions, most of which were open only to those who could afford to pay for them. In the South and in the mid-Atlantic states, most schools were run by religious groups. In New England, private academies were often more secular, many of them modeled on those founded by the Phillips family at Andover, Massachusetts, in 1778, and at Exeter, New Hampshire, three years later. By 1815, there were thirty such private secondary schools in Massachusetts, thirty-seven in New York, and several dozen more scattered throughout the country. Many were frankly aristocratic in outlook, training their students to become members of the nation's elite. There were a few educational institutions open to the poor, but not nearly enough to accommodate everyone; and the education they offered was usually clearly inferior to that provided for more prosperous students.

Private secondary schools such as those in New England generally accepted only male students; even many public schools excluded females from the classroom. Yet the late eighteenth and early nineteenth century did see some important advances in education for women. As Americans began to place a higher value on the importance of the "republican mother" who would help train the new generation, they had to ask how mothers could raise their children to be enlightened if they themselves were uneducated. Beginning as early as the 1770s and accelerating thereafter, such concerns helped speed the creation of female academies throughout the nation (usually for the daughters of affluent families). In 1789, Massachusetts required that its public schools serve females as well as males. Other states, although not all, soon followed.

Some women aspired to more. In 1784, Judith Sargent Murray published an essay defending the right of women to education, and defending it in terms very different from those used by most men. Men and women were equal in intellect and equal in potential, Murray argued. Women, therefore, should have precisely the same educational opportunities as men. What was more, they should have opportunities to earn their own livings and to establish a role for themselves in society apart from their husbands and families. Murray's ideas attracted relatively little support at the time.

Reformers who believed in the power of education to reform and redeem "backward" people spurred a growing interest in Indian education. Because Jefferson and his followers liked to think of Native Americans as "noble savages" (uncivilized but, unlike blacks, not necessarily innately inferior), they hoped that schooling the Indians in white culture would "uplift" the tribes. Although white governments did little to promote Indian education, missionaries and mission schools proliferated among the tribes. There were no comparable efforts to educate enslaved African-Americans, largely because their owners preferred that they remain ignorant and thus presumably less likely to rebel.

Higher education similarly diverged from Republican ideals. The number of colleges and universities in America grew substantially, from nine at the time of the Revolution to twenty-two in 1800, and the number increased steadily thereafter. None of the new schools, however, was truly public. Even universities established by state legislatures (in Georgia, North Carolina, Vermont, Ohio, and South Carolina, for example) relied on private contributions and tuition fees to survive. Scarcely more than one white man in a thousand (and virtually no women, blacks, or Indians) had access to any college education; and those few who did attend universities were almost without exception members of prosperous, propertied families.

Now that they had won their political independence, many Americans—Federalists and Republicans alike—aspired to a form of cultural independence. They dreamed of an American literary and artistic life that would rival the greatest achievements of Europe. A 1772 "Poem on the

Rising Glory of America" predicted that America was destined to become the "seat of empire" and the "final stage" of civilization, with "glorious works of high invention and of wond'rous art." The Connecticut schoolmaster and lawyer Noah Webster echoed such sentiments, arguing that the American schoolboy should be educated as a nationalist. "As soon as he opens his lips," Webster wrote, "he should rehearse the history of his own country; he should lisp the praise of liberty, and of those illustrious heroes and statesmen who have wrought a revolution in her favor."

Despite serious obstacles getting works by American writers published, a growing number of native authors began working to create a strong native literature. Among the most ambitious was the Philadelphia writer Charles Brockden Brown, who tried to use his novels to give voice to distinctively American themes, to convey the "soaring passions and intellectual energy" of his country. But his fascination with horror and deviance kept him from developing a popular audience. More successful was Washington Irving of New York, whose popular folk tales, recounting the adventures of such American rustics as Ichabod Crane and Rip Van Winkle, made him the widely acknowledged leader of American literary life in the early nineteenth century.

Religion and Revivalism

The American Revolution had weakened traditional forms of religious practice by detaching established churches from government and by elevating ideas of individual liberty and reason that challenged many ecclesiastical traditions. By the 1790s, only a small proportion of white Americans (perhaps as few as 10 percent) were members of formal churches, and ministers were complaining often about the "decay of vital piety."

Religious traditionalists were particularly alarmed about the emergence of new, "rational" religious doctrines—theologies that reflected modern, scientific attitudes and sharply de-emphasized the role of God in the world. "Deism," which had originated among Enlightenment philosophers in France, attracted such educated Americans as Jefferson and Franklin and by 1800 was reaching a moderately broad popular audience. Deists accepted the existence of God, but they considered Him a remote being who, after having created the universe, had withdrawn from direct involvement with the human race and its sins. Religious skepticism also produced the philosophies of "universalism" and "unitarianism," which emerged at first as dissenting views within the New England Congregational church. Disciples of these new ideas rejected the traditional Calvinist belief in predestination, arguing that salvation was available to all. They rejected, too, the idea of the Trinity. Jesus was only a great religious teacher, they claimed, not the son of God. So wide was the gulf between these dissenters and the Congregationalist establishment that a permanent schism finally occurred. The Universalist church was founded as a separate denomination in Gloucester, Massachusetts, in 1779, and the Unitarian church was established in Boston three years later.

Many Americans believed that the spread of rationalism foretold the end of traditional, evangelistic religion in the new nation. In reality, quite the contrary was true. Most Americans continued to hold strong religious beliefs; what had declined was their commitment to organized churches and denominations. Deism, Universalism, and Unitarianism appeared more powerful than they actually were, in part because those who clung to more traditional faiths were for a time confused and disorganized, unable to react effectively. Beginning in 1801, however, traditional religion staged a dramatic comeback in the form of a wave of revivalism known as the Second Great Awakening.

The origins of the awakening lay in the efforts of conservative theologians of the 1790s to fight the spread of religious rationalism and in the efforts of church establishments to revitalize their organizations. Presbyterians expanded their efforts on the Western fringes of white settlement, and conservatives became increasingly militant in response to dissenters. Methodism, founded in England by John Wesley, spread to America in the 1770s; authoritarian and hierarchical in structure, the Methodists sent itinerant preachers throughout the nation to win recruits for the new church, which soon became the fastest-growing denomination in America. Almost as successful were the Baptists, who were themselves relatively new to America; they found an especially fervent following in the South.

By 1800, the revivalist energies of all these denominations were combining to create the greatest surge of evangelical fervor since the first Great Awakening sixty years before. In only a few years, the revivalists mobilized a large proportion of the American people; and membership in those churches embracing revivalism—most prominently the Methodist, Baptist, and Presbyterian—was mushrooming. At Cane Ridge, Kentucky, in the summer of 1801, a group of evangelical ministers presided over the nation's first "camp meeting"—an extraordinary revival that lasted several days and impressed all who saw it with its size (some estimated that 25,000 people attended) and its fervor. Such events became common in subsequent years, as the Methodists in particular came to rely on them as a way to "harvest" new members.

The message of the Second Great Awakening was not entirely uniform, but its basic thrust was clear. Individuals must readmit God and Christ into their daily lives, must embrace a fervent, active piety, and must reject the skeptical rationalism that threatened traditional beliefs. Yet the wave of revivalism did not restore the religion of the past. Few denominations any longer accepted the idea of predestination; and the belief that a person could affect his or her own chances for salvation, rather than encouraging irreligion as many had feared, added intensity to the individual's search for salvation. The Awakening, in short, combined a more active piety with a belief in a God whose grace could be attained through faith and good works.

One of the striking features of the Awakening was the preponderance of women, particularly young women, within it. Female converts far outnumbered males. One reason for this was that women were more numerous in certain regions than men, who were more likely than women to strike out on their own and move west. Their marriage prospects thus diminished and their futures plagued with uncertainty, some women discovered in religion a foundation on which to build their lives. But even in areas where there was no shortage of men, women flocked to the revivals in enormous numbers,

THE CAMP MEETING Camp meetings became a popular feature of evangelical religion in America beginning in 1800. By the 1820s, there were about 1,000 such meetings a year, most of them in the South and the West. This lithograph, which dates from the 1830s, illustrates the central role of women in the religious revivals of the time.

which suggests that they may have been responding in part to changing economic roles as well. The movement of industrial work out of the home (where women had often contributed to the family economy through spinning and weaving) and into the factory—a process making rapid strides in the early nineteenth century—robbed women of one of their most important social roles. Religious enthusiasm helped compensate for the losses and adjustments these transitions produced; it also provided access to a new range of activities associated with the churches—charitable societies ministering to orphans and the poor, missionary organizations, and others—in which women came to play important roles.

Revivalism was not restricted to white society. In some areas of the country, revivals were open to people of all races. Many blacks not only attended the events but embraced the new religious fervor. Out of these revivals emerged a group of black preachers who became important figures within the slave community. Some of them translated the apparently egalitarian religious message of the Awakening—that salvation was available to all—into a similarly egalitarian message for blacks in the present world. Out of black revival meetings in Virginia, for example, arose an elaborate plan in 1800 (devised by Gabriel Prosser, the brother of a black preacher) for a slave rebellion and attack on Richmond. The plan was discovered and the rebellion forestalled by whites, but revivalism continued in subsequent years to create occasional racial unrest in the South.

The spirit of revivalism was particularly strong in these years among Native Americans, although its origins and the forms it took were very different from those in white or black society. The dislocations and military defeats Indians suffered in the aftermath of the American Revolution created a sense of crisis among many of the Eastern tribes in particular; as a result, the 1790s and early 1800s became an era of Indian religious fervor and prophecy. Presbyterian and Baptist missionaries were active among the Southern tribes and sparked a wave of conversions. But the most important revivalism came from the efforts of a great Indian prophet: Handsome Lake, a Seneca whose seemingly miraculous "rebirth" after years of alcoholism helped give him a special stature within his tribe. Handsome Lake, like the earlier Indian prophet Neolin, who had been active in the 1760s, called for a revival of traditional Indian ways. That meant repudiating the individualism of white society and restoring the communal quality of the Indian world. Handsome Lake's message spread through the scattered Iroquois communities that had survived the military and political setbacks of previous decades and inspired many Indians to give up whiskey, gambling, and other destructive customs derived from white society. But revivalism did not produce a restoration of traditional Iroquois culture. Handsome Lake encouraged Christian missionaries to become active within the tribes, and he urged Iroquois men to abandon their roles as hunters (partly because so much of their hunting land had been seized by whites) and become sedentary farmers instead. Iroquois women, who had traditionally done the farming, were to move into more domestic roles.

STIRRINGS OF INDUSTRIALISM

It was not only culturally and religiously that the nation was developing in ways unforeseen by Jefferson and his followers. Economically, the United States was taking the first, tentative steps toward a transformation that would ultimately shatter forever the vision of a simple, agrarian republic.

Technology and Transportation in America

While Americans were engaged in a revolution to win their independence, an even more important revolution was in progress in England: the emergence of modern industrialism. Power-driven machines were taking the place of hand-operated tools and were permitting manufacturing to become more rapid and extensive—with profound social and economic consequences. Not since the agrarian revolution thousands of years earlier, when humans had turned from hunting to farming for sustenance, had there been an economic change of a magnitude comparable to the industrial revolution. Centuries of traditions, of social patterns, of cultural and religious assumptions were challenged and often shattered.

Nothing even remotely comparable to the English industrial revolution occurred in America in the first two decades of the nineteenth century. Indeed, it was opposition to the kind of economic growth occurring in England that had helped the Republicans defeat the Federalists in 1800. Yet even while Jeffersonians warned of the dangers of rapid economic change, they were witnessing a series of technological advances that would ultimately help ensure that the United States too would be transformed.

Some of these technological advances were imported from England. Despite efforts by the British government to prevent the export of textile machinery or the emigration of skilled mechanics, a number of immigrants with advanced knowledge of English technology arrived in the United States eager to introduce the new machines to America. Samuel Slater, for example, used the knowledge he had acquired before leaving England to build a spinning mill in Pawtucket, Rhode Island, for the Quaker merchant Moses

Brown in 1790. It was generally recognized as the first modern factory in America.

More important than imported technology was that of purely domestic origin. America in the early nineteenth century produced several important inventors of its own. Among the most important was the Massachusetts-born, Yale-educated Eli Whitney. In 1793, Whitney, who was working as a tutor on a Georgia plantation, invented a machine that performed the arduous task of removing the seeds from short-staple cotton quickly and efficiently. It was dubbed the cotton gin ("gin" being a derivative of "engine"). With the device a single operator could clean as much cotton in a few hours as a group of workers had once needed a whole day to do. The results were profound. Soon cotton growing spread throughout the South. (Previously it had been restricted largely to the coast and the sea islands, the only places where "long-staple" cotton—easily cleaned without the cotton gin—could be grown.) Within a decade, the total cotton crop increased eightfold. African-American slavery, which with the decline of tobacco production had seemed for a time to be a dwindling institution, expanded and firmly fixed itself upon the South. The large supply of domestically produced fiber also served as a strong incentive to entrepreneurs in New England and elsewhere to develop a native textile industry.

One of the prerequisites for industrialization is a transportation system that allows the efficient movement of raw materials to factories and of finished goods to markets. The United States had no such system in the early years of the republic, and thus it had no domestic market extensive enough to justify large-scale production. But efforts were under way that would ultimately remove the transportation obstacle.

In river transportation, a new era began with the development of the steamboat. Oliver Evans's high-pressure engine, lighter and more efficient than the earlier steam engine created by James Watt in England in the 1760s, made steam more feasible for powering boats and, eventually, locomotives and mill machinery. The perfecting of the steamboat was chiefly the work of the inventor Robert Fulton and the promoter Robert R. Livingston. Their *Clermont*, equipped with paddle wheels and an English-built engine, sailed up the Hudson in the summer of 1807. In 1811, a partner of Livingston, Nicholas J. Roosevelt (a remote ancestor of Theodore Roosevelt), introduced the steamboat to the West by sending the *New Orleans* from Pittsburgh down the Ohio and Mississippi. The next year, the vessel began a profitable career of service between New Orleans and Natchez.

SLATER'S MILL Samuel Slater served as an apprentice in England in
the 1780s to Richard Arkwright, an inventor of machinery for the
new cotton mills that were driving the English industrial revolution.
In 1790 Slater designed the first successful cotton-spinning mill in the
United States at Pawtucket, Rhode Island. This drawing shows the
Pawtucket bridge, falls, and mill as they appeared sometime between
1810 and 1819.

Meanwhile, what was to become known as the turnpike era had begun.
In 1792, a corporation constructed a toll road running the sixty miles from
Philadelphia to Lancaster, with a hard-packed surface of crushed rock. This
venture proved so successful that similar turnpikes (so named from the kind
of tollgate frequently used) were laid out from other cities to neighboring
towns. But similar highways would not be extended over the mountains until
governments began to participate in the financing of the projects.

Despite all the changes and all the advances, America remained in the
early nineteenth century an overwhelmingly rural and agrarian nation. Only
3 percent of the population lived in towns of more than 8,000 in 1800. Ten
percent of the non-Indian population lived west of the Appalachian Mountains, far from what urban centers there were. Even the nation's largest cities
could not begin to compare, either in size or in cultural sophistication, with
such European capitals as London and Paris (although Philadelphia, with
70,000 residents, New York, with 60,000, and others were becoming centers
of commerce, learning, and urban culture comparable to many of the
secondary cities of Europe).

It was still possible in the early nineteenth century to believe that this small, half-formed nation might not become a complex modern society. But forces were already at work that, in time, would lastingly transform the United States. And Thomas Jefferson, for all his commitment to the agrarian ideal, found himself, as president, obliged to confront and accommodate them.

JEFFERSON THE PRESIDENT

Privately, Thomas Jefferson may well have considered his victory over John Adams in 1800 to be what he later termed it: a revolution "as real . . . as that of 1776." Publicly, however, he was restrained and conciliatory, attempting to minimize the differences between the two parties and calm the passions that the bitter campaign had aroused. There was no complete repudiation of Federalist policies, no true "revolution." Indeed, at times Jefferson seemed to outdo the Federalists at their own work—most notably in overseeing a remarkable expansion of the territory of the United States.

In some respects, however, the Jefferson presidency did indeed represent a fundamental change in the direction of the federal government. The new administration oversaw a drastic reduction in the powers of some national institutions, and it forestalled the development of new powers in areas where the Federalists would certainly have attempted to expand them.

The Federal City and the "People's President"

The relative unimportance of the federal government during the era of Jefferson was symbolized by the character of the newly founded national capital, the city of Washington. John Adams had moved to the new seat of government during the last year of his administration. And there were many at that time who envisioned that the raw, uncompleted town would soon emerge as a great and majestic city, a focus for the growing nationalism that the Federalists were promoting. The French architect Pierre L'Enfant had designed the capital on a grand scale, with broad avenues radiating from the uncompleted Capitol building. Many Americans believed Washington would become the Paris of the United States.

In reality, throughout Jefferson's presidency—indeed, throughout most of the nineteenth century—Washington remained little more than a straggling, provincial village. Although the population increased steadily from the 3,200 counted in the 1800 census, it never rivaled that of New York, Philadelphia, and the other major cities of the nation. The city remained a

raw, inhospitable community, with few public buildings of any consequence. Members of Congress viewed Washington not as a home but as a
place to visit briefly during sessions of the legislature and leave as quickly as
possible. Few owned houses there. Most lived in a cluster of simple boardinghouses in the vicinity of the Capitol. It was not unusual for a member of
Congress to resign his seat in the midst of a session to return home if he had
an opportunity to accept the more prestigious post of member of his state
legislature.

As president, Jefferson acted in a spirit of democratic simplicity appropriate to the frontierlike character of the unfinished federal city. He was a
wealthy and aristocratic planter by background, but he conveyed to the
public an image of plain, almost crude disdain for pretension. He walked
like an ordinary citizen to and from his inauguration at the Capitol, instead
of riding in a coach at the head of a procession. In the presidential mansion,
which had not yet acquired the name White House, he disregarded the
courtly etiquette of his predecessors. He did not always bother to dress up,
prompting the British ambassador to complain on one occasion of being
received by the president in clothes that were "indicative of utter slovenli-
ness and indifference to appearances."

Yet Jefferson managed nevertheless to impress most of those who knew
him. He was a brilliant conversationalist, a gifted writer, and one of the
nation's most intelligent and creative men, with a wider range of interests
and accomplishments than any public figure in American history with the
possible exception of Benjamin Franklin. In addition to politics and diplomacy, he was an active architect, educator, inventor, scientific farmer, and
philosopher-scientist.

Jefferson was, above all, a shrewd and practical politician. He went to
great lengths to eliminate the aura of majesty surrounding the presidency
that he believed his predecessors had created. But he also worked hard to
exert influence as the leader of his party, giving direction to Republicans in
Congress by quiet and sometimes even devious means. Although the Republicans had objected strenuously to the efforts of their Federalist predecessors to build a network of influence through patronage, Jefferson used
his powers of appointment as an effective political weapon. Like Washington before him, he believed that federal offices should be filled with men
loyal to the principles and policies of the administration. By the end of his
second term practically all federal jobs were held by loyal Republicans.

Jefferson was a popular president during his first term and had little
difficulty winning reelection against the Federalist Charles C. Pinckney.
The Republican ticket carried even the New England states (except Con-

THOMAS JEFFERSON This 1805 portrait by the noted American painter Rembrandt Peale shows Jefferson at the beginning of his second term as president. It also conveys (through the simplicity of dress and the slightly unkempt hair) the image of democratic simplicity that Jefferson liked to project as the champion of the "common man."

necticut), and Jefferson won by the overwhelming electoral majority of 162 to 14. Republican membership of both houses of Congress increased.

Dollars and Ships

Under Washington and Adams, the Republicans believed, the government had been needlessly extravagant. Yearly federal expenditures had nearly tripled between 1793 and 1800. The public debt had also risen, as Hamilton had intended. And an extensive system of internal taxation, including the hated whiskey excise tax, had been erected.

The Jefferson administration moved deliberately to reverse these trends. In 1802, the president persuaded Congress to abolish all internal taxes, leaving customs duties and the sale of Western lands as the only source of revenue for the government. Meanwhile, Secretary of the Treasury Albert Gallatin drastically reduced government spending, cutting the already small staffs of the executive departments to minuscule levels. Although Jefferson was unable entirely to retire the national debt as he had hoped, he did cut it almost in half (from $83 million to $45 million).

Jefferson also scaled down the armed forces. He reduced the already tiny army of 4,000 men to 2,500. He pared down the navy from twenty-five ships in commission to seven, cutting the number of officers and sailors accordingly. Anything but the smallest of standing armies, he argued, might menace civil liberties and civilian control of government. And a large navy, he feared, might be misused to promote overseas commerce, which Jefferson believed should remain secondary to agriculture. Yet Jefferson was not a pacifist. At the same time that he was reducing the size of the army and navy, he helped establish the United States Military Academy at West Point, founded in 1802. And when trouble began brewing overseas, he began again to build up the fleet.

Such trouble appeared first in the Mediterranean, off the coast of northern Africa. For years the Barbary states of North Africa—Morocco, Algiers, Tunis, and Tripoli—had been demanding money from all nations whose ships sailed the Mediterranean as protection against piracy. Even Great Britain gave regular contributions to the pirates. During the 1780s and 1790s the United States too had agreed to treaties providing for annual tribute to the Barbary states, but Jefferson showed reluctance to continue this policy of appeasement.

In 1801, the pasha of Tripoli forced Jefferson's hand. Unhappy with American responses to his demands, he ordered the flagpole of the American consulate chopped down—a symbolic declaration of war. Jefferson responded cautiously and built up American naval forces in the area over the next several years. Finally, in 1805, he agreed to terms by which the United States ended the payment of tribute to Tripoli but paid a substantial (and humiliating) ransom for the release of American prisoners.

Conflict with the Courts

Having won control of the executive and legislative branches of government, the Republicans looked with suspicion on the judiciary, which remained largely in the hands of Federalist judges. Soon after Jefferson's first inauguration, his followers in Congress launched an attack on this last preserve of the opposition. Their first step was the repeal of the Judiciary

Act of 1801, thus eliminating the judgeships to which Adams had made his "midnight appointments."

The debate over the courts led to one of the most important judicial decisions in the history of the nation. Federalists had long maintained that the Supreme Court had the authority to nullify acts of Congress (although the Constitution said nothing specifically to support the claim), and the Court itself had actually exercised the power of judicial review in 1796 when it upheld the validity of a law passed by Congress. But the Court's authority in this area would not be secure, it was clear, until it actually declared a congressional act unconstitutional.

In 1803, in the case of *Marbury* v. *Madison*, it did so. William Marbury, one of Adams's "midnight appointments," had been named a justice of the peace in the District of Columbia. But his commission, although signed and sealed, had not been delivered to him before Adams left office. When Jefferson took office, his secretary of state, James Madison, refused to hand over the commission. Marbury asked the Supreme Court to direct Madison to perform his official duty. But the Court ruled that while Marbury had a right to his commission, the Court had no authority to order Madison to deliver it. On the surface, therefore, the decision was a victory for the administration. But of much greater importance than the relatively insignificant matter of Marbury's commission was the Court's reasoning in the decision.

The original Judiciary Act of 1789 had given the Court the power to compel executive officials to act in such matters as the delivery of commissions, and it was on that basis that Marbury had filed his suit. But the Court ruled that Congress had exceeded its authority, that the Constitution defined the powers of the judiciary, and that the legislature had no right to expand them. The relevant section of the 1789 act was, therefore, void. In seeming to deny its own authority, the Court was in fact radically enlarging it. The justices had repudiated a relatively minor power (the power to force the delivery of a commission) by asserting a vastly greater one (the power to nullify an act of Congress).

The chief justice of the United States at the time of the ruling (and until 1835) was John Marshall, one of the towering figures in the history of American law. A leading Federalist and prominent Virginia lawyer, he had served John Adams as secretary of state. (It was Marshall, ironically, who had neglected to deliver Marbury's commission in the closing hours of the administration.) In 1801, just before leaving office, Adams had appointed him chief justice; and almost immediately Marshall established himself as the dominant figure on the Court, shaping virtually all its most important rulings—including, of course, *Marbury* v. *Madison*. Through a succession of Republican presidents, he battled to give the federal government unity and strength. And in so doing, he established the judiciary as a coequal branch of government with the executive and the legislature—a position that the founders of the republic had never clearly indicated it should occupy.

DOUBLING THE NATIONAL DOMAIN

In the same year Jefferson was elected president of the United States, Napoleon Bonaparte made himself ruler of France with the title of first consul. In the year Jefferson was reelected, Napoleon named himself emperor. The two men had little in common. Yet for a time they were of great assistance to each other in international politics—until Napoleon's ambitions moved from Europe to America and created conflict and estrangement.

Jefferson and Napoleon

Having failed in a grandiose plan to seize India from the British Empire, Napoleon began to dream of restoring French power in the New World. The territory east of the Mississippi, which France had ceded to Great Britain in 1763, was now part of the United States and lost forever. But Napoleon hoped to regain the lands west of the Mississippi, which belonged to Spain. Under the secret Treaty of San Ildefonso of 1800, France regained title to Louisiana, which included almost the whole of the Mississippi Valley to the west of the river, plus New Orleans near the river's mouth. The Louisiana Territory would, Napoleon hoped, become the heart of a great French Empire in America.

Jefferson was unaware at first of Napoleon's imperial ambitions in America, and for a time he pursued a foreign policy that reflected his well-known admiration for France. But he began to reassess American relations with the French when he heard rumors of the secret transfer of Louisiana. Particularly troubling to Jefferson was French control of New Orleans, the outlet through which the produce of the fast-growing Western regions of the United States was shipped to the markets of the world. If France should actually take and hold New Orleans, Jefferson said, then "we must marry ourselves to the British fleet and nation."

Jefferson was even more alarmed when, in the fall of 1802, he learned that the Spanish intendant at New Orleans (who still governed the city, since the French had not yet taken formal possession of the region) had announced a disturbing new regulation. American ships sailing the Mississippi River had for many years been accustomed to depositing their cargoes in New Orleans for transfer to ocean-going vessels. The intendant now forbade the practice, even though Spain had guaranteed Americans that right in the Pinckney Treaty of 1795; the prohibition effectively closed the lower Mississippi to American shippers.

Westerners demanded that the federal government do something to reopen the river, and the president faced a dilemma. If he yielded to the frontier clamor and tried to change the policy by force, he would run the risk of a major war with France. If he ignored the Westerners' demands, he might lose political support. But Jefferson saw another solution. He instructed Robert Livingston, the American minister in Paris, to negotiate for the purchase of New Orleans. Livingston on his own authority proposed that the French sell the United States the rest of Louisiana as well.

In the meantime, Jefferson persuaded Congress to appropriate funds for an expansion of the army and the construction of a river fleet, and he hinted that American forces might soon descend on New Orleans and that the United States might form an alliance with Great Britain if the problems with France were not resolved. Perhaps in response, Napoleon suddenly decided to offer the United States the entire Louisiana Territory.

Napoleon had good reasons for the decision. His plans for an American empire had already gone seriously awry, partly because a yellow fever epidemic had wiped out much of the French army in the New World and partly because the expeditionary force he wished to send to reinforce the troops and take possession of Louisiana had been icebound in a Dutch harbor through the winter of 1802–1803. By the time the harbor thawed in the spring of 1803, Napoleon was preparing for a renewed war in Europe. He would not, he realized, have the resources to secure an American empire.

The Louisiana Purchase

Faced with Napoleon's startling proposal, Livingston and James Monroe, whom Jefferson had sent to Paris to assist in the negotiations, had to decide whether they should accept it even if they had no authorization from their government to do so. But fearful that Napoleon might withdraw the offer, they decided to proceed without further instructions from home. After some haggling over the price, Livingston and Monroe signed an agreement with Napoleon on April 30, 1803.

By the terms of the treaty, the United States was to pay a total of 80 million francs ($15 million) to the French government. The United States was also to grant certain exclusive commercial privileges to France in the port of New Orleans and was to incorporate the residents of Louisiana into the Union with the same rights and privileges as other citizens. The boundaries of the purchase were not clearly defined; the treaty simply specified that Louisiana would consist of the same territory France and Spain had claimed.

In Washington, the president was both pleased and embarrassed when he received the treaty. He was pleased with the terms of the bargain; but because he believed the Constitution should be strictly observed, he was uncertain about his authority to accept it, since the Constitution said nothing about the acquisition of new territory. But Jefferson's advisers persuaded him that his treaty-making power under the Constitution would justify the purchase of Louisiana; and Congress promptly approved the treaty and appropriated money to implement it. Finally, late in 1803, General James Wilkinson, the commissioner of the United States and the commander of a small occupation force, took formal control of the territory on behalf of the United States. In New Orleans, beneath a bright December sun, the French tricolor was lowered and the American flag raised.

Before long, the Louisiana Territory was organized on the general pattern of the Northwest Territory, with the assumption that it would be divided into states. The first of these was admitted to the Union as the state of Louisiana in 1812.

Exploring the West

Meanwhile, a series of explorations was revealing the geography of the far-flung new territory to white Americans. In 1803, even before Napoleon's offer to sell Louisiana, Jefferson helped plan an expedition that was to cross the continent to the Pacific Ocean, gather geographical facts, and investigate prospects for trade with the Indians. He named as its leader his private secretary and Virginia neighbor, the thirty-two-year-old Meriwether Lewis, a veteran of Indian wars who was skilled in the ways of the wilderness. Lewis chose as a colleague the twenty-eight-year-old William Clark, who—like George Rogers Clark, his older brother—was an experienced frontiersman and Indian fighter. In the spring of 1804, Lewis and Clark, with a company of four dozen men, started up the Missouri River from St. Louis. With the Shoshone woman Sacajawea as their interpreter, they eventually crossed the Rocky Mountains, descended the Snake and Columbia rivers, and in the late autumn of 1805 camped on the Pacific coast. In September 1806, they were back in St. Louis with elaborate records of the geography and the Indian civilizations they had observed along the way.

While Lewis and Clark were on their journey, Jefferson dispatched other explorers to other parts of the Louisiana Territory. Lieutenant Zebulon Montgomery Pike, twenty-six years old, led an expedition in the fall of 1805 from St. Louis into the upper Mississippi Valley. In the summer of 1806, he set out again, proceeding up the valley of the Arkansas River and into what later became Colorado, where he encountered, but failed in his attempt to climb, the peak that now bears his name. His account of his Western travels created an enduring (and inaccurate) impression among most Americans that the land between the Missouri and the Rockies was a desert that farmers could never cultivate and that ought to be left forever to the nomadic Indian tribes.

The Burr Conspiracy

Jefferson's triumphant reelection in 1804 suggested that most of the nation approved the new acquisition. But some New England Federalists raged against it. They realized that the more the West grew and the more new states joined the Union, the less power the Federalists and their region would retain. In Massachusetts, a group of the most extreme Federalists, known as the Essex Junto, concluded that the only recourse for New England was to secede from the Union and form a separate "Northern Confederacy." If a Northern Confederacy was to have any hope for lasting success as a separate nation, the Federalists believed, it would have to include New York and New Jersey as well as New England. But the leading Federalist in New York, Alexander Hamilton, refused to support the secessionist scheme.

Federalists in New York then turned to Hamilton's greatest political rival: Vice President Aaron Burr, a politician without prospects in his own party, because Jefferson had never forgiven him for the 1800 election deadlock. Burr accepted a Federalist proposal that he become their candidate for governor of New York in 1804, and there were rumors (unsupported by any evidence) that he had also agreed to support the Federalist plans for secession. Hamilton accused Burr of plotting treason and made numerous private remarks, widely reported in the press, about Burr's "despicable" character. When Burr lost the election, he blamed his defeat on Hamilton's malevolence and challenged him to a duel. Hamilton feared that refusing

A M E R I C A N   V O I C E S

LEWIS AND CLARK

Exploring the Louisiana Territory,
1804–1806

NOV. 7, 1805. A cloudy foggey morning. Some rain. We set out early, proceeded under the stard. [starboard] side under high ruged hills with steep assent, the shore boalt and rockey, the fog so thick we could not see across the river. Two canos of Indians met and returned with us to their village which is situated on the stard. side behind a cluster of marshey islands, on a narrow chanl. of the river through which we passed to the village of 4 houses. They gave us to eate some fish, and sold us fish, *wap pa to* roots, three dogs and 2 otter skins for which we gave fish hooks principally, of which they were verry fond. . . .

After delaying at this village one hour and a half we set out piloted by an Indian dressed in a salors dress, to the main chanel of the river. . . . A large marshey island near the middle of the river near which several canoes came allong side with skins, roots, fish &c. to sell, and had a temporey residence on this island. . . .

Great joy in camp. We are in view of the ocian (in the morning when the fog cleared off just below the last village, first on leaving this village, of Warkiacum) this great Pacific Ocean which we been so long anxious to see, and the roreing or noise made by the waves brakeing on the rockey shores (as I suppose) may be heard distinctly.

SOURCE: From *Original Journals of the Lewis and Clark Expedition.*

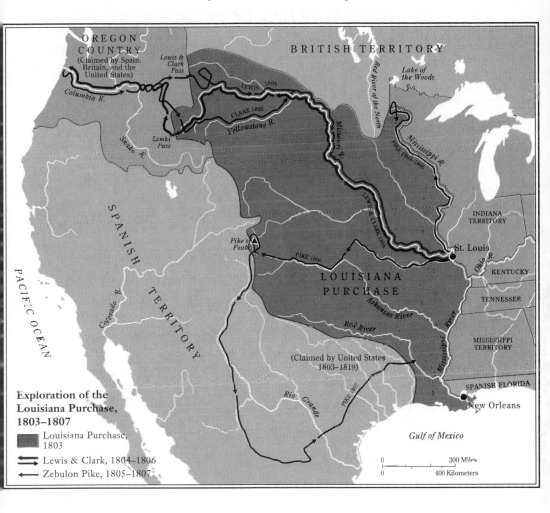

Exploration of the Louisiana Purchase, 1803–1807

■ Louisiana Purchase, 1803

⇔ Lewis & Clark, 1804–1806

← Zebulon Pike, 1805–1807

Burr's challenge would brand him a coward. And so, on a July morning in 1804, the two men met at Weehawken, New Jersey. Hamilton was mortally wounded; he died the next day.

The resourceful and charismatic Burr was now a political outcast, who had to flee New York to avoid an indictment for murder. He found new outlets for his ambitions in the West. Even before the duel, he had begun corresponding with prominent white settlers in the Southwest, especially with General James Wilkinson, now governor of the Louisiana Territory. Burr and Wilkinson, it seems clear, hoped to lead an expedition that would capture Mexico from the Spanish. But there were also rumors that they wanted to separate the Southwest from the Union and create a Western empire that Burr would rule. There is little evidence that these rumors were true.

Whether true or not, many of Burr's opponents chose to believe the rumors—including, ultimately, Jefferson himself. When Burr led a group of armed followers down the Ohio River by boat in 1806, disturbing reports flowed into Washington (the most alarming from Wilkinson, who had suddenly turned against Burr and who now informed the president that treason was afoot) that an attack on New Orleans was imminent. Jefferson ordered the arrest of Burr and his men as traitors. Burr was brought to Richmond for trial. Jefferson carefully managed the government's case from Washington. But Chief Justice Marshall, presiding over the case on circuit duty, limited the evidence the government could present and defined the charge in such a way that the jury had little choice but to acquit Burr.

The Burr conspiracy was in part the story of a single man's soaring ambitions and flamboyant personality. But it was also a symbol of the larger perils still facing the new nation. With a central government that remained deliberately weak, with vast tracts of land only nominally controlled by the United States, with ambitious political leaders willing, if necessary, to circumvent normal channels in their search for power, the legitimacy of the federal government—and indeed the existence of the United States as a stable and united nation—remained to be fully established.

CHAPTER EIGHT

War and Expansion

Causes of Conflict ~ The War of 1812 ~ Postwar Expansion

WO VERY DIFFERENT conflicts took shape in the early nineteenth century that would, together, draw the United States into a difficult and frustrating war. One was the continuing tension in Europe, which in 1803 escalated once again into a full-scale conflict (the Napoleonic Wars). As fighting between the British and the French increased, each side took steps to prevent the United States from trading with (and thus assisting) the other.

The other conflict occurred in North America itself. It was a result of the ceaseless westward expansion of white settlement, which was now stretching to the Mississippi River and beyond, colliding again with a native population committed to protecting its lands from intruders. In both the North and the South, the threatened tribes mobilized to resist white encroachments. They began as well to forge connections with British forces in Canada and Spanish forces in Florida. The Indian conflict on land, therefore, became intertwined with the European conflict on the seas.

Together, the conflict on the seas and the conflict in the Western lands drew the United States into a war with Great Britain—the War of 1812, an unpopular struggle with ambiguous results. But the more important war, in the long run, was the conflict with the Indians. And in that, white America won a series of decisive victories.

CAUSES OF CONFLICT

Politicians at the time and historians since have argued over whether the conflict in the West or the conflict on the seas was the real cause of the War of 1812. In fact, the war cannot be understood without considering both.

Neutral Rights

The early nineteenth century saw a dramatic expansion of American shipping in the Atlantic. Britain retained significant naval superiority, but the British merchant marine was preoccupied with commerce in Europe and Asia and devoted little energy to trade with America. Thus the United States stepped effectively into the void and developed one of the most important merchant marines in the world, one that soon controlled a large proportion of the trade between Europe and the West Indies.

In 1805, at the Battle of Trafalgar, a British fleet virtually destroyed what was left of the French navy. Because France could no longer challenge the British at sea, Napoleon now chose to pressure England through economic rather than naval means. The result was what he called the Continental System, which was designed to close the European continent to British trade. Accordingly, he issued a series of decrees (one in Berlin in 1806 and another in Milan in 1807) barring British ships and neutral ships touching at British ports from landing their cargoes at any European port controlled by France or its allies. The British government replied to Napoleon's decrees by establishing—through a series of "orders in council"—a blockade of the European coast. The blockade required that any goods being shipped to Napoleon's Europe be carried either in British vessels or in neutral vessels stopping at British ports—precisely what Napoleon's policies forbade.

American ships were caught between Napoleon's Berlin and Milan decrees and Britain's orders in council. If they sailed directly for the European continent, they risked being captured by the British navy. If they sailed by way of a British port, they ran the risk of seizure by the French. Both of the warring powers were violating America's rights as a neutral nation. But most Americans considered the British, with their greater sea power, the worse offender. British ships pounced on Yankee merchantmen all over the ocean; the French could do so only in European ports. In particular, British vessels stopped American ships on the high seas and seized sailors off the decks, making them victims of "impressment."

Impressment

The British navy—with its floggings, its low pay, and its terrible shipboard conditions—was a "floating hell" to its sailors. Few volunteered. Most had had to be "impressed" (forced) into the service. At every opportunity they deserted. By 1807, many of these deserters had joined the American merchant marine or the American navy. To check this loss of vital manpower, the British claimed the right to stop and search American merchantmen (although not naval vessels) and reimpress deserters. They did not claim the right to take native-born Americans, but they did insist on the right to seize naturalized Americans born on British soil. In practice, the British navy often made no careful distinctions, impressing British deserters and native-born Americans alike into their service. Thousands of American sailors were thus kidnapped.

In the summer of 1807, the British went to more provocative extremes in an incident involving a vessel of the American navy. Sailing from Norfolk, with several alleged deserters from the British navy among the crew, the American naval frigate *Chesapeake* was hailed by the British ship *Leopard*. When the American commander, James Barron, refused to allow the British to search the *Chesapeake*, the *Leopard* opened fire. Barron was compelled to surrender, and a boarding party from the *Leopard* dragged four men off the American frigate.

When news of the *Chesapeake-Leopard* incident reached the American public, there was great popular clamor for revenge. If Congress had been in session, it might have declared war. But Jefferson and Madison tried to maintain the peace. Jefferson expelled all British warships from American waters to lessen the likelihood of future incidents. Then he sent instructions to his minister in England, James Monroe, to demand from the British government the complete renunciation of impressment. The British government disavowed the action of the officer responsible for the *Chesapeake-Leopard* affair and recalled him; it offered compensation for those killed and wounded in the incident; and it promised to return three of the captured sailors (one of the original four had been hanged). But the British cabinet refused to renounce impressment and instead reasserted its right to recover deserting seamen. The impressment issue therefore prevented any permanent settlement of Anglo-American differences.

"Peaceable Coercion"

In an effort to prevent future incidents that might bring the nation again to the brink of war, Jefferson presented a drastic measure to Congress when it reconvened late in 1807. The Republican legislators promptly enacted it into law. It was known as the Embargo, and it became one of the most controversial political issues of its time. The Embargo prohibited American ships from leaving the United States for any foreign port anywhere in the world. (If it had specified only British and French ports, Jefferson reasoned, it could have been evaded by means of false clearance papers.) Congress also passed a "force act" to give the government power to enforce the Embargo.

The law was widely evaded, but it was effective enough to create a serious depression through most of the nation. Hardest hit were the merchants and shipowners of the Northeast, most of them Federalists. Their once lucrative shipping business was at a virtual standstill, and they were losing money every day. They became convinced that Jefferson had acted unconstitutionally.

The election of 1808 came in the midst of the Embargo-induced depression. James Madison, Jefferson's secretary of state and political ally, was elected president; but the Federalist candidate, Charles Pinckney again, ran much more strongly than he had in 1804. The Federalists gained seats in Congress, although the Republicans still controlled both houses. The Embargo was clearly a growing political liability, and Jefferson decided to back down. A few days before leaving office, he approved a bill ending his experiment with what he called "peaceable coercion."

To replace the Embargo, Congress passed the Non-Intercourse Act just before Madison took office. It reopened trade with all nations but Great Britain and France. A year later, in 1810, the Non-Intercourse Act expired and was replaced by Macon's Bill No. 2, which reopened free commercial relations with Britain and France but authorized the president to prohibit commerce with either belligerent if it should continue violating neutral shipping after the other had stopped. Napoleon, in an effort to induce the United States to reimpose the Embargo against Britain, announced that France would no longer interfere with American shipping. Madison announced that an embargo against Great Britain alone would automatically go into effect early in 1811 unless Britain renounced its restrictions on American shipping.

In time, this new, limited embargo, although less well enforced than the earlier one, hurt the economy of England enough that the government repealed its blockade of Europe. But the repeal was too late to prevent war. In any case, naval policies were only part of the reason for tensions between Britain and the United States.

The "Indian Problem" and the British

Given the ruthlessness with which white settlers in North America had dislodged Indian tribes to make room for expanding settlement, it was hardly surprising that ever since the Revolution most Indians had continued to look to England—which had historically attempted to limit Western expansion—for protection. The British in Canada, for their part, had relied on the Indians as partners in the lucrative fur trade and as potential military allies. Even so, there had been relative peace in the Northwest for over a decade after Jay's Treaty and Anthony Wayne's victory over the tribes at Fallen Timbers in 1794. But the 1807 war crisis following the *Chesapeake-Leopard* incident revived the conflict between Indians and white settlers. Two important (and very different) leaders emerged to lead it: William Henry Harrison and Tecumseh.

The Virginia-born Harrison, already a veteran Indian fighter at age twenty-six, went to Washington as the congressional delegate from the Northwest Territory in 1799. He was a committed advocate of growth and development in the Western lands, and he was largely responsible for the passage in 1800 of the so-called Harrison Land Law, which enabled white settlers to acquire farms from the public domain on much easier terms than before.

In 1801, Jefferson appointed Harrison governor of Indiana Territory to administer the president's proposed solution to the "Indian problem." Jefferson offered the Indians a choice: they could convert themselves into settled farmers and become a part of white society, or they could migrate to the west of the Mississippi. In either case, they would have to give up their claims to their tribal lands in the Northwest.

Jefferson considered the assimilation policy a benign alternative to the continuing conflict between Indians and white settlers, a conflict he assumed the tribes were destined to lose. But to the tribes, the new policy seemed far from benign, especially given the bludgeonlike efficiency with which Harrison set out to implement it. He played off one tribe against another and used threats, bribes, trickery, and whatever other tactics he felt would help him conclude treaties. By 1807, the United States had extracted treaty rights from reluctant tribal leaders to eastern Michigan, southern Indiana, and most of Illinois. Meanwhile, in the Southwest, white Americans were taking millions of acres from other tribes in Georgia, Tennessee, and Mississippi. The Indians wanted desperately to resist, but the separate tribes were helpless by themselves against the power of the United States. They might have accepted their fate passively but for the emergence of two new factors.

One factor was the policy of the British authorities in Canada. After the *Chesapeake* incident and the surge of anti-British feeling throughout the United States, the British colonial authorities began to expect an American invasion of Canada and took desperate measures for their own defense. Among those measures were efforts to renew friendship with the Indians and provide them with increased supplies.

Tecumseh and the Prophet

The second, and more important, factor intensifying the border conflict was the rise of two remarkable native leaders. One was Tenskwatawa, a charismatic religious leader and orator known as the Prophet. He had experienced a mystical awakening in the process of recovering from alcoholism. Having freed himself from what he considered the evil effects of white culture, he began to speak to his people of the superior virtues of Indian civilization and the sinfulness and corruption of the white world. In the process, he inspired a religious revival that spread through numerous tribes and helped unite them. The Prophet's headquarters at the confluence of Tippecanoe Creek and the Wabash River (known as Prophetstown) became a sacred place for people of many tribes and attracted thousands of Indians from throughout the Midwest. Out of their common religious experiences, they began to consider joint political and military efforts as well.

The Prophet's brother Tecumseh—"the Shooting Star," chief of the Shawnees—emerged as the leader of these more secular efforts. Tecumseh understood, as few other Indian leaders had, that only through united action could the tribes hope to resist the steady advance of white civilization. Beginning in 1809, after tribes in Indiana had ceded vast lands to the United States, he set out to unite all the tribes of the Mississippi Valley, north and south. Together, he promised, they would halt white expansion, recover the whole Northwest, and make the Ohio River the boundary between the United States and Indian country. He maintained that Harrison and others, by negotiating treaties with individual tribes, had obtained no real title to land. The land belonged to all the tribes; none of them could rightfully cede any of it without the consent of the others. In 1811, Tecumseh left Prophetstown and traveled down the Mississippi to visit the tribes of the South and persuade them to join the alliance. During his absence, Governor Harrison saw a chance to destroy the growing influence of the two Indian leaders. With 1,000 soldiers he camped near Prophetstown, and on November 7, 1811, he provoked an armed conflict. Although the white forces suffered losses as heavy as those of the natives, Harrison drove off the Indians and burned the town. The Battle of Tippecanoe (named for the creek near which it was fought) disillusioned many of the Prophet's followers, who had believed that his magic would protect them; and Tecumseh returned to find the confederacy in disarray. But there were still warriors eager for combat, and by spring of 1812 they were active along the frontier, from Michigan to Mississippi, raiding white settlements and terrifying settlers.

The bloodshed along the Western borders was largely a result of the Indians' own initiative, but Britain's agents in Canada had encouraged and helped to supply the uprising. To Harrison and most white residents of the regions, there seemed only one way to make the West safe for Americans. That was to drive the British out of Canada and annex that province to the United States—a goal that many Westerners had long cherished for other reasons as well.

The Lure of Florida

While white "frontiersmen" in the North demanded the conquest of Canada, those in the South looked to the acquisition of Spanish Florida (a territory that included the present state of Florida and the southern areas of what is now Alabama, Mississippi, and Louisiana). The territory was a continuing threat to whites in the Southern United States. Slaves escaped across the Florida border; Indians in Florida launched frequent raids north into white settlements along the border. But white Southerners also coveted Florida because through it ran rivers that could provide residents of the Southwest access to valuable ports on the Gulf of Mexico.

In 1810, American settlers in West Florida (the area presently part of Mississippi and Louisiana) seized the Spanish fort at Baton Rouge and asked the federal government to annex the territory to the United States. President Madison happily agreed and then began scheming to get the rest of Florida too. The desire for Florida became yet another motivation for war with Britain. Spain was Britain's ally, and a war with England might provide an excuse for taking Spanish as well as British territory.

By 1812, therefore, war fever was raging on both the Northern and Southern borders of the United States. The white residents of these outlying regions made up a relatively small proportion of the national population and were represented in Congress by only a few, nonvoting territorial delegates. But their demands found substantial support in Washington among a group of determined young congressmen who soon earned the name of "War Hawks."

In the congressional elections of 1810, voters elected a large number of representatives of both parties eager for war with Britain. They represented a new generation, aggressive and impatient. The most influential of them came from the new states in the West or from the back country of the old states in the South. Two of their leaders, both recently elected to the House of Representatives, were Henry Clay of Kentucky and John C. Calhoun of

South Carolina, men of great intellect, magnetism, and ambition who would play a large role in national politics for nearly forty years. Both were supporters of war with Great Britain.

Clay was elected Speaker of the House in 1811, and he filled committees with those who shared his eagerness for war. He appointed Calhoun to the crucial Committee on Foreign Affairs. Both men began agitating for the conquest of Canada. Madison still preferred peace but was losing control of Congress. On June 18, 1812, he approved a declaration of war against Britain.

THE WAR OF 1812

Preoccupied with their struggle against Napoleon in Europe, the British were not eager for an open conflict with the United States. Even after the Americans declared war, Britain largely ignored them for a time. But in the fall of 1812, Napoleon launched a catastrophic campaign against Russia that left his army in disarray and his power in Europe diminished. By late 1813, with the French empire on its way to final defeat, Britain was able to turn its military attention to America.

The Course of Battle

Americans entered the War of 1812 with great enthusiasm, but events on the battlefield soon cooled their ardor. In the summer of 1812, American forces invaded Canada by way of Detroit, as part of a planned three-pronged attack. They were soon forced to retreat back to Detroit and in August surrendered the fort there. Other invasion efforts also failed. In the meantime, Fort Dearborn (Chicago) fell before an Indian attack.

Things went only slightly better for the United States on the seas. At first, American frigates won some spectacular victories over British war-ships, and American privateers destroyed or captured many British merchant ships, occasionally braving the coastal waters of the British Isles and burning vessels within sight of the shore. But by 1813, the British navy was counterattacking effectively, driving the American frigates to cover and imposing a blockade on the United States.

The United States did, however, achieve significant early military successes on the Great Lakes. First, the Americans took command of Lake Ontario; this permitted them to raid and burn York (now Toronto), the capital of Canada, before returning to their own lands across the lake.

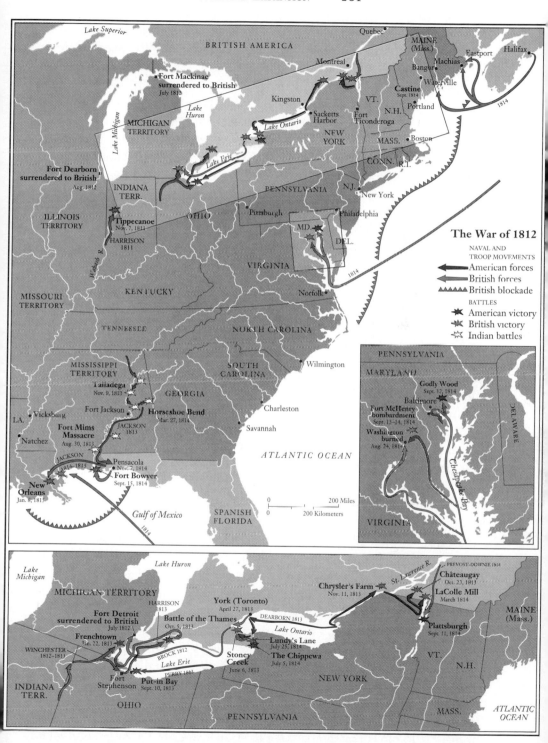

The War of 1812

NAVAL AND
TROOP MOVEMENTS
→ American forces
→ British forces
▲▲▲▲ British blockade
BATTLES
✳ American victory
✴ British victory
☆ Indian battles

American forces then seized control of Lake Erie, mainly through the work of the youthful Oliver Hazard Perry, who engaged and dispersed a British fleet at Put-in Bay on September 10, 1813. This made possible, at last, an invasion of Canada by way of Detroit, which Americans could now reach easily by water. William Henry Harrison, the American commander in the West, pushed up the river Thames into upper Canada and on October 5, 1813, won a victory notable for the death of Tecumseh, who was serving as a brigadier general in the British army. The Battle of the Thames resulted in no lasting occupation of Canada, but it weakened and disheartened the Indians of the Northwest and greatly diminished their ability to defend their claims to the region.

In the meantime, another white military leader was striking an even harder blow at the Indians of the Southwest. The Creeks, aroused by Tecumseh on a Southern visit and supplied by the Spaniards in Florida, had been attacking white settlers near the Florida border. Andrew Jackson, a wealthy Tennessee planter and a general in the state militia, temporarily abandoned plans for an invasion of Florida and set off in pursuit of the Creeks. On March 27, 1814, in the Battle of Horseshoe Bend, Jackson's men took terrible revenge on the Indians—slaughtering women and children along with warriors—and broke the resistance of the Creeks. The tribe agreed to cede most of its lands to the United States and retreated westward, farther into the interior. The battle also won Jackson a commission as major general in the United States Army, and in that capacity he led his men farther south into Florida. On November 7, 1814, he seized the Spanish fort at Pensacola.

But the victories over the tribes were not enough to win the war. After the surrender of Napoleon in 1814, England began to transfer part of its European army to America and prepared to invade the United States from three approaches—Chesapeake Bay, Lake Champlain, and the mouth of the Mississippi. A British armada sailed up the Patuxent River from Chesapeake Bay and landed an army that marched to nearby Bladensburg, on the outskirts of Washington, where it dispersed a more numerous but poorly trained force of American militiamen. On August 24, 1814, the British troops entered Washington and put the government to flight. Then they set fire to several public buildings, including the White House, in retaliation for the earlier American burning of the Canadian capital at York. This was the low point of American fortunes in the war.

Leaving Washington in partial ruins, the invading army proceeded up the bay toward Baltimore. But Baltimore, guarded by Fort McHenry, was prepared. To block the approaching fleet, the American garrison had sunk several ships in the Patapsco River (the entry to Baltimore's harbor), thus forcing the British to bombard the fort from a distance. Through the night of September 13, Francis Scott Key (a Washington lawyer on board one of the British ships, where he was trying to secure the release of an American prisoner) watched the bombardment. The next morning, "by the dawn's early light," he could see the flag on the fort still flying; he recorded his pride in the moment by scribbling a poem—"The Star-Spangled Banner"—on the back of an envelope. The British withdrew from Baltimore. Key's words were soon set to the tune of an old English drinking song. (In 1931, "The Star-Spangled Banner" became the official national anthem.)

Meanwhile, American forces repelled another British invasion in northern New York; at the Battle of Plattsburgh, on September 11, 1814, they

THE BATTLE OF NEW ORLEANS The Battle of New Orleans was the last major engagement and the greatest American victory on land of the War of 1812. General Andrew Jackson commanded about 4,500 troops and fended off superior British forces under the command of Sir Edward Pakenham (who was killed in the fighting). The artist Hyacinthe de Laclotte drew the sketch that became the basis of this painting while standing above the battlefield.

turned back a much more numerous British naval and land force and secured the Northern border of the United States. In the South, a formidable array of battle-hardened British veterans, fresh from the campaign against the French in Spain, landed below New Orleans and prepared to advance north up the Mississippi. Awaiting the British was Andrew Jackson with a motley collection of Tennesseans, Kentuckians, Creoles, blacks, pirates, and regular army troops drawn up behind earthen breastworks. On January 8, 1815, the redcoats advanced on the American fortifications, but the exposed British forces were no match for Jackson's well-protected men. After the Americans had repulsed several waves of attackers, the British finally retreated, leaving behind 700 dead (including their commander, Sir Edward Pakenham), 1,400 wounded, and 500 prisoners. Jackson's losses: 8 killed, 13 wounded. Only later did news reach North America that the United States and Britain had signed a peace treaty several weeks before the Battle of New Orleans. Even so, Americans long remembered the battle as a glorious victory, a sign of the rising power of the United States among the nations of the world.

The Revolt of New England

With a few notable exceptions, such as the battles of Put-in Bay and New Orleans, the military operations of the United States between 1812 and 1815 consisted of a series of humiliating failures. As a result, the American government faced increasing popular opposition as the contest dragged on. In New England, opposition both to the war and to the Republican government that was waging it was so extreme that some Federalists celebrated British victories. In Congress, in the meantime, the Republicans had continual trouble with the Federalist opposition, led by a young congressman from New Hampshire, Daniel Webster, who missed no opportunity to embarrass the administration.

By now the Federalists were very much in the minority in the country as a whole, but they were still the majority party in New England. Some of them began to dream of creating a separate nation in that region, which they could dominate and in which they could escape what they saw as the tyranny of slaveholders and backwoodsmen. Talk of secession revived and reached a climax in the winter of 1814–1815, when the republic appeared to be on the verge of ruin.

On December 15, 1814, delegates from the New England states met in Hartford, Connecticut, to discuss the grievances of their region against the Madison administration. The would-be seceders at the Hartford Convention were outnumbered by a comparatively moderate majority. But while the convention's report only hinted at secession, it reasserted the right of nullification and proposed seven amendments to the Constitution (presumably as the condition of New England's remaining in the Union)—amendments designed to protect New England from the growing influence of the South and the West.

Because the war was going badly and the government was becoming desperate, the New Englanders assumed that the Republicans would have to agree to their demands. Soon after the convention adjourned, however, the news of Jackson's smashing victory at New Orleans reached the cities of the Northeast. A day or two later, reports arrived from abroad of a treaty of peace. In the euphoria of this apparent triumph, the Hartford Convention and the Federalist party came to seem futile, irrelevant, even treasonable.

The Peace Settlement

Peace talks between the United States and Britain had begun even before the first battles of the War of 1812 were fought, but serious negotiations did not begin until August 1814, when American and British diplomats met in Ghent, Belgium. John Quincy Adams, Henry Clay, and Albert Gallatin led the American delegation.

Although both sides began with extravagant demands, the final treaty did very little except end the fighting itself. The Americans gave up their demand for a British renunciation of impressment and for the cession of Canada to the United States. The British abandoned their call for creation of an Indian buffer state in the Northwest and made other, minor territorial concessions. Other disputes were referred to arbitration. Hastily drawn up, the treaty was signed on Christmas Eve 1814.

Both sides had reason to accept this skimpy agreement. The British, exhausted and in debt from their prolonged conflict with Napoleon, were eager to settle the lesser dispute in North America. The Americans realized that with the defeat of Napoleon in Europe, the British would no longer have much incentive to interfere with American commerce. Indeed, by the end of 1815, impressment had all but ceased.

Other settlements followed the Treaty of Ghent and contributed to a long-term improvement in Anglo-American relations. A commercial treaty in 1815 gave Americans the right to trade freely with England and much of the British Empire. The Rush-Bagot agreement of 1817 provided for mutual disarmament on the Great Lakes; eventually (although not until 1872) the Canadian-American boundary became the longest "unguarded frontier" in the world.

For the other parties to the War of 1812, the Indian tribes east of the Mississippi, the Treaty of Ghent was of no lasting value. It required that the United States restore to the tribes lands seized by white Americans in the fighting, but those provisions were never enforced. Ultimately, the war was another disastrous blow to the capacity of Indians to resist white expansion. Tecumseh, their most important leader, was dead. The British, their most important allies, were gone from the Northwest. The inter-tribal alliance that Tecumseh and the Prophet had forged was in disarray. The end of the war served as a spur to white movement westward, and the Indians had lost much of their capacity to oppose the expansion.

No sooner did the war with England end in 1815 than Congress declared war again, this time against Algiers, which had taken advantage of the War of 1812 to resume sending its pirates out against American shipping in the Mediterranean. An American naval squadron under the command of Stephen Decatur sailed to the Mediterranean, captured a number of enemy ships, blockaded the coast of Algiers, and forced the dey (the Algerian ruler) to accept a treaty that not only ended the payment of tribute by the United States but required that Algiers pay reparations to America. Decatur then sailed on to Tunis and Tripoli and extracted similar concessions from them. This naval action in the Mediterranean did more to provide Americans with free access to the seas than the War of 1812 itself had done.

POSTWAR EXPANSION

In the aftermath of the war, American commerce revived and expanded, industry advanced rapidly, and westward expansion accelerated dramatically. It was a time of rapid economic growth—too rapid, as it turned out, for the boom was followed in 1819 by a disastrous bust. The collapse only temporarily slowed economic expansion, but it revealed clearly that the United States continued to lack some of the basic institutions necessary to sustain long-term growth.

Economic Growth and the Government

The aftermath of the war saw the emergence of political issues connected with national economic development: reestablishing the Bank of the United States (the first Bank's charter had not been renewed when it expired in 1811), protecting new industries, and building roads and waterways.

The wartime experience seemed to underline the need for another national bank. After the first Bank's charter expired, a large number of state banks sprang up and issued vast quantities of bank notes, often without a large enough reserve of gold or silver to support them. Soon there were many different kinds of notes, of widely varying value, in circulation at the same time, creating a confusion that made honest business difficult and counterfeiting easy.

Congress struck at the currency problem by chartering a second Bank of the United States in 1816. It was essentially the same institution as the one founded under Hamilton's leadership in 1791 except that it had more capital than its predecessor. The national bank could not prohibit state banks from issuing notes, but its size and power gave it the ability to dominate the state banks. It could compel them to issue only sound notes or risk being forced out of business.

American manufacturing had flourished during the war; with imports effectively blocked, native industry grew. Demand was so high that even with comparatively unskilled labor and poor management, new factories

THE UNITED STATES CAPITOL IN 1824 This slightly idealized view by the American artist Charles Burton shows the approach to the west front of the United States Capitol along Pennsylvania Avenue. The large, columned dome that today rises above the building was built in the 1860s to replace the simpler dome shown in this painting.

could make quick profits. The American textile industry had experienced particularly dramatic growth, spurred first by the Embargo of 1807 and then by the war. Between 1807 and 1815, the total number of cotton spindles increased more than fifteenfold, from 8,000 to 130,000. Until 1814, the textile factories—most of them in New England—produced only yarn and thread; the weaving of cloth was left to families operating handlooms at home. Then the Boston merchant Francis Cabot Lowell developed a power loom that was better than its English counterpart. In 1813, in Waltham, Massachusetts, Lowell founded the first mill in America to house spinning and weaving under a single roof. Lowell's company was an important step in revolutionizing American manufacturing.

As the War of 1812 came to an end, however, the prospects for American industry suddenly dimmed. British ships swarmed into American ports and unloaded cargoes of manufactured goods to be sold at prices much lower than those of domestic goods. The "infant industries" cried out for protection, arguing that they needed time to grow strong enough to withstand foreign competition. In 1816, protectionists in Congress won passage of a tariff law that effectively limited competition from abroad on cotton cloth and other items. There were objections from agricultural interests, who stood to pay higher prices for manufactured goods. But the nationalist dream of creating an important American industrial economy prevailed.

The nation's most pressing economic need in the aftermath of the war, however, was improvements in its transportation system that would provide manufacturers with access to raw materials and markets. An old debate resumed: Should the federal government help finance roads and other "internal improvements"? The idea of using government funds to finance road building was not a new one. When Ohio entered the Union in 1803, the federal government had allotted part of the proceeds from the sale of public lands there to building roads. In 1807, Congress enacted a law, proposed by the Jefferson administration, providing for construction of a national road, from the Potomac to the Ohio, financed partly by the Ohio land sales. The next year, it appropriated $20 million for another, more ambitious program of internal improvements. By 1818, the national road was completed to Wheeling, Virginia, on the Ohio River; and the Lancaster pike, funded in part by the state of Pennsylvania, extended west to Pittsburgh. The roads were heavily traveled and helped lower shipping rates across the mountains.

At the same time, on the rivers and the Great Lakes, steam-powered shipping was experiencing rapid expansion. By 1816, river steamers were beginning for the first time to journey up and down the Ohio River as far as Pittsburgh. Steamboats were soon carrying more cargo on the Mississippi than all the earlier forms of river transport combined. They stimulated the agricultural economy of the West and the South by providing access to markets at greatly reduced cost, and they enabled Eastern manufacturers to send their finished goods west much more readily.

But despite the progress with steamboats and turnpikes, there remained serious gaps in the nation's transportation network. In 1815, President Madison informed Congress of the "great importance of establishing throughout our country the roads and canals which can be best executed under the national authority." But when, shortly before Madison left office, Representative Calhoun steered to passage a bill that would have used the funds owed the government by the Bank of the United States to finance internal improvements, the president vetoed it. He supported the purpose of the bill, he explained, but he believed that Congress lacked authority to fund the improvements without a constitutional amendment. And so on the issue of internal improvements, at least, the nationalists fell short of their goals. For a time, the tremendous task of building the transportation network necessary for the growing American economy was left largely to state governments and private enterprise.

Westward Migration

One reason for the growing interest in internal improvements was the sudden and dramatic surge in westward expansion in the years following the War of 1812. By the time of the census of 1820, almost one of every four white Americans lived west of the Appalachians, compared with only one in seven a decade before.

The pressures driving Americans out of the East came in part from the continued growth of the population—both through natural increase and immigration. Between 1800 and 1820, the nation's population nearly doubled—from 5.3 million to 9.6 million. The growth of the nation's cities absorbed some of that increase; but most Americans were still farmers, and the agricultural lands of the East were by now largely occupied. In the South, the spread of the plantation system and its slave labor force limited opportunities for new white settlers.

Meanwhile, the West itself was becoming increasingly attractive to white settlers. The War of 1812 helped diminish one of the traditional inhibitions to Western expansion: fear of Indian opposition. In the aftermath

THE NATIONAL ROAD, 1827 This picture of heavy traffic along the National
Turnpike suggests the rapid acceleration of commerce in the Eastern United
States in the 1820s and the pressure that economic growth was placing on existing
means of transportation. The painting also shows the Fair View Inn, which stood
three miles from Baltimore, Maryland.

of the war, the federal government continued its policy of pushing the
remaining tribes farther and farther west. A series of treaties in 1815
wrested still more land from the Indians.

The fertile lands now secure for white settlement drew migrants from
throughout the East to what was then known as the Old Northwest (now
part of the Midwest). Settlers traveled west by river and over land, established land claims, built lean-tos or cabins, and then hewed clearings out of
the forests. Most grew corn to supplement the wild game they caught and
the domestic animals they had brought with them. It was a rough existence,
often plagued by loneliness, poverty, dirt, and disease. Men, women, and
children worked side by side in the fields. Some had virtually no contact for
weeks or months at a time with anyone outside their own families.

Life in the Northwest was not, however, always as solitary and individualistic as later myth suggested. Migrants often journeyed westward in
groups, which at times became the basis of new communities where schools,
churches, stores, and other shared institutions were built. The labor shortage in the interior meant that neighbors developed systems of mutual aid,

gathering periodically to raise a barn, clear land, harvest crops, or make quilts. Gradually, white settlers built a thriving farm economy based largely on family units of modest size and committed to growing grain and raising livestock.

In the Southwest, the new agricultural economy emerged along different lines—just as the economy of the Old South had long been different from that of the Northeast. The principal attraction of the region was cotton, the market for which continued to grow. In the Southwest, around the end of the Appalachian range, stretched a broad zone within which cotton could thrive—including what was to become known as the Black Belt of central Alabama and Mississippi, a vast prairie with dark, productive soil.

The advance of the Southern frontier meant the spread not just of cotton but also of slavery. Usually the first arrivals were ordinary frontier people like those farther north, small farmers who made rough clearings in the forest. Then came wealthier planters, who bought up the cleared or partially cleared land, while the original settlers moved farther west and started over again. The large planters made the westward journey in a style quite different from that of the first settlers, traveling in great caravans with herds of livestock, wagonloads of household goods, long lines of slaves, and—at the rear—the planter's family riding in carriages. Success in the wilderness was by no means assured, even for the wealthiest settlers. But many planters soon expanded small clearings into vast fields of cotton and replaced the cabins of the pioneers with more sumptuous log dwellings and ultimately with imposing mansions that demonstrated the rise of a newly rich class.

The rapid growth of the West resulted in the admission of four new states to the Union in the immediate aftermath of the War of 1812: Indiana in 1816, Mississippi in 1817, Illinois in 1818, and Alabama in 1819.

The Far West

The Far Western areas of the continent remained largely unknown to most white Americans. Only New Englanders who were engaged in Pacific whaling or the China trade were familiar with the Oregon coast. Only fur traders and trappers had any knowledge of the land between the Missouri and the Pacific.

Before the War of 1812, John Jacob Astor's American Fur Company had established Astoria as a trading post at the mouth of the Columbia River in Oregon. When war came, Astor sold his interests to a British company and moved his own operations to the Great Lakes area, from which he eventually extended them westward to the Rockies. Other companies carried on operations up the Missouri and its tributaries and in the Rocky Mountains. At first, fur traders did most of their business by purchasing pelts from the Indians. But beginning with Andrew and William Ashley's Rocky Mountain Fur Company, founded in 1822, more and more traders dispatched white trappers into the wilderness to travel with the Indians in pursuit of furs.

The trappers (or "mountain men") explored the Far West and gained an intimate knowledge of the region and its people; but few wrote books or drew maps, so their knowledge did not spread widely. Public awareness of the region increased more as a result of the explorations of Major Stephen H. Long, who in 1819–1820 led nineteen soldiers on a journey through what is now Nebraska and eastern Colorado. Long wrote an influential report on his trip, assessing the region's potential for future settlement and development: "We do not hesitate in giving the opinion that it is almost wholly unfit for cultivation, and of course uninhabitable by a people depending upon agriculture for their subsistence." On the published map of his expedition, he labeled the Great Plains the "Great American Desert"—strengthening the mistaken belief, first advanced by Pike and others, that the land beyond the Missouri River was unfit for cultivation.

The "Era of Good Feelings"

The expansion of the economy, the growth of the West, the creation of new states—all reflected the rising spirit of nationalism that was permeating the United States in the years following the war. That spirit found reflection, for a time, in the course of American politics.

Ever since 1800, the presidency had remained in the hands of Virginians. After two terms in office Jefferson helped his secretary of state, James Madison, to succeed him; and after two more terms, Madison secured the presidential nomination for his own secretary of state, James Monroe. Many in the North were already expressing their impatience with the so-called Virginia Dynasty, but the Republicans had no difficulty electing their candidate in the listless campaign of 1816. Monroe received 183 ballots in the electoral college; his Federalist opponent, Rufus King of New York, only 34—from Massachusetts, Connecticut, and Delaware.

Monroe was sixty-one years old when he became president. In the course of his long and varied career, he had served as a soldier in the Revolution, as a diplomat, and most recently as a cabinet officer. He entered office under what seemed to be remarkably favorable circumstances. With the decline of the Federalists, his party faced no serious opposition. With the conclusion of the War of 1812, the nation faced no important international threats. American politicians had dreamed since the first days of the republic of a time in which partisan divisions and factional disputes might come to an end, a time in which the nation might achieve the harmony and virtue the founders had envisioned. In the postwar years, Monroe attempted to use his office to realize that dream.

He made that clear, above all, in the selection of his cabinet. For secretary of state, he chose the New Englander and former Federalist John Quincy Adams. Jefferson, Madison, and Monroe had all served as secretary of state before becoming president; Adams, therefore, immediately became the heir apparent, suggesting that the "Virginia Dynasty" would soon come to an end. Monroe asked Henry Clay to be secretary of war, but Clay chose to remain as Speaker of the House, so he named John C. Calhoun instead. In his other appointments, too, Monroe took pains to include both Northerners and Southerners, Easterners and Westerners, Federalists and Republicans—to harmonize the various interests and sections of the country in a government of national unity.

Soon after his inauguration, Monroe did what no president since Washington had done: he made a goodwill tour through the country. In New England, so recently the scene of rabid Federalist discontent, he was greeted everywhere with enthusiastic demonstrations. The *Columbian Centinel*, a Federalist newspaper in Boston, commenting on the "Presidential Jubilee" in that city, observed that an "era of good feelings" had arrived. This phrase became a popular label for the presidency of Monroe. On the surface, at least, the years of Monroe's presidency did appear to be an "era of good feelings." In 1820, Monroe was re-elected without opposition. For all practical purposes, the Federalist party had now ceased to exist.

John Quincy Adams and Florida

Like his father, the second president of the United States, John Quincy Adams had spent much of his life in diplomatic service. He had represented the United States in Britain, Russia, the Netherlands, and Prussia. He had helped negotiate the Treaty of Ghent. And he had demonstrated in all his assignments a calmness and firmness that made him one of the great diplomats in American history. He was also a committed nationalist; and when he assumed the office of secretary of state, he considered his most important task to be the promotion of American expansion.

CAPTURING THE SEMINOLES A nineteenth-century woodcut illustrates American troops under the command of Andrew Jackson
taking two Seminole chiefs into captivity in Florida in 1816.

His first challenge was Florida. The United States had already annexed
West Florida, but that claim was in dispute. Most Americans, moreover, still
believed the nation should gain possession of the entire peninsula. In 1817,
Adams began negotiations with the Spanish minister, Luis de Onís, in hopes
of resolving the dispute and gaining the entire territory for the United States.

In the meantime, however, events were taking their own course in
Florida itself. Andrew Jackson, now in command of American troops along
the Florida frontier, had orders from Secretary of War Calhoun to "adopt
the necessary measures" to stop the continuing raids on American territory
by Seminole Indians south of the Florida border. Jackson used those orders
as an excuse to invade Florida, seize the Spanish forts at St. Marks and
Pensacola, and order the hanging of two British subjects on the charge of
supplying and inciting the Indians.

Instead of condemning Jackson's raid, Adams urged the government to
assume responsibility for it, because he saw a chance to win an important
advantage in his negotiations with Spain. The United States, he told the
Spanish, had the right under international law to defend itself against threats
from across its borders. Since Spain was unwilling or unable to curb those

threats, America had simply done what was necessary. Jackson's raid had demonstrated to the Spanish that the United States could easily take Florida by force. Adams implied that the nation might consider doing so.

Onís realized, therefore, that he had little choice but to come to terms with the Americans. Under the provisions of the Adams-Onís Treaty of 1819, Spain ceded all of Florida to the United States and gave up its claim to territory north of the 42nd parallel in the Pacific Northwest. In return, the American government gave up its claims to Texas.

The Panic of 1819

But the Monroe administration had little time to revel in its diplomatic successes. At the same time Adams was negotiating with Onís, the nation was experiencing a serious economic crisis that helped revive many of the political disputes that the "era of good feelings" had presumably settled.

The Panic of 1819 followed a period of high foreign demand for American farm goods (a result of the disruption of European agriculture by the Napoleonic Wars) and thus of exceptionally high prices for American farmers. The rising prices for farm goods stimulated a land boom in the Western United States. Fueled by speculative investments, land prices soared well above the government-established minimum of $2 an acre; some land in the Black Belt of Alabama and Mississippi went for $100 an acre and more.

The availability of easy credit to settlers and speculators—from the government (under the land acts of 1800 and 1804); from state banks and wildcat banks; even for a time from the rechartered Bank of the United States—fueled the land boom. Beginning in 1819, however, new management at the national bank began tightening credit, calling in loans and foreclosing mortgages. The new governors also collected state bank notes and demanded payment in cash from the banks, many of which could not meet the demand and hence failed. These bank failures launched a financial panic, which many Americans, particularly those in the West, blamed on the Bank of the United States. Thus began a process that would eventually make the Bank's existence one of the nation's most burning political issues.

Six years of depression followed. Prices for both manufactured goods and agricultural produce fell rapidly. Manufacturers secured passage of a new tariff in 1824 to protect them from foreign competition. Indebted farmers won some relief through the land law of 1820 and the relief act of 1821, which lowered the price of land and reduced existing debts while extending their payment schedules.

Some Americans saw the Panic of 1819 and the widespread distress that followed as a warning that rapid economic growth and territorial expansion would destabilize the nation and threaten its survival. But most Americans by 1820 were irrevocably committed to such growth and expansion. Public debate in the future would revolve less around the question of whether such growth was good or bad than around the question of how it should be encouraged and controlled. That debate, which the Panic of 1819 did much to encourage, created new factional divisions within the Republican party and ultimately brought the era of nonpartisanship—the "era of good feelings"—to an acrimonious end.

CHAPTER NINE

A Resurgence of Nationalism

America's Economic Revolution ~ Sectionalism and Nationalism
The Revival of Opposition

IKE A "FIRE BELL IN THE NIGHT," as Thomas Jefferson put it, the issue of slavery arose after the War of 1812 to threaten the unity of the nation. The specific question was whether the territory of Missouri should be admitted to the Union as a free or as a slaveholding state. But the larger issue, one that would arise again and again to plague the republic, was the question of whether the vast new Western regions of the United States would ultimately be controlled by the North or by the South.

Yet the Missouri crisis, which was settled by a compromise in 1820, was significant at the time not only because it was a sign of the sectional crises to come but because it stood in such sharp contrast to the rising American nationalism of the 1820s. Whatever forces might be working to pull the nation apart, stronger ones were acting for the moment to draw it together. The American economy was experiencing remarkable growth. The federal government was acting in both domestic and foreign policy to assert a vigorous nationalism. Above all, perhaps, the United States was bound together by a set of shared sentiments and ideals: the memory of the Revolution, the veneration of the Constitution and its framers, the widely held sense that America had a special destiny in the world. Events would prove that the forces of nationalism were not, in the end, strong enough to overcome the emerging sectional differences. For the time being, however, they permitted the republic to enter an era of unprecedented expansion confident and united.

AMERICA'S ECONOMIC REVOLUTION

In the 1820s and 1830s, America began to experience the economic revolution that would, by the end of the century, almost entirely transform it. By the mid-1820s, the nation's economy was growing more rapidly than its population.

The American Population, 1820–1840

Three trends characterized the American population in the 1820s and 1830s, all of them contributing in various ways to economic growth: The population was increasing rapidly. Much of it was moving westward. And much of it was moving to towns and cities.

The American population had stood at only 4 million in 1790. By 1820, it had reached 10 million; by 1830, nearly 13 million; and by 1840, 17 million. The United States was growing much more rapidly in population

FOURTH OF JULY PICNIC AT WEYMOUTH LANDING (C. 1845), BY SUSAN MERRETT
Celebrations of Independence Day, like this one in eastern Massachusetts, became major festive events throughout the United States in the early nineteenth century, a sign of rising American nationalism.

than Britain or Europe. By 1860 it had a larger population than did the United Kingdom and had nearly overtaken Germany and France.

Public health efforts gradually improved, and the number and ferocity of epidemics (such as the great cholera plague of 1832) slowly declined, as did the mortality rate as a whole. But the population increase was also a result of a high birth rate. In 1840, the birth rate for white women stood at 6.14, a decline from the very high rates of the eighteenth century but still substantial enough to produce rapid population increases.

The African-American population increased more slowly than the white. After 1808, when the importation of slaves became illegal, the proportion of blacks to whites in the nation as a whole steadily declined. In 1820, there was one African-American to every four whites; in 1840, one to every five. The slower increase of the black population was a result of its comparatively high death rate. Slave mothers had large families, but life was shorter for both slaves and free blacks than for whites—a result of the enforced poverty in which virtually all African-Americans lived.

Immigration, choked off by wars in Europe and economic crises in America, contributed little to the American population in the first three decades of the nineteenth century. Of the total population of nearly 13 million in 1830, the foreign-born numbered fewer than 500,000. Soon, however, immigration began to grow once again. It reached a total of 60,000 in 1832 and nearly 80,000 in 1837. Reduced transportation costs and increasing economic opportunities in America helped stimulate the immigration boom, which also introduced new groups to the United States. In particular, the number of immigrants arriving from the southern (Catholic) counties of Ireland began to grow, reflecting the beginning of a tremendous influx of Irish Catholics that was to occur over the next two decades.

The Northwest and the Southwest continued to grow much more rapidly than did the rest of the country. By 1830, more than a fourth of the American people lived west of the Appalachians; by 1850, nearly half. As a result, some of the seaboard states found themselves with a depleted labor supply. Year after year such eastern states as Vermont, New Hampshire, and the Carolinas lost nearly as many people through migration as they gained by natural increase; their populations remained almost static.

Not all the Eastern migrants sought the unsettled West; some moved instead to the rapidly growing cities. In 1790, one person in thirty lived in a city (defined as a community of 8,000 or more); in 1820, one in twenty; and in 1840, one in twelve. The rise of New York City was particularly dramatic. By 1810 it was the largest city in the United States. That was partly

THE PORT OF NEW YORK, 1828 This view of South Street in
Manhattan shows the East River lined with docks. Other docks,
similarly busy, lined the Hudson River on the opposite side of the
island. The population of New York City was approaching
150,000 by 1828.

a result of its superior natural harbor. It was partly a result of the Erie Canal
(completed in 1825), which gave the city unrivaled access to the interior.
And it was partly because of liberal state laws that made the city attractive
for both foreign and domestic commerce.

The Canal Age

From 1790 until the 1820s, the so-called turnpike era, the United States had
relied largely on roads for internal transportation. But roads alone were not
adequate for the nation's expanding needs. And so, in the 1820s and 1830s,
Americans began to construct other means of transportation as well.

The larger rivers, especially the Mississippi and the Ohio, became
increasingly useful as steamboats grew in number and improved in design.
New river boats carried to New Orleans the corn and other crops of
Northwestern farmers and the cotton and tobacco of Southwestern planters.
From New Orleans, ocean-going ships took the cargoes on to Eastern ports.

But neither the farmers of the West nor the merchants of the East were
satisfied with this pattern of trade. Farmers would get better prices for their

crops if they could ship them directly eastward to market, rather than by the roundabout river-sea route; and merchants could sell larger quantities of their manufactured goods if they could transport them more directly and economically to the West. New highways across the mountains provided a partial solution to the problem. But the costs of hauling goods overland, although lower than before the roads were built, were still too high for anything except the most compact and valuable merchandise. On a turnpike, four horses could haul one and a half tons eighteen miles in a day. But the same four horses could draw a boatload of a hundred tons twenty-four miles a day on a canal. Thus interest quickly grew in expanding the nation's water routes.

Canal building was too expensive for private enterprise, so the job of digging canals fell largely to the states. New York was the first to act. It had the natural advantage of a good route between the Hudson River and Lake Erie through the only break in the Appalachian chain. Yet the engineering tasks were still imposing. The distance was more than 350 miles, several times as long as any of the existing canals in America and interrupted by high ridges and a wilderness of woods. After a long public debate over whether the scheme was practical, canal advocates prevailed when De Witt Clinton, a late but ardent convert to the cause, became governor in 1817. Digging began on July 4, 1817.

The building of the Erie Canal was the greatest construction project Americans had ever undertaken. The canal itself was simple: basically a ditch, forty feet wide and four feet deep, with towpaths along the banks for the horses or mules that were to draw the canal boats. But it required hundreds of difficult cuts and fills, some of them enormous, to enable the canal to pass through hills and over valleys; stone aqueducts to carry it across streams; and eighty-eight locks, of heavy masonry with great wooden gates, to permit ascents and descents. The Erie Canal was not just an engineering triumph but an immediate financial success. It opened in October 1825, amid elaborate ceremonies and celebrations, and traffic was soon so heavy that, within about seven years, tolls had repaid the entire cost of construction. By providing access to the Great Lakes, the canal gave New York access to Chicago and the growing markets of the West.

The system of water transportation extended farther when the states of Ohio and Indiana, inspired by the success of the Erie Canal, provided water connections between Lake Erie and the Ohio River. These canals made it possible to ship goods by inland waterways all the way from New York to New Orleans, although it was still necessary to transfer cargoes several times among canal, lake, and river craft.

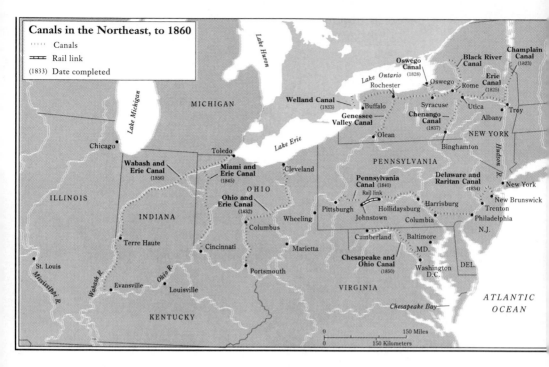

One of the immediate results of these new transportation routes was increased white settlement in the Northwest, because it had become easier for migrants to make the westward journey and to ship their produce back to markets. Although much of the Western produce continued to go downriver to New Orleans, an increasing proportion of it (including most of the wheat of the Northwest) went east to New York. And manufactured goods from throughout the East now moved in growing volume through New York and then by the new water routes to the West.

Rival cities along the Atlantic seaboard took alarm at the prospect of New York's acquiring so vast a hinterland, largely at their expense. But they had limited success in catching up. Boston, its way to the Hudson River blocked by the Berkshire Mountains, did not try to connect itself to the West by canal; its hinterland would remain confined largely to New England itself. Philadelphia and Baltimore had the still more formidable Allegheny Mountains to contend with. They made a serious effort at canal building, nevertheless, but with discouraging results. Pennsylvania's effort ended in an expensive failure. Maryland constructed part of the Chesapeake and Ohio Canal beginning in 1828, but only the stretch between Washington, D.C., and Cumberland, Maryland, was ever completed. In the South, Richmond and Charleston also aspired to build water routes to the Ohio Valley but never completed them.

For none of these rivals of New York did canals provide a satisfactory way to the West. Some cities, however, saw their opportunity in a different and newer means of transportation. Even before the canal age had reached its height, the era of the railroad was already beginning.

The Early Railroads

Railroads played no more than a secondary role in the nation's transportation system in the 1820s and 1830s; but railroad pioneers did lay the groundwork for the great surge of railroad building in midcentury that would link the nation together as never before. Railroads eventually became the primary transportation system for the United States and remained so until the construction of the interstate highway system in the mid-twentieth century.

Railroads emerged from a combination of technological and entrepreneurial innovations: the invention of tracks; the creation of steam-powered locomotives; and the development of trains as public carriers of passengers and freight. By 1804, both English and American inventors had experimented with steam engines for propelling land vehicles. In 1820, John Stevens ran a locomotive and cars around a circular track on his New Jersey estate. And in 1825, the Stockton and Darlington Railroad in England opened a short length of track and became the first line to carry general traffic.

American businessmen, especially in those seaboard cities that sought better communication with the West, quickly grew interested in the English experiment. The first company to begin actual operations was the Baltimore and Ohio, which opened a thirteen-mile stretch of track in 1830. In New York, the Mohawk and Hudson began running trains along the sixteen miles between Schenectady and Albany in 1831. By 1836, more than 1,000 miles of track had been laid in eleven states.

But there was not yet a true railroad system. Even the longest of the lines was comparatively short in the 1830s, and most of them served simply to connect water routes to one another, not to link one railroad to another. Even when two lines did connect, the tracks often differed in gauge (width), so cars from one line often could not fit onto the tracks of another. Schedules were erratic and wrecks were frequent. But railroads made some important advances in the 1830s and 1840s. Roadbeds were improved through the introduction of heavier iron rails. Steam locomotives became more flexible and powerful. Passenger cars were redesigned to be stabler, more comfortable, and larger.

Railroads and canals were soon competing bitterly with each other. For a time, the Chesapeake and Ohio Canal Company blocked the advance of the Baltimore and Ohio Railroad through the narrow gorge of the upper Potomac, which it controlled; and the state of New York prohibited railroads from hauling freight in competition with the Erie Canal and its branches. But railroads had so many advantages over canals that where free competition existed, they almost always prevailed.

The Expansion of Business

American business grew rapidly in the 1820s and 1830s, not only because of population growth and the transportation revolution but also because of the daring, imagination, and ruthlessness of a new generation of entrepreneurs.

One important change came in the retail distribution of goods, which was becoming increasingly systematic and efficient. In the larger cities, stores specializing in groceries, dry goods, hardware, and other lines appeared, although residents of smaller towns and villages still depended on the general store and did much of their business by barter. The organization of business was also changing. Most businesses continued to be operated by individuals or limited partnerships, and the dominating figures were still the great merchant capitalists, whose enterprises were generally owned by a

RACING ON THE RAILROAD Peter Cooper designed and built the first steam-powered locomotive in America in 1830 for the Baltimore and Ohio railroad. On August 28 of that year, he raced his locomotive (the "Tom Thumb") against a horse-drawn railroad car. This sketch depicts the moment when Cooper's engine overtook the horse-car.

single man. In some larger businesses, however, the individual merchant capitalist was giving way to the corporation. Corporations had the advantage of combining the resources of a large number of shareholders, and they began to develop particularly rapidly in the 1830s, when some legal obstacles to their formation were removed. Previously, a corporation could obtain a charter only by a special act of the state legislature—a cumbersome process that stifled corporate growth. By the 1830s, however, states were beginning to pass general incorporation laws, under which a group could secure a charter merely by paying a fee. The laws also established the privilege of limited liability, which meant that individual stockholders risked losing only the value of their own investment if a corporation should fail—they were not liable (as they had been in the past) for the corporation's larger losses. Corporations made possible the accumulation of much larger amounts of capital and hence the existence of much larger manufacturing and business enterprises.

But investment alone still provided too little capital to meet the demands of the most ambitious businesses. They relied on credit, which often created dangerous instability. Credit mechanisms remained very crude in the early nineteenth century. The government alone was permitted to issue currency, but the official currency was only gold and silver, not paper, and the amount was thus too small to support the demand for credit. Under pressure from corporate promoters, many banks issued large quantities of bank notes to provide capital for expanding business ventures. Many institutions issued notes far in excess of their own specie reserves. As a result, bank failures were frequent and bank deposits often insecure.

The Rise of the Factory

All of these changes—increasing population, improved transportation, and the expansion of business activity—contributed to perhaps the most profound economic development in mid-nineteenth-century America: the rise of the factory.

Before the War of 1812, most of what manufacturing there was in the United States took place within households or in small, individually operated workshops. Gradually, however, improved technology and increasing demand produced a fundamental change. It came first in the New England textile industry. There, beginning early in the nineteenth century, entrepreneurs were beginning to make use of new machines driven by waterpower that allowed them to bring textile operations together under a single roof. This factory system, as it came to be known, spread rapidly in the 1820s and began to make serious inroads into the old home-based system of spinning thread and weaving cloth. It also penetrated the shoe industry, concentrated in eastern Massachusetts. Shoemaking continued to be done largely by hand, but manufacturers were beginning to employ workers who specialized in one or another of the various tasks involved in production. Some factories began producing large numbers of identical shoes in ungraded sizes and without distinction as to rights and lefts. By the 1830s, factory production was spreading from textiles and shoes into other industries and from New England to other areas of the Northeast.

Machine technology advanced more rapidly in the United States in the mid-nineteenth century than in any other country in the world. Change was so rapid, in fact, that some manufacturers built their new machinery out of wood; by the time the wood wore out, they reasoned, improved technology would have made the machine obsolete. By the end of the 1830s, so advanced had American technology become—particularly in textile manufacturing—that industrialists in Britain and Europe were beginning to travel to the United States to learn new techniques, instead of the other way around.

Men and Women at Work

However advanced their technology, manufacturers still relied above all on a supply of labor. In later years, much of that supply would come from great waves of immigration from abroad. In the 1820s and 1830s, however, labor had to come primarily from the native population. Recruitment was not easy. City populations, although increasing, were still relatively small; 90 percent of the American people still lived and worked on farms. What produced the beginnings of an industrial labor supply was the transformation of American agriculture in the nineteenth century and a dramatic increase in food production. No longer did each region have to feed itself entirely from its own farms; it could import food from other regions—and particularly from the fertile lands of the newly settled West. As a result, the Northeastern agricultural economy slowly declined, and rural people began to look for work in the factories.

Two systems of recruitment emerged to bring this new labor supply to the expanding textile mills. One, common in the mid-Atlantic states and in parts of New England, brought whole families from the farm to the mill, where parents and children worked together tending the looms. The second system, common in Massachusetts, enlisted young women (mostly from farm families) in their late teens and early twenties. It was known as the Lowell or Waltham system, after the factory towns in which it first emerged.

A M E R I C A N V O I C E S

MARY PAUL

Letter from the Lowell Mills, 1845

DEAR FATHER,

I received your letter on Thursday the 14th with much pleasure. I am well which is one comfort. My life and health are spared while others are cut off. Last Thursday one girl fell down and broke her neck, which caused instant death. She was going in or coming out of the mill and slipped down it being very icy. The same day a man was killed by the cars. Another had nearly all his ribs broken. Another was nearly killed by . . . having a bale of cotton fall on him. Last Tuesday we were paid. In all I had six dollars and sixty cents paid $4.68 for board. With the rest I got me a pair of rubbers and a pair of 50.cts shoes. Next payment I am to have a dollar a week beside my board. . . . Perhaps you would like something about our regulations about going in and coming out of the mill. At 5 o'clock in the morning the bell rings for the folks to get up and get breakfast. At half past six it rings for the girls to get up and at seven they are called into the mill. At half past 12 we have dinner are called back again at one and stay till half past seven. I get along very well with my work. I can doff as fast as any girl in our room. . . . I think that the factory is the best place for me and if any girl wants employment I advise them to come to Lowell.

SOURCE: Thomas Dublin, ed., *Farm to Factory: Women's Letters, 1830–1860* (New York: Columbia University Press, 1981), pp. 103–104.

THE ASSORTING ROOM Well-dressed young women work in the assorting room of a New England textile factory in the 1830s, while a young male supervisor oversees them. Eventually the relatively benign conditions portrayed in this drawing deteriorated considerably.

Most of these women worked in the factories for only a few years. Some saved their wages and returned home to marry and raise children. Others married men they met in the factories or in town and remained part of the industrial world, but even they often stopped working in the mills after marriage.

Labor conditions in these early years of the factory system were significantly better than those in English industry and better too than they would ultimately become in the United States. The employment of young children was a harsh practice, but usually less so than in Europe, since working children in American factories generally remained under the supervision of their parents.

Even more distinctive from the European labor system was the lot of working women in the mills in Lowell and factory towns like it. In England, woman workers in coal mines and other heavy industries were employed in unimaginably wretched conditions. English visitors to America considered the Lowell mills a female paradise by contrast. The Lowell workers lived in clean boardinghouses and dormitories maintained for them by the factory owners. They were well fed and closely supervised. Because many New Englanders considered the employment of women to be vaguely immoral, the factory owners were careful to guard the environment in which their employees lived, enforcing strict curfews and requiring regular church attendance. Wages for the Lowell workers were generous by the modest standards of the time. The women even found time to write and publish a monthly magazine, the *Lowell Offering*.

Yet even these relatively well-treated workers often found the transition from farm life to factory work difficult, even traumatic. They shared with men the shock of moving from a seasonal, relatively informal rural work schedule to the rigid, time-bound pattern of factory work. And female mill workers also suffered from a special disadvantage, since unlike men they had very few employment options. They had no access to construction work; they could not become sailors or dockworkers; only with great difficulty could they travel the country alone, as many men did, in search of opportunities.

The paternalistic factory system of Lowell and Waltham did not survive for long. In the highly competitive textile market that developed in the 1830s and 1840s—a market especially vulnerable to the booms and busts that afflicted the American economy as a whole—manufacturers were eager to reduce labor costs and hence reluctant to maintain the high living standards and reasonably attractive working conditions with which they had begun. Wages declined; the hours of work lengthened; the conditions of the boardinghouses deteriorated as the buildings decayed and overcrowding increased. In 1834, mill workers in Lowell organized a union—the Factory Girls Association—which staged a strike to protest a 25 percent wage cut. Two years later, the association struck again—against a rent increase in the boardinghouses. Both strikes failed, and a recession in 1837 virtually destroyed the organization. Eight years later, led by the militant Sarah Bagley, the Lowell women created the Female Labor Reform Association and began agitating for a ten-hour day and for improvements in conditions in the mills. By then, however, the character of the factory work force was changing again. Textile manufacturers were turning to a less rebellious labor supply: immigrants.

Immigrant workers had even less leverage than the women they at times displaced; thus they often encountered far worse working conditions. Construction gangs, made up increasingly of Irish immigrants, performed heavy, unskilled work on turnpikes, canals, and railroads under often terrible conditions. Because most of these workers had no marketable skills and because of native prejudice against them, they received wages so low—and received them so intermittently, since the work was seasonal and uncertain— that they generally did not earn enough to support their families in even minimal comfort.

By the 1840s, Irish workers predominated in the New England textile mills as well, and their arrival accelerated the deterioration of working conditions there. There was far less social pressure on owners to provide a decent environment for Irish workers than for native women. Employers began paying piece rates rather than a daily wage and employed other devices to speed up production and exploit the labor force more efficiently.

The factory system gradually displaced many of the skilled artisans who had once been the backbone of American manufacturing. In the face of competition from industrial capitalists, craftsmen began early in the nineteenth century to form organizations—the first American labor unions—to protect their endangered positions. In Philadelphia, Baltimore, Boston, New York, and other cities, the skilled workers of each craft formed societies for mutual aid. During the 1820s and 1830s, the craft societies began to combine on a citywide and then a national basis through organizations known as trade unions. In 1834, delegates from six cities founded the National Trades' Union; and in 1836, the printers and the cordwainers set up their own national craft unions. But this early labor movement soon collapsed in the face of hostile laws, hostile courts, and the Panic of 1837.

SECTIONALISM AND NATIONALISM

For a brief but alarming moment in 1819–1820, the increasing differences between the nation's two leading sections threatened the unity of the United States. But once a sectional crisis was averted with the Missouri Compromise, the forces of nationalism continued to assert themselves; and the federal government began to assume the role of promoter of economic growth.

The Missouri Compromise

When Missouri applied for admission to the Union as a state in 1819, slavery was already well established there. Even so, Representative James Tallmadge, Jr., of New York, proposed an amendment to the Missouri statehood bill that would prohibit the further introduction of slaves into Missouri and provide for the gradual emancipation of those already there. The Tallmadge Amendment provoked a controversy that was to rage for the next two years.

Since the beginning of the republic, partly by chance and partly by design, new states had come into the Union more or less in pairs, one from the North, another from the South. In 1819, there were eleven free states and eleven slave states; the admission of Missouri would upset that balance and establish a precedent that in the future might increase the political power of one section over another—hence the interest of both the North and the South in the question of slavery and freedom in Missouri.

The Missouri question was soon complicated by the application of Maine (previously the northern part of Massachusetts) for admission as a new state. Speaker of the House Henry Clay informed Northern members that if they blocked Missouri from entering the Union as a slave state, Southerners would block the admission of Maine. But Maine ultimately offered a way out of the impasse, as the Senate agreed to combine the Maine and Missouri proposals into a single bill. Maine would be admitted as a free state, Missouri as a slave state. Then Senator Jesse B. Thomas of Illinois proposed an amendment prohibiting slavery in the rest of the Louisiana Purchase territory north of the southern boundary of Missouri (the 36°30′

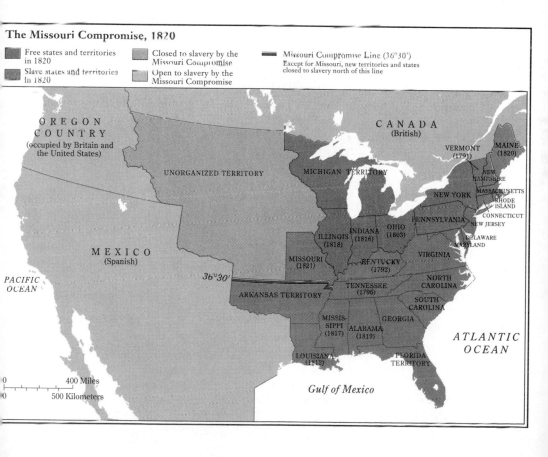

The Missouri Compromise, 1820

Free states and territories in 1820

Slave states and territories in 1820

Closed to slavery by the Missouri Compromise

Open to slavery by the Missouri Compromise

Missouri Compromise Line (36°30′)
Except for Missouri, new territories and states closed to slavery north of this line

parallel). The Senate adopted the Thomas Amendment, and Speaker Clay, although with great difficulty, guided the amended Maine-Missouri bill through the House.

Nationalists in both North and South hailed the Missouri Compromise as a happy resolution of a danger to the Union. But the debate over it had revealed a strong undercurrent of sectionalism that was competing with—although at the moment failing to derail—the powerful tides of nationalism.

Marshall and the Court

John Marshall served as chief justice of the United States for almost thirty-five years, from 1801 to 1835, and dominated the Court as no one

JOHN MARSHALL Marshall became Chief Justice of the United States Supreme Court in 1801 after establishing himself as one of the leaders of the Federalist party. He served as Chief Justice for thirty-five years, longer than anyone else in American history.

else before or since. Republican presidents filled vacancies with one after another Republican justice, but so influential was Marshall with his colleagues that he continued to carry a majority with him in most of the Court's decisions. More than anyone but the framers themselves, he molded the development of the Constitution itself: strengthening the judicial branch at the expense of the executive and legislature; increasing the power of the federal government at the expense of the states; and advancing the interests of the propertied and commercial classes.

Committed to promoting commerce, the Marshall Court firmly strengthened the inviolability of contracts as a cornerstone of American law. In *Fletcher* v. *Peck* (1810), which arose out of the notorious Yazoo land frauds, the Court had to decide whether the Georgia legislature of 1796 could rightfully repeal the act of the previous legislature granting lands under shady circumstances to the Yazoo Land Companies. In a unanimous decision, Marshall held that a land grant was a valid contract and could not be repealed even if corruption was involved. *Dartmouth College* v. *Woodward* (1819) expanded further the meaning of the contract clause of the Constitution. Having gained control of the New Hampshire state government, Republicans tried to revise Dartmouth's charter (granted by King George III in 1769) to convert the private college into a state university. The college trustees (represented by Daniel Webster, a Dartmouth graduate) persuaded the court to rule that the legislature had unconstitutionally violated the original charter. By proclaiming that corporation charters were contracts and that contracts were inviolable, the decision also placed important restrictions on the ability of state governments to control corporations.

In overturning not only the act of the legislature but the decisions of New Hampshire courts, the *Dartmouth College* case seemed to establish the right of the Supreme Court to override the decisions of state courts. But some advocates of states' rights, notably in the South, continued to challenge its right to do so. In *Cohens* v. *Virginia* (1821), Marshall explicitly affirmed the constitutionality of federal review of state court decisions. The states had given up part of their sovereignty in ratifying the Constitution, he explained, and their courts must submit to federal jurisdiction; otherwise, the federal government would be prostrated "at the feet of every state in the Union."

Meanwhile, in *McCulloch* v. *Maryland* (1819), Marshall confirmed the "implied powers" of Congress by upholding the constitutionality of the Bank of the United States. The Bank had become so unpopular in the South and the West that several of the states tried to drive branches out of business by outright prohibition or by prohibitory taxes. This case presented two constitutional questions to the Supreme Court: Could Congress charter a bank? And if so, could individual states ban it or tax it? Daniel Webster, one of the Bank's attorneys, argued that establishing such an institution came within the "necessary and proper" clause of the Constitution, and he added that the power to tax involved a "power to destroy." If the states could tax the Bank at all, they could tax it to death. Marshall adopted Webster's words in deciding for the Bank.

In the case of *Gibbons* v. *Ogden* (1824), the Court strengthened Congress's power to regulate interstate commerce. The state of New York had granted Robert Fulton and Robert Livingston's steamboat company the exclusive right to carry passengers on the Hudson River to New York City. Fulton and Livingston then gave Aaron Ogden the business of carrying passengers across the river between New York and New Jersey. But Thomas Gibbons, with a license granted under an act of Congress, went into competition with Ogden, who brought suit against him and was sustained by the New York courts. When Gibbons appealed to the Supreme Court, the justices faced the twofold question of whether "commerce" included navigation and whether Congress alone or Congress and the states together could regulate interstate commerce. Marshall replied that "commerce" was a broad term embracing navigation as well as the buying and selling of goods and asserted that the power of Congress to regulate such commerce was "complete in itself" and might be "exercised to its utmost extent." The state-granted monopoly, therefore, was void.

The lasting significance of *Gibbons* v. *Ogden* was that it freed transportation systems from restraints by the states and helped pave the way for unfettered capitalist growth. But its more immediate effect was that it headed off a movement to weaken the Supreme Court. Influential Republicans, mostly from the South and the West, were arguing that the Marshall Court was not merely interpreting the Constitution but illegitimately changing it. In Congress, they proposed measures to curb the Court's power. One senator suggested making the Senate, not the Court, the agency for deciding the constitutionality of state laws and settling interstate disputes. Other members introduced bills proposing to increase the size of the Court (from seven to ten justices) and to require more than a simple majority to declare a state law unconstitutional. Still others argued for "codification": for making legislative statutes the basis of the law, rather than the common-law precedents that judges used. Such a reform, codifiers argued, would limit the power of the judiciary and prevent "judge-made" law. The Court reformers failed to pass any of their measures; and after *Gibbons* v. *Ogden*, with its popular stand against monopoly power, hostility to the judicial branch of the government gradually died down.

The decisions of the Marshall Court established the primacy of the federal government over the states in regulating the economy and opened the way for an increased federal role in promoting economic growth. They protected corporations and other private economic institutions from local government interference. They were, in short, highly nationalistic decisions, designed to promote the growth of a strong, unified, and economically developed United States.

The Court and the Tribes

The nationalist inclinations of the Marshall Court were visible as well in a series of decisions concerning the legal status of Indian tribes within the United States. But these decisions not only affirmed the supremacy of the United States; they carved out a distinctive position for Native Americans within the constitutional structure.

The first of the crucial Indian decisions was in the case of *Johnson* v. *McIntosh* (1823). Leaders of the Illinois and Pinakeshaw tribes had sold parcels of their land to a group of white settlers (including Johnson), but they later signed a treaty with the federal government ceding to the United States territory that included those same parcels. The government proceeded to grant settlement rights to new white residents of the area (among them McIntosh) on the land claimed by Johnson. The Court was asked to decide which claim had precedence. Marshall's ruling, not surprisingly, favored the United States. But in explaining it, he offered a preliminary definition of the place of Indians within the nation. The tribes had a basic right to their tribal lands, he said, that preceded all other American law. Individual American citizens could not buy or take land from the tribes; only the federal government could do that.

Eight years later, in *Cherokee Nation* v. *Georgia*, the Marshall Court refused to hear a case filed by the Cherokees against a Georgia law abolishing their tribal legislature and courts. The Cherokee argued that because the tribe was a "foreign nation," the Supreme Court (which had constitutional responsibility for mediating disputes between the states and foreign nations) had jurisdiction. Marshall disagreed. The tribes were not foreign nations, he said. They did, however, have a special status within the nation. "Their relation to the United States resembles that of a ward to his guardian," he wrote. This was the origin of what became known as the "trust relationship," by which the United States claimed broad powers over the tribes but accepted substantial responsibility for protecting their welfare.

Most important was the Court's 1832 decision in *Worcester v. Georgia*. The Georgia state government had passed a law requiring that any United States citizen desiring to enter Cherokee territory obtain permission from the governor. Two missionaries (one of them named Worcester) sued, claiming the state was encroaching on the federal government's constitutionally mandated role to regulate trade with the tribes. Marshall invalidated the Georgia law, another important step in consolidating federal authority over the states. In doing so, he defined further the nature of the Indian nations. The tribes, he explained, were sovereign entities in much the same way Georgia was a sovereign entity, "distinct political communities, having territorial boundaries within which their authority is exclusive." In defending the power of the federal government, he was also affirming, indeed expanding, tribal authority.

The Marshall decisions, therefore, did what the Constitution itself had not done: they defined a place for Indian tribes within the American political system. The tribes had basic property rights. They were sovereign entities not subject to the authority of state governments. But the federal government, like a "guardian" governing its "ward," had ultimate authority over tribal affairs—even if that authority was, according to the Court, limited by the government's obligation to protect Indian welfare. These provisions were seldom enough to defend Indians from the steady westward march of white civilization. But they formed the basis of what legal protections the Indians have had.

The Latin American Revolution and the Monroe Doctrine

Just as the Supreme Court was asserting American nationalism in the shaping of the country's economic life, so the Monroe administration was asserting nationalism in foreign policy. As always, American diplomacy was principally concerned with Europe. But in dealing with Europe, Americans were forced in the 1820s to develop a policy toward Latin America, which was suddenly winning its independence.

Americans looking southward in the years following the War of 1812 beheld a gigantic spectacle: the Spanish Empire in its death throes, a whole continent in revolt, new nations in the making. Already the United States had developed a profitable commerce with Latin America and was rivaling Great Britain as the principal trading nation there. Many believed the success of the anti-Spanish revolutions would further strengthen America's position in the region.

In 1815, the United States proclaimed neutrality in the wars between Spain and its rebellious colonies, a position which implied a partial recognition of the rebels' status as nations. Moreover, the United States sold ships and supplies to the revolutionaries, clearly indicating that it was not genuinely neutral but was trying to help the insurgents. But Secretary of State John Quincy Adams and President James Monroe hesitated at first to take the risky step of formally recognizing the new governments unless Great Britain agreed to do so at the same time. The British declined. Finally, in 1822, nationalist impulses in the United States prevailed, and President Monroe decided to proceed alone. In defiance of the rest of the world, he established diplomatic relations with five new nations—La Plata (later Argentina), Chile, Peru, Colombia, and Mexico—making the United States the first country to recognize them.

In 1823, Monroe went further and announced a policy that would ultimately be known (beginning some thirty years later) as the "Monroe Doctrine." "The American continents," Monroe declared, ". . . are henceforth not to be considered as subjects for future colonization by any European powers." The United States would consider any foreign challenge to the sovereignty of existing American nations as an unfriendly act. At the same time, he proclaimed, "Our policy in regard to Europe . . . is not to interfere in the internal concerns of any of its powers."

The Monroe Doctrine emerged directly out of America's relations with Europe in the 1820s. After Napoleon's defeat, the nations of Europe combined in a "concert" to prevent future challenges to the "legitimacy" of established governments. Great Britain soon withdrew from the concert, leaving Russia and France the strongest of its four remaining members. In 1823, the four allies authorized France to intervene in Spain to restore the Bourbon dynasty, which a revolution had toppled. Some in England and the Americas feared that the allies might next support a French effort to retake the lost Spanish Empire in America.

To most Americans, and certainly to the secretary of state, an even greater threat was Great Britain, which Adams suspected had designs on Cuba. Adams feared the transfer of Cuba from Spain, a weak power, to Britain. He thought Cuba eventually should belong to the United States and wanted to keep it in Spanish hands until it fell to the United States. For a time, Monroe and Adams considered making their pronouncements about Latin America part of a joint statement with Great Britain. But Adams soon came to believe that the American government should act alone instead of following along like a "cock-boat in the wake of a British man-of-war." When the British lost interest in a joint statement, they only strengthened an already growing inclination within the administration to make its own pronouncement.

Monroe and Adams hoped the message would rally the people of Latin America to resist foreign intervention. They also hoped that by appealing to national pride, the message would help arouse the United States from a business depression, divert it from sectional politics, and increase its interest in the otherwise lackluster administration of Monroe. It did neither. But the Monroe Doctrine was important nevertheless for several reasons. It was an expression of the growing spirit of nationalism in the United States in the 1820s. It was an expression of concern about the forces that were already gathering to threaten that spirit. And it established the idea of American hegemony in the Western Hemisphere that later United States governments would invoke at will to justify policies in Latin America.

THE REVIVAL OF OPPOSITION

After 1816, the Federalist party offered no presidential candidate and soon ceased to exist as a national political force. National politics was now conducted wholly within the Republican party, which considered itself not a party at all but an organization representing the whole of the population.

Yet the policies of the federal government continued to spark opposition, and by the late 1820s partisan divisions were emerging once again. In some respects, the division mirrored the schism that had produced the first party system in the 1790s. The Republicans had in many ways come to resemble the early Federalist regimes in their promotion of economic growth and centralization. And the opposition, like the opposition in the 1790s, stood opposed to the federal government's expanding role in the economy. There was, however, a crucial difference. At the beginning of the century, the opponents of centralization had also often been opponents of economic growth. Now, in the 1820s, the controversy involved not whether but how the nation should continue to expand.

The "Corrupt Bargain"

Until 1820, when the Federalist party ceased effective operations and James Monroe ran for reelection unopposed, presidential candidates were nominated by caucuses of the two parties in Congress. In 1824, had the caucus system prevailed, Republicans in Congress would have produced a candidate who would have run unopposed again.

But in 1824, "King Caucus" was overthrown. The Republican caucus did nominate a candidate: William H. Crawford of Georgia, the secretary of the treasury. But other candidates received nominations from state legislatures and endorsements from irregular mass meetings throughout the country. One of them was Secretary of State John Quincy Adams, who held the office that was the traditional stepping stone to the presidency but who had little popular appeal. Another contender was Henry Clay, the Speaker of the House, who had a devoted personal following and a definite and coherent program: the "American System," which proposed creating a great home market for factory and farm producers by raising the protective tariff, strengthening the national bank, and financing internal improvements. Andrew Jackson, the fourth major candidate, had no significant legislative record, but he was a military hero and had the help of shrewd political allies from his home state of Tennessee.

Jackson received a plurality, although not a majority, of both the popular and the electoral vote. In the electoral college, he had 99 votes to Adams's 84, Crawford's 41, and Clay's 37. The final decision was left to the House of Representatives, which was to choose among the candidates with the three highest electoral votes. Clay was out of the running, but he was in a strong position to influence the result, both because he had carried several states and because he was Speaker of the House.

Supporters of Jackson, Crawford, and Adams all wooed Clay as the congressional vote approached. But Clay's course was already set. Crawford was no longer a serious candidate, since he was suffering from a paralyzing disease. And Jackson was Clay's most dangerous political rival in the West and had not supported Clay's legislative program. Adams was no friend of Clay either; but alone among the candidates, he was an ardent nationalist and a likely supporter of the American System. Clay gave his support to Adams, and the House elected him.

The Jacksonians were enraged enough at this, but they became much angrier when the new president announced that Clay was to be secretary of state. The State Department was the well-established route to the presidency, and Adams thus appeared to be naming Clay as his own successor. To the Jacksonians, it seemed clear that Clay and Adams must have agreed to make each other president—Adams now, Clay next; and they expressed outrage at this "corrupt bargain." Very likely there had been some sort of understanding between Clay and Adams; and although there was nothing corrupt, or even unusual, about it, it proved to be politically costly for both men.

The Second President Adams

Throughout his term in the White House, Adams and his policies were thoroughly frustrated by the political bitterness arising from the "corrupt bargain." In his inaugural address and in his first message to Congress, Adams recommended "laws promoting the improvement of agriculture, commerce, and manufactures, the cultivation of the mechanic and of the elegant arts, the advancement of literature, and the progress of the sciences, ornamental and profound"—a nationalist program reminiscent of Clay's American System. But Jacksonians in Congress prevented him from securing appropriations for most of these goals. He did win several million dollars to improve rivers and harbors and to extend the National Road westward from Wheeling; this was more than Congress had appropriated for internal improvements under all his predecessors together, but it was far less than he and Clay had envisioned.

Adams also experienced diplomatic frustrations. He appointed delegates to an international conference that the Venezuelan liberator, Simón Bolívar, had called in Panama in 1826. But Southerners in Congress opposed the idea of white Americans mingling with black delegates from Haiti, which would be represented in Panama. And supporters of Jackson charged that Adams intended to sacrifice American interests and involve the nation in an entangling alliance. Congress delayed approving the Panama mission so long that the American delegation did not arrive until after the conference was over.

Adams also lost a contest with the state of Georgia, which wished to remove the remaining Creek and Cherokee Indians from the state to gain their land as additional soil for cotton planters. The United States government, in a 1791 treaty, had guaranteed that land to the Creeks; but in 1825, white Georgians had extracted a new treaty from William McIntosh, the leader of one faction in the tribe and a long-time advocate of Indian cooperation with the United States. In the new treaty, the Creeks ceded their tribal lands in Georgia and Alabama and agreed to move west. The president believed the new treaty had no legal force, since McIntosh clearly did not represent the wishes of the tribe. Adams refused to enforce the treaty, setting up a direct conflict between the president and the state. The governor of Georgia defied the president and went ahead with plans for Indian removal. In 1827, the Creeks succumbed to pressure from Georgia and agreed to still another treaty, in which they again yielded their land, thus undercutting Adams's position.

Even more damaging to the administration was its support for a new tariff on imported goods in 1828. This measure originated in the demands of Massachusetts and Rhode Island woolen manufacturers, who complained that the British were dumping textiles on the American market at prices with which the domestic mill owners could not compete. They won support from the middle and Western states, but at the cost of provisions that antagonized the original New England supporters of the bill. The Western provisions placed high duties not only on woolens, as the New Englanders had wanted, but also on items the West produced. That distressed New England manufacturers; the benefits of protecting their manufactured goods from foreign competition now had to be weighed against the prospects of having to pay more for raw materials. The bill presented Adams with a dilemma, for he would lose friends whether he signed or vetoed it. Adams signed it, earning the animosity of Southerners, who cursed it as the "tariff of abominations."

Jackson Triumphant

By the time of the 1828 presidential election, a new two-party system had begun to emerge as a result of the divisions among the Republicans. On one side stood the supporters of John Quincy Adams, who called themselves the National Republicans and who supported the economic nationalism of the preceding years. Opposing them were the followers of Andrew Jackson, who took the name Democratic Republicans and who called for an assault on privilege and a widening of opportunity. Adams attracted the support of most of the remaining Federalists; Jackson appealed to a broad coalition that opposed the "economic aristocracy." But issues seemed to count for little in the end, as the campaign degenerated into a war of personal invective.

Jackson's victory was decisive, if sectional. He won 56 percent of the popular vote and an electoral majority of 178 votes to 83. But Adams swept virtually all of New England, and he showed significant strength in the mid-Atlantic region. Nevertheless, the Jacksonians considered their victory as complete and as important as Jefferson's in 1800. Once again, they believed, the forces of privilege had been driven from Washington. Once again, a champion of democracy would occupy the White House and restore liberty to the society and the economy. America had entered, some Jacksonians claimed, the "era of the common man."

CHAPTER TEN

Jacksonian America

The Advent of Mass Politics ~ "Our Federal Union" ~ Jackson and the Bank War
The Emergence of the Second Party System ~ Politics After Jackson

M ANY AMERICANS WERE growing apprehensive about the future of their republic in the 1820s and 1830s, as the nation expanded both economically and territorially. Some feared that the rapid growth of the United States would produce social chaos; they insisted that the country's first priority must be to establish order and a clear system of authority. Others argued that the greatest danger facing the nation was the growth of inequality and privilege; they believed that society's goal should be to eliminate the favored status of powerful elites and make opportunity more widely available. Advocates of this latter vision seized control of the federal government in 1829 with the inauguration of Andrew Jackson.

Despite their enthusiasm for the idea of democracy, Jackson and his followers were imperfect democrats. They did nothing to challenge (and indeed much to support) the existence of slavery; they supervised one of the most vicious assaults on American Indians in the nation's history; and they readily accepted economic, social, and gender inequality. Jackson himself was a frontier aristocrat, and most of those who served him were people of wealth and standing. But the Jacksonians were not usually aristocrats by birth. Convinced that they had risen to prominence on the basis of their own talents and energies, their goal in public life was to ensure that others like themselves would have the opportunity to do the same.

THE ADVENT OF MASS POLITICS

On March 4, 1829, thousands of Americans from all regions of the country—including many farmers, laborers, and others of humble rank—crowded before the United States Capitol to watch the inauguration of

Andrew Jackson. After the ceremonies, the crowd poured into a public reception at the White House, where, in their eagerness to shake the new president's hand, the people filled the state rooms to overflowing, trampled one another, soiled the carpets, and ruined the upholstery. "It was a proud day for the people," wrote Amos Kendall, one of Jackson's closest political associates. But Supreme Court Justice Joseph Story, a friend and colleague of John Marshall, looked on the inaugural levee, as it was called, and remarked with disgust: "The reign of King 'Mob' seems triumphant."

In fact, the "age of Jackson" was less a triumph of the people than Kendall hoped and Story feared. But it did mark a transformation of American politics that extended power widely to new groups. Once restricted to a relatively small group of property owners, politics now became open to virtually all the nation's white male citizens. In a political sense at least, the era had at least some claim to the title the Jacksonians gave it: the "age of the common man."

The Expanding Electorate

Until the 1820s, relatively few Americans had been permitted to vote; most states restricted the franchise to white male property owners or taxpayers or both, effectively removing a great mass of the less affluent from the voting roles. But even before Jackson's election, the franchise began to expand. Change came first in Ohio and other new states of the West, which, on joining the Union, adopted constitutions that guaranteed all adult white males the right to vote and permitted all voters the right to hold public office. Older states, concerned about the loss of their population to the West, began to grant similar political rights to their citizens, dropping or reducing their property ownership or taxpaying requirements. Eventually, every state democratized its electorate to some degree, although some later and less fully than others.

The wave of state reforms was generally peaceful, but in Rhode Island democratization efforts created considerable instability. The Rhode Island constitution (which was still basically the old colonial charter) barred more than half the adult males in the state from voting in the 1830s. The conservative legislature, chosen by this restricted electorate, consistently blocked all efforts at reform. In 1840, the lawyer and activist Thomas L. Dorr and a group of his followers formed a "People's party," held a convention, drafted a new constitution, and submitted it to a popular vote. It was overwhelmingly approved. The existing legislature rejected the Dorr docu-

JACKSON'S INAUGURAL LEVEE, 1829 Even in the relatively rustic days of the early republic, presidential inaugurations often took place amid almost monarchical grandeur. But when Andrew Jackson entered office in 1829, having won election as the champion of democratic simplicity, he avoided formal trappings and threw the White House open to the public.

ment and submitted a new constitution of its own to the voters. It was narrowly defeated. The Dorrites, in the meantime, had begun to set up a new government, under their own constitution, with Dorr as governor; and so, in 1842, two governments were laying claims to legitimacy in Rhode Island. The old state government proclaimed that Dorr and his followers were rebels and began to imprison them. The Dorrites, in the meantime, made a brief and ineffectual effort to capture the state arsenal. The Dorr Rebellion, as it was known, quickly failed, and Dorr himself surrendered and was briefly imprisoned. But the episode helped spur the old guard to draft a new constitution, which greatly expanded the suffrage.

The democratization process was far from complete. In much of the South, election laws continued to favor the planters and politicians of the older counties and to limit the influence of more newly settled Western areas. Free blacks could not vote anywhere in the South and hardly anywhere in the North. Pennsylvania, in fact, amended its state constitution in 1838 to strip blacks of the right to vote, which they had previously enjoyed. In no state could women vote. Nowhere was the ballot secret, and often it was cast as a spoken vote rather than a written one, which meant that voters could be, and often were, bribed or intimidated.

Despite the persisting limitations, however, the number of voters increased at a much more rapid rate than did the population as a whole. Indeed, one of the most striking political trends of the early nineteenth century was the change in the method of choosing presidential electors and the dramatic increase in popular participation in the process. In 1800, the legislature had chosen the presidential electors in ten states, and the people in only six. By 1828, electors were chosen by popular vote in every state but South Carolina. In the presidential election of 1824, fewer than 27 percent of adult white males had voted. In the election of 1828, the figure was 58 percent; and in 1840, 80 percent.

The high level of voter participation was only in part the result of an expanded electorate. It was also the result of a growing popular interest in politics and a strengthening of party organization.

The Legitimation of Party

Although party competition was part of American politics almost from the beginning of the republic, acceptance of the *idea* of party was not. For more than thirty years, most Americans who had opinions about the nature of government considered parties evils to be avoided and thought the nation should seek a broad consensus in which permanent factional lines would not exist. But in the 1820s and 1830s, those assumptions gave way to a new view: that permanent, institutionalized parties were a desirable part of the political process, that indeed they were essential to democracy.

The elevation of the idea of party occurred first at the state level, most prominently in New York. There, Martin Van Buren led a dissident political faction (known as the "Bucktails" or the "Albany Regency"). In the years after the War of 1812 this group began to challenge the established political elite—led by the aristocratic governor, De Witt Clinton—that had dominated the state for years. Factional rivalries were not new, of course; what was new about this one was the way in which Van Buren and his followers posed their challenge. Refuting the traditional view of a political party as undemocratic, they argued that only an institutionalized party, based in the populace at large, could ensure genuine democracy. The alternative was the sort of closed elite that Clinton had created. In this new kind of party, ideological commitments would be less important than loyalty to the party itself. Above all, for a party to survive, it must have a permanent opposition. Competing parties would give each political faction a sense of purpose; they would force politicians to remain continually sensitive to the will of the people; and they would check and balance each other in much the same way that the different branches of government checked and balanced one another.

By the late 1820s, this new idea of party was spreading beyond New York. The election of Jackson in 1828, the result of a popular movement that stood apart from the usual political elites, seemed further to legitimize it. In the 1830s, finally, a fully formed two-party system began to operate at the national level, with each party committed to its own existence as an institution and willing to accept the legitimacy of its opposition. The anti-Jackson forces began to call themselves the Whigs. Jackson's followers called themselves Democrats, thus giving a permanent name to the nation's oldest political party.

President of the Common Man

The Democratic party may have had no single ideological position, but Andrew Jackson himself did embrace a distinct, if simple, theory of democracy. Government, he said, should offer "equal protection and equal benefits" to all its white male citizens and favor no one region or class over another. In practice, that meant an assault on what Jackson and his associates considered the citadels of the Eastern aristocracy and an effort to extend opportunities to the rising classes of the West and the South.

Jackson's first target was the entrenched officeholders in the federal government, many of whom had been in place for a generation or more. Jackson bitterly denounced what he considered a "class" of permanent officeholders. Offices, he said, belonged to the people, not to a self-serving bureaucracy. Equally important, a large turnover in the bureaucracy would give him enormous patronage; it would allow him to reward his own supporters with offices.

One of his henchmen, William L. Marcy of New York, once explained, "To the victors belong the spoils"; and the process of giving out jobs as political rewards became known as the "spoils system." In the end, during the eight years of his presidency Jackson removed no more than one-fifth of the federal officeholders. But by embracing the philosophy of the "spoils system," a system already well entrenched in a number of state governments, the Jackson administration helped fix it firmly upon American politics.

Jackson supporters also worked to transform the process by which presidential candidates were selected. They had long resented the congressional caucus, which Jackson himself had avoided in 1828. In 1832, the president's followers staged a national convention to renominate him. In later generations, some would come to see the party convention as the source of corruption and political exclusivity, but those who created it in the 1830s considered it a great triumph for democracy. Through the convention, they believed, power in the party would arise directly from the people rather than from such elite political institutions as the caucus.

The spoils system and the political convention did limit the power of two entrenched elites—permanent officeholders and the exclusive party caucus. Yet neither really transferred power to the common people. Appointments to office almost always went to prominent political allies of the president and his associates. Delegates to national conventions were less often common men than members of local party elites. Political opportunity within the party was expanding, but much less so than Jacksonian rhetoric suggested.

"OUR FEDERAL UNION"

Jackson's belief in extending power beyond entrenched elites led him to want to reduce the functions of the federal government. A concentration of power in Washington would, he believed, restrict opportunity to those favored few with political connections. But Jackson also believed in forceful presidential leadership and was strongly committed to the preservation of the Union. Thus at the same time that Jackson was promoting an economic program to reduce the power of the national government, he was asserting the supremacy of the Union in the face of a potent challenge. For no sooner had he entered office than his own vice president—John C. Calhoun—began to champion a controversial (and, Jackson believed, dangerous) constitutional theory: nullification.

Calhoun and Nullification

Calhoun was forty-six years old in 1828, with a distinguished past and an apparently promising future. Running for vice president with Andrew Jackson, he could, it seemed, look forward to the presidency itself.

But the smoldering issue of the tariff created a dilemma for him. Once he had been an outspoken protectionist, strongly supporting the tariff of 1816. But by the late 1820s, many South Carolinians had come to believe that the tariff was responsible for the stagnation of their state's economy. In fact, that stagnation was largely a result of the exhaustion of South Carolina's farmland, which could no longer compete effectively with the newly opened and fertile lands of the Southwest. But most Carolinians blamed the "tariff of abominations" of 1828. Some exasperated Carolinians were ready to consider a drastic remedy—secession.

Calhoun's future political hopes rested on how he met this challenge in his home state. He did so by developing a theory that he believed offered a more moderate alternative to secession: the theory of nullification. Drawing from the ideas of Madison and Jefferson and their Virginia and Kentucky Resolutions of 1798–1799 and citing the Tenth Amendment to the Constitution, Calhoun argued that since the federal government was a creation of the states, the states—not the courts or Congress—were the final arbiters of the constitutionality of federal laws. If a state concluded that Congress had passed an unconstitutional law, then it could hold a special convention and declare the federal law null and void within the state. The nullification doctrine—and the idea of using it to nullify the 1828 tariff—quickly attracted broad support in South Carolina.

Calhoun's real hope was that the nullification theory would never be put to the test but would simply pressure the federal government to reduce

JOHN C. CALHOUN John Wesley Jarvis painted this portrait of a relatively young John C. Calhoun—before his identification with Southern nationalism destroyed what had once seemed his bright prospects for election to the presidency.

tariff rates. But Calhoun did not, he soon discovered, have as much influence in the new administration as he had hoped. For he had a powerful rival in Martin Van Buren.

The Rise of Van Buren

Van Buren was about the same age as Calhoun and equally ambitious. As leader of the Democratic party organization of New York, he had helped carry the state for Jackson in 1828 while getting himself elected governor. Van Buren resigned the governorship and went to Washington in 1829 when Jackson called him to head the new cabinet as secretary of state.

Jackson relied for advice on an unofficial circle of political allies who came to be known as the "Kitchen Cabinet," which included such Democratic newspaper editors as Isaac Hill of New Hampshire and Amos Kendall and Francis P. Blair of Kentucky. Van Buren alone was a member of both the official cabinet and this unofficial circle; so his influence with the president was unmatched. The two men grew closer still through a curious quarrel over etiquette that drove a wedge between the president and Calhoun.

Peggy O'Neale was the attractive daughter of a Washington tavern keeper with whom both Andrew Jackson and his friend John H. Eaton had taken lodgings while serving as senators from Tennessee. O'Neale was married, but rumors circulated in Washington in the mid-1820s that she and Senator Eaton were having an affair. O'Neale's husband died in 1828, and she and Eaton were soon married. A few weeks later, Jackson named Eaton secretary of war and thus made the new Mrs. Eaton a cabinet wife. The rest of the administration wives, led by Mrs. Calhoun, refused to receive her. Jackson (remembering the effects of public slander directed against his own late wife) was furious and demanded that the members of the cabinet accept her into their social world. Calhoun, under pressure from his wife, refused. Van Buren, a widower, befriended the Eatons and thus ingratiated himself with Jackson.

By 1831, partly as a result of the Peggy Eaton affair, Jackson had chosen Van Buren to succeed him in the White House. Calhoun's dreams of the presidency had all but vanished.

The Webster-Hayne Debate

In January 1830, a great debate in the United States Senate dramatically revealed the degree to which sectional issues were intruding into national politics. The controversy grew out of a seemingly routine Senate discussion of federal policy toward the public lands in the West. In the midst of the debate, a senator from Connecticut suggested that all land sales and surveys be temporarily discontinued. Senator Thomas Hart Benton of Missouri, the Jacksonian leader in the Senate, attacked the proposal, charging that it would serve the economic needs of the Northeast at the expense of the West.

Robert Y. Hayne, a young senator from South Carolina, took up Benton's argument. He had no direct interest in the Western lands, but he and other Southerners saw the issue as a way to win Western support for their drive to lower the tariff. Hayne argued that the South and the West were both victims of the tyranny of the Northeast and hinted that the two regions might combine to defend themselves against that tyranny.

Daniel Webster, now a senator from Massachusetts, took the floor the day after Hayne's speech. Although once an advocate of states' rights and an opponent of the tariff, he had changed his own position as the sectional passions of his own region had ebbed. Now he attacked Hayne, and through him Calhoun, for what he considered their challenge to the integrity of the Union. He was, in effect, challenging Hayne to a debate not on public lands and the tariff but on the issue of states' rights versus national power. Hayne, coached by Calhoun, responded with a defense of the theory of nullification. Webster then spent two full afternoons delivering what became known as his "Second Reply to Hayne," a speech that Northerners quoted and revered for years to come. He concluded with the ringing appeal: "Liberty *and* Union, now and for ever, one and inseparable!"

Calhoun's followers believed Hayne had the better of the argument, but their main concern was what President Jackson thought. The answer became clear at the annual Democratic party banquet in honor of Thomas Jefferson. After dinner, guests delivered a series of toasts. The president arrived with a written text in which he had underscored certain words: "Our *Federal* Union—*It must be preserved.*" While he spoke, he looked directly at Calhoun. The diminutive Van Buren, who stood on his chair to see better, thought he saw Calhoun's hand shake and a trickle of wine run down his glass as he responded to the president's toast with his own: "The Union— next to our liberty most dear." Sharp lines had been drawn.

The Nullification Crisis

In 1832, finally, the controversy over nullification produced a crisis when South Carolinians responded angrily to a congressional tariff bill that offered them no relief from the 1828 "tariff of abominations." Some militant South Carolinians were ready to secede from the Union, but Calhoun persuaded them to turn to nullification instead. The supporters of nullification won a substantial victory in the state elections of 1832. Almost immediately, the newly elected legislature summoned a state convention, which voted to nullify the tariffs of 1828 and 1832 and to forbid the collection of duties within the state. At the same time, South Carolina elected Hayne to serve as governor and Calhoun (who resigned as vice president) to replace Hayne as senator.

Jackson insisted that nullification was treason and that its adherents were traitors. He strengthened the federal forts in South Carolina and ordered a warship and several revenue ships to Charleston. When Congress convened early in 1833, Jackson's followers won approval of a force bill authorizing the president to use the military to see that acts of Congress were obeyed. Violence seemed a real possibility early in 1833.

Calhoun faced a predicament as he took his place in the Senate. Not a single state had come to South Carolina's support. Even South Carolina itself was divided and could not hope to prevail in a showdown with the federal government. Calhoun was saved by the timely intervention of Henry Clay, newly elected to the Senate, who devised a compromise by which the tariff would be lowered gradually until in 1842 it would reach approximately the same level as in 1816. The compromise and the force bill were passed on the same day, March 1, 1833. Jackson signed them both.

In South Carolina, the convention reassembled and repealed its nullification of the tariffs. But unwilling to allow Congress to have the last word, the convention nullified the force act—a purely symbolic act, since the tariff toward which the force act was directed had already been repealed. Calhoun and his followers claimed a victory for nullification, which had, they insisted, forced the revision of the tariff. They had some justification for doing so. But the episode taught Calhoun and his allies an important lesson: No state could defy the federal government alone.

The Removal of the Indians

Jackson's presidency coincided with a new and decisive phase in the long struggle between white settlement and Indian rights in the lands east of the Mississippi River. Jackson approached the conflict with a deep antipathy toward the tribes. That was in part a result of his earlier experiences leading military attacks against them; but it was also a result of a now widely shared view of Indians somewhat different from the view many Americans had embraced in the past.

In the eighteenth century, many whites had shared Thomas Jefferson's view of the Indians as "noble savages," peoples without real civilization but with an inherent dignity that made civilization possible among them. By the first decades of the nineteenth century, this vaguely philanthropic attitude was fading, particularly among the whites in the West. They were coming to view Native Americans simply as "savages," not only uncivilized but uncivilizable. Hence one reason for the growing white commitment to removing the Indians from all the lands east of the Mississippi was the belief that whites should not be expected to live in close proximity to savages. White Westerners also favored removal to put an end to violence and conflict in the Western areas of white settlement. Most of all, however, they favored Indian removal because the tribes still possessed valuable acreage that whites wanted.

The federal government had already removed many Indians from the East before Jackson became president, but substantial tribal enclaves remained. In the Old Northwest, the long process of expelling the woodland Indians culminated in a last battle in 1831–1832. An alliance of Sauk (or Sac) and Fox Indians under the fabled and now aged warrior Black Hawk fought white settlers in Illinois in an effort to overturn a treaty ceding tribal lands in that state to the United States; Black Hawk and his followers considered the agreement, signed by a rival tribal faction, illegal. The Illinois state militia and federal troops defeated the Indians. The Black Hawk War was notable for the viciousness of the white military efforts. White forces attacked the Indians even when they attempted to surrender, pursued them as they retreated, and slaughtered many of them.

More troubling to the government in the 1830s were the remaining Indian tribes of the South. In western Georgia, Alabama, Mississippi, and Florida lived what were known as the "Five Civilized Tribes"—the Cherokee, Creek, Seminole, Chickasaw, and Choctaw—most of whom had established settled and productive agricultural societies. They were, therefore, even more closely tied to their lands than many of the more nomadic tribes to the north.

The federal government had worked steadily through the first decades of the nineteenth century to negotiate treaties with the Southern Indians that would remove them to the West and open their lands for white settlement. But the negotiating process did not proceed fast enough to satisfy the region's whites. In 1830, finally, Congress passed the Removal Act, which appropriated new funds for negotiating treaties with the Southern tribes and relocating them in the West. By then, several Southern state governments were taking measures of their own to speed the removal. Most

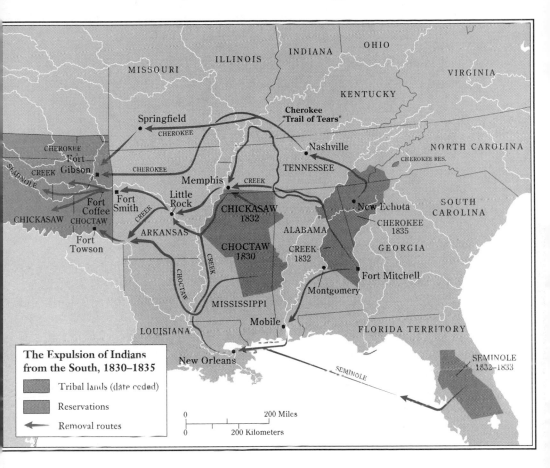

The Expulsion of Indians
from the South, 1830–1835

Tribal lands (date ceded)

Reservations

Removal routes

0   200 Miles

0   200 Kilometers

tribes were too weak to resist white pressures and ceded their lands in return for only token payments. Some, however, resisted.

The Cherokees tried to stop the encroachments by the state of Georgia through an appeal in the Supreme Court, and the Court's decisions in *Cherokee Nation v. Georgia* and *Worcester v. Georgia* (see pp. 235–236) supported the tribe's contention that the state had no authority to negotiate with tribal representatives. But the Jackson administration refused to enforce the decisions.

In 1835, the United States government extracted a treaty from a minority faction of the Cherokees that ceded to Georgia the tribe's land in that state in return for $5 million and a reservation west of the Mississippi. The great majority of the 17,000 Cherokees did not recognize the treaty as legitimate and refused to leave their homes. But Jackson sent an army of 7,000 under General Winfield Scott to round them up and drive them westward. About 1,000 fled to North Carolina, where eventually the federal government provided them with a reservation in the Smoky Mountains that survives today. But most of the rest made a long, forced trek to Oklahoma beginning in the winter of 1838. Thousands, perhaps a quarter or more of the émigrés, perished before reaching their unwanted destination. In the harsh new reservations in which they were now forced to live, the survivors remembered the terrible journey as "The Trail Where They Cried," the Trail of Tears.

Between 1830 and 1838, virtually all the Five Civilized Tribes were expelled from the Southern states and forced to travel along their own Trail of Tears to "Indian Territory" (formally created by the Indian Intercourse Act of 1834), in what later became Oklahoma. The new territory seemed safely removed from existing white settlements and embraced land that most whites considered undesirable. It had the additional advantage, the government believed, of being bordered on the west by what explorers such as Edwin James and Stephen H. Long had christened the "Great American

THE TRAIL OF TEARS This twentieth-century painting by Robert Lindneux shows the forced evacuation of 18,000 Cherokee Indians from their ancestral lands in Georgia beginning in 1838. An epidemic of smallpox, along with starvation and exposure, cost thousands of Indians their lives. Here the Cherokees, guarded by soldiers carrying guns and bayonets, cross the Missouri River on their way to their new and unfamiliar homes in what is now Oklahoma.

Desert," land deemed unfit for habitation. Whites seemed unlikely ever to settle along the western borders of the Indian Territory, which meant that further conflict might be avoided. The Choctaws of Mississippi and western Alabama were the first to make the trek, beginning in 1830. The army moved out the Creeks of eastern Alabama and western Georgia in 1836. The Chickasaw in northern Mississippi began the long march westward a year later, and the Cherokees, finally, a year after that.

Only the Seminoles in Florida managed to resist the pressures, and even their success was limited. Like other tribes, the Seminoles had agreed under pressure to a settlement (the 1832–1833 treaties of Payne's Landing) by which they ceded their lands and agreed to move to Indian Territory within three years. Most did move west, but a substantial minority, under the leadership of the chieftain Osceola, balked and staged an uprising beginning in 1835 to defend their lands. (Joining the Indians in their struggle was a group of runaway black slaves, who had been living with the tribe.) The Seminole War dragged on for years. Jackson sent troops to Florida, but the Seminoles with their black associates were masters of guerrilla warfare in the jungle-like Everglades. Finally, in 1842, the government abandoned the war. By then, many of the Seminoles had been either killed or forced westward. But the relocation of the Seminoles, unlike the relocation of most of the other tribes, was never complete.

By the end of the 1830s, virtually all the important Indian societies east of the Mississippi (with a few exceptions such as the Seminoles and Cherokees) had been removed to the West. The tribes had ceded over 100 million acres of Eastern land to the federal government; they had received in return about $68 million and 32 million acres in the far less hospitable lands west of the Mississippi. There they lived, divided by tribe into a series of separate reservations, in a territory surrounded by a string of United States forts to keep them in (and to keep most whites out), in a region whose climate and topography bore little relation to anything they had known before. Eventually, even this forlorn enclave would face encroachments from white civilization.

JACKSON AND THE BANK WAR

Jackson was quite willing to use federal power against the Indian tribes. Where white Americans were concerned, however, he was consistently opposed to concentrating power either in the federal government or in elite institutions associated with it. An early example of that was his 1830 veto of a congressional measure providing a subsidy to the proposed Maysville Road in Kentucky. The bill was unconstitutional, Jackson argued, because the road in question lay entirely within Kentucky and was not, therefore, a part of "interstate commerce." But the bill was also unwise, because it committed the government to what Jackson considered extravagant expenditures. A similar resistance to federal power lay behind the most celebrated episode of Jackson's presidency: the war against the Bank of the United States.

Biddle's Institution

With its headquarters in Philadelphia and its branches in twenty-nine other cities, the Bank of the United States had a monopoly on the deposits of the federal government, which owned one-fifth of the Bank's stock; it also did a tremendous business in general banking. It provided credit to growing enterprises; it issued bank notes which served as a dependable medium of exchange throughout the country; and it exercised a restraining effect on the less well managed state banks. Nicholas Biddle, president of the Bank from 1823 on, had done much to put the institution on a sound and prosperous basis. Nevertheless, Andrew Jackson was determined to destroy it, convinced that it was a citadel of privilege that benefited Eastern elites and impeded the rise of aspiring capitalists in the West and elsewhere.

Opposition to the Bank came from two very different groups: the "soft-money" faction and the "hard-money" faction. Advocates of soft money consisted largely of state bankers and their allies. They objected to the Bank of the United States because it restrained the state banks from issuing notes freely. The hard-money people believed that coin was the only safe currency, and they condemned all banks that issued bank notes, including the Bank of the United States. The soft-money advocates were believers in rapid economic growth and speculation; the hard-money forces embraced older ideas of "public virtue" and looked with suspicion on expansion and speculation. Jackson himself supported the hard-money position, but he was also sensitive to the complaints of his many soft-money supporters in the West and the South. He made it clear that he would not favor renewing the charter of the Bank of the United States, which was due to expire in 1836.

Biddle was a Philadelphia aristocrat, unaccustomed to politics. But in his efforts to save the Bank, he began granting banking favors to influential men. In particular, he relied on Senators Clay and Webster, the latter of whom was connected with the Bank as legal counsel, director of the Boston branch, a frequent, heavy borrower, and Biddle's personal friend. Clay, Webster, and other advisers persuaded Biddle to apply to Congress for a recharter bill in 1832, four years ahead of the expiration date. Congress passed the recharter bill; Jackson vetoed it; and the Bank's supporters in Congress failed to override the veto. The Bank question then emerged as the paramount issue of the 1832 election, just as Clay had hoped.

In 1832, Clay ran for president as the unanimous choice of the National Republicans, who held a nominating convention in Baltimore late in 1831. But the "Bank War" failed to provide Clay with the winning issue for which he had hoped. Jackson, with Van Buren as his running mate, overwhelmingly defeated Clay (and several minor-party candidates) with 55 percent of the popular vote and 219 electoral votes (more than four times as many as Clay received). The results were a defeat not only for Clay but for Biddle.

The "Monster" Destroyed

Jackson was now more determined than ever to destroy the "monster." He could not legally abolish the institution before the expiration of its charter, but he could weaken it. He decided to remove the government's deposits from the Bank. His secretary of the treasury believed that such an action would destabilize the financial system and refused to give the order. Jackson removed him and appointed a replacement. When the new secretary similarly procrastinated, Jackson named a third: Roger B. Taney, the attorney general, a close friend and loyal ally of the president.

Taney began drawing on the government's deposits in the Bank of the United States and placing incoming receipts in a number of state banks (which Jackson's enemies called "pet banks"). When the administration began to transfer funds directly from the Bank of the United States to the pet banks (as opposed to the initial practice of simply depositing new funds in those banks), Biddle called in loans and raised interest rates, explaining that without the government deposits the Bank's resources were stretched too thin. He realized his actions were likely to cause financial distress, and he reasoned that a short recession would cause Congress to recharter the Bank.

As financial conditions worsened in the winter of 1833–1834, supporters of the Bank organized meetings around the country and sent petitions to Washington urging a rechartering of the Bank. But the Jacksonians blamed the recession on Biddle and refused to budge. The banker finally carried his contraction of credit too far and had to reverse himself to appease the business community. His hopes of winning a recharter of the Bank died in the process.

Jackson had won a considerable political victory. But when the Bank of the United States died in 1836, the country lost an important financial institution and was left with a fragmented and chronically unstable banking system that would plague the economy for many years.

The Taney Court

In the aftermath of the Bank War, Jackson moved against the most powerful institution of economic nationalism: the Supreme Court. In 1835, when John Marshall died, the president appointed as the new chief justice his trusted ally Roger B. Taney. Taney did not bring a sharp break in constitutional interpretation, but he did help modify Marshall's vigorous nationalism.

Perhaps the clearest indication of the new judicial mood was the celebrated case of *Charles River Bridge* v. *Warren Bridge* of 1837. The case involved a dispute between two Massachusetts companies over the right to build a bridge across the Charles River between Boston and Cambridge. One company had a longstanding charter from the state to operate a toll bridge, a charter that the firm claimed guaranteed it a monopoly of the bridge traffic. Another company had applied to the legislature for authorization to construct a second, competing bridge that would—since it would be toll-free—greatly reduce the value of the first company's charter. The first company contended that in granting the second charter, the legislature was engaging in a breach of contract; and it noted that the Marshall Court, in the *Dartmouth College* case and other decisions, had ruled that states had no right to abrogate contracts. But now Taney, speaking for the Democratic majority on the Court, supported the right of Massachusetts to award the second charter. The object of government, Taney maintained, was to promote the general happiness, an object that took precedence over the rights of property. A state, therefore, had the right to amend or abrogate a contract if such action was necessary to advance the well-being of the community. The decision reflected one of the cornerstones of the Jacksonian idea: that the key to democracy was an expansion of economic opportunity, which would not occur if older corporations could maintain monopolies and choke off competition from newer companies.

THE EMERGENCE
OF THE SECOND PARTY SYSTEM

Jackson's forceful—some claimed tyrannical—tactics in crushing first the nullification movement and then the Bank of the United States helped galvanize a growing opposition coalition that by the mid-1830s was ready to assert itself in national politics. It began as a gathering of national political leaders opposed to Jackson's use of power. Denouncing the president as "King Andrew I," they began to refer to themselves as Whigs, after the party in England that traditionally worked to limit the power of the king. As the new party began to develop as a national organization with constituencies in every state, its appeal became more diffuse. Nevertheless, both in its philosophy and in the nature of its membership, the Whig party was different from the party of Jackson.

With the emergence of the Whigs, the nation once again had two competing political parties. What scholars now call the "second party system" had begun what would turn out to be its relatively brief life.

The Two Parties

The philosophy of the Democratic party in the 1830s bore the stamp of Andrew Jackson, but it drew from many older traditions as well. Democrats envisioned a future of steadily expanding opportunities. The function of government, therefore, was to remove artificial obstacles to that expansion and to avoid creating new obstacles of its own. The federal government should be limited in power, except to the degree that it worked to eliminate social and economic arrangements that entrenched privilege and stifled opportunity. The rights of states should be protected except to the extent that state governments interfered with social and economic mobility. Jacksonian Democrats celebrated "honest workers," "simple farmers," and "forthright businessmen" and contrasted them to the corrupt, monopolistic, aristocratic forces of established wealth.

The Jacksonians were not hostile to wealth. Most Democrats believed in material progress, and many party leaders—including Jackson himself—were wealthy men. Yet Democrats tended to look with suspicion on government efforts to stimulate commercial and industrial growth. These efforts, they believed, generally produced such menacing institutions of power as the Bank of the United States. Democrats were less likely than Whigs to support chartered banks and corporations, state-supported internal improvements, even public schools. They were more likely than Whigs to support territorial expansion, which would, they believed, widen opportunities for aspiring Americans. Among the most radical members of the party—the so-called Locofocos, mainly workingmen and small businessmen and professionals in the Northeast—sentiment was strong for a vigorous, perhaps even violent, assault on monopoly and privilege far in advance of anything Jackson himself ever contemplated.

The political philosophy that became known as Whiggery favored expanding the power of the federal government, encouraging industrial and commercial development, and knitting the country together into a consolidated economic system. Whigs embraced material progress enthusiastically, but they were cautious about westward expansion, fearful that rapid territorial growth would produce instability. Their vision of America was of a nation embracing the industrial future and rising to world greatness as a commercial and manufacturing power. And although Whigs insisted that their vision would result in increasing opportunities for all Americans, they tended to attribute particular value to the elites they considered the enterprising, modernizing forces in society—the entrepreneurs and institutions that most effectively promoted economic growth. Thus while Democrats were inclined to oppose legislation establishing banks, corporations, and other modernizing institutions, Whigs generally favored such measures.

To some extent, the constituencies of the two major parties were reflections of these diffuse philosophies. The Whigs were strongest among the more substantial merchants and manufacturers of the Northeast; the wealthier planters of the South (those who favored commercial development and the strengthening of ties with the North); and the ambitious farmers and rising commercial class of the West—usually migrants from the Northeast—who advocated internal improvements, expanding trade, and rapid economic progress. The Democrats drew more support from smaller merchants and the workingmen of the Northeast; from Southern planters suspicious of industrial growth; and from Westerners—usually with Southern roots—who favored a predominantly agrarian economy and opposed the development of powerful economic institutions in their region. Whigs tended to be wealthier than Democrats, tended to have more aristocratic backgrounds, and tended to be more commercially ambitious.

But Whigs and Democrats alike were more interested in winning elections than in maintaining philosophical purity. And both parties made adjustments from region to region in order to attract the largest possible number of voters, often at the sacrifice of party philosophy. In New York, for example, the Whigs developed a popular following through a movement known as Anti-Masonry. The Anti-Mason party had emerged in the 1820s in response to widespread resentment against the secret and exclusive, hence supposedly undemocratic, Society of Freemasons. Such resentments increased in 1826 when a former Mason, William Morgan, mysteriously disappeared from his home in Batavia, New York, shortly before he was scheduled to publish a book purporting to expose the secrets of Freemasonry. The assumption was widespread that Morgan had been abducted and murdered by the vengeful Masons. Whigs seized on the Anti-Mason frenzy to launch spirited attacks on Jackson and Van Buren (both Freemasons), implying that the Democrats were connected with the antidemocratic conspiracy. By embracing Anti-Masonry, Whigs were portraying themselves as opponents of aristocracy and exclusivity. They were, in other words, attacking the Democrats with the Democrats' own issues. (Later, Anti-Masonry grew powerful enough to become the basis of a new political party.)

Religious and ethnic divisions also played an important role in determining the constituencies of the two parties. Irish and German Catholics, among the largest of the recent immigrant groups, tended to support the Democrats, who appeared to share their own vague aversion to commercial development and entrepreneurial progress and who seemed to respect and protect their cultural values and habits. Evangelical Protestants gravitated toward the Whigs because they associated the party with constant development and improvement, goals their own religion embraced. They envisioned a society progressing steadily toward unity and order, and they looked on the new immigrant communities as a threat to that progress—as groups that needed to be disciplined and taught "American" ways. In many communities, these and other local ethnic, religious, and cultural tensions were far more influential in determining party alignments than any concrete political or economic proposals.

The Whig party was more successful at defining its positions and attracting a constituency than it was in uniting behind a national leader. No one person was ever able to command the loyalties of the party in the way Jackson commanded the loyalties of the Democrats. Instead, Whigs tended to divide among three major figures: Henry Clay, Daniel Webster, and John Calhoun. Clay won support from many of those who favored internal improvements and economic development, what he called the American System; but his image as a devious political operator and his identification with the West proved an insuperable liability. He ran for president three times and never won. Daniel Webster, the greatest orator of his era, won broad support with his passionate speeches in defense of the Constitution and the Union; but his close connection with the Bank of the United States and the protective tariff, his reliance on rich men for financial support, and his excessive fondness for brandy prevented him from developing enough of a national constituency to win him the office he so desperately wanted. John C. Calhoun, the third member of what became known as the Great Triumvirate, never considered himself a true Whig, and his identification with the nullification controversy in effect disqualified him from national leadership in any case. Yet he sided with Clay and Webster on the issue of the national bank. And he shared with them a strong animosity toward Andrew Jackson.

The Whigs, in other words, were able to marshal an imposing array of national leaders, each with his own powerful constituency. Yet for many years they were unable to find a way to merge those constituencies into a single winning combination. The result was that while Whigs competed relatively evenly with the Democrats in congressional, state, and local races, they managed to win only two presidential elections in the more than twenty years of their history.

Their problems became particularly clear in 1836. The Democrats were united behind Andrew Jackson's personal choice for president, Martin Van Buren. The Whigs could not even agree on a single candidate. Instead, they ran several candidates, hoping to profit from the regional strength of each. Webster represented the party in New England; Hugh Lawson White of Tennessee ran in the South; and the former Indian fighter and hero of the War of 1812 from Ohio, William Henry Harrison, was the candidate in the middle states and the West. None of the three candidates could expect to get a majority in the electoral college, but party leaders hoped they might separately draw enough votes from Van Buren to prevent his getting a majority and throw the election to the House of Representatives, where the Whigs might be better able to elect one of their candidates. In the end, however, the three Whigs were no match for the one Democrat. Van Buren won easily, with 170 electoral votes to 124 for all his opponents.

POLITICS AFTER JACKSON

Andrew Jackson retired from public life in 1837, the most beloved political figure of his age. Martin Van Buren was very different from his predecessor and far less fortunate. He was never able to match Jackson's personal popularity; and his administration was plagued with economic difficulties that hurt the Democrats and helped the Whigs.

The Panic of 1837

Van Buren's success in the 1836 election was a result in part of a nationwide economic boom that was reaching its height in that year. Canal and railroad builders were at a peak of activity. Prices were rising, money was plentiful, and credit was easy as banks increased their loans and notes with little regard to their reserves of cash. The land business, in particular, was booming.

Between 1835 and 1837 nearly 40 million acres of public land were sold, nearly three-fourths of it to speculators, who purchased large tracts in hopes of reselling them at a profit. These land sales, along with revenues the government received from the tariff of 1833, created a series of substantial federal budget surpluses and made possible a steady reduction of the national debt (something Jackson had always advocated). From 1835 to 1837, the government for the first and only time in its history was out of debt, with a substantial surplus in the Treasury.

Congress and the administration now faced the question of what to do with the Treasury surplus. Reducing the tariff was not an option, since no one wanted to raise that touchy issue again. Instead, support began to build for returning the federal surplus to the states. An 1836 "distribution" act required that the federal government pay its surplus funds to the states each year in four quarterly installments as interest-free, unsecured loans. No one expected the "loans" to be repaid. The states spent the money quickly, mainly to encourage construction of highways, railroads, and canals. The distribution of the surplus thus gave further stimulus to the economic boom. At the same time, the withdrawal of federal funds strained the state (or "pet") banks in which they had been deposited by the government; they had to call in their own loans to make the transfer of funds to the state governments.

Congress did nothing to check the speculative fever, with which many congressmen themselves were badly infected. Webster, for one, was buying up thousands of acres in the West. But Jackson, always suspicious of paper currency, was unhappy that the government was selling good land and receiving in return various state bank notes worth no more than the credit of the issuing bank. In 1836, not long before leaving office, he issued a presidential order, the "specie circular," which stipulated that only gold or silver coins or currency backed by gold or silver could be accepted in payment for public lands. Jackson was right to fear the speculative fever but wrong in thinking the specie circular would cure it. On the contrary, it produced a financial panic that began in the first months of Van Buren's presidency. Hundreds of banks and hundreds of businesses failed. Unemployment grew. There were bread riots in some of the larger cities. Prices fell, especially the price of land. Many railroad and canal schemes were abandoned; several of the debt-burdened state governments ceased to pay interest on their bonds, and a few repudiated their debts, at least temporarily. It was the worst depression in American history to that point, and it lasted for five years. It was a political catastrophe for Van Buren and the Democrats.

Both parties bore some responsibility for the panic. The distribution of the Treasury surplus, which had weakened the state banks and helped cause the crash, had been a Whig measure. Jackson's specie circular, which had started a run on the banks as land buyers rushed to trade in their bank notes for specie, was also to blame. But the depression was only partly a result of federal policies. England and western Europe were facing panics of their own, which meant that European (and especially English) investors had been withdrawing funds from America, putting an added strain on American banks. A succession of crop failures on American farms reduced the purchasing power of farmers and required increased imports of food, which sent more money out of the country. Whatever its actual causes, the Panic of 1837 occurred during a Democratic administration. The Democrats paid the political price for it.

WHIG HEADQUARTERS The Whig Party managed in 1840 to disguise its relatively elitist roots by portraying its presidential candidate, the patrician General William Henry Harrison, as a product of a log cabin who enjoyed drinking hard cider from a jug. Pictures of log cabins abounded in Whig campaign posters, as seen in this drawing of a Harrison rally in Philadelphia.

The Van Buren Program

The Van Buren administration, which strongly opposed government intervention in the economy, did little to fight the depression. Some of the steps it took—borrowing money to pay government debts and accepting only specie for payment of taxes—may have made things worse. Other efforts failed in Congress: a "preemption" bill that would have given settlers the right to buy government land near them before it was opened for public sale, and another bill that would have lowered the price of land. Van Buren did succeed in establishing a ten-hour workday on all federal projects by issuing a presidential order, but he had few other legislative achievements.

The most important and controversial measure in the president's program was a proposal for a new financial system to replace the Bank of the United States. Under Van Buren's plan, known as the "independent treasury" or "subtreasury" system, government funds would be placed in an independent treasury at Washington and in subtreasuries in other cities. No private banks would have the government's money or name to use as a basis for speculation; the government and the banks would be "divorced." Van Buren called a special session of Congress in 1837 to consider the proposal, which failed in the House. In 1840, the administration finally succeeded in driving the measure through both houses of Congress. As a result, the American banking system remained highly decentralized, and almost entirely free of federal regulation, until the Federal Reserve Act of 1913.

The Log Cabin Campaign

As the campaign of 1840 approached, the Whigs realized that they would have to settle on one candidate for president. Accordingly, they held their first national nominating convention in Harrisburg, Pennsylvania, in December 1839. Passing over Henry Clay, who expected the nomination, the convention chose William Henry Harrison and, for vice president, John Tyler of Virginia. Harrison was a descendant of the Virginia aristocracy but had spent his adult life in the Northwest. He was a renowned soldier and a popular national figure. The Democrats nominated Van Buren. But because their party was, in some respects, no more united than the Whigs, they failed to nominate a vice presidential candidate, leaving the choice of that office to the electors.

The 1840 campaign illustrated how fully the ethos of party competition (the subordination of ideology to immediate political needs) had established itself in America. The Whigs—who had emerged as a party largely because of their opposition to Andrew Jackson's common-man democracy, who in most regions represented the more affluent elements of the population, who favored government policies that would aid business—presented themselves in 1840 as the party of the common people. So, of course, did the Democrats. Both parties used the same techniques of mass voter appeal, the same evocation of simple, rustic values. What mattered now was not the philosophical purity of the party but its ability to win votes. The Whig campaign was particularly effective in portraying William Henry Harrison, a wealthy man with a considerable estate, as a simple man of the people who loved log cabins and hard cider. Against such techniques and the effects of the depression the Democrats could not win. Harrison won the election with 234 electoral votes to 60 for Van Buren and with a popular majority of 53 percent.

The Frustration of the Whigs

Despite their decisive victory, the Whigs were to find the next four years frustrating and divisive ones. In large part, that was because their appealing new president, "Old Tippecanoe," William Henry Harrison, died of pneumonia one month after taking office. John Tyler now became the first vice president to succeed a fallen president. He moved quickly to establish a full claim to the office, despite objections from some that he should be considered no more than "acting president." Control of the administration had fallen to a man with whom the Whig party leadership had relatively weak ties. Harrison had generally deferred to Henry Clay and Daniel Webster, whom he named secretary of state. Under Tyler, things soon changed.

Tyler was a former Democrat who had left the party in reaction to what he considered Jackson's excessively egalitarian program and his imperious methods. But there were still signs of his Democratic past in his approach to public policy. The president did agree to bills abolishing the independent treasury system and raising tariff rates. But he refused to support Clay's attempt to recharter the Bank of the United States. And he vetoed several internal improvement bills sponsored by Clay and other congressional Whigs. Finally, a conference of congressional Whigs (many of whom referred scornfully to the new president as "His Accidency") read Tyler out of the party. Every cabinet member but Webster resigned; five former Democrats took their places. When Webster, too, left the cabinet, Tyler appointed Calhoun, who had rejoined the Democratic party, to replace him.

A new political alignment was taking shape. Tyler and a small band of conservative Southern Whigs were preparing to rejoin the Democrats. Into the common man's party of Jackson and Van Buren was arriving a faction with decidedly aristocratic political ideas, men who thought that government had an obligation to protect and even expand the institution of slavery and who believed in states' rights with almost fanatical devotion.

Whig Diplomacy

In the midst of these domestic controversies, a series of incidents brought Great Britain and the United States to the brink of war in the late 1830s.

Residents of the eastern provinces of Canada launched a rebellion against the British colonial government in 1837, and some of the rebels chartered an American steamship, the *Caroline*, to ship them supplies across the Niagara River from New York. British authorities in Canada seized the *Caroline* and burned it, killing one American in the process. The British government refused either to disavow the attack or to provide compensation for it, and resentment in the United States was high.

At the same time, tensions flared over the boundary between Canada and Maine, which had been in dispute since the treaty of 1783. In 1838, groups of Americans and Canadians, mostly lumberjacks, began moving into the Aroostook River region in the disputed area, precipitating a violent brawl between the two groups that became known as the "Aroostook War."

Several years later, there were yet more Anglo-American problems. In 1841, an American ship, the *Creole*, sailed from Virginia for New Orleans with more than 100 slaves aboard. En route the slaves mutinied, seized possession of the ship, and took it to the Bahamas. British officials there declared the slaves free, and the English government refused to overrule them. Many Americans, especially Southerners, were infuriated.

At this critical juncture a new government came to power in Great Britain; eager to reduce the tensions with the United States, it sent Lord Ashburton, an admirer of Americans, to negotiate an agreement on the Maine boundary and other matters. The result was the Webster-Ashburton Treaty of 1842, under which the United States received slightly more than half the disputed area and agreed to a revised Northern boundary as far west as the Rocky Mountains. Ashburton also eased the memory of the *Caroline* and *Creole* affairs by expressing regret and promising no future "officious interference" with American ships. The Webster-Ashburton Treaty was popular in America, and Anglo-American relations suddenly looked better than they had for many years.

During the Tyler administration, the United States established its first diplomatic relations with China as part of an effort to win a share in the newly emerging China trade. In the Treaty of Wang Hya, concluded in

1844, American diplomats secured the same trading privileges as the English. In the next ten years, American trade with China steadily increased.

In their diplomatic efforts, at least, the Whigs were able to secure some important successes. But by the end of the Tyler administration, the party could look back on few other victories. In the election of 1844, the Whigs lost the White House. They were to win only one more national election in their history before a great sectional crisis would arise that would shatter their party and, for a time, the Union.

DEBATING THE PAST

Jacksonian Democracy

T O MANY AMERICANS in the 1820s and 1830s, Andrew Jackson was a champion of democracy, a symbol of the spirit of antielitism and egalitarianism that was sweeping American life. Historians, however, have disagreed sharply not only in their assessments of Jackson himself but in their portrayal of American society in his era.

The "progressive" historians of the early twentieth century tended to see Jacksonian politics as a forebear of their own battles against economic privilege and political corruption. Frederick Jackson Turner encouraged scholars to see Jacksonianism as the product of the democratic West: a protest by the people of the frontier against the conservative aristocracy of the East, which they believed was restricting their own freedom and opportunity. Jackson represented those who wanted to make government responsive to the will of the people rather than to the power of special interests. The culmination of this progressive interpretation of Jacksonianism was the publication in 1945 of Arthur M. Schlesinger, Jr.'s *The Age of Jackson.* Schlesinger was less interested in the regional basis of Jacksonianism than the disciples of Turner had been. Jacksonian Democracy, he argued, was the effort "to control the power of the capitalist groups, mainly Eastern, for the benefit of non-capitalist groups, farmers and laboring men, East, West, and South." He portrayed Jacksonianism as an early version of modern reform efforts (in the progressive era and the New Deal) to "restrain the power of the business community."

Richard Hofstadter, in an influential 1948 essay, sharply disagreed. Jackson, he argued, was the spokesman of rising entrepreneurs—aspiring businessmen who saw the road to opportunity blocked by the monopolistic power of Eastern aristocrats. The Jacksonians opposed special privileges only to the extent that those privileges blocked their own road to success. They were less sympathetic to the aspirations of those below them. Bray Hammond, writing in 1957, argued similarly that the Jacksonian cause was "one of enterpriser against capitalist," of rising elites against entrenched

(continued on next page)

ones. Other historians, exploring the ideological origins of the movement, saw Jacksonianism less as a democratic reform movement than as a nostalgic effort to restore a lost (and largely imagined) past. Marvin Meyers's *The Jacksonian Persuasion* (1957) argued that Jackson and his followers looked with misgivings on the new industrial society emerging around them and yearned instead for a restoration of the agrarian, republican virtues of an earlier time.

Historians of the 1960s began examining Jacksonianism in entirely new ways: looking less at Jackson and his supporters and more at the nature of American society in the early nineteenth century—and the ways in which it challenged the rhetoric of the politics of the time. Lee Benson's *The Concept of Jacksonian Democracy* (1961) used new quantitative techniques to challenge those historians who tried to explain political alignments in the 1830s on the basis of region, class, occupation, or even ideology. Local and cultural factors—religion and ethnicity in particular—were, he argued, the crucial determinants of party divisions. If there was an egalitarian spirit alive in America in those years, he claimed, it extended well beyond the Democratic party and the followers of Jackson. Edward Pessen's *Jacksonian America* (1969) revealed that the democratic rhetoric of the age disguised the reality of an increasingly stratified society, in which inequality was growing more, not less, severe. Alan Dawley went further in 1977, arguing that the extension of political rights in the 1820s and 1830s not only failed to advance economic democracy, but undermined the ability of workers and other exploited groups to articulate and act upon their grievances.

Scholars in more recent years have continued to pay less attention to Jackson and the Democratic party than to the origins and character of democratic ideas generally. In *Chants Democratic* (1984), Sean Wilentz identified the rise in the 1820s of a powerful working-class identity, expressed through a set of ideas known as "republicanism" and stimulated (although not fundamentally shaped) by the democratic rhetoric of party politics at the time. Workers in New York, he showed, were attracted less to Jackson himself than to the idea that power in a republic should be widely dispersed. They were raising a genuinely radical challenge to the rise of laissez-faire capitalism and to an emerging wage-labor system that threatened to reduce once-independent artisans into factory laborers unable to control their own livelihoods.

CHAPTER ELEVEN

The North and the South: Diverging Societies

The Developing North ~ The Expanding South
The "Peculiar Institution"

AMERICANS IN THE first half of the nineteenth century were a highly nationalistic people. Yet in many respects the United States in those years was not truly a nation at all—at least not in the way nations would be defined in later times. It was, rather, a highly decentralized confederation of states, many of which had little in common with one another. Those states remained together in part because the union was so loose, and the central authority of the nation so weak, that the differences among them did not often have to be confronted. But when the United States began to move in the direction of greater national unity in the 1840s, it had to confront the reality of sharp sectional differences that threatened to tear the country apart.

There had been sectional differences among the American colonies as early as the seventeenth century. By the 1840s and 1850s, however, sectionalism had changed. Socially and economically, there were now four quite distinct regions: the Northeast, with a growing industrial and commercial economy based on free labor; the Northwest, a rapidly expanding agricultural region; the Southeast, with a settled, slave labor plantation system and (in some areas) declining economic fortunes; and the Southwest, a booming frontierlike region with an expanding cotton economy. Politically, however, many Americans soon came to view their nation as divided into two sections, each with a distinctive and relatively homogeneous culture: the North and the South.

THE DEVELOPING NORTH

The most conspicuous change in American life in the 1840s and 1850s was the rapid industrialization of the Northeast. Factories proliferated. Urban centers grew rapidly. New industrial capitalists and financiers accumulated great fortunes. The urban middle class grew in size and importance. And a rapidly expanding industrial labor force created a distinct working class. The Northeast, in partnership with its new economic ally the Northwest, was developing a complex, modern society, one that would greatly increase the differences that had always existed between that region and the South.

Northeastern Industry

Between 1840 and 1860, American industry experienced a steady and, in some fields, spectacular growth. In 1840, the total value of manufactured goods produced in the United States was $483 million; ten years later the figure had climbed to over $1 billion; and in 1860 it was almost $2 billion. The bulk of this growth occurred in New England and the mid-Atlantic states. Although the Northeast had only a little more than half the mills and factories of the nation, it produced more than two-thirds of the manufactured goods and employed more than two-thirds of the industrial workers.

Technological advances sped the growth of industry. The machine tools used in the factories of the Northeast were by the 1840s already better than those in European factories. The principle of interchangeable parts, first applied decades earlier in gun factories, was being introduced into many other industries. Coal was replacing wood as an industrial fuel and was being used to drive new steam engines, which were in turn replacing water power in northeastern factories. That made it possible to locate mills away from running streams and thus permitted industry to expand still more widely.

In an earlier period, the dominant economic figures in the Northeast had been the great merchant traders. They remained figures of substance in the 1840s, particularly those in New York, Philadelphia, and Boston who invested in the China trade and who dispatched the famous and beautiful clipper ships to Asia and Europe. But international trade was becoming relatively less important in these years than manufacturing; and the new economic leaders of the Northeast, therefore, were the factory owners, some of whom were merchant capitalists who had shifted their resources into manufacturing.

By the 1840s, the corporate form of organization was spreading rapidly to manufacturing, particularly in the textile industry. Ownership of American enterprise was moving away from individuals and families and toward its highly dispersed modern form: many stockholders, each owning a relatively small proportion of the total. The discovery of new and more flexible forms of financing was, along with the technological innovations of the era, a crucial factor in the advancement of industrialization.

Transportation and Communications

Transportation was essential to the new industrial economy, above all for forging ties between the industrial Northeast and the Northwest. In the 1830s, the Erie Canal had been the most important transportation route between the two regions. But after 1840, in the more populated areas east of the Mississippi, railroads gradually took over. In 1840, the total railroad trackage of the country was only 2,818 miles; by the end of the decade, the trackage figure had risen to 9,021 miles; and between 1850 and 1860, trackage tripled again. The Northeast had twice as much trackage per square mile as the Northwest and four times as much as the South. Railroads were even reaching west of the Mississippi, although no extensive system had yet emerged there.

In the South, such towns as Charleston, Atlanta, Savannah, Richmond, and Norfolk had rail connections with Memphis, and thus with the Mississippi River and the Northwest. Much of the South, however, remained unconnected to a national railroad system. Most lines in the region were short, local ones. In the North, by contrast, short lines were being consolidated into trunk lines; and extensive rail connections with the Northwest were already in place by the 1850s, when Chicago emerged as the rail center of the West. The great trunk lines diverted traffic from the Mississippi River, weakening further the connection between the Northwest and the South.

The construction of railroads was the single greatest economic project in American history to that point and required massive amounts of capital. Much of it came from private investors, but much of it also came from government. State and local governments contributed capital because they were eager to have railroad service. Even greater assistance came from the federal government. In 1850, Senator Stephen A. Douglas of Illinois and other railroad-minded politicians persuaded Congress to grant federal lands to Illinois to aid the Illinois Central Railroad, which was building toward the Gulf of Mexico. By 1860, Congress had allotted over 30 million acres to eleven states to subsidize other railroad lines.

Crucial to the operation of railroads, and important in other ways to the transformation of American life, was the telegraph, which burst into

The Growth of the Railroads, 1850–1860

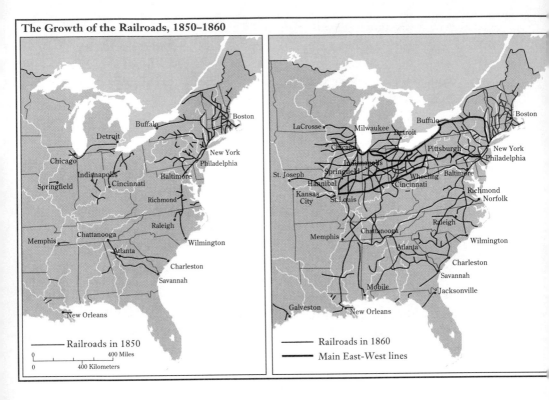

Railroads in 1850
400 Miles
400 Kilometers

Railroads in 1860
Main East-West lines

American life in 1844, when Samuel F. B. Morse, after several years of experimentation, succeeded in transmitting from Baltimore to Washington the news of James K. Polk's nomination for the presidency. By 1860, more than 50,000 miles of wire connected most parts of the country (although far more extensively in the North than in the South); and a year later, the Pacific telegraph, with 3,595 miles of wire, was operating between New York and San Francisco. By then, nearly all the independent lines had been absorbed into one organization, the Western Union Telegraph Company.

Cities and Immigrants

One of the most profound changes in the nature of Northeastern society in the antebellum period occurred in the character and distribution of the population, above all the growing size of cities. The populations of New York, Philadelphia, and Boston, for example, all nearly tripled between 1840 and 1860; New York's population was 1.2 million in 1860 if Brooklyn (then a separate municipality) is included. By 1860, 26 percent of the population of the free states was living in towns or cities (places of 2,500 people or more), a figure up from 14 percent in 1840. (In the South, by contrast, the increase of urban residents rose only from 6 percent in 1840 to 10 percent in 1860.)

The enlarged urban population was in part simply a reflection of the growth of the national population as a whole, which rose by more than a third—from 23 million to over 31 million—in the 1850s alone. But it was more directly a result of the flow of people into the cities from two sources: the native farmers of the Northeast, who were being forced off their lands by Western competition; and even more significantly by the 1850s, immigrants from Europe. Only 500,000 foreign immigrants had arrived in the United States in the 1830s (partly because of the serious depression in those years). But between 1840 and 1850, more than 1.5 million Europeans moved to America; in the 1850s, the number rose to 2.5 million. Almost half the population of New York City in the 1850s was foreign-born. In St. Louis, Chicago, and Milwaukee, the foreign born outnumbered the native born. Few immigrants settled in the South. Only 500,000 lived in the slave states in 1860, a third of them in Missouri.

The newcomers came from many different countries, but the overwhelming majority came from Ireland and Germany, where widespread poverty and political upheaval were driving many people out. By 1860, there were more than 1.5 million Irish-born and approximately 1 million German-born people in the United States. The great majority of the Irish remained in the Eastern cities where they landed and swelled the ranks of unskilled labor. Germans generally moved on to the Northwest, where they became farmers or went into business in the Western towns. The difference in settlement patterns was in part because Germans tended to arrive with at least some money, while the Irish generally arrived with none. But it was also because most German immigrants were members of family groups or were single men, for whom movement to the agricultural frontier was both possible and attractive, while the largest number of Irish immigrants consisted of single women, for whom movement west was much less plausible. Single women were more likely to stay in the Eastern cities, where factory and domestic work was available.

The Rise of Nativism

The new foreign-born population almost immediately became a major factor in American political life. Many politicians saw in the immigrant population a source of important potential support. They pushed state

LEAVING FOR AMERICA Irish emigrants bid friends and family goodbye as they board the mail coach from Cahirciveen in County Kerry, the first step in the long journey to the United States.

governments to liberalize their laws to allow unnaturalized immigrants to vote, and they eagerly courted the support of the new arrivals. Others, however, viewed the growing foreign population with alarm. Some argued that the immigrants were mentally and physically inferior and politically corrupt. Others complained that because the foreign born were willing to work for low wages, they were stealing jobs from the native work force. Protestants warned that the Catholic church was becoming a force in American government through the growing Irish population. Older-stock Americans feared that immigrants would become a radical force in politics. Out of these fears and prejudices emerged a number of secret societies to combat the "alien menace."

The first was the Native American Association, founded in 1837, which in 1845 was transformed into the Native American party. In 1850, nativist groups combined to form the Supreme Order of the Star-Spangled Banner, whose demands included banning Catholics or aliens from holding public office, enacting more restrictive naturalization laws, and establishing literacy tests for voting. The order adopted a strict code of secrecy, which included a secret password, used in lodges across the country: "I know nothing." Ultimately, members of the movement were labeled the "Know-Nothings."

After the 1852 elections, the Know-Nothings created a new political organization they called the American party. It scored an immediate and astonishing success in the elections of 1854. The Know-Nothings made a strong showing in Pennsylvania and New York and actually won control of the state government in Massachusetts. Outside the Northeast, however, their progress was more modest. And after 1854, the strength of the Know-Nothings declined. The party's most lasting impact was its contribution to the collapse of the second party system and the creation of new national political alignments.

Labor in the Northeast

In the early years of industrial growth, when mills were relatively few, the work force of the Northeastern factories had remained both small and for the most part impermanent. By the 1840s, however, the need for factory workers was such that a large, permanent laboring class was beginning to emerge, drawn from the new urban, immigrant population.

Working conditions quickly grew much worse than they had been for the Lowell and Waltham factory girls in the 1830s. Employers maintained no neat boardinghouses and dormitories for the new workers; they were left to find whatever accommodations they could in the squalid factory towns that were rapidly springing up. The factories themselves were becoming large, noisy, unsanitary, and often dangerous places to work; the average workday extended to twelve, often fourteen hours; and wages declined for all workers, but for women and children most of all.

Workers attempted at times to improve their lot. They tried, with little success, to persuade state legislatures to pass laws setting a maximum workday. Two states—New Hampshire in 1847 and Pennsylvania in 1848—actually passed laws barring employers from forcing employees to work more than ten hours without their consent; but the measures had little effect, since employers could require that workers agree to extended workdays as a condition of hiring. Three states—Massachusetts, New Hampshire, and Pennsylvania—passed laws regulating child labor. But the laws simply limited the workday to ten hours for children unless their parents agreed to something longer; again, employers had little difficulty persuading parents to consent to additional hours.

NEW ENGLAND TEXTILE WORKERS Women continued to constitute the majority of the work force in the cotton mills of New England even after the carefully monitored life of the "Lowell girls" became a thing of the past— as this 1868 engraving by Winslow Homer suggests.

Perhaps the greatest legal victory for industrial workers came when the Massachusetts supreme court ruled in 1842, in *Commonwealth* v. *Hunt*, that unions were lawful organizations and that the strike was a lawful weapon. Other state courts gradually followed suit. But the union movement of the 1840s and 1850s remained, on the whole, feeble and ineffective.

What organization there was among laborers usually occurred among limited groups of skilled workers. Their primary purpose was usually to protect the favored position of their members in the labor force by restricting admission to the skilled trades. Virtually all the early craft unions excluded women, even though female workers were numerous in almost every industry. As a result, women themselves created several women's protective unions in the 1850s, often with the support of middle-class female reformers. Like the male craft unions, however, the female protective unions had little power in dealing with employers.

Many factors combined to inhibit the growth of effective labor resistance in America, some of them the result of the growing number of immigrants in the work force. The newcomers were usually willing to work for lower wages than native workers; and because they were so numerous, manufacturers had little difficulty replacing disgruntled or striking native workers with eager immigrants. Ethnic divisions and tensions—both between natives and immigrants and among the various immigrant groups themselves—often caused working-class resentments to be channeled into internal bickering rather than into complaints against employers. Many immigrants expected to return to their original homes once they had earned enough money (and some actually did), which meant that they did not feel a strong stake in the long-term structure of the workplace. There was, finally, the sheer strength of the industrial capitalists, who had not only economic but political and social power and could usually triumph over even the most militant challenges.

Wealth and Mobility

The commercial and industrial growth of the United States greatly increased national wealth in the 1840s and 1850s and elevated the average income of the American people. But this increasing wealth was not widely or equally distributed. Some groups of the population, of course, shared hardly at all in the economic growth: enslaved African-Americans, Indians, landless farmers, and unskilled workers on the fringes of the manufacturing system. But even among the rest of the population, disparities of income were becoming ever more conspicuous. Wealth had always been unequally distributed in the United States, to be sure. But by the mid-nineteenth century, the concentration of wealth had become more pronounced than ever before. In 1860, 5 percent of the families in the United States possessed more than 50 percent of the wealth.

Why did this inequality not produce more resentment? There are several possible answers. First, however much the economic position of American workers was declining relative to that of other Americans, the absolute living standard of most laborers was improving. Factory workers generally ate better, were better clothed and housed, and had greater access to consumer goods than they had had on the farms or in the European societies from which they had migrated.

Second, there were opportunities for social mobility, for working one's way up the economic ladder, even if they were limited ones. A few workers managed to move from poverty to riches by dint of work, ingenuity, and luck—enough to support the dreams of those who watched them. A much larger number managed to move at least one notch up the ladder—for example, becoming in the course of a lifetime a skilled, rather than an unskilled, laborer. Such people could envision their children and grandchildren moving up even further.

Third, and more important than social mobility, was geographical mobility. Some workers saved their money and moved west to the new lands the government was opening; to some degree, the West became what the historian Frederick Jackson Turner later called a "safety valve" for discontent. Most workers, however, had neither the money nor the expertise to make such a move. Far more frequent was the migration of laborers, many of them victims of layoffs, from one industrial town to another looking for better opportunities. The rootlessness of this large segment of the work force—perhaps the most distressed segment—made effective organization and protest more difficult.

There was, finally, another "safety valve" for working-class discontent: politics. Economic opportunity may not have greatly expanded in the nineteenth century, but opportunities to participate in politics had. And to many working people, access to the ballot seemed to offer a way to help guide their society and to feel like a significant part of their communities.

Women and the "Cult of Domesticity"

Industrialization also produced profound changes in the nature and function of the American family. In the early decades of the nineteenth century (and for many years before that), the family itself had been the principal unit of economic activity. And among the farming population, which was still the majority, the family often remained a close-knit economic unit. But in the industrial economy of the rapidly growing cities, there was a marked erosion of the traditional economic function of the family. The urban household itself was seldom a center of production any longer. Instead, most income earners left home each day to work elsewhere. A sharp distinction began to emerge between the public world of the workplace— the world of commerce and industry—and the private world of the family— a world now dominated by housekeeping, child rearing, and other primarily domestic concerns.

The emerging distinction between the public and private worlds, between the workplace and the home, was accompanied by increasingly sharp distinctions between the social roles of men and women—distinctions that affected not just workers and farmers but the growing middle class as well. Traditional inequalities remained. Women had many fewer legal and political rights than did men, and within the family they remained under the virtually absolute authority of their husbands. Women were seldom encouraged—and in most cases were effectively barred—from pursuing education above the primary level. Not until 1837 did any college or university accept women students: Oberlin in Ohio, which educated both women and men; and Mt. Holyoke in Massachusetts, founded by Mary Lyon as an academy for women. Not until much later in the century were there more than a handful of others.

But however unequal the positions of men and women in the preindustrial era, those positions had generally been defined within the context of a household in which all members played important economic roles. In the middle-class family of the new industrial society, however, the husband was assumed to be the principal, usually the only, income producer. The wife was now expected to remain in the home and to engage in largely domestic activities. The image of women changed from one of contributors to the family economy to one of guardians of the "domestic virtues." Middle-class women, no longer producers, now became more important as consumers. They learned to place a higher value on keeping a clean, comfortable, and well-appointed home; on entertaining; on dressing elegantly and stylishly.

Within their own separate sphere, women began to develop a distinctive female culture. A "lady's" literature began to emerge to meet the demands of middle-class women. There were romantic novels (many of them by female writers), which focused on the private sphere that women now inhabited. There were women's magazines, which focused on fashions, shopping, homemaking, and other purely domestic concerns.

Most middle-class men—and many middle-class women—considered the new female sphere a vehicle for expressing special qualities that made women in some ways superior to men. Women were to be the custodians of morality and benevolence; they were to provide religious and moral instruction to their children and to counterbalance the acquisitive, secular impulses of their husbands. This "cult of domesticity," as some scholars have called it, gave many women greater material comfort than they had had in the past and placed a higher value on their "female virtues" and on their roles as wives and mothers. At the same time, it left women increasingly detached from the public world, with few outlets for their interests and energies.

Except for teaching and nursing—the favored occupations of unmarried middle-class women—work by women outside the household gradually came to be seen as a lower-class preserve. Working-class women continued to work in factories and mills, but under conditions far worse than those that the original, more "respectable" women workers of Lowell and Waltham had experienced. Domestic service became another frequent source of female employment. Now that production had moved outside the household, women who needed to earn money had to move outside their own homes to do so.

The Old Northwest

Agriculture was in steady decline in the states of the Northeast in the mid-nineteenth century. Some Eastern farmers continued to thrive by raising vegetables and fruits or producing dairy products to supply the growing urban population of the region. But the great staple crops became less and less important to the Northeastern economy—largely because of the dramatic agricultural growth in the states of what was then known as the Northwest (and is now called the Midwest).

There was more industry in this region than in the South; and in the two decades before the Civil War, the section experienced steady industrial growth, especially around Cleveland, Cincinnati, and Chicago. But for the white (and occasionally black) settlers who populated the lands that had by now been largely wrested from the natives, the Northwest was primarily an agricultural region.

The typical white citizen of the Northwest was not an industrial worker or a poor, marginal farmer, as was the case in the Northeast, but the owner of a reasonably prosperous family farm. The average size of Western farms was 200 acres, the great majority of them owned by the people who worked them; the farmers concentrated on corn, wheat, cattle, sheep, and hogs. Even relatively small farmers generally prospered, since the growing demand for farm products—both from the urban centers of the United States and from the industrial cities of Europe—resulted in steadily rising farm prices.

The growth of the agricultural economy of the Northwest had profound effects on sectional alignments in the United States. The Northwest sold most of its products to the residents of the Northeast. Eastern industry, in turn, found an important market for its products in the prospering West. Hence a strong economic relationship was emerging between the two regions that was profitable to both—and that was increasing the isolation of the South within the Union.

To meet the increasing demand for their products, farmers in the Northwest worked strenuously, and often frantically, to increase its productive capacities. One way they did so was by enlarging the area under cultivation during the 1840s. By 1850, the growing Western population had settled the prairie regions east of the Mississippi and was pushing beyond the river. But another way the Northwest increased production was by adopting more advanced (if at times wasteful and exploitive) agricultural techniques. New varieties of seed, notably Mediterranean wheat, which was hardier than the native type, were introduced in some areas. Better breeds of animals, such as hogs and sheep from England and Spain, were imported to take the place of native stock. More efficient grain drills, harrows, mowers, and hay rakes were developed and marketed. A steel plow, more durable than the older, iron ones, was introduced by John Deere in 1847.

Two new machines heralded a revolution in grain production. The most important was the automatic reaper, invented by Cyrus H. McCormick of Virginia, which replaced the hand-operated sickle and enabled small crews to harvest grain much more quickly than larger crews using sickles had been able to do. McCormick established a factory at Chicago, in the heart of the grain belt, in 1847. By 1860, more than 100,000 reapers were in use on Western farms. Almost as important to the grain grower was the thresher—a machine that separated the grain from the wheat stalks—which appeared in large numbers after 1840. Before then, grain was generally flailed by hand (seven bushels a day was a good average for a farm) or trodden by farm animals (twenty bushels a day on the average). A threshing machine could thresh twenty-five bushels or more in an hour.

Large portions of the Northwest—most of the upper third of the Great Lakes states—continued to be populated mainly by Indians until after the Civil War. In those areas, hunting and fishing, along with some sedentary agriculture, remained the principal economic activities. But the tribes never became fully integrated into the commercialized economy that was emerging elsewhere in the Northwest.

THE EXPANDING SOUTH

The South, like the North, experienced dramatic growth in the middle years of the nineteenth century. Southerners fanned out into the new territories of the Southwest and established new communities, new states, and new markets. The Southern agricultural economy grew increasingly productive and increasingly prosperous. Trade in such staples as sugar, rice, tobacco, and above all cotton made the South a major force in international commerce and created substantial wealth within the region.

Yet for all the expansion and change, the South experienced a much less fundamental transformation in these years than did the North. It had begun the nineteenth century as a primarily agricultural region; it remained overwhelmingly agrarian in 1860. It had begun the century with few important cities and little industry; and so it remained sixty years later. In 1800, the economy of the South had been dominated by a plantation system

Slavery and Cotton: The South in 1820 and 1860

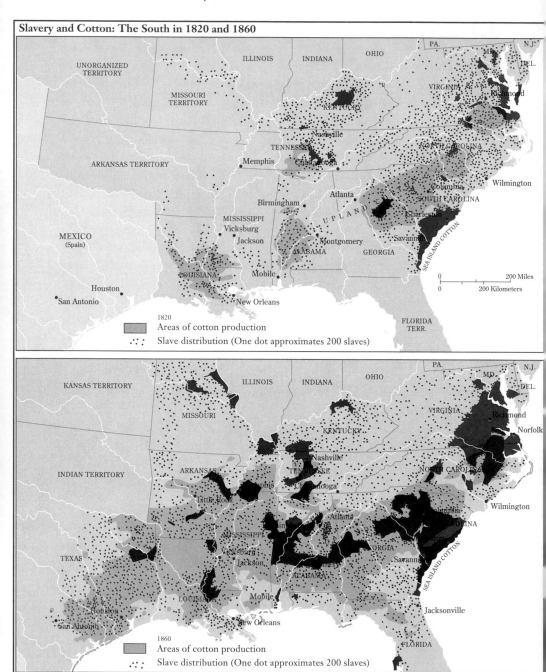

1820
Areas of cotton production
Slave distribution (One dot approximates 200 slaves)

1860
Areas of cotton production
Slave distribution (One dot approximates 200 slaves)

dependent on slave labor; by 1860, that system had only strengthened its grip on the region. As one historian has written, "The South grew, but it did not develop." As a result, it became increasingly unlike the North and increasingly sensitive to what it considered as threats to its distinctive way of life.

The Rise of King Cotton

The most important economic development in the South of the mid-nineteenth century was the shift of economic power from the "upper South"—such older and more developed states as Virginia, North Carolina, Maryland, and Kentucky—to the "lower South"—the expanding agricultural regions in the new states of the Southwest. That shift reflected above all the growing dominance of cotton in the Southern economy.

The decline of the tobacco economy in the upper South (a result of falling prices and soil exhaustion) and the natural limits of the sugar, rice, and long-staple cotton economies farther south might have forced the region to shift its attention to other, nonagricultural pursuits in the nineteenth century had it not been for the growing importance of a new product, which soon overshadowed all else: short-staple cotton. This hardier and coarser strain of cotton could be grown effectively in a variety of climates and in a variety of soils. It was more difficult to clean than the long-staple strain, but the invention of the cotton gin had largely solved that problem. By the 1820s, therefore, cotton production was spreading rapidly. From the western areas of South Carolina and Georgia, production moved into Alabama and Mississippi and then into northern Louisiana, Texas, and Arkansas. By the 1850s, cotton had come to be the linchpin of the Southern economy. By the time of the Civil War, it constituted nearly two-thirds of the total export trade of the United States and was bringing in nearly $200 million a year. The annual value of the rice crop, in contrast, was $2 million. It was little wonder that white Southerners now proclaimed: "Cotton is king!"

The prospect of tremendous profits from cotton quickly drew settlers by the thousands to the Southwest. Some were wealthy planters from the older states. Most were small slaveholders or slaveless farmers who hoped to become great planters. A similar shift occurred in the slave population. According to some estimates, 410,000 slaves moved from the upper South to the cotton states between 1840 and 1860—either accompanying masters who were themselves migrating to the Southwest or (more often) sold to planters already there. Indeed, the sale of slaves to the Southwest became an important economic activity in the upper South and helped the troubled planters of that region compensate for the declining value of tobacco and their other crops.

Southern Trade and Industry

In comparison to this booming agricultural expansion, other forms of economic activity developed slowly in the South. There was growing activity in flour milling and in textile and iron manufacturing, particularly in the upper South. The Tredegar Iron Works in Richmond, for example, compared favorably with the best iron mills in the Northeast. But industry remained an insignificant force relative to agriculture in the South, and it was even more insignificant when compared with the industry of the North.

To the degree that the South developed a nonfarm commercial sector, it was largely to serve the needs of the plantation economy. Brokers, or factors, marketed the planters' crops and provided planters with manufactured goods; they became figures of considerable influence in the region and established merchant communities in such towns as New Orleans, Charleston, Mobile, and Savannah. The South had only a very rudimentary financial system, and the factors often also served as bankers, providing planters with credit. There were also substantial groups of professional people in the South—lawyers, editors, doctors, and others; they too were closely tied to and dependent on the plantation economy.

These manufacturers, merchants, and professionals were, moreover, relatively insubstantial compared with the manufacturers, merchants, and professionals of the North, on whom Southerners were coming increasingly (and increasingly unhappily) to depend. Perceptive Southerners recognized the economic subordination of their region. As a result, there were calls for promoting Southern economic independence. Among the leading advocates was James B. D. De Bow of New Orleans, who published *De Bow's Review* from 1846 until 1860. The magazine warned constantly of the dangers of the "colonial" relationship between the sections. Yet *De Bow's Review* was itself evidence of the dependency of the South on the North. It was printed in New York, because no New Orleans printer had facilities adequate to the task; it was filled with advertisements from Northern manufacturing firms; and its circulation was always modest in comparison with those of Northern publications. In Charleston, for example, it sold an average of 173 copies per issue; *Harper's Magazine* of New York regularly sold 1,500 copies there.

Despite this awareness of the region's "colonial dependency," the South made few serious efforts to develop an economy that might challenge that dependency. An important question about antebellum Southern history, therefore, is why the region did so little to develop a larger industrial and commercial economy of its own.

One reason was the great profitability of the region's agricultural system, and particularly of cotton production. Another reason was that wealthy Southerners had so much capital invested in their land and in their slaves that they had little left for other investments. Some historians have suggested that the Southern climate—with its long, hot, steamy summers— was less suitable for industrial development than the climate of the North. Still others have gone so far as to claim that Southern work habits impeded industrialization; some white Southerners appeared—at least to many Northern observers—not to work very hard, to lack the strong work ethic that fueled Northern economic development.

But the Southern failure to create a flourishing commercial or industrial economy was also in part the result of a set of values distinctive to the South that discouraged the growth of cities and industry. White Southerners liked to think of themselves as representatives of a special way of life: one based on traditional values of chivalry, leisure, and elegance. Southerners were, some argued, "cavaliers," people happily free from the base, acquisitive instincts of Northerners and more concerned with creating a refined and gracious civilization than with rapid growth and development. But as appealing as the "cavalier" image was to Southern whites, it did not conform to the reality of most of Southern society.

Plantation Society

Only a small minority of Southern whites owned slaves. In 1850, when the total white population of the South was over 6 million, the number of slaveholders was only 347,525. Each slaveholder was normally the head of a family averaging five members. But even with all members of slaveowning families included in the figures, those owning slaves still amounted to perhaps no more than one-quarter of the white population. And of the minority of whites holding slaves, only a small proportion owned them in substantial numbers.

How, then, did the South come to be seen—both by the outside world and by many Southerners themselves—as a society dominated by great plantations and wealthy landowning planters? In large part, it was because the planter aristocracy—the cotton magnates, the sugar, rice, and tobacco nabobs, the whites who owned at least forty or fifty slaves and 800 or more acres—exercised power and influence far in excess of their numbers. They stood at the apex of society, determining the political, economic, and even social life of their region. Enriched by vast annual incomes, dwelling in palatial homes, surrounded by broad acres and many black servants, they became a class to which others paid deference.

Southerners liked to compare their planter class to the old upper classes of England and Europe: true aristocracies long entrenched. In fact, however, the Southern upper class was in most cases not at all similar to the landed aristocracies of the Old World. In the upper South—the tidewater region of Virginia, for example—some of the great aristocrats were people whose families had occupied positions of wealth and power for generations. In most of the South, however, there was no longstanding landed aristocracy. As late as the 1850s, most of the great landowners in the lower South were still first-generation settlers who had only relatively recently begun to live in anything like aristocratic style. Large areas of the "Old South" (as Americans later called the South of the pre–Civil War era) had been settled and cultivated for less than two decades at the time of the Civil War.

Nor was the world of the planter nearly as leisured and genteel as the "cavalier" myth would suggest. Growing staple crops was a business—often a big and highly profitable business; it was in its own way just as competitive and just as risky as the industrial enterprises of the North. Thus planters were, in many respects, as much capitalists as the industrialists of the North whose life styles they claimed to hold in contempt.

Wealthy Southern whites sustained their image of themselves as aristocrats in many ways. They adopted an elaborate code of "chivalry," which obligated white men to defend their "honor" (often through dueling). They avoided such "coarse" occupations as trade and commerce; those who did not become planters often gravitated toward the military, a "suitable" career for men raised in a culture in which medieval knights (as portrayed in the novels of Walter Scott) were a powerful and popular image. Above all, perhaps, the aristocratic ideal found reflection in the definition of a special role for Southern white women.

The "Southern Lady"

In some respects, affluent white women in the South occupied roles very similar to those occupied by middle-class white women in the North. Their lives were centered in the home, where they served as companions to (and hostesses for) their husbands and as nurturing mothers for their children. Seldom did "genteel" Southern white women engage in public activities or find income-producing employment.

But the life of the "Southern lady" was also in many ways very different from that of her Northern counterpart. For one thing, the cult of honor in the region meant that Southern white men attributed particular importance to the "defense" of women. In practice, this generally meant that white women were even more subordinate to men in Southern culture than they were in the North. George Fitzhugh, one of the South's most important social theorists, wrote in the 1850s: "Women, like children, have but one right, and that is the right to protection. The right to protection involves the obligation to obey."

The vast majority of females in the region lived on farms, relatively isolated from people outside their own families, with virtually no access to the "public world" and thus few opportunities to look beyond their roles as wives and mothers. For some white women, living on farms of modest size meant a fuller engagement in the economic life of the family than was becoming typical for middle-class women in the North. These women engaged in spinning, weaving, and other production; they participated in agricultural tasks; they helped supervise the slave work force. On the larger plantations, however, even these limited roles were often considered unsuitable for white women; and the "plantation mistress" became, in some cases, more an ornament for her husband than a meaningful part of the economy or the society.

Southern white women also had less access to education than their Northern counterparts. Nearly a quarter of all white women over twenty were completely illiterate; relatively few women had more than a rudimentary exposure to schooling. Even wealthy planters were not particularly interested in extensive schooling for their daughters. The few female "academies" in the South were designed largely to train women to be suitable wives.

Southern white women had other special burdens as well. The Southern white birth rate remained nearly 20 percent higher than that of the nation as a whole, and infant mortality in the region remained higher than elsewhere; nearly half the children born in the South in 1860 died before they reached five years of age. Male slaveowners had frequent sexual relationships with the female slaves on their plantations; the children of those unions became part of the plantation labor force and served as a constant reminder to white women of their husbands' infidelity. Black women (and men) were obviously the most important victims of such practices. But white women suffered too. However much they might resent their husbands' liaisons with slaves, the social code under which they lived generally prevented them from venting their anger (except toward slave women, whom plantation mistresses often treated very harshly), or even openly acknowledging that the relationships existed at all.

The "Plain Folk"

The typical white Southerner was not a great planter and slaveholder, but a modest yeoman farmer. Some owned a few slaves, with whom they worked and lived far more closely than did the larger planters. Most (in fact, two-thirds of all white families) owned no slaves at all. These "plain folk," most of whom owned their own land, devoted themselves largely to subsistence farming. There were occasional examples of poor farmers moving into the ranks of the planter class, but such cases were rare. Most yeomen knew they had little prospect of substantially bettering their lot.

One reason was the Southern educational system, which provided poor whites with few opportunities to learn and thus limited their chances of advancement. For the sons of wealthy planters, Southern colleges and universities were by 1860 enrolling more students than in any other region. But such institutions were open only to relatively wealthy people. And below the college level, where the white lower classes more often looked, the schools of the South were not only fewer but also inferior to those of the Northeast. The South had more than 500,000 white illiterates, over half the country's total.

In a few areas of the South, poor whites resented and set themselves apart from the plantation elite. These were mainly the Southern highlanders, the "hill people," who lived in the Appalachian ranges east of the Mississippi and in the Ozarks to the west of it. Of all Southern whites, they were the most isolated from the mainstream of the region's life. They practiced a crude form of subsistence agriculture, owned practically no slaves, and had a proud sense of seclusion. Such whites frequently expressed animosity toward the planter aristocracy of the other regions of the South and misgivings about (although seldom moral objections to) the system of slavery. The mountain region was the only part of the South to resist the movement toward secession when it developed. Even during the Civil War, many hill people refused to support the Confederacy; some fought for the Union.

But most nonslaveowning whites lived in the midst of the plantation system and did relatively little to oppose or resist it. Many, perhaps most of them, accepted that system because they were tied to it in important ways. Small farmers depended on the local plantation aristocracy for many things:

for access to cotton gins, for markets for their modest crops and their livestock, for financial assistance in time of need. In many areas, there were also extensive networks of kinship linking lower- and upper-class whites. The poorest resident of a county might easily be a cousin of the richest aristocrat.

There were other white Southerners, however, who did not share in the plantation economy in even these limited ways and yet continued to accept its premises. These were the members of that degraded class—numbering perhaps a half-million in 1850—known variously as "crackers," "sand hillers," or "poor white trash." Occupying the infertile lands of the pine barrens, the red hills, and the swamps, they lived in utter squalor. They often suffered from dietary deficiencies, resorted at times to eating clay, and were afflicted by pellagra, hookworm, and malaria. In some material respects, their plight was worse than that of the black slaves (who themselves often looked down on the poor whites).

Even among these Southerners—the true outcasts of white society in the region—there was no real opposition to the plantation system or slavery. In part, this was probably because these men and women were so benumbed by poverty that they had little strength to protest. But it resulted also from perhaps the single greatest unifying factor among the Southern white population—the one force most responsible for reducing tensions among the various classes. That force was race. However poor and miserable white Southerners might be, they could still consider themselves members of a ruling race; they could still look down on the black population of the region and feel a bond with their fellow whites born of a determination to maintain their racial supremacy. As Frederick Law Olmsted, a Northerner who visited the South and chronicled Southern society in the 1850s, wrote: "From childhood, the one thing in their condition which has made life valuable to the mass of whites has been that the niggers are yet their inferiors."

THE "PECULIAR INSTITUTION"

White Southerners often referred to slavery as the "peculiar institution." By that, they meant not that the institution was odd but that it was distinctive. And American slavery was distinctive indeed. The South in the mid-nineteenth century was the only area in the Western world except for Brazil and Cuba where slavery still existed; and Southern slavery differed even from its Caribbean and South American counterparts. Slavery, more than any other single factor, isolated the South from the rest of American society. And as that isolation increased, so did the commitment of Southerners to defend the institution.

Within the South itself, the institution of slavery had paradoxical results. On the one hand, it isolated blacks from whites, drawing a sharp and inviolable line between the races. As a result, blacks under slavery developed a distinct society and culture of their own. On the other hand, slavery created a unique bond between blacks and whites—masters and slaves—in the South. The two races may have maintained separate spheres, but each sphere was deeply influenced by, indeed dependent on, the other.

Varieties of Slavery

Slavery was an institution established and regulated in detail by law. The slave codes of the Southern states forbade slaves to hold property, to leave their masters' premises without permission, to be out after dark, to congregate with other slaves except at church, to carry firearms, or to strike a white person even in self-defense. The codes prohibited whites from teaching slaves to read or write, and they denied slaves the right to testify in court against white people. They contained no provisions to legalize slave marriages or divorces. If an owner killed a slave while punishing him, the act was generally not considered a crime. Slaves, however, faced the death penalty for killing or even resisting a white person or for inciting to revolt. The codes also contained extraordinarily rigid provisions for defining a person's race. Anyone with even a trace of African ancestry was considered black.

These and dozens of other regulations suggest that slaves lived under a uniformly harsh and dismal regime. In fact, however, the laws were unevenly applied. Sometimes slaves did acquire property, did learn to read and write, and did assemble with other slaves, in spite of laws to the contrary. There was, in short, considerable variety within the slave system. Some blacks lived in almost prisonlike conditions, rigidly and harshly controlled by their masters. Many (probably most) others enjoyed a certain flexibility and (at least in comparison to the regimen prescribed by law) a striking degree of autonomy.

Small farmers generally supervised their workers directly and often worked closely alongside them. On such farms, blacks and whites developed a form of intimacy unknown on larger plantations. The paternal relationship between such masters and their slaves could, like relationships between fathers and children, be warm and in some respects benevolent. It could also be tyrannical and cruel. In general, the evidence suggests, blacks themselves preferred to live on larger plantations, where they had more opportunities for privacy and for a social world of their own.

Although most slaveowners were small farmers, most slaves lived on plantations of medium or large size, with substantial African-American work forces. There the relationship between master and slave was not usually intimate. Substantial planters often hired overseers and even assistant overseers to represent them. "Head drivers," trusted and responsible slaves often assisted by several subdrivers, acted under the overseer as foremen. On most plantations, slaves worked under the gang system, in which slaves were divided up into groups, each directed by a driver, and worked for as many hours as the overseer considered a reasonable workday.

Masters usually provided slaves with an adequate if rough diet, consisting mainly of corn meal, salt pork, and molasses. Many slaves were allowed to raise gardens for their own use and were issued fresh meat on special

RETURNING FROM THE COTTON FIELD In this photograph, South Carolina field workers return after a day of picking cotton, some of their harvest carried in bundles on their heads. A black slave driver leads the way.

occasions. They were given cheap clothing and shoes. They lived in rude cabins, called slave quarters, usually clustered together near the master's house. The plantation mistress or a doctor retained by the owner provided some medical care, but slave women themselves were the more important source.

Slaves worked hard, beginning with light tasks as children. Slave women worked particularly hard. They generally toiled in the fields with the men and then did traditional "women's chores"—cooking, cleaning, and child rearing—as well. Because slave families were often divided, with husbands and fathers living on neighboring plantations (or, at times, sold to plantation owners far away), many black women found themselves acting in effect as single parents. Black women thus acquired a higher measure of authority within their families than did most white women.

The conditions of American slavery were less severe than those of slavery in the Caribbean and South America. In those regions, the slave supply was constantly replenished well into the nineteenth century by the African slave trade, giving owners less incentive to protect their existing laborers. In the United States, newly imported slaves were in short supply, and thus there were strong economic incentives to maintain a healthy slave population. Some masters even hired Irish workers and other whites to do such dangerous or unhealthy tasks as clearing malarial swamps or handling cotton bales at the bottom of long chutes. Still, cruel or rash masters might forget their pocketbooks in the heat of anger. And slaves were often left to the discipline of overseers, who had no financial stake in their well-being; overseers were paid in proportion to the amount of work they could get out of the slaves they supervised.

Household servants had a somewhat easier life—physically at least—than did field hands. On large plantations, there was generally a domestic staff of nursemaids, housemaids, cooks, butlers, and coachmen. These people lived close to the master and his family, eating the leftovers from the family table and in some cases even sleeping in the "big house." Between the blacks and whites of such households affectionate, almost familial, relationships might develop. More often, however, house servants resented their isolation from their fellow slaves and the lack of privacy that came with living in such close proximity to the family of the master. Female household servants were especially vulnerable to sexual abuse by their masters. When emancipation came after the Civil War, it was often the house servants who were the first to leave the plantations of their former owners.

Slavery in the cities differed significantly from slavery in the country. On the relatively isolated plantations, slaves had little contact with free

A M E R I C A N   V O I C E S

JAMES L. BRADLEY

An African-American Describes His Bondage, 1835

I THINK I was between two and three years old when the soul-destroyers tore me from my mother's arms, somewhere in Africa, far back from the sea. They carried me a long distance to a ship; all the way I looked back, and cried. The ship was full of men and women loaded with chains; but I was so small they let me run about on deck.

After many long days, they brought us into Charleston, South Carolina. A slaveholder bought me, and took me up into Pendleton County. I suppose that I staid with him about six months. He sold me to a Mr. Bradley, by whose name I have ever since been called. This man was considered a wonderfully kind master; and it is true that I was treated better than most of the slaves I knew. I never suffered for food, and never was flogged with the whip; but oh, my soul! I was tormented with kicks and knocks more than I can tell. . . .

I used to work very hard. I was always obliged to be in the field by sunrise, and I labored till dark stopping only at noon long enough to eat dinner. . . . My master had kept me ignorant of everything he could. . . . Yet from the time I was fourteen years old, I used to think a great deal about freedom. It was my heart's desire; I could not keep it out of my mind. Many a sleepless night I have spent in tears, because I was a slave. I looked back on all I had suffered—and when I looked ahead, all was dark and hopeless bondage.

SOURCE: John W. Blassingame, ed., *Slave Testimony* (Baton Rouge: Louisiana State University Press, 1977), pp. 687–688.

blacks and lower-class whites; a deep and seemingly unbridgeable chasm yawned between slavery and freedom. In the cities, however, masters could not supervise their slaves so closely if they hoped to use them profitably. Some—particularly skilled workers such as blacksmiths or carpenters— were hired out; after hours they often fended for themselves, neither their owners nor their employers bothering to supervise them. Thus urban slaves gained numerous opportunities to mingle with free blacks and with whites. In the cities, the line between slavery and freedom remained, but it grew less and less distinct.

Indeed, white Southerners generally considered slavery to be incompatible with city life; and as Southern cities grew, the relative number of slaves in them declined. Fearing conspiracies and insurrections, urban slaveowners sold off much of their male "property" to the countryside. The cities were left with an excess of black women while they continued to have an excess of white men (a situation that certainly helped to account for the birth of many mulattoes). While slavery in the cities declined, segregation of blacks, both free and slave, increased. Segregation was a means of social control intended to make up for the loosening of the discipline of slavery itself.

The Slave Trade

Although the importing of slaves from outside the United States largely ceased in 1808 (except for illegal smuggling), a flourishing slave trade continued through the 1850s. What sustained it was the great population movement from the upper South to the lower South and the great demand for slaves in the newly cultivated areas. Professional traders transported slaves from the tidewater region and the Carolinas over long distances to the Southwest, using trains and river or ocean steamers. On shorter journeys, the slaves moved on foot, trudging in coffles of hundreds along dusty highways. Eventually they arrived at such central markets as Natchez, New Orleans, Mobile, or Galveston, where purchasers collected to bid for them. At the auction, the bidders checked the slaves like livestock, watching them as they were made to walk or trot, inspecting their teeth, feeling their arms and legs, looking for signs of infirmity or age. Buyers were careful, because traders were known to deceive them by blacking gray hair, oiling withered skin, and concealing physical defects in other ways.

The domestic slave trade dehumanized all who were involved in it. It separated children from parents, and parents from each other. Even families kept together by scrupulous masters might be broken up in the division of the estate after the master's death. Planters who bought or sold slaves eased their consciences by holding the traders in contempt and assigning them a low social position.

Slave Resistance

Few issues have sparked as much debate among historians as the effects of slavery on the slaves themselves. Slaveowners, and many white Americans in later generations, liked to argue that the slaves were generally content, "happy with their lot." That may have been true in some cases. But it is clear that the vast majority of Southern blacks were not content with being slaves, that they yearned for freedom even though most realized there was little they could do to secure it. Evidence for that conclusion comes, if from nowhere else, from the reaction of slaves when emancipation finally came. Virtually all Southern blacks reacted to freedom with great joy, and relatively few chose to remain in the service of the whites who had owned them

HARRIET TUBMAN WITH ESCAPED SLAVES Harriet Tubman (c. 1820–1913) was born into slavery in Maryland. In 1849, when her master died, she escaped to Philadelphia to avoid being sold out of state. Over the next ten years, she assisted first members of her own family and then up to 300 other slaves to escape from Maryland to freedom. During the Civil War, she served alternately as a nurse and as a spy for Union forces in South Carolina. She is shown here, on the left, with some of the slaves she had helped to free.

before the Civil War (although most blacks, of course, remained for many years subservient to whites in one way or another).

The dominant response of African-Americans to slavery was a complex one: a combination of adaptation and resistance. At the extremes, slavery could produce two opposite reactions—each of which served as the basis for a powerful stereotype in white society. One extreme was what became known as the "Sambo"—the shuffling, grinning, head-scratching, deferential slave who acted out the role the white world expected. More often than not, the "Sambo" pattern of behavior was a charade, a façade assumed in the presence of whites. The other extreme was the slave rebel—the black who could not accommodate himself or herself to slavery. Rebellious slaves faced terrible consequences if they acted on their impulses, but many revolted, in large ways or small, nevertheless.

Actual slave revolts were extremely rare, but fear of them gripped white Southerners everywhere. In 1800, Gabriel Prosser gathered 1,000 rebellious slaves outside Richmond; but two blacks gave the plot away, and the Virginia militia was called out in time to head it off. Prosser and thirty-five others were executed. In 1822, the Charleston free black Denmark Vesey and his followers—rumored to total 9,000—made preparations for revolt; but again the word leaked out, and retribution followed. In 1831, Nat Turner, a slave preacher, led a band of blacks who armed themselves with guns and axes and, on a summer night, went from house to house in Southampton County, Virginia. They killed sixty white men, women, and children before being overpowered by state and federal troops. More than a hundred blacks were executed in the aftermath. Nat Turner's was the only actual slave insurrection in the nineteenth-century South.

Resistance to slavery usually took other, less drastic forms. In some cases, slaves worked "within the system" to free themselves from it—earning money with which they bought their own and their families' freedom. Some slaves were set free by their masters' wills, although state laws made it more and more difficult, and in some cases practically impossible, for owners to do that after the 1830s. By 1860, there were about 250,000 free blacks in the slaveholding states, more than half of them in Virginia and Maryland. A few (generally on the northern fringes of the slaveholding regions) bought land and prospered. Some owned slaves themselves, usually relatives whom they had bought in order to ensure their ultimate emancipation. Most, however, lived in urban areas in abject poverty. Law or custom closed many occupations to them, forbade them to assemble without white supervision, and placed numerous other restraints on them. Yet great as were the hardships of freedom, blacks usually preferred them to slavery.

Some blacks attempted to resist slavery by running away. A few escaped to the North or to Canada, especially after sympathetic whites began organizing the so-called underground railroad to assist them in flight. But the obstacles to a successful escape, particularly from the Deep South, were almost impossibly great. They included the hazards of distance, the slaves' ignorance of geography, and the white "slave patrols," which stopped wandering blacks on sight throughout the South demanding to see travel permits or pursued runaways through the woods using bloodhounds. Despite the obstacles, however, blacks continued to run away from their masters in large numbers. Some did so repeatedly, undeterred by the whippings and other penalties inflicted on them when captured.

But perhaps the most important method of slave resistance was simply a pattern of everyday behavior by which blacks defied their masters. That whites so often considered blacks to be lazy and shiftless suggests one means of resistance: refusal to work hard. Slaves might also steal from their masters or from neighboring whites. They might perform isolated acts of sabotage: losing or breaking tools (Southern planters gradually began to buy unusually heavy hoes because so many of the lighter ones got broken), performing tasks improperly, mistreating livestock, or faking illness. Some slaves deliberately maimed themselves. Others engaged in arson, which slaveowners feared almost as much as they feared insurrections.

Slave Religion and the Black Family

Resistance was only one aspect of the slave response to slavery. The other was an elaborate process of adaptation—a process that implied not contentment with bondage but recognition that there was no realistic alternative. One of the ways blacks adapted was by developing a rich and complex culture, one that enabled them to sustain a sense of racial pride and unity. In many areas, they retained a language of their own, sometimes incorporating African speech patterns into English. They developed a distinctive music, establishing in the process one of the greatest of all American musical traditions. The most important features of African-American culture, however, were embodied in the development of two powerful institutions: religion and the family.

A separate slave religion was not supposed to exist. Almost all blacks were Christians, and their masters expected them to worship under the supervision of white ministers—often in the same chapels as whites. Indeed, autonomous black churches were banned by law. Nevertheless, blacks throughout the South developed their own version of Christianity, at times incorporating such African practices as voodoo but more often simply bending religion to the special circumstances of bondage. Natural leaders emerging within the slave community rose to the rank of preacher; and when necessary, blacks would hold services in secret, often at night.

Black religion was more emotional than its white counterparts, and it reflected the influence of African customs and practices. Slave prayer meetings routinely involved fervent chanting, spontaneous exclamations from the congregation, and ecstatic conversion experiences. Black religion was also more joyful and affirming than that of many white denominations. And above all, black religion emphasized the dream of freedom and deliverance. In their prayers and songs and sermons, black Christians talked and sang of the day when the Lord would "call us home," "deliver us to freedom," "take us to the Promised Land." And while their white masters generally chose to interpret such language merely as the expression of hopes for life after death, blacks themselves used the images of Christian salvation to express their own dream of freedom in the present world.

The slave family was the other crucial institution of black culture in the South. The nuclear family was the dominant kinship model among African-Americans. But such families did not always operate according to white customs. Black women generally began bearing children at younger ages than most whites, often as early as age fourteen or fifteen. Slave communities did not condemn premarital pregnancy in the way white society did, and black couples would often begin living together before marrying. It was customary, however, for couples to marry soon after conceiving a child. Family ties were no less strong than those of whites, and many slave marriages lasted throughout the course of long lifetimes. When marriages did not survive, it was often because of circumstances over which blacks had no control. Up to a third of all black families were broken up by the slave trade.

The need for the black family to adapt itself to its own uncertain future accounted for some of its other distinctive characteristics. Networks of kinship—which grew to include not only spouses and their children but aunts, uncles, grandparents, even distant cousins—remained strong and important and often served to compensate for the breakup of nuclear families. A slave suddenly moved to a new area, far from his or her family, might create "fictional" kinship ties and become "adopted" by a family in the new community. Even so, the impulse to maintain contact with a spouse and children remained strong long after the breakup of a family. One of the most frequent causes of flight from the plantation was a slave's desire to find a husband, wife, or child who had been sent elsewhere.

In addition to establishing social and cultural institutions of their own, slaves adapted themselves to slavery by forming complex relationships with their masters. However much blacks resented their lack of freedom, they often found it difficult to maintain an entirely hostile attitude toward their owners. Not only were they dependent on whites for the material means of existence—food, clothing, and shelter; they also often derived from their masters a sense of security and protection. There was, in short, a paternal relationship between slave and master—sometimes harsh, sometimes kindly, but almost invariably important. That paternalism, in fact, became (even if not always consciously) a vital instrument of white control. By creating a sense of mutual dependence, whites helped reduce resistance to an institution that, in essence, was designed solely for the benefit of the ruling race.

D E B A T I N G   T H E   P A S T

The Nature of Plantation Slavery

N O ISSUE IN American history has produced a richer literature or a more spirited debate than the nature of plantation slavery. The debate began even before the Civil War, when abolitionists strove to expose slavery to the world as a brutal, dehumanizing institution, while Southern defenders of slavery tried to depict it as a benevolent, paternalistic system. That same debate continued for a time after the Civil War; but by the late nineteenth century, with white Americans eager for sectional conciliation, most Northern and Southern chroniclers of slavery began to accept a romanticized and unthreatening picture of the Old South and its peculiar institution.

The first major scholarly examination of slavery was fully within this romantic tradition. Ulrich B. Phillips's *American Negro Slavery* (1918) portrayed slavery as an essentially benign institution in which kindly masters looked after submissive, childlike, and generally contented African-Americans. Phillips's apologia for slavery remained the authoritative work on the subject for nearly thirty years.

In the 1940s, as concern about racial injustice increasingly engaged the attention of white Americans, challenges to Phillips began to emerge. In 1941, for example, Melville J. Herskovits challenged Phillips's contention that black Americans retained little of their African cultural inheritance. In 1943, Herbert Aptheker published a chronicle of slave revolts as a way of challenging Phillips's claim that blacks were submissive and content.

A somewhat different challenge to Phillips emerged in the 1950s from historians who emphasized the brutality of the institution. Kenneth Stampp's *The Peculiar Institution* (1956) and, even more powerfully, Stanley Elkins's *Slavery* (1959) described a labor system that did serious physical and psychological damage to its victims. Stampp and Elkins portrayed slavery as something like a prison, in which men and women had virtually no space to develop their own social and cultural lives. Elkins compared the system to Nazi concentration camps during World War II and likened the childlike "Sambo" personality of slavery to the tragic distortions of character produced by the Holocaust.

In the early 1970s, an explosion of new scholarship on slavery shifted the emphasis away from the damage the system inflicted on African-Americans and toward the striking success of the slaves themselves in building a culture of their own despite their enslavement. John Blassingame in 1973, echoing Herskovits's claims of thirty years earlier, argued that "the most remarkable aspect of the whole process of enslavement is the extent to which the American-born slaves were able to retain their ancestors' culture." Herbert Gutman, in *The Black Family in Slavery and Freedom* (1976), challenged the prevailing belief that slavery had weakened and even destroyed the African-American family. On the contrary, he argued, the black family survived slavery with impressive strength, although with some significant differences from the prevailing form of the white family. Eugene Genovese's *Roll, Jordan, Roll* (1974) revealed how African-Americans manipulated the paternalist assumptions that lay at the heart of slavery to build a large cultural space of their own, within the system, where they could develop their own family life, social traditions, and religious patterns. That same year, Robert Fogel and Stanley Engerman published their controversial *Time on the Cross*, a highly quantitative study that supported some of the claims of Gutman and Genovese about black achievement but that went much further in portraying slavery as a successful and reasonably humane (if ultimately immoral) system. Slave workers, they argued, were better treated and lived in greater comfort than most Northern industrial workers of the same era. Their conclusions produced a storm of criticism.

Some of the most important recent scholarship on slavery has focused on the role of gender in shaping plantation society. Elizabeth Fox-Genovese, for example, argues in *Within the Plantation Household* (1988) that the world of black women was in many ways distinctive, defined by their dual roles as members of the plantation work force and anchors of the black family. She rejects the contention of some scholars that slave women formed special bonds, born of shared female experiences, with the plantation mistresses. But the role of gender, she argues, was nevertheless as important as the role of race in determining the nature of the "peculiar institution."

CHAPTER TWELVE

An Age of Reforms

The Romantic Impulse ~ Remaking Society
The Crusade Against Slavery

HE UNITED STATES in the mid-nineteenth century was growing rapidly in geographical extent, in the size and diversity of its population, and in the dimensions and complexity of its economy. And like any people faced with such rapid and fundamental change, Americans reacted with ambiguity. On the one hand, they were excited by the new possibilities that economic growth was providing. On the other hand, they were painfully aware of the dislocations that it was creating: the challenges to traditional values and institutions, the social instability, the uncertainty about the future.

One result of these conflicting attitudes was the emergence of movements to "reform" the nation. Such movements were highly diverse, but most reflected one of two basic impulses, and at times elements of both. Some rested on an optimistic faith in human nature, a belief that within every individual resided a spirit that was basically good and that society should attempt to unleash. This assumption—which produced in both Europe and America a movement known as romanticism—stood in marked contrast to the traditional Calvinist assumption that human desires and instincts were sinful and needed to be repressed.

A second impulse was a desire for order and control. With their society changing so rapidly, with their traditional values and institutions being challenged and eroded, many Americans yearned above all for a restoration of stability and discipline to their nation. Often, this impulse embodied a conservative nostalgia for better, simpler times. But it also inspired efforts to create new institutions of social control, suited to the realities of the new age.

Reform efforts took many forms and could be found in every part of the nation. By the end of the 1840s, however, one issue—slavery—had come to overshadow all others. And one group of reformers—the abolitionists— had become the most influential of all. At that point, the reform impulse became another wedge between the North and the South.

THE ROMANTIC IMPULSE

"In the four quarters of the globe," wrote the English wit Sydney Smith in 1820, "who reads an American book? or goes to an American play? or looks at an American picture or statue?" The answer, he assumed, was obvious— no one.

American intellectuals were painfully aware of the low regard in which their culture was held by Europeans, and they tried in the middle decades of the century to create an American artistic life that would express their own nation's special virtues. At the same time, many of the nation's cultural leaders were striving for another kind of liberation, which was—ironically— largely an import from Europe: the spirit of romanticism. In literature, in philosophy, in art, even in politics and economics, American intellectuals were committing themselves to the liberation of the human spirit.

An American Literature

The effort to create a distinctively American literature, which Washington Irving and others had begun in the first decades of the century, made important advances in the 1820s through the work of the first great American novelist: James Fenimore Cooper. What most distinguished his work was its evocation of the American West. Cooper had a lifelong fascination with man's relationship to nature and with the challenges (and dangers) of America's expansion westward. His most important novels—among them *The Last of the Mohicans* (1826) and *The Deerslayer* (1841)—explored the experience of rugged white frontiersmen with Indians, pioneers, violence, and the law. Cooper not only celebrated the American spirit and landscape; he also evoked, through the character of Natty Bumppo, the ideal of the independent individual with a natural inner goodness—an ideal that many Americans feared was in jeopardy in the expanding, industrializing world of the East.

Another, slightly later group of American writers displayed more clearly the appeal of romanticism to the nation's artists and intellectuals. In 1855, Walt Whitman published his first book of poems, *Leaves of Grass*, and established himself as one of the nation's most important writers. These and later poems were celebrations of democracy, of the liberation of the individual spirit, and of the pleasures of the flesh. Whitman helped liberate verse from traditional, restrictive conventions; he also expressed a personal yearning for emotional and physical release and personal fulfillment—a yearning perhaps rooted in part in his personal experience as a homosexual living in a society profoundly intolerant of unconventional sexuality.

Less exuberant was Herman Melville, probably the greatest American writer of his era. The most important of his novels was *Moby Dick*, published in 1851—the story of Ahab, the powerful, driven captain of a whaling vessel, who was obsessed with his search for Moby Dick, the great white whale that had once maimed him. It was a story of courage and of the strength of human will. But it was also a tragedy of pride and revenge, and a metaphor for the harsh, individualistic, achievement-driven culture of nineteenth-century America.

The Transcendentalists

One of the outstanding expressions of the romantic impulse in America came from a group of New England writers and philosophers known as the transcendentalists. Borrowing heavily from German and English writers and philosophers, the transcendentalists embraced a theory of the individual that rested on a distinction between what they called "reason" and "understanding." Reason, as they defined it, was the highest human faculty; it was the individual's innate capacity to grasp beauty and truth by giving full expression to the instincts and emotions. Understanding, by contrast, was the use of intellect in the narrow, artificial ways imposed by society; it involved the repression of instinct and the victory of externally imposed learning. Every person's goal, therefore, should be liberation from the confines of "understanding" and cultivation of "reason." Each individual should strive to "transcend" the limits of the intellect and allow the emotions, the "soul," to create an "original relation to the Universe."

Transcendentalist philosophy emerged first among a small group of intellectuals centered in Concord, Massachusetts, and led by Ralph Waldo Emerson. A Unitarian minister in his youth, Emerson left the clergy in 1832 to devote himself to writing, teaching, and lecturing. In "Nature" (1836),

WALT WHITMAN This picture of the youthful, jaunty,
bearded poet was the frontispiece for the first edition
of *Leaves of Grass* (1855). It is an engraving from a
painting by Francis B. Carpenter, one of the
most successful portrait painters of the
mid-nineteenth century.

Emerson wrote that in the quest for self-fulfillment, individuals should work
for a communion with the natural world: "in the woods, we return to reason
and faith. . . . Standing on the bare ground,—my head bathed by the
blithe air, and uplifted into infinite space,—all mean egotism vanishes. . . .
I am part and particle of God." In other essays, he was even more explicit in
advocating a commitment of the individual to the full exploration of inner
capacities. "Nothing is at last sacred," he wrote in "Self-Reliance" (1841),
perhaps his most famous essay, "but the integrity of your own mind."

Almost as influential as Emerson was another Concord transcendentalist, Henry David Thoreau. Thoreau went even further than his friend
Emerson in repudiating the repressive forces of society, which produced, he
said, "lives of quiet desperation." Each individual should work for self-
realization by resisting pressures to conform to society's expectations and
responding instead to his or her own instincts. Thoreau's own effort to free
himself—immortalized in *Walden* (1854)—led him to build a small cabin in

the Concord woods on the edge of Walden Pond, where he lived alone for two years as simply as he could, attempting to liberate himself from repressive convention and from what he considered society's excessive interest in material comforts. "I went to the woods," he explained, "because I wished to live deliberately, to front only the essential facts of life, and see if I could not learn what it had to teach, and not, when I came to die, discover that I had not lived." Thoreau's rejection of what he considered the artificial constraints of society extended to his relationship with government. In 1846, he went to jail (briefly) rather than agree to pay a poll tax. He would not, he insisted, give financial support to a government that permitted the existence of slavery. In his 1849 essay "Resistance to Civil Government," he explained his refusal by arguing that a government which required an individual to violate his or her own morality had no legitimate authority. The proper response was "civil disobedience," or "passive resistance"—a public refusal to obey unjust laws.

Visions of Utopia

Although transcendentalism was at its heart an individualistic philosophy, it helped spawn the most famous of all nineteenth-century experiments in communal living: Brook Farm. The dream of the Boston transcendentalist George Ripley, Brook Farm was established in 1841 as an experimental community in West Roxbury, Massachusetts. There, according to Ripley, individuals would gather to create a new society that would permit every member to have full opportunity for self-realization. All residents would share equally in the labor of the community so that all could share too in the leisure, which was essential for cultivation of the self. (Ripley was one of the first Americans to attribute positive connotations to the idea of leisure; most of his contemporaries equated it with laziness and sloth.) The tension between the ideal of individual freedom and the demands of a communal society took their toll on Brook Farm. Many residents became disenchanted and left. When a fire destroyed the central building of the community in 1847, the experiment dissolved.

Among the original residents of Brook Farm was the writer Nathaniel Hawthorne, who expressed his disillusionment with the experiment and, to some extent, with transcendentalism in a series of novels voicing some of the same concerns that his contemporary Herman Melville was articulating. In *The Blithedale Romance* (1852), he wrote scathingly of Brook Farm itself. In other novels—most notably *The Scarlet Letter* (1850) and *The House of the*

Seven Gables (1851)—he wrote equally passionately about the price individuals pay for cutting themselves off from society. Egotism, he claimed (in an indirect challenge to the transcendentalist faith in the self), was the "serpent" that lay at the heart of human misery.

The failure of Brook Farm did not, however, prevent the formation of other experimental communities. The Scottish industrialist and philanthropist Robert Owen founded an experimental community in Indiana in 1825, which he named New Harmony. It was to be a "Village of Cooperation," in which every resident worked and lived in total equality. The community was an economic failure, but the vision that had inspired it continued to enchant Americans. Dozens of other "Owenite" experiments began in other locations in the ensuing years.

Redefining Gender Roles

Many of the new utopian communities (and many of the new social philosophies on which they rested) were centrally concerned with the relationship between men and women. Some experimented with a radical redefinition of gender roles.

Such a redefinition was central to one of the most enduring of the utopian colonies of the nineteenth century: the Oneida Community, established in 1848 in upstate New York by John Humphrey Noyes. The Oneida "Perfectionists," as residents of the community called themselves, rejected traditional notions of family and marriage. All residents, Noyes declared, were "married" to all other residents; there were to be no permanent conjugal ties. But Oneida was not, as horrified critics often claimed, an experiment in unrestrained "free love." It was a place where the community carefully monitored sexual behavior; where women were protected from unwanted childbearing; and where children were raised communally, often seeing little of their own parents. The Oneidans took pride in what they considered their liberation of women from the demands of male "lust" and from the traditional bonds of family.

The Shakers, too, made a redefinition of traditional gender roles central to their society. Founded by "Mother" Ann Lee in the 1770s, the society of the Shakers survived into the twentieth century. (Only a tiny remnant is left today.) But the Shakers attracted a particularly large following in the mid-nineteenth century and established more than twenty communities throughout the Northeast and Northwest in the 1840s. They derived their name from a unique religious ritual—a sort of dance, in which members of a congregation would "shake" themselves free of sin while performing a loud chant.

The most distinctive feature of Shakerism, however, was its commitment to complete celibacy—which meant, of course, that no one could be born to Shakerism; all Shakers had to choose the faith voluntarily. Shaker communities attracted about 6,000 members in the 1840s, more women than men. They lived in communities where contacts between men and women were strictly limited, and they endorsed the idea of sexual equality. Within Shaker society, women exercised the most power. Shakerism, one observer wrote in the 1840s, was a refuge from the "perversions of marriage" and "the gross abuses which drag it down."

The Shakers were not, however, motivated only by a desire to escape the burdens of traditional sexual roles. They were trying as well to create a society separated and protected from the chaos and disorder that they believed had come to characterize American life as a whole. In that, they were much like other dissenting religious sects and other utopian communities of their time.

The Mormons

Perhaps the most important effort to create a new and more ordered society within the old was that of the Church of Jesus Christ of Latter Day Saints, whose members are known as Mormons. Mormonism began in upstate New York as a result of the efforts of Joseph Smith, an energetic but economically unsuccessful man, who had spent most of his twenty-four years moving restlessly through New England and the Northeast. Then, in 1830, he published a remarkable document—the *Book of Mormon*—which he claimed was a translation of a set of golden tablets he had found in the hills of New York after a revelation by an angel of God. The *Book of Mormon* told the story of an ancient civilization in America, whose now vanished kingdom could become a model for a new holy community in the United States.

Gathering a small group of believers around him, Smith began in 1831 to seek a sanctuary for his new community of "saints," an effort that would continue, unhappily, for more than twenty years. Time and again, the Mormons attempted to establish their "New Jerusalem." Time and again, they met with persecution from surrounding communities suspicious of their radical religious doctrines—which included polygamy (the right of men to take several wives), a rigid form of social organization, and an intense secrecy that gave rise to wild rumors among their critics of conspiracy and depravity.

Driven from their original settlements in Independence, Missouri, and Kirtland, Ohio, the Mormons founded Nauvoo, Illinois, which in the early 1840s became an imposing and economically successful community. In 1844, however, Joseph Smith was arrested, charged with treason (for conspiring against the government to win foreign support for a new Mormon colony in the Southwest), and imprisoned in nearby Carthage, Illinois. There an angry mob attacked the jail, forced Smith from his cell, and shot and killed him. The Mormons now abandoned Nauvoo and, under the leadership of Smith's successor, Brigham Young, traveled across the desert—a society of 12,000 people, one of the largest group migrations in American history—and established a new settlement in Utah, the present Salt Lake City. There, at last, the Mormons were able to create a permanent settlement.

Like other experiments in social organization of the era, Mormonism reflected a belief in human perfectibility. God had once been a man, the church taught; and thus every man or woman could aspire to become, in effect, a god—as Joseph Smith had done. But the Mormons did not celebrate individual liberty. Instead, they created a highly organized, centrally directed, almost militarized social structure as a refuge against the disorder and uncertainty of the secular world. They placed particular emphasis on the structure of the family. The original Mormons were, for the most part, men and women who felt displaced in their rapidly changing society—economically marginal people left behind by the material growth and social progress of their era. In the new religion, they found security and order.

REMAKING SOCIETY

The reform impulse also helped create new movements to remake mainstream society—movements in which, to a striking degree, women formed both the rank and file and the leadership. By the 1830s, such movements had taken the form of organized reform societies. The new organizations worked on behalf of a wide range of goals: temperance; education; peace; the care of the poor, the handicapped, and the mentally ill; the treatment of criminals; the rights of women; and many more. Few eras in American history have witnessed as wide a range of reform efforts. And few eras have exposed more clearly the simultaneous attraction of Americans to the ideas of personal liberty and social order.

Revivalism, Morality, and Order

The philosophy of reform arose in part from the optimistic vision of those such as the transcendentalists who preached the divinity of the individual. But another, and in many respects more important, source was Protestant revivalism—the movement that had begun with the Second Great Awakening early in the century and had, by the 1820s, evolved into a powerful force for social reform.

The New Light evangelicals embraced the optimistic belief that every individual was capable of salvation through his or her own efforts. (Hence the term "Free Will Baptists," by which some described themselves.) Partly as a result, revivalism soon became not only a means of personal salvation but a mandate for the reform of the larger society. In particular, revivalism produced a crusade against personal immorality. "The church," said Charles Grandison Finney, the leading revivalist of his time, "must take right ground on the subject of Temperance, the Moral Reform, and all the subjects of practical morality which come up for decision from time to time."

THE DRUNKARD'S PROGRESS This 1846 lithograph by Nathaniel Currier shows what temperance advocates argued was the inevitable consequence of alcohol consumption. Beginning with an apparently innocent "glass with a friend," the young man rises step by step to the summit of drunken revelry, then declines to desperation and suicide while his abandoned wife and child grieve.

Evangelical Protestantism added major strength, therefore, to one of the most influential reform movements of the era: the crusade against drunkenness. No social vice, temperance advocates argued, was more responsible for crime, disorder, and poverty than the excessive use of alcohol. Women, who were particularly active in the temperance movement, complained that men spent money their families needed on alcohol and that drunken husbands often beat and abused their wives. Temperance also appealed to those who were alarmed by immigration; drunkenness, many nativists believed, was responsible for violence and disorder in immigrant communities and temperance was a way to discipline them. By 1840, temperance had become a major national movement, with powerful organizations and more than a million followers who had signed a formal pledge to forgo hard liquor.

As the movement gained in strength, it became divided in purpose. Some demanded legislation to restrict the sale and consumption of alcohol (Maine passed such a law in 1851); others insisted that temperance must rely on the conscience of the individual. Whatever their disagreements, however, most temperance advocates shared similar motives. By promoting abstinence, reformers were attempting to promote individual moral self-improvement. They were also trying to impose discipline on a disordered society.

Education and Rehabilitation

One of the most important reform movements of the mid-nineteenth century was the effort to produce a system of universal public education. As of 1830, no state had such a system, although some—such as Massachusetts—were supporting limited versions. Now, however, interest in public education grew rapidly.

The greatest of the educational reformers was Horace Mann, the first secretary of the Massachusetts Board of Education, which was established in 1837. To Mann and his followers, education was the only way to "counterwork this tendency to the domination of capital and the servility of labor." It was also the only way to protect democracy, for an educated electorate was essential to the workings of a free political system. Mann reorganized the Massachusetts school system, lengthened the academic year (to six months), doubled teachers' salaries (although he did not eliminate the large disparities between the salaries of male and female teachers), broadened the curriculum, and introduced new methods of professional training for teachers. Other states followed similar courses: building new schools, creating teachers' colleges, and offering many children access to education for the first time. By the 1850s, the principle (although not yet the reality) of tax-supported elementary schools was established in every state.

Yet the quality of public education continued to vary widely. In some places—Massachusetts, for example—educators were generally capable men and women, often highly trained, who had an emerging sense of themselves as career professionals. In other areas, however, teachers were often barely literate, and funding for education was severely limited. In much of the West, where the population was highly dispersed, many children had no access to schools at all. In the South, all African-Americans were barred from education (although approximately 10 percent of them managed to achieve literacy anyway), and only about a third of all white children of school age were actually enrolled in schools in 1860. In the North, 72 percent were enrolled; but even there, many students attended classes only briefly and casually.

The interest in education (and, implicitly, in the unleashing of individual talents that could result from it) was visible too in the growing movement to educate American Indians in the antebellum period. Some reformers, even many who considered black people inferior and unredeemable, believed that Indians could be "civilized" if only they could be taught the ways of the white world. Efforts by missionaries and others to educate Indians and encourage them to assimilate were particularly prominent in such areas of the Far West as Oregon, where substantial numbers of whites were beginning to settle in the 1840s and where conflicts with the natives had not yet become acute. Nevertheless, the great majority of Native Americans remained outside the reach of educational reform, either by choice or by circumstance or both.

Despite limitations and inequities, the achievements of the school reformers were impressive. By the beginning of the Civil War, the United States had one of the highest literacy rates of any nation of the world: 94 percent of the population of the North, 83 percent of the white population (and 58 percent of the total population) of the South.

The conflicting impulses that underlay the movement for school reform were visible in some of the different educational institutions that emerged. The belief in the potential of the individual sparked the creation of new institutions to help the handicapped, institutions that formed part of a great network of charitable activities known as the Benevolent Empire. Among them was the Perkins School for the Blind in Boston, the first such school in America. Nothing better exemplified the romantic spirit of the era than the belief of those who founded Perkins that even society's least-favored members—the unsighted and otherwise handicapped—could be helped to discover their own inner strength and wisdom.

More typical of educational reform, however, were efforts to use schools to impose a set of social values on children—values that reformers and others believed were appropriate for their new, industrializing society. These values included thrift, order, discipline, punctuality, and respect for authority. Horace Mann, for example, spoke of the role of public schools in extending democracy and expanding individual opportunity. But he spoke, too, of their role in creating social order: "The unrestrained passions of men are not only homicidal, but suicidal. . . . Train up a child in the way he should go, and when he is old he will not depart from it."

Similar impulses produced another powerful movement of reform: the creation of "asylums" for criminals and the mentally ill. In advocating prison and hospital reform, Americans were reacting against one of society's most glaring ills: antiquated jails and mental institutions whose inmates lived in almost inhuman conditions. Beginning in the 1820s, many states built new penitentiaries and mental asylums. New York built the first penitentiary at Auburn in 1821. In Massachusetts, the reformer Dorothea Dix began a national movement for new methods of treating the mentally ill.

But the creation of asylums for social deviants was not simply an effort to curb the abuses of the old system. It was also an attempt to reform and rehabilitate the inmates. New forms of prison discipline were designed to rid criminals of the "laxness" that had presumably led them astray. Solitary confinement and the imposition of silence on work crews (both instituted in Pennsylvania and New York in the 1820s) were meant to give prisoners opportunities to meditate on their wrongdoings and develop "penitence" (hence the name "penitentiary"). Some reformers argued that the discipline of the asylum could serve as a model for other potentially disordered environments—for example, factories and schools. Before long, however, penitentiaries and many mental hospitals fell victim to overcrowding, and the original reform ideal was gradually lost. Most prisons and many mental hospitals ultimately degenerated into little more than warehouses for inmates, with scant emphasis on rehabilitation.

Some of the same impulses that produced asylums underlay the emergence in the 1840s and 1850s of a new "reform" approach to the problems of Native Americans: the idea of the reservation. For several decades, the dominant thrust of the United States policy toward the Indians in areas of white settlement had been relocation. The principal motive behind reloca-

316 ~ The Unfinished Nation

tion was simple: getting the tribes out of the way of white civilization. But among some whites there had also been another, if secondary, intent: to move the Indians to a place where they would be protected from whites and allowed to develop to a point at which assimilation might be possible. Even Andrew Jackson, whose animus toward Indians was legendary, once described the removals as part of the nation's "moral duty . . . to protect and if possible to preserve and perpetuate the scattered remnants of the Indian race."

It was a small step from the idea of relocation to the idea of the reservation, the notion of creating an enclosed region in which Indians would live in isolation from white society. Again, the reservations served white economic purposes above all, as they involved moving Native Americans out of good lands that white settlers wanted. But they also had a reform purpose. Just as prisons, asylums, and orphanages would provide society with an opportunity to train and uplift misfits and unfortunates within white society, so the reservations might provide a way to undertake what one official called "the great work of regenerating the Indian race."

The Rise of Feminism

The reform ferment of the antebellum period had a particular meaning for American women. As they played central roles in reform movements, women began to confront the problems they themselves faced in a male-dominated society. The result was the emergence of the first important American feminist movement.

Many of the women who became involved in reform movements in the 1820s and 1830s came to resent the social and legal restrictions that limited their participation. Some began to defy them. Sarah and Angelina Grimké, sisters born in South Carolina who had become active and outspoken abolitionists, ignored attacks by men who claimed that their activism was inappropriate to their gender. "Men and women were *CREATED EQUAL*," they argued. "They are both moral and accountable beings, and whatever is right for man to do, is right for women to do." Other reformers— Catharine Beecher, Harriet Beecher Stowe (her sister), Lucretia Mott, Elizabeth Cady Stanton, and Dorothea Dix—similarly pressed at the boundaries of "acceptable" female behavior, chafing at the restrictions placed on women by men.

In 1840, American female delegates arrived at a world antislavery convention in London, only to be turned away by the men who controlled the proceedings. Angered at the rejection, several of the delegates—notably Lucretia Mott and Elizabeth Cady Stanton—became convinced that their first duty as reformers should now be to elevate the status of women. Over the next several years, Mott, Stanton, and others began drawing pointed parallels between the plight of women and the plight of slaves; and in 1848, in Seneca Falls, New York, they organized a convention to discuss the question of women's rights. Out of the meeting came the "Declaration of Sentiments and Resolutions" (patterned on the Declaration of Independence), which stated that "all men and women are created equal," that women no less than men are endowed with certain inalienable rights. In demanding the right to vote, they launched a movement for woman suffrage that would survive until the battle was finally won in 1920. But the Seneca Falls document was at least equally important for its rejection of the whole notion that men and women should be assigned separate "spheres" in society.

Many of the women involved in these feminist efforts were Quakers. Quakerism had long embraced the ideal of sexual equality and had tolerated, indeed encouraged, the emergence of women as preachers and community leaders. Quakers had also been among the leaders of the antislavery movement, and Quaker women had played a leading role within those efforts. Not all Quakers went so far as to advocate full sexual equality in American society, but enough Quaker women coalesced around such demands to cause a schism in the yearly meeting of Friends in Genesee, New York, in 1848. That dissident faction formed the core of the group that organized the Seneca Falls convention. Of the women who drafted the Declaration of Sentiments there, all but Elizabeth Cady Stanton were Quakers. Stanton, joined two years later by Susan B. Anthony, led the movement to implement the Seneca Falls resolutions in the 1850s and beyond. Together, they ultimately transformed it into a powerful force for change.

Progress toward feminist goals was limited in the antebellum years, but certain individual women did manage to break the social barriers to advancement. Elizabeth Blackwell, born in England, gained acceptance and fame as a physician. Her sister-in-law Antoinette Brown Blackwell became the first ordained woman minister in the United States; and another sister-in-law, Lucy Stone, took the revolutionary step of retaining her maiden name after marriage. She became a successful and influential lecturer on women's rights. Emma Willard, founder of the Troy Female Seminary in 1821, and Catharine Beecher, who founded the Hartford Female Seminary in 1823, worked on behalf of women's education.

Feminists benefited greatly from their association with other reform movements, most notably abolitionism; but they also suffered as a result. The demands of women were usually assigned—even by some women themselves—a secondary position to what many considered the far greater issue of the rights of slaves.

THE CRUSADE AGAINST SLAVERY

The antislavery movement was not new to the mid-nineteenth century. But only in 1830 did it begin to gather the force that would ultimately enable it to overshadow virtually all other efforts at social reform.

Early Opposition to Slavery

In the early years of the nineteenth century, those who opposed slavery were, for the most part, a calm and genteel lot, expressing moral disapproval but doing little else. To the extent that there was an organized antislavery movement, it centered on the concept of colonization—the effort to resettle American blacks in Africa or the Caribbean. In 1817, a group of prominent white Virginians organized the American Colonization Society (ACS), which tried to challenge slavery without challenging property rights or Southern sensibilities. The ACS proposed a gradual freeing of slaves, with masters receiving compensation. The liberated blacks would then be transported out of the country and helped to establish a new society of their own. The ACS was not without impact. It received some funding from private donors, some from Congress, some from the legislatures of Virginia and Maryland. And it arranged to have several groups of blacks transported out of the United States, some of them to the west coast of Africa, where in 1830 they established the nation of Liberia. (In 1846, Liberia became an independent black republic, with its capital, Monrovia, named for the American president who had presided over the initial settlement.) But the ACS was in the end a negligible force. Neither private nor public funding was nearly enough to carry out the vast projects its supporters envisioned. In the space of a decade, they managed to "colonize" fewer slaves than were born in the United States in a month. Nothing, in fact, would have been enough; there were far too many blacks in America in the nineteenth century to be transported to Africa by any conceivable program. And the ACS met resistance, in any case, from blacks themselves, many of whom were now three or more generations removed from Africa and despite their loathing of slavery, had no wish to emigrate.

By 1830, colonization was failing rapidly, particularly since the cotton boom in the Deep South was increasing the commitment of planters to their labor system. Those opposed to slavery had reached what appeared to be a dead end.

Garrison and Abolitionism

At this crucial juncture, with the antislavery movement seemingly on the verge of collapse, a new figure emerged to transform it: William Lloyd Garrison. Born in Massachusetts in 1805, Garrison was in the 1820s an assistant to the New Jersey Quaker Benjamin Lundy, who published the leading antislavery newspaper of the time. Garrison grew impatient with his employer's moderate tone and mild proposals for reform. In 1831, therefore, he returned to Boston to found his own weekly newspaper, the *Liberator*.

Garrison's philosophy was so simple as to be genuinely revolutionary. Opponents of slavery, he said, should not, as earlier reformers had done, talk about the evil influence of slavery on white society; they should talk about the damage the system did to blacks. And they should, therefore, reject "gradualism" and demand the immediate, unconditional, universal abolition of slavery and the extension to blacks of all the rights of American citizenship. Garrison wrote in a relentless, uncompromising tone. "I am aware," he wrote in the very first issue of the *Liberator*, "that many object to the severity of my language; but is there not cause for severity? I will be as harsh as truth, and as uncompromising as justice. . . . I am in earnest—I will not equivocate—I will not excuse—I will not retreat a single inch—*and I will be heard*."

Garrison soon attracted a large group of followers throughout the North, enough to enable him to found the New England Antislavery Society in 1832 and a year later, after a convention in Philadelphia, the American Antislavery Society. By 1835, there were more than 400 local societies; by 1838, there were 1,350, with more than 250,000 members.

Abolitionists were very much a part of the larger spirit of reform of their era. Like other reformers, they were calling for an unleashing of the individual human spirit, the elimination of artificial social barriers to fulfillment. Who, after all, was more in need of assistance in realizing individual potential than the enslaved blacks?

Black Abolitionists

Abolitionism had a particular appeal, perhaps needless to say, to the free black population of the North, which in 1850 numbered about 250,000, mostly concentrated in cities. These free blacks lived in conditions of poverty and oppression at times worse than those of their slave counterparts in the South. They were often the victims of mob violence; they had virtually no access to education; they could vote in only a few states; and they were barred from all but the most menial of occupations. Most worked either as domestic servants or as sailors in the American merchant marine, and their wages were so low that most lived in squalor. Some were kidnapped by whites and forced back into slavery.

For all their problems, however, Northern blacks were fiercely proud of their freedom and sensitive to the plight of those members of their race who remained in bondage; they were aware that their own position in society would remain precarious as long as slavery existed. Many in the 1830s came to support Garrison. But they also rallied to leaders of their own.

The greatest of the black abolitionists was Frederick Douglass, one of the most electrifying orators of his time. Born a slave in Maryland, Douglass

FREDERICK DOUGLASS Frederick Douglass was the most prominent African-American of the nineteenth century. Born in Maryland to an unknown white father and a slave mother, he escaped from slavery into the North in 1838. He quickly became a leader in the abolitionist movement.

escaped to Massachusetts in 1838, became an outspoken leader of antislavery sentiment, and spent two years lecturing in England, where he was lionized by members of that country's vigorous antislavery movement. On his return to the United States in 1847, Douglass purchased his freedom from his Maryland owner and founded an antislavery newspaper, the *North Star*, in Rochester, New York. He achieved wide renown as well for his autobiography, *Narrative of the Life of Frederick Douglass* (1845), in which he presented a damning picture of slavery. Douglass demanded not only freedom but full social and economic equality.

Antiabolitionism

The rise of abolitionism was a powerful force, but it provoked a powerful opposition as well. Almost all white Southerners, of course, were bitterly hostile to the movement. But even in the North, abolitionists were a small, dissenting minority whom most whites viewed as dangerous radicals. Some feared that abolitionism would produce a destructive war between the sections. Others feared that it would lead to a great influx of free blacks into the North.

The result of such fears was an escalating wave of violence directed against abolitionists in the 1830s. A mob in Philadelphia attacked the abolitionist headquarters there in 1834, burned it to the ground, and began a bloody race riot. Another mob seized Garrison on the streets of Boston in 1835 and threatened to hang him. He was saved from death only by being locked in jail. Elijah Lovejoy, the editor of an abolitionist newspaper in Alton, Illinois, was victimized repeatedly by mob violence and finally killed when he tried to defend his press from attack.

That so many men and women continued to embrace abolitionism in the face of such vicious opposition from within their own communities suggests that abolitionists were not people who made their political commitments lightly or casually. They were strong-willed, passionate crusaders who displayed not only enormous courage and moral strength but at times a fervency that many of their contemporaries (and some later historians) found disturbing. The mobs were only the most violent expression of a hostility to abolitionism that many, perhaps most, other white Americans shared.

Abolitionism Divided

By the mid-1830s, the abolitionist crusade had begun to experience serious internal strains and divisions. One reason was the violence of the antiabolitionists, which persuaded some members of the movement that a more moderate approach was necessary. Another reason was the growing radicalism of William Lloyd Garrison, who shocked even many of his own allies (including Frederick Douglass) by attacking not only slavery but the government itself. The Constitution, he said, was "a covenant with death and an agreement with hell." The nation's churches, he claimed, were bulwarks of slavery. In 1840, Garrison precipitated a formal division within the American Antislavery Society by insisting that women, who had always been central to the organization's work, be permitted to participate in the movement on terms of full equality. He continued after 1840 to arouse controversy with new and even more radical stands: an extreme pacifism that rejected even defensive wars; opposition to all forms of coercion—not just slavery but prisons and asylums; and finally, in 1843, a call for Northern disunion from the South. The nation could, he suggested, purge itself of the sin of slavery by expelling the slave states from the Union.

From 1840 on, therefore, abolitionism moved in many channels and spoke with many different voices. The Garrisonians, with their radical and uncompromising moral stance, remained influential. But others operated in more moderate ways, arguing that abolition could be accomplished only as the result of a long, patient, peaceful struggle—"immediate abolition gradually accomplished," as they called it. At first, they depended on "moral suasion." They appealed to the conscience of the slaveholders, attempting to convince them that their institution was sinful. When that produced no results, they turned to political action, seeking to induce the Northern states and the federal government to aid the cause. They joined the Garrisonians in helping runaway slaves find refuge in the North or in Canada through what became known as the underground railroad (although their efforts were never as highly organized as the name suggests). After the Supreme Court (in *Prigg* v. *Pennsylvania*, 1842) ruled that states need not aid in enforcing the 1793 law requiring the return of fugitive slaves to their owners, abolitionists won passage in several Northern states of "personal liberty laws," which forbade state officials to assist in the capture and return of runaways. And the antislavery societies petitioned Congress to abolish slavery in places where the federal government had jurisdiction—in the territories and in the District of Columbia—and to prohibit the interstate slave trade. But few members of the movement believed that Congress could constitutionally interfere with a "domestic" institution such as slavery within the individual states themselves.

Antislavery sentiment underlay the formation in 1840 of the Liberty party, which ran Kentucky antislavery leader James G. Birney for president.

But this party and its successors never campaigned for outright abolition (an illustration of the important fact that "antislavery" and "abolitionism" were not always the same thing). They stood instead for "free soil," for keeping slavery out of the territories. Some free-soilers were concerned about the welfare of blacks; others were people who cared nothing about slavery but simply wanted to keep the West a country for whites. Garrison dismissed free-soilism as "white-manism." But the free-soil position would ultimately do what abolitionism never could: attract the support of large numbers, even a majority, of the white population of the North.

The frustrations of political abolitionism drove some critics of slavery to embrace more drastic measures. A few began to advocate violence; it was a group of prominent abolitionists in New England, for example, who funneled money and arms to John Brown for his bloody uprisings in Kansas and Virginia. Others attempted to arouse public anger through propaganda. The most powerful of all abolitionist propaganda was Harriet

UNCLE TOM'S CABIN This poster (advertising, among other things, a German edition of Harriet Beecher Stowe's novel) did not exaggerate when it described *Uncle Tom's Cabin* as "The Greatest Book of the Age." There were, to be sure, greater literary accomplishments; but no American book of the nineteenth century had so profound a political impact.

Beecher Stowe's novel *Uncle Tom's Cabin*, published as a book in 1852. It rocked the nation. It sold more than 300,000 copies within a year of publication and was later issued again and again, becoming one of the most remarkable best sellers in American history. And it succeeded in bringing the message of abolitionism to an enormous new audience—not only those who read the book but those who watched dramatizations of its story by countless theater companies throughout the nation. Reviled throughout the South, Stowe became a hero to many in the North. And in both regions, her novel helped inflame sectional tensions to a new level of passion. Few books in American history have had so great an impact on the course of public events.

Even divided, therefore, abolitionism remained a powerful influence on the life of the nation. Only a relatively small number of people before the Civil War ever accepted the abolitionist position that slavery must be entirely eliminated in a single stroke. But the crusade that Garrison had launched, and that thousands of committed men and women kept alive for three decades, was a constant, visible reminder of how deeply the institution of slavery was dividing America.

CHAPTER THIRTEEN

The Impending Crisis

Expansion and War ~ *A New Sectional Crisis*
The Crises of the 1850s

U NTIL THE 1840s, the tensions between North and South remained relatively contained. Had no new sectional issues arisen, it is possible that the United States would have avoided a civil war, that the two sections might have resolved their differences peaceably over time. But new issues did arise, centered around the expansion of slavery. From the North came the strident and increasingly powerful abolitionist movement, which kept the issue alive in the public mind and increased sectional animosities. And from the West, more significantly, came a series of controversies that would ultimately destroy the fragile Union. For ironically, the vigorous nationalism that was in some ways helping to keep the United States together was also producing a desire for territorial expansion that would tear the nation apart.

EXPANSION AND WAR

More than a million square miles of new territory came under the control of the United States during the 1840s—the greatest wave of expansion since the Louisiana Purchase nearly forty years before. By the end of the decade, the nation possessed all the territory of the present-day United States except Alaska, Hawaii, and a few relatively small areas acquired later through border adjustments. Many factors accounted for this great new wave of expansion, but one of the most important was a set of ideas—an ideology known as "Manifest Destiny."

Manifest Destiny

Manifest Destiny reflected both the burgeoning pride that characterized American nationalism in the mid-nineteenth century and the idealistic vision of social perfection that fueled so much of the reform energy of the time. It rested on the idea that America was destined—by God and by history—to expand its boundaries over a vast area, an area that included, but was not necessarily restricted to, the continent of North America. American expansion was not selfish, its advocates insisted; it was an altruistic attempt to extend American liberty to new realms.

By the 1840s, the idea of Manifest Destiny had spread throughout the nation, publicized by the new "penny press," which made newspapers available to a far greater proportion of the population than ever before, and fanned by the rhetoric of nationalist politicians. Advocates of Manifest Destiny disagreed, however, about how far and by what means the nation should expand. Some had relatively limited territorial goals; others envisioned a vast new "empire of liberty" that would include Canada, Mexico, Caribbean and Pacific islands, and ultimately, a few dreamed, much of the rest of the world. Some believed that America should use force to achieve its expansionist goals, others that the nation should expand peacefully or not at all.

Not everyone embraced the idea of Manifest Destiny. Henry Clay and other prominent politicians feared, correctly as it turned out, that territorial expansion would reopen the painful controversy over slavery and threaten the stability of the Union. Their voices, however, were all but drowned out in the enthusiasm over expansion in the 1840s, which began with the issues of Texas and Oregon.

Texas and Oregon

The United States had once claimed Texas—which, as the 1830s began, was part of the republic of Mexico—as a part of the Louisiana Purchase, but it had renounced the claim in 1819. Twice thereafter, the United States had offered to buy Texas, only to meet with indignant Mexican refusals. But in the early 1820s, the Mexican government launched an ill-advised experiment. It began encouraging Americans to move into Texas in hopes of strengthening the economy of the territory and increasing its own tax revenues. Thousands of Americans, attracted by the rich soil in Texas, took advantage of Mexico's welcome. The great majority were white Southerners, and the slaves they brought with them. By 1835, approximately 35,000 Americans, white and black, were living in Texas.

Almost from the beginning, there was friction between the new settlers and the Mexicans. Finally the Mexican government, feeling threatened by the new settlers, tried to exert control. A new law increased the powers of the national government of Mexico at the expense of the state governments, a measure that Texans from the United States assumed was aimed specifically at them. In 1836, the American settlers defiantly proclaimed their independence from Mexico.

The Mexican dictator, Antonio de Santa Anna, advanced with a large army into Texas, where the American settlers were having difficulty organizing a resistance. Their garrison at the Alamo mission in San Antonio was annihilated after a famous, if futile, defense by a group of Texas "patriots," a group that included, among others, the renowned frontiersman Davy Crockett; another garrison at Goliad suffered substantially the same fate when the Mexicans murdered most of the force after it had surrendered. But General Sam Houston kept a small army together, and on April 21, 1836, at the Battle of San Jacinto (near present-day Houston), he defeated the Mexican army and took Santa Anna prisoner. Texas had effectively won its independence.

The new republic of Texas, through its first president, Sam Houston, immediately requested annexation by the United States. But many American Northerners opposed acquiring a large new slave territory, and others opposed increasing the Southern votes in Congress and in the electoral college. President Jackson feared annexation might cause an ugly sectional controversy and even a war with Mexico. He did not, therefore, support annexation, and he even delayed recognizing the new republic until 1837. Martin Van Buren also refrained from pressing the issue.

Spurned by the United States, Texas cast out on its own. Its leaders sought money and support from Europe. They dreamed of creating a vast southwestern nation, stretching to the Pacific, that would rival the United States—a dream that appealed to European nations eager to counter the growing power of the United States. England and France quickly recognized and concluded trade treaties with Texas. Observing this, President Tyler persuaded Texas to apply again for admission to the United States in 1844. But when Secretary of State Calhoun presented an annexation treaty to Congress as if its only purpose were to extend slavery, Northern senators rebelled and defeated it. The Texas question quickly became the central issue in the election of 1844.

Control of what was known as the Oregon Country, in the Pacific Northwest, was another major political issue in the 1840s. Its half-million square miles included the present states of Oregon, Washington, and Idaho, parts of Montana and Wyoming, and half of British Columbia. Both Britain and the United States claimed sovereignty in the region; and unable to resolve their claims diplomatically, they agreed in an 1818 treaty to allow citizens of each country equal access to the territory. This arrangement, known as "joint occupation," continued for twenty years, until it, too, broke down in the face of growing immigration.

The Westward Migration

Throughout the 1840s, 1850s, and 1860s, hundreds of thousands of white and black Americans moved to the Far Western regions of the continent, settling in areas that had previously been inhabited almost entirely by Indians and a few missionaries. Many were white planters from the Southern states, most of whom settled in Texas and brought slaves with them. But the largest number came from the Old Northwest (what we now know as the Midwest)—white men and women, and a few blacks, who undertook arduous journeys in search of new opportunities. Most traveled in family groups, until the early 1850s, when the great gold rush attracted many single men. Most were reasonably young people. Most had experienced earlier, if usually shorter, migrations in the past.

All were in search of a new life, but they harbored many different visions of what the new life would bring. Some (particularly after the discovery of gold in California in 1849) hoped for quick riches. Others wanted to acquire property for farming or speculation and planned to take advantage of the vast public lands the federal government was selling at modest prices. Still others hoped to establish themselves as merchants and serve the new white communities developing in the West. Some (among them the Mormons) were on religious missions or were attempting to escape hardships or oppression in the East.

Most migrants traveled west along the great overland trails. They generally gathered in one of several major depots in Iowa and Missouri (Independence, St. Joseph, or Council Bluffs), joined a wagon train led by hired guides, and set off with their belongings piled in covered wagons and their livestock trailing behind. The major route west was the 2,000-mile Oregon Trail, which stretched from Independence across the Great Plains and through the South Pass of the Rocky Mountains. From there, migrants

THE OREGON TRAIL Trappers and merchants had used the Oregon Trail to reach the Far West since early in the nineteenth century, but settlers traveling by wagon train dominated traffic along the trail beginning in the 1840s. This drawing by William Henry Jackson suggests both the ruggedness of the journey and the large dimensions of the migration.

moved north into Oregon or south (along the California Trail) to the northern California coast. Other migrations moved along the Santa Fe Trail, which extended southwest from Independence into New Mexico.

However they traveled, overland migrants faced great dangers and hardships. The mountain and desert terrain in the later portions of the trip were particularly difficult. Most journeys lasted five or six months (from May to November), and there was always pressure to get through the Rockies before the snows began, not always an easy task given the very slow pace of most wagon trains (about fifteen miles a day). There was also the danger of disease; many groups were decimated by cholera. And there were encounters with Indians.

In reality, Indians were usually more helpful than dangerous to the white migrants. They often served as guides through difficult terrain or aided travelers in crossing streams or herding livestock. They maintained an extensive trade with the white travelers in horses, clothing, and fresh food. But occasional Indian attacks on isolated travelers and small wagon trains frightened the white migrants into considering all Indians a threat. In the end, whites probably inflicted more violence on Indians during these overland journeys than the Indians did on whites. In any case, the number of deaths in such conflicts was relatively small in relation to the size of the migrations; fewer than 1,000 whites and Indians combined died in such conflicts between 1840 and 1860.

Even when migrants avoided disaster (as most did), the strains of the long journey caused significant changes in ordinary life. Conventional gender roles soon gave way to pressing necessities, and women began performing such traditionally "male tasks" as driving cattle and loading wagons. And despite the traditional image of westward migrants as rugged individualists, travelers found the journey an intensely collective experience. Indeed, one of the most frequent causes of disaster for travelers was the breakdown of the necessarily communal character of the migratory companies. Those who made the journey successfully generally learned the value of cooperation.

Polk and Expansion

By the mid-1840s, there were already substantial numbers of Americans living in settlements up and down the Pacific coast and more than 5,000 in Oregon. These new settlers (along with advocates of Manifest Destiny in the East) were urging the United States government to take possession of the disputed Oregon Territory. Such demands quickly became a factor in national politics.

The election of 1844 was widely expected to be a contest between two old foes: the Whig Henry Clay and the Democrat and former president Martin Van Buren. Both men tried to avoid taking a stand on the controversial issue of the annexation of Texas. Their separate statements on the question were so similar that many suspected they had collaborated in preparing them. Both favored annexation, but only with the consent of Mexico. Since such consent was unlikely, the statements meant virtually nothing.

Because sentiment for expansion was mild within the Whig party, Clay had no difficulty securing the nomination despite his noncommittal position. Among the Democrats, however, there were many supporters of annexation, particularly in the South; and they resented Van Buren's equivocal stand. The expansionists took control of the Democratic convention and nominated a strong supporter of annexation, James K. Polk—the first "dark horse" to win the presidential nomination of his party.

Polk was not as obscure as his Whig critics claimed, but neither was he a genuinely major figure within his party. Beginning in 1825, he had represented Tennessee in the House of Representatives for fourteen years, four of them as Speaker. Subsequently, he had been governor of Tennessee.

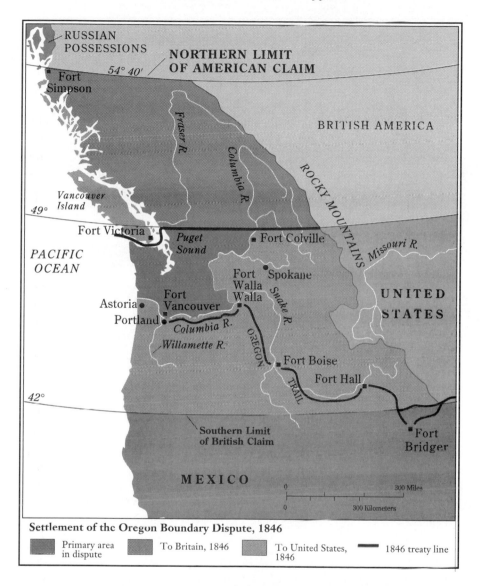

Settlement of the Oregon Boundary Dispute, 1846

| Primary area in dispute | | To Britain, 1846 | | To United States, 1846 | | 1846 treaty line |

But by 1844, he had been out of public office—and for the most part out of the public mind—for three years. What made his victory possible was the belief, expressed in the Democratic platform, "that the re-occupation of Oregon and the re-annexation of Texas at the earliest practicable period are great American measures." By combining the Oregon and Texas questions, the Democrats hoped to appeal to both Northern and Southern expansionists.

Western Trails to 1860

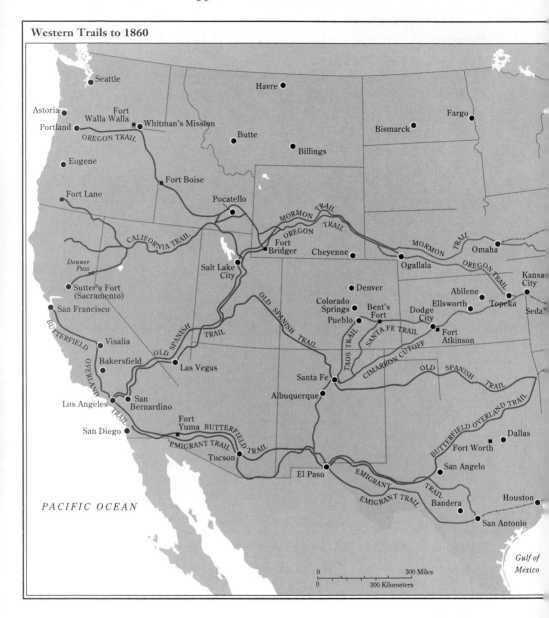

In a belated effort to catch up with public sentiment, Clay announced his qualified support for annexing Texas in midcampaign. But his tardy straddling probably cost him more votes than it gained. Polk carried the election by 170 electoral votes to 105, although his popular majority was less than 40,000. The Liberty party, running James G. Birney a second time, polled 62,000 votes (as compared with 7,000 in 1840), mainly from antislavery Whigs who had turned against Clay.

Polk may have been obscure, but he was intelligent and energetic; and he entered office with a clear set of goals and plans for attaining them. John Tyler accomplished the first of Polk's goals for him in the last days of his own presidency. Interpreting the election returns as a mandate for the annexation of Texas, the outgoing president won congressional approval for it in February 1845. Polk accepted the settlement Tyler had arranged, and in December 1845 Texas became a state.

Polk himself resolved the Oregon question, although not without difficulty and not without disappointing some of his supporters. Although publicly he seemed to support American title to all of the Oregon Territory, privately he was willing to compromise and set the boundary at the 49th parallel. But when the British minister in Washington rejected Polk's offer without even referring it to London, Polk again asserted the American claim to all of Oregon. There was loose talk of war on both sides of the Atlantic—talk that in the United States often took the form of the bellicose slogan "Fifty-four forty or fight!" (a reference to where the Americans hoped to draw the northern boundary of their part of Oregon). But neither country really wanted war. Finally, the British government offered to accept Polk's original proposal and divide the territory at the 49th parallel. The president, reluctant to alienate nationalists who wanted more, submitted the British proposal to the Senate without supporting it. No doubt to his relief, the Senate accepted the agreement; and on June 15, 1846, a treaty was signed fixing the boundary at the 49th parallel, where it remains today.

The Southwest and California

One of the reasons the Senate and the president had agreed so readily to the British proposal for settling the Oregon question was that new tensions were emerging in the Southwest—tensions that threatened to lead (and ultimately did lead) to a war with Mexico. As soon as the United States admitted Texas to statehood in 1845, the Mexican government broke diplomatic relations with Washington. To make matters worse, a dispute now developed over the boundary between Texas and Mexico. Texans claimed the Rio Grande as their western and southern border, a claim that would have added much of what is now New Mexico to Texas. Mexico still refused formally to concede the loss of Texas but argued nevertheless that the border had always been the Nueces River, to the north of the Rio Grande.

Polk recognized the Texas claim, and in the summer of 1845 he sent a small army under General Zachary Taylor to the Nueces line—to protect Texas, he claimed, against a possible Mexican invasion.

Only a few people lived in New Mexico, part of the area in dispute. Its trading center was the town of Santa Fe, 300 miles from the nearest settlements to the south and more than 1,000 miles from Mexico City and Vera Cruz. In the 1820s, the Mexican government had invited American traders into the region (just as it was inviting American settlers into Texas), hoping to speed development of the province. New Mexico, like Texas, soon began to become more American than Mexican. A flourishing commerce soon developed between Santa Fe and Independence, Missouri, with long caravans moving back and forth along the Santa Fe Trail, carrying manufactured goods west and bringing gold, silver, furs, and mules east in return. The Santa Fe trade, as it was called, further increased the American presence in New Mexico and signaled to advocates of expansion another direction for their efforts.

Americans were also increasing their interest in an even more distant province of Mexico: California. In this vast region lived members of several Western Indian tribes and perhaps 7,000 Mexicans, mostly descendants of Spanish colonists. Gradually, however, white Americans began to arrive: first maritime traders and captains of Pacific whaling ships, who stopped to barter goods or buy supplies; then merchants, who established stores, imported merchandise, and developed a profitable trade with the Mexicans and Indians; and finally pioneering farmers, who entered California from the east, by land, and settled in the Sacramento Valley. Some of these new settlers began to dream of bringing California into the United States.

President Polk soon came to share their dream and committed himself to acquiring both New Mexico and California for the United States. At the same time that he dispatched the troops under Taylor to the Nueces in Texas, he sent secret instructions to the commander of the Pacific naval squadron to seize the California ports if Mexico declared war. Representatives of the president quietly informed Americans in California that the United States would respond sympathetically to revolt against Mexican authority there.

Having appeared to prepare for war, Polk turned once more to diplomacy and dispatched a special minister, John Slidell, to try to buy off the Mexicans. But Mexican leaders rejected Slidell's offer to purchase the disputed territories. And on January 13, 1846, as soon as he heard the news, Polk ordered Taylor's army in Texas to move across the Nueces to the Rio Grande. For months, the Mexicans refused to fight. But finally, according to the accounts of American commanders, some Mexican troops crossed the Rio Grande and attacked a unit of American soldiers. Polk, who had been planning to request a declaration of war even without a military provocation, now told Congress: "War exists by the act of Mexico herself." On May 13, 1846, Congress declared war by votes of 40 to 2 in the Senate and 174 to 14 in the House.

The Mexican War

The war was not universally popular in the United States. Whig critics charged from the beginning that Polk had deliberately maneuvered the country into the conflict and that the border incident that had precipitated the declaration had been staged. Many argued that the hostilities with Mexico were draining resources and attention away from the more important issue of the Pacific Northwest; and when the United States finally reached its agreement with Britain on the Oregon question, opponents claimed that Polk had settled for less than he should have because he was preoccupied with Mexico. Opposition intensified as the war continued and as the public became aware of the casualties and expense.

American forces were generally successful in their campaigns against the Mexicans, but final victory did not come nearly as quickly as Polk had hoped. Through most of the war, the president himself planned the military strategy. He ordered Taylor to cross the Rio Grande and seize parts of northeastern Mexico, beginning with the city of Monterrey. Polk apparently thought Taylor could move south from Monterrey and, if necessary, threaten Mexico City itself. Taylor attacked Monterrey in September 1846 and, after a hard fight, captured it. But he let the Mexican garrison evacuate without pursuit. Polk now began to doubt the feasibility of his plan to move toward Mexico City. He feared that Taylor lacked the tactical skill for the campaign, and he became convinced that an advance south through the mountains would involve impossible supply problems. (He also feared Taylor's political ambitions, which extending the war might help advance.)

In the meantime, Polk ordered other offensives against New Mexico and California. In the summer of 1846, a small army under Colonel Stephen W. Kearny made the long march to Santa Fe and occupied the town with no opposition. Then he proceeded with a few hundred soldiers to California. There he joined a conflict already in progress that was being staged jointly by American settlers, a well-armed exploring party led by John C. Frémont, and the American navy: the so-called Bear Flag Revolution. Kearny brought

SCOTT'S ARMY IN MEXICO CITY General Winfield Scott leads an American army
into the capital of Mexico in September 1847, marking final U.S. victory in the
Mexican War. George W. Kendall of the New Orleans *Picayune* accompanied
Scott throughout the assault on the city.

the disparate American forces together under his command, and by the
autumn of 1846 he had completed the conquest of California.

The United States now controlled the two territories for which it had
gone to war. But Mexico still refused to end the hostilities or cede the
conquered territories. At this point, Polk and General Winfield Scott, the
commanding general of the army and its finest soldier, devised a plan to
force peace on the Mexicans—and, perhaps, gain even more new territory
for the United States. Scott would assemble an army at Tampico, and the
navy would transport it down the Mexican coast to Vera Cruz, where the
Americans would establish a base. From Vera Cruz, Scott would move west
along the National Highway to Mexico City. Scott conducted the campaign
brilliantly. He took Vera Cruz and began moving inland. With an army that
never numbered more than 14,000, he advanced 260 miles into enemy
territory, kept casualties low by making flanking movements instead of

frontal assaults, and finally achieved his objective without losing a battle. He inflicted a crushing defeat on the Mexican army at Cerro Gordo in the mountains and met no further resistance until he was within a few miles of Mexico City. After a hard fight on the outskirts of the capital, Americans occupied the city. A new Mexican government now took power and announced its willingness to negotiate a peace treaty.

President Polk was now growing thoroughly unclear about his objectives. He continued to encourage those who demanded that the United States annex much of Mexico itself. At the same time, concerned about the approaching presidential election, he was growing anxious to get the war finished quickly. Polk had sent to Mexico with the army a special presidential envoy who was authorized to negotiate a settlement. The agent, Nicholas Trist, concluded an agreement with the new Mexican government on February 2, 1848: the Treaty of Guadalupe Hidalgo. Mexico agreed to cede California and New Mexico to the United States and acknowledge the Rio Grande as the boundary of Texas. In return, the United States promised to assume the claims of its citizens against Mexico and pay the Mexicans $15 million. When the treaty reached Washington, Polk faced a dilemma. Trist had obtained most of Polk's original demands, but he had not satisfied the new, more expansive dreams of acquiring additional territory in Mexico itself. Polk angrily claimed that Trist had violated his instructions, but he soon realized that he had no choice but to accept the treaty. Some ardent expansionists were demanding that he hold out for annexation of—in a phrase widely bandied about at the time—"All Mexico!" Antislavery leaders, in the meantime, were charging that the demands for acquisition of Mexico were part of a Southern scheme to extend slavery to new realms. To silence this bitter and potentially destructive debate, Polk submitted the Trist treaty to the Senate, which approved it by a vote of 38 to 14. The war was over, and America had gained a vast new territory. But it had also acquired a new set of troubling and divisive issues.

A NEW SECTIONAL CRISIS

James Polk tried to be a president whose policies transcended sectional divisions. But conciliating the sections was becoming an ever more difficult task, and Polk gradually earned the enmity of Northerners and Westerners alike, who believed his policies (and particularly his enthusiasm for territorial expansion in the Southwest) favored the South at their expense.

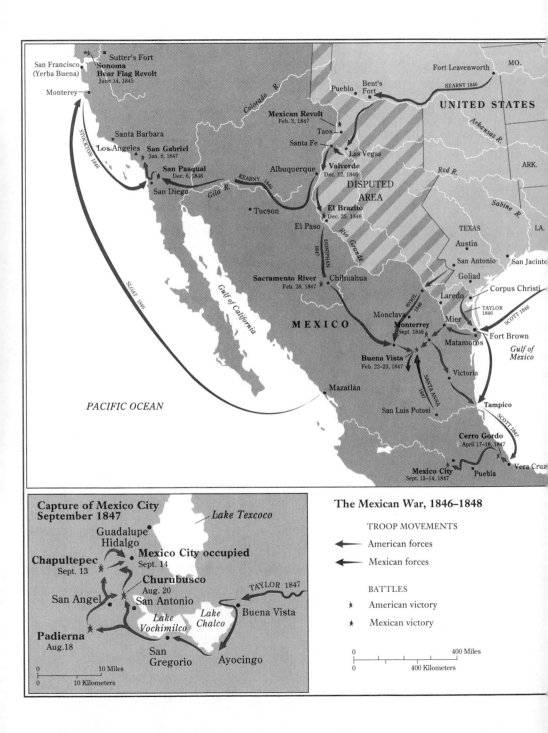

The Mexican War, 1846–1848

The Sectional Debate

In August 1846, while the Mexican War was still in progress, Polk asked Congress to appropriate $2 million for purchasing peace with Mexico. Representative David Wilmot of Pennsylvania, an antislavery Democrat, introduced an amendment to the appropriation bill prohibiting slavery in any territory acquired from Mexico. The so-called Wilmot Proviso passed the House but failed in the Senate. It would be called up, debated, and voted on repeatedly for years. Southern militants, in the meantime, had a plan of their own. They contended that since the territories belonged to the entire nation, all Americans had equal rights in them, including the right to move their slaves (which they considered property) into them.

President Polk supported a proposal to extend the Missouri Compromise (36°30′) through the new territories to the Pacific coast, banning slavery north of the line and permitting it south of the line. Others supported another compromise, originally called "squatter sovereignty" and later awarded the more dignified title of "popular sovereignty," which would allow the people of each territory (acting through their legislature) to decide the status of slavery there. The debate over these various proposals dragged on for many months. By the time Polk left office in 1849, nothing had been resolved.

The presidential campaign of 1848 dampened the controversy for a time as both Democrats and Whigs tried to avoid the slavery question. When Polk declined to run again, the Democrats nominated Lewis Cass of Michigan, a dull, aging party regular. The Whigs nominated a military hero with no political record, General Zachary Taylor of Louisiana. Opponents of slavery found the choice of candidates unsatisfying, and out of their discontent emerged the Free-Soil party, which drew from the existing Liberty party and the antislavery wings of the Whig and Democratic parties and which endorsed the Wilmot Proviso. Its candidate was former president Martin Van Buren.

Taylor won a narrow victory. But while Van Buren failed to carry a single state, he polled an impressive 291,000 votes (10 percent of the total), and the Free-Soilers elected ten members to Congress. Van Buren probably drew enough Democratic votes away from Cass, particularly in New York, to throw the election to Taylor.

Taylor and the Territories

Zachary Taylor was a Southerner and a slaveholder, but from his long years in the army he had acquired a national outlook. He recognized the impor-

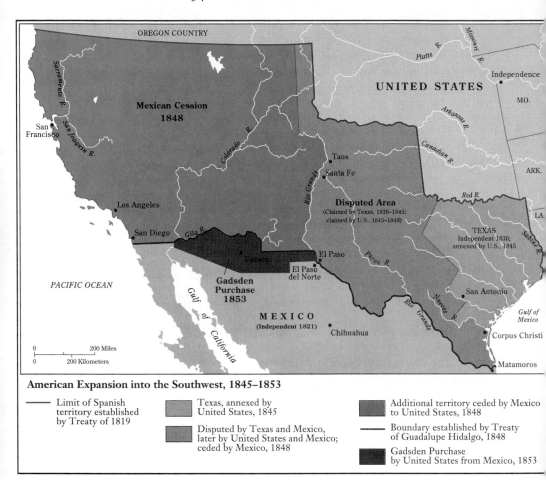

American Expansion into the Southwest, 1845–1853

—— Limit of Spanish territory established by Treaty of 1819	▨ Texas, annexed by United States, 1845
	▨ Disputed by Texas and Mexico, later by United States and Mexico; ceded by Mexico, 1848
▨ Additional territory ceded by Mexico to United States, 1848	
—— Boundary established by Treaty of Guadalupe Hidalgo, 1848	
▨ Gadsden Purchase by United States from Mexico, 1853	

tance of dealing with the problems of the newly acquired territories, which—in the absence of territorial governments—were still being administered by military officials. There was particular pressure to establish a new government in California, for that territory was experiencing a remarkable boom. In January 1848, gold was accidentally discovered in the Sacramento Valley. As word of the strike spread, thousands of Westerners, fired by dreams of quick riches, moved to the area to stake claims. By the end of the summer of 1848, news of the strike had reached the Eastern states and Europe and sparked an even greater gold rush. From all over the United States and from throughout the world, thousands of "forty-niners" poured into California—more than 80,000 in 1849 alone. By the end of that year, the territory had a population of roughly 100,000, enough to qualify it for statehood.

President Taylor believed statehood could become the solution to the issue of slavery in the territories. As long as the new lands were territories, the federal government was responsible for deciding the fate of slavery within them. But once they became states, their own governments would be able to settle the slavery question. Taylor ordered military officials in California and New Mexico to speed up the statehood movements. California promptly adopted a constitution that prohibited slavery, and in December 1849 Taylor asked Congress to admit California as a free state. New Mexico, he said, should be granted statehood when it was ready and should, like California, be permitted to decide for itself what it wanted to do about slavery. But Congress balked.

That was partly because of several other controversies concerning slavery that were complicating the debate over the territories. One was the effort of antislavery forces to abolish slavery in the District of Columbia, a movement bitterly resisted by Southerners. Another was the emergence of personal liberty laws in Northern states, which barred courts and police officers from helping to return runaway slaves to their owners. In response, Southerners demanded a stringent national fugitive slave law. Still another controversy involved a border dispute between Texas and New Mexico, as well as Texas's resentment at the failure of the federal government to take over the debts it had accumulated during its brief independence. But the biggest obstacle to the president's program was the white South's fear that two new free states would be added to the Northern majority. The number of free and slave states was equal in 1849—fifteen each. But the admission of California would upset the balance; and New Mexico, Oregon, and Utah might upset it further, leaving the South in a minority in the Senate, as it already was in the House.

Tempers were now rising to dangerous levels. Even many otherwise moderate Southern leaders were beginning to talk about secession from the Union. In the North, every state legislature but one adopted a resolution demanding the prohibition of slavery in the territories.

The Compromise of 1850

Faced with this unprecedented crisis, moderates and unionists spent the winter of 1849–1850 trying to frame a great compromise. The aging Henry Clay, who was spearheading the effort, believed that no compromise could last unless it settled all the issues in dispute between the sections. As a result, he took several measures which had been proposed separately, combined them into a single piece of legislation, and presented it to the Senate on January 29, 1850. The bill had five provisions. It proposed (1) that California be admitted as a free state; (2) that, in the rest of the lands acquired from Mexico, territorial governments be formed without restrictions on slavery; (3) that Texas yield in its boundary dispute with New Mexico and that the federal government compensate it by taking over its public debt; (4) that the slave trade, but not slavery itself, be abolished in the District of Columbia; and (5) that a new and more effective fugitive slave law be passed. These resolutions launched a debate that raged for seven months—both in Congress and throughout the nation. The debate occurred in two phases, the differences between which revealed much about how American politics was changing in the 1850s.

In the first phase of the debate, the dominant voices in Congress were those of old men—national leaders who still remembered Jefferson, Adams, and other founders—who argued for or against the compromise on the basis of broad ideals. Clay himself, seventy-three years old in 1850, was the most prominent of these spokesmen. He made a broad plea for sectional conciliation and appealed to shared sentiments of nationalism.

Early in March, another of the older leaders—John C. Calhoun, sixty-eight years old and so ill that he had to sit grimly in his seat while a colleague read his speech for him—joined the debate. Calhoun insisted that the North grant the South equal rights in the territories, that it agree to observe the laws concerning fugitive slaves, that it cease attacking slavery, and that it accept an amendment to the Constitution guaranteeing a balance of power between the sections. The amendment would provide for the election of dual presidents, one from the North and one from the South, each possessing a veto power. Calhoun was making radical demands that had no chance of passage. But he was expressing his belief in the importance of saving the Union; and like Clay, he was offering what he considered a comprehensive, permanent solution to the sectional problem—even if that solution would have required an abject surrender by the North.

After Calhoun came the third of the elder statesmen, the sixty-eight-year-old Daniel Webster. His "Seventh of March Address" was probably the greatest oratorical effort of his long career. Still nourishing presidential ambitions, he sought to calm angry passions and to rally Northern moderates to support Clay's compromise.

After six months of debate, however—six months dominated by ringing appeals to the memory of the founders, to nationalism, to idealism—the effort to win approval of the compromise failed. In July, Congress defeated the Clay proposal. And with that, the controversy moved into its second phase, in which a very different cast of characters would predominate. Clay, ill and tired, left Washington to spend the summer resting in the mountains. He would return, but never with his old vigor; he died in 1852. Calhoun had died even before the vote in July. And Webster in the course of the summer accepted a new appointment as secretary of state, thus removing himself from the Senate and from the debate.

In place of these leaders, a new, younger group now emerged. There was William H. Seward of New York, forty-nine years old, a wily political operator who staunchly opposed the proposed compromise. The ideals of Union were to him less important than the issue of eliminating slavery. There was Jefferson Davis of Mississippi, forty-two years old, a representative not of the old aristocratic South of Calhoun but of the new, cotton South—a hard, newly settled, and rapidly growing region. To him, the slavery issue was not only one of principles and ideals but also one of economic self-interest.

Most important of all, there was Stephen A. Douglas, a thirty-seven-year-old Democratic senator from Illinois. A Westerner from a rapidly growing state, he was an open spokesman for the economic needs of his section—and especially for the construction of railroads. His was a career devoted not to any broad national goals, as Clay's, Webster's, and even Calhoun's had often been, but devoted frankly to sectional gain and personal self-promotion.

The new leaders of the Senate were able, where the old leaders were not, to produce a compromise in 1850. In part, they were assisted by the great prosperity of the early 1850s, the result of expanding foreign trade, the flow of gold from California, and a boom in railroad construction. Conservative economic interests everywhere wanted to end the sectional dispute and concentrate on economic growth. Progress toward the compromise was also furthered by the disappearance of the most powerful obstacle to it: the president. President Taylor had been adamant that only after California and possibly New Mexico were admitted as states could other measures be discussed. He had threatened not only to veto any measure that diverged from this proposal but to use force against the South (even to lead the troops in person) if they attempted to secede. But on July 9, 1850, Taylor suddenly died—the victim of a violent stomach disorder following an attack of heat prostration. He was succeeded by Millard Fillmore of New York—a dull, handsome, dignified man who understood the political importance of

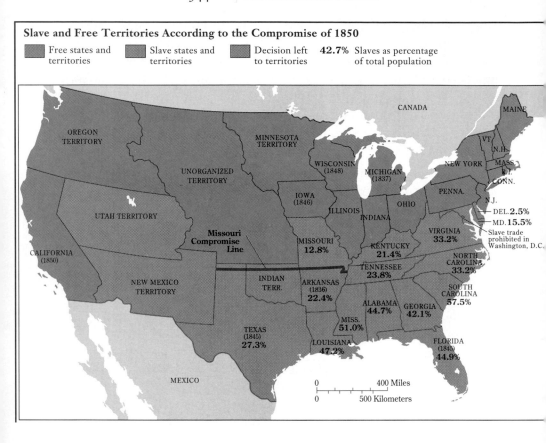

Slave and Free Territories According to the Compromise of 1850

Free states and territories | Slave states and territories | Decision left to territories | 42.7% Slaves as percentage of total population

flexibility. He supported the compromise and used his powers of persuasion to swing Northern Whigs into line.

The new leaders also benefited, however, from their own pragmatic tactics. Douglas's first step, after the departure of Clay, was to break up the "omnibus bill" that Clay had envisioned as a great, comprehensive solution to the sectional crisis and introduce instead a series of separate measures to be voted on one by one. Thus representatives of different sections could support those elements of the compromise favorable to them and could abstain from voting on or could vote against those they opposed. Douglas also gained support by avoiding the grand appeals to patriotism of Clay and Webster and resorting instead to complicated backroom deals linking the compromise to such nonideological matters as the sale of government bonds and the construction of railroads. As a result of his efforts, by mid-September all the components of the compromise had been enacted by both houses of

Congress and signed by the president. The outcome was a great if clouded victory for Douglas and the forces of conciliation. The Compromise of 1850, unlike the Missouri Compromise thirty years before, was not a product of widespread agreement on common national ideals. It was, rather, a triumph of self-interest that had not resolved the underlying problems. Still, members of Congress hailed the measure as a triumph of statesmanship; and Millard Fillmore, signing it, called it a just settlement of the sectional problem, "in its character final and irrevocable."

THE CRISES OF THE 1850S

For a few years after the Compromise of 1850, the sectional conflict seemed briefly to be forgotten amid booming prosperity and growth. But the tensions between North and South remained, and the crisis continued to smolder until—in 1854—it once more burst into the open.

The Uneasy Truce

Both major parties endorsed the Compromise of 1850 in their platforms in 1852, and both parties nominated presidential candidates unlikely to arouse passionate opposition in either North or South. The Democrats chose the obscure New Hampshire politician Franklin Pierce and the Whigs the military hero General Winfield Scott, a man whose political views were so undefined that no one knew what he thought about the Compromise.

The gingerly way in which party leaders dealt with the sectional question could not prevent its divisive influence from intruding on the election. The Whigs were the principal victims. Already plagued by the defections of those antislavery Northerners who had formed the Free-Soil party in 1846, they alienated still more party members—the "Conscience" Whigs—by straddling the issue of slavery and refusing openly to condemn it. In the meantime, the Free-Soil party was gaining in numbers and influence in the North; its presidential candidate, John P. Hale, repudiated the Compromise of 1850. The divisions among the Whigs helped produce a victory for the Democrats in 1852.

Franklin Pierce, a charming, amiable man of no particular distinction, attempted to maintain party—and national—harmony by avoiding divisive issues, and particularly by avoiding the issue of slavery. But those issues arose despite him. They arose, in particular, because of Northern opposition to the Fugitive Slave Act, opposition which intensified after 1850 when Southerners began appearing occasionally in Northern states to pursue fugitives or to claim as slaves blacks who had been living for years in Northern communities. So fervently did many opponents of slavery resent such efforts that mobs formed in many cities to prevent enforcement of the law. Several Northern states also passed new personal liberty laws, which attempted to use state authority to interfere with the deportation of fugitive slaves. The supreme court of Wisconsin, in *Ableman* v. *Booth* (1857), even declared the federal Fugitive Slave Act void and ignored the United States Supreme Court when it overruled the Wisconsin ruling. White Southerners watched with growing anger and alarm as the one element of the Compromise of 1850 that they had considered a victory became virtually meaningless as a result of the extralegal device of mobs and through legal efforts of dubious constitutionality.

"Young America"

One of the ways Franklin Pierce hoped to dampen sectional controversy was through his support of a movement in the Democratic party known as "Young America." Its adherents saw the expansion of American democracy throughout the world as a diversion from what they considered the transitory issue of slavery. The great liberal and nationalist revolutions of 1848 in Europe stirred them to dream of a republican Europe with governments based on the model of the United States. They dreamed as well of expanding American commerce in the Pacific and acquiring new territories in the Western Hemisphere.

Few Americans in either section objected to displays of nationalism. But efforts to extend the nation's domain could not avoid becoming entangled with the sectional crisis. Pierce had been pursuing unsuccessful diplomatic attempts to buy Cuba from Spain (efforts begun in 1848 by Polk). But in 1854 a group of his envoys sent him a private document from Ostend, Belgium, making the case for seizing Cuba by force. When the Ostend Manifesto, as it became known, was leaked to the public, it enraged many antislavery Northerners, who charged the administration with conspiring to bring a new slave state into the Union.

The South, for its part, opposed all efforts to acquire new territory that would not support a slave system. The kingdom of Hawaii agreed to join the United States in 1854, but the treaty died in the Senate because it contained a clause prohibiting slavery in the islands. A powerful movement to annex Canada to the United States—a movement that had the support of many Canadians eager for access to American markets—similarly foundered, at least in part because of slavery.

The Kansas-Nebraska Controversy

What fully revived the sectional crisis, however, was the same issue that had produced it in the first place: slavery in the territories. By the 1850s, the line of white settlement had moved west to the great bend of the Missouri River. Beyond the boundaries of Missouri, Iowa, and what is now Minnesota stretched a great expanse of plains, which most white Americans had always believed was unfit for cultivation (it was widely known as the Great American Desert) and which the nation had therefore assigned to the Indian tribes it had dislodged from the more fertile lands to the east. Now it was becoming apparent that large sections of this region were, in fact, suitable for farming. In the states of the Old Northwest, therefore, prospective settlers urged the government to open the area to them, provide territorial governments, and—despite the solemn assurance the United States had earlier given the Indians of the sanctity of their reservations—dislodge the tribes so as to make room for white settlers. There was relatively little opposition from any segment of white society to the violation of Indian rights proposed by these demands. But the interest in further settlement raised two issues that did prove highly divisive and that gradually became entwined with each other: railroads and slavery.

As the nation expanded westward and as the problem of communication between the older states and the so-called trans-Mississippi West (the areas west of the Mississippi River) became more and more critical, broad support began to emerge for building a transcontinental railroad. The problem was where to place it—and in particular, where to locate the railroad's eastern terminus. Northerners favored Chicago, the rapidly growing capital of the free states of the Northwest. Southerners supported St. Louis, Memphis, or New Orleans—all located in slave states. The transcontinental railroad, in other words, was—like nearly everything else in the 1850s—becoming entangled in sectionalism. It had become a prize that both North and South were struggling to secure.

Pierce's secretary of war, Jefferson Davis of Mississippi, removed one obstacle to a Southern route. Surveys indicated that a road with a Southern terminus would have to pass through an area in Mexican territory. But Davis dispatched James Gadsden, a Southern railroad builder, to buy the region in question from Mexico. In 1853 Gadsden persuaded the Mexican government to accept $10 million in exchange for a strip of land that today comprises part of Arizona and New Mexico, the so-called Gadsden Purchase. But the acquisition simply intensified the sectional debate.

Stephen Douglas's strong interest in a transcontinental railroad led him to introduce in Congress a fateful legislative act that finally destroyed the Compromise of 1850. As a senator from Illinois, a resident of Chicago, and the acknowledged leader of Northwestern Democrats, Douglas naturally wanted the transcontinental railroad for his own city and section. He also realized the strength of the principal argument against the Northern route: that west of the Mississippi it would run mostly through country largely inhabited by Indians. As a result, he introduced a bill in January 1854 to organize (and thus open to white settlement) a huge new territory, known as Nebraska, west of Iowa and Missouri.

Douglas knew the South would oppose his bill because it would prepare the way for a new free state; the proposed territory was in the area of the Louisiana Purchase north of the Missouri Compromise line (36°30′) and hence closed to slavery. In an effort to make the measure acceptable to Southerners, Douglas inserted a provision that the status of slavery in the territory would be determined by the territorial legislature—that is, according to popular sovereignty. In theory, the region could choose to open itself to slavery (although few believed it actually would). When Southern Democrats demanded more, Douglas agreed to two changes in the bill: an additional clause explicitly repealing the antislavery provision of the Missouri Compromise (which the popular-sovereignty provision of his original bill had done implicitly), and a modification creating two territories, Nebraska and Kansas, instead of one, hence establishing a new territory (Kansas) that might become a slave state. In its final form the measure was known as the Kansas-Nebraska Act. President Pierce supported the bill; and after a strenuous debate, it became law in May 1854 with the unanimous support of the South and the partial support of Northern Democrats.

No piece of legislation in American history produced so many immediate, sweeping, and ominous changes. It destroyed the Whig party, which disappeared almost entirely by 1856, and along with it a conservative, nationalistic influence in American politics. It divided the Northern Democrats (many of whom were appalled at the repeal of the Missouri Compromise, which they considered an almost sacred part of the fabric of the Union) and drove many of them from the party.

Most important of all, it spurred the creation of a new party that was frankly sectional in composition and creed. People in both major parties who opposed Douglas's bill began to call themselves Anti-Nebraska Democrats and Anti-Nebraska Whigs. In 1854, they formed a new organization and named it the Republican party. In the elections of that year, the Republicans won enough seats in Congress to be able to organize the House of Representatives (with the help of the Know-Nothings) and won control of several Northern state governments.

"Bleeding Kansas"

Events in Kansas itself in the next two years increased the popular excitement in the North. White settlers from both the North and the South began moving into the territory almost immediately after the passage of the Kansas-Nebraska Act, and in the spring of 1855, elections were held for a territorial legislature. There were only about 1,500 legal voters in Kansas by then, but more than 6,000 people voted. That was because thousands of Missourians, some traveling in armed bands, had crossed into Kansas to vote. The result was that the proslavery forces elected a majority to the legislature, which proceeded immediately to enact a series of laws legalizing slavery. Outraged free-staters defied the legislature and elected delegates to a constitutional convention, which met at Topeka and adopted a constitution excluding slavery. They then chose their own governor and legislature and petitioned Congress for statehood. President Pierce denounced them as traitors and threw the full support of the federal government behind the proslavery territorial legislature.

A few months later a proslavery federal marshal assembled a large posse, consisting mostly of Missourians, to arrest the free-state leaders, who had set up their headquarters in Lawrence. The posse made the arrests and looted the town, killing several free-staters in the melee. Retribution came quickly. Among the most fervent opponents of slavery in Kansas was John Brown, a fiercely committed zealot who considered himself an instrument of God's will to destroy slavery. He gathered six followers and in one night murdered five proslavery settlers (as retribution for the five free-staters killed in Lawrence); he left their mutilated bodies to discourage other supporters of slavery from entering Kansas. The episode was known as the Pottawatomie Massacre; and its result was more civil strife in Kansas—irregular, guerrilla warfare conducted by armed bands, some of them more interested in land claims or loot than in ideologies. People in each section—Northerners and Southerners alike—came to believe that the events in

Kansas illustrated (and were caused by) the aggressive designs of the other section. Thus "Bleeding Kansas" became a symbol of the sectional controversy.

Another symbol soon appeared, in the United States Senate. In May 1856, Charles Sumner of Massachusetts rose to give a speech entitled "The Crime Against Kansas." Handsome, eloquent, humorless, and passionately doctrinaire, Sumner was a militant opponent of slavery. And in his speech, he gave particular attention to his colleague, Senator Andrew P. Butler of South Carolina, an outspoken defender of slavery. The South Carolinian was, Sumner claimed, the "Don Quixote" of slavery, having "chosen a mistress . . . who, though ugly to others, is always lovely to him, though polluted in the sight of the world, is chaste in his sight . . . the harlot slavery."

The pointedly sexual references and the general viciousness of the speech enraged Butler's nephew, Preston Brooks, a member of the House of Representatives from South Carolina, who resolved to deliver a public chastisement. Several days after the speech, Brooks approached Sumner at his desk in the Senate chamber during a recess, raised a heavy cane, and began beating him repeatedly on the head and shoulders. Sumner, trapped in his chair, rose in agony with such strength that he tore the desk from the bolts holding it to the floor; then he collapsed, bleeding and unconscious. So severe were his injuries that he was unable to return to the Senate for four years, during which time his state refused to replace him. He became a potent symbol throughout the North—a martyr to the barbarism of the South. Preston Brooks became a symbol too. Censured by the House, he resigned his seat, returned to South Carolina, and stood successfully for reelection. He had become a Southern hero. Like Sumner, he served as evidence of how strong the antagonism between North and South had become.

The Free-Soil Ideology

What had happened to produce such deep hostility between the two sections? There were, obviously, important social and economic differences between the North and the South and important disagreements, particularly over slavery in the territories. But neither the differences nor the disagreements would have been enough to disrupt the Union if they had not become tied up with other, larger concerns on both sides. As the nation expanded and political power grew more dispersed, the North and the South each became concerned with ensuring that its vision of America's future would be the dominant one. And those visions were becoming—partly as a result of internal developments within the sections themselves, partly because of each region's conceptions (and misconceptions) of what was happening outside it—increasingly distinct and increasingly rigid.

In the North, assumptions about the proper structure of society came to center on the belief in "free soil" and "free labor." The abolitionists generated some support for their argument that slavery was a moral evil and must be eliminated. Theirs, however, was never the dominant voice of the North. Instead, an increasing number of Northerners, gradually becoming a majority, came to believe that the existence of slavery was dangerous not because of what it did to blacks but because of what it threatened to do to whites. At the heart of American democracy, they argued, was the right of all citizens to own property, to control their own labor, and to have access to opportunities for advancement. The ideal society, in other words, was one of small-scale capitalism, in which everyone could aspire to a stake and to upward mobility. According to this vision, the South was the antithesis of democracy. It was a closed, static society, in which the slave system preserved an entrenched aristocracy and common whites had no opportunity to improve themselves. More than that, the South was a backward society—decadent, lazy, dilapidated. While the North was growing and prospering, displaying thrift, industry, and a commitment to progress, the South was stagnating, rejecting the Northern values of individualism and progress. The South was, Northern free-laborites further maintained, engaged in a conspiracy to extend slavery throughout the nation and thus to destroy the openness of Northern capitalism and replace it with the closed, aristocratic system of the South. This "slave power conspiracy," as it came to be known, threatened the future of every white laborer and property owner in the North. The only solution was to fight the spread of slavery and work for the day when the nation's democratic (i.e., free-labor) ideals would extend to all sections of the country—the day of the victory of what Northerners called "Freedom National."

This ideology lay at the heart of the new Republican party. There were abolitionists and others in the party who sincerely believed in the rights of blacks to freedom and citizenship. More important, however, were those who cared principally about the threat they believed slavery posed to white labor and to individual opportunity. This ideology also strengthened the commitment of Republicans to the Union. Since the idea of continued growth and progress was central to the free-labor vision, the prospect of dismemberment of the nation—a diminution of America's size and economic power—was unthinkable.

The Proslavery Argument

In the South, in the meantime, a very different ideology was emerging—one that was entirely incompatible with the free-labor ideology in the North. It emerged out of a rapid hardening of position among Southern whites on the issue of slavery.

As late as the early 1830s, a substantial number of Southern whites had harbored reservations about slavery. By the mid-1830s, however, this ambivalence about slavery was beginning to be replaced by a militant defense of the system. In part, the change was a result of events in the South. The Nat Turner uprising in 1831 terrified whites throughout the region, and they grew more determined than ever to make slavery secure. There was also an economic incentive to defend the system. With the expansion of the cotton economy into the Deep South, slavery—which had begun to seem unprofitable in many areas of the upper South—now became lucrative once again.

But the change was also a result of events in the North, and particularly of the growth of the Garrisonian abolitionist movement, with its strident attacks on Southern society. The popularity of Harriet Beecher Stowe's *Uncle Tom's Cabin* (see p. 324) was perhaps the most glaring evidence of the success of those attacks, but other abolitionist writings had been antagonizing white Southerners for years.

In response to these pressures, a number of white Southerners elaborated an intellectual defense of slavery. It began as early as 1832, when Professor Thomas R. Dew of the College of William and Mary outlined the case for slavery. It matured in 1852, when apologists for slavery summarized their views in an anthology that gave their ideology its name: *The Pro-Slavery Argument*. John C. Calhoun had stated the essence of their argument in 1837: Southerners should stop apologizing for slavery as a necessary evil and defend it as "a good—a positive good." It was good for the slaves, the Southern apologists argued, because, as inferior people, blacks needed the guidance of white masters; the slaves were, moreover, better off—better fed, clothed, and housed, and more secure—than Northern factory workers. Slavery was good for Southern society as a whole because it was the only way the two races could live together in peace. It was good for the entire country because the Southern economy, based on slavery, was the key to the prosperity of the nation.

Above all, Southern apologists argued, slavery was good because it served as the basis for the Southern way of life—a way of life superior to any other in the United States, perhaps in the world. White Southerners looking at the North saw a society that they believed was abandoning traditional American values and replacing them with a spirit of greed, debauchery, and destructiveness. "The masses of the North are venal, corrupt, covetous, mean and selfish," wrote one Southerner. Others wrote with horror of the factory system and the crowded, pestilential cities filled with unruly immigrants. The South, in contrast, was a stable, orderly society, operating at a slow and human pace. It had a labor system that avoided the feuds between capital and labor plaguing the North, a system that protected the welfare of its workers, a system that allowed the aristocracy to enjoy a refined and accomplished cultural life. It was, in short, as nearly perfect as any human civilization could become, an ideal social order in which all elements of the population were secure and content.

The defense of slavery rested, too, on increasingly elaborate arguments about the biological inferiority of African-Americans, who were, white Southerners argued, inherently unfit to take care of themselves, let alone exercise the rights of citizenship. And just as abolitionist arguments drew strength from Protestant theology in the North, the proslavery defense mobilized the Protestant clergy in the South to give the institution a religious and biblical justification.

By the 1850s, Southern leaders had not only committed themselves to a militant proslavery ideology. They had also become convinced that they must silence their opponents. Some Southern critics of slavery found it advisable to leave the region. Beginning in 1835 (when a Charleston mob destroyed sacks containing abolitionist literature in the city post office), Southern postmasters generally refused to deliver antislavery mail. Southern state legislatures passed resolutions demanding that Northern states suppress the "incendiary" agitation of the abolitionists. Southern representatives even managed for a time to impose a "gag rule" (adopted in 1836, repealed in 1844) on Congress, according to which all antislavery petitions would be tabled without being read. This growing intolerance of criticism of slavery further encouraged those Northerners who warned of the "slave power conspiracy" against their liberties.

Buchanan and Depression

It was in this unpromising climate—with the nation aroused by the Brooks assault and the continuing violence in Kansas, and with each section becoming increasingly militant in support of its own ideology—that the presidential campaign of 1856 began. Democratic party leaders wanted a candidate who had not made many enemies and who was not closely associated with the explosive question of "Bleeding Kansas." They chose James Puchanan of Pennsylvania, a reliable party stalwart who as minister to England had been safely out of the country during the recent controversies. The Republicans, participating in their first presidential contest, denounced the Kansas-Nebraska Act and the expansion of slavery but approved a program of internal improvements, thus combining the idealism of antislavery with the economic aspirations of the North. As eager as the Democrats to present a safe candidate, the Republicans nominated John C. Frémont, who had made a national reputation as an explorer of the Far West and who had no political record. In the meantime, the Native American, or Know-Nothing, party was beginning to break apart. At its convention, many Northern delegates withdrew because the platform was not sufficiently firm in opposing the expansion of slavery. The remaining delegates nominated former president Millard Fillmore. His candidacy was endorsed as well by a sad remnant of the Whig party, those who could not bring themselves to support either Buchanan or Frémont.

After a heated, even frenzied campaign, Buchanan won a narrow victory. He polled a plurality but not a majority of the popular votes: 1,833,000 to 1,340,000 for Frémont and 872,000 for Fillmore. A slight shift of votes in Pennsylvania and Illinois would have thrown those states into the Republican column and elected Frémont. More significant, perhaps, was that Frémont, who attracted virtually no votes at all in the South, received a third of all votes cast. In the North, he had outpolled all other candidates.

Buchanan had been in public life for more than forty years at the time of his inauguration; he was, at age sixty-five, the oldest president, except for William Henry Harrison, ever to have taken office. Whether because of age and physical infirmities or because of a more fundamental weakness of character, he became a painfully timid and indecisive president at a time when the nation cried out for strong, effective leadership.

In the year Buchanan took over, a financial panic struck the country, followed by a depression that lasted several years. European demand for American food had risen during the Crimean War of 1854–1856. When that demand fell off, agricultural prices declined. In the North, the depression strengthened the Republican party. Distressed manufacturers and farmers came to believe that the hard times were the result of the unsound policies of Southern-controlled Democratic administrations. They advocated a high protective tariff (the tariff had been lowered again in 1857), a homestead act, and internal improvements—all measures the South opposed. The frustrated economic interests of the North were being drawn into an alliance with antislavery elements and thus into the Republican party.

The Dred Scott *Decision*

The Supreme Court of the United States now projected itself into the sectional controversy with one of the most controversial decisions in its history—its ruling in the case of *Dred Scott* v. *Sanford*, handed down two days after Buchanan was inaugurated. Dred Scott was a Missouri slave, once owned by an army surgeon who had taken Scott with him to Illinois, a free state, and to a part of Wisconsin Territory where slavery was forbidden by the Missouri Compromise. Scott was persuaded by some abolitionists to bring suit in the Missouri courts for his freedom on the ground that residence in a free territory had made him a free man. The state supreme court decided against him. By then, the surgeon had died and ownership of Scott had been transferred to his widow's brother, J. F. A. Sanford, an abolitionist who lived in New York. Now Scott's lawyers could get the case into the federal courts on the ground that the suit lay between citizens of different states. Regardless of the final decision, Scott would be freed; his abolitionist owners would not keep him a slave. The case was intended not to determine Scott's future but to secure a federal decision on the status of slavery in the territories.

The Supreme Court was so divided that it was unable to issue a single ruling on the case. It released separate decisions on each of the major issues it had considered. Each of the justices, moreover, wrote a separate opinion. The thrust of the rulings, however, was a defeat for the antislavery movement and an affirmation of the South's argument that the Constitution guaranteed the existence of slavery. Chief Justice Roger Taney, who wrote one of the majority opinions, declared that Scott was not a citizen of Missouri or of the United States and hence could not bring a suit in the federal courts. According to Taney, no black could qualify as a citizen; indeed, blacks had virtually no rights at all under the Constitution. He went on to argue that Scott's sojourn in the North had not affected his status as a slave. Slaves were property, said Taney, and the Fifth Amendment prohibited Congress from taking property without "due process of law." Consequently, Congress possessed no authority to pass a law depriving persons of their slave property in the territories. The Missouri Compromise, therefore, had always been unconstitutional.

The ruling did nothing to challenge the right of an individual state to prohibit slavery within its borders, but the statement that the federal government was powerless to act on the issue was a drastic and startling one. Few judicial opinions have stirred as much popular excitement. Southern whites were elated: the highest tribunal in the land had sanctioned parts of the most extreme Southern argument. In the North, the decision produced widespread dismay. Republicans threatened that when they won control of the national government, they would reverse the decision—by "packing" the Court with new members.

Deadlock over Kansas

President Buchanan, who endorsed the *Dred Scott* decision, believed that the best solution to the controversy was to admit Kansas to the Union as a slave state. In response to his urgings, the proslavery territorial legislature called an election for delegates to a constitutional convention. The free-state residents refused to participate, claiming that the legislature had discriminated against them in drawing district lines. As a result, the proslavery forces won control of the convention, which met in 1857 at Lecompton, framed a constitution legalizing slavery, and refused to give voters a chance to reject it. When an election for a new territorial legislature was called, the antislavery groups turned out to vote and won a majority. The new legislature promptly submitted the Lecompton constitution to the voters, who rejected it by more than 10,000 votes.

Both sides had resorted to fraud and violence, but it was clear nevertheless that a majority of the people of Kansas opposed slavery. Buchanan, however, ignored the evidence and pressured Congress to admit Kansas under the Lecompton constitution. Stephen A. Douglas and other Western Democrats refused to support the president; and while Buchanan's proposal passed the Senate, Western Democrats helped block it in the House. Finally, in April 1858, Congress approved a compromise: the Lecompton constitution would be submitted to the voters of Kansas again. If the document won approval, Kansas would be admitted to the Union; if it was rejected, statehood would be postponed until the population of the territory reached the level required for a representative in Congress. Again, Kansas voters decisively rejected the Lecompton constitution. Not until the closing months of Buchanan's administration in 1861, when a number of Southern states had withdrawn from the Union, did Kansas enter the Union—as a free state.

The Emergence of Lincoln

Given the gravity of the sectional crisis, the congressional elections of 1858 took on a special importance. Of particular note was the United States Senate election in Illinois, which pitted Stephen A. Douglas, the most prominent Northern Democrat, against Abraham Lincoln, the most skillful politician in the Republican party.

THE LINCOLN-DOUGLAS DEBATES, ILLINOIS, 1858 The still clean-shaven Abraham Lincoln lost in his 1858 bid to replace Stephen Douglas as United States senator from Illinois, but he gained wide national recognition for his performance in the debates between the two candidates during the campaign.

Lincoln had been the leading Whig in Illinois and was now the state's leading Republican. But since he was not a national figure comparable to Douglas, he sought to increase his visibility by engaging Douglas in a series of debates. The Lincoln-Douglas debates attracted enormous crowds and received wide attention. By the time they ended, Lincoln had become nationally prominent.

The content of the debates revealed the deep disagreements between the two parties in the North. Douglas, defending popular sovereignty, accused the Republicans of promoting a war of sections, of wishing to interfere with slavery in the South, and of advocating social equality of the races. Lincoln denied these charges (properly, since neither he nor his party had ever advocated any of these things). He, in turn, accused the Democrats of conspiring to extend slavery into the territories and possibly into the free states as well (a charge that was equally unfounded).

At the heart of the debates, however, was a basic difference on the issue of slavery. Douglas appeared to have no moral position on the issue and, Lincoln claimed, did not care whether slavery was "voted up, or voted down." Lincoln's opposition to slavery was more fundamental. If the nation could accept that blacks were not entitled to basic human rights, he argued, then it could accept that other groups—immigrant laborers, for example—could be deprived of rights too. And if slavery were to extend into the Western territories, he argued, opportunities for poor white laborers to better their lots there might be lost. The nation's future, he argued (reflecting the central idea of the Republican party), rested on the spread of free labor.

Lincoln believed slavery was morally wrong, but he was not an abolitionist. That was in part because he could not envision an easy alternative to it in the areas where it already existed. He shared the prevailing view among Northern whites that the black race was not prepared (and perhaps never would be) to live on equal terms with whites. He and his party would "arrest the further spread" of slavery, that is, prevent its expansion into the territories; they would not directly challenge it where it already existed, but would trust that the institution would gradually die out there of its own accord.

Yet the implications of Lincoln's argument were more sweeping than this relatively moderate formula suggests, for both he and other Republicans believed that by restricting slavery to the South, they would be consigning slavery to its "ultimate extinction." As he said in the most famous speech of the campaign:

A house divided against itself cannot stand. I believe this government cannot endure permanently half slave and half free. I do not expect the

Union to be dissolved—I do not expect the house to fall—but I do expect it will cease to be divided. It will become all one thing, or all the other.

In the debate at Freeport, Lincoln asked Douglas if the people of a territory could exclude slavery prior to the formation of a state constitution. In other words, was popular sovereignty still workable despite the *Dred Scott* decision? Douglas replied that the people of a territory could legally exclude slavery before forming a state constitution simply by refusing to pass laws recognizing the right of slave ownership. Without such laws, he claimed, slavery could not exist. Douglas's reply became known as the Freeport Doctrine or, in the South, the Freeport Heresy. It satisfied his followers sufficiently to win him reelection to the Senate, but it aroused little enthusiasm and did nothing to enhance his national political ambitions.

Outside Illinois, the elections went heavily against the Democrats, who lost ground in almost every Northern state. The party retained control of the Senate but lost its majority in the House, with the result that the congressional sessions of 1858 and 1859 were bitterly deadlocked.

John Brown's Raid

The battles in Congress, however, were almost entirely overshadowed by a spectacular event that enraged and horrified the entire South and greatly hastened the rush toward disunion. In the fall of 1859, John Brown, the antislavery zealot whose bloody actions in Kansas had inflamed the crisis there, staged an even more dramatic episode, this time in the South itself. With private encouragement and financial aid from some prominent Eastern abolitionists (a group sometimes known as the "Secret Six"), he made elaborate plans to seize a mountain fortress in Virginia from which, he believed, he could foment a slave insurrection in the South. On October 16, he and a group of eighteen followers attacked and seized control of a United States arsenal in Harpers Ferry, Virginia. But the slave uprising Brown hoped to inspire did not occur, and he quickly found himself besieged in the arsenal by citizens, local militia companies, and before long United States troops under the command of Robert E. Lee. After ten of his men were killed, Brown surrendered. He was promptly tried in a Virginia court for treason against the state, found guilty, and sentenced to death. On December 2, 1859, he was hung. Six of his followers met a similar fate.

Probably no other single event did as much as the Harpers Ferry raid to convince white Southerners that they could not live safely in the Union. Despite their defiant defense of slavery, many were consumed with one great, if often secret, fear: the possibility of a general slave insurrection. And John Brown's raid, which many Southerners believed (incorrectly) had the support of the Republican party, suggested that the North was now committed to producing just such an insurrection. When abolitionists such as Wendell Phillips and Ralph Waldo Emerson began to glorify Brown as a new saint, and when his execution made him a martyr to thousands of Northerners, the white South reacted with shock and alarm (even though the great majority of Northerners denounced Brown and his actions).

The Election of Lincoln

The presidential election of 1860 had the most momentous consequences of any in American history. It was also among the most complex.

The Democratic party was torn apart by a battle between Southerners, who demanded a strong endorsement of slavery, and Westerners, who supported the idea of popular sovereignty. When the party convention met, inopportunely, in Charleston, South Carolina (a hotbed of secessionist

JOHN BROWN Even in this formal photographic portrait (taken in 1859, the last year of his life), John Brown conveys the fierce sense of righteousness that fueled his extraordinary activities in the fight against slavery.

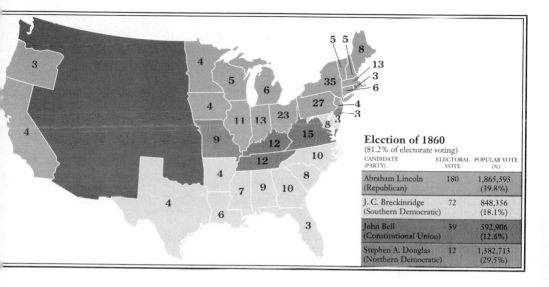

Election of 1860
(81.2% of electorate voting)

CANDIDATE (PARTY)	ELECTORAL VOTE	POPULAR VOTE (%)
Abraham Lincoln (Republican)	180	1,865,593 (39.8%)
J. C. Breckinridge (Southern Democratic)	72	848,356 (18.1%)
John Bell (Constitutional Union)	39	592,906 (12.6%)
Stephen A. Douglas (Northern Democratic)	12	1,382,713 (29.5%)

sentiment) in April, it endorsed the Western position. Delegates from eight states in the lower South walked out. The remaining delegates could not agree on a presidential candidate and finally adjourned the convention to meet again two months later in Baltimore. By the time the Democrats reconvened in June, some disenchanted Southerners had organized an alternative meeting in Richmond. The decimated convention at Baltimore nominated Stephen Douglas for president. The Southern Democrats in Richmond nominated John C. Breckinridge of Kentucky.

The Republican leaders, in the meantime, were working to broaden the base of their party. No longer content to present themselves simply as opponents of slavery, they tried now to appeal to every major interest group in the North that feared the South was blocking its economic aspirations. The platform endorsed such traditional Whig measures as a high tariff, internal improvements, a homestead bill, and a Pacific railroad to be built with federal financial assistance. It supported the right of each state to decide the status of slavery within its borders. But it also insisted that neither Congress nor territorial legislatures could legalize slavery in the territories. Passing over better known candidates, the Republican convention chose Abraham Lincoln as the party's presidential nominee. Lincoln was prominent enough to be respectable but obscure enough to have made few enemies. He was radical enough to please the antislavery faction in the party but conservative enough to satisfy the ex-Whigs.

But the Republicans were not yet conservative enough to satisfy all the former Whigs. In May, a group of them—mostly conservative elder states-men—met in Baltimore and formed the Constitutional Union party in an effort to transcend sectional passions and create a truly national political movement. They nominated John Bell of Tennessee for president and Edward Everett of Massachusetts for vice president. They endorsed the Constitution and the Union and avoided taking a clear stand on the issue of slavery.

In the November election, Lincoln won the presidency with a majority of the electoral votes but only about two-fifths of the fragmented popular vote. The Republicans, moreover, failed to win a majority in Congress; and, of course, they did not control the Supreme Court. Even so, the election of Lincoln became the final signal to many white Southerners that their position in the Union was hopeless. And within a few weeks of Lincoln's victory, the process of disunion began—a process that would quickly lead to a prolonged and bloody war between two groups of Americans, both heirs to more than a century of struggling toward nationhood, each now con-vinced that it shared no common ground with the other.

CHAPTER FOURTEEN

The Civil War

The Secession Crisis ∼ *The Mobilization of the North*
The Mobilization of the South ∼ *Strategy and Diplomacy*
Campaigns and Battles

B Y THE END of 1860, the cords that had once bound the Union together seemed to have snapped. The almost mystical veneration of the Constitution and its framers was no longer working to unite the nation; residents of the North and South—particularly after the controversial *Dred Scott* decision—now differed fundamentally over what the Constitution said and what the framers had meant. The romantic vision of America's great national destiny had ceased to be a unifying force; the two sections now defined that destiny in different and apparently irreconcilable terms. The stable two-party system could not dampen sectional conflict any longer; that system had collapsed in the 1850s, to be replaced by a new one that accentuated rather than muted regional controversy. Above all, the federal government was no longer the remote, unthreatening presence it once had been; the need to resolve the status of the territories had made it necessary for Washington to deal with sectional issues in a direct and forceful way. And thus, beginning in 1860, the divisive forces that had always existed within the United States were no longer counterbalanced by unifying forces. As a result, the Union began to dissolve.

THE SECESSION CRISIS

Almost as soon as the news of Abraham Lincoln's election reached the South, the militant leaders of the region—the champions of the new concept of Southern "nationalism," men known both to their contemporaries and to history as the "fire-eaters"—began to demand an end to the Union.

The Withdrawal of the South

South Carolina, long the hotbed of Southern separatism, went first. It called a special convention, at which the delegates voted unanimously on December 20, 1860, to withdraw the state from the Union. By the time Lincoln took office, six other Southern states—Mississippi (January 9, 1861), Florida (January 10), Alabama (January 11), Georgia (January 19), Louisiana (January 26), and Texas (February 1)—had seceded. In February 1861, representatives of the seven seceded states met at Montgomery, Alabama, and formed a new nation—the Confederate States of America. The re-

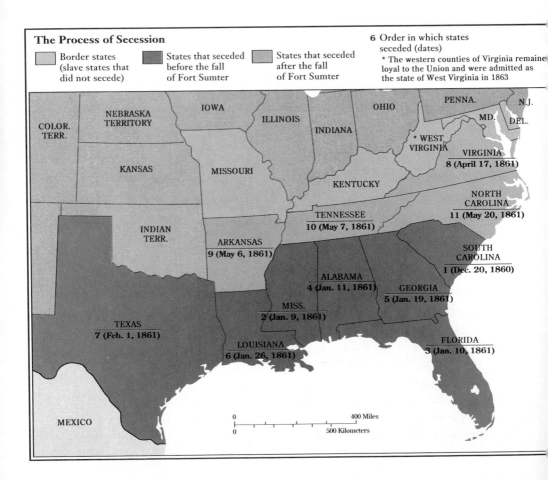

The Process of Secession

Border states (slave states that did not secede)

States that seceded before the fall of Fort Sumter

States that seceded after the fall of Fort Sumter

6 Order in which states seceded (dates)
* The western counties of Virginia remained loyal to the Union and were admitted as the state of West Virginia in 1863

sponse from the North was confused and indecisive. President James Buchanan told Congress in December 1860 that no state had the right to secede from the Union, but he suggested that the federal government had no authority to stop a state if it did.

The seceding states immediately seized the federal property—forts, arsenals, government offices—within their boundaries. But they did not at first have sufficient military power to seize two fortified offshore military installations: Fort Sumter, on an island in the harbor of Charleston, South Carolina, garrisoned by a small force under Major Robert Anderson; and Fort Pickens, in the harbor of Pensacola, Florida. South Carolina sent commissioners to Washington to ask for the surrender of Sumter; but Buchanan, timid though he was, refused to yield it. Indeed, in January 1861, he ordered an unarmed merchant ship to proceed to Fort Sumter with additional troops and supplies. Confederate guns on shore fired at the vessel (the first shots between North and South) and turned it back. Still, neither section was yet ready to concede that war had begun. And in Washington, efforts began once more to forge a compromise.

The Failure of Compromise

Gradually, the compromise efforts came together around a proposal first submitted by Senator John J. Crittenden of Kentucky and known as the Crittenden Compromise. It called for several constitutional amendments, which would guarantee the permanent existence of slavery in the slave states and would satisfy Southern demands on such issues as fugitive slaves and slavery in the District of Columbia. But the heart of Crittenden's plan was a proposal to reestablish the Missouri Compromise line in all the present and future territory of the United States: slavery would be prohibited north of the line and permitted south of it. Southerners in the Senate seemed willing to accept the plan, but the Republicans were not. The compromise would have required that the Republicans abandon their most fundamental position: that slavery not be allowed to expand.

And so nothing had been resolved when Abraham Lincoln arrived in Washington for his inauguration—sneaking into the city in disguise on a night train to avoid assassination as he passed through the slave state of Maryland. In his eloquent inaugural address, Lincoln laid down several basic principles: Since the Union was older than the Constitution, no state could leave it. Acts of force or violence to support secession were insurrectionary. And the government would "hold, occupy, and possess" federal property in the seceded states—a clear reference to Fort Sumter.

Conditions at Fort Sumter were deteriorating quickly. Union forces there were running short of supplies; unless they received fresh provisions, the fort would have to be evacuated. Lincoln believed that if he surrendered Sumter, his commitment to maintaining the Union would no longer be credible. So he sent a relief expedition to the fort, carefully informing the South Carolina authorities that there would be no attempt to send troops or munitions unless the supply ships met with resistance. The new Confederate government now faced a dilemma. Permitting the expedition to land would seem to be a tame submission to federal authority. Firing on the ships or the fort would seem (to the North at least) to be aggression. Confederate leaders finally decided that to appear cowardly would be worse than to appear belligerent; they ordered General P. G. T. Beauregard, commander of Confederate forces at Charleston, to take the fort, by force if necessary. When Anderson refused to give up, the Confederates bombarded it for two days, April 12–13, 1861. On April 14, Anderson surrendered. The Civil War had begun.

Almost immediately, Lincoln began mobilizing the North for war. Equally promptly, four more slave states seceded from the Union and joined the Confederacy: Virginia (April 17, 1861), Arkansas (May 6), Tennessee (June 8), and North Carolina (May 20). The four remaining slave states, Maryland, Delaware, Kentucky, and Missouri, cast their lot with the Union (under heavy political and even military pressure from Washington).

The Opposing Sides

As the war began, only one thing was clear: all the important material advantages lay with the North. Its population was more than twice as large as that of the South (and more than four times as large as the nonslave population of the South), so the Union had a much greater manpower reserve both for its armies and its work force. The North had an advanced industrial system and was able by 1862 to manufacture almost all its own war materials. The South had almost no industry at all and had to rely on imports from Europe throughout the war.

In addition, the North had a much better transportation system than did the South, and in particular more and better railroads: twice as much trackage as the Confederacy had, and a much better integrated system of lines. In the course of the war, moreover, the already inferior Confederate railroad system steadily deteriorated, and by the beginning of 1864 it had almost collapsed.

At the start of the war, however, the material advantages of the North were not as decisive as they now appear to have been. The South was, for the most part, fighting a defensive war on its own land and thus had the advantage of local support and familiarity with the territory. The Northern armies, on the other hand, were fighting mostly within the South on unfamiliar ground, and amid hostile local populations; they had to maintain long lines of communications and had access only to the South's own inadequate transportation system. The commitment of the white population of the South to the war was, with limited exceptions, clear and firm. In the North, opinion about the war was more divided and support for it remained shaky until very near the end. A major Southern victory at any one of several crucial moments might have proved decisive by breaking the North's will to continue the struggle. Finally, many Southerners believed that the dependence of the English and French textile industries on American cotton would force them to intervene on the side of the Confederacy.

THE MOBILIZATION OF THE NORTH

In the North, the war produced considerable discord, frustration, and suffering. But it also produced prosperity and economic growth by giving a major stimulus to both industry and agriculture.

Economic Measures

With Southern forces now gone from Congress, the Republican party could exercise almost unchallenged supremacy. During the war, it enacted an aggressively nationalistic program to promote economic development.

The Homestead and Morrill Acts of 1862 promoted the rapid development of the West. The Homestead Act permitted any citizen or prospective citizen to claim 160 acres of public land and to purchase it for a small fee after living on it for five years. The Morrill Act transferred substantial public acreage to the state governments; they were to sell the land and use the proceeds to finance public education. This act led to the creation of many new state colleges and universities, the so-called land-grant institutions. Congress also passed a series of tariff bills that by the end of the war had raised duties to the highest level in the nation's history—a great boon to domestic industries eager for protection from foreign competition.

Congress also moved to complete the dream of a transcontinental railroad. It created two new federally chartered corporations: the Union Pacific Railroad Company, which was to build westward from Omaha, and the Central Pacific, which was to build eastward from California. The two projects were to meet in the middle and complete the link. The government provided free public lands and generous loans to the companies.

The National Bank Acts of 1863–1864 created a new national banking system. Existing or newly formed banks could join the system if they had enough capital and were willing to invest one-third of it in government securities. In return, they could issue United States Treasury notes as currency. The new system eliminated much of the chaos and uncertainty in the nation's currency and created a uniform system of national bank notes.

More difficult than promoting economic growth was financing the war itself. The government tried to do so in three ways: levying taxes, issuing paper currency, and borrowing. Congress levied new taxes on almost all goods and services; and in 1861 the government levied an income tax for the first time, with rates that eventually rose to 10 percent on incomes above $5,000. But taxation raised only a small proportion of the funds necessary for financing the war, and strong popular resistance prevented the government from raising the rates.

At least equally controversial was the printing of paper currency, or "greenbacks." The new currency was backed not by gold or silver but simply by the good faith and credit of the government (much like today's currency). The value of the greenbacks fluctuated according to the fortunes of the Northern armies. Early in 1864, with the war effort bogged down, a greenback dollar was worth only 39 percent of a gold dollar. Even at the close of the war, it was worth only 67 percent of a gold dollar. Because of the difficulty of making purchases with this uncertain currency, the government used greenbacks sparingly. The Treasury issued only $450 million worth of paper currency—a small proportion of the cost of the war but enough to produce serious inflation which raised prices by over 80 percent by the close of the war.

By far the largest source of financing for the war was loans. In previous wars, the government had sold bonds only to banks and to a few wealthy investors. Now, however, the Treasury persuaded ordinary citizens to buy over $400 million worth of bonds—the first example of mass financing of a war in American history. But public bond purchases constituted only a small part of the government's borrowing, which in the end totaled $2.6 billion, most of it from banks and large financial interests.

Raising the Union Armies

Over 2.1 million men served in the Union military forces during the course of the Civil War. But at the beginning of 1861, the regular army of the United States consisted of only 16,000 troops, many of them stationed in the West to protect white settlers from Indians. So the Union, like the Confederacy, had to raise its army mostly from scratch. Lincoln called for an increase of 23,000 in the regular army, but the bulk of the fighting, he knew, would have to be done by the volunteers in state militias. When Congress convened in July 1861, it authorized enlisting 500,000 volunteers for three-year terms (as opposed to the customary three-month terms).

But this voluntary system of recruitment produced adequate forces only briefly, during the first flush of enthusiasm for the war. By March 1863, Congress was forced to pass a national draft law. Virtually all young adult males were eligible to be drafted; but a man could escape service by hiring someone to go in his place or by paying the government a fee of $300. Although only about 46,000 men were ever actually conscripted, the draft greatly increased voluntary enlistments.

To a people accustomed to a remote and inactive national government, conscription was strange and threatening. Opposition to the law was widespread, particularly among laborers, immigrants, and Democrats opposed to the war (known as "Peace Democrats"). Occasionally it erupted into violence. Demonstrators against the draft rioted in New York City for four days in July 1863, killed over 100 people, mostly blacks (whom many opponents of the war blamed for the conflict), and burned down African-American homes, businesses, and even an orphanage. It was the bloodiest riot in American history. Only the arrival of federal troops halted the violence.

The Politics of Wartime

When Abraham Lincoln arrived in Washington early in 1861, many Republicans—noting his lack of national experience and his folksy, unpretentious manner—considered him a minor politician from the prairies, a man who would be easily controlled by the real leaders of his party. But the new president moved quickly to establish his own authority. He assembled a cabinet representing every faction of the Republican party and every segment of Northern opinion—men of exceptional prestige, influence, and in some cases arrogance, several of whom believed that they, not Lincoln, should be president. Lincoln moved boldly as well to use the war powers of the presidency, blithely ignoring inconvenient parts of the Constitution because, he said, it would be foolish to lose the whole by being afraid to disregard a part. He sent troops into battle without asking Congress for a declaration of war, arguing that the conflict was a domestic insurrection and that no congressional authorization was necessary. He increased the size of the regular army without receiving legislative authority to do so. He unilaterally proclaimed a naval blockade of the South.

Lincoln's greatest political problem was the widespread popular opposition to the war, mobilized by factions in the Democratic party. The Peace Democrats (or, as their enemies called them, "Copperheads") feared that agriculture and the Northwest were losing influence to industry and the East and that Republican nationalism was eroding states' rights. Lincoln used extraordinary methods to suppress them. He ordered military arrests of civilian dissenters and suspended the right of habeas corpus (the right of an arrested person to receive a speedy trial). At first, Lincoln used these methods only in sensitive areas such as the border states; but in 1862, he proclaimed that all persons who discouraged enlistments or engaged in disloyal practices were subject to martial law. In all, more than 13,000 persons were arrested and imprisoned for varying periods.

By the time of the presidential election of 1864, the North was rife with political dissension. The Republicans had suffered heavy losses in 1862, and in response leaders of the party tried to create a broad coalition of all the groups that supported the war. They called the new organization the Union party; but it was, in reality, little more than the Republican party and a small faction of War Democrats. The Union party nominated Lincoln for another term as president and Andrew Johnson of Tennessee, a War Democrat who had opposed his state's decision to secede, for the vice presidency.

The Democrats nominated George B. McClellan, a celebrated former Union general who had been relieved of his command by Lincoln, and adopted a platform denouncing the war and calling for a truce. McClellan repudiated that demand, but the Democrats were clearly the peace party in the campaign, trying to profit from growing war weariness and from the Union's discouraging military position in the summer of 1864.

At this crucial moment, however, several Northern military victories, particularly the capture of Atlanta, Georgia, early in September, rejuvenated Northern morale and boosted Republican prospects. Lincoln won reelection comfortably, with 212 electoral votes to McClellan's 21; the president carried every state except Kentucky, New Jersey, and Delaware. But Lincoln's lead in the popular vote was a more modest 10 percent. Had Union victories not occurred when they did, and had Lincoln not made special arrangements to allow Union troops to vote, the Democrats might have won.

The Politics of Emancipation

Despite their surface unity in 1864 and their general agreement on most economic matters, the Republicans disagreed sharply with one another on the issue of slavery. Radicals—led in Congress by such men as Representative Thaddeus Stevens of Pennsylvania and Senators Charles Sumner of Massachusetts and Benjamin Wade of Ohio—wanted to use the war to abolish slavery immediately and completely. Conservatives favored a slower, more gradual, and, they believed, less disruptive process for ending slavery. In the beginning, at least, they had the support of the president.

Despite the president's cautious view of emancipation, momentum began to gather behind it early in the war. In 1861, Congress passed the Confiscation Act, which declared that all slaves used for "insurrectionary" purposes (that is, in support of the Confederate military effort) would be considered freed. Subsequent laws in the spring of 1862 abolished slavery in the District of Columbia and in the Western territories and provided for the compensation of owners. In July 1862, the Radicals pushed through Congress the second Confiscation Act, which declared free the slaves of persons aiding and supporting the insurrection (whether or not the slaves themselves were doing so) and authorized the president to employ blacks, including freed slaves, as soldiers.

As the war progressed, the North seemed slowly to accept emancipation as a central war aim; nothing less, many believed, would justify the enormous sacrifices of the struggle. As a result, the Radicals gained increasing influence within the Republican party—a development that did not go unnoticed by the president, who decided to seize the leadership of the rising antislavery sentiment himself.

On September 22, 1862, after the Union victory at the Battle of Antietam, the president announced his intention to use his war powers to issue an executive order freeing all slaves in the Confederacy. And on January 1, 1863, he formally signed the Emancipation Proclamation, which declared forever free the slaves in all areas of the Confederacy except those already under Union control: Tennessee, western Virginia, and southern Louisiana. The proclamation did not apply to the border slave states, which had never seceded from the Union and which were not, therefore, subject to the president's war powers.

The immediate effect of the proclamation was limited, since it applied only to slaves still under Confederate control. But the document was of great importance nevertheless, because it clearly and irrevocably established that the war was being fought not only to preserve the Union but also to eliminate slavery. Eventually, as federal armies occupied much of the South, the proclamation became a practical reality and led directly to the freeing of thousands of slaves. About 186,000 of these emancipated blacks served as soldiers, sailors, and laborers for the Union forces. Even in areas not directly affected by the proclamation, the antislavery impulse gained strength. By the end of the war, slavery had been abolished in two Union slave states, Maryland and Missouri, and in three Confederate states occupied by Union forces: Tennessee, Arkansas, and Louisiana. The final step came in 1865, when Congress approved and the necessary states ratified the Thirteenth Amendment, which abolished slavery as an institution in all parts of the United States, not just the areas covered by the Emancipation Proclamation. After more than two centuries, legalized slavery finally ceased to exist in the United States.

The War and Society

The Civil War did not, as some historians used to claim, transform the North from an agrarian to an industrial society. Industrialization was already far advanced when the war began; and in some areas, the war actually retarded growth by diverting labor and resources to military purposes.

On the whole, however, the war sped the economic development of the North. That was in part a result of the political dominance of the Republican party and its promotion of nationalistic economic legislation. But it was also because the war itself required the expansion of certain sectors of the economy. Coal production increased by nearly 20 percent during the war. Railroad facilities improved—mainly through the adoption of a standard gauge (track width) on new lines. The loss of farm labor to the military forced many farmers to increase the mechanization of agriculture.

The war was a difficult experience for many American workers. Industrial laborers suffered a substantial loss of purchasing power, as prices in the North rose by more than 70 percent during the war while wages rose only about 40 percent. That was partly because liberalized immigration laws permitted a flood of new workers to enter the labor market and thus helped keep wages low. It was also because the increasing mechanization of production eliminated the jobs of many skilled workers. One result was a

THE U.S. SANITARY COMMISSION Matthew Brady took this photograph of female nurses and Union soldiers standing before an infirmary at Brandy Station, Virginia, near Petersburg, in 1864. The infirmary was run by the U.S. Sanitary Commission, the government-supported nursing corps that became indispensable to the medical care of wounded soldiers during the Civil War.

substantial increase in union membership in many industries and the creation of several national unions, for coal miners, railroad engineers, and others—organizations bitterly opposed and rigorously suppressed by employers.

Women found themselves, either by choice or by necessity, thrust into new and often unfamiliar roles. They took over positions vacated by men as teachers, retail salesclerks, office workers, and mill and factory hands. They were responding not only to the needs of employers for additional labor but to their own, often desperate, need for money. With husbands and fathers away in the army, many women were left destitute—particularly since military pay was small and erratic. Above all, women entered nursing, a field previously dominated by men. The United States Sanitary Commission, an organization of civilian volunteers led by Dorothea Dix, mobilized large numbers of female nurses to serve in field hospitals. By the end of the war, women were the dominant force in nursing; by the end of the century, nursing had become an almost entirely female profession.

THE MOBILIZATION OF THE SOUTH

Early in February 1861, representatives of the seven states that had seceded from the Union met at Montgomery, Alabama, to create a new Southern nation. When Virginia seceded several months later, the government of the Confederacy moved to Richmond—one of the few Southern cities large enough to house a government.

Southerners boasted loudly of the differences between their new nation and the nation they had left. Those differences were real. But there were also important similarities between the Union and the Confederacy, which became particularly clear as the two sides mobilized for war: similarities in their political systems, in the methods they used for financing the war and conscripting troops, and in the way they fought.

The Confederate Government

The Confederate constitution was almost identical to the Constitution of the United States, but with several significant exceptions. It explicitly acknowledged the sovereignty of the individual states (although not the right of secession). And it specifically sanctioned slavery and made its abolition (even by one of the states) practically impossible.

The constitutional convention at Montgomery named a provisional president and vice president: Jefferson Davis of Mississippi and Alexander H. Stephens of Georgia, who were later chosen by the general electorate, without opposition, for six-year terms. Davis had been a moderate, not an extreme, secessionist before the war. Stephens had argued against secession. The Confederate government, like the Union government, was dominated throughout the war by men of the center. It was also, like the Union government, dominated less by the old aristocracy of the East than by the newer aristocrats of the West, of whom Davis was the most prominent example.

Davis was, in the end, an unsuccessful president. He was a reasonably able administrator and the dominating figure in his government, encountering little interference from the generally tame members of his unstable cabinet and serving, in effect, as his own secretary of war. But he rarely provided genuinely national leadership. He spent too much time on routine items; and unlike Lincoln, he displayed a punctiliousness about legal and constitutional niceties inappropriate to the needs of a new nation at war. One shrewd Confederate official wrote: "All the revolutionary vigor is with the enemy. . . . With us timidity—hair splitting."

There were no formal political parties in the Confederacy, but its congressional and popular politics were badly divided nevertheless. Some white Southerners (and most blacks who were aware of the course of events) opposed secession and war altogether. Many white people in poorer "back-country" and "upcountry" regions, where slavery was limited, refused to recognize the new Confederate government or to serve in the Southern army; some worked or even fought for the Union. Most white Southerners supported the war, but as in the North many were openly critical of the government and the military, particularly as the tide of battle turned against the South and the Confederate economy decayed.

Money and Manpower

Financing the Confederate war effort was a monumental and ultimately impossible task. It involved creating a national revenue system in a society unaccustomed to large tax burdens. It depended on a small and unstable banking system that had little capital to lend. Because most wealth in the South was invested in slaves and land, liquid assets were scarce; and the Confederacy's only specie—seized from United States mints located in the South—was worth only about $1 million.

The Confederate Congress tried at first not to tax the people directly but to requisition funds from the individual states; but most of them were also unwilling to tax their citizens and paid their shares, when they paid them at all, with bonds or notes of dubious worth. In 1863, therefore, Congress enacted an income tax. But taxation never provided the Confederacy with very much revenue; it produced only about 1 percent of the government's total income. Borrowing was not much more successful. The Confederate government issued bonds in such vast amounts that the public lost faith in them and stopped buying them, and efforts to borrow money in Europe using cotton as collateral fared no better.

As a result, the Confederacy had to pay for the war through the least stable, most destructive form of financing: paper currency, which it began issuing in 1861. By 1864, the Confederacy had issued the staggering total of $1.5 billion in paper money, more than twice what the Union had produced. And unlike the Union, the Confederacy did not establish a uniform currency system; the national government, states, cities, and private banks all issued their own notes, producing widespread chaos and confusion. The result was a disastrous inflation—a 9,000 percent increase in prices in

CONFEDERATE VOLUNTEERS Smiling and apparently
confident, young southern soldiers pose for a photograph in 1861, shortly before the first Battle of Bull
Run. The Civil War was one of the first military conflicts extensively chronicled by photographers.

the course of the war (in contrast to 80 percent in the North)—with
devastating effects on the new nation's morale.

Like the United States, the Confederacy first raised armies by calling
for volunteers. And as in the North, by the end of 1861 voluntary enlistments
were declining. In April 1862, therefore, Congress enacted a Conscription
Act, which subjected all white males between the ages of eighteen and
thirty-five to military service for three years. As in the North, a draftee could
avoid service if he furnished a substitute. But since the price of substitutes
was high, the provision aroused such opposition from poorer whites that it
was repealed in 1863. Even more controversial were other exemptions that
had no counterparts in the North, especially the exemption of one white
man on each plantation with twenty or more slaves, a provision that caused
smaller farmers to complain: "It's a rich man's war but a poor man's fight."

Even so, conscription worked for a time. At the end of 1862, about
500,000 soldiers were in the Confederate army. That number did not
include the many slave men and women recruited by the military to perform

such services as cooking, laundry, and manual labor, hence freeing additional white manpower for fighting. After 1862, however, conscription began producing fewer men, and the armed forces steadily decreased in size.

As 1864 opened, the government faced a critical manpower shortage. In a desperate move, Congress began trying to draft men as young as seventeen and as old as fifty. But in a nation suffering from intense war weariness, where many had concluded that defeat was inevitable, nothing could attract or retain an adequate army any longer. In 1864–1865, there were 100,000 desertions. In a frantic final attempt to raise men, Congress authorized the conscription of 300,000 slaves; but the war ended before this incongruous experiment could be attempted.

States' Rights Versus Centralization

The greatest source of division in the South, however, was not differences of opinion over the war, which most white Southerners generally supported, but the doctrine of states' rights. States' rights had become such a cult among many white Southerners that they resisted virtually all efforts to exert national authority, even those necessary to win the war. States' rights enthusiasts obstructed the conduct of the war in many ways. They restricted Davis's ability to impose martial law and suspend habeas corpus. They obstructed conscription. Recalcitrant governors such as Joseph Brown of Georgia and Zebulon M. Vance of North Carolina tried at times to keep their own troops apart from the Confederate forces and insisted on hoarding surplus supplies for their own states' militias.

The Confederate government still made substantial strides in centralizing power in the South; and by the end of the war, the Confederate bureaucracy was larger than its counterpart in Washington. The national government experimented, successfully for a time, with a "food draft"— which permitted soldiers to feed themselves by seizing crops from farms in their path. The government impressed slaves, often over the objections of their owners, to work as laborers on military projects. The Confederacy seized control of the railroads and shipping; it imposed regulations on industry; it limited corporate profits. States' rights sentiment was a significant handicap, but the South nevertheless took dramatic steps in the direction of centralization—becoming in the process increasingly like the region whose institutions it was fighting to escape.

Social Effects of the War

The war worked to transform Southern society in many of the same ways that it was changing the society of the North. It was particularly significant for Southern women. Because so many men left the farms and plantations to fight, the task of keeping families together and maintaining agricultural production fell increasingly to women. Slaveowners' wives often became responsible for managing large slave work forces; the wives of more modest farmers learned to plow fields and harvest crops. Substantial numbers of females worked in government agencies in Richmond. Even larger numbers chose nursing, both in hospitals and in temporary facilities set up to care for wounded soldiers. Others became schoolteachers.

The principal social effect of the war on the South, however, was widespread suffering and privation. Once the Northern naval blockade became effective, the South experienced massive shortages of almost everything. The region was overwhelmingly agricultural; but since it had concentrated so single-mindedly on producing cotton and other export crops, it did not grow enough food to meet its own needs. And despite the efforts of women to keep farms functioning, the departure of male workers seriously diminished the region's ability to keep up what food production there had been. Doctors were conscripted in large numbers to serve the needs of the military, leaving many communities without any medical care. Blacksmiths, carpenters, and other craftsmen were similarly in short supply.

As the war continued, the shortages, the inflation, and the suffering created increasing instability in Southern society. There were major food riots (some led by women) in cities in Georgia, North Carolina, and Alabama in 1863, as well as a large demonstration in Richmond that quickly turned violent. Resistance to conscription, food impressment, and taxation increased throughout the Confederacy.

STRATEGY AND DIPLOMACY

Militarily, the initiative in the Civil War lay mainly with the North, since it needed to defeat the Confederacy while the South needed only to avoid defeat. Diplomatically, however, the initiative lay with the South. It needed to enlist the recognition and support of foreign governments; the Union wanted only to preserve the status quo.

The Commanders

The most important Union military commander was Abraham Lincoln, whose previous military experience consisted only of brief service in his state militia. Lincoln was a successful commander in chief because he realized that numbers and resources were on his side and because he took advantage of the North's material advantages. He realized, too, that the proper objective of his armies was the destruction of the Confederate armies and not the occupation of Southern territory.

It was fortunate that Lincoln had a good grasp of strategy, because many of his generals did not. The problem of finding adequate commanders for the troops in the field plagued him throughout the first three years of the war.

From 1861 to 1864, Lincoln tried time and again to find a chief of staff capable of orchestrating the Union war effort. He turned first to General Winfield Scott, the aging hero of the Mexican War. But Scott was unprepared for the magnitude of the new conflict and retired on November 1, 1861. Lincoln then appointed the young George B. McClellan, who was the

ULYSSES S. GRANT One observer said of Grant (photographed here during the Wilderness campaign of 1864): "He habitually wears an expression as if he had determined to drive his head through a brick wall, and was about to do it." It was an apt metaphor for Grant's military philosophy, which relied on constant, unrelenting assault.

commander of the Union forces in the East, the Army of the Potomac; but the proud, arrogant McClellan had a wholly inadequate grasp of strategy and in any case returned to the field in March 1862. For most of the rest of the year, Lincoln had no chief of staff at all. And when he eventually appointed General Henry W. Halleck to the post, he found him an ineffectual strategist who left all substantive decision making to the president. Not until March 1864 did Lincoln finally find a general he trusted to command the war effort: Ulysses S. Grant, who shared Lincoln's belief in making enemy armies and resources, not enemy territory, the target of military efforts. Lincoln gave Grant a relatively free hand, but the general always submitted at least the broad outlines of his plans to the president for advance approval.

Lincoln's (and later Grant's) handling of the war effort faced constant scrutiny from the Committee on the Conduct of the War, a joint investigative committee of the two houses of Congress and the most powerful voice the legislative branch has ever had in formulating war policies. Established in December 1861 and chaired by Senator Benjamin F. Wade of Ohio, it complained constantly of the inadequate ruthlessness of Northern generals, which Radicals on the committee attributed (largely inaccurately) to a secret sympathy among the officers for slavery. The committee's efforts often seriously interfered with the conduct of the war.

Southern command arrangements centered on President Davis, who unlike Lincoln was a trained professional soldier but who, also unlike Lincoln, failed ever to create an effective central command system. Early in 1862, Davis named General Robert E. Lee as his principal military adviser. But in fact, Davis had no intention of sharing control of strategy with anyone. After a few months, Lee left Richmond to command forces in the field, and for the next two years Davis planned strategy alone. In February 1864, he named General Braxton Bragg as a military adviser, but Bragg never provided much more than technical advice. Not until February 1865 did the Confederate Congress create the formal position of general in chief. Davis named Lee to the post but made clear that he expected to continue to make all basic decisions. In any case, the war ended before the new command structure had time to take shape.

At lower levels of command, men of markedly similar backgrounds controlled the war in both the North and the South. Many of the professional officers on both sides were graduates of the United States Military Academy at West Point and the United States Naval Academy at Annapolis and thus had been trained in similar ways. Many were closely acquainted, even friendly, with their counterparts on the other side. Amateur officers played an important role in both armies as commanders of volunteer regiments. In both North and South, such men were usually economic or social leaders in their communities who appointed themselves officers and rounded up troops to lead. Although occasionally this system produced officers of real ability, more often it did not.

The Role of Sea Power

The Union had an overwhelming advantage in naval power, and it gave its navy two important roles in the war. One was enforcing a blockade of the Southern coast, which the president ordered on April 19, 1861. The other was assisting the Union armies in field operations.

The blockade of the South was never fully effective. The United States Navy could generally keep ocean-going ships out of Confederate ports, but for a time small blockade runners continued to slip through. Gradually, however, federal forces tightened the blockade by seizing the ports themselves. The last important port in Confederate hands—Wilmington, North Carolina—fell to the Union early in 1865.

The Confederates made bold attempts to break the blockade with new weapons. Foremost among them was an ironclad warship, constructed by plating with iron a former United States frigate, the *Merrimac*, which the Yankees had scuttled in Norfolk harbor when Virginia seceded. On March 8, 1862, the refitted *Merrimac*, renamed the *Virginia*, left Norfolk to attack a blockading squadron of wooden ships at nearby Hampton Roads. It destroyed two of the ships and scattered the rest. But the federal government had already built ironclads of its own. And one of them, the *Monitor*, arrived off the coast of Virginia only a few hours after the *Virginia*'s dramatic foray. The next day, it met the *Virginia* in the first battle between ironclad ships. Neither vessel was able to sink the other, but the *Monitor* put an end to the *Virginia*'s raids and preserved the blockade.

As a supporter of land operations, the Union navy was particularly important in the Western theater of war—the vast region between the Appalachian Mountains and the Mississippi River—where the larger rivers were navigable by large vessels. The navy transported supplies and troops and joined in attacking Confederate strong points. The South had no significant navy of its own and could defend against the Union gunboats only with fixed land fortifications, which proved no match for the mobile land-and-water forces of the Union.

Europe and the Disunited States

Judah P. Benjamin, the Confederate secretary of state for most of the war, was a clever and intelligent man, but he lacked strong convictions and confined most of his energy to routine administrative tasks. William Seward, his counterpart in Washington, gradually became one of the outstanding American secretaries of state. He had invaluable assistance from Charles Francis Adams, the American minister to London, who had inherited the considerable diplomatic talents of his father, John Quincy Adams, and his grandfather, John Adams.

At the beginning of the war, the sympathies of the ruling classes of England and France, the two nations whose support was most crucial to both sides, lay largely with the Confederacy. That was partly because the two nations imported much Southern cotton; but it was also because they were eager to weaken the United States, an increasingly powerful rival to them in world commerce, and because many admired the South's defense of aristocracy. But France was unwilling to take sides in the conflict unless England did so first. And in England, the government was reluctant to act

ROBERT E. LEE Lee provided a sharp contrast to his Northern counterpart, Ulysses S. Grant. Grant was slightly built, slouching, disheveled, and gruff. Lee was tall, dignified, and elegant in both dress and manner. He admired George Washington and attempted to emulate him in his conduct both of the war and of his life.

because there was powerful popular support for the Union. Important English liberals such as John Bright and Richard Cobden considered the war a struggle between free and slave labor and urged their followers to support the Union cause. The politically conscious but largely unenfranchised workers in Britain expressed their sympathy for the North frequently and unmistakably—in mass meetings, in resolutions, and through their champions in Parliament. After Lincoln issued the Emancipation Proclamation, these groups worked particularly avidly for the Union.

Southern leaders hoped to counter the strength of the British antislavery forces by arguing that access to Southern cotton was vital to the English and French textile industries. But this "King Cotton diplomacy," on which the Confederacy had staked so many of its hopes, was a failure. English manufacturers had a surplus of both raw cotton and finished goods on hand in 1861 and could withstand a temporary loss of access to American cotton. Later, as the supply of cotton began to diminish, both England and France managed to keep at least some of their mills open by importing cotton from Egypt, India, and other sources. Equally important, English workers, the people most seriously threatened by the cotton shortage, did not clamor to have the blockade broken. Even the 500,000 English textile workers thrown out of jobs as a result of mill closings continued to support the North. In the end, therefore, no European nation offered diplomatic recognition to the Confederacy or intervened in the war. No nation wanted to antagonize the United States unless the Confederacy seemed likely to win, and the South never came close enough to victory to convince its potential allies to support it.

Even so, there was considerable tension, and on occasion near hostilities, between the United States and Britain, beginning in the first days of the war. Great Britain declared itself neutral as soon as the fighting began; it was followed by France and other nations. The Union government was furious. Neutrality implied that the two sides to the conflict had equal stature, but Washington was insisting that the conflict was simply a domestic insurrection, not a war between two legitimate governments.

A more serious crisis, the so-called *Trent* affair, began in late 1861. Two Confederate diplomats, James M. Mason and John Slidell, had slipped through the then ineffective Union blockade to Havana, Cuba, where they boarded an English steamer, the *Trent*, for England. Waiting in Cuban waters was the American frigate *San Jacinto*, commanded by the impetuous Charles Wilkes. Acting without authorization, Wilkes stopped the British vessel, arrested the diplomats, and carried them in triumph to Boston. The British government demanded the release of the prisoners, reparations, and an apology. Lincoln and Seward, aware that Wilkes had violated maritime law and unwilling to risk war with England, spun out the negotiations until American public opinion had cooled off; then they released the diplomats with an indirect apology.

A second diplomatic crisis produced problems that lasted for years. Unable to construct large ships itself, the Confederacy bought six ships, known as commerce destroyers, from British shipyards. The best known of them were the *Alabama*, the *Florida*, and the *Shenandoah*. The United States protested that this sale of military equipment to a belligerent violated the laws of neutrality, and the protests became the basis, after the war, of damage claims by the United States against Great Britain.

CAMPAIGNS AND BATTLES

In the absence of direct intervention by the European powers, the two contestants in North America were left to resolve the conflict between themselves. They did so in four long years of bloody combat that produced more carnage than any war in American history, before or since. More than 618,000 Americans died in the course of the Civil War, far more than the 115,000 who perished in World War I or the 318,000 who died in World War II—more, indeed, than died in all other American wars through Vietnam combined. There were nearly 2,000 deaths for every 100,000 of population during the Civil War. In World War I, the comparable figure was only 109; in World War II, 241.

Despite the gruesome cost, the Civil War has become the most romanticized and the most intently studied of all American wars. In part, that is because the conflict produced—in addition to hideous fatalities—a series of military campaigns of classic strategic interest and a series of military leaders who displayed unusual brilliance and daring.

The Opening Clashes, 1861

The Union and the Confederacy fought their first major battle of the war in northern Virginia. A Union army of over 30,000 men under the command of General Irvin McDowell was stationed just outside Washington. About thirty miles away, at Manassas, was a slightly smaller Confederate army under P. G. T. Beauregard. If the Northern army could destroy the Southern one, Union leaders believed, the war might end at once. In mid-July, McDowell marched his inexperienced troops toward Manassas. Beauregard moved his troops behind Bull Run, a small stream north of Manassas, and called for reinforcements, which reached him the day before the battle. The two armies were now approximately the same size.

On July 21, in the First Battle of Bull Run, or First Battle of Manassas, McDowell almost succeeded in dispersing the Confederate forces. But the Southerners managed to stop a last strong Union assault and then began a savage counterattack. The Union troops, exhausted after hours of hot, hard fighting, suddenly panicked. They broke ranks and retreated chaotically. McDowell was unable to reorganize them, and he had to order a retreat to Washington—a disorderly withdrawal complicated by the presence along the route of many civilians, who had ridden down from the capital, picnic baskets in hand, to watch the battle from nearby hills. The Confederates, as disorganized by victory as the Union forces were by defeat, and short of supplies and transportation, did not pursue. The battle was a severe blow to Union morale and to the president's confidence in his officers. It also dispelled the illusion that the war would be a quick one.

Elsewhere, Union forces were achieving some small but significant victories in 1861. In Missouri, rebel forces gathered behind Governor Claiborne Jackson and other state officials who wanted to take the state out of the Union. Nathaniel Lyon, who commanded a small regular army force in St. Louis, moved his troops into southern Missouri to face the secessionists. On August 10, at the Battle of Wilson's Creek, he was defeated and killed—but not before he had seriously weakened the striking power of the Confederates. Union forces were subsequently able to hold most of the state.

Meanwhile, a Union force under George B. McClellan moved east from Ohio into western Virginia. By the end of 1861, it had "liberated" the antisecession mountain people of the region, who created their own state government loyal to the Union; the state was admitted to the Union as West Virginia in 1863. The occupation of western Virginia was of limited military value, since the mountains cut the area off from the rest of Virginia. It was, however, an important propaganda victory for the North.

The Western Theater

After the battle at Bull Run, military operations in the East settled into a long and frustrating stalemate. The first decisive operations in 1862 occurred, therefore, in the Western theater. Here the Union forces were trying to seize control of the southern part of the Mississippi River; this would divide the Confederacy and give the North easy transportation into the heart of the South. Northern soldiers advanced on the southern Mississippi from both the north and south, moving down the river from Kentucky and up from the Gulf of Mexico toward New Orleans.

In April, a Union squadron of ironclads and wooden vessels commanded by David G. Farragut gathered in the Gulf of Mexico, then smashed past weak Confederate forts near the mouth of the Mississippi, and from there sailed up to New Orleans. The city was virtually defenseless because

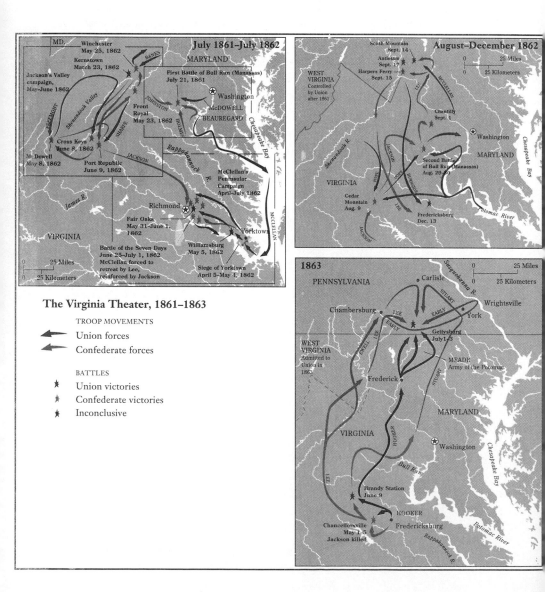

The Virginia Theater, 1861–1863

TROOP MOVEMENTS

Union forces

Confederate forces

BATTLES

* Union victories

* Confederate victories

* Inconclusive

the Confederate high command had expected the attack to come from the north. The surrender of New Orleans on April 25, 1862, was the first major Union victory and an important turning point in the war. From then on, the mouth of the Mississippi was closed to Confederate trade, and the South's largest city and most important banking center was in Union hands.

Farther north in the Western theater, Confederate troops under the command of Albert Sidney Johnston were stretched out in a long defensive line, whose center was at two forts in Tennessee, Fort Henry and Fort Donelson, on the Tennessee and Cumberland rivers respectively. But the forts were located well behind the main Southern flanks, a fatal weakness that Union commanders recognized and exploited. Early in 1862, Ulysses S. Grant attacked Fort Henry, whose defenders, awed by the ironclad river boats accompanying the Union army, surrendered with almost no resistance on February 6. Grant then moved both his naval and ground forces to Fort Donelson, where the Confederates put up a stronger fight but finally, on February 16, had to surrender. By cracking the Confederate center, Grant had gained control of river communications and forced Confederate forces out of Kentucky and half of Tennessee.

With about 40,000 men, Grant now advanced south along the Tennessee River to seize control of railroad lines vital to the Confederacy. From Pittsburg Landing, he marched to nearby Shiloh, Tennessee, where a force almost equal to his own and commanded by Albert Sidney Johnston and P. G. T. Beauregard caught him by surprise. The result was the Battle of Shiloh, April 6–7. In the first day's fighting (during which Johnston was killed), the Southerners drove Grant back to the river. But the next day, reinforced by 25,000 fresh troops, Grant recovered the lost ground and forced Beauregard to withdraw. After the narrow Union victory at Shiloh, Northern forces occupied Corinth, Mississippi, the hub of several important railroads, and took control of the Mississippi River as far south as Memphis.

Braxton Bragg, now in command of the Confederate army in the West, gathered his forces at Chattanooga, in eastern Tennessee, which the Confederacy still controlled. He hoped to win back the rest of the state and then move north into Kentucky. But first he had to face a Union army (commanded first by Don Carlos Buell and then by William S. Rosecrans), whose assignment was to capture Chattanooga. The two armies maneuvered for advantage inconclusively in northern Tennessee and southern Kentucky for several months until they finally met, on December 31–January 2, in the Battle of Murfreesboro, or Stone's River. Bragg was forced to withdraw to the south, his campaign a failure.

By the end of 1862, Union forces had made considerable progress in the West. But the major conflict remained in the East, and they were having much less success there.

The Virginia Front, 1862

Union operations were being directed in 1862 by George B. McClellan, commander of the Army of the Potomac and the most controversial general of the war. McClellan was a superb trainer of men, but he often seemed reluctant to commit his troops to battle. Opportunities for important engagements came and went, and McClellan seemed never to take advantage of them—claiming always that his preparations were not yet complete or that the moment was not right.

During the winter of 1861–1862, McClellan concentrated on training his army of 150,000 men near Washington. Finally, he designed a spring campaign whose purpose was to capture the Confederate capital at Richmond. But instead of heading overland directly toward Richmond, McClellan chose a complicated, roundabout route that he thought would circumvent the Confederate defenses. The navy would carry his troops down the Potomac to a peninsula east of Richmond, between the York and James rivers; the army would approach the city from there. The combined operations became known as the Peninsular campaign.

McClellan began the campaign with only part of his army. Approximately 100,000 men accompanied him down the Potomac. Another 30,000, under General Irvin McDowell, remained behind to protect Washington. McClellan insisted that Washington was safe as long as he was threatening Richmond, and he finally persuaded Lincoln to send him the additional men. But before the president could do so, a Confederate army under Thomas J. ("Stonewall") Jackson changed his plans. Jackson staged a rapid march north through the Shenandoah Valley, as if he were planning to cross the Potomac and attack Washington. Alarmed, Lincoln dispatched McDowell's corps to head off Jackson. In the brilliant Valley campaign of May 4–June 9, 1862, Jackson defeated two separate Union forces and slipped away before McDowell could catch him.

Meanwhile, Confederate troops under Joseph E. Johnston were attacking McClellan's advancing army outside Richmond. But in the two-day Battle of Fair Oaks, or Seven Pines (May 31–June 1), they could not repel the Union forces. Johnston, badly wounded, was replaced by Robert E. Lee, who then recalled Stonewall Jackson from the Shenandoah Valley. With a combined force of 85,000 to face McClellan's 100,000, Lee launched a new

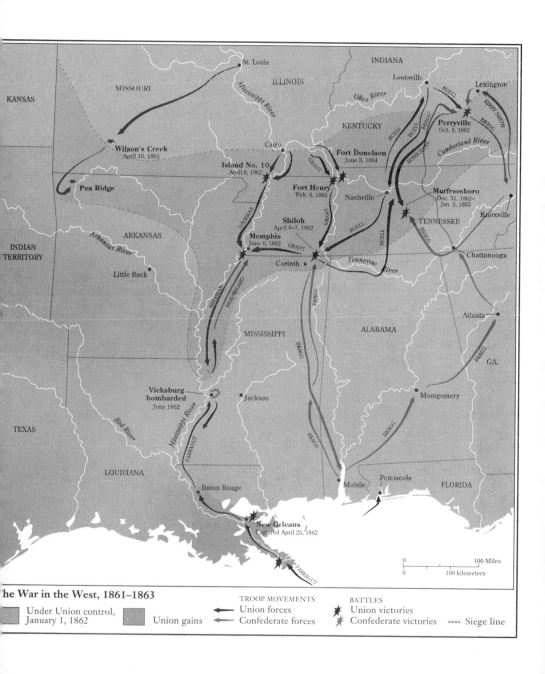

KANSAS

MISSOURI

St. Louis

ILLINOIS

INDIANA

Louisville

Lexington

Mississippi River

Ohio River

BUELL

KIRBY SMITH

KENTUCKY

Perryville
Oct. 8, 1862

BRAGG

Wilson's Creek
April 10, 1861

Cairo

BUELL

BUELL

BRAGG

Pea Ridge

Island No. 10
April 8, 1862

GRANT

Fort Donelson
June 3, 1864

ROSECRANS

Cumberland River

Nashville

Fort Henry
Feb. 6, 1862

Murfreesboro
Dec. 31, 1862–
Jan. 2, 1863

Knoxville

SHERMAN

Arkansas River

ARKANSAS

Shiloh
April 6–7, 1862

Memphis
June 6, 1862

GRANT

BUELL

TENNESSEE

BRAGG

INDIAN
TERRITORY

Little Rock

BEAUREGARD

GRANT

Corinth

Tennessee River

Chattanooga

SHERMAN

MISSISSIPPI

ALABAMA

Atlanta

BRAGG

BRAGG

GA.

TEXAS

Red River

**Vicksburg
bombarded**
June 1862

Jackson

Montgomery

Mississippi River

BRAGG

BRAGG

LOUISIANA

FARRAGUT

Baton Rouge

Mobile

Pensacola

FLORIDA

New Orleans
Captured April 25, 1862

FARRAGUT

0   100 Miles
0   100 kilometers

he War in the West, 1861–1863

Under Union control,
January 1, 1862

Union gains

TROOP MOVEMENTS
Union forces
Confederate forces

BATTLES
Union victories
Confederate victories   Siege line

offensive, known as the Battle of the Seven Days (June 25–July 1). Lee wanted to cut McClellan off from his base on the York River and then destroy the isolated Union army. But McClellan fought his way across the peninsula and set up a new base on the James. There, with naval support, the Army of the Potomac was safe.

It was also only twenty-five miles from Richmond, with a secure line of water communications, and thus in a good position to renew the campaign. Time and again, however, McClellan found reasons for delay. Lincoln, instead of replacing McClellan with a more aggressive commander, finally ordered the army to move back to northern Virginia and join a smaller force under John Pope. The president hoped to begin a new offensive against Richmond on the direct overland route that he himself had always preferred.

As the Army of the Potomac left the peninsula by water, Lee moved north with the Army of Northern Virginia to strike Pope before McClellan could join him. Pope was as rash as McClellan was cautious, and he attacked the approaching Confederates without waiting for the arrival of all of McClellan's troops. In the ensuing Second Battle of Bull Run, or Second Battle of Manassas (August 29–30), Lee threw back the assault and routed Pope's army, which fled to Washington. With hopes for an overland campaign against Richmond now in disarray, Lincoln removed Pope from command and put McClellan in charge of all the federal forces in the region.

Lee soon went on the offensive again, heading north through western Maryland, and McClellan moved out to meet him. McClellan had the good luck to get a copy of Lee's orders, which revealed that a part of the Confederate army, under Stonewall Jackson, had separated from the rest to attack Harpers Ferry. But instead of attacking quickly before the Confederates could recombine, McClellan stalled and gave Lee time to pull most of his forces together behind Antietam Creek, near the town of Sharpsburg. There, on September 17, in the bloodiest engagement of the war, McClellan's 87,000-man army repeatedly attacked Lee's force of 50,000, with staggering casualties on both sides. In all, 6,000 men were killed, 17,000 wounded. Late in the day, just as the Confederate line seemed ready to break, the last of Jackson's troops arrived from Harpers Ferry to reinforce it. McClellan might have broken through with one more assault. Instead, he allowed Lee to retreat into Virginia. Technically, Antietam was a Union victory; but in reality, it was an opportunity squandered. In November, Lincoln finally removed McClellan from command for good.

McClellan's replacement, Ambrose E. Burnside, was a short-lived mediocrity. He tried to move toward Richmond by crossing the Rappahannock River at Fredericksburg, the strongest defensive point on the river. There, on December 13, he launched a series of attacks against Lee, all of them bloody, all of them hopeless. After losing a large part of his army, he withdrew to the north bank of the Rappahannock. He was relieved at his own request.

1863: Year of Decision

By the beginning of 1863, General Joseph Hooker was commanding the still formidable Army of the Potomac, whose 120,000 troops remained north of the Rappahannock, opposite Fredericksburg. But despite his formidable reputation (his popular nickname was "Fighting Joe"), Hooker showed little resolve as he launched his own campaign in the spring. Taking part of his army, Hooker crossed the river above Fredericksburg and moved toward the town and Lee's army. But at the last minute, he apparently lost his nerve and drew back to a defensive position in a desolate area of brush and scrub trees known as the Wilderness. Lee had only half as many men as Hooker had, but he boldly divided his forces for a dual assault on the Union army. In the Battle of Chancellorsville, May 1–5, Stonewall Jackson attacked the Union right and Lee himself charged the front. Hooker barely managed to escape with his army. Lee had frustrated Union objectives, but it was not an entirely happy victory. He had not destroyed the Union army. And his ablest officer, Jackson, was fatally wounded in the course of the battle.

While the Union forces were suffering repeated frustrations in the East, they were winning some important victories in the West. In the spring of 1863, Ulysses S. Grant was driving at Vicksburg, Mississippi, one of the Confederacy's two remaining strongholds on the southern Mississippi River. Vicksburg was well protected, surrounded by rough country on the north and low, marshy ground on the west, and had good artillery coverage of the river itself. But in May, Grant boldly moved men and supplies—over land and by water—to an area south of the city, where the terrain was better. He then attacked Vicksburg from the rear. Six weeks later, on July 4, Vicksburg—whose residents were by then literally starving as a result of a prolonged siege—surrendered. At almost the same time, the other Confederate strong point on the river, Port Hudson, Louisiana, also surrendered—to a Union force that had moved north from New Orleans. The Union had achieved one of its basic military aims: control of the whole length of the Mississippi. The Confederacy was split in two, with Louisiana, Arkansas, and Texas cut off from the other seceded states. The victories on the Mississippi were one of the great turning points of the war.

Early in the siege of Vicksburg, Lee proposed an invasion of Pennsylvania, which would, he argued, divert Union troops north and remove the pressure on the lower Mississippi. Further, he argued, if he could win a major victory on Northern soil, England and France might come to the Confederacy's aid. The war-weary North might even quit the war before Vicksburg fell.

In June 1863, Lee moved up the Shenandoah Valley into Maryland and then entered Pennsylvania. The Union Army of the Potomac, commanded first by Hooker and then by George C. Meade, moved north too, paralleling the Confederates' movement and staying between Lee and Washington. The two armies finally encountered one another at the small town of Gettysburg, Pennsylvania. There, on July 1–3, 1863, they fought the most celebrated battle of the war.

Meade's army established a strong, well-protected position on the hills south of the town. The confident and combative Lee attacked, even though his army of 75,000 was outnumbered by Meade's 90,000. His first assault on the Union forces on Cemetery Ridge failed. A day later, he ordered a second, larger effort. In what is remembered as Pickett's Charge, a force of 15,000 Confederate soldiers advanced for almost a mile across open country while being swept by Union fire. Only about 5,000 made it up the ridge, and this remnant finally had to surrender or retreat. By now, Lee had lost nearly a third of his army. On July 4, the same day as the surrender of Vicksburg, he withdrew from Gettysburg. The retreat was another major turning point in the war. Never again were the weakened Confederate forces able seriously to threaten Northern territory.

Before the end of the year, there was another important turning point, this one in Tennessee. After occupying Chattanooga on September 9, Union forces under William Rosecrans began an unwise pursuit of Bragg's retreating Confederate forces. Bragg was waiting for them just across the Georgia line, with reinforcements from Lee's army. The two armies engaged in the Battle of Chickamauga (September 19–20), one of the few battles in which the Confederates enjoyed a numerical superiority (70,000 to 56,000). Union forces could not break the Confederate lines and retreated back to Chattanooga.

Bragg now began a siege of Chattanooga itself, seizing the heights nearby and cutting off fresh supplies to the Union forces. Grant came to the rescue. In the Battle of Chattanooga (November 23–25), the reinforced Union army drove the Confederates back into Georgia. Northern troops then occupied most of eastern Tennessee. Union forces had now achieved a second important objective: control of the Tennessee River. Four of the

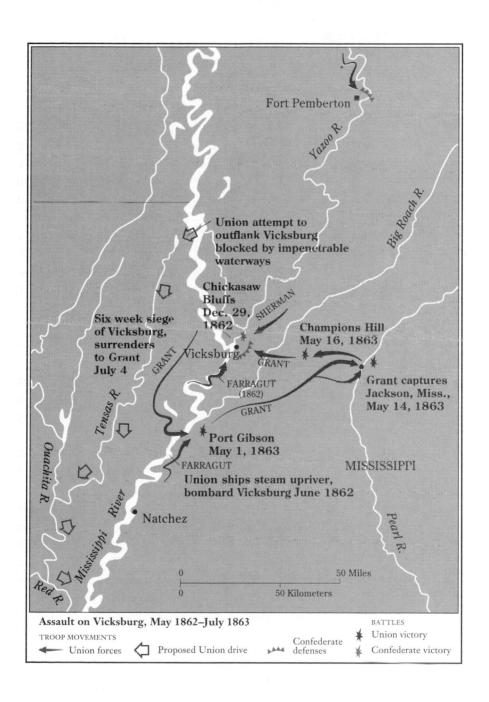

Fort Pemberton

Yazoo R.

Big Roach R.

Union attempt to outflank Vicksburg blocked by impenetrable waterways

Chickasaw Bluffs Dec. 29, 1862

SHERMAN

Champions Hill May 16, 1863

Six week siege of Vicksburg, surrenders to Grant July 4

GRANT

Vicksburg

GRANT

Grant captures Jackson, Miss., May 14, 1863

FARRAGUT (1862)

Tensas R.

GRANT

Port Gibson May 1, 1863

FARRAGUT

Union ships steam upriver, bombard Vicksburg June 1862

MISSISSIPPI

Ouachita R.

Natchez

Mississippi River

Pearl R.

Red R.

| 0 | 50 Miles |
| 0 | 50 Kilometers |

Assault on Vicksburg, May 1862–July 1863

TROOP MOVEMENTS

⬅ Union forces   ⬜ Proposed Union drive   ▶▶▶ Confederate defenses

BATTLES

✸ Union victory

✸ Confederate victory

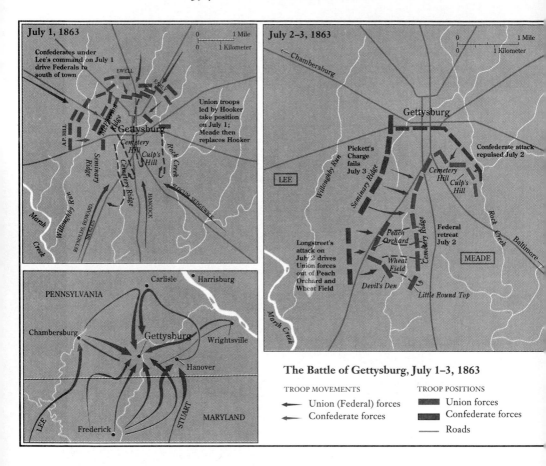

The Battle of Gettysburg, July 1–3, 1863

TROOP MOVEMENTS
- ← Union (Federal) forces
- ← Confederate forces

TROOP POSITIONS
- ▬ Union forces
- ▬ Confederate forces
- —— Roads

eleven Confederate states were now effectively cut off from the Southern nation. No longer could the Confederacy hope to win independence through a decisive military victory. They could hope to win only by holding on and exhausting the Northern will to fight.

The Last Stage, 1864–1865

By the beginning of 1864, Ulysses S. Grant had become general in chief of all the Union armies. At long last, the president had found a general whom he could rely on to pursue the war doggedly and tenaciously. Grant was not a subtle strategic or tactical general; he simply believed in using the North's great advantage in troops and material resources to overwhelm the South. He was not afraid to absorb massive casualties as long as he was inflicting similar casualties on his opponents.

Grant planned two great offensives for 1864. In Virginia, the Army of the Potomac (technically under Meade's command, but really now under Grant's) would advance toward Richmond and force Lee into a decisive battle. In Georgia, the Western army, under William T. Sherman, would

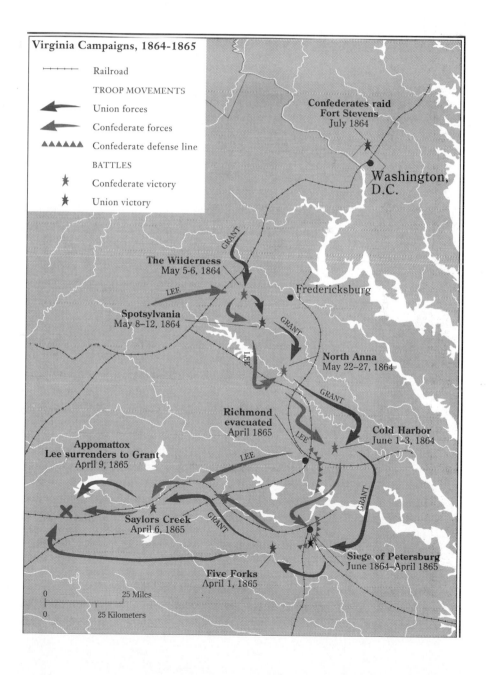

Virginia Campaigns, 1864-1865

Railroad

TROOP MOVEMENTS

Union forces

Confederate forces

Confederate defense line

BATTLES

Confederate victory

Union victory

Confederates raid Fort Stevens July 1864

Washington, D.C.

The Wilderness May 5-6, 1864

Fredericksburg

Spotsylvania May 8-12, 1864

North Anna May 22-27, 1864

Richmond evacuated April 1865

Cold Harbor June 1-3, 1864

Appomattox Lee surrenders to Grant April 9, 1865

Saylors Creek April 6, 1865

Five Forks April 1, 1865

Siege of Petersburg June 1864-April 1865

0   25 Miles

0   25 Kilometers

advance east toward Atlanta and destroy the remaining Confederate force, which was now under the command of Joseph E. Johnston.

The northern campaign began when the Army of the Potomac, 115,000 strong, plunged into the rough, wooded Wilderness area of northwestern Virginia in pursuit of Lee's 75,000-man army. After avoiding an engagement for several weeks, Lee turned Grant back in the Battle of the Wilderness (May 5–7). But Grant was undeterred. Without stopping to rest or reorganize, he resumed his march toward Richmond. He met Lee again in the bloody, five-day Battle of Spotsylvania Court House, in which 12,000 Union troops and a large, but unknown, number of Confederates fell. Despite the enormous losses, Grant kept moving. But victory continued to elude him. Lee kept his army between Grant and the Confederate capital and on June 1–3 repulsed the Union forces again, just northeast of Richmond, at Cold Harbor. The month-long Wilderness campaign had cost Grant 55,000 men (killed, wounded, or captured) compared with Lee's 31,000. And Richmond still had not fallen.

Grant now changed his strategy. He moved his army east of Richmond, bypassing the capital altogether, and headed south toward the railroad center at Petersburg. If he could seize Petersburg, he could cut off the capital's communications with the rest of the Confederacy. But Petersburg had strong defenses; and once Lee came to the city's relief, the assault became a prolonged siege, which lasted nine months.

In Georgia, meanwhile, Sherman was facing a less ferocious resistance. With 90,000 men, he confronted Confederate forces of 60,000 under Johnston, who was unwilling to risk a direct engagement. As Sherman advanced, Johnston tried to delay him by maneuvering. The two armies fought only one real battle—Kennesaw Mountain, northwest of Atlanta, on June 27—where Johnston scored an impressive victory. Even so, he was unable to stop the Union advance toward Atlanta. Davis replaced Johnston with the combative John B. Hood, who twice daringly attacked Sherman's army but accomplished little except seriously weakening his own forces. Sherman took Atlanta on September 2. News of the victory electrified the North and helped unite the previously divided Republican party behind President Lincoln.

Hood now tried unsuccessfully to draw Sherman out of Atlanta by moving back up through Tennessee and threatening an invasion of the North. Sherman did not take the bait. But he did send Union troops to reinforce Nashville. In the Battle of Nashville on December 15–16, 1864, Northern forces practically destroyed what was left of Hood's army.

Meanwhile, Sherman had left Atlanta to begin his soon-to-be-famous "March to the Sea." Living off the land, destroying supplies it could not use, his army cut a sixty-mile-wide swath of desolation across Georgia. "War is all hell," Sherman had once said. By that he meant not that war is terrible, and to be avoided, but that it should be made as horrible and costly as possible for the opponent. He sought not only to deprive the Confederate army of war materials and railroad communications but also to break the will of the Southern people by burning towns and plantations along his route. By December 20, he had reached Savannah, which surrendered two days later. Sherman offered it to President Lincoln as a Christmas gift. Early in 1865, Sherman continued his destructive march, moving northward through South Carolina. He was virtually unopposed until he was well inside North Carolina, where a small force under Johnston could do no more than cause a brief delay.

In April 1865, Grant's Army of the Potomac—still engaged in the prolonged siege at Petersburg—finally captured a vital railroad junction southwest of the town. Without rail access to the South, cut off from other Confederate forces, plagued by heavy casualties and massive desertions, Lee

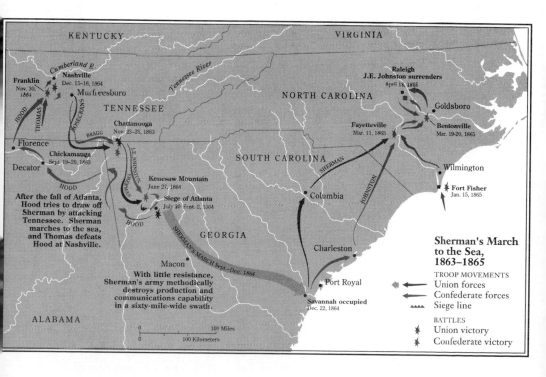

AMERICAN VOICES

J. J. HILL

The 29th Connecticut Colored Infantry Enters Richmond, April 1865

ALL WAS QUIET here until the 1st of April, when all was in readiness, and the order was given to strike tents and move on to Richmond. . . . On our march to Richmond, we captured 500 pieces of artillery, some of the largest kind, 6,000 stand of small arms, and the prisoners I was not able to number. The road was strewed with all kinds of obstacles, and men were lying all along the distance of seven miles. The main body of the army went up the New Market road. The 29th skirmished all the way, and arrived in the city at 7 a.m., and were the first infantry that entered the city. . . .

The 3rd [of April] President Lincoln visited the city. No triumphal march of a conqueror could have equalled in moral sublimity the humble manner in which he entered Richmond. I was standing on the bank of the James River viewing the scene of desolation when a boat, pulled by twelve sailors, came up the stream. It contained President Lincoln and his son. In some way the colored people on the bank of the river ascertained that the tall man wearing the black hat was President Lincoln. . . . As he approached, I said to a woman, "Madam, that is the man that made you free." . . . She gazed at him with clasped hands and said, "Glory to God, Give him the praise for his goodness," and she shouted till her voice failed her. . . . It was a man of the people among the people. It was a great deliverer among the delivered. No wonder tears came to his eyes. . . . After visiting Jeff Davis's Mansion, he proceeded to the rebel capital and from the steps delivered a short speech to the colored people as follows: ". . . God has made you free. Although you have been deprived of your God-given rights by your so-called masters, you are now as free as I am, and if those that claim to be your superiors do not know that you are free, take the sword and bayonet and teach them that you are—for God created all men free, giving to each the same rights of life, liberty, and the pursuit of happiness."

informed the Confederate government that he could no longer defend Richmond. Within hours, Jefferson Davis, his cabinet, and as much of the white population as could find transportation fled along with Lee's soldiers. That night, mobs roamed the city, setting devastating fires. And the next morning, Northern forces (led by an African-American infantry brigade) entered the Confederate capital. With them was Abraham Lincoln, who walked through the streets of the burned-out city surrounded by black men and women cheering him as the "Messiah" and "Father Abraham." In one particularly stirring moment, the president turned to a former slave kneeling on the street before him and said: "Don't kneel to me. . . . You must kneel to God only, and thank Him for the liberty you will enjoy hereafter."

With the remnant of his army, now about 25,000 men, Lee began moving west in the forlorn hope of finding a way around the Union forces so that he could move south and link up with Johnston in North Carolina. But the Union army pursued him and blocked his escape route. Lee finally recognized that further bloodshed was futile. He arranged to meet Grant at a private home in the small town of Appomattox Courthouse, Virginia, where on April 9 he surrendered what was left of his forces. Nine days later, near Durham, North Carolina, Johnston surrendered to Sherman.

In military terms, at least, the long war was now effectively over, even though Jefferson Davis refused to accept defeat. He moved south after leaving Richmond, hoping to reach Texas and continue the struggle from there. He was finally captured in Georgia. A few Southern diehards continued to fight, but even their resistance collapsed before long. And well before the last shot was fired, the difficult process of reuniting the shattered nation had begun.

Debating the Past

The Causes of the Civil War

THE OUTLINES OF the scholarly debate over the causes of the Civil War became visible even before the war itself began. In 1858, Senator William H. Seward of New York took note of the two competing explanations of the sectional tensions that were then inflaming the nation. On one side, he said, stood those who believed the conflicts to be "accidental, unnecessary, the work of interested or fanatical agitators." Opposing them stood those (among them Seward himself) who believed there to be "an irrepressible conflict between opposing and enduring forces." Without realizing it, Seward had identified a division of opinion that would survive among historians for more than a century.

The irrepressible-conflict argument dominated historical discussion of the war from the 1860s to the 1920s. War was inevitable, some historians claimed, because there was no room for compromise on the central issue of slavery. Others de-emphasized slavery and pointed to the economic differences between the agrarian South and the industrializing North. Charles and Mary Beard, for example, wrote in 1927 of the "inherent antagonisms" between the interests of planters and those of industrialists. Each group was seeking to control the federal government to promote its own economic interests. Still others cited social and cultural differences between the two sections as the source of an irrepressible conflict. Slavery, the historian Allan Nevins argued, was only one factor in the cultural divergence that was making residents of the North and South "separate peoples." There were fundamental differences in "assumptions, tastes, and cultural aims" that made it virtually impossible for the two societies to live together in peace.

More recent proponents of "irrepressible-conflict" arguments similarly emphasize culture and ideology but define the concerns of the North and the South in different terms. Eric Foner, writing in 1970, argued that the moral concerns of abolitionists and the economic concerns of industrialists were less important in explaining Northern hostility to the South than was the broad-based "free-labor" ideology of the region. Northerners opposed slavery because they feared it might spread into their own region and threaten the position of free white laborers. Hence their insistence that it not be allowed to expand into the West.

Other historians have taken a very different view of the Civil War. Rather than arguing over what factors made the war inevitable, they have suggested that the differences between North and South were not so great as to require a conflict. The modern version of this position began to emerge in the 1920s, among a group known as the "revisionists." James G. Randall, for example, saw in the social and economic systems of the North and the South no differences so fundamental as to require a war. By the time the war began, he argued, slavery was already "crumbling in the presence of nine-teenth century tendencies." The failures of a "blundering generation" of political leaders, not irrepressible differences, caused the Civil War. Avery Craven, writing in 1942, argued similarly that slavery was on the road to "ultimate extinction" and that skillful and responsible leaders could have produced a compromise solution that would have avoided war. David Donald, writing in 1960, agreed with Randall and Craven that compromise should have been possible. He was less critical than they of the political leaders of the 1850s; he argued, rather, that the rapid extension of democracy in both North and South had made it more difficult for "statesmen" to guard against popular passions. Michael Holt revived the "revisionist" argument in a 1978 book, in which he too emphasized the partisan ambitions of politicians who used sectional rivalries to advance their own aims. "Much of the story of the coming of the Civil War," he argued, "is the story of the successful efforts of Democratic politicians in the South and Republican politicians in the North to keep the sectional conflict at the center of the political debate."

Like the proponents of the "irrepressible conflict" interpretation, the "revisionists" have differed among themselves in important ways. But the explanation of the coming of the Civil War continues, more than a century later, to reflect the two schools of thought William Seward identified in 1858.

CHAPTER FIFTEEN

Reconstructing the Nation

The Problems of Peacemaking ~ *Radical Reconstruction*
The South in Reconstruction ~ *The Grant Administration*
The Abandonment of Reconstruction

EW PERIODS in the history of the United States have produced as much bitterness or created such enduring controversy as the era of Reconstruction—the years following the Civil War during which Americans attempted to reunite their shattered nation. Those who lived through the experience viewed it in sharply different ways. To many white Southerners, Reconstruction was a vicious and destructive experience—a period when vindictive Northerners inflicted humiliation and revenge on the prostrate South and unnecessarily delayed a genuine reunion of the sections. Northern defenders of Reconstruction, in contrast, argued that their policies were the only way to prevent unrepentant Confederates from restoring Southern society as it had been before the war; without forceful federal intervention, there would be no way to forestall the reemergence of a backward aristocracy and the continued subjugation of blacks—no way, in other words, to prevent the same sectional problems that had produced the Civil War in the first place.

To most black Americans at the time, and to many people of all races since, Reconstruction was notable for other reasons. Neither a vicious tyranny, as white Southerners charged, nor a drastic and necessary reform, as many Northerners claimed, it was, rather, an essentially moderate, even conservative program that fell far short of providing the newly freed slaves with the protection they needed. Reconstruction, in other words, was significant less for what it did than for what it failed to do. And when it came to an end, finally, in the late 1870s, black Americans found themselves once again abandoned.

CHARLESTON, 1865 Not until 1864 did substantial fighting and destruction begin to take place in the urban South. But in the last year of the war, several major cities (and many towns and smaller communities) experienced devastation at the hands of the Northern armies—among them Richmond, Atlanta, and (as seen here) Charleston.

THE PROBLEMS OF PEACEMAKING

In 1865, when the Confederacy finally surrendered to the North, no one in Washington knew quite what to do in response. Abraham Lincoln could not negotiate a treaty with the defeated government; he continued to insist that that government had no legal right to exist. Yet neither could he simply readmit the Southern states into the Union as if nothing had happened.

The Aftermath of War

The South after the Civil War was a desolate place. Towns had been gutted, plantations burned, fields neglected, bridges and railroads destroyed. Many white Southerners—stripped of their slaves through emancipation and stripped of the capital they had invested in now worthless Confederate bonds and currency—had no personal property. More than 258,000 Confederate soliders had died in the war, and thousands more returned home wounded or sick. Many families had to rebuild their fortunes without the help of adult males. Many white Southerners faced starvation and homelessness.

If conditions were bad for Southern whites, they were far worse for Southern blacks—the 4 million men and women now emerging from bondage. As soon as the war ended, hundreds of thousands of them—young and old, many of them ill and feeble—left the plantations in search of a new life in freedom. But most had nowhere to go. They trudged to the nearest town or city or roamed the countryside, camping at night on the bare ground. Few had any possessions except the clothes they wore.

The response of many white Southerners to this desolation was an effort to restore their society to its antebellum form. Slavery had been abolished in some areas in 1863 by the Emancipation Proclamation and in all areas as of December 1865 by the Thirteenth Amendment. But many white planters wanted to continue slavery in an altered form by keeping black workers legally tied to the plantations. Blacks, of course, had a very different vision of the postwar South. They wanted, above all, to know and feel their freedom and to be assured that they were not again to lose it. They wanted to own land, to educate their children, and to gain the right to vote. The struggle between Southern blacks and whites over these competing visions was an unequal one, but for a time blacks had the benefit of at least some support from the federal government.

The government kept troops in the South to preserve order and protect the freedmen. And in March 1865, Congress established the Freedmen's Bureau, an agency of the army directed by General Oliver O. Howard. The Freedmen's Bureau distributed food to millions of former slaves. It established schools, staffed by missionaries and teachers who had been sent to the South by Freedmen's Aid Societies and other private and church groups in the North. It tried to settle blacks on lands of their own. (The bureau also offered considerable assistance to poor whites, many of whom were similarly destitute and homeless after the war.)

But the Freedmen's Bureau was not a permanent solution. It had authority to operate for only one year; and it was, in any case, far too small to deal effectively with the enormous problems facing Southern society. It remained up to the federal government to determine whether the hopes of Southern whites or those of Southern blacks would prevail.

Issues of Reconstruction

The terms by which the Southern states rejoined the Union had important implications for both major political parties. The Republican victories in 1860 and 1864 had been a result, in large part, of divisions within the Democratic party and, later, the removal of the South from the electorate. Leaders of both parties believed that readmitting the South would reunite the Democrats and weaken the Republicans. In addition, the Republican party had taken advantage of the absence of the South from Congress to pass a program of nationalistic economic legislation—railroad subsidies, protective tariffs, and other measures of benefit to Northern business leaders and industrialists. Should the Democratic party regain power with heavy Southern support, these programs would be in jeopardy. Complicating these practical questions were emotional concerns. Many Northerners believed the South should be punished for the suffering and sacrifice its rebellion had caused. And many Northerners believed, too, that the South should be transformed, made over in the North's urban-industrial image.

Even among the Republicans in Congress, there was considerable disagreement about the proper approach to Reconstruction—disagreement that reflected the same factional division (between the party's Conservatives and Radicals) that had created disputes during the war over emancipation. Conservatives insisted that the South accept the abolition of slavery, but they proposed few other conditions for the readmission of the seceded states. The Radicals, led by Representative Thaddeus Stevens of Pennsylvania and Senator Charles Sumner of Massachusetts, urged that the civil and military chieftains of the late Confederacy be punished, that large numbers of Southern whites be disenfranchised, that the legal rights of blacks be protected, and that the property of wealthy white Southerners who had aided the Confederacy be confiscated and distributed among the freedmen. Some Radicals favored granting suffrage to the former slaves. Others hesitated, since few Northern states permitted blacks to vote. Between the Radicals and the Conservatives stood a faction of uncommitted Republicans, the Moderates, who rejected the punitive goals of the Radicals but supported extracting at least some concessions from the South on black rights.

Plans for Reconstruction

President Lincoln's sympathies lay with the Moderates and Conservatives of his party. He believed that a lenient Reconstruction policy would encourage Southern Unionists and other former Whigs to join the Republican party and thus prevent the readmission of the South from strengthening the Democrats. More immediately, the Southern Unionists could become the nucleus of new, loyal state governments in the South. Lincoln was not uninterested in the fate of the freedmen, but he was willing to defer questions about race relations for the sake of rapid reunification.

Lincoln's Reconstruction plan, which he announced in December 1863, offered a general amnesty to those white Southerners—other than high officials of the Confederacy—who would pledge loyalty to the government and accept the elimination of slavery. When 10 percent of the number of voters in 1860 took the oath in any state, those loyal voters could set up a state government. Lincoln also hoped to extend suffrage to those blacks who were educated, owned property, and had served in the Union army. Three Southern states—Louisiana, Arkansas, and Tennessee, all under Union occupation—reestablished loyal governments under the Lincoln formula in 1864.

The Radical Republicans were astonished at the mildness of Lincoln's program. They persuaded Congress to deny seats to representatives from

ABRAHAM LINCOLN Lincoln was the subject of many photographic portraits, of which this one, by Matthew Brady, is one of the most famous.

the three "reconstructed" states and refused to count the electoral vote of those states in the election of 1864. But for the moment, the Radicals were uncertain about what form their own Reconstruction plan should take.

Their first effort to resolve that question was the Wade-Davis Bill, passed by Congress in July 1864. By its provisions, the president would appoint a provisional governor for each conquered state. When a majority (not Lincoln's ten percent) of the white males of the state pledged their allegiance to the Union, the governor could summon a state constitutional convention, whose delegates were to be elected by voters who had never borne arms against the United States (again, a major departure from Lincoln's plan). The new state constitutions would be required to abolish slavery, disenfranchise Confederate civil and military leaders, and repudiate debts accumulated by the state governments during the war. After these conditions were met, Congress would readmit the states to the Union. Like the president's proposal, the Wade-Davis Bill left up to the states the question of political rights for blacks.

Congress passed the bill a few days before it adjourned in 1864, and Lincoln disposed of it with a pocket veto. His action enraged the Radical leaders, and the pragmatic Lincoln realized he would have to accept at least some of the Radical demands. As a result, he began to move toward a new approach to Reconstruction.

The Death of Lincoln

What plan he might have produced no one can say. On the night of April 14, 1865, Lincoln and his wife attended a play at Ford's Theater in Washington. As they sat in the presidential box, John Wilkes Booth, an unsuccessful actor obsessed with aiding the Southern cause, entered the box from the rear and shot Lincoln in the head. Early the next morning, the president died.

The circumstances of Lincoln's death earned him immediate martyrdom. They also produced something close to hysteria throughout the North. There were accusations that Booth had acted as part of a great conspiracy—accusations that contained some truth. Booth did indeed have associates, one of whom shot and wounded Secretary of State William Seward the night of the assassination, another of whom abandoned at the last moment a scheme to murder Vice President Andrew Johnson. Booth himself escaped on horseback into the Maryland countryside, where, on April 26, he was cornered by Union troops and shot to death in a blazing barn. Eight other people were convicted by a military tribunal of participating in the conspiracy (at least two of them on the basis of virtually no evidence). Four were hanged.

To many Northerners, however, the murder of the president seemed evidence of an even greater conspiracy—one masterminded and directed by the unrepentant leaders of the defeated South. Militant Republicans exploited such suspicions relentlessly in the ensuing months, ensuring that Lincoln's death would help doom his plans for a relatively generous peace.

Johnson and "Restoration"

Leadership of the Moderates and Conservatives fell to Lincoln's successor, Andrew Johnson, who was not well suited, either by circumstance or personality, for the task. A Democrat until he had joined the Union ticket with Lincoln in 1864, he became president at a time of growing partisan passions. And Johnson himself was an intemperate and tactless man, filled with resentments and insecurities.

Johnson revealed his plan for Reconstruction—or "Restoration," as he preferred to call it—soon after he took office, and he implemented it during the summer of 1865 when Congress was in recess. Like Lincoln, he offered amnesty to those Southerners who would take an oath of allegiance. (High-ranking Confederate officials and all white Southerners with land worth $20,000 or more would have to apply to the president for individual pardons.) In most other respects, however, his plan resembled that of the Wade-Davis Bill. For each state, the president appointed a provisional governor, who would invite qualified voters to elect delegates to a constitutional convention. Johnson did not specify how many qualified voters were necessary, but he implied that he would require a majority (as had the Wade-Davis Bill). In order to win readmission to Congress, a state had to revoke its ordinance of secession, abolish slavery and ratify the Thirteenth Amendment, and repudiate Confederate and state war debts—essentially the same stipulations that had been laid down in Wade-Davis. The final procedure before restoration was that a state would elect a state government and send representatives to Congress.

By the end of 1865, all the seceded states had formed new governments—some under Lincoln's plan, some under Johnson's—and were ready to rejoin the Union, *if* Congress chose to recognize them when it met in December 1865. But Radicals in Congress vowed not to recognize the Johnson governments, just as they had previously refused to recognize the Lincoln regimes; for by now, Northern opinion had become more hostile toward the South than it had been a year earlier when Congress passed the

Wade-Davis Bill. Many Northerners were disturbed by the apparent reluctance of some delegates to the Southern conventions to abolish slavery and by the refusal of all the conventions to grant suffrage to any blacks. They were astounded that states claiming to be "loyal" should elect as state officials and representatives to Congress prominent leaders of the recent Confederacy. Particularly hard to accept was Georgia's choice of Alexander H. Stephens, former vice president of the Confederacy, as a United States senator.

RADICAL RECONSTRUCTION

Reconstruction under Johnson's plan—often known as "presidential Reconstruction"—continued only until Congress reconvened in December 1865. At that point, Congress refused to seat the senators and representatives of the states the president had "restored." Instead, it set up a new Joint Committee on Reconstruction to investigate conditions in the South and to advise Congress in devising a Reconstruction policy of its own. The period of "congressional" or "Radical" Reconstruction had begun.

The Black Codes

Meanwhile, events in the South were driving Northern opinion in even more radical directions. Throughout the South in 1865 and early 1866, state legislatures were enacting sets of laws known as the Black Codes, modeled in many ways on the codes that had regulated free blacks in the prewar South and designed to guarantee white supremacy. Although there were variations from state to state, all codes authorized local officials to apprehend unemployed blacks, fine them for vagrancy, and hire them out to private employers to satisfy the fine. Some of the codes forbade blacks to own or lease farms or to take any jobs other than as plantation workers or domestic servants. To the white South, the Black Codes were a realistic approach to a great social problem. To the North, and to most African-Americans, they represented a return to slavery in all but name.

Congress first responded to the Black Codes by passing an act extending the life of the Freedmen's Bureau and widening its powers. The bureau could now establish special courts for settling labor disputes; the courts could nullify work agreements forced on freedmen under the Black Codes. In April, Congress struck again at the Black Codes by passing the first Civil Rights Act, which declared blacks to be citizens of the United States and empowered the federal government to intervene in state affairs when necessary to protect the rights of citizens. Johnson vetoed both the Freedmen's Bureau and Civil Rights Acts, but Congress eventually overrode him.

The Fourteenth Amendment

In April 1866, the Radicals acted again. The Joint Committee on Reconstruction submitted a proposed Fourteenth Amendment to the Constitution, which Congress approved in early summer and sent to the states for ratification. Eventually, it became one of the most important of all the provisions in the Constitution.

The amendment offered the first constitutional definition of American citizenship. Everyone born in the United States, and everyone naturalized, was automatically a citizen and entitled to all the "privileges and immunities" guaranteed by the Constitution, including equal protection of the laws by both the state and national governments. There could be no other requirements. The amendment also imposed penalties—reduction of representation in Congress and in the electoral college—on states that denied suffrage to any adult male inhabitants. (This was the first time the Constitution had made reference to gender, and the wording clearly reflected the prevailing view in Congress and elsewhere that the franchise was properly restricted to men.) Finally, it prohibited those who had aided the Confederacy after having taken an oath to support the Constitution (that is, members of Congress and other federal officials) from holding any state or federal office unless two-thirds of Congress voted to pardon them.

Congressional Radicals made it clear that if Southern legislatures ratified the Fourteenth Amendment, their states would be readmitted to the Union. But of the former Confederate states, only Tennessee did so. The refusal of others to ratify, along with the refusal of Kentucky and Delaware, denied the amendment the necessary approval of three-fourths of the states and temporarily derailed it.

In the meantime, however, the Radicals were growing stronger, in part because of Northern anger at the South's and Johnson's recalcitrance. When bloody race riots broke out in New Orleans and other Southern cities—riots in which blacks were the principal victims—Radicals cited the incidents as evidence of the inadequacy of Johnson's policy. In the 1866 congressional elections, Johnson actively campaigned for Conservative candidates; but he did his own cause more harm than good with his intemperate speeches. The voters returned an overwhelming majority of Republicans, most of them Radicals, to Congress. In the Senate, there were now 42 Republicans to 11

Democrats; in the House, 143 Republicans to 49 Democrats. (The South remained largely unrepresented in both chambers.) Nothing now prevented the Republicans in Congress from devising a Reconstruction plan of their own.

The Congressional Plan

The Radicals passed three Reconstruction bills early in 1867. Johnson vetoed them all, but Congress overrode him. Finally, nearly two years after the end of the war, the federal government had established a coherent plan for Reconstruction.

That two-year delay had important effects on the way the South reacted to the program. In 1865, with the South reeling from its defeat and nearly prostrate, the federal government could probably have imposed almost any plan on the region without provoking much resistance. But by 1867, the South had already begun to reconstruct itself under the reasonably generous terms Lincoln and Johnson had extended. Measures that might once have seemed moderate now seemed radical, and the congressional Reconstruction plan created deep resentments and continuing resistance.

Under the congressional plan, Tennessee, which had ratified the Fourteenth Amendment, was promptly readmitted. But Congress rejected the Lincoln-Johnson governments of the other ten Confederate states and, instead, combined them into five military districts. Each was assigned a military commander who—in preparation for the readmission of the states—was to register qualfied voters, defined as all adult black males and those white males who had not participated in the rebellion. After the registration was completed, voters would elect a convention to prepare a new state constitution, which had to include provisions for black suffrage. Once voters ratified the new constitution, elections for a state government could be held. Finally, if Congress approved the constitution, if the state legislature ratified the Fourteenth Amendment, and if enough states ratified the amendment to make it part of the Constitution, then the state was to be restored to the Union.

By 1868, seven of the eleven former Confederate states (Arkansas, North Carolina, South Carolina, Louisiana, Alabama, Georgia, and Florida) had fulfilled these conditions (including ratification of the Fourteenth Amendment, which now became part of the Constitution) and were readmitted to the Union. Conservative whites held up the return of Virginia and Texas until 1869 and Mississippi until 1870. By then, Congress had added an additional requirement for readmission—ratification of another constitutional amendment, the Fifteenth, which forbade the states and the federal government to deny the suffrage to any citizen on account of "race, color, or previous condition of servitude." Several Northern and border states refused to approve the Fifteenth Amendment, and it was adopted only with the support of the four Southern states that had to ratify it in order to be readmitted to the Union.

To stop the president from interfering with their designs, the congressional Radicals passed two remarkable laws in 1867. One, the Tenure of Office Act, forbade the president to remove civil officials, including members of his cabinet, without the consent of the Senate. The principal purpose of the law was to protect the job of Secretary of War Edwin M. Stanton, who was the only Lincoln appointee still in Johnson's cabinet and who was cooperating with the Radicals. The other law, the Command of the Army Act, prohibited the president from issuing military orders except through the commanding general of the army (General Grant), whose headquarters were to be in Washington and who could not be relieved or assigned elsewhere without the consent of the Senate.

The congressional Radicals also took action to stop the Supreme Court from interfering with their plans. In 1866, the Court had declared in the case of *Ex parte Milligan* that military tribunals were unconstitutional in places where civil courts were functioning, a decision that seemed to threaten the system of military government the Radicals were planning for the South. Radicals in Congress immediately proposed legislation to require a two-thirds majority of the justices to overrule a law of Congress, to deny the Court jurisdiction in Reconstruction cases, to reduce its membership to three, and even to abolish it. The justices apparently took the hint. Over the next two years, the Court refused to accept jurisdiction in any cases involving Reconstruction.

The Impeachment of the President

Although President Johnson had long since ceased to be a serious obstacle to the passage of Radical legislation, he was still the official charged with administering the Reconstruction programs; and as such, the Radicals believed, he was a serious impediment to their plans. Early in 1867, they began looking for a way to get rid of him. According to the Constitution, only "high crimes or misdemeanors" in office were grounds for impeaching a president and removing him from office. Republicans could find nothing on which to base such charges until Johnson gave them what they considered a plausible reason for action. He deliberately violated the Tenure of

Office Act—in hopes of bringing a test case of the law before the courts. He dismissed Secretary of War Stanton even though the Senate had already refused to consent to the removal.

In the House of Representatives, elated Radicals impeached the president on eleven charges and sent the case to the Senate for trial. The first nine counts dealt with the violation of the Tenure of Office Act. The tenth and eleventh charged Johnson with slandering Congress and with not enforcing the Reconstruction Acts.

The trial before the Senate lasted throughout April and May 1868. The president's accusers argued that Johnson had defied Congress and was indeed guilty of high crimes and misdemeanors. His defenders claimed that he had acted properly in challenging what he considered an unconstitutional law. The Radicals put heavy pressure on all the Republican senators, but the Moderates (who were losing faith in the Radical program) vacillated. On the first three charges to come to a vote, seven Republicans joined the twelve Democrats to support acquittal. The vote was 35 to 19, one short of the constitutionally required two-thirds majority. After that, the Radicals dropped the impeachment campaign.

THE SOUTH IN RECONSTRUCTION

When white Southerners spoke bitterly in later years of the effects of Reconstruction, they referred most frequently to the governments Congress imposed on them—governments that were, they claimed, both incompetent and corrupt, that saddled the region with enormous debts, and that trampled on the rights of citizens. When black Southerners and their defenders condemned Reconstruction, in contrast, they spoke of its failure to guarantee to freedmen even the most elemental rights of citizenship—a failure that resulted in a new and cruel system of economic subordination. Both complaints had some justification, but most historians would now agree that the black criticisms of Reconstruction had a much stronger basis than the white ones.

The Reconstruction Governments

In the ten states of the South that were reorganized under the congressional plan, approximately one-fourth of the white males were at first excluded from voting or holding office, which produced black majorities among voters in South Carolina, Mississippi, and Louisiana (where blacks were also a majority of the population) and in Alabama and Florida (where they were not). But most suffrage restrictions were soon lifted so that nearly all white males could soon vote. After that, Republicans maintained control only with the support of many Southern whites.

Critics labeled these Southern white Republicans with the derogatory term "scalawags." Many were former Whigs who had never felt comfortable in the Democratic party. Some were wealthy (or once wealthy) planters or businessmen. Others were farmers who lived in remote areas where there had been little or no slavery and who hoped the Republican program of internal improvements would help end their economic isolation. White men from the North, known to their opponents as "carpetbaggers" (after the cheap suitcases some of them carried as they moved into the region), also served as Republican leaders in the South. Most of the carpetbaggers were veterans of the Union army who looked on the South as a new frontier, more

THE BURDENED SOUTH This Reconstruction-era cartoon expresses the South's sense of its oppression at the hands of Northern Republicans. President Grant rides in comfort in a carpetbag as the South staggers under the burden in chains.

promising than the West. They had settled there at war's end as hopeful planters, businessmen, or professionals.

The most numerous Republicans in the South were the black freedmen, most of whom had no previous experience in politics and tried, therefore, to build institutions through which they could learn to exercise their power. In several states, African-American voters held their own conventions to chart their future course. One such "colored convention," as Southern whites called it, assembled in Alabama in 1867 and announced: "We claim exactly the same rights, privileges and immunities as are enjoyed by white men—we ask nothing more and will be content with nothing less." Black churches also helped give unity and political self-confidence to the former slaves. After emancipation, most blacks withdrew from the white churches they had been compelled to attend on the plantations and formed their own—institutions based on the elaborate religious practices they had developed (occasionally surreptitiously) under slavery.

African-Americans played a significant role in the politics of the Reconstruction South. They served as delegates to the constitutional conventions. They held public offices of practically every kind. Between 1869 and 1901, twenty blacks served in the United States House of Representatives, two in the Senate. They served, too, in state legislatures and in various other state offices. Southern whites complained loudly (both at the time and for generations to come) about "Negro rule" during Reconstruction, but no such thing ever actually existed in any of the states. No black man was ever elected governor of a Southern state (although P. B. S. Pinchback, the African-American lieutenant governor of Louisiana, was acting governor briefly). Blacks never controlled any of the state legislatures (although African-Americans did once win a majority of seats in South Carolina's lower house). In the South as a whole, the percentage of black officeholders was far lower than the percentage of blacks in the population.

Expanding Budgets and Services

The record of the Reconstruction governments was mixed. Critics at the time and since have denounced them for corruption and financial extravagance, and there is some truth to both charges. Officeholders in many states enriched themselves through graft and other illicit activities. State budgets expanded to hitherto unknown totals, and state debts soared to previously undreamed-of heights. In South Carolina, for example, the public debt increased from $7 million to $29 million in eight years.

The corruption in the South, real as it was, was hardly unique to the

Reconstruction governments. Corruption was at least as rampant in the Northern states. The end of Reconstruction, moreover, did not end corruption in Southern state governments. In many states, in fact, corruption grew worse. And the state expenditures of the Reconstruction years were huge only in comparison with the meager budgets of the antebellum era. They represented an effort to provide the South with desperately needed services that antebellum governments had never offered: public education, public works programs, poor relief, and other costly new commitments. There were, to be sure, graft and extravagance in Reconstruction governments; there were also positive and permanent accomplishments.

Perhaps the most important of those accomplishments was a dramatic improvement in Southern education—an improvement that benefited both whites and blacks. In the first years of Reconstruction, much of the impetus for educational reform in the South came from outside groups—from the Freedmen's Bureau, from Northern private philanthropic organizations, from many Northern white women who traveled to the South to teach in freedmen's schools—and from African-Americans themselves. Over the opposition of many Southern whites, who feared that education would give blacks "false notions of equality," these reformers established a large network of schools for former slaves—4,000 schools by 1870, staffed by 9,000 teachers (half of them black), teaching 200,000 students (about 12 percent of the total school-age population of the freedmen). In the 1870s, Reconstruction governments began to build a comprehensive public school system in the South. By 1876, more than half of all white children and about 40 percent of all black children were attending schools in the South. Several black "academies," offering more advanced education, also began operating. Gradually, these academies grew into an important network of black colleges and universities.

Landownership

The most ambitious goal of the Freedmen's Bureau, and of some Republican Radicals in Congress, was to make Reconstruction the vehicle for a fundamental reform of landownership in the South. The effort failed. In the last years of the war and the first years of Reconstruction, the Freedmen's Bureau did oversee the redistribution of substantial amounts of land to freedmen in a few areas. By June 1865, the bureau had settled nearly 10,000 black families on their own land—most of it drawn from abandoned plantations. By the end of that year, however, the experiment was already collapsing. Southern plantation owners were returning and demanding the

AFTER SLAVERY Although many freed slaves remained agricultural laborers after Emancipation, a considerable number moved off the land
in search of new occupations and new homes. For many, that meant living for some time without stable employment or a permanent home.
This photograph from the late 1860s shows a group of former slaves at
a county almshouse in the South.

restoration of their property, and President Johnson was supporting their
demands. Despite the resistance of the Freedmen's Bureau, most of the
confiscated land was eventually returned to the original white owners.
Congress, moreover, never had much stomach for the idea of land redistribution. Very few Northern Republicans believed that the federal government had the right to confiscate property. Even so, the distribution of
landownership in the South changed considerably in the postwar years.
Among whites, there was a striking decline in landownership, from 80
percent before the war to 67 percent by the end of Reconstruction. Some
whites lost their land because of unpaid debt or increased taxes; some left
the marginal lands they had owned to move to more fertile areas, where
they rented. Among blacks, during the same period, the proportion who
owned land rose from virtually none to more than 20 percent.

Still, most blacks, and a growing minority of whites, did not own their
own land during Reconstruction; and some who acquired land in the 1860s
had lost it by the 1890s. Instead, they worked for others in one form or
another. Many black agricultural laborers—perhaps 25 percent of the to-

tal—simply worked for wages. Most, however, became tenants of white landowners—that is, they worked their own plots of land and paid their landlords either a fixed rent or a share of their crop (hence the term "sharecropping"). The new system represented a repudiation by blacks of the gang-labor system of the antebellum plantation, in which slaves had lived and worked together under the direction of a master. As tenants and sharecroppers, blacks enjoyed at least a physical independence from their landlords and had the sense of working their own land, even if in most cases they could never hope to buy it. But tenantry also benefited landlords in some ways, relieving them of the cost of purchasing slaves and of any responsibility for the physical well-being of their workers.

Incomes and Credit

In some respects, the postwar years were a period of remarkable economic progress for blacks. If the material benefits they had received under slavery are calculated as income, then prewar blacks had earned about a 22 percent share of the profits of the plantation system. By the end of Reconstruction, they were earning 56 percent. Measured another way, the per capita income of blacks rose 46 percent between 1857 and 1879, while the per capita income of whites declined 35 percent. This represented one of the most significant redistributions of income in American history.

But these figures are somewhat misleading. For one thing, while the black share of profits was increasing, the total profits of Southern agriculture were declining—a result of the dislocations of the war and a reduction in the world market for cotton. For another thing, while blacks were earning a greater return on their labor than they had under slavery, they were working less. Women and children were less likely to labor in the fields than in the past. Adult men tended to work shorter days. In all, the black labor force worked about one-third fewer hours during Reconstruction than it had been compelled to do under slavery—a reduction that brought the working schedule of blacks roughly into accord with that of white farm laborers. Nor did the income redistribution of the postwar years lift many blacks out of poverty. Black per capita income rose from about one-quarter of white per capita income to about one-half in the first few years after the war. After this initial increase, it rose hardly at all.

For blacks and poor whites alike, whatever gains there might have been as a result of land and income redistribution were often overshadowed by the ravages of the crop lien system. Few of the traditional institutions of credit in the South—the "factors" and banks—returned after the war. In their stead emerged a new system of credit, centered in large part on local country stores—some of them owned by planters, others owned by independent merchants. Blacks and whites, landowners and tenants—all depended on these stores for such necessities as food, clothing, seed, and farm implements. And since farmers do not have the same steady cash flow as other workers, customers usually had to rely on credit from these merchants in order to purchase what they needed. Most local stores had no competition (and went to great lengths to ensure that things stayed that way). As a result, they were able to set interest rates as high as 50 or 60 percent. Farmers had to give the merchants a lien (or claim) on their crops as collateral for the loans (thus the term "crop-lien system," generally used to describe Southern farming in this period). If a farmer suffered a few bad years in a row, as often happened, he could become trapped in a cycle of debt from which he could never escape.

This burdensome credit system had a number of effects on the region, almost all of them unhealthy. One was that some blacks who had acquired land during the early years of Reconstruction gradually lost it as they fell into debt. So, to a lesser extent, did white small landowners. Another was that Southern farmers became almost wholly dependent on cash crops—and most of all on cotton—because only such marketable commodities seemed to offer any possibility of escape from debt. Thus Southern agriculture, never sufficiently diversified even in the best of times, became more one-dimensional than ever. The relentless planting of cotton, moreover, was contributing to an exhaustion of the soil. The crop-lien system, in other words, was not only helping to impoverish small farmers; it was also contributing to a general decline in the Southern agricultural economy.

The African-American Family in Freedom

One of the most striking features of the black response to Reconstruction was the effort to build or rebuild family structures and to protect them from the interference they had experienced under slavery. A major reason for the rapid departure of so many blacks from plantations was the desire to find lost relatives and reunite families. Thousands of blacks wandered through the South looking for husbands, wives, children, or other relatives from whom they had been separated. Former slaves rushed to have their marriages, previously without legal standing, sanctified by church and law. Black families resisted living in the former slave quarters and moved instead to small cabins scattered widely across the countryside, where they could enjoy at least some privacy.

Within the black family, the definition of male and female roles quickly came to resemble that within white families. Many women and children ceased working in the fields. Such work, they believed, was a badge of slavery. Instead, many women restricted themselves largely to domestic tasks—cooking, cleaning, gardening, raising children, attending to the needs of their husbands. Still, economic necessity often compelled black women to engage in income-producing activities: working as domestic servants, taking in laundry, or helping their husbands in the field. By the end of Reconstruction, half of all black women over the age of sixteen were working for wages. And unlike white working women, most black female income earners were married.

THE GRANT ADMINISTRATION

Exhausted by the political turmoil of the Johnson administration, American voters in 1868 yearned for a strong, stable figure to guide them through the troubled years of Reconstruction. They did not find one. Instead, they turned trustingly to General Ulysses S. Grant, the hero of the war and, by 1868, a revered national idol. Grant was a disastrous president. During his two terms in office, he faced problems that would have taxed the abilities of a master of statecraft. Grant, however, was a dull and unimaginative man with few political skills and little vision.

The Soldier President

Grant could have had the nomination of either party in 1868. But believing that Republican Reconstruction policies were more attuned to public opinion than the Democratic alternatives, he accepted the Republican nomination. The Democrats nominated former governor Horatio Seymour of New York. The campaign was a bitter one, and Grant's triumph was surprisingly modest. He carried twenty-six states, Seymour eight. But Grant's popular majority was a scant 310,000 votes, a result of some 500,000 black votes in the reconstructed states of the South.

Grant entered the White House with no political experience of any kind, and his performance in office was clumsy and ineffectual from the start. Except for Hamilton Fish, whom Grant appointed secretary of state and who served for eight years with great distinction, most members of the cabinet were as dull and inept as the president. Grant relied chiefly, and increasingly, on the machine leaders in the party—the group most ardently devoted to the spoils system.

Grant used the spoils system even more blatantly than most of his predecessors. In doing so, he provoked the opposition of Senator Charles Sumner and other Republican leaders, who joined with reformers to agitate for a new civil-service system to limit the president's appointive powers. Nothing came of their efforts. Grant soon attracted the hostility of other Republicans as well. Many Northerners were growing disillusioned with Reconstruction. Disgusted by stories of corruption, extravagance, and incompetence in the South, they opposed Grant's continuing support of Radical programs there. Some Republicans suspected, too, that there was also corruption in the Grant administration itself. Still others criticized Grant because he did not support a tariff reduction.

By the end of Grant's first term, therefore, members of a substantial faction of the party—who referred to themselves as Liberal Republicans—had come to oppose what they called "Grantism." In 1872, hoping to prevent Grant's reelection, they bolted the party and nominated their own presidential candidate: Horace Greeley, veteran editor and publisher of the New York *Tribune*. The Democrats, somewhat reluctantly, named Greeley their candidate as well, hoping that the alliance with the Liberals would enable them to defeat Grant. But the effort was in vain. Grant won a substantial victory, polling 286 electoral votes and 3,597,000 popular votes to Greeley's 66 and 2,834,000. Greeley had carried only two Southern and four border states. Three weeks later, apparently crushed by his defeat, Greeley died.

The Grant Scandals

During the 1872 campaign, the first of a series of political scandals came to light that would plague Grant and the Republicans for the next eight years. It involved the French-owned Crédit Mobilier construction company, which had helped build the Union Pacific Railroad. The heads of Crédit Mobilier had used their positions as Union Pacific stockholders to steer large and fraudulent contracts to the construction company, thus bilking the Union Pacific (and the federal government, which provided large subsidies to the railroad) of millions. To prevent investigations, the directors had transferred some Crédit Mobilier stock to key members of Congress. But in 1872, Congress did conduct an investigation, which revealed that some highly placed Republicans—including Schuyler Colfax, now Grant's vice president—had accepted stock.

One dreary episode followed another in Grant's second term. Benjamin H. Bristow, Grant's third Treasury secretary, discovered that some of his officials and a group of distillers operating as a "whiskey ring" were cheating the government out of taxes by filing false reports. Then a House investigation revealed that William W. Belknap, secretary of war, had accepted bribes to retain an Indian-post trader in office (the so-called Indian ring). Other, lesser scandals added to the growing impression that "Grantism" had brought rampant corruption to government.

The Greenback Question

Compounding Grant's, and the nation's, problems was the financial crisis known as the Panic of 1873. It began with the failure of a leading investment banking firm, Jay Cooke and Company, which had invested too heavily in postwar railroad building. There had been panics before—in 1819, 1837, and 1857—but this was the worst one yet. The depression it produced lasted four years.

Debtors now pressured the government to inflate the value of their currency, which would have made it easier for them to pay their debts. More specifically, they urged the government to redeem its war bonds with greenbacks, paper currency of the sort printed during the Civil War, which would increase the amount of money in circulation. But Grant and most Republicans wanted a "sound" currency—based solidly on gold reserves—which would favor the interests of banks and other creditors.

The greenback question would not go away. There was, for one thing, the approximately $356 million in paper currency issued during the Civil War that was still in circulation. And in 1873, when the Supreme Court ruled in *Knox* v. *Lee* that greenbacks were legal, the Treasury issued more in response to the panic. The following year, Congress voted to raise the total further. But Grant, under pressure from Eastern financial interests, vetoed the measure.

In 1875, Republican leaders in Congress, in an effort to crush the greenback movement for good, passed the Specie Resumption Act. This law provided that after January 1, 1879, the greenback dollars, whose value constantly fluctuated, would be redeemed by the government and replaced with new certificates, firmly pegged to the price of gold. The law satisfied creditors, who had worried that debts would be repaid in debased paper currency. But "resumption" did little for debtors, because the gold-based money supply was never able to expand as much as they wanted.

In 1875, the "greenbackers," as the inflationists were called, formed their own political organization: the National Greenback party. Active in the next three presidential elections, it failed to gain widespread support. But it did keep the money issue alive. And in the 1880s, the greenback forces began to merge with another, more powerful group of currency reformers— those who favored silver as the basis of currency—to help produce a political movement that would ultimately attain enormous strength. The question of the proper composition of the currency was to remain one of the most controversial and enduring issues in late-nineteenth-century American politics.

Republican Diplomacy

The Johnson and Grant administrations achieved their greatest success in foreign affairs. The accomplishments were the work not of the presidents themselves, who displayed little aptitude for diplomacy, but of two outstanding secretaries of state: William H. Seward, who had served Lincoln and who remained in office until 1869; and Hamilton Fish, who served throughout the two terms of the Grant administration.

An ardent expansionist and advocate of a vigorous foreign policy, Seward acted with as much daring as the demands of Reconstruction politics and the Republican hatred of President Johnson would permit. Seward agreed to a Russian offer to sell Alaska to the United States for $7.2 million. Only with great difficulty was he able to persuade Congress to authorize the purchase, and he faced criticism from many who considered Alaska a useless frozen wasteland and derided it as "Seward's Folly" or "Seward's icebox." But Seward knew that Alaska was an important fishing center and a potential source of valuable resources such as gold. In 1867, Seward also engineered the American annexation of the tiny Midway Islands west of Hawaii.

In contrast with its often shambling course in domestic politics, the diplomatic performance of the Grant administration under Hamilton Fish was generally decisive and firm. Fish's first major challenge was resolving a burning controversy with England. Many Americans believed that the British government had violated the neutrality laws during the Civil War by permitting English shipyards to build ships (among them the *Alabama*) for the Confederacy. American demands that England pay for the damage these vessels had caused became known as the "Alabama claims."

Seward had tried to settle the Alabama claims through the Johnson-Clarendon Convention of 1869, which would have submitted the matter to arbitration. But the Senate rejected it because it contained no British apology. In 1871, Fish succeeded in forging a new agreement, the Treaty of Washington, which provided for international arbitration and in which Britain expressed regret for the escape of the *Alabama* from England.

THE ABANDONMENT OF RECONSTRUCTION

As the North grew increasingly preoccupied with its own political and economic problems, interest in Reconstruction began to wane. The Grant administration continued to protect Republican governments in the South, but less because of any interest in ensuring the position of freedmen than because of a desire to prevent the reemergence of a strong Democratic party in the region. But even the presence of federal troops was not enough to prevent white Southerners from overturning the Reconstruction regimes. By the time Grant left office, Democrats had taken back (or, as white Southerners liked to put it, "redeemed") seven of the governments of the former Confederate states.

For three other states—South Carolina, Louisiana, and Florida—the end of Reconstruction had to wait for the withdrawal of the last federal troops in 1877, a withdrawal that was the result of a long process of political bargaining and compromise at the national level.

The Southern States "Redeemed"

In the states where whites constituted a majority—the states of the upper South—overthrowing Republican control was relatively simple. By 1872, all but a handful of Southern whites had regained suffrage. Now a clear majority, they needed only to organize and elect their candidates.

In other states, where blacks were a majority or the populations of the two races were almost equal, whites used intimidation and violence to undermine the Reconstruction regimes. Secret societies—the Ku Klux Klan, the Knights of the White Camellia, and others—used terrorism to frighten or physically bar blacks from voting or otherwise exercising citizenship. Paramilitary organizations—the Red Shirts and White Leagues—armed themselves to "police" elections and worked to force all white males to join the Democratic party and to exclude all blacks from meaningful political activity. Strongest of all, however, was the simple weapon of economic pressure. Some planters refused to rent land to Republican blacks; storekeepers refused to extend them credit; employers refused to give them work.

In the meantime, Southern blacks were losing the support of many of their former advocates in the North. After the adoption of the Fifteenth Amendment in 1870, some reformers convinced themselves that their long campaign in behalf of black people was now over; that with the vote, blacks ought to be able to take care of themselves. Former Radical leaders such as Charles Sumner and Horace Greeley now began calling themselves Liberals, cooperating with the Democrats, and at times outdoing even the Democrats in denouncing what they viewed as black-and-carpetbag misgovernment. Within the South itself, many white Republicans joined the Liberals and moved into the Democratic party.

The Panic of 1873 further undermined support for Reconstruction. In the congressional elections of 1874, the Democrats won control of the House of Representatives for the first time since 1861. Grant took note of the changing temper of the North and stopped using military force to prop up the Republican regimes that were still standing in the South.

By the end of 1876, only three states were left in the hands of the Republicans—South Carolina, Louisiana, and Florida. In the state elections that year, Democrats (after using terrorist tactics) claimed victory in all three. But the Republicans claimed victory as well and were able to remain in office because of the presence of federal troops. If the troops were to be withdrawn, the last of the Republican regimes would fall.

The Compromise of 1877

Grant had hoped to run for another term in 1876, but most Republican leaders—shaken by recent Democratic successes, afraid of the scandals with which Grant was associated, and worried about the president's failing health—resisted. Instead, they sought a candidate not associated with the problems of the Grant years, one who might entice Liberals back and unite the party again. They settled on Rutherford B. Hayes, a former Union army officer and congressman, three times governor of Ohio, and a champion of civil-service reform. The Democrats united behind Samuel J. Tilden, the reform governor of New York, who had been instrumental in overthrowing the corrupt Tweed Ring of New York City's Tammany Hall.

Although the campaign was a bitter one, there were few differences of principle between the candidates, both of whom were conservatives committed to moderate reform. The November election produced an apparent Democratic victory. Tilden carried the South and several large Northern states, and his popular margin over Hayes was nearly 300,000 votes. But disputed returns from Louisiana, South Carolina, Florida, and Oregon, whose total electoral vote was 20, threw the election in doubt. Tilden had undisputed claim to 184 electoral votes, only one short of the majority. But Hayes could still win if he managed to receive all 20 disputed votes.

The Constitution had established no method to determine the validity of disputed returns. It was clear that the decision lay with Congress, but it was not clear with which house or through what method. (The Senate was Republican, and the House was Democratic.) Members of each party naturally supported a solution that would yield them the victory.

Finally, late in January 1877, Congress tried to break the deadlock by creating a special electoral commission to judge the disputed votes. The commission was to be composed of five senators, five representatives, and five justices of the Supreme Court. The congressional delegation would consist of five Republicans and five Democrats. The Court delegation would include two Republicans, two Democrats, and the only independent, Justice David Davis. But when the Illinois legislature elected Davis to the United States Senate, the justice resigned from the commission. His seat went instead to a Republican justice. The commission voted along straight party lines, 8 to 7, awarding every disputed vote to Hayes. Congress accepted the verdict on March 2. Two days later, Hayes was inaugurated.

Behind the resolution of the deadlock, however, lay a series of elaborate compromises among leaders of both parties. When a Democratic filibuster threatened to derail the commission's report, Republican Senate leaders met secretly with Southern Democratic leaders to work out terms by which the Democrats would support Hayes. According to traditional accounts, Republicans and Southern Democrats met at Washington's Wormley Hotel. In return for a Republican pledge that Hayes would withdraw the last federal troops from the South, thus permitting the overthrow of the last Republican governments there, the Southerners agreed to abandon the filibuster.

Actually, the story behind the "Compromise of 1877" is somewhat more complex. Hayes was already on record as favoring withdrawal of the troops. The real agreement, the one that won the Southern Democrats over, was reached before the Wormley meeting. As the price of their cooperation, the Southern Democrats (among them some former Whigs) exacted several pledges from the Republicans: the appointment of at least one Southerner to the Hayes cabinet, control of federal patronage in their areas, generous internal improvements, federal aid for the Texas and Pacific Railroad, and withdrawal of the troops. Many powerful Southern Democrats supported industrializing the region. They believed that Republican programs of federal support for business would aid their region more than the states' rights policies of the Democrats.

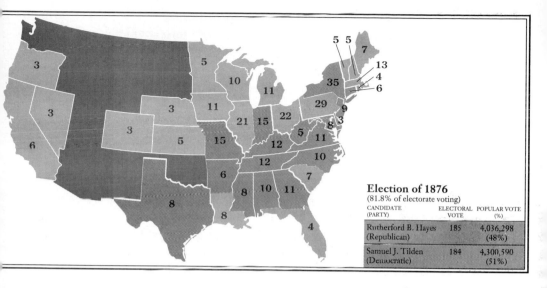

Election of 1876
(81.8% of electorate voting)

CANDIDATE (PARTY)	ELECTORAL VOTE	POPULAR VOTE (%)
Rutherford B. Hayes (Republican)	185	4,036,298 (48%)
Samuel J. Tilden (Democratic)	184	4,300,590 (51%)

In his inaugural address, Hayes announced that the South's most pressing need was the restoration of "wise, honest, and peaceful local self-government"—a signal that he planned to withdraw the troops and let white Democrats take over the state governments. The statement, and Hayes's subsequent actions, supported the widespread charges that he was paying off the South for acquiescing in his election and strengthened those who referred to him as "His Fraudulency." But the election had already created such bitterness that there was probably nothing Hayes could have done to mollify his critics, not even his promise to serve only one term.

The president and his party hoped to build up a "new Republican" organization in the South drawn from Whiggish conservative white groups and committed to modest support for black rights. But all such efforts failed. Although many white Southern leaders sympathized with Republican economic policies, resentment of Reconstruction was so deep that supporting the party was politically impossible. The "solid" Democratic South, which would survive until the mid-twentieth century, was taking shape. And the withdrawal of federal troops was a signal that the national government was giving up its attempt to control Southern politics and to improve the lot of blacks in Southern society.

The Legacy of Reconstruction

Reconstruction was not a complete failure in its effort to help African-Americans. There was a significant redistribution of income, from which blacks benefited. There was a more limited but not unimportant redistribution of landownership, which enabled some former slaves to acquire property. There was both a relative and an absolute improvement in the economic circumstances of most African-Americans.

Nor was Reconstruction as disastrous an experience for Southern whites as most believed at the time. The region had emerged from a prolonged and bloody war defeated and devastated; and yet within little more than a decade, the white South had regained control of its own institutions and, to a great extent, restored its traditional ruling class to power. Former Confederate leaders received no severe punishments. The federal government imposed no drastic economic reforms on the region and indeed few lasting political changes of any kind other than the abolition of slavery. Not many conquered peoples fare as well.

Yet for all that, Americans of the twentieth century cannot help but look back on Reconstruction as a tragic era. For in those years the United States failed in its first serious effort to resolve its oldest and deepest social problem—the problem of race. What was more, the experience so disappointed, disillusioned, and embittered white Americans that it would be nearly a century before they would try again in any serious way.

Why did this great assault on racial injustice end so badly? In part, it was because of the weaknesses and errors of the people who directed it. But in greater part, it was because attempts to produce solutions ran up against conservative obstacles so deeply embedded in the nation's life that they could not be dislodged. Veneration of the Constitution sharply limited the willingness of national leaders to infringe on the rights of states and individuals. A profound respect for private property and free enterprise prevented any real assault on economic privilege in the South. Above all, perhaps, a pervasive belief among many of even the most liberal whites that the black race was inherently inferior served as an obstacle to equality. Given the context within which Americans of the 1860s and 1870s were working, what is surprising, perhaps, is not that Reconstruction did so little but that it accomplished even as much as it did.

Given the odds confronting them, therefore, African-Americans had reason for pride in the limited gains they were able to make during Reconstruction. And future generations had reason for gratitude for two great charters of freedom—the Fourteenth and Fifteenth amendments to the Constitution—which, although largely ignored at the time, would one day serve as the basis for a "Second Reconstruction" that would renew the drive to bring freedom and equality to all Americans.

D E B A T I N G   T H E   P A S T

Reconstruction

D EBATE OVER THE nature of Reconstruction has been unusually intense, not only among historians but among much of the larger public as well. Indeed, few issues in American history have raised such deep and enduring passions.

Beginning in the late nineteenth century and continuing well into the twentieth, a relatively uniform and highly critical view of Reconstruction prevailed among historians—a reflection of a broad consensus among white Americans about the inferiority of blacks and of a yearning in both the North and the South for sectional reconciliation. William A. Dunning's *Reconstruction, Political and Economic* (1907) was the principal scholarly expression of this prevailing view. Dunning portrayed Reconstruction as a corrupt and oppressive outrage imposed on a prostrate South by a vindictive group of Northern Republican radicals. Unscrupulous carpetbaggers flooded the South and plundered the region. Ignorant African-Americans were thrust into political offices for which they were unfit. Reconstruction governments were awash in corruption and compiled enormous levels of debt. The Dunning interpretation dominated several generations of historical scholarship. It also helped shape such popular images of Reconstruction as those in the novel and film *Gone with the Wind*.

Among historians, at least, the Dunning interpretation gradually lost credibility in the face of a series of challenges. W. E. B. Du Bois, the great African-American scholar, offered one of the first alternative views in *Black Reconstruction* (1935). To Du Bois, Reconstruction was an effort by freed blacks (and their white allies) to create a more democratic society in the

(continued on next page)

South, and it was responsible for many valuable social innovations. In the early 1960s, John Hope Franklin and Kenneth Stampp, building on a generation of work by other scholars, published new histories of Reconstruction that replaced, and radically revised, the Dunning interpretation. Reconstruction, they argued, was a genuine, if flawed, effort to solve the problem of race in the South. The Reconstruction governments were not perfect, but they were bold experiments in interracial politics. Congressional radicals were not saints, but they were genuinely concerned with protecting the rights of former slaves. Reconstruction had brought important, if temporary, progress to the South and had created no more corruption there than governments were creating in the North at the same time. What was tragic about Reconstruction, the revisionists claimed, was not what it did to Southern whites but what it failed to do for Southern blacks. It was, in the end, too weak and too short-lived to guarantee African-Americans genuine equality.

In more recent years, some historians have begun to question the assessment of the first revisionists that, in the end, Reconstruction accomplished relatively little. Leon Litwack argued in *Been in the Storm So Long* (1979) that former slaves used the protections Reconstruction offered them to carve out a certain level of independence for themselves within southern society: strengthening churches, reuniting families, and resisting the efforts of white planters to revive the gang labor system.

Eric Foner's *Reconstruction: America's Unfinished Revolution* (1988) also emphasized how far African-Americans moved toward freedom and independence in a short time, how much of lasting value they were able to accomplish despite imposing obstacles, and how important they were in shaping the execution of Reconstruction policies. Reconstruction, he argues, "can only be judged a failure" as an effort to secure "blacks' rights as citizens and free laborers." But it "closed off even more oppressive alternatives. . . . The post-Reconstruction labor system embodied neither a return to the closely supervised gang labor of antebellum days, nor the complete dispossession and immobilization of the black labor force and coercive apprenticeship systems envisioned by white Southerners in 1865 and 1866. Nor were blacks, as in twentieth-century South Africa, barred from citizenship, herded into labor reserves, or prohibited by law from moving from one part of the country to another. . . . The doors of economic opportunity that had opened could never be completely closed."

APPENDICES

CANADA

Puget
Sound
Seattle
Olympia
Spokane
WASHINGTON
Portland Columbia River
Salem
Eugene
OREGON

MONTANA
Missouri   River
Helena
Yellowstone   River

Lake
Sakakawea
Minot
NORTH
DAKOTA
Bismarck

Boise
IDAHO
Snake   River

WYOMING

Pierre
SOUTH
DAKOTA
Sioux F

Great Salt
Lake
Salt Lake
City
Reno
Carson City
NEVADA

UTAH

Cheyenne
N. Platte River
S. Platte River
NEBRASKA
Platte River
Li

Sacramento
Oakland
Stockton
Modesto
San Jose
San Francisco
Fresno
CALIFORNIA
Bakersfield
Las Vegas
Colorado River

Denver
Colorado
Springs
COLORADO

KANSAS
Arkansas
Wichita

Pasadena
San
Bernardino
Los Angeles
Long Beach
Santa Ana
San Diego
Colorado River

ARIZONA
Phoenix
Tucson

Santa Fe
Albuquerque
NEW
MEXICO
Rio Grande
El Paso

Amarillo
Lubbock
Abilene
OKLAHOMA
Oklahoma
City
Red River
Dallas
Fort Worth
Waco

PACIFIC
OCEAN

TEXAS
Au

60°N
RUSSIA
ARCTIC
OCEAN
Bering
Strait
ALASKA
Yukon River
Bering Sea
ALEUTIAN ISLANDS
PACIFIC OCEAN
Anchorage
Gulf of Alaska
Juneau
CANADA

MEXICO
Rio Grande
Nueces
River
Laredo
San Anto
Co
Ch
Brown

Kauai PACIFIC OCEAN
Niihau Oahu Molokai HAWAII
Honolulu Lanai Maui
Kahoolawe
Hawaii

0   400 Miles
0   400 Kilometers

0   200 Miles
0   200 Kilometers

A-2

CANADA

Lake of the Woods

MINNESOTA

Lake Superior

MAINE

*Augusta

MICHIGAN

VERMONT

Montpelier NEW
HAMPSHIRE

*Concord

NEW YORK

Lake Ontario

Albany

*Boston

Minneapolis
St. Paul

WISCONSIN

Milwaukee

Lansing

Rochester

Buffalo

MASSACHUSETTS

Providence

Hartford

RHODE ISLAND

New Haven

CONNECTICUT

IOWA

Madison

Grand
Rapids

Detroit Cleveland

PENNSYLVANIA

Newark

New York

NEW JERSEY

Cedar
Rapids

Chicago

Gary

Fort Wayne

Toledo Akron

Harrisburg

Trenton

Philadelphia

Mississippi River

Illinois River

Peoria

INDIANA

Columbus

OHIO

Pittsburgh

Baltimore

Dover

DELAWARE

Omaha

Des
Moines

ILLINOIS

Springfield

Indianapolis

Dayton

Cincinnati

Washington,
D.C.

Annapolis

MARYLAND

Kansas
City

St. Louis

Louisville

Frankfort

Charleston

WEST
VIRGINIA

VIRGINIA

Chesapeake
Bay

Jefferson
City

Lexington

Richmond

Norfolk

ATLANTIC
OCEAN

MISSOURI

KENTUCKY

Cape
Hatteras

Greensboro

Raleigh

NORTH CAROLINA

ARKANSAS

Nashville

Knoxville

TENNESSEE

Chattanooga

Charlotte

Little
Rock

Memphis

Huntsville

Columbia

SOUTH
CAROLINA

Cape
Fear

Atlanta

Shreveport

MISSISSIPPI

ALABAMA

Birmingham

Macon

Charleston

Columbus

Jackson

Montgomery

GEORGIA

Savannah

Baton Rouge

Mobile

LOUISIANA

New Orleans

Jacksonville

Tallahassee

FLORIDA

Houston

Gulf of Mexico

Orlando

Cape
Canaveral

Tampa

St. Petersburg

Lake Okeechobee

Fort
Lauderdale

Hollywood

Miami

The United States in 1990	
National Capital	
State Capitals	
URBAN POPULATION CENTERS	
Over 5,000,000	
3,000,000–5,000,000	
1,000,000–3,000,000	
500,000–1,000,000	
100,000–500,000	
Less than 100,000 (selected)	

0   300 Miles
0   400 Kilometers

A-3

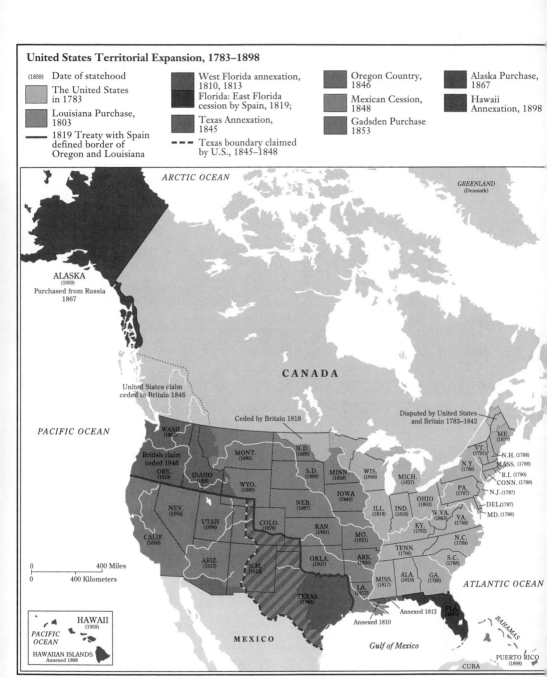

United States Territorial Expansion, 1783–1898

(1859) Date of statehood

The United States in 1783

Louisiana Purchase, 1803

─── 1819 Treaty with Spain defined border of Oregon and Louisiana

West Florida annexation, 1810, 1813

Florida: East Florida cession by Spain, 1819;

Texas Annexation, 1845

─ ─ ─ Texas boundary claimed by U.S., 1845–1848

Oregon Country, 1846

Mexican Cession, 1848

Gadsden Purchase 1853

Alaska Purchase, 1867

Hawaii Annexation, 1898

ARCTIC OCEAN

GREENLAND (Denmark)

ALASKA (1959) Purchased from Russia 1867

PACIFIC OCEAN

CANADA

United States claim ceded to Britain 1846

Ceded by Britain 1818

Disputed by United States and Britain 1783–1842

British claim ceded 1846

WASH. (1889)

MONT. (1889)

N.D. (1889)

ME. (1820)

VT. (1791)

N.H. (1788)

ORE. (1859)

IDAHO (1890)

S.D. (1889)

MINN. (1858)

WIS. (1848)

MICH. (1837)

N.Y. (1788)

MASS. (1788)

R.I. (1790)

CONN. (1788)

WYO. (1890)

IOWA (1846)

PA. (1787)

N.J. (1787)

NEV. (1864)

UTAH (1856)

NEB. (1867)

ILL. (1818)

IND. (1816)

OHIO (1803)

W.VA. (1863)

VA. (1788)

DEL.(1787)

MD. (1788)

CALIF. (1850)

COLO. (1876)

KAN. (1861)

MO. (1821)

KY. (1792)

N.C. (1789)

TENN. (1796)

ARIZ. (1912)

N.M. (1912)

OKLA. (1907)

ARK. (1836)

S.C. (1788)

ATLANTIC OCEAN

TEXAS (1845)

MISS. (1817)

ALA. (1819)

GA. (1788)

LA. (1812)

Annexed 1813

FLA. (1845)

0   400 Miles

0   400 Kilometers

Annexed 1810

BAHAMAS

HAWAII (1959)

PACIFIC OCEAN

MEXICO

Gulf of Mexico

PUERTO RICO (1898)

HAWAIIAN ISLANDS Annexed 1898

CUBA

A-4

Documents and Tables

THE DECLARATION OF INDEPENDENCE

In Congress, July 4, 1776,

THE UNANIMOUS DECLARATION OF THE THIRTEEN UNITED STATES OF AMERICA

When, in the course of human events, it becomes necessary for one people to dissolve the political bands which have connected them with another, and to assume, among the powers of the earth, the separate and equal station to which the laws of nature and of nature's God entitle them, a decent respect to the opinions of mankind requires that they should declare the causes which impel them to the separation.

We hold these truths to be self-evident, that all men are created equal; that they are endowed by their Creator with certain unalienable rights; that among these, are life, liberty, and the pursuit of happiness. That, to secure these rights, governments are instituted among men, deriving their just powers from the consent of the governed; that, whenever any form of government becomes destructive of these ends, it is the right of the people to alter or to abolish it, and to institute a new government, laying its foundation on such principles, and organizing its powers in such form, as to them shall seem most likely to effect their safety and happiness. Prudence, indeed, will dictate that governments long established, should not be changed for light and transient causes; and, accordingly, all experience hath shown, that mankind are more disposed to suffer, while evils are sufferable, than to right themselves by abolishing the forms to which they are accustomed. But, when a long train of abuses and usurpations, pursuing invariably the same object, evinces a design to reduce them under absolute despotism, it is their right, it is their duty, to throw off such government and to provide new guards for their future security. Such has been the patient sufferance of these colonies, and such is now the necessity which constrains them to alter their former systems of government. The history of the present King of Great Britain is a history of repeated injuries and usurpations, all having, in direct object, the establishment of an absolute tyranny over these States. To prove this, let facts be submitted to a candid world:

He has refused his assent to laws the most wholesome and necessary for the public good.

He has forbidden his governors to pass laws of immediate and pressing importance, unless suspended in their operation till his assent should be obtained; and, when so suspended, he has utterly neglected to attend to them.

He has refused to pass other laws for the accommodation of large districts of people, unless those people would relinquish the right of representation in the legislature; a right inestimable to them, and formidable to tyrants only.

He has called together legislative bodies at places unusual, uncomfortable, and distant from the depository of their public records, for the sole purpose of fatiguing them into compliance with his measures.

He has dissolved representative houses repeatedly for opposing, with manly firmness, his invasions on the rights of the people.

He has refused, for a long time after such dissolutions, to cause others to be elected; whereby the legislative powers, incapable of annihilation, have returned to the people at large for their exercise; the state remaining, in the meantime, exposed to all the danger of invasion from without, and convulsions within.

He has endeavored to prevent the population of these States; for that purpose, obstructing the laws for naturalization of foreigners, refusing to pass others to encourage their migration hither, and raising the conditions of new appropriations of lands.

He has obstructed the administration of justice, by refusing his assent to laws for establishing judiciary powers.

He has made judges dependent on his will alone, for the tenure of their offices, and the amount and payment of their salaries.

He has erected a multitude of new offices, and sent hither swarms of officers to harass our people, and eat out their substance.

He has kept among us, in time of peace, standing armies, without the consent of our legislatures.

He has affected to render the military independent of, and superior to, the civil power.

He has combined, with others, to subject us to a jurisdiction foreign to our Constitution, and unacknowledged by our laws; giving his assent to their acts of pretended legislation:

For quartering large bodies of armed troops among us:

For protecting them by a mock trial, from punishment, for any murders which they should commit on the inhabitants of these States:

For cutting off our trade with all parts of the world:

For imposing taxes on us without our consent:

For depriving us, in many cases, of the benefit of trial by jury:

For transporting us beyond seas to be tried for pretended offences:

For abolishing the free system of English laws in a neighboring province, establishing therein an arbitrary government, and enlarging its boundaries, so as to render it at once an example and fit instrument for introducing the same absolute rule into these colonies:

For taking away our charters, abolishing our most valuable laws, and altering, fundamentally, the powers of our governments:

For suspending our own legislatures, and declaring themselves invested with power to legislate for us in all cases whatsoever.

He has abdicated government here, by declaring us out of his protection, and waging war against us.

He has plundered our seas, ravaged our coasts, burnt our towns, and destroyed the lives of our people.

He is, at this time, transporting large armies of foreign mercenaries to complete the works of death, desolation, and tyranny, already begun, with circumstances of cruelty and perfidy scarcely paralleled in the most barbarous ages, and totally unworthy the head of a civilized nation.

He has constrained our fellow citizens, taken captive on the high seas, to bear arms against their country, to become the executioners of their friends, and brethren, or to fall themselves by their hands.

He has excited domestic insurrections amongst us, and has endeavored to bring on the inhabitants of our frontiers, the merciless Indian savages, whose known rule of warfare is an undistinguished destruction of all ages, sexes, and conditions.

In every stage of these oppressions, we have petitioned for redress, in the most humble terms; our repeated petitions have been answered only by repeated injury. A prince, whose character is thus marked by every act which may define a tyrant, is unfit to be the ruler of a free people.

Nor have we been wanting in attention to our British brethren. We have warned them, from time to time, of attempts made by their legislature to extend an unwarrantable jurisdiction over us. We have reminded them of the circumstances of our emigration and settlement here. We have appealed to their native justice and magnanimity, and we have conjured them, by the ties of our common kindred, to disavow these usurpations, which would inevitably interrupt our connections and correspondence. They, too, have been deaf to the voice of justice and consanguinity. We must, therefore, acquiesce in the necessity which denounces our separation, and hold them as we hold the rest of mankind, enemies in war, in peace, friends.

We, therefore, the representatives of the United States of America, in general Congress assembled, appealing to the Supreme Judge of the world for the rectitude of our intentions, do, in the name, and by the authority of the good people of these colonies, solemnly publish and declare, that these united colonies are, and of right ought to be, free and independent states: that they are absolved from all allegiance to the British Crown, and that all political connection between them and the state of Great Britain is, and ought to be, totally dissolved; and that, as free and independent states, they have full power to levy war, conclude peace, contract alliances, establish commerce, and to do all other acts and things which independent states may of right do. And, for the support of this declaration, with a firm reliance on the protection of Divine Providence, we mutually pledge to each other our lives, our fortunes, and our sacred honor.

The foregoing Declaration was, by order of Congress, engrossed, and signed by the following members:

John Hancock

New Hampshire
Josiah Bartlett
William Whipple
Matthew Thornton

Massachusetts Bay
Samuel Adams
John Adams
Robert Treat Paine
Elbridge Gerry

Rhode Island
Stephen Hopkins
William Ellery

Connecticut
Roger Sherman
Samuel Huntington
William Williams
Oliver Wolcott

New York
William Floyd
Philip Livingston
Francis Lewis
Lewis Morris

New Jersey
Richard Stockton
John Witherspoon
Francis Hopkinson
John Hart
Abraham Clark

Pennsylvania
Robert Morris
Benjamin Rush
Benjamin Franklin
John Morton
George Clymer
James Smith
George Taylor
James Wilson
George Ross

Delaware
Caesar Rodney
George Read
Thomas M'Kean

Maryland
Samuel Chase
William Paca
Thomas Stone
Charles Carroll,
   of Carrollton

Virginia
George Wythe
Richard Henry Lee
Thomas Jefferson
Benjamin Harrison
Thomas Nelson, Jr.
Francis Lightfoot Lee
Carter Braxton

North Carolina
William Hooper
Joseph Hewes
John Penn

South Carolina
Edward Rutledge
Thomas Heyward, Jr.
Thomas Lynch, Jr.
Arthur Middleton

Georgia
Button Gwinnett
Lyman Hall
George Walton

Resolved, That copies of the Declaration be sent to the several assemblies, conventions, and committees, or councils of safety, and to the several commanding officers of the continental troops; that it be proclaimed in each of the United States, at the head of the army.

THE CONSTITUTION OF THE UNITED STATES[1]

We the People of the United States, in Order to form a more perfect Union, establish Justice, insure domestic Tranquility, provide for the common defence, promote the general Welfare, and secure the Blessings of Liberty to ourselves and our Posterity, do ordain and establish this CONSTITUTION for the United States of America.

Article I

Section 1.
All legislative Powers herein granted shall be vested in a Congress of the United States, which shall consist of a Senate and House of Representatives.

Section 2.
The House of Representatives shall be composed of Members chosen every second Year by the People of the several States, and the Electors in each State shall have the Qualifications requisite for Electors of the most numerous Branch of the State Legislature.

No Person shall be a Representative who shall not have attained to the Age of twenty-five Years, and been seven Years a Citizen of the United States, and who shall not, when elected, be an Inhabitant of that State in which he shall be chosen.

[Representatives and direct Taxes[2] shall be apportioned among the several States which may be included within this Union, according to their respective Numbers, which shall be determined by adding to the whole Number of free Persons, including those bound to Service for a Term of Years, and excluding Indians not taxed, three fifths of all other Persons.][3] The actual Enumeration shall be made within three Years after the first Meeting of the Congress of the United States, and within every subsequent Term of ten Years, in such Manner as they shall by Law

---

[1] This version, which follows the original Constitution in capitalization and spelling, was published by the United States Department of the Interior, Office of Education, in 1935.
[2] Altered by the Sixteenth Amendment.
[3] Negated by the Fourteenth Amendment.

direct. The Number of Representatives shall not exceed one for every thirty Thousand, but each State shall have at Least one Representative; and until such enumeration shall be made, the State of New Hampshire shall be entitled to chuse three, Massachusetts eight, Rhode-Island and Providence Plantations one, Connecticut five, New York six, New Jersey four, Pennsylvania eight, Delaware one, Maryland six, Virginia ten, North Carolina five, South Carolina five, and Georgia three.

When vacancies happen in the Representation from any State, the Executive Authority thereof shall issue Writs of Election to fill such Vacancies.

The House of Representatives shall chuse their Speaker and other Officers; and shall have the sole Power of Impeachment.

Section 3.

The Senate of the United States shall be composed of two Senators from each State, chosen by the Legislature thereof, for six Years; and each Senator shall have one Vote.

Immediately after they shall be assembled in Consequence of the first Election, they shall be divided as equally as may be into three Classes. The Seats of the Senators of the first Class shall be vacated at the Expiration of the second Year, of the second Class at the Expiration of the fourth Year, and of the third Class at the Expiration of the sixth Year, so that one-third may be chosen every second Year; and if Vacancies happen by Resignation, or otherwise, during the Recess of the Legislature of any State, the Executive thereof may make temporary Appointments until the next Meeting of the Legislature, which shall then fill such Vacancies.

No Person shall be a Senator who shall not have attained to the Age of thirty Years, and been nine Years a Citizen of the United States, and who shall not, when elected, be an Inhabitant of that State for which he shall be chosen.

The Vice President of the United States shall be President of the Senate, but shall have no vote, unless they be equally divided.

The Senate shall chuse their other Officers, and also a President pro tempore, in the absence of the Vice President, or when he shall exercise the Office of President of the United States.

The Senate shall have the sole Power to try all Impeachments. When sitting for that purpose they shall be on Oath or Affirmation. When the President of the United States is tried, the Chief Justice shall preside: And no person shall be convicted without the Concurrence of two thirds of the Members present.

Judgment in Cases of Impeachment shall not extend further than to removal from Office, and disqualification to hold and enjoy any Office of honor, Trust, or Profit under the United States: but the Party convicted shall nevertheless be liable and subject to Indictment, Trial, Judgment, and Punishment, according to Law.

Section 4.

The Times, Places and Manner of holding Elections for Senators and Representatives, shall be prescribed in each State by the Legislature thereof; but the

Congress may at any time by Law make or alter such Regulations, except as to the Places of Chusing Senators.

The Congress shall assemble at least once in every Year, and such Meeting shall be on the first Monday in December, unless they shall by Law appoint a different Day.

Section 5.

Each House shall be the Judge of the Elections, Returns and Qualifications of its own Members, and a Majority of each shall constitute a Quorum to do Business; but a smaller number may adjourn from day to day, and may be authorized to compel the Attendance of absent Members, in such Manner, and under such Penalties, as each House may provide.

Each House may determine the Rules of its Proceedings, punish its Members for disorderly Behaviour, and, with the Concurrence of two thirds, expel a Member.

Each House shall keep a Journal of its Proceedings, and from time to time publish the same, excepting such Parts as may in their Judgment require Secrecy; and the Yeas and Nays of the Members of either House on any question shall, at the Desire of one fifth of those Present, be entered on the Journal.

Neither House, during the Session of Congress, shall, without the Consent of the other, adjourn for more than three days, nor to any other Place than that in which the two Houses shall be sitting.

Section 6.

The Senators and Representatives shall receive a Compensation for their Services, to be ascertained by Law, and paid out of the Treasury of the United States. They shall in all Cases, except Treason, Felony, and Breach of the Peace, be privileged from Arrest during their Attendance at the Session of their respective Houses, and in going to and returning from the same; and for any Speech or Debate in either House, they shall not be questioned in any other Place.

No Senator or Representative shall, during the Time for which he was elected, be appointed to any civil Office under the Authority of the United States, which shall have been created, or the Emoluments whereof shall have been increased, during such time; and no Person holding any Office under the United States shall be a Member of either House during his continuance in Office.

Section 7.

All Bills for raising Revenue shall originate in the House of Representatives; but the Senate may propose or concur with Amendments as on other bills.

Every Bill which shall have passed the House of Representatives and the Senate, shall, before it become a Law, be presented to the President of the United States; If he approve he shall sign it, but if not he shall return it, with his Objections, to that House in which it shall have originated, who shall enter the Objections at large on their Journal, and proceed to reconsider it. If after such Reconsideration two thirds of that House shall agree to pass the bill, it shall be sent, together with the objections, to the other House, by which it shall likewise be reconsidered, and if approved by two thirds of that House, it shall become a Law. But in all such Cases the Votes of both Houses shall be determined by Yeas and Nays, and the Names of the Persons voting for and against the Bill shall be entered on the Journal of each House respectively. If any Bill shall not be returned by the President within ten Days (Sundays excepted) after it shall have been presented to him, the Same shall be a Law, in like Manner as if he had signed it, unless the Congress by their Adjournment prevent its Return, in which Case it shall not be a Law.

Every Order, Resolution, or Vote to which the Concurrence of the Senate and House of Representatives may be necessary (except on a question of Adjournment) shall be presented to the President of the United States; and before the Same shall take Effect, shall be approved by him, or being disapproved by him, shall be repassed by two thirds of the Senate and House of Representatives, according to the Rules and Limitations prescribed in the Case of a Bill.

Section 8.

The Congress shall have Power To lay and collect Taxes, Duties, Imposts and Excises, to pay the Debts and provide for the common Defence and general Welfare of the United States; but all Duties, Imposts and Excises shall be uniform throughout the United States;

To borrow money on the credit of the United States;

To regulate Commerce with foreign Nations, and among the several States, and with the Indian Tribes;

To establish an uniform rule of Naturalization, and uniform Laws on the subject of Bankruptcies throughout the United States;

To coin Money, regulate the Value thereof, and of foreign Coin, and fix the Standard of Weights and Measures;

To provide for the Punishment of counterfeiting the Securities and current Coin of the United States;

To establish Post Offices and post Roads;

To promote the Progress of Science and useful Arts, by securing for limited Times to Authors and Inventors the exclusive Right to their respective Writings and Discoveries;

To constitute Tribunals inferior to the Supreme Court;

To define and punish Piracies and Felonies committed on the high Seas, and Offenses against the Law of Nations;

To declare War, grant Letters of Marque and Reprisal, and make Rules concerning Captures on Land and Water;

To raise and support Armies, but no Appropriation of Money to that Use shall be for a longer Term than two Years;

To provide and maintain a Navy;

To make Rules for the Government and Regulation of the land and naval forces;

To provide for calling forth the Militia to execute the Laws of the Union, suppress Insurrections and repel Invasions;

To provide for organizing, arming, and disciplining the Militia, and for governing such Part of them as may be employed in the Service of the United States, reserving to the States respectively, the Appointment of the Officers, and the Authority of training the Militia according to the discipline prescribed by Congress;

To exercise exclusive Legislation in all Cases whatsoever, over such District (not exceeding ten Miles square) as may, by Cession of particular States, and the acceptance of Congress, become the Seat of the Government of the United States, and to exercise like Authority over all Places purchased by the Consent of the Legislature of the State in which the Same shall be, for the Erection of Forts, Magazines, Arsenals, Dock-yards, and other needful Buildings;—And

To make all Laws which shall be necessary and proper for carrying into Execution the foregoing Powers, and all other Powers vested by this Constitution in the Government of the United States, or in any Department or Officer thereof.

Section 9.

The Migration or Importation of such Persons as any of the States now existing shall think proper to admit, shall not be prohibited by the Congress prior to the Year one thousand eight hundred and eight, but a tax or duty may be imposed on such Importation, not exceeding ten dollars for each Person.

The privilege of the Writ of Habeas Corpus shall not be suspended, unless when in Cases of Rebellion or Invasion the public Safety may require it.

No bill of Attainder or ex post facto Law shall be passed.

No capitation, or other direct, Tax shall be laid unless in Proportion to the Census or Enumeration herein before directed to be taken.

No Tax or Duty shall be laid on Articles exported from any State.

No Preference shall be given by any Regulation of Commerce or Revenue to the Ports of one State over those of another: nor shall Vessels bound to, or from, one State, be obliged to enter, clear, or pay Duties in another.

No Money shall be drawn from the Treasury, but in Consequence of Appropriations made by Law; and a regular Statement and Account of the Receipts and Expenditures of all public Money shall be published from time to time.

No Title of Nobility shall be granted by the United States: And no Person holding any Office of Profit or Trust under them, shall, without the Consent of the Congress, accept of any present, Emolument, Office, or Title, of any kind whatever, from any King, Prince, or foreign State.

Section 10.

No State shall enter into any Treaty, Alliance, or Confederation; grant Letters of Marque and Reprisal; coin Money; emit Bills of Credit; make any Thing but gold and silver Coin a Tender in Payment of Debts; pass any Bill of Attainder, ex post facto Law, or Law impairing the Obligation of Contracts, or grant any Title of Nobility.

No State shall, without the Consent of the Congress, lay any Imposts or Duties on Imports or Exports, except what may be absolutely necessary for executing its inspection Laws; and the net Produce of all Duties and Imposts, laid by any State on Imports or Exports, shall be for the use of the Treasury of the United States; and all such Laws shall be subject to the Revision and Control of the Congress.

No state shall, without the Consent of Congress, lay any duty of Tonnage, keep Troops, or Ships of War in time of Peace, enter into any Agreement or Compact with another State, or with a foreign Power, or engage in War, unless actually invaded, or in such imminent Danger as will not admit of delay.

Article II

Section 1.

The executive Power shall be vested in a President of the United States of America. He shall hold his Office during the Term of four years, and, together with the Vice President, chosen for the same Term, be elected, as follows:

Each State shall appoint, in such Manner as the Legislature thereof may direct, a Number of Electors, equal to the whole Number of Senators and Representatives to which the State may be entitled in the Congress: but no Senator or Representative, or Person holding an Office of Trust or Profit under the United States, shall be appointed an Elector.

[The Electors shall meet in their respective States, and vote by Ballot for two persons, of whom one at least shall not be an Inhabitant of the same State with themselves. And they shall make a List of all the Persons voted for, and of the Number of Votes for each; which List they shall sign and certify, and transmit sealed to the Seat of the Government of the United States, directed to the President of the Senate. The President of the Senate shall, in the Presence of the Senate and House of Representatives, open all the Certificates, and the Votes shall then be counted. The Person having the greatest Number of Votes shall be the President, if such Number be a Majority of the whole Number of Electors appointed; and if there be more than one who have such Majority, and have an equal Number of Votes, then the House of Representatives shall immediately chuse by Ballot one of them for President; and if no Person have a Majority, then from the five highest on the List the said House shall in like Manner chuse the President. But in chusing the President, the Votes shall be taken by States, the Representation from each State having one Vote; a quorum for this Purpose shall consist of a Member or Members from two-thirds of the States, and a Majority of all the States shall be necessary to a Choice. In every Case, after the Choice of the President, the Person having the greatest Number of Votes of the Electors shall be the Vice President. But if there should remain two or more who have equal votes, the Senate shall chuse from them by Ballot the Vice President.][4]

The Congress may determine the Time of chusing the Electors, and the Day

---

[4] Revised by the Twelfth Amendment

on which they shall give their Votes; which Day shall be the same throughout the United States.

No person except a natural-born Citizen, or a Citizen of the United States, at the time of the Adoption of this Constitution, shall be eligible to the Office of President; neither shall any Person be eligible to that Office who shall not have attained to the Age of thirty-five years, and been fourteen Years a Resident within the United States.

In Case of the Removal of the President from Office, or of his Death, Resignation, or Inability to discharge the Powers and Duties of the said Office, the same shall devolve on the Vice President, and the Congress may by Law provide for the Case of Removal, Death, Resignation, or Inability, both of the President and Vice President, declaring what Officer shall then act as President, and such Officer shall act accordingly, until the disability be removed, or a President shall be elected.

The President shall, at stated Times, receive for his Services a Compensation, which shall neither be increased nor diminished during the Period for which he shall have been elected, and he shall not receive within that Period any other Emolument from the United States, or any of them.

Before he enter on the execution of his Office, he shall take the following Oath or Affirmation:—"I do solemnly swear (or affirm) that I will faithfully execute the Office of President of the United States, and will, to the best of my Ability, preserve, protect, and defend the Constitution of the United States."

Section 2.

The President shall be Commander in Chief of the Army and Navy of the United States, and of the Militia of the several States, when called into the actual Service of the United States; he may require the Opinion, in writing, of the principal Officer in each of the executive Departments, upon any subject relating to the Duties of their respective Offices, and he shall have Power to Grant Reprieves and Pardons for Offenses against the United States, except in Cases of Impeachment.

He shall have Power, by and with the Advice and Consent of the Senate, to make Treaties, provided two-thirds of the Senators present concur; and he shall nominate, and by and with the Advice and Consent of the Senate, shall appoint Ambassadors, other public Ministers and Consuls, Judges of the supreme Court, and all other Officers of the United States, whose Appointments are not herein otherwise provided for, and which shall be established by Law: but the Congress may by Law vest the Appointment of such inferior Officers, as they think proper, in the President alone, in the Courts of Law, or in the Heads of Departments.

The President shall have Power to fill up all Vacancies that may happen during the Recess of the Senate, by granting Commissions which shall expire at the End of their next Session.

Section 3.

He shall from time to time give to the Congress Information of the State of the Union, and recommend to their Consideration such Measures as he shall judge necessary and expedient; he may, on extraordinary occasions, convene both Houses, or either of them, and in Case of Disagreement between them, with respect to the Time of Adjournment, he may adjourn them to such Time as he shall think proper; he shall receive Ambassadors and other public Ministers; he shall take care that the Laws be faithfully executed, and shall Commission all the Officers of the United States.

Section 4.

The President, Vice President and all civil Officers of the United States, shall be removed from Office on Impeachment for, and Conviction of, Treason, Bribery, or other high Crimes and Misdemeanors.

Article III

Section 1.

The judicial Power of the United States, shall be vested in one supreme Court, and in such inferior Courts as the Congress may from time to time ordain and establish. The Judges, both of the supreme and inferior Courts, shall hold their Offices during good Behaviour, and shall, at stated Times, receive for their Services, a Compensation, which shall not be diminished during their Continuance in Office.

Section 2.

The judicial Power shall extend to all Cases, in Law and Equity, arising under this Constitution, the Laws of the United States, and Treaties made, or which shall be made, under their Authority;—to all Cases affecting ambassadors, other public ministers and consuls;—to all cases of admiralty and maritime Jurisdiction;—to Controversies to which the United States shall be a Party;—to Controversies between two or more States;—between a State and Citizens of another State;[5]—between Citizens of different States—between Citizens of the same State claiming Lands under Grants of different States, and between a State, or the Citizens thereof, and foreign States, Citizens, or Subjects.

In all Cases affecting Ambassadors, other public Ministers and Consuls, and those in which a State shall be Party, the supreme Court shall have original Jurisdiction. In all the other Cases before mentioned, the supreme Court shall have appellate Jurisdiction, both as to Law and Fact, with such Exceptions, and under such Regulations as the Congress shall make.

The trial of all Crimes, except in Cases of Impeachment, shall be by Jury; and such Trial shall be held in the State where the said Crimes shall have been committed; but when not committed within any State, the Trial shall be at such Place or Places as the Congress may by Law have directed.

---

[5] Qualified by the Eleventh Amendment.

Section 3.

Treason against the United States, shall consist only in levying War against them, or in adhering to their Enemies, giving them Aid and Comfort. No Person shall be convicted of Treason unless on the Testimony of two Witnesses to the same overt Act, or on Confession in open Court.

The Congress shall have power to declare the Punishment of Treason, but no Attainder of Treason shall work Corruption of Blood, or Forfeiture except during the Life of the Person attained.

Article IV

Section 1.

Full Faith and Credit shall be given in each State to the public Acts, Records, and judicial Proceedings of every other State. And the Congress may by general Laws prescribe the Manner in which such Acts, Records and Proceedings shall be proved, and the Effect thereof.

Section 2.

The Citizens of each State shall be entitled to all Privileges and Immunities of Citizens in the several States.

A Person charged in any State with Treason, Felony, or other Crime, who shall flee from Justice, and be found in another State, shall on demand of the executive Authority of the State from which he fled, be delivered up, to be removed to the State having Jurisdiction of the crime.

No Person held to Service or Labour in one State, under the Laws thereof, escaping into another, shall, in Consequence of any Law or Regulation therein, be discharged from such Service or Labour, but shall be delivered up on Claim of the Party to whom such Service or Labour may be due.

Section 3.

New States may be admitted by the Congress into this Union; but no new State shall be formed or erected within the Jurisdiction of any other State; nor any State be formed by the Junction of two or more States, or parts of States, without the Consent of the Legislatures of the States concerned as well as of the Congress.

The Congress shall have Power to dispose of and make all needful Rules and Regulations respecting the Territory or other Property belonging to the United States; and nothing in this Constitution shall be so construed as to Prejudice any Claims of the United States, or of any particular State.

Section 4.

The United States shall guarantee to every State in this Union a Republican Form of Government, and shall protect each of them against Invasion; and on Application of the Legislature, or of the Executive (when the Legislature cannot be convened) against domestic Violence.

Article V

The Congress, whenever two-thirds of both Houses shall deem it necessary, shall propose Amendments to this Constitution, or, on the Application of the Legislatures of two-thirds of the several States, shall call a Convention for proposing Amendments, which, in either Case, shall be valid to all Intents and Purposes, as part of this Constitution, when ratified by the Legislatures of three-fourths of the several States, or by Conventions in three-fourths thereof, as the one or the other Mode of Ratification may be proposed by the Congress; Provided that no Amendment which may be made prior to the Year One thousand eight hundred and eight shall in any Manner affect the first and fourth Clauses in the Ninth Section of the first Article; and that no State, without its Consent, shall be deprived of its equal Suffrage in the Senate.

Article VI

All Debts contracted and Engagements entered into, before the Adoption of this Constitution, shall be as valid against the United States under this Constitution, as under the Confederation.

This Constitution, and the Laws of the United States which shall be made in Pursuance thereof; and all Treaties made, or which shall be made, under the Authority of the United States, shall be the supreme Law of the Land; and the Judges in every State shall be bound thereby, any Thing in the Constitution or Laws of any State to the Contrary notwithstanding.

The Senators and Representatives before mentioned, and the Members of the several State Legislatures, and all executive and judicial Officers, both of the United States and of the several States, shall be bound by Oath or Affirmation to support this Constitution; but no religious Tests shall ever be required as a qualification to any Office or public Trust under the United States.

Article VII

The Ratification of the Conventions of nine States shall be sufficient for the Establishment of this Constitution between the States so ratifying the same.

Done in Convention by the Unanimous Consent of the States present the Seventeenth Day of September in the Year of our Lord one thousand seven hundred and Eighty seven, and of the Independence of the United States of America the Twelfth. In Witness whereof We have hereunto subscribed our Names.[6]

George Washington
President and deputy and deputy from Virginia

New Hampshire
John Langdon
Nicholas Gilman

Massachusetts
Nathaniel Gorham
Rufus King

Connecticut
William Samuel
  Johnson
Roger Sherman

New York
Alexander Hamilton

New Jersey
William Livingston
David Brearley
William Paterson
Jonathan Dayton

Pennsylvania
Benjamin Franklin
Thomas Mifflin
Robert Morris
George Clymer
Thomas FitzSimons
Jared Ingersoll
James Wilson
Gouverneur Morris

Delaware
George Read
Gunning Bedford, Jr.
John Dickinson
Richard Bassett
Jacob Broom

Maryland
James McHenry
Daniel of
  St. Thomas Jenifer
Daniel Carroll

Virginia
John Blair
James Madison, Jr.

North Carolina
William Blount
Richard Dobbs
  Spaight
Hugh Williamson

South Carolina
John Rutledge
Charles Cotesworth
  Pinckney
Charles Pinckney
Pierce Butler

Georgia
William Few
Abraham Baldwin

Articles in Addition to, and Amendment of, the Constitution of the United States of America, Proposed by Congress, and Ratified by the Legislatures of the Several States, Pursuant to the Fifth Article of the Original Constitution.[7]

[Article I]

Congress shall make no law respecting an establishment of religion, or prohibiting the free exercise thereof; or abridging the freedom of speech, or of the press; or the right of the people peaceably to assemble, and to petition the Government for a redress of grievances.

---

[6] These are the full names of the signers, which in some cases are not the signatures on the document.

[7] This heading appears only in the joint resolution submitting the first ten amendments.

[Article II]

A well regulated Militia, being necessary to the security of a free State, the right of the people to keep and bear Arms shall not be infringed.

[Article III]

No Soldier shall, in time of peace, be quartered in any house, without the consent of the Owner, nor in time of war, but in a manner to be prescribed by law.

[Article IV]

The right of the people to be secure in their persons, houses, papers, and effects, against unreasonable searches and seizures, shall not be violated, and no Warrants shall issue, but upon probable cause, supported by Oath or affirmation, and particularly describing the place to be searched, and the persons or things to be seized.

[Article V]

No person shall be held to answer for a capital or otherwise infamous crime, unless on a presentment or indictment of a Grand Jury, except in cases arising in the land or naval forces, or in the Militia, when in actual service in time of War or public danger; nor shall any person be subject for the same offence to be twice put in jeopardy of life or limb; nor shall be compelled in any criminal case to be a witness against himself, nor be deprived of life, liberty, or property, without due process of law; nor shall private property be taken for public use, without just compensation.

[Article VI]

In all criminal prosecutions, the accused shall enjoy the right to a speedy and public trial, by an impartial jury of the State and district wherein the crime shall have been committed, which district shall have been previously ascertained by law, and to be informed of the nature and cause of the accusation; to be confronted with the witnesses against him; to have compulsory process for obtaining witnesses in his favour, and to have the Assistance of Counsel for his defense.

[Article VII]

In suits at common law, where the value in controversy shall exceed twenty dollars, the right of trial by jury shall be preserved, and no fact tried by a jury, shall be otherwise reexamined in any Court of the United States, than according to the rules of the common law.

[Article VIII]

Excessive bail shall not be required, nor excessive fines imposed, nor cruel and unusual punishments inflicted.

[Article IX]

The enumeration of the Constitution, of certain rights, shall not be construed to deny or disparage others retained by the people.

[Article X]

The powers not delegated to the United States by the Constitution, nor prohibited by it to the States, are reserved to the States respectively, or to the people.

[Amendments I–X, in force 1791.]

[Article XI][8]

The Judicial power of the United States shall not be construed to extend to any suit in law or equity, commenced or prosecuted against one of the United States by Citizens of another State, or by Citizens or Subjects of any Foreign State.

[Article XII][9]

The Electors shall meet in their respective States and vote by ballot for President and Vice-President, one of whom, at least, shall not be an inhabitant of the same State with themselves; they shall name in their ballots the person voted for as President, and in distinct ballots the person voted for as Vice-President, and they shall make distinct lists of all persons voted for as President, and of all persons voted for as Vice-President, and of the number of votes for each, which lists they shall sign and certify, and transmit sealed to the seat of the government of the United States, directed to the President of the Senate;—The President of the Senate shall, in the presence of the Senate and House of Representatives, open all the certificates and the votes shall then be counted;—The person having the greatest number of votes for President, shall be the President, if such number be a majority of the whole number of Electors appointed; and if no person have such majority, then from the persons having the highest numbers not exceeding three on the list of those voted for as President, the House of Representatives shall choose immediately, by ballot,

[8] Adopted in 1798.
[9] Adopted in 1804.

the President. But in choosing the President, the votes shall be taken by states, the representation from each state having one vote; a quorum for this purpose shall consist of a member or members from two-thirds of the states, and a majority of all the states shall be necessary to a choice. And if the House of Representatives shall not choose a President whenever the right of choice shall devolve upon them, before the fourth day of March next following, then the Vice-President shall act as President, as in the case of the death or other constitutional disability of the President.—The person having the greatest number of votes as Vice-President, shall be the Vice-President, if such number be a majority of the whole number of Electors appointed, and if no person have a majority, then from the two highest numbers on the list, the Senate shall choose the Vice-President; a quorum for the purpose shall consist of two-thirds of the whole number of Senators, and a majority of the whole number shall be necessary to a choice. But no person constitutionally ineligible to the office of President shall be eligible to that of Vice-President of the United States.

[Article XIII][10]

Section 1.
Neither slavery nor involuntary servitude, except as a punishment for crime whereof the party shall have been duly convicted, shall exist within the United States, or any place subject to their jurisdiction.

Section 2.
Congress shall have power to enforce this article by appropriate legislation.

[Article XIV][11]

Section 1.
All persons born or naturalized in the United States, and subject to the jurisdiction thereof, are citizens of the United States and of the State wherein they reside. No State shall make or enforce any law which shall abridge the privileges or immunities of citizens of the United States; nor shall any State deprive any person of life, liberty, or property, without due process of law; nor deny to any person within its jurisdiction the equal protection of the laws.

Section 2.
Representatives shall be apportioned among the several States according to their respective numbers, counting the whole number of persons in each State, excluding

[10] Adopted in 1865.
[11] Adopted in 1868.

Indians not taxed. But when the right to vote at any election for the choice of electors for President and Vice-President of the United States, Representatives in Congress, the Executive and Judicial officers of a State, or the members of the Legislature thereof, is denied to any of the male inhabitants of such State, being twenty-one years of age, and citizens of the United States, or in any way abridged, except for participation in rebellion, or other crime, the basis of representation therein shall be reduced in the proportion which the number of such male citizens shall bear to the whole number of male citizens twenty-one years of age in such State.

Section 3.

No person shall be a Senator or Representative in Congress, or elector of President and Vice-President, or hold any office, civil or military, under the United States, or under any State, who, having previously taken an oath, as a member of Congress, or as an officer of the United States, or as a member of any State legislature, or as an executive or judicial officer of any State, to support the Constitution of the United States, shall have engaged in insurrection or rebellion against the same, or given aid or comfort to the enemies thereof. But Congress may by a vote of two-thirds of each House, remove such disability.

Section 4.

The validity of the public debt of the United States, authorized by law, including debts incurred for payment of pensions and bounties for services in suppressing insurrection or rebellion, shall not be questioned. But neither the United States nor any State shall assume or pay any debts or obligation incurred in aid of insurrection or rebellion against the United States, or any claim for the loss or emancipation of any slave; but all such debts, obligations, and claims shall be held illegal and void.

Section 5.

The Congress shall have the power to enforce, by appropriate legislation, the provisions of this article.

[Article XV][12]

Section 1.

The right of citizens of the United States to vote shall not be denied or abridged by the United States or by any State on account of race, color, or previous condition of servitude—

Section 2.

The Congress shall have power to enforce this article by appropriate legislation.

[12] Adopted in 1870.

[Article XVI][13]

The Congress shall have power to lay and collect taxes on incomes, from whatever source derived, without apportionment among the several States, and without regard to any census or enumeration.

[Article XVII][14]

The Senate of the United States shall be composed of two Senators from each State, elected by the people thereof, for six years; and each Senator shall have one vote. The electors in each State shall have the qualifications requisite for electors of the most numerous branch of the State legislatures.

When vacancies happen in the representation of any State in the Senate, the executive authority of such State shall issue writs of election to fill such vacancies: *Provided*, That the legislature of any State may empower the executive thereof to make temporary appointments until the people fill the vacancies by election as the legislature may direct.

This amendment shall not be so construed as to affect the election or term of any Senator chosen before it becomes valid as part of the Constitution.

[Article XVIII][15]

Section 1.

After one year from the ratification of this article the manufacture, sale, or transportation of intoxicating liquors within, the importation thereof into, or the exportation thereof from the United States and all territory subject to the jurisdiction thereof for beverage purposes is hereby prohibited.

Section 2.

The Congress and the several States shall have concurrent power to enforce this article by appropriate legislation.

Section 3.

This article shall be inoperative unless it shall have been ratified as an amendment to the Constitution by the legislatures of the several States, as provided in the Constitution, within seven years from the date of the submission hereof to the States by the Congress.

[13] Adopted in 1913.
[14] Adopted in 1913.
[15] Adopted in 1918.

[Article XIX][16]

The right of citizens of the United States to vote shall not be denied or abridged by the United States or by any State on account of sex.

Congress shall have power to enforce this article by appropriate legislation.

[Article XX][17]

Section 1.

The terms of the President and Vice-President shall end at noon on the 20th day of January, and the terms of Senators and Representatives at noon on the 3d day of January, of the years in which such terms would have ended if this article had not been ratified; and the terms of their successors shall then begin.

Section 2.

The Congress shall assemble at least once in every year, and such meeting shall begin at noon on the 3d day of January, unless they shall by law appoint a different day.

Section 3.

If, at the time fixed for the beginning of the term of the President, the President elect shall have died, the Vice-President elect shall become President. If a President shall not have been chosen before the time fixed for the beginning of his term or if the President elect shall have failed to qualify, then the Vice-President elect shall act as President until a President shall have qualified; and the Congress may by law provide for the case wherein neither a President elect nor a Vice-President elect shall have qualified, declaring who shall then act as President, or the manner in which one who is to act shall be selected, and such person shall act accordingly until a President or Vice-President shall have qualified.

Section 4.

The Congress may by law provide for the case of the death of any of the persons from whom the House of Representatives may choose a President whenever the right of choice shall have devolved upon them, and for the case of the death of any of the persons from whom the Senate may choose a Vice-President whenever the right of choice shall have devolved upon them.

[16] Adopted in 1920.
[17] Adopted in 1933.

Section 5.
Sections 1 and 2 shall take effect on the 15th day of October following the ratification of this article.

Section 6.
This article shall be inoperative unless it shall have been ratified as an amendment to the Constitution by the legislatures of three-fourths of the several States within seven years from the date of its submission.

[Article XXI][18]

Section 1.
The eighteenth article of amendment to the Constitution of the United States is hereby repealed.

Section 2.
The transportation or importation into any State, Territory, or possession of the United States for delivery or use therein of intoxicating liquors, in violation of the laws thereof, is hereby prohibited.

Section 3.
This article shall be inoperative unless it shall have been ratified as an amendment to the Constitution by conventions in the several States, as provided in the Constitution, within seven years from the date of the submission hereof to the States by the Congress.

[Article XXII][19]

No person shall be elected to the office of the President more than twice, and no person who has held the office of President, or acted as President, for more than two years of a term to which some other person was elected President shall be elected to the office of the President more than once.

But this Article shall not apply to any person holding the office of President when this Article was proposed by the Congress, and shall not prevent any person who may be holding the office of President, or acting as President, during the term within which this Article becomes operative from holding the office of President or acting as President during the remainder of such term.

[18] Adopted in 1933.
[19] Adopted in 1961.

This article shall be inoperative unless it shall have been ratified as an amendment to the Constitution by the legislatures of three-fourths of the several states within seven years from the date of its submission to the states by the Congress.

[Article XXIII][20]

Section 1.
The District constituting the seat of Government of the United States shall appoint in such manner as the Congress may direct:

A number of electors of President and Vice-President equal to the whole number of Senators and Representatives in Congress to which the District would be entitled if it were a State, but in no event more than the least populous State; they shall be in addition to those appointed by the States, but they shall be considered, for the purposes of the election of President and Vice-President, to be electors appointed by a State; and they shall meet in the District and perform such duties as provided by the twelfth article of amendment.

Section 2.
The Congress shall have power to enforce this article by appropriate legislation.

[Article XXIV][21]

Section 1.
The right of citizens of the United States to vote in any primary or other election for President or Vice President, for electors for President or Vice President, or for Senator or Representative in Congress, shall not be denied or abridged by the United States or any state by reason of failure to pay any poll tax or other tax.

Section 2.
The Congress shall have the power to enforce this article by appropriate legislation.

[Article XXV][22]

Section 1.
In case of the removal of the President from office or of his death or resignation, the Vice President shall become President.

[20] Adopted in 1961.
[21] Adopted in 1964.
[22] Adopted in 1967.

Section 2.

Whenever there is a vacancy in the office of the Vice President, the President shall nominate a Vice President who shall take office upon confirmation by a majority vote of both Houses of Congress.

Section 3.

Whenever the President transmits to the President Pro Tempore of the Senate and the Speaker of the House of Representatives his written declaration that he is unable to discharge the powers and duties of his office, and until he transmits to them a written declaration to the contrary, such powers and duties shall be discharged by the Vice President as Acting President.

Section 4.

Whenever the Vice President and a majority of either the principal officers of the executive departments or of such other body as Congress may by law provide, transmit to the President Pro Tempore of the Senate and the Speaker of the House of Representatives their written declaration that the President is unable to discharge the powers and duties of his office, the Vice President shall immediately assume the powers and duties of the office as Acting President.

Thereafter, when the President transmits to the President Pro Tempore of the Senate and the Speaker of the House of Representatives his written declaration that no inability exists, he shall resume the powers and duties of his office unless the Vice President and a majority of either the principal officers of the executive departments or of such other body as Congress may by law provide, transmit within four days to the President Pro Tempore of the Senate and the Speaker of the House of Representatives their written declaration that the President is unable to discharge the powers and duties of his office. Thereupon Congress shall decide the issue, assembling within forty-eight hours for that purpose if not in session. If the Congress, within twenty-one days after receipt of the latter written declaration, or, if Congress is not in session, within twenty-one days after Congress is required to assemble, determines by two-thirds vote of both Houses that the President is unable to discharge the powers and duties of his office, the Vice President shall continue to discharge the same as Acting President; otherwise, the President shall resume the powers and duties of his office.

[Article XXVI][23]

Section 1.

The right of citizens of the United States, who are eighteen years of age or older, to vote shall not be denied or abridged by the United States or by any State on account of age.

Section 2.

The Congress shall have power to enforce this article by appropriate legislation.

[23] Adopted in 1971.

PRESIDENTIAL ELECTIONS

Year	Candidates	Parties	Popular Vote	Percentage of Popular Vote	Electoral Vote	Percentage of Voter Participation
1789	**GEORGE WASHINGTON (Va.)***				69	
	John Adams				34	
	Others				35	
1792	**GEORGE WASHINGTON (Va.)**				132	
	John Adams				77	
	George Clinton				50	
	Others				5	
1796	**JOHN ADAMS (Mass.)**	Federalist			71	
	Thomas Jefferson	Democratic-Republican			68	
	Thomas Pinckney	Federalist			59	
	Aaron Burr	Dem.-Rep.			30	
	Others				48	
1800	**THOMAS JEFFERSON (Va.)**	Dem.-Rep.			73	
	Aaron Burr	Dem.-Rep.			73	
	John Adams	Federalist			65	
	C. C. Pinckney	Federalist			64	
	John Jay	Federalist			1	
1804	**THOMAS JEFFERSON (Va.)**	Dem.-Rep.			162	
	C. C. Pinckney	Federalist			14	

Year	Candidate	Party	Popular Vote	%	Electoral Vote	%
1808	JAMES MADISON (Va.)	Dem.-Rep.			122	
	C. C. Pinckney	Federalist			47	
	George Clinton	Dem.-Rep.			6	
1812	JAMES MADISON (Va.)	Dem.-Rep.			128	
	De Witt Clinton	Federalist			89	
1816	JAMES MONROE (Va.)	Dem.-Rep.			183	
	Rufus King	Federalist			34	
1820	JAMES MONROE (Va.)	Dem.-Rep.			231	
	John Quincy Adams	Dem.-Rep.			1	
1824	JOHN Q. ADAMS (Mass.)	Dem.-Rep.	108,740	30.5	84	26.9
	Andrew Jackson	Dem.-Rep.	153,544	43.1	99	
	William H. Crawford	Dem.-Rep.	46,618	13.1	41	
	Henry Clay	Dem.-Rep.	47,136	13.2	37	
1828	ANDREW JACKSON (Tenn.)	Democratic	647,286	56.0	178	57.6
	John Quincy Adams	National Republican	508,064	44.0	83	
1832	ANDREW JACKSON (Tenn.)	Democratic	687,502	55.0	219	55.4
	Henry Clay	National Republican	530,189	42.4	49	
	John Floyd	Independent			11	
	William Wirt	Anti-Mason	33,108	2.6	7	

* State of residence at time of election.

PRESIDENTIAL ELECTIONS *(cont.)*

Year	Candidates	Parties	Popular Vote	Percentage of Popular Vote	Electoral Vote	Percentage of Voter Participation
1836	**MARTIN VAN BUREN (N.Y.)**	Democratic	765,483	50.9	170	57.8
	W. H. Harrison	Whig			73	
	Hugh L. White	Whig	739,795	49.1	26	
	Daniel Webster	Whig			14	
	W. P. Magnum	Independent			11	
1840	**WILLIAM H. HARRISON (Ohio)**	Whig	1,274,624	53.1	234	80.2
	Martin Van Buren	Democratic	1,127,781	46.9	60	
	J. G. Birney	Liberty	7,069		—	
1844	**JAMES K. POLK (Tenn.)**	Democratic	1,338,464	49.6	170	78.9
	Henry Clay	Whig	1,300,097	48.1	105	
	J. G. Birney	Liberty	62,300	2.3	—	
1848	**ZACHARY TAYLOR (La.)**	Whig	1,360,967	47.4	163	72.7
	Lewis Cass	Democratic	1,222,342	42.5	127	
	Martin Van Buren	Free-Soil	291,263	10.1	—	
1852	**FRANKLIN PIERCE (N.H.)**	Democratic	1,601,117	50.9	254	69.6
	Winfield Scott	Whig	1,385,453	44.1	42	
	John P. Hale	Free-Soil	155,825	5.0	—	
1856	**JAMES BUCHANAN (Pa.)**	Democratic	1,832,955	45.3	174	78.9
	John C. Frémont	Republican	1,339,932	33.1	114	
	Millard Fillmore	American	871,731	21.6	8	
1860	**ABRAHAM LINCOLN (Ill.)**	Republican	1,865,593	39.8	180	81.2
	Stephen A. Douglas	Democratic	1,382,713	29.5	12	
	John C. Breckinridge	Democratic	848,356	18.1	72	
	John Bell	Union	592,906	12.6	39	

Year	Candidate	Party	Popular Vote	%	Electoral Vote	Participation %
1864	**ABRAHAM LINCOLN (Ill.)**	Republican	2,213,655	55.0	212	73.8
	George B. McClellan	Democratic	1,805,237	45.0	21	
1868	**ULYSSES S. GRANT (Ill.)**	Republican	3,012,833	52.7	214	78.1
	Horatio Seymour	Democratic	2,703,249	47.3	80	
1872	**ULYSSES S. GRANT (Ill.)**	Republican	3,597,132	55.6	286	71.3
	Horace Greeley	Democratic; Liberal Republican	2,834,125	43.9	66	
1876	**RUTHERFORD B. HAYES (Ohio)**	Republican	4,036,298	48.0	185	81.8
	Samuel J. Tilden	Democratic	4,300,590	51.0	184	
1880	**JAMES A. GARFIELD (Ohio)**	Republican	4,454,416	48.5	214	79.4
	Winfield S. Hancock	Democratic	4,444,952	48.1	155	
1884	**GROVER CLEVELAND (N.Y.)**	Democratic	4,874,986	48.5	219	77.5
	James G. Blaine	Republican	4,851,981	48.2	182	
1888	**BENJAMIN HARRISON (Ind.)**	Republican	5,439,853	47.9	233	79.3
	Grover Cleveland	Democratic	5,540,309	48.6	168	
1892	**GROVER CLEVELAND (N.Y.)**	Democratic	5,556,918	46.1	277	74.7
	Benjamin Harrison	Republican	5,176,108	43.0	145	
	James B. Weaver	People's	1,041,028	8.5	22	
1896	**WILLIAM McKINLEY (Ohio)**	Republican	7,104,779	51.1	271	79.3
	William J. Bryan	Democratic-People's	6,502,925	47.7	176	
1900	**WILLIAM McKINLEY (Ohio)**	Republican	7,207,923	51.7	292	73.2
	William J. Bryan	Dem.-Populist	6,358,133	45.5	155	
1904	**THEODORE ROOSEVELT (N.Y.)**	Republican	7,623,486	57.9	336	65.2
	Alton B. Parker	Democratic	5,077,911	37.6	140	
	Eugene V. Debs	Socialist	402,283	3.0	—	

PRESIDENTIAL ELECTIONS (cont.)

Year	Candidates	Parties	Popular Vote	Percentage of Popular Vote	Electoral Vote	Percentage of Voter Participation
1908	**WILLIAM H. TAFT (Ohio)**	Republican	7,678,908	51.6	321	65.4
	William J. Bryan	Democratic	6,409,104	43.1	162	
	Eugene V. Debs	Socialist	420,793	2.8	—	
1912	**WOODROW WILSON (N.J.)**	Democratic	6,293,454	41.9	435	58.8
	Theodore Roosevelt	Progressive	4,119,538	27.4	88	
	William H. Taft	Republican	3,484,980	23.2	8	
	Eugene V. Debs	Socialist	900,672	6.0	—	
1916	**WOODROW WILSON (N.J.)**	Democratic	9,129,606	49.4	277	61.6
	Charles E. Hughes	Republican	8,538,221	46.2	254	
	A. L. Benson	Socialist	585,113	3.2	—	
1920	**WARREN G. HARDING (Ohio)**	Republican	16,152,200	60.4	404	49.2
	James M. Cox	Democratic	9,147,353	34.2	127	
	Eugene V. Debs	Socialist	919,799	3.4	—	
1924	**CALVIN COOLIDGE (Mass.)**	Republican	15,725,016	54.0	382	48.9
	John W. Davis	Democratic	8,386,503	28.8	136	
	Robert M. LaFollette	Progressive	4,822,856	16.6	13	
1928	**HERBERT HOOVER (Calif.)**	Republican	21,391,381	58.2	444	56.9
	Alfred E. Smith	Democratic	15,016,443	40.9	87	
	Norman Thomas	Socialist	267,835	0.7	—	
1932	**FRANKLIN D. ROOSEVELT (N.Y.)**	Democratic	22,821,857	57.4	472	56.9
	Herbert Hoover	Republican	15,761,841	39.7	59	
	Norman Thomas	Socialist	881,951	2.2	—	

Year	Candidate	Party	Popular Vote	%	Electoral Vote	%
1936	**FRANKLIN D. ROOSEVELT** (N.Y.)	Democratic	27,751,597	60.8	523	61.0
	Alfred M. Landon	Republican	16,679,583	36.5	8	
	William Lemke	Union	882,479	1.9	—	
1940	**FRANKLIN D. ROOSEVELT** (N.Y.)	Democratic	27,244,160	54.8	449	62.5
	Wendell L. Willkie	Republican	22,305,198	44.8	82	
1944	**FRANKLIN D. ROOSEVELT** (N.Y.)	Democratic	25,602,504	53.5	432	55.9
	Thomas E. Dewey	Republican	22,006,285	46.0	99	
1948	**HARRY S. TRUMAN** (Mo.)	Democratic	24,105,695	49.5	304	53.0
	Thomas E. Dewey	Republican	21,969,170	45.1	189	
	J. Strom Thurmond	State-Rights Democratic	1,169,021	2.4	38	
	Henry A. Wallace	Progressive	1,156,103	2.4	—	
1952	**DWIGHT D. EISENHOWER** (N.Y.)	Republican	33,936,252	55.1	442	63.3
	Adlai E. Stevenson	Democratic	27,314,992	44.4	89	
1956	**DWIGHT D. EISENHOWER** (N.Y.)	Republican	35,575,420	57.6	457	60.6
	Adlai E. Stevenson	Democratic	26,033,066	42.1	73	
	Other	—	—		1	
1960	**JOHN F. KENNEDY** (Mass.)	Democratic	34,227,096	49.9	303	62.8
	Richard M. Nixon	Republican	34,108,546	49.6	219	
	Other	—	—		15	
1964	**LYNDON B. JOHNSON** (Tex.)	Democratic	43,126,506	61.1	486	61.7
	Barry M. Goldwater	Republican	27,176,799	38.5	52	

PRESIDENTIAL ELECTIONS (cont.)

Year	Candidates	Parties	Popular Vote	Percentage of Popular Vote	Electoral Vote	Percentage of Voter Participation
1968	RICHARD M. NIXON (N.Y.)	Republican	31,770,237	43.4	301	60.6
	Hubert H. Humphrey	Democratic	31,270,533	42.7	191	
	George Wallace	American Independent	9,906,141	13.5	46	
1972	RICHARD M. NIXON (N.Y.)	Republican	47,169,911	60.7	520	55.2
	George S. McGovern	Democratic	29,170,383	37.5	17	
	Other				1	
1976	JIMMY CARTER (Ga.)	Democratic	40,828,587	50.0	297	53.5
	Gerald R. Ford	Republican	39,147,613	47.9	241	
	Other		1,575,459	2.1		
1980	RONALD REAGAN (Calif.)	Republican	43,901,812	50.7	489	52.6
	Jimmy Carter	Democratic	35,483,820	41.0	49	
	John B. Anderson	Independent	5,719,722	6.6	—	
	Ed Clark	Libertarian	921,188	1.1	—	
1984	RONALD REAGAN (Calif.)	Republican	54,455,075	59.0	525	53.3
	Walter Mondale	Democratic	37,577,185	41.0	13	
1988	GEORGE BUSH (Texas)	Republican	47,946,422	54.0	426	50.2
	Michael S. Dukakis	Democratic	41,016,429	46.0	112	
1992	BILL CLINTON (Ark.)	Democratic	43,728,375	43.0	370	55
	George Bush	Republican	38,167,416	38.0	168	
	Ross Perot	Independent	19,237,247	19.0	0	

POPULATION OF THE UNITED STATES,
1790–1990

Year	Population	Percent Increase	Population per Square Mile	Percent Urban/ Rural	Percent White/ Nonwhite	Median Age
1790	3,929,214		4.5	5.1/94.9	80.7/19.3	NA
1800	5,308,483	35.1	6.1	6.1/93.9	81.1/18.9	NA
1810	7,239,881	36.4	4.3	7.3/92.7	81.0/19.0	NA
1820	9,638,453	33.1	5.5	7.2/92.8	81.6/18.4	16.7
1830	12,866,020	33.5	7.4	8.8/91.2	81.9/18.1	17.2
1840	17,069,453	32.7	9.8	10.8/89.2	83.2/16.8	17.8
1850	23,191,876	35.9	7.9	15.3/84.7	84.3/15.7	18.9
1860	31,443,321	35.6	10.6	19.8/80.2	85.6/14.4	19.4
1870	39,818,449	26.6	13.4	25.7/74.3	86.2/13.8	20.2
1880	50,155,783	26.0	16.9	28.2/71.8	86.5/13.5	20.9
1890	62,947,714	25.5	21.2	35.1/64.9	87.5/12.5	22.0
1900	75,994,575	20.7	25.6	39.6/60.4	87.9/12.1	22.9
1910	91,972,266	21.0	31.0	45.6/54.4	88.9/11.1	24.1
1920	105,710,620	14.9	35.6	51.2/48.8	89.7/10.3	25.3
1930	122,775,046	16.1	41.2	56.1/43.9	89.8/10.2	26.4
1940	131,669,275	7.2	44.2	56.5/43.5	89.8/10.2	29.0
1950	150,697,361	14.5	50.7	64.0/36.0	89.5/10.5	30.2
1960	179,323,175	18.5	50.6	69.9/30.1	88.6/11.4	29.5
1970	203,302,031	13.4	57.4	73.5/26.5	87.6/12.4	28.0
1980	226,545,805	11.4	64.0	73.7/26.3	86.0/14.0	30.0
1990	248,709,873	9.9	70.3	77.5/22.5	80.3/19.7	32.9

NA = Not available.

EMPLOYMENT, 1870–1990

Year	Number of Workers (in millions)	Male/Female Employment Ratio	Percentage of Workers in Unions
1870	12.5	85/15	—
1880	17.4	85/15	—
1890	23.3	83/17	—
1900	29.1	82/18	3
1910	38.2	79/21	6
1920	41.6	79/21	12
1930	48.8	78/22	7
1940	53.0	76/24	27
1950	59.6	72/28	25
1960	69.9	68/32	26
1970	82.1	63/37	25
1980	108.5	58/42	23
1985	108.9	57/43	19
1988	114.9	55/45	17
1990	124.8	54/46	16

PRODUCTION, TRADE, AND FEDERAL SPENDING/DEBT, 1790–1990

Year	Gross National Product (GNP) (in billions $)	Balance of Trade (in millions $)	Federal Budget (in billions $)	Federal Surplus/Deficit (in billions $)	Federal Debt (in billions $)
1790	—	-3	.004	+0.00015	.076
1800	—	-20	.011	+0.0006	.083
1810	—	-18	.008	+0.0012	.053
1820	—	-4	.018	-0.0004	.091
1830	—	+3	.015	+0.100	.049
1840	—	+25	.024	-0.005	.004
1850	—	-26	.040	+0.004	.064
1860	—	-38	.063	-0.01	.065
1870	7.4	-11	.310	+0.10	2.4
1880	11.2	+92	.268	+0.07	2.1
1890	13.1	+87	.318	+0.09	1.2
1900	18.7	+569	.521	+0.05	1.2
1910	35.3	+273	.694	-0.02	1.1
1920	91.5	+2,880	6.357	+0.3	24.3
1930	90.7	+513	3.320	+0.7	16.3
1940	100.0	-3,403	9.6	-2.7	43.0
1950	286.5	+1,691	43.1	-2.2	257.4
1960	506.5	+4,556	92.2	+0.3	286.3
1970	992.7	+2,511	196.6	+2.8	371.0
1980	2,631.7	+24,088	579.6	-59.5	914.3
1990	5,465.1	-100,997.1	1,251.8	-220.3	3,223.3

Suggested Readings

CHAPTER 1 THE MEETING OF CULTURES

American Indians. Wilcomb E. Washburn, *The Indian in America* (1975); James H. Merrell, *The Indians' New World* (1989); Bruce G. Trigger, *Natives and Newcomers* (1985); Carl Sauer, *Sixteenth-Century North America* (1985); Francis Jennings, *The Invasion of America: Indians, Colonialism, and the Cant of Conquest* (1975); Neal Salisbury, *Manitou and Providence: Indians, Europeans, and the Making of New England* (1982); Nathan Wachtel, *The Vision of the Vanquished* (1977); Kenneth MacGowan and J. A. Hester, Jr., *Early Man in the New World* (1950); Harold E. Driver, *Indians of North America*, 2nd ed. (1970); Francisco Guerra, *The Pre-Columbian Mind* (1971); Gary B. Nash, *Red, White, and Black*, rev. ed. (1982); Alfred W. Crosby, Jr., *The Columbian Exchange: Biological and Cultural Consequences of 1492* (1972); Henry Warner Bowden, *American Indians and Christian Missions* (1982); James Axtell, *The European and the Indian: Essays in the Ethnohistory of Colonial North America* (1981) and *The Invasion Within: The Contest of Cultures in Colonial North America* (1983); R. F. Spencer, J. D. Jennings, et al., *The Native Americans* (1978); Christopher L. Miller, *Prophetic Worlds: Indians and Whites on the Columbia Plateau* (1985).

European Explorations and Spanish America. Samuel Eliot Morison, *Admiral of the Ocean Sea*, 2 vols. (1942), *The European Discovery of America: The Northern Voyages* (1971), and *The European Discovery of America: The Southern Voyages* (1974); J. H. Parry, *The Age of Reconnaissance* (1963); David B. Quinn, *North America from Earliest Discovery to First Settlements* (1977); Charles Gibson, *Spain in America* (1966); James Lockhart, *Spanish Peru, 1532–1560: A Colonial Society* (1968); James Lang, *Conquest and Commerce: Spain and England in the Americas* (1975); J. H. Elliott, *The Old World and the New, 1492–1650* (1970); William H. Prescott, *History of the Conquest of Mexico*, 3 vols. (1843).

England Looks West. W. H. McNeill, *The Rise of the West* (1963); J. H. Parry, *Europe and the New World, 1415–1715* (1949) and *The Age of Reconnaissance* (1963); Wallace Notestein, *The English People on the Eve of Colonization, 1603–1630* (1954); Peter Laslett, *The World We Have Lost* (1965); Carl Bridenbaugh, *Vexed and Troubled Englishmen, 1590–1642* (1968); Patrick Collinson, *The Elizabethan Puritan Movement* (1967); C. H. George and Katherine George, *The Protestant Mind of the English Reformation* (1961); Michael Walzer, *The Revolution of the Saints* (1965); Keith Thomas, *Religion and the Decline of Magic* (1971); David Quinn, *The Elizabethans and the Irish* (1966); Nicholas Canny, *The Elizabethan Conquest of Ireland* (1976) and *Kingdom and Colony: Ireland in the Atlantic World* (1988); Lawrence Stone, *The Crisis of the Aristocracy* (1965); Margaret Spufford, *Contrasting Communities* (1974); David Underdown, *Pride's Purge* (1985); Christopher Hill, *The Century of Revolution, 1603–1714* (1961).

First English Colonies. Keith Wrightson, *English Society, 1580–1680* (1982); David B. Quinn, *The Roanoke Voyages, 1584–1590*, 2 vols. (1955), *Raleigh and the British Empire* (1947), and *Set Fair for Roanoke* (1985); Karen Ordahl Kupperman, *Roanoke: The Abandoned Colony* (1984).

CHAPTER 2 THE ENGLISH "TRANSPLANTATIONS"

General Histories. Charles M. Andrews, *The Colonial Period in American History*, 4 vols. (1934–1938); Clarence L. Ver Steeg, *The Formative Years, 1607–1763* (1964); John E. Pomfret and F. M. Shumway, *Founding the American Colonies, 1583–1660* (1970).

Jamestown. Philip L. Barbour, ed., *The Complete Works of Captain John Smith*, 3 vols. (1986); Bradford Smith, *Captain John Smith* (1953); Philip L. Barbour, *The Three Worlds of Captain John Smith* (1964); Alden T. Vaughn, *American Genesis* (1975).

The Chesapeake. Darret B. and Anita H. Rutman, *A Place in Time* (1984); Allan Kulikoff, *Tobacco and Slaves* (1986); Fredrick F. Siegel, *The Roots of Southern Distinctiveness* (1987); Suzanne Lebsock, *A Share of Honour* (1984); Aubrey Land et al., *Law, Society, and Politics in Early Maryland* (1977); T. H. Breen, *Tobacco Culture* (1985); Wesley Frank Craven, *The Dissolution of the Virginia Company* (1932), *The Southern Colonies in the Seventeenth Century* (1949), and *White, Red, and Black: The Seventeenth Century Virginian* (1971); Edmund S. Morgan, *American Slavery, American Freedom* (1975); Richard L. Morton, *Colonial Virginia*, 2 vols. (1960); Wilcomb E. Washburn, *The Governor and the Rebel* (1958); David W. Jordon, *Foundations of Representative Government: Maryland, 1632–1715* (1987); David B. Quinn, ed., *Early Maryland in a Wider World* (1982); Gloria Main, *Tobacco Colony: Life in Early Maryland, 1650–1720* (1982); Lois G. Carr and David W. Jordan, *Maryland's Revolution of Government, 1689–1692* (1974); Thad Tate and David L. Ammerman, eds., *The Chesapeake in the Seventeenth Century* (1979).

Plymouth and Massachusetts Bay. William Bradford, *Of Plymouth Plantation* (1952); George Langdon, *Pilgrim Colony* (1966); John Demos, *A Little Commonwealth* (1970); William Cronon, *Changes in the Land: Indians, Colonists, and the Ecology of New England* (1983); Samuel Eliot Morison, *Builders of the Bay Colony* (1930); Darrett Rutman, *Winthrop's Boston* (1965); R. E. Wall, *Massachusetts Bay: The Crucial Decade, 1640–1650* (1972); Edmund S. Morgan, *The Puritan Dilemma: The Story of John Winthrop* (1962); Alden T. Vaughn, *New England Frontier: Puritans and Indians* (1965); Bernard Bailyn, *The New England Merchants in the Seventeenth Century* (1955); Harold Selesky, *War and Society in Colonial Connecticut* (1990).

New England Puritanism. Perry Miller, *The New England Mind: The Seventeenth Century* (1939), *The New England Mind: From Colony to Province* (1953), *Orthodoxy in Massachusetts* (1933), and *Errand into the Wilderness* (1956); Edmund S. Morgan, *Visible Saints* (1963), *The Puritan Family* (1966), and *Roger Williams: The Church and the State* (1967); Kenneth Silverman, *The Life and Times of Cotton Mather* (1984); Charles Hambrick-Stowe, *The Practice of Piety* (1982); Philip F. Gura, *A Glimpse of Sion's Glory* (1984); Harry S. Stout, *The New England Soul* (1986); Norman Pettit, *The Heart Prepared: Grace and Conversion in Puritan Spiritual Life* (1989); Sacvan Bercovitch, *The American Jeremiad* (1978) and *The Puritan Origins of the American Self* (1975); Andrew Delbanco, *The Puritan Ordeal* (1989); David Hall, *The Faithful Shepherd* (1972) and *Worlds of Wonder, Days of Judgment* (1989); Robert Middlekauff, *The Mathers* (1971); Larzer Ziff, *Puritanism in America* (1973); Kai Erikson, *Wayward Puritans* (1966); W. K. B. Stoever, *A Faire and Easy Way to Heaven* (1978); J. V. James, *Colonial Rhode Island* (1975); M. J. A. Jones,

Congregational Commonwealth: Connecticut, 1636–1662 (1968); Paul R. Lucas, *Valley of Discord* (1976).

The Restoration Colonies. Christopher Hill, *The World Turned Upside Down* (1972); H. T. Merrens, *Colonial North Carolina* (1964); M. E. Sirmans, *Colonial South Carolina* (1966); Clarence L. Ver Steeg, *Origins of a Southern Mosaic* (1975); Robert Weir, *Colonial South Carolina* (1983); Roger Ekirch, *Poor Carolina* (1981); Peter H. Wood, *Black Majority* (1974); Oliver A. Rink, *Holland on Hudson* (1986); Thomas J. Archdeacon, *New York City, 1664–1710* (1976); Michael Kammen, *Colonial New York* (1975); Thomas J. Condon, *New York Beginnings* (1968); Van Cleaf Bachman, *Peltries or Plantations* (1969); George L. Smith, *Religion and Trade in New Netherland* (1973); Patricia Bonomi, *A Factious People* (1971); Barry Levy, *Quakers and the American Family* (1988); Alan Tully, *William Penn's Legacy* (1977); Edwin B. Bronner, *William Penn's Holy Experiment* (1962); Mary Maples Dunn, *William Penn: Politics and Conscience* (1967); James T. Lemmon, *The Best Poor Man's Country* (1972); J. E. Pomfret, *The Province of East and West New Jersey, 1609–1702* (1956) and *The Province of East New Jersey* (1962); T. R. Reese, *Colonial Georgia: A Study in British Imperial Policy in the Eighteenth Century* (1963); K. Coleman, *Colonial Georgia* (1976).

The Development of Empire. Lawrence Gipson, *The British Empire Before the American Revolution*, 15 vols. (1936–1970); Stephen S. Webb, *The Governors-General* (1979) and *1676: The End of American Independence* (1984); Leonard Labaree, *Royal Government in America* (1964); Michael Kammen, *Empire and Interest* (1970); Thomas C. Barrow, *Trade and Empire* (1967); I. K. Steele, *The Politics of Colonial Policy* (1968); James Henretta, *Salutary Neglect* (1972); Michael Hall, *Edward Randolph and the American Colonies* (1960); Viola Barnes, *The Dominion of New England* (1923); Lawrence Harper, *The English Navigation Laws* (1939); David S. Lovejoy, *The Glorious Revolution in America* (1972); J. M. Sosin, *English America and the Revolution of 1688* (1982) and *English America and the Restoration Monarchy of Charles II* (1980).

CHAPTER 3 LIFE IN PROVINCIAL AMERICA

General Social Histories. James A. Henretta and Gregory Nobles, *The Evolution of American Society, 1700–1815*, rev. ed. (1987); Richard Hofstadter, *America at 1750: A Social Portrait* (1971); David Hackett Fischer, *Albion's Seed* (1989).

Population and Family. Robert V. Wells, *The Population of the British Colonies in America Before 1776* (1975); Philip Greven, *Four Generations* (1970) and *The Protestant Temperament: Patterns of Child-Rearing, Religious Experience, and the Self in Early America* (1977); John Putnam Demos, *Past, Present, and Personal: The Family and Life Course in American History* (1986); Helena Wall, *Fierce Communion: Family and Community in Early America* (1990); Edmund S. Morgan, *The Puritan Family* (1966); J. William Frost, *The Quaker Family in Colonial America* (1972); Christopher Jedrey, *The World of John Cleaveland: Family and Community in Eighteenth-Century New England* (1979); Joan M. Jensen, *Loosening the Bonds: Mid-Atlantic Farm Women, 1750–1850* (1986); Laura Thatcher Ulrich, *Good Wives: Image and Reality in the Lives of Women in Northern New England, 1650–1750* (1982); Roger Thompson, *Women in Stuart England and America*

(1974); Lyle Koehler, *A Search for Power: 'The Weaker Sex' in Seventeenth-Century New England* (1982); Daniel Blake Smith, *Inside the Great House: Planter Family Life in Eighteenth Century Chesapeake Society* (1980); Judith Walzer Leavitt, *Brought to Bed: Child Bearing in America, 1750–1950* (1986).

Immigration. Bernard Bailyn, *The Peopling of British North America: An Introduction* (1986) and *Voyagers to the West: A Passage in the Peopling of America on the Eve of the Revolution* (1986); Albert B. Faust, *The German Element in the United States*, 2 vols. (1909); Ian C. C. Graham, *Colonists from Scotland: Emigration to North America, 1707–1783* (1956); James G. Leyburn, *The Scotch-Irish: A Social History* (1962); Frederic Klees, *The Pennsylvania Dutch* (1950); R. J. Dickson, *Ulster Immigration to the United States* (1966); Marcus L. Hanson, *The Atlantic Migration, 1607–1860* (1940); James Kettner, *The Development of American Citizenship* (1978).

Society and Slavery in the Colonial South. Edmund S. Morgan, *American Slavery, American Freedom* (1975); Peter Wood, *Black Majority* (1974); Winthrop Jordan, *White over Black* (1968); David Brion Davis, *The Problem of Slavery in Western Culture* (1966); Mechal Sobel, *The World They Made Together: Black and White Values in Eighteenth-Century Virginia* (1987); David W. Galenson, *Traders, Planters, and Slaves: Market Behavior in Early English America* (1986); Rhys Isaac, *The Transformation of Virginia, 1740–1790* (1982); Jean E. Friedman, *The Enclosed Garden: Women and Community in the Evangelical South* (1985); Jack P. Greene, *Pursuits of Happiness* (1988); Allan Kulikoff, *Tobacco and Slaves* (1986); Philip D. Curtin, *The Atlantic Slave Trade* (1969); Daniel Littlefield, *Rice and Slaves: Ethnicity and the Slave Trade in Colonial South Carolina* (1981); David Eltis, *Economic Growth and the Ending of the Transatlantic Slave Trade* (1987); Jay Coughtry, *The Notorious Triangle: Rhode Island and the African Slave Trade, 1799–1807* (1981); Abbot E. Smith, *Colonists in Bondage* (1947); Gerald Mullin, *Flight and Rebellion* (1972); Eugene Genovese, *From Rebellion to Revolution* (1979); Gary B. Nash, *Red, White, and Black*, rev. ed. (1982); Charles Joyner, *Down by the Riverside: A South Carolina Slave Community* (1984); T. H. Breen and Stephen Innes, *'Myne Own Ground,' Race and Freedom on Virginia's Eastern Shore* (1980); T. H. Breen, *Tobacco Culture* (1985); Julia C. Spruill, *Women's Life and Work in the Southern Colonies* (1972); J. Leitch Wright, Jr., *Anglo-Spanish Rivalry in North America* (1971) and *The Only Land They Knew: The Tragic Story of the American Indians in the Old South* (1981).

Society and Town in Colonial New England. Kenneth Lockridge, *A New England Town* (1970); Michael Zuckerman, *Peaceable Kingdoms* (1970); Darrett Rutman, *Winthrop's Boston* (1965); Charles Grant, *Democracy in the Connecticut Frontier Town of Kent* (1961); Paul Boyer and Stephen Nissenbaum, *Salem Possessed* (1974); John Putnam Demos, *Entertaining Satan: Witchcraft and the Culture of Early New England* (1982); Carol Karlsen, *The Devil in the Shape of a Woman: Witchcraft in Colonial New England* (1987); E. M. Cook, Jr., *The Fathers of Towns* (1975); Sumner Chilton Powell, *Puritan Village* (1963); Steven Foster, *The Long Argument: English Puritanism and the Shaping of New England Culture, 1570–1700* (1991); Richard Bushman, *From Puritan to Yankee* (1967); Robert Gross, *The Minutemen and Their World* (1976).

The Colonial Economy. Alice Hanson Jones, *Wealth of a Nation to Be* (1980); Jackson Turner Main, *The Social Structure of Revolutionary America* (1965); Stuart Bruchey, *Roots* *of American Economic Growth, 1607–1861* (1965); John J. McCusker and Russell R. Menard, *The Economy of British America, 1607–1787* (1985); Carl Bridenbaugh, *Myths and Realities: Societies of the Colonial South* (1963); Paul G. E. Clemens, *The Atlantic Economy and Colonial Maryland's Eastern Shore: From Tobacco to Grain* (1980); Edmund S. Morgan, *Virginians at Home* (1952); Jacob M. Price, *France and the Chesapeake*, 2 vols. (1973), *The Tobacco Adventure to Russia* (1961), and *Capital and Credit in the British Overseas Trade: The View from the Chesapeake, 1700–1776* (1980); Harry R. Merrens, *Colonial North Carolina in the Eighteenth Century* (1964); Stephen Innes, *Labor in a New Land: Economy and Society in Seventeenth Century Springfield* (1983); Stephen Innes, ed., *Work and Labor in Early America* (1988); David W. Galenson, *White Servitude in Colonial America: An Economic Analysis* (1982); Sharon U. Salinger, *"To Serve Well and Faithfully": Labor and Indentured Servants in Pennsylvania, 1692–1800* (1987).

Cities and Commerce. Carl Bridenbaugh, *Cities in the Wilderness* (1938) and *Cities in Revolt* (1955); Gary B. Nash, *The Urban Crucible* (1979) and *Forging Freedom: The Formation of Philadelphia's Black Community, 1720–1840* (1988); G. B. Warden, *Boston, 1687–1776* (1970); Stephanie G. Wolf, *Urban Village* (1976); Stuart Bruchey, *The Colonial Merchant* (1966); J. F. Shepherd and G. M. Walton, *The Economic Rise of Early America* (1979); James B. Hedges, *The Browns of Providence Plantation*, vol. 1 (1952); Frederick B. Tolles, *Meeting House and Counting House: The Quaker Merchants of Colonial Philadelphia, 1682–1763* (1948); Thomas M. Doerflinger, *A Vigorous Spirit of Enterprise: Merchants and Economic Development in Revolutionary Philadelphia* (1986); Bernard Bailyn, *The New England Merchants in the Seventeenth Century* (1955); Marcus Rediker, *Between the Devil and the Deep Sea: Merchant Seamen, Pirates, and the Anglo-American Maritime World, 1700–1750* (1987); Arthur Jensen, *The Maritime Commerce of Colonial Philadelphia* (1963); Randolph S. Klein, *Portrait of an Early American Family* (1975).

Colonial Religion. For studies of Puritanism, see Suggested Readings for Chapter 2. Patricia U. Bonomi, *Under the Canopy of Heaven: Religion, Society, and Politics in Colonial America* (1986); Sidney Ahlstrom, *A Religious History of the American People* (1972); W. W. Sweet, *Religion in Colonial America* (1942); Carl Bridenbaugh, *Mitre and Sceptre: Transatlantic Faiths, Ideas, Personalities, and Politics, 1689–1775* (1962); Sidney Mead, *The Lively Experiment: The Shaping of Christianity in America* (1963); J. T. Ellis, *Catholics in America* (1965); J. R. Marcus, *Early American Jewry* (1951); Janet Whitman, *John Woolman, American Quaker* (1942); William C. McLoughlin, *New England Dissent, 1630–1833*, 2 vols. (1971); Marilyn Westerkamp, *Triumph of Laity* (1988); J. William Frost, *A Perfect Freedom: Religious Liberty in Pennsylvania* (1990); Edwin S. Gaustad, *The Great Awakening in New England* (1957); J. M. Bumsted and John E. Van de Wetering, *What Must I Do to Be Saved? The Great Awakening in Colonial America* (1976); Alan Heimert, *Religion and the American Mind* (1966); Perry Miller, *Jonathan Edwards* (1949); Ola Winslow, *Jonathan Edwards* (1940); Patricia Tracy, *Jonathan Edwards: Pastor* (1980); Conrad Wright, *The Beginnings of Unitarianism in America* (1955); J. W. Davidson, *The Logic of Millennial Thought* (1977).

Education. Lawrence A. Cremin, *American Education: The Colonial Experience, 1607–1783* (1970); Bernard Bailyn, *Education in the Forming of American Society* (1960); James Axtell, *The School upon a Hill: Education and Society in Colonial New England* (1974); Robert Middlekauff, *Ancients and Axioms* (1963); Samuel Eliot Morison, *The Founding of Harvard*

College (1935); Jurgen Herbst, *From Crisis to Crisis* (1982); Kenneth Lockridge, *Literacy in Colonial New England* (1974).

Culture and the Enlightenment. Jack Greene, *Pursuits of Happiness* (1988); Louis B. Wright, *The Cultural Life of the American Colonies* (1957); Daniel J. Boorstin, *The Americans: The Colonial Experience* (1958); Richard Beale Davis, *Intellectual Life in the Colonial South*, 2 vols. (1978); Henry May, *The Enlightenment in America* (1976); Howard Mumford Jones, *O Strange New World* (1964); Jean-Christophe Agnew, *Worlds Apart: The Market and the Theater in Anglo-American Thought, 1550–1750* (1986); Brook Hindle, *The Pursuit of Science in Revolutionary America* (1956); Carl Van Doren, *Benjamin Franklin* (1941); V. W. Crane, *Benjamin Franklin and a Rising People* (1954); H. Leventhal, *In the Shadow of Enlightenment* (1976).

Law and Politics. Bernard Bailyn, *The Origins of American Politics* (1968); Jack P. Greene, *The Quest for Power* (1963); J. R. Pole, *Political Representation in England and the Origins of the American Republic* (1966); Michael Kammen, *Spheres of Liberty: Changing Perceptions of Liberty in American Culture* (1986); Thomas Curry, *The First Freedoms: Church and State in America to the Passage of the First Amendment* (1986); Leonard W. Labaree, *Royal Government in America* (1930); Robert Zemsky, *Merchants, Farmers, and River Gods* (1971); Caroline Robbins, *The Eighteenth-Century Commonwealthman* (1959); J. G. A. Pocock, *The Machiavellian Moment* (1975); Robert Ferguson, *Law and Letters in American Culture* (1984); Marylynn Salmon, *Women and the Law of Property in Early America* (1986); Gerald W. Gawalt, *The Promise of Power: The Emergence of the Legal Profession in Massachusetts, 1760–1840* (1979); A. G. Roeber, *Faithful Magistrates and Republican Lawyers: Creators of Virginia Legal Culture, 1680–1810* (1981).

CHAPTER 4 THE EMPIRE UNDER STRAIN

General Histories. Robert Middlekauff, *The Glorious Cause: The American Revolution, 1763–1789* (1982); Edward Countryman, *The American Revolution* (1985); Alfred E. Young, Jr., ed., *The American Revolution* (1976); John C. Miller, *Origins of the American Revolution* (1957); Merrill Jensen, *The Founding of a Nation* (1968); Edmund S. Morgan, *The Birth of the Republic* (1956); J. R. Alden, *A History of the American Revolution* (1969); Charles M. Andrews, *The Colonial Background of the American Revolution* (1924, rev. 1931); Lawrence Henry Gipson, *The Coming of the Revolution, 1763–1775* (1954); Ian R. Christie and Benjamin W. Labaree, *Empire or Independence, 1760–1776* (1976); Ian R. Christie, *Crisis of Empire* (1966).

The British Imperial System. Lawrence Henry Gipson, *The British Empire Before the American Revolution*, 15 vols. (1936–1970); Robert C. Newbold, *The Albany Congress and Plan of Union of 1754* (1955); Richard Pares, *War and Trade in the West Indies, 1739–1763* (1936); Howard H. Peckham, *The Colonial Wars, 1689–1762* (1963); Alan Rogers, *Empire and Liberty* (1974); Lewis B. Namier, *England in the Age of the American Revolution*, rev. ed. (1961) and *The Structure of Politics at the Accession of George III*, rev. ed. (1961); John Brewer, *Party Ideology and Popular Politics at the Accession of George III* (1967); Bernard Donoughue, *British Politics and the American Revolution: The Path to War, 1773–1775* (1965); John Brooke, *King George III* (1972); Michael Kammen, *A Rope of Sand* (1968).

The French and the Indians. Fred Anderson, *A People's Army: Massachusetts Soldiers and Society in the Seven Years War* (1984); Thomas P. Abernethy, *Western Lands and the American Revolution* (1937); J. M. Sosin, *Whitehall and the Wilderness* (1961); David H. Corkran, *The Cherokee Frontier* (1962); R. S. Cotterill, *The Southern Indians* (1954); Howard H. Peckham, *Pontiac and the Indian Uprising* (1947); William Pencak, *War, Politics, and Revolution in Provincial Massachusetts* (1981); Francis Jennings, *Empire of Fortune* (1988) and *The Ambiguous Iroquois Empire* (1984).

Merchants and the Empire. Joseph Ernst, *Money and Politics in America, 1755–1775* (1973); Arthur M. Schlesinger, *The Colonial Merchants and the American Revolution* (1917); Oliver M. Dickinson, *The Navigation Acts and the American Revolution* (1951); Thomas Doerflinger, *A Vigorous Spirit of Enterprise: Merchants and Economic Development in Revolutionary Philadelphia* (1986).

American Resistance. David Ammerman, *In the Common Cause* (1974); Hiller B. Zobel, *The Boston Massacre* (1970); Edmund S. Morgan and Helen M. Morgan, *The Stamp Act Crisis* (1953); Benjamin W. Labaree, *The Boston Tea Party* (1964); John Shy, *Toward Lexington* (1965); Pauline Maier, *From Resistance to Revolution* (1972); Dirk Hoerder, *Crowd Action in Revolutionary Massachusetts* (1977); Paul A. Gilje, *The Road to Mobocracy: Popular Disorder in New York City, 1763–1834* (1987).

Revolutionary Ideology. Bernard Bailyn, *The Ideological Origins of the American Revolution* (1967); Ian R. Christie, *Wilkes, Wyvil, and Reform* (1962); George Rudé, *Wilkes and Liberty* (1962); Isaac Kramnick, *Bolingbroke and His Circle* (1968); Clinton Rossiter, *Seedtime of the Republic* (1953); Nathan Hatch, *The Sacred Cause of Liberty* (1977); Richard Merritt, *Symbols of American Community, 1735–1775* (1966); Gary B. Nash, *The Urban Crucible* (1979); Rhys Isaac, *The Transformation of Virginia, 1740–1790* (1982); David Brion Davis, *Revolutions: Reflections on American Equality and Foreign Liberations* (1990).

Revolutionary Politics. Carl Becker, *The History of Political Parties in the Province of New York* (1909); Richard D. Brown, *Revolutionary Politics in Massachusetts* (1970); David Lovejoy, *Rhode Island Politics and the American Revolution* (1958); L. R. Gerlach, *Prologue to Independence* (1976); Theodore Thayer, *Pennsylvania Politics and the Growth of Democracy* (1953); Ronald Hoffman, *A Spirit of Dissension* (1973); R. E. Brown and B. K. Brown, *Virginia, 1705–1786* (1964); Charles S. Sydnor, *Gentlemen Freeholders* (1952).

CHAPTER 5 THE AMERICAN REVOLUTION

General Histories. Robert Middlekauff, *The Glorious Cause: The American Revolution, 1763–1789* (1985); Edward Countryman, *The American Revolution* (1985); Alfred E. Young, Jr., ed., *The American Revolution* (1976); Merrill Jensen, *The Founding of a Nation, A History of the American Revolution, 1763–1789* (1968); Edmund S. Morgan, *The Birth of the Republic, 1763–1789* (1956); Michael Kammen, *A Season of Youth: The American Revolution and the Historical Imagination* (1978).

The Road to Independence. Carl Becker, *The Declaration of Independence* (1922); Morton White, *The Philosophy of the American Revolution* (1978); Gary Wills, *Inventing*

America (1978); Eric Foner, *Tom Paine and Revolutionary America* (1976); David Hawke, *Paine* (1974); Peter Shaw, *The Character of John Adams* (1976) and *American Patriots and the Rituals of Revolution* (1981); John R. Howe, Jr., *The Changing Political Thought of John Adams* (1966); Edmund S. Morgan, *The Meaning of Independence* (1976).

The War. Willard Wallace, *Appeal to Arms* (1950); John R. Alden, *The American Revolution* (1964); Piers Mackesy, *The War for America* (1964); Don Higginbotham, *The American War for Independence* (1971) and *George Washington and the American Military Tradition* (1985); Howard H. Peckham, *The War for Independence* (1958); Christopher Ward, *The War of the Revolution*, 2 vols. (1952); John Shy, *A People Numerous and Armed* (1976); Charles Royster, *A Revolutionary People at War* (1979); G. W. Allen, *Naval History of the American Revolution*, 2 vols. (1913); Samuel Eliot Morison, *John Paul Jones* (1959); T. G. Frothingham, *Washington: Commander in Chief* (1930); Douglas Southall Freeman, *George Washington*, 7 vols. (1948–1957); James T. Flexner, *George Washington in the American Revolution* (1968); Charles Royster, *Light-Horse Harry Lee and the Legacy of the American Revolution* (1981); E. Wayne Carp, *To Starve the Army at Pleasure: Continental Army Administration and American Political Culture, 1775–1783* (1984).

Revolutionary Diplomacy. Samuel F. Bemis, *The Diplomacy of the American Revolution* (1935); Richard B. Morris, *The Peacemakers* (1965); Gerald Stourzh, *Benjamin Franklin and American Foreign Policy*, rev. ed. (1969); Jonathan R. Dull, *A Diplomatic History of the American Revolution* (1985); L. S. Kaplan, *Colonies into Nation: American Diplomacy, 1763–1801* (1972); Clarence L. Ver Steeg, *Robert Morris* (1954); E. J. Ferguson, *The Power of the Purse* (1961).

The Loyalists. Wallace Brown, *The King's Friends* (1965); Robert M. Calhoon, *The Loyalists in Revolutionary America* (1973); Mary Beth Norton, *The British Americans: The Loyalist Exiles in England 1774–1789* (1972); William H. Nelson, *The American Tory* (1962); Bernard Bailyn, *The Ordeal of Thomas Hutchinson* (1974); Paul H. Smith, *Loyalists and Redcoats* (1964); James W. St. G. Walker, *The Black Loyalists* (1976).

Women, Family, and the Revolution. Mary Beth Norton, *Liberty's Daughters* (1980); Linda K. Kerber, *Women of the Republic* (1980); Linda Grant DePauw, *Founding Mothers* (1975); Joan Jensen, *Loosening the Bonds: Mid-Atlantic Farm Women, 1750–1850* (1986); Joy Day Buel and Richard Buel, Jr., *The Way of Duty: A Woman and Her Family in Revolutionary America* (1984); Jay Fliegelman, *Prodigals and Pilgrims* (1982).

Indians and Blacks in the Revolution. James H. O'Donnell, III, *Southern Indians in the American Revolution* (1973); Barbara Graymont, *The Iroquois in the American Revolution* (1973); Isabel T. Kelsay, *Joseph Brant, 1743–1807* (1984); Anthony F. C. Wallace, *The Death and Rebirth of the Seneca* (1969); Benjamin Quarles, *The Negro in the American Revolution* (1961); Duncan McLeod, *Slavery, Race and the American Revolution* (1974); Ira Berlin and Ronald Hoffman, eds., *Slavery in the Revolutionary Era* (1982); David Brion Davis, *The Problem of Slavery in the Age of Revolution* (1975); Edmund S. Morgan, *American Slavery, American Freedom* (1975); Arthur Zilversmit, *The First Emancipation* (1967).

Social Effects. Gordon S. Wood, *The Radicalism of the American Revolution* (1992); J. F. Jameson, *The American Revolution Considered as a Social Movement* (1962); Staughton Lynd, *Class Conflict, Slavery and the United States Constitution* (1968); Merrill Jensen, *The American Revolution Within America* (1974); Richard McCormick, *Experiment in Independence* (1950); Jackson Turner Main, *The Social Structure of Revolutionary America* (1965); Jerome J. Nadlehaft, *The Disorders of War: The Revolution in South Carolina* (1981); Robert Gross, *The Minutemen and Their World* (1976); Charles G. Steffen, *The Mechanics of Baltimore: Workers and Politics in the Age of Revolution, 1763–1812* (1984); Edward Countryman, *A People in Revolution* (1981).

State Governments. Gordon S. Wood, *The Creation of the American Republic* (1969); Stephen E. Patterson, *Political Parties in Revolutionary Massachusetts* (1973); Irwin Polishook, *Rhode Island and the Union, 1774–1795* (1969); Willi Paul Adams, *The First American Constitutions* (1980); Jackson Turner Main, *Political Parties Before the Constitution* (1973), *The Sovereign States, 1775–1783* (1973), and *The Upper House in Revolutionary America, 1763–1788* (1967).

The Articles of Confederation. John Fiske, *The Critical Period of American History, 1783–1789* (1883); Jack N. Rakove, *The Beginnings of National Politics* (1979); Merrill Jensen, *The New Nation* (1950) and *The Articles of Confederation*, rev. ed. (1959); H. James Henderson, *Party Politics in the Continental Congress* (1974); Jack Eblen, *The First and Second United States Empires* (1968); David Szatmary, *Shays' Rebellion: The Making of an Agrarian Insurrection* (1980); Andrew R. L. Cayton, *The Frontier Republic: Ideology and Politics in the Ohio Country, 1780–1825* (1986); Steven Watts, *The Republic Reborn: War and the Making of Liberal America, 1790–1800* (1987).

CHAPTER 6 THE CONSTITUTION AND THE
NEW REPUBLIC

The Constitution. Max Farrand, ed., *Records of the Federal Convention of 1787*, 4 vols. (1911–1937); Max Ferrand, *The Framing of the Constitution of the United States* (1913); Michael Kammen, *A Machine that Would Go of Itself: The Constitution in American Culture* (1986) and *Sovereignty and Liberty: Constitutional Discourse in American Culture* (1988); Charles A. Beard, *An Economic Interpretation of the Constitution of the United States* (1913); Forrest McDonald, *We the People: The Economic Origins of the Constitution* (1958), *E Pluribus Unum: The Formation of the American Republic, 1776–1790* (1965) and *Novus Ordo Seclorum: The Intellectual Origins of the Constitution* (1985); Robert E. Brown, *Charles Beard and the Constitution* (1956); Leonard Levy, *Constitutional Opinions: Aspects of the Bill of Rights* (1986) and *Original Intent and the Framers' Constitution* (1988); Thomas Curry, *The First Freedom: Church and State in America to the Passage of the First Amendment* (1986); William L. Miller, *The First Liberty: Religion and the American Republic* (1986); Richard B. Morris, *The Forging of the Union, 1781–1789* (1987); Clinton Rossiter, *1787: The Grand Convention* (1965); Christopher Collier and James Lincoln Collier, *Decision: Philadelphia: The Constitutional Convention of 1787* (1986); Douglas Adair, *Fame and the Founding Fathers* (1974); Jackson Turner Main, *The Anti-Federalists* (1961); Alpheus T. Mason, *The State Rights Debate* (1964); J. E. Cooke, ed., *The Federalist* (1961); Garry Wills, *Explaining America* (1981); Linda G. DePauw, *The Eleventh Pillar: New York State and* *the Federal Constitution* (1966); Gerald Stourzh, *Alexander Hamilton and the Idea of Republican Government* (1970); Robert A. Rutland, *The Ordeal of the Constitution* (1966); Michael Lienesch, *New Order of the Ages: Time, the Constitution, and the Making of Modern American Political Thought* (1988); Edmund S. Morgan, *Inventing the People: The Rise of Popular Sovereignty in England and America* (1988).

The Federalist Era. John C. Miller, *The Federalist Era, 1789–1801* (1960); Leonard D. White, *The Federalists* (1948); Forrest McDonald, *The Presidency of George Washington* (1974); Ralph Adams Brown, *The Presidency of John Adams* (1975); Stephen Kurtz, *The Presidency of John Adams* (1957); John R. Howe, *The Changing Political Thought of John Adams* (1966); Manning Dauer, *The Adams Federalists* (1953); Richard Kohn, *Eagle and Sword: The Federalists and the Creation of the Military Establishment in America, 1783–1802* (1975); Carl E. Prince, *The Federalists and the Origins of the U.S. Civil Service* (1978); Ralph Ketchum, *Presidents Above Party: The First American Presidency, 1789–1829* (1984); Leonard Levy, *Legacy of Suppression: Freedom of Speech and Press in Early American History*, rev. ed. (1985); James M. Smith, *Freedom's Fetters: The Alien and Sedition Laws and American Civil Liberties* (1956); Leland D. Baldwin, *The Whiskey Rebels* (1939); Thomas P. Slaughter, *The Whiskey Rebellion: Frontier Epilogue to the American Revolution* (1986); Irving Brant, *The Bill of Rights* (1965); John C. Miller, *Crisis in Freedom* (1951).

The Jeffersonian Republicans. Charles A. Beard, *The Economic Origins of the Jeffersonian Opposition* (1915); Joseph Charles, *The Origins of the American Party System* (1956); Noble Cunningham, *The Jeffersonian Republicans* (1957); Merrill D. Peterson, *Thomas Jefferson and the New Nation* (1970); Richard Hofstadter, *The Idea of a Party System* (1970); Norman K. Risjord, *Chesapeake Politics, 1781–1800* (1978); Alfred F. Young, *The Democratic-Republicans of New York* (1967); William N. Chambers, *Political Parties in a New Nation* (1963); Patricia Watlington, *The Partisan Spirit* (1972); John Zvesper, *Political Philosophy and Rhetoric: A Study of the Origins of American Party Politics* (1977); Richard W. Buel, Jr., *Securing the Revolution: Ideology in American Politics, 1789–1815* (1972); Joyce Appleby, *Capitalism and a New Social Order: The Republican Vision of the 1790s* (1984); Drew McCoy, *The Elusive Republic: Political Economy in Jeffersonian America* (1980) and *The Last of the Fathers: James Madison and the Republican Legacy* (1989).

Federalist Diplomacy. Felix Gilbert, *To the Farewell Address* (1961); Samuel F. Bemis, *Jay's Treaty* (1923) and *Pinckney's Treaty* (1926, rev. 1960); Alexander DeConde, *Entangling Alliance* (1958) and *The Quasi-War* (1966); Lawrence S. Kaplan, *Jefferson and France* (1967); Harry Ammon, *The Genêt Mission* (1973); Louis M. Sears, *George Washington and the French Revolution* (1960); Bradford Perkins, *The First Rapprochement: England and the United States* (1967); Charles Ritcheson, *Aftermath of Revolution: British Policy Toward the United States, 1783–1795* (1969); Paul A. Varg, *Foreign Policies of the Founding Fathers* (1963).

The Founders. Douglas Southall Freeman, *George Washington*, 7 vols. (1948–1957); Garry Wills, *Cincinnatus: George Washington and the Enlightenment* (1984); Barry Schwartz, *George Washington: The Making of a Symbol* (1987); Esmond Wright, *Franklin of Philadelphia* (1986); Dumas Malone, *Jefferson and His Time*, 6 vols. (1948–1981); Merrill Peterson, *Thomas Jefferson and the New Nation* (1970); Irving Brant, *James Madison* (1950); James T. Flexner, *George Washington*, 4 vols. (1965–1972); Page Smith, *John Adams*

(1962); John C. Miller, *Alexander Hamilton* (1959); Milton Lomask, *Aaron Burr*, 2 vols. (1979, 1982); Richard B. Morris, *Witnesses at the Creation: Hamilton, Madison, Jay, and the Constitution* (1985).

CHAPTER 7 THE JEFFERSONIAN ERA

General Histories. Henry Adams, *History of the United States During the Administration of Jefferson and Adams*, 9 vols., (1889–1891); Marcus Cunliffe, *The Nation Takes Shape, 1789–1832* (1959); Charles Mayfield, *The New Nation* (1981); Marshall Smelser, *The Democratic Republicans, 1801–1815* (1968).

Society and Culture. Joseph J. Ellis, *After the Revolution: Profiles of Early American Culture* (1979); Russel B. Nye, *The Cultural Life of the New Nation* (1960); Kenneth Silverman, *A Cultural History of the American Revolution* (1976); Lawrence A. Cremin, *American Education: The National Experience* (1981); Carl F. Kaestle, *The Evolution of an Urban School System* (1973); Harry Warfel, *Noah Webster, Schoolmaster to America* (1936); Priscilla F. Clement, *Welfare and the Poor in the Nineteenth-Century City* (1985); William W. Sweet, *Revivalism in America* (1944); William G. McLoughlin, *Revivals, Awakenings, and Reform* (1978); Sydney Ahlstrom, *A Religious History of the American People* (1972); Whitney R. Cross, *The Burned Over District* (1950); John Boles, *The Great Revival in the South* (1972); Cathy Davidson, *The Revolution and the Word* (1986); Terry D. Bilhartz, *Urban Religion and the Second Great Awakening* (1986); Jan Lewis, *The Pursuit of Happiness: Family and Values in Jefferson's Virginia* (1983); Richard Slotkin, *Regeneration Through Violence* (1973).

Economic Growth. Stuart Bruchey, *The Roots of American Economic Growth* (1965); Thomas C. Cochran, *Frontiers of Change: Early Industrialization in America* (1981); Douglas C. North, *The Economic Growth of the United States, 1780–1860* (1961); W. Elliot Brownlee, *Dynamics of Ascent* (1979); Nathan Rosenberg, *Technology and American Economic Growth* (1972); Merritt Roe Smith, *Harpers Ferry Armory and the New Technology* (1977); Anthony F. C. Wallace, *Rockdale* (1978); Arthur H. Cole, *The American Wool Manufacture*, 2 vols. (1926); Caroline F. Ware, *Early New England Cotton Manufacture* (1931); C. M. Green, *Eli Whitney and the Birth of American Technology* (1956); W. J. Rorabaugh, *The Craft Apprentice: From Franklin to the Machine Age in America* (1986); Barbara M. Tucker, *Samuel Slater and the Origins of the American Textile Industry, 1790–1860* (1984); George R. Taylor, *The Transportation Revolution* (1951); James Henretta and Gregory Nobles, *The Evolution of American Society, 1700–1815*, rev. ed. (1987).

Politics and Government. Morton Borden, *Parties and Politics in the Early Republic* (1967); Noble Cunningham, *The Jeffersonian Republicans in Power* (1963) and *The Process of Government Under Jefferson* (1978); Robert Dawidoff, *The Education of John Randolph* (1979); James S. Young, *The Washington Community* (1966); David Hackett Fischer, *The Revolution of American Conservatism* (1965); Linda Kerber, *Federalists in Dissent* (1970); James M. Banner, *To the Hartford Convention* (1967); Leonard White, *The Jeffersonians* (1951); Alexander Balinky, *Albert Gallatin: Fiscal Theories and Policy* (1958); Robert M. Johnstone, Jr., *Jefferson and the Presidency* (1978); Dumas Malone, *Jefferson the President:*

First Term (1970) and *Jefferson the President: Second Term* (1974); Richard Ellis, *The Jeffersonian Crisis* (1971); Leonard Baker, *John Marshall: A Life in Law* (1974).

Jeffersonian Thought. Adrienne Koch, *The Philosophy of Thomas Jefferson* (1943); Charles M. Wiltse, *The Jeffersonian Tradition in American Democracy* (1935); Merrill Peterson, *The Jeffersonian Image in the American Mind* (1960); Leonard W. Levy, *Jefferson and Civil Liberties: The Darker Side* (1963); Drew McCoy, *The Elusive Republic: Political Economy in Jeffersonian America* (1980) and *The Last of the Fathers: James Madison and the Republican Legacy* (1989).

Foreign Policy. Irving Brant, *James Madison: Secretary of State* (1953); Bradford Perkins, *Prologue to War: England and the United States, 1805–1812* (1961); Alexander DeConde, *The Affair of Louisiana* (1976); Arthur P. Whitaker, *The Mississippi Question* (1934); George Dangerfield, *Chancellor Robert R. Livingston of New York* (1960); Harry Ammon, *James Monroe and the Quest for National Identity* (1971); Bernard deVoto, *Course of Empire* (1952); Bernard deVoto, ed., *The Journals of Lewis and Clark* (1953); Nathan Schachner, *Aaron Burr* (1937); Thomas P. Abernethy, *The Burr Conspiracy* (1954); Milton Lomask, *Aaron Burr*, 2 vols. (1979, 1982).

Indians and the West. B. W. Sheehan, *Seeds of Extinction* (1973); Francis S. Philbrick, *The Rise of the New West* (1965); Ray Allen Billington and Martin Ridge, *Westward Expansion*, rev. ed. (1982); Richard White, *The Roots of Dependency* (1983); James P. Ronda, *Lewis and Clarke Among the Indians* (1984); Charles Wilkinson, *American Indians, Time, and the Law*, rev. ed. (1987); Francis P. Prucha, *American Indian Policy in the Formative Years* (1962); Reginald Horsman, *Expansion and American Indian Policy, 1783–1812* (1962) and *Matthew Elliott, British Indian Agent* (1964); R. David Edmunds, *The Shawnee Prophet* (1983) and *Tecumseh and the Quest for Indian Leadership* (1984).

CHAPTER 8 WAR AND EXPANSION

The War of 1812. J. C. A. Stagg, *Mr. Madison's War: Politics, Diplomacy, and Warfare in the Early American Republic, 1783–1830* (1983); Julius W. Pratt, *Expansionists of 1812* (1925); Reginald Horsman, *The Causes of the War of 1812* (1962) and *The War of 1812* (1969); Bradford Perkins, *Prologue to War: England and the United States, 1805–1812* (1961); A. L. Burt, *The United States, Great Britain, and British North America* (1940); Roger H. Brown, *The Republic in Peril: 1812* (1964); Harry L. Coles, *The War of 1812* (1965); F. F. Beirne, *The War of 1812* (1949); John Mahon, *The War of 1812* (1975); William Wood, *The War with the United States* (1915); Irving Brant, *James Madison: Commander-in-Chief* (1961); Robert V. Remini, *Andrew Jackson and the Course of American Empire* (1977); Alfred T. Mahan, *Sea Power in Its Relation to the War of 1812*, 2 vols. (1905); Samuel F. Bemis, *John Quincy Adams and the Foundations of American Foreign Policy* (1949); Bradford Perkins, *Castlereagh and Adams* (1964); R. David Edmunds, *The Shawnee Prophet* (1983) and *Tecumseh and the Quest for Indian Leadership* (1984).

Postwar Expansion. George Dangerfield, *The Awakening of American Nationalism* (1965) and *The Era of Good Feelings* (1952); Shaw Livermore, Jr., *The Twilight of Federalism*

(1962); Bray Hammond, *Banks and Politics in America from the Revolution to the Civil War* (1957); Murray N. Rothbard, *The Panic of 1819* (1962).

The West.   Francis S. Philbrick, *The Rise of the West, 1745–1830* (1965); Thomas P. Abernethy, *The South in the New Nation* (1961); Frederick Jackson Turner, *The Rise of the New West* (1906) and *The Frontier in American History* (1920); Ray Allen Billington, *The Far Western Frontier* (1965); Ray Allen Billington and Martin Ridge, *Westward Expansion*, rev. ed. (1982); John A. Hawgood, *America's Western Frontier* (1967); David J. Wishart, *The Fur Trade of the American West* (1979); Frederick Merk, *History of the Westward Movement* (1978); Dale Van Every, *The Final Challenge* (1964); Julie Roy Jeffrey, *Frontier Women: The Trans-Mississippi West* (1979); Glenda Riley, *The Female Frontier* (1988); Colin Calloway, *Crown and Calumet* (1987).

CHAPTER 9 A RESURGENCE OF NATIONALISM

The Economic Revolution.   See Suggested Readings for Chapter 7. W. Elliot Brownlee, *Dynamics of Ascent* (1974); Stuart Bruchey, *The Growth of the Modern American Economy* (1975); George R. Taylor, *The Transportation Revolution* (1951); Nathan Miller, *The Enterprise of a Free People* (1962); R. E. Shaw, *Erie Water West* (1966); Harry N. Scheiber, *Ohio Canal Era* (1969); Albert Fishlow, *American Railroads and the Transformation of the Ante-Bellum Economy* (1965); E. P. Douglas, *The Coming of Age of American Business* (1971); Thomas C. Cochran and William Miller, *The Age of Enterprise* (1942); Thomas C. Cochran, *Business in American Life* (1972); Richard D. Brown, *Modernization: The Transformation of American Life, 1600–1865* (1976); Diane Lindstrom, *Economic Development in the Philadelphia Region, 1810–1850* (1978); Merritt Roe Smith, *Harpers Ferry Armory and the New Technology* (1977); David J. Jeremy, *Transatlantic Industrial Revolution: The Diffusion of Textile Technologies Between Britain and America, 1780–1830* (1981); H. J. Habbakuk, *American and British Technology in the Nineteenth Century* (1962); Nathan Rosenberg, *Technology and American Economic Growth* (1972).

Factories and the Working Class.   Arthur H. Cole, *The American Wool Manufacture*, 2 vols. (1926); Caroline Ware, *The Early New England Cotton Manufacture* (1931); Barbara M. Tucker, *Samuel Slater and the Origins of the American Textile Industry, 1790–1860* (1985); Thomas Dublin, *Women at Work* (1979); Alan Dawley, *Class and Community: The Industrial Revolution in Lynn* (1976); Alice Kessler-Harris, *Out to Work: A History of Wage-Earning Women in the United States* (1982); Mary Blewett, *Men, Women, and Work* (1988); Christine Stansell, *City of Women: Sex and Class in New York, 1789–1860* (1986); Bruce Laurie, *Working People of Philadelphia* (1980); Susan E. Hirsch, *Roots of the American Working Class: The Industrialization of Crafts in Newark, 1800–1860* (1978); Steven J. Ross, *Workers on the Edge: Work, Leisure, and Politics in Industrializing Cincinnati, 1788–1890* (1985); Sean Wilentz, *Chants Democratic: New York City and the Rise of the American Working Class, 1788–1850* (1984).

Political Affairs.   George Dangerfield, *The Awakening of American Nationalism* (1965) and *The Era of Good Feelings* (1952); Glover Moore, *The Missouri Compromise* (1953); Paul C. Nagle, *One Nation Indivisible: The Union in American Thought, 1815–1828* (1965); Glyndon Van Deusen, *The Life of Henry Clay* (1937); Harry Ammon, *James Monroe: The*

Quest for National Identity (1971); Charles M. Wiltse, *John C. Calhoun: American Nationalist* (1944); Wesley Frank Craven, *The Legend of the Founding Fathers* (1956); Shaw Livermore, *The Twilight of Federalism* (1962); Samuel F. Bemis, *John Quincy Adams and the Union* (1956); Robert V. Remini, *The Election of Andrew Jackson* (1963); Norman K. Risjord, *The Old Republicans: Southern Conservatism in the Age of Jefferson* (1965).

The Courts. Albert J. Beveridge, *The Life of John Marshall*, 4 vols. (1916–1919); Leonard Baker, *John Marshall: A Life in Law* (1974); Francis N. Stites, *John Marshall: Defender of the Constitution* (1981); Richard E. Ellis, *The Jeffersonian Crisis: Courts and Politics in the Young Republic* (1971); R. Kent Newmyer, *The Supreme Court Under Marshall and Taney* (1968); Charles G. Haines, *The Role of the Supreme Court in American Government and Politics, 1789–1835* (1970); D. O. Dewey, *Marshall Versus Jefferson: The Political Background of* Marbury v. Madison (1970); Alexander M. Bickel, *Justice Joseph Story and the Rise of the Supreme Court* (1971); James McClellan, *Joseph Story and the American Constitution* (1971).

The Monroe Doctrine. Arthur P. Whitaker, *The United States and the Independence of Latin America* (1941); Dexter Perkins, *The Monroe Doctrine* (1927) and *Hands Off: A History of the Monroe Doctrine* (1941); Ernest R. May, *The Making of the Monroe Doctrine* (1975); Samuel F. Bemis, *John Quincy Adams and the Foundations of American Foreign Policy* (1940); Bradford Perkins, *Castlereagh and Adams: England and the United States, 1812–1823* (1964); Frank Thistlethwaite, *The Anglo-American Connection in the Early Nineteenth Century* (1959).

CHAPTER 10 JACKSONIAN AMERICA

General History. Glyndon Van Deusen, *The Jacksonian Era* (1959); John Mayfield, *The New Nation, 1800–1845* (1981); James C. Curtis, *Andrew Jackson and the Search for Vindication* (1976); Edward Pessen, *Jacksonian America*, rev. ed. (1979).

Democracy. Alexis de Tocqueville, *Democracy in America*, 2 vols. (1835); Moisie Ostrogorskii, *Democracy and the Organization of Political Parties*, 2 vols. (1902); Chilton Williamson, *American Suffrage from Property to Democracy, 1760–1860* (1960); Louis Hartz, *The Liberal Tradition in America* (1955); Michael Kammen, *Spheres of Liberty: Changing Perceptions of Liberty in American Culture* (1986); Marvin E. Gettleman, *The Dorr-Rebellion* (1973); Patrick T. Conley, *Democracy in Decline* (1977); Alexander Sexton, *The Rise and Fall of the Republic: Class Politics and Mass Culture in Nineteenth-Century America* (1990).

Jacksonian Society. Edward Pessen, *Riches, Class, and Power Before the Civil War* (1973); Douglas T. Miller, *Jacksonian Aristocracy* (1967); Sean Wilentz, *Chants Democratic: New York City and the Rise of the American Working Class, 1788–1850* (1984); Mary Ryan, *Cradle of the Middle Class: The Family in Oneida County, New York, 1790–1865* (1981); Christine Stansell, *City of Women: Sex and Class in New York, 1789–1860* (1986); Nancy Hewitt, *Women's Activism and Social Change: Rochester, New York, 1822–1872* (1984); Carroll Smith-Rosenberg, *Religion and the Rise of the City* (1971).

Jacksonian Politics. Arthur M. Schlesinger, Jr., *The Age of Jackson* (1945); Marvin Meyers, *The Jacksonian Persuasion* (1960); Richard Hofstadter, *The American Political Tradition* (1948); John William Ward, *Andrew Jackson: Symbol for an Age* (1955); Lee Benson, *The Concept of Jacksonian Democracy* (1961); Leonard White, *The Jacksonians: A Study in Administrative History* (1954); Richard B. Latner, *The Presidency of Andrew Jackson: White House Politics, 1829–1837* (1979); Richard B. McCormick, *The Second American Party System: Party Formation in the Jacksonian Era* (1966); Ronald P. Formisano, *The Birth of Mass Political Parties: Michigan, 1827–1861* (1971); Harry L. Watson, *Jacksonian Politics and Community Conflict: The Emergence of the Second Party System in Cumberland County, North Carolina* (1981); C. B. Swisher, *Roger B. Taney* (1936); Morton Horwitz, *The Transformation of American Law, 1780–1860* (1977).

Andrew Jackson. Robert V. Remini, *Andrew Jackson and the Course of American Empire: 1767–1821* (1977), *Andrew Jackson and the Course of American Freedom: 1822–1832* (1981), *Andrew Jackson and the Course of American Democracy* (1984), and *Andrew Jackson* (1966); Marquis James, *Andrew Jackson*, 2 vols. (1933–1937); James Parton, *Life of Andrew Jackson*, 3 vols. (1860).

Nullification. William V. Freehling, *Prelude to Civil War: The Nullification Controversy in South Carolina* (1966) and *The Road to Disunion. I. Secessionists at Bay, 1776–1854* (1990); Charles S. Sydnor, *The Development of Southern Sectionalism 1819–1848* (1948); Merrill D. Peterson, *Olive Branch and Sword: The Compromise of 1833* (1983).

Indian Policies. Ronald N. Satz, *American Indian Policy in the Jacksonian Era* (1975); Michael Rogin, *Fathers and Children: Andrew Jackson and the Destruction of American Indians* (1975); Grant Foreman, *Indian Removal: The Emigration of the Five Civilized Tribes* (1932) and *Indians and Pioneers: The Story of the American Southwest Before 1830* (1936); Arthur H. DeRosier, Jr., *The Removal of the Choctaw Indians* (1970); Theda Perdue, *Slavery and the Evolution of Cherokee Society, 1540–1866* (1979); Daniel F. Littlefield, Jr., *Africans and Seminoles: From Removal to Emancipation* (1976) and *Africans and Creeks: From the Colonial Period to the Civil War* (1979); Thurman Wilkins, *Cherokee Tragedy* (1970); Michael D. Green, *The Politics of Indian Removal: Cherokee Government and Society in Crisis* (1982); Richard White, *The Roots of Dependency* (1983); Angie Debo, *A History of the Indians of the United States* (1970), *The Road to Disappearance: A History of the Creek Indians* (1941), and *And Still the Waters Run: The Betrayal of the Five Civilized Tribes* (1973); Wilcomb E. Washburn, *The Indian in America* (1975); William Brandon, *The Last Americans* (1974); B. W. Sheehan, *Seeds of Extinction: Jeffersonian Philanthropy and the American Indian* (1973); Francis P. Prucha, *American Indian Policy in the Formative Years* (1962); Cecil Elby, *"That Disgraceful Affair"* (1973).

The Bank War. Robert V. Remini, *Andrew Jackson and the Bank War* (1967); Bray Hammond, *Banks and Politics in America from the Revolution to the Civil War* (1957); Peter Temin, *The Jacksonian Economy* (1969); J. M. McFaul, *The Politics of Jacksonian Finance* (1972); William G. Shade, *Banks or No Banks: The Money Issue in Western Politics, 1832–1865* (1972); J. A. Wilburn, *Biddle's Bank* (1967); T. P. Govan, *Nicholas Biddle; Nationalist and Public Banker* (1959); Reginald C. McGrane, *The Panic of 1837* (1924); J. R. Sharp, *The Jacksonians Versus the Banks* (1970).

Post-Jacksonian Politics. Robert V. Remini, *Martin Van Buren and the Making of the Democratic Party* (1959); James C. Curtis, *The Fox at Bay: Martin Van Buren and the Presidency* (1970); John Niven, *Martin Van Buren: The Romantic Age of American Politics* (1983); Paul Goodman, *Toward a Christian Republic: Anti-Masonry and the Great Transition in New England, 1826–1836* (1988); E. M. Carroll, *Origins of the Whig Party* (1925); Daniel Walker Howe, *The Political Culture of the American Whigs* (1979); Thomas Brown, *Politics and Statesmanship: Essays on the American Whig Party* (1985); Claude M. Fuess, *Daniel Webster*, 2 vols. (1930); Richard N. Current, *Daniel Webster and the Rise of National Conservatism* (1955); Irving Bartlett, *Daniel Webster* (1978); Norman D. Brown, *Daniel Webster and the Politics of Availability* (1969); Sydney Nathans, *Daniel Webster and Jacksonian Democracy* (1973); Robert Dalzell, *Daniel Webster and the Trial of American Nationalism* (1973); Maurice C. Baxter, *One and Inseparable: Daniel Webster and the Union* (1984); Clement Eaton, *Henry Clay and the Art of American Politics* (1957); George R. Poage, *Henry Clay and the Whig Party* (1936); Merrill D. Peterson, *The Great Triumvirate: Webster, Clay, and Calhoun* (1987); Thomas H. O'Connor, *Lords of the Loom: The Cotton Whigs and the Coming of the Civil War* (1968); William Preston Vaughn, *The Anti-Masonic Party in the United States, 1826–1843* (1983); Oscar D. Lambert, *Presidential Politics in the United States, 1841–1844* (1936); R. G. Gunderson, *The Log Cabin Campaign* (1957); Oliver P. Chitwood, *John Tyler: Champion of the Old South* (1939); Howard Jones, *To the Webster-Ashburton Treaty* (1977); A. B. Corey, *The Crisis of 1830–1842 in Canadian-American Relations* (1941); John B. Brebner, *North Atlantic Triangle* (1945).

CHAPTER 11 THE NORTH AND THE SOUTH: DIVERGING SOCIETIES

The Northern Economy. See Suggested Readings for Chapters 7 and 9. Thomas C. Cochran, *Frontiers of Change: Early Industrialization in America* (1981); David A. Hounshell, *From the American System to Mass Production, 1800–1932: The Development of Manufacturing Technology in the United States* (1985); Paul W. Gates, *The Farmer's Age* (1960); Peter Temin, *Iron and Steel in Nineteenth-Century America* (1964); Alfred D. Chandler, Jr., *The Visible Hand: The Managerial Revolution in American Business* (1977); James Norris, *R.G. Dun & Co., 1841–1900* (1978); Joseph E. Walker, *Hopewell: A Social and Economic History of an Ironmaking Community* (1966); Robert W. Fogel, *Railroads and American Economic Growth* (1964); Carter Goodrich, *Government Promotion of Canals and Railroads, 1800–1890* (1960); John F. Stover, *The Life and Decline of the American Railroad* (1970) and *Iron Road to the West: American Railroads in the 1850s* (1978); R. L. Thompson, *Wiring a Continent* (1947).

Immigration. John Bodnar, *The Transplanted: A History of Immigrants in America* (1985); Marcus Hansen, *The Immigrant in American History* (1940) and *The Atlantic Migration, 1607–1860* (1940); Maldwyn A. Jones, *American Immigration* (1960); Oscar Handlin, *The Uprooted* (1951, rev. 1973) and *Boston's Immigrants* (1941); Charlotte Erickson, *Invisible Immigrants* (1972); Philip Taylor, *The Distant Magnet* (1971); Robert Ernst, *Immigrant Life in New York City, 1825–1863* (1949); Kathleen N. Conzen, *Immigrant Milwaukee: 1836–1860* (1976); Carl Wittke, *We Who Built America*, rev. ed.

(1964), *Refugees of Revolution: The German Forty-Eighters in America* (1952), and *The Irish in America* (1956); Hasia Diner, *Erin's Daughters in America* (1983); Harold Runblom and Hans Norman, *From Sweden to America* (1976); Theodore C. Blegen, *Norwegian Migration to America*, 2 vols. (1931–1940); Stuart C. Miller, *The Unwelcome Immigrant* (1969); Rowland T. Berthoff, *British Immigrants in Industrial America, 1790–1950* (1953); Jay P. Dolan, *The Immigrant Church: New York's Irish and German Catholics* (1975); Ray Billington, *The Protestant Crusade, 1800–1860* (1938); I. M. Leonard and R. D. Parmet, *American Nativism, 1830–1860* (1971); T. J. Curran, *Xenophobia and Immigration* (1975); Allan Nevins, *The Ordeal of the Union*, 2 vols. (1947).

Northern Labor, Society, and Culture. Susan E. Hirsch, *Roots of the American Working Class: The Industrialization of Crafts in Newark, 1800–1860* (1978); W. J. Rorabaugh, *The Craft Apprentice: From Franklin to the Machine Age* (1986); Bruce Laurie, *Working People of Philadelphia* (1980); Norman Ware, *The Industrial Worker, 1840–1860* (1924); Henry Pelling, *American Labor* (1960); Hannah Josephson, *The Golden Threads* (1949); David Thelen, *Paths of Resistance: Tradition and Dignity in Industrializing Missouri* (1986); Mary Ryan, *Cradle of the Middle Class: The Family in Oneida County, New York, 1790–1865* (1981); Christine Stansell, *City of Women: Sex and Class in New York, 1789–1860* (1986); Carroll Smith-Rosenberg, *Disorderly Conduct: Visions of Gender in Victorian America* (1985); Alan Dawley, *Class and Community: The Industrial Revolution in Lynn* (1976), John Brooke, *The Heart of the Commonwealth: Society and Political Culture in Worcester County, Massachusetts, 1713–1861* (1990); Michael Frisch, *Town into City: Springfield, Massachusetts, and the Meaning of Community, 1840–1880* (1972); Elizabeth Blackmar, *Manhattan for Rent* (1989); Peter Knights, *The Plain People of Boston, 1830–1860* (1971); Christopher Clark, *The Roots of Rural Capitalism: Western Massachusetts, 1780–1860* (1990); Don Doyle, *The Social Order of a Frontier Community: Jacksonville, Illinois, 1825–1870* (1978); Stuart Blumin, *The Urban Threshold: Growth and Change in a Nineteenth-Century Community* (1976); Sam Bass Warner, Jr., *The Urban Wilderness* (1972); Richard C. Wade, *The Urban Frontier, 1790–1830* (1957); Raymond A. Mohl, *Poverty in New York, 1783–1825* (1971); Edward Pessen, *Riches, Classes, and Power Before the Civil War* (1973); Stephan Thernstrom, *Poverty and Progress* (1964); Frank Luther Mott, *American Journalism* (1950); Glyndon Van Deusen, *Horace Greeley* (1953).

The Southern Mind. W. J. Cash, *The Mind of the South* (1941); Avery Craven, *The Growth of Southern Nationalism* (1953); James Oakes, *Slavery and Freedom: An Interpretation of the Old South* (1990); John McCardell, *The Idea of a Southern Nation* (1979); Charles S. Sydnor, *The Development of Southern Sectionalism, 1819–1848* (1948); Clement Eaton, *Freedom of Thought in the Old South* (1940) and *The Growth of Southern Nationalism, 1848–1861* (1961); William R. Taylor, *Cavalier and Yankee: The Old South and American National Character* (1961); Rollin G. Osterweis, *Romanticism and Nationalism in the Old South* (1949); John Hope Franklin, *The Militant South* (1956); Drew Gilpin Faust, *A Sacred Circle: The Dilemma of the Intellectual in the Old South* (1977) and *James Henry Hammond and the Old South: A Design for Mastery* (1982); Bertram Wyatt-Brown, *Southern Honor: Ethics and Behavior in the Old South* (1982) and *Yankee Saints and Southern Sinners* (1985); Edward L. Ayers, *Vengeance and Justice* (1984); Donald G. Mathews, *Religion in the Old South* (1977); Ann C. Loveland, *Southern Evangelicals and the Social*

Order, 1800–1860 (1980); Frank Freidel, *Francis Lieber* (1947); Don Fehrenbacher, *Constitutions and Constitutionalism in the Slaveholding South* (1989).

The Plantation Economy. Gavin Wright, *The Political Economy of the Cotton South: Households, Markets, and Wealth in the Nineteenth Century* (1978); Lewis C. Gray, *History of Agriculture in the Southern United States to 1860*, 2 vols. (1933); Ulrich B. Phillips, *Life and Labor in the Old South* (1929); R. R. Russel, *Economic Aspects of Southern Sectionalism, 1840–1861* (1924); Frank L. Owsley, *Plain Folk of the Old South* (1949); Ralph A. Wooster, *Politicians, Planters, and Plain Folk* (1975); J. William Harris, *Plain Folk and Gentry in a Slave Society* (1985); Peter Kolchin, *Unfree Labor: American Slavery and Russian Serfdom* (1987).

The Planters. Robert Manson Myers, ed., *The Children of Pride* (1972); Mary D. Robertson, ed., *Lucy Breckinridge of Grove Hill* (1979); Carol Bleser, *The Hammonds of Redcliffe* (1981); Frances Ann Kemble, *Journal of a Residence on a Georgian Plantation in 1838–1839* (1863); Eugene Genovese, *The Political Economy of Slavery* (1965) and *The World the Slaveholders Made* (1969); James Oakes, *The Ruling Race: A History of American Slaveholders* (1982); Kenneth S. Greenberg, *Masters and Statesmen: The Political Culture of American Slavery* (1985).

Southern White Women. Anne Firor Scott, *The Southern Lady* (1970); Catherine Clinton, *The Plantation Mistress: Woman's World in the Old South* (1982); Mary Boykin Chesnut, *A Diary from Dixie* (1981, ed. by C. Vann Woodward); Suzanne Lebsock, *The Free Women of Petersburg: Status and Culture in a Southern Town* (1984); Jane Turner Censer, *North Carolina Planters and Their Children, 1800–1860* (1984); Elizabeth Fox-Genovese, *Within the Plantation Household* (1988).

Slavery. Kenneth Stampp, *The Peculiar Institution* (1955); Stanley Elkins, *Slavery* (1959); Herbert Aptheker, *American Negro Slave Revolts* (1943); Melville J. Herskovits, *The Myth of the Negro Past* (1941); John Blassingame, *The Slave Community* (1973); Eugene Genovese, *Roll, Jordan, Roll: The World the Slaves Made* (1974); Herbert Gutman, *The Black Family in Slavery and Freedom* (1976); Judith Chase, *Afro-American Art and Craft* (1971); Dena Epstein, *Sinful Tunes and Spirituals* (1977); Lawrence W. Levine, *Black Culture and Black Consciousness: Afro-American Folk Thought from Slavery to Freedom* (1977); Michael P. Johnson and James L. Roark, *Black Masters* (1984); G. P. Rawick, *From Sundown to Sunup: The Making of the Black Community* (1973); Leslie Howard Owens, *This Species of Property* (1976); Robert Fogel and Stanley Engerman, *Time on the Cross*, 2 vols. (1974); Herbert Gutman, *Slavery and the Numbers Game* (1975); P. A. David et al., *Reckoning with Slavery* (1976); Barbara Jean Fields, *Slavery and Freedom on the Middle Ground* (1985); Jacqueline Jones, *Labor of Love, Labor of Sorrow* (1985); Deborah G. White, *Ar'n't I a Woman?* (1985); Robert Starobin, *Industrial Slavery in the Old South* (1970); Richard C. Wade, *Slavery in the Cities* (1964); Stephen B. Oates, *The Fires of Jubilee* (1974); Robert Starobin, *Denmark Vesey* (1970); Carl Degler, *Neither Black nor White* (1971); Joel Williamson, *New People: Miscegenation and Mulattoes in the United States* (1980); Ira Berlin, *Slaves Without Masters* (1974); Leon Litwack, *North of Slavery* (1961); Orlando Patterson, *Slavery and Social Death: A Comparative Study* (1982); David Brion Davis, *Slavery and Human Progress* (1984).

CHAPTER 12 AN AGE OF REFORMS

Antebellum Literature. Vernon L. Parrington, *The Romantic Revolution in America,
1800–1860* (1927); F. O. Matthiessen, *American Renaissance* (1941); David Reynolds,
*Beneath the American Renaissance: The Subversive Imagination in the Age of Emerson and
Melville* (1988); Leo Marx, *The Machine and the Garden* (1964); Henry F. May, *The
Enlightenment in America* (1976); Van Wyck Brooks, *The Flowering of New England,
1815–1865* (1936); Neil Harris, *Humbug: The Art of P. T. Barnum* (1973); Mary Kelley,
The Limits of Sisterhood (1988).

Social Philosophies and Utopias. Ann Rose, *Transcendentalism as a Social Movement*
(1981); P. F. Boller, Jr., *American Transcendentalism, 1830–1860: An Intellectual Inquiry*
(1974); Gay Wilson Allen, *Waldo Emerson* (1981); Arthur M. Schlesinger, Jr., *Orestes A.
Brownson: A Pilgrim's Progress* (1939); Henry Steele Commager, *Theodore Parker* (1936);
Richard Lebeaux, *Young Man Thoreau* (1977); Perry Miller, *The Transcendentalists* (1950)
and *The Life of the Mind in America: From the Revolution to the Civil War* (1966); Arthur
Bestor, *Backwoods Utopias: The Sectarian and Owenite Phases of Communitarian Socialism
in America, 1663–1829* (1950); M. L. Carden, *Oneida: Utopian Community to Modern
Corporation* (1971); Raymond Muncy, *Sex and Marriage in Utopian Communities* (1973);
Priscilla Brewer, *Shaker Communities and Shaker Lives* (1986); R. D. Thomas, *The Man
Who Would Be Perfect: John Humphrey Noyes and the Utopian Impulse* (1977); Fawn Brodie,
No Man Knows My Name: The Life of Joseph Smith (1945); Klaus J. Hansen, *Quest for
Empire* (1967); Wallace Stegner, *The Gathering of Zion* (1964).

Antebellum Reforms. Alice Felt Tyler, *Freedom's Ferment* (1944); Ronald G. Walters,
American Reformers, 1815–1860 (1978); William G. McLoughlin, *Revivals, Awakenings
and Reform* (1978); Whitney R. Cross, *The Burned-Over District* (1950); Paul Johnson, *A
Shopkeeper's Millennium* (1978); Timothy L. Smith, *Revivalism and Social Reform in
Mid-Nineteenth Century America* (1957); William W. Sweet, *Revivalism in America* (1949);
Charles A. Johnson, *The Frontier Camp Meeting* (1955); C. C. Cole, Jr., *The Social Ideas
of the Northern Evangelists, 1826–1860* (1954); W. J. Rorabaugh, *The Alcoholic Republic*
(1979); Ian R. Tyrrell, *Sobering Up: From Temperance to Prohibition in Antebellum America,
1800–1860* (1979); David Rothman, *The Discovery of the Asylum* (1971); Estelle Freedman,
Their Sister's Keepers: Women's Prison Reform in America, 1830–1930 (1981).

Education. Michael Katz, *The Irony of Early School Reform* (1968); Lawrence A. Cremin,
American Education: The National Experience (1980); Stanley K. Schultz, *The Culture
Factory: Boston's Public Schools, 1789–1860* (1973); Paul Monroe, *The Founding of the
American Public School System* (1949); Carl Bode, *The American Lyceum* (1956); Jonathan
Messerli, *Horace Mann* (1972); Robert Trennert, *Alternatives to Extinction: Federal Indian
Policy and the Beginning of the Reservation System* (1975).

Feminism. Barbara J. Berg, *The Remembered Gate: Origins of American Feminism. The
Woman and the City* (1977); Ellen C. Du Bois, *Feminism and Suffrage: The Emergence of
an Independent Woman's Movement in America, 1848–1860* (1978); Mary Ryan, *Women in
Public: Between Banners and Ballots, 1825–1880* (1990); Nancy Cott, *The Bonds of Wom-*

anhood: "Woman's Sphere" in New England, 1780–1835 (1977); Nancy A. Hewitt, Women's Activism and Social Change: Rochester, New York, 1822–1872 (1988); Ann Douglas, The Feminization of American Culture (1977); Margaret H. Bacon, Mothers of Feminism: The Story of Quaker Women in America (1986); Jean Fagan Yellin, Women and Sisters: The Antislavery Feminists in American Culture (1989); Lois Banner, Elizabeth Cady Stanton (1980); Kathleen Barry, Susan B. Anthony (1988); Kathryn K. Sklar, Catharine Beecher: A Study in American Domesticity (1973); William L. O'Neill, Everyone Was Brave: The Rise and Fall of Feminism in the United States (1970); Eleanor Flexner, Century of Struggle, rev. ed. (1975); Barbara Leslie Epstein, The Politics of Domesticity: Women, Evangelism, and Temperance in Nineteenth-Century America (1981).

Antislavery and Abolitioni m. Louis Filler, The Crusade Against Slavery (1960); Gerald Sorin, Abolitionism (1972); M. L. Dillon, The Abolitionists (1974); Blanche G. Hersh, Slavery of Sex: Feminist Abolitionists in America (1978); John McKivigan, The War Against Proslavery Religion (1984); Alan Kraut, ed., Crusaders and Compromisers (1983); J. B. Stewart, Holy Warriors (1976); Peter F. Walker, Moral Choices: Memory, Desire, and Imagination in Nineteenth Century Abolition (1978); Lawrence J. Friedman, Gregarious Saints: Self and Community in American Abolitionism (1982); Lewis Perry and Michael Fellman, eds., Antislavery Reconsidered: New Perspectives on the Abolitionists (1979); Aileen Kraditor, Means and Ends in American Abolitionism: Garrison and His Critics on Strategy and Tactics, 1834–1850 (1967); G. H. Barnes, The Antislavery Impulse (1933); Gerda Lerner, The Grimké Sisters of South Carolina: Rebels Against Slavery (1967); John L. Thomas, The Liberator (1963); James Brewer Stewart, Wendell Phillips (1987); Bertram Wyatt-Brown, Lewis Tappan and the Evangelical War Against Slavery (1969); Robert Abzug, Theodore Dwight Weld (1980); Irving Bartlett, Wendell Phillips (1962); Betty Fladeland, James Gillespie Birney (1955); Martin Duberman, ed., The Anti-Slavery Vanguard (1965); Benjamin Quarles, Black Abolitionists (1969); William H. Pease and Jane H. Pease, They Would Be Free (1974); Arna Bontemps, Free at Last: The Life of Frederick Douglass (1971); William McFeely, Frederick Douglass (1991); Nathan Huggins, Slave and Citizen (1980); Leonard Richards, Gentlemen of Property and Standing (1970); George Fredrickson, The Black Image in the White Mind: The Debate on Afro-American Character and Destiny, 1817–1914 (1971).

CHAPTER 13 THE IMPENDING CRISIS

Westward Expansion. Ray Allen Billington, Westward Expansion, rev. ed. (1974) and The Far Western Frontier, 1830–1860 (1956); John D. Unruh, The Plains Across: The Overland Emigrants and the Trans-Mississippi West, 1840–1860 (1979); John M. Faragher, Women and Men on the Overland Trail (1979); Frederick Merk, History of the Westward Movement (1978), Manifest Destiny and Mission in American History (1963), Fruits of Propaganda in the Tyler Administration (1971), Slavery and the Annexation of Texas (1972), The Oregon Question (1967), and The Monroe Doctrine and American Expansionism, 1843–1849 (1966); Albert K. Weinberg, Manifest Destiny (1935); William H. Goetzmann, Exploration and Empire (1966); Henry Nash Smith, Virgin Land (1950); Norman A. Graebner, Empire of the Pacific (1955); E. C. Barker, Mexico and Texas, 1821–1835 (1928); William C. Binkley, The Texas Revolution (1952); Francis Parkman, The Oregon Trail (1849); R. L. Duffus, The Santa Fe Trail (1930); R. G. Cleland, From Wilderness to Empire:

A History of California, 1542–1900 (1944); R. W. Paul, *California Gold* (1947); J. S. Holliday, *The World Rushed In* (1981); O. O. Winther, *The Great Northwest*, rev. ed. (1950).

Expansion and the Mexican War. David J. Weber, *The Mexican Frontier, 1821–1846: The American Southwest Under Mexico* (1982); Charles G. Sellers, *James K. Polk: Continentalist, 1843–1846* (1966); J. S. Reeves, *American Diplomacy Under Tyler and Polk* (1907); David M. Pletcher, *The Diplomacy of Annexation: Texas, Oregon, and the Mexican War* (1973); G. M. Brack, *Mexico Views Manifest Destiny, 1821–1846* (1975); K. Jack Bauer, *The Mexican-American War, 1846–1848* (1974); John H. Schroeder, *Mr. Polk's War: American Opposition and Dissent* (1973); Otis A. Singletary, *The Mexican War* (1960); S. V. Conner and O. B. Faulk, *North America Divided* (1971); Holman Hamilton, *Zachary Taylor, Soldier of the Republic* (1941); C. W. Elliott, *Winfield Scott* (1937); Samuel F. Bemis, ed., *American Secretaries of State*, vols. 5 and 6 (1928); Basil Rauch, *American Interest in Cuba, 1848–1855* (1948); Robert E. May, *The Southern Dream of a Caribbean Empire, 1854–1861* (1973); Robert W. Johnson, *To the Halls of Montezuma: The Mexican War in the American Imagination* (1985).

The Sectional Crisis: General Studies. Allan Nevins, *The Ordeal of the Union*, 2 vols. (1947) and *The Emergence of Lincoln*, 2 vols. (1950); Michael Holt, *The Political Crisis of the 1850s* (1978); Roy F. Nichols, *The Disruption of American Democracy* (1948); Avery Craven, *The Coming of the Civil War* (1942); David Potter, *The Impending Crisis, 1848–1861* (1976); William J. Cooper, *The South and the Politics of Slavery, 1828–1856* (1978) and *Liberty and Slavery* (1983); James G. Randall and David Donald, *The Civil War and Reconstruction*, rev. ed. (1969); Richard H. Sewell, *A House Divided: Sectionalism and the Civil War, 1848–1865* (1988); James M. McPherson, *Ordeal by Fire* (1981) and *Battle Cry of Freedom* (1988).

The Compromise of 1850. Holman Hamilton, *Prologue to Conflict: The Crisis and Compromise of 1850* (1964); Chaplain W. Morrison, *Democratic Politics and Sectionalism: The Wilmot Proviso Controversy* (1973); Kinley J. Bauer, *Cotton Versus Conscience: Massachusetts Whig Politics and Southern Expansion, 1843–1858* (1967); Robert W. Johannsen, *Stephen A. Douglas* (1973); Charles M. Wiltse, *John C. Calhoun: Sectionalist, 1840–1850* (1951); Holman Hamilton, *Zachary Taylor: Soldier in the White House* (1951); Richard N. Current, *Daniel Webster and the Rise of National Conservatism* (1955); Robert F. Dalzell, Jr., *Daniel Webster and the Trial of American Nationalism, 1843–1852* (1973).

Sectional Crises in the 1850s. Kenneth Stampp, *America in 1857: A Nation on the Brink* (1990); Gerald Wolff, *The Kansas-Nebraska Bill* (1977); James C. Malin, *The Nebraska Question* (1953); Paul W. Gates, *Fifty Million Acres: Conflict over Kansas Land Policy, 1854–1890* (1954); Stephen Oates, *To Purge This Land with Blood: A Biography of John Brown* (1970); R. O. Boyer, *The Legend of John Brown* (1973); Truman Nelson, *The Old Man: John Brown at Harpers Ferry* (1973); J. C. Furnas, *The Road to Harpers Ferry* (1959); Benjamin Quarles, *Allies for Freedom* (1974); Eric Foner, *Free Soil, Free Labor, Free Men* (1970) and *Politics and Ideology in the Age of the Civil War* (1980); William E. Gienapp, *The Origins of the Republican Party, 1852–1856* (1987); David Donald, *Charles Sumner and the Coming of the Civil War* (1960); Dale Baum, *The Civil War Party System: The Case of Massachusetts, 1848–1876* (1984); William Jenkins, *Pro-Slavery Thought in the*

Old South (1935); Harvey Wish, *George Fitzhugh: Propagandist of the Old South* (1943); Don E. Fehrenbacher, *The Dred Scott Case* (1978).

The Emergence of Lincoln. Richard N. Current, *The Lincoln Nobody Knows* (1958); David Donald, *Lincoln Reconsidered* (1956); Don E. Fehrenbacher, *Prelude to Greatness: Lincoln in the 1850's* (1962); George B. Forgie, *Patricide in the House Divided* (1979).

CHAPTER 14 THE CIVIL WAR

General Studies. James M. McPherson, *Battle Cry of Freedom* (1988) and *Ordeal by Fire*, rev. ed. (1985); James G. Randall and David Donald, *The Civil War and Reconstruction*, rev. ed. (1969); Allan Nevins, *The War for the Union*, 4 vols. (1959–1971); Shelby Foote, *The Civil War: A Narrative*, 3 vols. (1958–1974); Bruce Catton, *This Hallowed Ground* (1956); Philip Shaw Paludan, *"A People's Contest": The Union and the Civil War, 1861–1865* (1988).

The Secession Crisis. Ralph A. Wooster, *The Secession Conventions of the South* (1962); David Potter, *Lincoln and His Party in the Secession Crisis* (1942); William L. Barney, *The Road to Secession* (1972) and *The Secessionist Impulse: Alabama and Mississippi in 1860* (1974); Kenneth M. Stampp, *And the War Came* (1950); Richard N. Current, *Lincoln and the First Shot* (1963); Steven A. Channing, *Crisis of Fear* (1970); Michael P. Johnson, *Toward a Patriarchal Republic* (1977).

Lincoln. Benjamin Thomas, *Abraham Lincoln* (1952); Stephen B. Oates, *With Malice Toward None* (1979); James G. Randall, *Lincoln the President*, 4 vols. (1945–1955), the final volume with Richard N. Current; Carl Sandburg, *Abraham Lincoln*, 6 vols. (1929–1939); T. Harry Williams, *Lincoln and the Radicals* (1941) and *Lincoln and His Generals* (1952); William B. Hesseltine, *Lincoln and the War Governors* (1948); Robert V. Bruce, *Lincoln and the Tools of War* (1956); Harry J. Carman and Reinhard Luthin, *Lincoln and the Patronage* (1943); LaWanda Cox, *Lincoln and Black Freedom* (1981).

Politics and Society in the North. David Donald, *Charles Sumner and the Rights of Man* (1970); Benjamin P. Thomas and Harold M. Hyman, *Stanton* (1962); Glyndon Van Deusen, *William Henry Seward* (1967); Martin Duberman, *Charles Francis Adams* (1961); James G. Randall, *Constitutional Problems Under Lincoln* (1926); Robert P. Sharkey, *Money, Class, and Party* (1959); Wood Gray, *The Hidden Civil War* (1942); Frank Klement, *The Copperheads in the Middle West* (1960); Mark Neely, Jr., *The Fate of Liberty: Abraham Lincoln and Civil Liberties* (1990); George Fredrickson, *The Inner Civil War* (1965); Daniel Aaron, *The Unwritten War* (1973); Edmund Wilson, *Patriotic Gore* (1962); John P. Bugardt, ed., *Civil War Nurse* (1980); Susan M. Reverby, *Ordered to Care: The Dilemma of American Nursing, 1850–1945* (1987); Iver Bernstein, *The New York City Draft Riots* (1990); J. Matthew Gallman, *Mastering Wartime: A Social History of Philadelphia During the Civil War* (1990).

Blacks and Emancipation. Ira Berlin, Leslie Rowland, et al., eds., *Freedom: A Documentary History of Emancipation, 1861–1867*, Series II: *The Black Military Experience* (1982); Clarence L. Mohr, *On the Threshold of Freedom: Masters and Slaves in Civil War*

Georgia (1986); Benjamin Quarles, *Lincoln and the Negro* (1962) and *The Negro in the Civil War* (1953); James M. McPherson, *The Struggle for Equality* (1964) and *The Negro's Civil War* (1965); Peter Kolchin, *First Freedom* (1972); John W. Blassingame, *Black New Orleans* (1973); Dudley T. Cornish, *The Sable Arm* (1966).

The Confederacy. Emory Thomas, *The Confederate Nation* (1979) and *The Confederate State of Richmond* (1971); Clement Eaton, *A History of the Southern Confederacy* (1954); Charles P. Roland, *The Confederacy* (1960); E. Merton Coulter, *The Confederate States of America* (1950); Clement Eaton, *Jefferson Davis* (1978); Hudson Strode, *Jefferson Davis*, 3 vols. (1955–1964); Thomas B. Alexander and Richard E. Beringer, *The Anatomy of the Confederate Congress* (1972); W. Buck Yearns, *The Confederate Congress* (1960); Emory Thomas, *The Confederacy as a Revolutionary Experience* (1971); Drew Gilpin Faust, *The Creation of Confederate Nationalism* (1988); Frank L. Owsley, *State Rights in the Confederacy* (1952); Bell I. Wiley, *The Life of Johnny Reb* (1943) and *The Plain People of the Confederacy* (1943); Paul D. Escott, *After Secession* (1978), *Slavery Remembered* (1979), and *Many Excellent People* (1985); James L. Roark, *Masters Without Slaves* (1977); Georgia Lee Tatum, *Disloyalty in the Confederacy* (1934); Ella Lonn, *Desertion During the Civil War* (1928); C. Vann Woodward, ed., *Mary Chestnut's Civil War* (1982).

Diplomacy. David P. Crook, *Diplomacy During the American Civil War* (1975) and *The North, the South, and the Powers, 1861–1865* (1974); Frank L. Owsley and Harriet Owsley, *King Cotton Diplomacy*, rev. ed. (1959); Gordon H. Warren, *Fountain of Discontent: The Trent Affair and Freedom of the Seas* (1981); Stuart L. Bernath, *Squall Across the Atlantic: American Civil War Prize Cases and Diplomacy* (1970).

Military Histories. Douglas Southall Freeman, *Robert E. Lee*, 4 vols. (1934–1935); Thomas L. Connelly, *The Marble Man* (1977); John Carpenter, *Ulysses S. Grant* (1976); Williams McFeely, *Grant* (1981); Bruce Catton, *Mr. Lincoln's Army* (1951), *Glory Road* (1952), *A Stillness at Appomattox* (1954), *America Goes to War* (1958), *Banners at Shenandoah* (1956), and *Grant Moves South* (1960); Bell Wiley, *The Life of Billy Yank* (1952); Kenneth P. Williams, *Lincoln Finds a General*, 4 vols. (1949–1952); Richard S. West, Jr., *Mr. Lincoln's Navy* (1957); C. E. MacCartney, *Mr. Lincoln's Admirals* (1956); John Niven, *Gideon Welles, Lincoln's Secretary of the Navy* (1973); William N. Still, Jr., *Iron Afloat: The Story of the Confederate Armorclads* (1971) and *Confederate Shipbuilding* (1969); T. Harry Williams, *McClellan, Sherman, and Grant* (1962) and *P. G. T. Beauregard, Napoleon in Gray* (1955); Burke Davis, *Sherman's March* (1980); Thomas L. Livermore, *Numbers and Losses in the Civil War in America* (1957); Herman Hattaway and Archer Jones, *How the North Won* (1983); Archer Jones et al., *Why the South Lost the Civil War* (1986).

CHAPTER 15 RECONSTRUCTING THE NATION

General Studies. Eric Foner, *Reconstruction: America's Unfinished Revolution, 1863–1877* (1988); Kenneth Stampp, *The Era of Reconstruction* (1965); John Hope Franklin, *Reconstruction After the Civil War* (1961); William A. Dunning, *Reconstruction, Political and Economic, 1865–1877* (1907); W. E. B. Du Bois, *Black Reconstruction* (1935); E. Merton Coulter, *The South During Reconstruction* (1947); Rembert Patrick, *The Reconstruction of the Nation* (1967).

Early Reconstruction. Herman Belz, *Reconstructing the Union* (1969); William B. Hesseltine, *Lincoln's Plan of Reconstruction* (1960); Willie Lee Rose, *Rehearsal for Reconstruction: The Port Royal Experiment* (1964); Louis S. Gerteis, *From Contraband to Freedman* (1973); Richard H. Abbott, *The First Southern Strategy* (1986).

Congressional Reconstruction. William R. Brock, *An American Crisis* (1963); Howard K. Beale, *The Critical Year: A Study of Andrew Johnson and Reconstruction* (1930); Eric McKitrick, *Andrew Johnson and Reconstruction* (1960); Hans Trefousse, *Andrew Johnson* (1989); Michael Les Benedict, *A Compromise of Principle: Congressional Republicans and Reconstruction, 1863–1869* and *The Impeachment and Trial of Andrew Johnson* (1973); Hans L. Trefousse, *The Radical Republicans* (1963) and *The Impeachment of a President* (1975); David Donald, *The Politics of Reconstruction* (1965); La Wanda Cox and John H. Cox, *Politics, Principles, and Prejudice, 1865–1867* (1963); Richard N. Current, *Old Thad Stevens* (1942); Fawn Brodie, *Thaddeus Stevens* (1959); David Donald, *Charles Sumner and the Rights of Man* (1970); Harold Hyman, *A More Perfect Union* (1973); Stanley Kutler, *The Judicial Power and Reconstruction Politics* (1968); Mark W. Summers, *Railroads, Reconstruction, and the Gospel of Prosperity* (1984); Charles Fairman, *Reconstruction and Reunion* (1971); Herman Belz, *A New Birth of Freedom* (1976) and *Emancipation and Equal Rights* (1978); William Gillette, *The Right to Vote* (1965).

The South in Reconstruction. Dan T. Carter, *When the War Was Over: The Failure of Self-Reconstruction in the South, 1865–1867* (1985); Michael Perman, *Reunion Without Compromise* (1973) and *The Road to Redemption: Southern Politics, 1869–1879* (1984); Joel G. Taylor, *Louisiana Reconstructed* (1974); Vernon Wharton, *The Negro in Mississippi, 1865–1890* (1965); Peyton McCrary, *Abraham Lincoln and Reconstruction* (1978); Joel Williamson, *After Slavery: The Negro in South Carolina During Reconstruction* (1965); Thomas Holt, *Black over White* (1977); Roberta Alexander, *North Carolina Faces the Freedmen: Race Relations During Presidential Reconstruction, 1865–1867* (1985); C. Peter Ripley, *Slaves and Freedmen in Civil War Louisiana* (1976); Barbara Fields, *Slavery and Freedom on the Middle Ground* (1985); Michael Wayne, *The Reshaping of Plantation Society: The Natchez District* (1983); William Gillette, *Retreat from Reconstruction* (1980); James D. Anderson, *The Education of Blacks in the South* (1989); Roger Ransom and Richard Sutch, *One Kind of Freedom* (1977); Robert Higgs, *Competition and Coercion* (1977); Crandall A. Shifflett, *Patronage and Poverty in the Tobacco South: Louisa County, Virginia 1860–1900* (1982); Leon Litwack, *Been in the Storm So Long* (1979); Eric Foner, *Nothing but Freedom: Emancipation and Its Legacy* (1983); Peter Kolchin, *First Freedom* (1972); Allen Trelease, *White Terror* (1967); William S. McFeely, *Yankee Stepfather: General O. O. Howard and the Freedmen* (1968); George Bentley, *A History of the Freedmen's Bureau* (1955); Otto Olsen, *Carpetbagger's Crusade: Albion Winegar Tourgée* (1965); L. N. Powell, *New Masters: Northern Planters During the Civil War and Reconstruction* (1980); William Harris, *Day of the Carpetbagger* (1979); Elizabeth Jacoway, *Yankee Missionaries in the South* (1979); Richard N. Current, *Those Terrible Carpetbaggers* (1988); William C. Harris, *The Day of the Carpetbagger: Republican Reconstruction in Mississippi, 1867–1875* (1979); Sarah Wiggins, *The Scalawag in Alabama Politics, 1865–1881* (1977); Jacqueline Jones, *Soldiers of Light and Love* (1980) and *Labor of Love, Labor of Sorrow: Black Women, Work, and the Family from Slavery to the Present* (1985); James Sefton, *The United States Army and Reconstruction* (1967).

The Grant Administration. Williams McFeely, *Grant* (1981); Margaret S. Thompson, *The "Spider Web": Congress and Lobbying in the Age of Grant* (1985); Allan Nevins, *Hamilton Fish* (1936); William B. Hesseltine, *U. S. Grant, Politician* (1935); David Loth, *Public Plunder* (1938); John G. Sproat, *"The Best Men"* (1968); Ari Hoogenboom, *Outlawing the Spoils* (1961); Irwin Unger, *The Greenback Era* (1964); C. Vann Woodward, *Reunion and Reaction* (1951); K. I. Polakoff, *The Politics of Inertia* (1973); Edwin C. Rozwenc, ed., *Reconstruction in the South*, rev. ed. (1952).

Illustration Credits

Index

Note: *Pages followed by the letter* m *refer to maps.*